SOCIAL PSYCHOLOGY
AND
CONTEMPORARY SOCIETY

SECOND EDITION

EDWARD E. SAMPSON

CLARK UNIVERSITY

JOHN WILEY & SONS, INC.
NEW YORK   LONDON   SYDNEY   TORONTO

Library of Congress Cataloging in Publication Data

Sampson, Edward E
Social psychology and contemporary society.

Bibliography: p.
1. Social psychology. I. Title [DNLM: 1. Psychology, Social. 2. Social change. 3. Social problems. HM251 S192s]

HM251.S262 1976   301.1   75-30225

Printed in the United States of America
10 9 8 7 6 5 4 3 2

SOCIAL PSYCHOLOGY
AND
CONTEMPORARY SOCIETY

PREFACE

The preface to the previous edition opened with an interview purportedly between myself and an unnamed interviewer. Through probing questions, the interviewer wrested from me the truth behind that book and its writing. No comparable interview is included here.

The cover on the first edition (of which I was particularly fond and had a hand in choosing) was an interesting test for those who proclaim that you can't tell a book by its cover; some people never went beyond that unclad couple on the outside to check out the book's interior. No comparable cover adorns this edition.

However, much more than these surface features has been changed. I almost completely reformulated, reorganized, and rewrote the original. This new edition is about ninety percent different, so much so that it was tempting to change the title or to consider it a second volume rather than call it a second edition. I made these extensive revisions less because of my dissatisfaction with the material of the original work than from a deeply felt need to provide a more clearly focused and integrated view of contemporary social psychology. I was especially eager to help the student learn how to think and view social psychologically; therefore, I devoted considerable space to the social psychological perspective (Chapters 1 and 2).

To see and understand within the purview of a discipline's perspective offers an enriching, often exciting, view of human social life. I compare it to the sense that a botanist can have when walking through the woods and seeing much more than just plants and trees; or the sense that a musician has in listening to music and hearing more than sweet sounds. To see the social world around us with the vision that a particular perspective provides can involve many things: it can involve taking what might otherwise be mundane, little-noticed events and placing them within a larger context that lets us see their meaning and significance; it can involve simply organizing and focusing our everyday experience, offering us new insights about familiar scenes; or it can provide us with a fresh vision about ourselves and the social worlds in which we live.

But I wanted to do more than simply present a perspective and guide the student's learning of it; I also felt it important to focus this perspective and this edition more sharply on fundamental themes, issues, and dilemmas of human life and to show what social psychology can contribute to our understanding of these basic matters.

Although these issues are clearly contemporary—a critical part of our own lives and experience—they are fundamental matters that have plagued and puzzled people and societies since our early beginnings. They involve questions of knowledge and understanding (Chapters 3 and 4); questions of language, communication, and interaction (Chapter 5); of identity (Chapter 6); of freedom and authority (Chapter 7); of responsibility and morality (Chapter 8); of altruism (Chapter 9); of justice (Chapter 10); of the impact of modernism on our lives and wellbeing (Chapter 11).

I suspect that occasionally this book will seem complex. Some will think it is too advanced for the beginning student, although I would use it for my own freshman classes. I have tried not to oversimplify what are complex matters nor to make straightforward matters unduly complex. My goal throughout, however, has been to show the enrichment and illumination that the theory and research of social psychology can bring to bear on matters basic to human life and experience. Reaching this goal often requires that we consider the more classic work and thought of the field; at other times, we must consider material still fresh and even now undergoing growth and development. I have not tried to update the text as an end in itself; material is introduced insofar as it contributes to our understanding of the basic issues examined. Fortunately, social psychology is a living, growing field; its direction has been such that these basic issues are becoming more and more important, permitting me to include some of the most recent writings of the field while not sacrificing my aim of grappling with issues of basic human significance.

To approach the understanding of such fundamental matters requires that we be interdisciplinary, covering in our social psychology both parental disciplines of sociology and psychology plus other relevant social sciences. I still believe that social psychology does not reside comfortably as a branch of either psychology or sociology alone; thus this edition continually attempts to create an integration of these perspectives and to call upon the ideas and research of both fields.

The instructor who is searching for a nonprovocative, simple text that will amuse more than instruct might be apprehensive about this edition. Our business is serious; our aspirations and hopes are high. There are important lessons to be learned, key concepts to be understood, vital issues to be confronted.

The instructor who is searching for a catalogue of the latest selections in social psychology also might have misgivings about this book. I have tried to go beyond a catalogue approach that surveys the field, that presents often dissociated bits and pieces of everything there is; I have attempted to present a synthesized, more unified approach to social behavior. I willingly sacrificed completeness of coverage in order to increase the clarity, comprehensibility and depth of understanding that a more theoretically integrated, thematic-and-issue-focused approach allows.

The author of a textbook never knows whether the audience that he writes for will actually be his audience. The population of potential users is vast and quite heterogeneous. So I write with my own classes in mind. I try the ideas and the material on my students, using their feedback and response as an important ingredient in my decisions about what material to include and how to include it. The material of this revision has been pretested on my own classes, and it generally has met with their approval.

These are bright students who usually have not had any previous course work in the social sciences. The introductory course in social psychology is often their first course as freshmen. They are students who aren't yet sure what purposes their own education will serve, although they have a vague, restless feeling that they want to do something with people and with helping.

I hope that this text will help to focus students' vague feelings and give direction and guidance to their desires to be helpful. I hope it will help them to understand that one can be relevant and deal with significant human issues without sacrificing critical thinking and scholarship; that one can be up to date without losing sight of the roots of our contemporary concerns; and that one can be more helpful with a firm base of knowledge than with the still unsharpened focus of the dreamer.

This volume carries a good part of me within it: some of my own dreams and hopes and my own vague, restless feelings of wanting to help.

Edward E. Sampson

Littleton, Massachusetts, 1976

CONTENTS

SOCIAL PSYCHOLOGY
AND
CONTEMPORARY SOCIETY

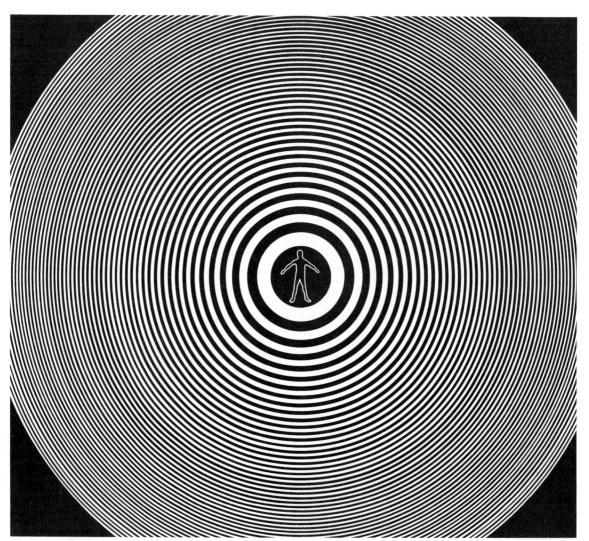

LAURI PROVENCHER.

PERSON, SITUATION, INTERACTION: AN INTRODUCTION TO THE SOCIAL PSYCHOLOGICAL PERSPECTIVE

1

How we formulate a field of inquiry such as social psychology plays an important role in determining the questions we ask about life and in the answers we seek or find acceptable. A field provides a perspective or framework from which to view everyday reality; it directs our attention to things, events, processes, and relationships that are considered important, emphasizing some aspects of the world in which we live while playing down or ignoring others.

Learning a new field involves in great measure learning its terms, concepts, and approaches—that is, its perspective—for grasping the great variety that is human life. It is important, therefore, for our own introduction to the field of social psychology, to obtain a good understanding of its perspective, its manner of comprehending the world, of asking questions of it, of finding answers, and of recommending solutions to the problems that we individually and collectively experience. Our study of social psychology requires that we view life through its perspective, perhaps to learn that it serves to organize and test what we take to be common sense; or perhaps to discover things that we might otherwise have passed over had we not immersed ourselves in its way of seeing and understanding.

ROSS AND MCDOUGALL: TWO EARLY VERSIONS OF SOCIAL PSYCHOLOGY

The year was 1908. Two authors, one a sociologist, Edward Ross, the other a psychologist, William McDougall, published their separate introductory textbooks in social psychology. Both were concerned with understanding the relationships between person and society and therefore their field was called social psychology; how-

ever, each offered a different analysis. Ross emphasized the important role that social and situational factors played in shaping the
person; McDougall stressed the role that person factors played in
shaping social interaction and society.

Ross argued that characteristics of the person arose through the
social processes of interaction, suggestion, and imitation; anyone
interested in understanding, predicting, or controlling (e.g., changing) human behavior would necessarily have to focus upon those
social or situational conditions (e.g., social interaction) that give rise
to it. We can say that Ross' theory of social psychology lay in a
tradition captured by the following statement:

$$\text{Human Behavior} = f \text{ (Situational Factors)}$$

This view calls our attention to the situation in which behavior
occurs in order to understand the causes of that behavior. For example, we are all aware that behavior appropriate to a job interview is
different from behavior appropriate at a football game. If we are
interested in understanding the causes of a person's (P's) behavior,
we must examine the situation in which he or she is located as well
as the people with whom he or she interacts.

For those students familiar with the approaches of behavioral
psychologists ranging from Watson (1919; 1925) through Skinner
(e.g., 1948; 1971), the thrust of this point of view is quite familiar.
Obviously, the behavioral approach is neither restricted to the sociologist Ross nor to the year 1908; an emphasis on situational factors
is very much with us today, though it would take us too far afield to
do more than take note of it at this point in our discussion.

McDougall's version of social psychology, influenced by the Dar-
winian conception of instinct, was concerned with internal factors
that motivated and directed a person's behavior. McDougall's perspective is contained within the following statement:

$$\text{Human Behavior} = f \text{ (Person Factors)}$$

Specifically, McDougall argued that a small set of innate instincts
—flight, repulsion, curiosity, self-abasement/self-assertion, and the
parental instinct—were the person factors that led P to perceive and
attend to objects of a certain class in the environment, to experience
a particular kind of emotion in response to these objects, and finally,
to act in a particular manner in regard to these objects. In other
words, P's behavior, as indexed by what P saw, felt, and did, was
assumed to be a function of these internal factors of instinct. Although McDougall's emphasis upon instincts as the key to under-

standing human behavior fell into disrepute shortly after its introduction in 1908—in part because situational determinants were becoming increasingly important to the discipline—the approach that maintains that person-factors (e.g., motives, personality traits, attitudes, etc.) play a major role in determining behavior, remains a basic point of view in contemporary theories of social psychology. The search for personality or character traits that produce consistent behavior across diverse situations is only one example of this perspective. For example, one seeks to understand conformity behavior by trying to uncover the "conformist personality"; one attempts to understand aggression by trying to uncover the "character" of the aggressive personality; and one hopes to understand prejudice by trying to uncover the personality of the bigot.

A convenient summary of these two perspectives is presented in Figure 1.

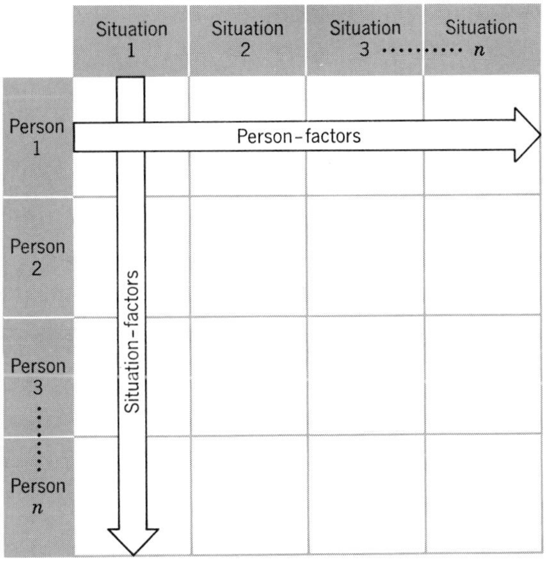

Figure 1

The chart is composed of various situations (1 through n) and various persons (1 through n). A person-centered perspective seeks those "broad underlying dispositions which pervasively influence the individual's behavior across many situations and lead to consistency in his behavior" (Mischel, 1973, p.253); the situation-centered perspective, on the other hand seeks its explanations for behavior in those aspects of situations that evoke common behaviors across persons. The person-centered approach asks: "What is there about people's motives, personalities, attitudes, and so forth, that helps explain why they act as they do?" The situation-centered approach asks: "What is there about the situation that evokes and maintains that kind of behavior thereby helping explain why people act as they do?"

Both perspectives can rightly be said to characterize historical and present day work within social psychology; thus each perspective is important for us to consider. I think it important to suggest, however, that the fundamental contribution of social psychology lies in its effort to examine the interaction between person and situation in explaining human behavior. But we shall have more to say about this after we first separately examine in more detail the person-centered and the situation-centered points of view.

The Person-Centered Perspective

To argue that behavior is a function of some enduring aspects or qualities of the person is simply to suggest that the consistencies we observe in P's behavior are to be attributed to some underlying disposition, trait, attitude, or *whatever* that P possesses. Our goal is to assess those underlying dispositions and establish their relationship to P's behavior. This perspective does not violate most of our everyday, intuitive, commonsense formulations. We have an extensive vocabulary of trait terms; one estimate suggests a lexicon of some 18,000 terms descriptive of trait-like concepts (Allport & Odbert, 1936). Thus, when each of us intuitively tries to explain P's behavior, we find a rich vocabulary of terms to direct us towards underlying qualities that P seems to possess and which thereby explains P's actions. We attribute P's refusal to lie or cheat to the trait of honesty; we attribute P's pleasing manner to the trait of friendliness, and so on. Our own intuitive theories of human behavior make us prone to use a person-centered approach. The 18,000 trait terms both reflect and facilitate this tendency. In Chapter 4, we examine this attributional process in more detail.

In psychology proper, many personality theorists employ a form of this person-centered perspective. Batteries of personality tests have been created to assess the wide variety of traits that persons are assumed to have and which presumably give us clues as to why they behave as they do. Most of us are familiar with such tests; many versions often appear in the popular press. We are also generally familiar with projective tests in which we are presented with a relatively ambiguous stimulus array, such as an inkblot, and asked to tell what we see; the analysis is said to provide a portrait of our inner world of motives, traits, and conflicts. Knowledge of that inside is assumed to be essential to understanding the reasons why we behave as we do.

The basic model assumes that our behaviors can best be understood by focusing on underlying dispositions that lead us to behave in a particular manner. Theorists who are more psychoanalytically oriented employ a similar perspective as they search for the basic, underlying aspects of *character* which explains a wide range of seemingly disparate behaviors. For example, to evaluate P as having an "oral character" is to provide a picture of a fundamental aspect of personality that is thought to be helpful in explaining such diverse behaviors as why P smokes, eats a great deal, talks considerably, seems to be dependent on others, and so forth. In this regard, a distinction is often drawn between a *phenotype,* which refers to observed surface behaviors (e.g., eating, talking, etc.) and a *genotype* (e.g., oral character), which refers to an assumed underlying disposition that explains diverse phenotypic behaviors. Thus, although we may observe that P behaves differently in different situations, rather than attributing these differences to specific situational factors, we continue to search for the underlying genotypic trait within the person that explains what on the surface appear to be such disparate behaviors.

IMPLICIT PERSONALITY THEORY

Another example of a person-centered approach involves the analysis of person perception and the concept of implicit personality theory (e.g., Cronbach, 1958; Schneider, 1973). Each of us has a set of trait-like terms by which we define other people; we also have a set of assumptions and hypotheses about psychology and human nature. In many respects, we are all commonsense psychologists complete with our theories of human behavior and data from our experiences that support the theories. We use these implicit theories in our encounters with others. On meeting strangers for the first time, we form impressions, many of which are highly resistant to later modification. Thereby we contribute significantly to the apparent consistency and stability of our interpersonal world; our implicit personality theory helps organize data about others, making others perhaps more consistent than in fact they may be.

Research reported in 1966 by Passini and Norman is instructive in demonstrating how these implicit personality theories operate to influence the impressions we form of others. The data suggest that in many respects our theory is a more important determinant of what impression we form of others than the actual characteristics of those others: a clear person-centered determinant. Passini and Norman asked students in their introductory psychology classes who had been together for less than 15 minutes to make trait ratings of others in their class. Data from ratings made by a different sample of persons who had known one another for much longer periods, from three days to three years, were available for purposes of comparison with these 15-minute impression ratings. The authors report that the ratings made by strangers (15-minute contact) and those made by persons who had been together even up to three years were very similar in their overall structure. All ratings could be summarized by five clusters of traits:

1. Extroversion: for example, talkative versus silent;
2. Agreeableness: for example, good-natured versus irritable;
3. Conscientiousness: for example, responsible versus irresponsible;
4. Emotional stability: for example, calm versus anxious;
5. Culture: for example, intellectual versus unreflective and narrow.

In other words, the rater's implicit personality theory involving these five key trait-clusters was a primary source of his perception of other persons; therefore, it mattered relatively little whether persons were rating strangers or long-term acquaintances in that their perception of others was more influenced by their implicit theory than by the actual characteristics of the other.

Research reported by Dornbusch, Hastorf, Richardson, Muzzy, and Vreeland (1965) supports a similar person-centered conclusion: "our findings indicate that the most powerful influence on interpersonal description is the manner in which the perceiver structures his interpersonal world" (p. 440). It is the person doing the perceiving rather than the object being perceived that seems most influential in determining the characteristics of what is seen; thus an analysis of the person who does the perceiving would seem warranted—that is, a person-centered perspective.

In 1973, Kahneman and Tversky reported the results of an investigation of persons' intuitive psychological theories that sheds additional light on this important matter. They addressed themselves to studying the extent to which person's intuitive (commonsense) predictions regarding others follows or deviates from the kind of prediction that a statistical or more scientific analysis would provide. For example, a statistical prediction about a future event uses information regarding the prior probabilities of occurrence of that event under the conditions specified. Do our intuitive predictions also use these prior probabilities? Kahneman and Tversky's data suggest the answer to be no.

Persons are given some information about others and asked to make predictions about those others. Their intuitive predictions are then compared with the kinds of predictions that one would make from a statistical utilization of the data. Results showed that persons made their intuitive predictions about another's likely behavior by selecting an outcome that seemed most representative of the input information they were given, ignoring prior probabilities and even questions regarding the reliability of the input information. Persons acted as though each piece of input information was representative of the other person's personality.

For example, subjects were given a brief personality sketch about a hypothetical other, Tom W., and asked to make a prediction about Tom's likely graduate field of study. Subjects tended to make these predictions on the basis of their evaluations of how similar Tom's personality was to that of others in various fields, ignoring information involving prior probabilities about *any* person's entering a given graduate field. While many more students enter the humanities or education than computer sciences, a fact which a statistical prediction of Tom's likely major field would consider, subjects ignored this information and rather made their predictions that he would more likely be a computer science student entirely from the personality sketch. Thus, their prediction was representative of the input (i.e., personality sketch) but ignored prior probabilities regarding the likelihood of given outcomes: that is, given no personality sketch one might reasonably predict that Tom is more likely to enter education than computer sciences; the sketch led subjects to make predictions representative of it rather than of a broader base of facts. Furthermore, subjects also tended to ignore the reliability of the personality input data in making their predictions. Kahneman and Tversky report, for example, that their subjects agreed that personality data obtained from projective tests would be a poor basis for making predictions about major fields of study, yet they made their predictions by using such data.

Khaneman and Tversky also report that persons tend to become highly confident about their judgments (they term this the *illusion of validity*), building this confidence on the consistency of input information even though such consistency may itself be unrelated to the outcome being predicted. For example, we may conduct an interview with someone in which they behave consistently in an aggressive manner; thus with great confidence we predict that they will not do well in a particular college even though the interview itself may be an unreliable assessment device and behavior in interviews may have little to do with the outcome of success in college. Our intuitive modes of prediction ignore these matters, even though we are aware of them; thus we make judgments that primarily represent the input (i.e., the interview) data by itself.

ATTITUDES

The social psychologist who employs a person-centered perspective often joins with the personality theorist in searching for underlying personality dispositions or intuitive modes of perception that account for behavior. However, much social psychological inquiry has been directed towards another kind of internal, person-centered determinant—P's *attitudes.* Basically, an attitude is an underlying positive or negative evaluation of some object; the person with a particular attitude is assumed to be disposed to behave favorably or unfavorably towards that object. Objects can refer to almost anything, ranging from other persons (e.g., political candidates, parents, minorities, etc.) to issues (e.g., abortion, euthanasia, energy conservation, school busing, etc.). The assumption is made that by understanding the underlying attitudes we will be able to explain P's behavior. If we can assess P's positive or negative evaluation of blacks, for example, then we can make predictions about P's behavior when faced with a black person.

The personality psychologists have invested much of their time and effort in devising techniques to measure P's underlying traits; the social psychologists have spent much of their time in seeking ways to evaluate P's attitudes towards particular persons, groups, and issues. Social surveys obtained around election time as well as throughout the year offer us examples of this concern; efforts to assess attitudes of prejudice towards various racial and ethnic minorities, provide another.

Because of the assumed link between attitudes and behavior, the social psychologist who is concerned with changing P's behavior, let us say from greater to lesser prejudice, focuses not only upon an assessment of P's existing attitudes but in addition upon techniques whereby those existing attitudes can be changed. If attitudes as an internal determinant of P's behavior can be changed, then presumably P's behavior accordingly will be changed. The history of social psychology is replete with examples of such efforts.

Toward the end of World War II, under the guidance of Carl Hovland at Yale University, an extensive series of investigations of persuasive communications was undertaken (e.g., Hovland, Janis, & Kelley, 1953; Hovland & Janis, 1959; Hovland, Lumsdaine, & Sheffield, 1949; Hovland & Weiss, 1951). Hovland's group sought to relate qualities of the communicator, the message, and the audience to P's attitude change in response to persuasive communications.

This research contributes to our understanding of how a communicator's prestige, expertise, and objectivity contribute to his or her effectiveness in changing attitudes; how the attributes of the persuasive message itself, whether it is one-sided or presents both sides of the issue, whether it is fear-arousing or neutral, likewise are effective in changing attitudes; how the audience, in particular its intellectual level and its degree of self-esteem play a role in their likelihood of being influenced to adopt the advocated attitude.

Work at Harvard (Smith, Bruner, & White, 1956) and at Michigan (Katz, 1960) examined the functions that attitudes were thought to serve in the life of the person and the implications of this functional view for producing attitude change. Attitudes were seen to serve the following functions:

1. Attitudes provide a way of organizing knowledge about the environment: for example, by holding a positive or a negative attitude towards a group, P has a shorthand way of responding to members of that group, of appraising them and of knowing how P should feel and respond to them.
2. Attitudes are instrumental in gaining benefits or avoiding costs: for example, P develops a positive attitude towards a political party that appears to offer the promise of security and satisfaction of P's economic needs.
3. Attitudes express important values that affirm P as being a particular kind of person: for example, political radicals affirm themselves as radicals by adopting and expressing extreme attitudes.
4. Attitudes serve ego-defensive functions, protecting the person from real and imagined threats: for example, P may be prejudiced towards others by projecting onto them P's own internal conflicts about sex and aggression.

Those who are interested in producing attitude change in order to produce behavior change would benefit from an awareness of the function a particular attitude serves in the life of the individual. For example, using persuasive messages with a rational appeal to change ego-defensive attitudes would not seem reasonable. Rather, as Katz, Sarnoff, and McClintock (1956) demonstrated, a technique that sought to provide people with insight into the defensive bases of their attitudes would be more effective. On the other hand, if people's attitudes serve primarily instrumental functions, then changing those instrumentalities (rather than providing psychological insight) would be the preferred approach to changing their attitudes. For example, if the reason that people hold antiblack attitudes is because by so doing they are more in line with the normative expectations of the community (i.e., it is instrumental to believe as other community members do), then actions that change community norms, for example legal rulings that provide people with an-

with another base for their instrumentality (e.g., good citizens must support the law of the land), can effect a change in attitude.

Attitudes and Behavior.   As we have noted, the person-centered perspective argues that our understanding of P's behavior derives primarily from understanding its internal determinants, in this instance, P's attitudes. Thus changing attitudes becomes an important way both of changing behavior and of insuring that once behavior is changed it will remain that way. Unfortunately, the conclusion to be reached from an examination of many studies that have sought to relate people's attitudes with their behaviors parallels the conclusion reached involving the relation between personality and behavior: low levels of predictability seem to be the rule (e.g., see Mischel, 1968; 1969; 1971 for a discussion and summary of the personality-behavior relationship and Wicker, 1969; 1971 for the attitude-behavior relationship).

The oft-cited classic case in point was the work of La Piere reported in 1934. La Piere traveled around the country with a Chinese couple, stopping at a variety of restaurants and hotels. Later, he sent a questionnaire to the manager of each place asking whether they would accommodate Chinese people. Approximately 92 percent said that they would not, yet all but one had actually served the couple. While his study can be critiqued on methodological grounds, it nevertheless points up the problem that has emerged in most attitude-behavior studies (see Dillehay, 1973). Here we have a case in which attitudes were rejecting but the behavior was accepting.

In what manner, then, can we maintain that people's behavior is a direct function of their attitudes or some other person-centered factor? It would seem that our explanations would have to search elsewhere. Other variables must be considered in addition to people's attitudes on only one issue, including for example, their attitudes on other, related issues; the situation in which they find themselves at the time the attitude was assessed and at the time the behavior was observed; the presence and potency of social norms; the degree to which the attitude as measured was overly general while the behavior observed was highly specific. As this last point suggests, asking persons their general attitudes towards Chinese may not be specific enough to the behaviors that are to be observed, namely the serving of an actual Chinese couple. We shall have more to say about these other factors and about the attitude-behavior relationship in a later section of this chapter. For the present, it would seem that an entirely person-centered perspective is not adequate to understanding the complexities of human behavior; but as we have noted (e.g., implicit personality theory), nor can person-factors be discounted as irrelevant.

COGNITIVE FACTORS

The concern with person-centered determinants of behavior finds one of its major expressions in contemporary social psychology in the form of cognitive theories and approaches, as our consideration of implicit personality theories and intuitive modes of prediction have already suggested. We consider cognitive determinants in Chapters 3 and 4 and thus will delay any detailed discussion until that time. We note, however, that a cognitive orientation emphasizes the role that the person's perception and thinking processes play in affecting the impact of external situations. The argument is that to understand P's behavior we must understand the processes whereby P gives meaning and structure to external situations: for example, how P's implicit theory affects the perception of other people.

Although a cognitive approach need not invariably be person-centered (as we note in Chapter 3), insofar as efforts are directed towards determining enduring styles of cognition that characterize persons, there is a clear parallel with the trait-type, person-centered approach. For example, in Chapter 3 we introduce Larry, a member of a sensitivity group who seemed to resist disclosing anything about himself to others in the group. We might explain this behavior by searching for an underlying trait that characterizes him, perhaps insecurity or low self-esteem. On the other hand, we might seek to understand Larry's characteristic way of dealing with input from his environment; we would inquire about the structure of his thinking and the kinds of constructs he has available for developing his impressions of other people. We may discover that our understanding of Larry's behavior is helped once we can grasp the manner by which he defines situations. We see that his evasiveness is a response to a situation that he has defined as highly dangerous and threatening: as he sees it, other people are out to hurt him. But more on this later; for now it is better that we examine the situation-centered perspective in order to sharpen our sensitivity to these two major, contrasting emphases in social psychology.

The Situation-Centered Perspective

The situation-centered perspective argues that behavior is a function of the circumstances in which it occurs. Whereas a person-centered perspective, for example, searches for the trait of honesty as a stable characteristic in order to explain a person's truth-telling behavior, the situation-centered approach searches for the conditions under which truth-telling is typically evoked in most persons. Given this emphasis, it is as important to develop a systematic approach to understanding situations as it has been to develop systematic ways of analyzing person-factors. Yet, in spite of the fact that much social psychological research has been concerned with the effects of specific situational conditions on persons' behavior, and in spite of the fact that behavioral psychologists interested in psychophysics have long been concerned with studying the relationship between physical aspects of stimuli (e.g., intensity) and behavior, a systematic analysis of situations or environments (we will use these terms interchangeably) still remains a relatively unexplored territory (Frederikson, 1972; Moos, 1973; Sells, 1963a; 1963b).

At this point, it will be helpful for us to outline and briefly review several approaches that have been developed for understanding situations or environments and their relationship to life and behavior. The outline is by no means exhaustive; rather, it is primarily an effort to suggest both the importance and several meanings of a situation-centered point of view. In our examination of these approaches, we will be confronted with several more general issues and distinctions.

1. Does situation refer to something relatively objective and external to a person's understanding of it or does situation refer to the setting as perceived by the person? (Ekehammar (1974) summarizes and gives a valuable historical perspective on this distinction.) Kurt Lewin, among others we will examine, places his major emphasis on the environment as the person perceives it. He notes, for example, that while a physicist might describe the environment in which the adult and the child are presently located as identical, the situation as they experience it can differ extensively. According to Lewin, it is this psychological rather than the purely physical environment that is of our greatest interest. We should note, by way of anticipating our later discussion, that by defining *situation* with reference to P's perception of it, we are really dealing with more of an interactionist than a purely situation-centered analysis. That is, we should rightly suppose that the situation as P perceives it contains both information about "what *it* is" and what internally influences P's perception of *it.* We return to this point in our consideration of the interactionist perspective in social psychology. In contrast to this emphasis on the psychological environment—the situation as perceived and defined by the person—we find those analysts who place their major emphasis on the relatively more objective physical or social environment.

2. Does situation refer to physical events and processes or to social events and processes involving other persons and forms of social organization? Some emphasize the physical environment of geo-

graphic, climatic, and architectural conditions; others stress the social environment including, for example, organizational and group structure, the characteristics of the population involved in a given setting, the behavior of others, and so forth. For the most part, social psychologists are interested primarily in this latter, social conception of environment.

3. Does situation refer to stimuli immediately present and directly affecting the person or does it refer to the general background and setting in which activities occur? The former view stresses stimuli in the situation that directly reinforce specific responses; the latter sees the environment as "reducing and shaping the potential variability in human behavior" (Moos, 1973, p. 659). In this latter view, the situation defines possibilities for behavior, introduces or constrains opportunities, supports or inhibits activities, and defines what P must adapt to and cope with. If we follow the lead of Zajonc (1968) whose research shows that frequent exposure to a stimulus can make a person's attitude towards the stimulus more positive, environmental influence can be seen as a function of the range of stimulus attributes presented and of the frequency of such presentations.

The following outline conveniently summarizes and organizes several different ways of conceptualizing situations and environments (adapted from Ekehammar, 1974; Moos, 1973; and Sells, 1963a; 1963b).

OUTLINE OF SITUATIONAL AND ENVIRONMENTAL FACTORS

I. emphasis primarily upon relatively objective aspects of the environment

   A. ecological factors

      1. geographic factors

      2. climate and meterological factors

   B. architectural and design factors

   C. temporal factors

   D. behavior setting analysis

    E. technological factors

    F. social factors

        1. organizational structures

        2. role systems

        3. group structures

        4. population characteristics

            a. density

            b. average characteristics of milieu inhabitants

II. emphasis primarily upon the psychosocial environment as perceived and defined by persons

    A. organizational and group climate

    B. institutional and cultural climate and ethos

III. emphasis primarily upon eliciting and reinforcing stimuli

    A. other persons

    B. behavior evoking properties

This outline should be understood primarily as a preliminary road-map that is intended to provide a helpful guide to the territory of situational analysis. We will now briefly examine several of these approaches so that we may better understand this perspective and its importance in social psychology.

Ecological Factors. A strict environmental determinist would argue that factors of geography and climate, for example, determine life style and behavior. Sells (1963b) reports several examples of physical and psychological adaptations of persons who live in extremely hot or cold climates where heat control is important, or who live in dry climates where finding and retaining water (e.g., in the stomach) is necessary for adaptation. Cultural traditions and forms of social organization have also been seen to be derivatives of geographic and other ecological necessities. One need not take an extreme determinist view, however, to note the important relationships that have been posited and in some cases empirically supported relating ecological factors to human behavior. Concerns have focused upon such things, for example, as the effects of temperature on violence and aggression (e.g., Berke & Wilson, 1951; Wolfgang, 1958); observations reported by the United States Riot Commission (1968) likewise suggest a correspondence between temperature and the eruption of violent demonstrations. Other kinds of interpersonal behavior, such as attraction or liking have also been related to temperature (e.g., Griffitt, 1970; Griffitt & Veitch, 1971). Others have focused on such ecological factors as ozone concentration, barometric pressure, solar disturbances, magnetic disturbances, cosmic rays, fog (e.g., and depressive moods) and so forth (see Moos, 1973 and Moos & Insel, 1974 for a selective but helpful review of several such works).

Architectural and Design Factors.   Over the last several years, a growing interest has emerged in relating architectural and design features of man-made environments to the behavior of the inhabitants and participants of those settings. Do some architectural arrangements, for example, promote better mental health, more intense interaction and better communication as compared with other arrangements? Early interest in such factors appeared in a study by Festinger, Schachter, and Back (1950) who found that residential housing arrangements helped to explain a significant amount of the pattern of communication and influence among residents. Interest also developed in the use of space in constraining behavior and in promoting opportunities for certain kinds of behavior. Osmond (1957) for one and Sommer (1967; 1969) for another, have examined space that brings people towards it to interact (sociopetal), in contrast to spatial arrangements with design features that seem to drive persons away from interacting within it (sociofugal). These kinds of spatial arrangements among others have been related to the kinds of behavior that takes place. We examine some aspects of this further in Chapter 5. Craik (1970), and Proshansky, Ittelson, and Rivlin (1970) provide helpful reviews of this developing field of situational analysis.

Temporal Factors.   Environments are not only structured spatially, but temporally as well. Internal body rhythms of both humans and animals have come under systematic study; but these involve primarily person-centered, very likely biological factors. On the environmental side, time has been used mainly to refer to the temporal organization of activities, including for example, the structure of work-time and of rest-time; the effects of shift work on psychological and physical functioning; an analysis of peak load usage of resources and facilities: "Problems of congestion and scarcity arise not solely because many want the same things but because they want the same things at the same time" (Lynch, 1972, p. 72).

The scheduling of activities creates an important temporal organization to our experience; we awake, go to work or school, return home, take our rest, schedule our vacations, do our shopping or do not (e.g., Sunday blue laws, closing hours, etc.), all as a function of environmental time scheduling. During the energy crisis of the early 1970s, a new time schedule was put into effect in order to save energy. In some countries, to discourage peak load usage of electricity, higher cost rates are imposed until 11 P.M. at which time lower rates come into effect; thus many households do their laundry late at night to take advantage of lower rates. Increasingly, some businesses are experimenting with self-imposed time schedules for workers who have a range of time, say from 10 A.M. to 3 P.M. when all must be present, but individuals determine whether they will work their eight hours starting at 8 A.M. or at 10 A.M.

Animal research has suggested several important interactions between the temperal structure of the environment and the animal's naturally occurring rhythms. Loud noises, for example, are experienced as more stressful at certain times than at others. Perhaps similar effects occur among persons whose biological rhythms are placed in conflict with man-made temporal organization (e.g., as in shift work). As Lynch (1972) notes, the temporal synchronization of one person's activities to another's, so necessary for coordinated living, may also provide a stressful weight, a temporal restriction on our independence and freedom.

While our understanding of internal clocks is growing, our understanding of the temporal structure and organization of settings remains a relatively unexplored field. Yet, settings differ in their time demands and in their pacing for activities; furthermore, social interaction is temporally organized such that the temporal placement of behavior engenders a different meaning for that behavior (See Rausch, pp. 35 to 39 of this chapter for an example). Thus, not only *where* something occurs makes a difference in our behavior and understanding, but also *when* it occurs. There is also reason to believe that cultures differ in their temporal organization of experience (e.g., Kluckhohn, 1956); some are more past oriented, others more concerned with the future. Furthermore, as we note in our discussion of self and identity (Chapter 6), cultures likewise vary in their organization of persons' life cycles. Environments also vary with respect to their temporal stability; new cities or buildings spring up over night. Might they not also disappear as quickly? In contrast, some live in temporally more stable environments, ones that convey a sense of a long past as well as a stable, living present.

Perhaps employee turnover rates in organizations also provide us with temporal cues about environmental stability and instability. What would be our experience of security if we worked in a setting in which every few months 30 percent of our fellow workers were transferred out?

As the Bible informs us and as our everyday experience affirms, there is a season for each thing; perhaps we should be guided by these clues in seeking a more systematic understanding of the temporal organization of environments and its effects upon human behavior.

Behavior Settings. As we shall see in Chapter 11, Roger Barker's efforts in the field of psychological ecology have been directed towards the analysis of situational units that he terms *behavior settings* and which involve such locations-and-activities as a restaurant, a street corner, a drug store, a bowling alley, a classroom, to name but several such settings. It is Barker's thesis that the major contributor to a person's behavior lies in the behavior setting. In one research program, for example, Barker and Wright (1955) suggested that 95 percent of the behavior of the children they observed could be accounted for by knowing the setting they were in; settings elicited the same or similar behavior from different children. We will deal in more detail with Barker's ideas later in Chapter 11 and so only mention them briefly at this point.

Technology. Technology is another man-made environmental factor that plays an important role as a determinant of behavior. The impact of new technology ranges from its immediate effect upon the worker who must now engage in new kinds of behaviors in order to adapt to different working conditions (for an example, see Coch & French, p. 329 of this text) to the longer term effects upon the organization of society in general. Development of the automobile, for example, made it possible for persons to be more mobile, thereby to live further from their places of work, to create new communities with a host of new jobs and new behavior settings, to affect the organization and life of the family (e.g., commuting parents), and so forth. In addition, different technologies provide different structures for the work environment itself. Some technologies promote interaction among and between workers, while others are more restrictive in this regard; some require high skill levels for workers, necessitating greater formal training. Technology can also change the population requirements for staffing work settings; for example, fewer workers may be required to operate an automated production line (see Chapter 11 for more on this point). Likewise, the societal structure of expertise and authority may shift as those most knowledgeable become an elite of technical experts, while others are relegated to lesser positions of influence over now highly technical and specialized decision making: in such cases alienation as a sense of powerlessness may be the resultant psychological state.

Insofar as much human behavior is a result of adapting to the environment, including the technological environment, changes in that environment trigger adaptive changes in persons, including both long-term transformations and short-term adjustments (e.g., Sells, 1963a; 1963b).

Role Systems. A society and its parts (e.g., an organization) can be viewed as a structural arrangement composed of various positions and the relationships between those positions. Each position defines the actions expected of its occupant. Two positions in an office, for example, are secretary and boss; each position has a set of actions or behaviors that define it as well as its interactions with the other positions with which it is related. These positions and their corresponding behavioral expectations are referred to as *roles.* Roles vary in the explicitness of the actions that define them and in the sanctions that occur for failure to enact them properly. For example, there is a fair degree of leeway in defining the actions appropriate to the respective roles of boss and secretary, whereas the role of undertaker usually contains a lesser degree of leeway for appropriate behavior. The roles of lecturer and student may be so strictly defined in certain respects that deviation, as when a lecturer refuses to lecture or a student insists on taking over the class, brings about sanctions, if only of social approbation or rejection.

Few, if any situations involving persons-in-interaction occur without the involvement of some form of role definition. Roles not only provide a situational definition for the behavior expected of P, but also suggest appropriate behavior for others whose roles exist in a relationship with P's: for example, the lecturer-student example just noted. A significant amount of research in social psychology has sought to analyze the specific characteristics of various roles and the implications of those characteristics for potential occupants (see Biddle & Thomas, 1966; and Sarbin & Allen, 1968 for summaries).

Stouffer and his many associates (Stouffer et al., 1949a; b), for example, studied various military roles, focusing in particular upon the conflict that exists for the occupant of a role (e.g., noncommissioned officer) that is defined differently by those subordinate to and superior to it in the military hierarchy. Note that a description of such role conflict refers to an attribute of a situation that presumably affects the behavior of the person who occupies that position and who is thereby subjected to conflicting expectations. Others have analyzed role, role conflict, and conflict resolution for the position of school superintendent (Gross, Mason, & McEachern, 1957). In another effort, Hemphill (1959) provided an analysis of the role of executive, attempting to develop a classification of the various aspects of the role. At several points throughout the text we will note further analyses employing the concept of role, especially in our consideration of sex roles, in Chapter 6.

Organizational and Group Structures.   Several efforts have been directed towards an analysis of organizational structures and their effects on behavior. Porter and Lawler (1964), for example, differentiated organizations in terms of their size and their structure, speaking of tall versus flat structures. A tall structure has a number of levels of responsibility in a hierarchial arrangement; a flat structure is less complex and more decentralized with respect to control over decision making. Their research sought to relate size and structure to worker satisfaction. Some results suggested how a tall structure was more satisfying to worker needs for security while a flat structure seemed to better satisfy needs for personal growth and self-fulfillment. Morse and Reimer's (1956) research provided a parallel analysis of organizational decision-making structures, comparing hierarchical structures with those that permitted greater worker autonomy in decision making (see Chapter 7). Other structural variables—including, for example, formalization of procedures, specialization of functions and standardization of regulations, among others—have also been studied (e.g., James & Jones, 1974). Throughout the text we will note other efforts to study the objective structure as well as the psychosocial climate of organizations: e.g., Chapter 11. In each case, the model focuses our attention on those aspects of the larger situation that play a significant role in eliciting and in maintaining P's behavior.

In addition to concerns with business and industrial organizations, substantial interest has also been invested in analyzing the structure of colleges and universities. Austin (1962), for example, examined such structural variables as selectivity of admissions, number of books in the library, percentage of males in the university, number of Ph.D.s on the faculty, among others, as descriptive attributes that differentiated colleges in ways that influenced the experience and development of the student in attendance. We return to a related analysis shortly when we examine efforts to understand the organizational climate as perceived by the person.

At the level of the small group (in contrast to the larger organization), similar efforts to provide a structural analysis have been made. In the specific area of communication, for example, several noteworthy structural analyses demonstrate how different arrangements of communication between persons can either facilitate or inhibit effective problem solving and the individual's sense of satisfaction (e.g., Bavelas, 1950; Leavitt, 1958). A communication structure termed the circle, for example, permits each person to communicate with two other persons directly. In the diagram that follows, C can directly communicate with B and D in the circle pattern. A wheel pattern, on the other hand, restricts communication to only one other person: for example, B can communicate only with C. Some early research employing these and other structures (Leavitt, 1958) suggested how the wheel in comparison with the circle promoted greater efficiency in solving problems that required a sharing of information among all five group members. On the other hand, the circle pattern, permitting greater participation between all members, was experienced as generally more satisfying than the more isolating pattern of the wheel.

Again, at various points throughout this text we will be introduced to other aspects of group structure and communication patterns that while not always as restrictive as in the proceeding cases, nevertheless significantly constrain behavior; from a situation-centered perspective, these structural features of group situations are vital to understanding behavior. In Chapter 2 we consider another aspect of group structure, its cooperative or competitive organization; in Chapter 7 we examine the structure of authority and leadership in small groups. In these and other cases, we examine how these structural aspects of the situation in which P is involved evoke and maintain a particular pattern of behavior.

Population Characteristics.   As the world has become increasingly populated and as the concentration of persons in urban areas has intensified, there has been a corresponding interest in relating population density and crowding to behavioral outcomes. We examine several of these research programs in Chapter 11.

In addition to its density and concentration another population-related aspect of situations involves the average characteristics of

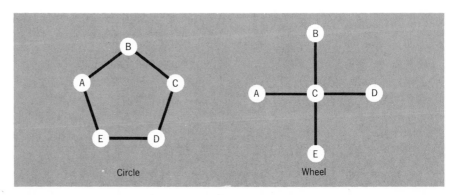

Circle   Wheel

the persons participating in the setting. Sells (1963a) has outlined several relevant clusters of characteristics of the milieu inhabitants, including among others:

1. age, sex, intelligence, skill level;
2. biological characteristics including height, weight, body type, race, physical condition;
3. social characteristics including rural or urban residence, occupation, income, education;
4. group membership characteristics including number of group associations, types of group membership, status of group memberships.

The basic idea is that the composition that typifies the persons in a given setting creates a particular kind of interpersonal climate that affects the persons involved in that setting. A lone female in an all male setting, for example, will experience a different kind of environmental pressure than a female in a setting that is half male and half female. Formulations of this sort have been applied to the sibling composition of families as well as to other kinds of groups. It has been suggested, for example, that a male child growing up with several female siblings may thereby tend to be more concerned with issues of traditional masculinity than a male growing up with brothers and sisters or even all brothers (e.g., Leventhal, 1968; Parsons, 1955).

There have been several efforts to study this situational determinant of behavior in larger contexts, including among others the work of Austin and Holland (1961) who described college environments in terms of the characteristics of their members: for example, size of institution, intelligence level of student body, and personal orientation of student body as assessed by choice of major. This last characteristic was grouped into several categories including realistic, (e.g., engineering), intellectual, (e.g., philosophy) social, (e.g., education), conventional, (e.g., accounting), enterprising, (e.g., political science) and artistic (e.g., fine arts). This population characteristic of the college environment—that is, its climate as assessed by a census of student occupations (majors)—not only played an instrumental role in determining who entered a particular college, but also the kinds of pressures and influences experienced by the person while attending the college. For example, a college characterized by its realistic orientation as defined by a preponderance of engineering, agriculture, physical education, and industrial arts majors is characterized by minimal concerns with humanistic and abstract theoretical matters. This is assumed to be a characteristic of the environment that a student faces and either adapts to or departs from.

If we extend our consideration of the characteristics of milieu inhabitants to include their attitudes, values, beliefs, or even their typical personality traits, we can see how lengthy and complex a listing of these situational factors could emerge. The logic of this kind of situational analysis should maintain, however, whether we are dealing with a person's physical, social, or psychological attributes; the average composition of the participants in a setting is assumed to provide an array of stimuli that affects persons' behaving in that setting. Thus, for example, the climate created by a group composed of persons who are all highly domineering should be different from the climate created by a group composed of persons who are all submissive. And though we are dealing with a personality variable, the assumption is made that the typical personality in a setting is a feature of that setting. P's behavior is explained by reference to the characteristics of the inhabitants of the milieu in which P is also behaving.

Although the emphasis has been upon average characteristics of milieu inhabitants, we can readily compute other indices of the participants' characteristics, for instance a rate computed from the individual incidence of some attribute or behavior, or a measure of the variation of the attribute within a given setting's population (e.g., Kendall & Lazarsfeld, 1955; Lazarsfeld & Menzel, 1969). The unemployment rate of a community, for example, can be computed and compared with the rate of another community. Our assumption would be that this difference in rates characterizes different environments for the inhabitants of those communities. A person living in community A with a 10 percent rate might thereby feel greater personal insecurity than a person living in community B with a 3 percent rate. Often, the social boundaries of the relevant milieu are not clearly marked; thus a national rate of unemployment might become a salient environmental input for many individuals whose attention is drawn to it by the mass media as well as by their own personal experiences or knowledge of persons who contribute to that rate.

Measures of the variability of an attitude or behavior within the population of a milieu can likewise be informative about the setting's characteristics. Thus, for example, two neighborhoods can have the same average number of children living in them, but in Neighborhood A the average is based on every household having between two and three children, while in Neighborhood B the average is based on several households with no children and several with six to eight children. As with other measures of milieu characteristics, variation measures can likewise be employed to describe a feature of the environment that the person living within the milieu may experience.

Psychosocial Aspects of the Environment. In 1938, in his analysis of personality and behavior, H. A. Murray introduced the concept of *press* to refer to the role of the stimulus situation in behavior. Press was defined as the "kind of effect an object or situation is exerting or could exert upon the S [person]. It . . . usually appears in the guise of a *threat of harm* or *promise of benefit* to the organism" (p. 748). While this definition seems to classify situations as either harmful or beneficial, Murray developed a more detailed analysis by employing the same terms he used to classify personality traits to classify situational press. Thus, for example, we can refer to the trait or need for affiliation and also to the *affiliative press,* referring to situations involving a sociable companion; we can speak not only of a need for aggression, but also of an *aggressive press,* referring to situations involving fight or conflict or their potential.

Pace and Stern (1958) employed this conceptual approach in their analysis of the press of college environments. In developing the items to ask persons for their perception of their college's characteristics, Pace and Stern asked themselves what the characteristics of an environment would be that satisfied or frustrated persons' needs for order, autonomy, affiliation, and so forth. They were able to develop a test to describe college environments consisting of some 300 items; these items were then presented to students and faculty members at several different institutions. An analysis suggested that the climate of the colleges dramatically differed, providing different kinds of environmental press: for example, one college climate emphasized orderliness and helpfulness; another had an environmental press that was more theoretical and intellectual. The point is that the experience the individual encounters will vary as a function of the psychosocial climate of the institution. Employing a somewhat different technique, Astin (see Moos, 1973) gives the following illustration, taking the case of a new student entering

> *an institution with high academic standards in which*
> *certain environmental stimuli occur relatively frequently:*
> *classroom examinations, discussions among students about*
> *grades, studying, intellectual arguments among students,*
> *and debates between faculty and students. The new student*
> *would be exposed to these and related stimuli and thus*
> *might feel anxiety about possible academic failure . . .*
> *experience increased fear of or hostility toward fellow*
> *students, or have increased feelings of competitiveness*
> *and/or feelings of inferiority. Presumably the student might*
> *be affected differently if he attended a different college. In*
> *terms of short-term behavioral effects, the student may*
> *increase the time he devotes to studying, reduce the time he*
> *devotes to social activities, and perhaps increase his*

*intellectual aggression. He may consequently experience
greater feelings of loneliness and isolation. Finally, there
may be longer lasting alterations in his self-concept and/or
relatively permanent changes in behavior which may persist
beyond college (e.g., devoting a great deal of time to the job
or competing constantly with others),* (Moos, 1973, p. 656).

Peterson and his associates (1970) developed an institutional climate questionnaire directed towards college faculty and administrators in order to obtain an evaluation of the work environment of different colleges. Such environment press dimensions as the following were included: freedom, both academic and personal, for all individuals in the campus community; diversity and heterogeneity of the student body; concern for undergraduate learning; institutional commitment to experimentation with new educational ideas; a shared sense of purpose and high morale. Not only can universities be differentiated along these dimensions, but these institutional distinctions create different working and learning environments that presumably have important consequences for the behavior of the individuals participating in the setting. To attempt to explain P's behavior without a consideration of these kinds of environmental factors, would seem to miss an important set of determinants.

Moos has employed a similar approach to understanding the press or climate of psychiatric wards and of community treatment programs. The treatment environment the person perceives "tends to define what he must adapt to and cope with and indicates the direction his behavior should take if he is to be adequately satisfied within the environment" (Moss and Insel, 1974, p. 471). Community treatment programs were characterized with respect to such perceived environmental dimensions as involvement of members in program activities; the degree to which members are encouraged to be open and spontaneous; the degree to which persons are encouraged to be self-sufficient and independent; the degree to which members are allowed or encouraged to express feelings, especially hostility; and the degree to which staff determines rules. This analysis of the psychosocial climate of the treatment program was then used to differentiate kinds of programs and to relate these various climate or press factors to program success as measured for example by drop-out rate and release rate (Moos, 1972).

Analyses of organizational climates in business and industry have also been based upon person's perceptions of their organizations; this contrasts with our earlier focus upon relatively more objective features of organizational structure and process. One such effort sought to integrate several others' works (Campbell, Dunnette, Lawler, and Weick, 1970), presenting four key dimensions of an organization's psychosocial climate:

1. individual autonomy: for example, the degree of individual responsibility and opportunities for exercising individual initiative;
2. imposed structure: for example, closeness of supervision over specific positions;
3. orientation towards reward: for example, promotion and achievement orientation;
4. consideration, warmth, and support: for example, the degree to which persons are given support and encouragement.

Organizational climate has been assumed to influence the way in which members of the organization define the stimuli presented to them, the constraints on their behaviors, and the reward and punishment process, especially with respect to setting goals and approving the means to attain them (James & Jones, 1974). Thus, for example, organizations that do not reward individual initiative and autonomy decrease the likelihood that the worker will take any self-directed action. In the context of the small group, the interesting early work of Lewin, Lippitt, and White (see Chapter 7 for a fuller discussion), suggested how the style of the groups' leader created a climate that served either to encourage or to discourage a member taking the initiative to keep working when the leader was absent. Presumably, organizational climates function in a similar manner.

Although the term *climate* tends not to be employed as the situational context expands beyond the organization and into the society or culture at large, a similar conception can be applied to a society's ethos or dominant cultural spirit, its ideologies, its norms and values: all are significant features of the larger social environment in which persons live. Benedict's view which we briefly consider in Chapter 2, the approach known as the sociology of knowledge (which we discuss in Chapter 4), and several other works which we consider throughout this text (for example, Titmuss's analysis of societal altruism), all emphasize, in one way or another, this larger environmental press that is presumed to play an important part in the individual's life.

The climate of a culture may be assessed by means of relatively objective approaches, or as with organizational climate, by an analysis of persons' perceptions of their cultural milieu. The former, for example, may involve an analysis of the major themes and characteristics employed in children's stories or on the mass media in order to determine dimensions of male and female sex role that are being inculcated into children (see p. 300 for an example of this approach) and adults. The latter perceptual approach would endeavor to examine person's own conceptions regarding their culture's emphasis on certain attributes of sex roles, for example.

Other Persons.   An obvious aspect of social situations involves the presence of other persons whose behaviors play a role in evoking and maintaining P's behavior. We have already considered one aspect of "others" in attributing an important situational role to the characteristics of the milieu inhabitants. Many major approaches within social psychology that we will examine later focus upon other persons as the key situational factor: for example, social comparison theory (Chapters 4 & 6), symbolic interactionism (Chapters 2 & 6), self-attribution theory (Chapter 4). In each case, P's behavior and internal states (for example, attitudes, self-perception) are viewed as outcomes of the actions or presence of others. It is not an exaggeration to note that the central focus of social psychology, in fact, is on this influence or affect of others on P.

The early work of F. Allport (1920; 1924) demonstrating what he termed *social facilitation* provides us with an important systematic demonstration and interpretation of the effects of other persons as our environment. Building on the observation of some European researchers that student assistants' work improved under scrutiny by their major professor, Allport demonstrated this facilitative effect in his laboratory. He showed how the quantity of subjects' performance on routine tasks (e.g., multiplication problems) done in the presence of others was greater than comparable work done under solitary conditions: for example, more multiplication problems were done in the group as compared with the solitary conditions. The presence of others, their sights and sounds, had a facilitative effect on person's own work. In later reflecting upon this work, Allport (1962) suggested that the mere presence of others leads persons to adjust their performance or actions with others so as "to establish some sort of a give-and-take, *structural,* relation with one's fellows—to be 'not left adrift' but included as a part of a present collectivity; or to help create, if necessary, such a structural relationship so that one *can* be a part of it" (p. 14). In this view, the presence of other persons in P's environment causes the adjustment of P's behavior with theirs so that they form or maintain a relationship or structure. As Allport notes, these mutual adjustments of structuring are all the more important when in order for P (or O) to achieve what he or she wants, O (or P) must act in a certain way; thus P (or O) adjusts to O's behavior (or O's to P's) so that together they both may accomplish their respective ends. The presence of others creates a structure that binds them together, even if neither party is aware of this effect or of these mutual adjustments.

Kelley and his associates (Kelley, Thibaut, Radloff & Mundy, 1962) provide some evidence affirming the idea that persons will make adjustments to one another's behavior resulting in a relatively stable structure of relationships even under conditions in which awareness of the other's presence is minimal or nonexistent; they also suggest one likely mechanism for these mutual adjustments. The basic research design, modeled after some earlier work of Sidowski (1957; Sidowski, Wyckoff and Tabory, 1956), brings two persons into separate rooms where they are unaware either of the presence of the other person or that their behavior is in any way influenced by the behavior of the other; this is termed a *minimal social situation.* The behavior called for is simply for each person to move a switch when a signal light goes on; if the move causes a red light to come on, the person loses 10 points; if a green light comes on, they win 10 points. They engage in such behavior over a series of trials, where a trial consists of the starting signal, their behavior, and its outcome of +10 or –10 points. Subjects are urged to try to accumulate as many points as possible. Unknown to either subject, the experimenter gives or takes away points from P as a function of O's behavior and gives or takes away points from O as a function of P's behavior. Recall that neither subject knows of the presence of the other or that his or her behavior is somehow dependent on the other's behavior—that is, they are unaware of their interdependence. The question is whether under these very minimal conditions of awareness, pairs would nevertheless produce a collective structure—that is, whether they will evolve a stable regularized adjustment of each person's behavior to the other's, the give-and-take that Allport discusses when persons are in the actual presence of others.

The answer to that question is yes. The data demonstrate how in the majority of pairs over half of the responses made are positive, delivering rewards to one's partner. In other words, persons under these minimal conditions nevertheless learn to cooperate, adjusting their behavior to the behavior of the other person, even though they remain unaware that another person exists or has anything to do with their behavior.

The explanation offered for such mutual adjustments was termed the win-stay, lose-change pattern. That is, if P's behavior won points on a given trial, P presumably would stay with the same behavior; if it lost points, presumably P would change. For example, if on the first trial, P's behavior led to a loss of 10 points for O, whereas O's behavior produced 10 points for P, on the second trial, P will stay with the winning behavior while O will change. O's change will result in a loss of points for P and P's staying will continue to lose for O. Thus on this trial, both P and O are being hurt by their choices. This would mean that on the next trial, both P and O would change. And this change now results in a gain for each. Presumably, now that each is being rewarded 10 points, each will stick with the winning behavior and will have created "thereby without knowing it, a kind of cooperative relationship" (Kelley et al., p. 2).

While admittedly this experimental situation is unusual because much of the time persons adjust their behavior to another's with more awareness than in the present context, it is a useful characterization of the kinds of influence that persons have over the behavior of others, establishing a give-and-take cooperative relationship that is entirely implicit. Allport stresses how a relationship may evolve and be explicit or implicit when others are actually known and present. As Kelley and his associates note,

> *It does seem possible . . . that underneath . . . more explicitly attained social arrangements the mechanism illustrated by our experiments [the win-stay, lose-change principle] provides a primitive and pervasive set of interpersonal adjustments of which the participants are hardly aware. These are likely to be in some respects unique to each pair of persons and consequently may explain the vague feelings a person often experiences that there is something mildly incompatible and inconsistent between the way he behaves toward one friend and the mannerisms he adopts toward another* (p. 17).

The preceding paragraph contains the situation-centered emphasis upon the circumstances in which behavior takes place and its important role in determining that behavior. In this instance, the situation involves the adjustment P makes to O whose presence is unknown but whose behavior is linked with P's.

We will shortly review the important research of Raush (1965) which further demonstrates the kinds of behavioral adjustments that tie P and O together. Raush's work shows how a major part of P's behavior can be understood by observing the immediately preceding act of O to which P's behavior is a response. For example, if we wish to understand why P acts aggressively, we would do well to note O's aggressive behavior to which P's own aggression is a response. But here we again anticipate an interactionist view; to speak of mutual adjustments and give-and-take is already to suggest how person and other are linked such that each one's behavior plays a part in determining the situation for the other.

BEHAVIOR EVOKING SITUATIONAL PROPERTIES

One approach to developing a systematic taxonomy of situations has examined situations with respect to "their tendency to elicit similar behaviors" (Frederiksen, 1972, p. 120). In 1974, Price and Bouffard reported the results of an investigation of what they termed "behavioral appropriateness" and "situational constraint." They suggest that specific behaviors—for example, talking, kissing, and writing —can be examined in terms of their appropriateness to given situations. Situations, in turn, can be examined with respect to how constraining they are, either requiring particular behaviors or being open to a wider range of possible behaviors.

Price and Bouffard asked one group of subjects (introductory psychology students) to keep a diary of their day's activities, noting what kinds of behavior they engaged in and in what kinds of situations. From these diaries Price and Bouffard were able to select a set of fifteen behaviors and fifteen situations (see Table 1.1). A matrix of behaviors-by-situations was formed by combining each behavior with each situation to create 225 items (i.e., 15 X 15): for example, running in class; reading on a bus; belching in church. A second group of subjects was given these 225 items and asked to rate each for its appropriateness: "Your task in each case is simply to rate, on a scale from 0 through 9, the appropriateness of the particular behavior in the situation given" (p.580).

It is possible to analyze the results in such a way that one can determine the separate influence of behaviors or situations upon the ratings of appropriateness. In this manner, it is possible to arrange behaviors according to their overall degree of appropriateness across all situations, and to arrange situations according to their

Table 1.1. Mean Rating of Appropriateness for Behaviors Collapsed Across Situations and for Situations Collapsed Across Behaviors*

Behavior		Situation	
Fight	1.96	Church	2.19
Belch	3.27	Job Interview	2.47
Run	3.46	Elevator	3.58
Shout	3.68	Family Dinner	3.85
Sleep	3.69	Class	3.88
Jump	3.74	Movies	3.95
Argue	3.97	Restroom	3.97
Cry	4.00	Sidewalk	4.39
Mumble	4.56	Bus	4.51
Write	4.83	Date	4.87
Kiss	5.00	Bar	4.87
Read	5.09	Football Game	5.33
Eat	5.85	Dorm Lounge	5.66
Laugh	7.01	Park	6.58
Talk	7.48	Own Room	7.50

0 = Extremely inappropriate.
9 = Extremely appropriate.
*Adapted from Price, R. H. & Bouffard, D. L. Behavioral appropriateness and situational constraint as dimensions of social behavior. *Journal of Personality and Social Psychology*, 1974, **30**, 579–586. Copyright 1974 by the American Psychological Association. Reprinted by permission.

overall degree of constraint across behaviors (see Table 1.1). To interpret the values in the "behavior column," note that a low number suggests that the given behavior is generally seen to be inappropriate in any of the fifteen situations examined. This column therefore indicates an overall judgment of behavioral appropriateness across the situations sampled. As we can see, fighting is seen to be the behavior that is least appropriate in any of the fifteen situations, with belching coming in second; on the other hand, laughing and talking are two behaviors that are felt to be generally appropriate in a greater number of situations.

Values in the "situation column" indicate the degree to which a given situation can be characterized as either permissive to or constraining of behaviors. A low value here indicates that few of the behaviors sampled are seen to be appropriate to that situation; thus the situation is relatively constraining. For example, the low ratings of church and of job interview suggest that few behaviors sampled are seen to be appropriate in those situations. A high value, on the other hand, indicates a situation that is relatively more permissive with regard to the range of appropriate behaviors. Here we see that the situations of a park or one's own room, receiving high ratings, are generally more open to a wide range of behaviors.

A followup report by Price and Bouffard (1974) sought further clarification of behavioral appropriateness and situational constraint by asking a new group of subjects information about the eliciting properties of situations with respect to such things as: Does the situation seem likely to produce embarassment? Does the situation require that people watch what they do? Is the approval of others important in this situation? Does the situation demand certain behaviors and not others? These results confirmed the meaning of a low situational rating. Price and Bouffard report, for example, that situations rated low in overall appropriateness (e.g., church and job interview) are indeed constraining, eliciting concerns with potential embarassment, increased monitoring of own behavior, concern with approval or disapproval of others, and demanding of certain behaviors rather than others.

As the authors note, the rating of situations according to their appropriateness provides us with an important tool in developing a classification of situations based on their behavior-eliciting properties. For example, situations with similar mean ratings share the same constraint properties. Thus we have an empirical technique for establishing some of the common properties of situations, a necessary first step in the process of developing as rich and analytic a vocabulary for understanding situations as we presently have for understanding persons. That this approach is but a first step is readily apparent as we note that while "movies" and "restroom" both have similar eliciting properties (i.e., mean scores), the actual behaviors appropriate to those situations differ dramatically.

Person X Situation: An Interactionist Perspective

Intuition and everyday experience inform us of the importance of person-centered factors in accounting for behavior. We are sensitive to the fact that what is ostensibly the "same" situation is responded to differently by different people. Surely, then, factors within persons must be important. Yet, we are also intuitively sensitive to the import of circumstances in eliciting behavior. We know that the same person behaves differently in different situations; that people reared in different environments are different. In fact, from an evolutionary perspective it is this ability to be responsive to different situational conditions that makes persons successfully adaptive. We would be in sorry shape as a species as well as in our individual lives if we always acted in the same way wherever we were, disregarding the specific circumstances.

Although much existing social psychological research and theory emphasizes either a person-centered or a situation-centered perspective, and thus will be important for us to examine in this text, it seems to me that it is both more fruitful and indeed more truly social and psychological to adopt an interactionist perspective. But what is this perspective? A brief consideration of the statistical concept of interaction will be instructive in providing us with an answer.

THE STATISTICAL CONCEPT OF INTERACTION

Using an example from Hays (1963), let us suppose that we are interested in evaluating two methods of golf instruction. Let us suppose further that we have selected one hundred persons to be our students, fifty men and fifty women. Twenty-five of each sex will be instructed according to Method I, while twenty-five of each sex will be instructed according to Method II. After a reasonable period of instruction, all 100 students are given a test designed to measure their proficiency, with a low score, as in golf, indicating good performance. Average scores for each method for each group are shown on the following table, as are overall averages for methods and for sex.

The results of this hypothetical teaching study are informative about the concept of statistical interaction. The table indicates that

	Method I	Method II	Overall
Males	55	65	60
Females	75	45	60
Overall	65	55	—

there is no overall effect for the factor of sex, in that the average score for males and for females is the same. However, there is an effect attributable to the methods: overall, Method II leads to better performance than Method I—that is, a score of 55 versus a score of 65, where low score indicates good golfing. An instructor who did not know the sex of his potential student population, therefore, would be more effective by selecting Method II over Method I. But a closer examination of these results indicates an *interaction effect.* The two methods work differently in their effectiveness according to the sex of the student. Female students do better when instructed by Method II whereas male students do better when instructed by Method I.

To speak of a statistical interaction effect is to note that a given factor (e.g., method) does not operate in the same manner across all levels of the other factor (e.g., sex of student). It is to note therefore that the behavior we are interested in, golfing performance in this case, is a joint function of two factors, method of instruction and sex of student, rather than any one factor by itself.

To generalize this concept of statistical interaction, let us use the following terms:

Let X be factor 1 (e.g., sex)
Let Z be factor 2 (e.g., method)
Let Y be behavior (e.g., golfing performance)

Interaction is said to exist if the relationship between Z and Y depends on X (or if the relationship between X and Y depends on Z). If interaction exists, the "functional relationship between X or Z and Y involves (X, Z) *pairs* in relation to Y" (Hays, 1963, p. 391). Neither X-factor nor Z-factor by itself is adequate for an interaction effect to take place; both are required because the effect, Y, is an outcome of the interaction between X and Z.

Now, let us employ the same two factors of our earlier concern, namely person (P) and situation (S):

Let P be factors attributable to the person
Let S be factors attributable to the situation
Let B be the behavioral events of interest

A statistical interaction is present when the relationship between P and B is dependent on S or the relationship between S and B is dependent on P. In other words, B is jointly determined by P and S.

To say that a statistical interaction effect exists in theory is to argue therefore that the behavioral event we are interested in exists in the pairing of P and S rather than in either P or S independently of the other.

Think about the previous point for a moment: it is crucial to an interactionist perspective in social psychology. Unlike the person-centered view or the situation-centered view, each of which maintains that behavior is primarily a function of either P or S, the interactionist perspective maintains that behavior is a joint outcome of P, S. As we shall see in Chapter 2 and at several other points throughout this text, this interactionist perspective goes by several different names. Although details of each view differ in certain respects, whether it is referred to as field theory or as systems theory, the emphasis is upon the joint determination of the behavioral effects being studied.

Before we leave this brief excursion into statistical interaction, several additional points are necessary for us to consider. The table of results that shows the interaction between sex of student and method of instruction not only reveals an *interaction effect* but also a *main effect* attributable to method. The point is that in arguing that behavioral events are the result of the pairing of two factors, we do not thereby require that each factor enter with equal weight in the determination of the effect. To apply this point to our P X S example, we may find behavioral events in which P-factors are relatively more important to their determination than S-factors; similarly, we may find behavioral events in which S-factors are relatively more important to their determination than P-factors. For example, we can think of situations that so constrain behavior that few persons would react inconsistently with a situational analysis; in this case, therefore, S-factors may weigh more heavily than P-factors. We can also think of persons, however, who for example seem hostile in most settings; in this case, P-factors may weigh more heavily than S-factors.

Let us consider two further points before we move on. In the first place, our concept of statistical interaction has thus far emphasized two factors and their pairing in determining behavior. However, the behavioral events we wish to understand may be the outcome of multiple factors. The two-factor example we chose was helpful primarily in illuminating the statistical concept of interaction; reality is usually more complex, involving the interaction of multiple factors.

In the second place, the example we selected of instructional method and sex of student involves two relatively independent factors. To say that two factors are independent is to note that one may be varied without influencing the state of the other. In a strict interactionist version of social psychology the factors that interact to determine behavior are usually understood to be interdependent. To say that two factors are interdependent is to note how variations in the state of one affects the state of the other. Person and situation, in a strict interactionist view, are of this latter sort: thus the state of the person affects his or her conception of the situation and the structure of the situation affects the state of the person. In social psychology, *situation* usually refers to other persons. To say that person and situation (i.e., other persons) are interdependent factors is to emphasize how P's behavior affects O's behavior and how O's behavior affects P's (the mutual adjustment and give-and-take of our earlier reference). These points are amplified in Chapters 2 and 3; our brief discussion of Lewin's field theory and of systems theory later in this chapter also expands somewhat on this approach. The strict version does not alter the basis for our understanding the causes of behavior; joint effects are the determinants. What is changed, however, is our conception of person and of situation as interacting elements that result in the behavioral events under study. Rather than viewing these as separate entities, each is seen as an interdependent part of a total field that includes the other as well. And behavior is a resultant of this total field.

Person X Situation: Some Research Results

The question is not really whether person or situation is a more important determinant of behavior, but rather within given settings and with particular persons, what is their unique and their joint contribution to the effects being studied. One typical research design for examining the main and the interactive effects of person and situation is the one used by Endler and Hunt (1968) in their study of hostility. Subjects were asked to complete a self-report questionnaire in which they are presented with ten modes of response to hostility (e.g., heart beats faster, want to strike something or someone, curse, etc.) and fourteen situations (e.g., talking to someone who does not answer, store closes as you are about to enter, someone makes an error and blames it on you); the subjects were then asked to rate the extent to which each item described them. The design permitted the researchers to separate person, situation, and their interaction as contributors to the ratings of hostility. (Other factors contributing to hostility are also possible to determine from this design, but these are not of relevance to our present concern with person, situation, and person-situation interaction.)

Results based on several different subject samples suggest that between 15 percent and 19 percent of hostility can be attributed to the person, between 5 percent and 7 percent to the situation, and between 10 percent and 11 percent to the person-by-situation interaction. Endler and Hunt (1966) previously reported findings from a study of anxiety. Those results suggest about 4 percent attributable to persons, between 4 percent and 8 percent to situations, and about 9 percent to the person-by-situation interaction. Both studies demonstrate the importance of the person-by-situation interaction effect for understanding hostility and anxiety. In particular, these studies demonstrate how person-factors seem to be a more important contributor to hostility than to anxiety. On the basis of such results it is not reasonable to make any broadly abstract statement that maintains that either P or S are the primary determinants of behavior. In this case not only is the interaction between factors important, but also, as we have seen, anxiety seems more situationally linked than does hostility. Another investigator, Moos (1969) makes the point even more clearly in noting how 42 percent of the smoking behavior of his sample of persons could be accounted for by person-factors and only 7 percent by the situation, while talking behavior was 68 percent situationally linked and only 10 percent attributable to person-factors.

Bowers (1973) offers a helpful summary of research in the interactionist perspective. He reviewed eleven studies reported between 1959 and 1972 that, like Endler and Hunt's work, permitted an analysis of person, situation, and person-by-situation interactions. Bowers' review suggests that on the average across these eleven studies, person-factors account for 12.71 percent of the behavioral events examined while situation-factors account for some 10.17 percent; the person-by-situation interaction, however, accounts for an average of 20.77 percent. In other words, if we were to use these studies as the empirical basis for our preferring a person-centered, a situation-centered, or an interactionist perspective, we would find more support for the interactionist view than either a person or a situation perspective.

A STUDY OF ONGOING SOCIAL INTERACTION: AN INTERACTIONIST EXAMPLE

Research methods for studying person-situation interactions range from the self-report variety (e.g., Endler & Hunt's work) to more directly observational approaches in which the person's behavior in a variety of settings is actually observed (e.g., Moos research). The study of social interaction conducted by Raush (1965) is of this latter sort. Because it is particularly helpful in further affirming the importance and the meaning of the interactionist perspective in social psychology, we will examine this one study in some detail.

Raush chose three different groups for his sample of persons: a group of hyperaggressive boys undergoing residential treatment who were observed both early and later in treatment; groups of normal, relatively well-adjusted American boys; a group of Norwegian, well-adjusted boys. While the specific characteristics that differentiate these three groups are not reported, group differences that emerge are nevertheless informative about the importance of person-factors in social interaction.

Raush selected six situations in which to make his observations of the boys' behavior: breakfasts, other mealtimes, games, unstructured group settings, group instructional settings, and snacks before bed. Acts of friendliness or unfriendliness were observed. The analysis of data permitted Raush to evaluate the determinants of the boys' behavior according to three sources:
1.   situational factors;
2.   group or person-factors;
3.   immediately antecedent acts.
Interactions among these sources were also studied. Source 3, antecedent acts, needs further explanation. As an example, take two persons, P and O. Our observation is of P's behavior. We know from which group P comes and in which of the six situations our observation is made. We also have one other piece of information about P's behavior, namely O's immediately preceding behavior to which P's act may be a response. When our concern is with ongoing social interaction between persons, as we noted, an important situational factor to examine involves the behavior of others in the setting.

In summarizing his analysis of the data, Raush reports that 12 percent of the boys' behavior can be attributed to the situation, 10 percent to their group, and 30 percent to the immediately preceding act. Let us look more closely at some examples of these results based on *main* effects rather than upon statistical interaction effects. By knowing the situation in which the behavior occurs, one can make informed statements about the kind of behavior that is likely to occur. For instance, in the American normal group, 42 percent of the acts in game settings were unfriendly, but only 5 percent were so at mealtimes. By knowing the group membership of the person behaving, we can also make statements about the likely behaviors. While 89 percent of the behavior of American normals and 85 percent of Norwegian normals was friendly, only 58 percent was friendly for the hyperaggressive group. As noted, the best predictor of all involves the immediately preceding behavior: "That is, if you want to know what Child B will do, the best single predictor is what Child A did to B the moment before" (p. 492).

In addition to these main effects, Raush was also concerned with interaction effects. An interaction effect involving *situations* would occur, for example, if the same antecedent act of O led to a different observed behavior in P as a function of the situation in which it occurred. Raush noted several of these effects. For instance among the American normal group friendly acts led to an unfriendly response 31 percent of the time in game situations but only 4 percent at meals. A similar pattern was noted among Norwegian boys. As Raush comments, the situation not only constrained the initial acts that occurred (that is, the main effects for situations previously discussed), but also influenced the subsequent response patterns. One is not only unfriendlier in game situations than at mealtimes (the main effect) but in addition, a friendly act is more likely to be met with an unfriendly reply in game settings as compared with mealtimes (an interaction effect).

Interaction effects involving group factors would occur, for example, if what is ostensibly the same stimulus situation were responded to differently by the different groups of boys. Raush reports that an unfriendly act was responded to with an unfriendly act by the hyperaggressive boys 80 percent of the time and 77 percent of the time by the normals. However, when the initial act was friendly, 8 percent of the responses were unfriendly among the normals, 19 percent were unfriendly among the hyperaggressives later in treatment, and 45 percent were unfriendly among the hyperaggressives early in treatment.

To restate these results, note that whereas all groups were able to respond to unfriendly acts with unfriendly replies, the hyperaggressives were less able than the normals to differentiate unfriendly from friendly overtures by others and thereby responded inappropriately—that is, with unfriendliness to both a friendly and an unfriendly overture. To repeat, this is an example of an interaction effect in which the relationship between variable 1 and behavior is jointly determined by variable 1 and variable 2. In this case, variable 1 involves O's initial act towards P while variable 2 involves the group to which P belongs; the same initial act of O evokes a different response from P as a function of P's group. The main effect of antecedent (i.e., initiating) acts, which we already noted, must thereby be tempered by our realization of this interactive effect.

This analysis also provides us with a sense of the difficulty that the hyperaggressive boys face: they reject friendly overtures thereby creating an interpersonal situation that increases the likelihood of unfriendly exchanges. Given the main effect that shows how O's acts influence P's subsequent behavior, the hyperaggressive boys' unfriendly response to O's friendly overture is likely to produce an unfriendly response from O, thereby diminishing the possibility for friendliness to characterize their relationship. This is the conclusion that Raush reached by examining sequences of interactions. He reports that for the hyperaggressive boys early in treatment there is a definite tendency for hostile responses to increase: "It is as though in this group of very disturbed aggressive children, as interaction continues, the course of hostility is progressively accelerated" (p. 495).

The later patient group to a certain extent, but particularly both groups of normal, display a sequential pattern with a corrective mechanism that seems to return a potentially progressive hostile interchange back to a more friendly level. Raush suggests that because the normal boys are able to anticipate the increasing hostility in their interactions, they can correct this trend; hyperaggressive boys, by contrast seem trapped by a sequence that once initiated runs its disasterous course.

From the interactionist perspective, Raush's results suggest that social interaction is extremely complex, being controlled and organized as a multiple function of person-factors, general situational factors, antecedent behaviors within the situation, and indeed as the preceding suggests, the temporal sequencing of the ongoing flow of interaction itself. Research of this sort leaves little doubt about the necessity of an interactionist perspective; each main effect, whether it focuses on factors within the person or on factors within situations, does not adequately capture the determinants of the observed behavior.

There are two additional aspects of the interactionist perspective that Raush's findings illuminate. The first involves the interdependence of person and situation as determinants of behavior. The findings show:

1. how the state of the person affects his or her perception of the situation (e.g., the hyperaggressives do not differentiate friendly from unfriendly acts whereas the normal groups do);
2. how the general structure of the situation affects the person (e.g., more unfriendly acts occur in games than at mealtimes); and
3. how events arising within the specific P–O encounter, as P and O mutually adjust their behavior to the behavior of the other, affect the course of their social interaction.

Thereby social interaction is a resultant of the total field created by person and situation.

In the second place, Raush's data point out the problems involved in a traditional kind of causal analysis that sees A to be the cause and B to be the effect. What is the cause and what is the effect in an ongoing sequence of social interaction? With other factors controlled, if we find that P's behavior is in response to O's preceding act and that O's act in turn has been in response to P's preceding act, then do we call O's act the cause of P's behavior, the effect of P's behavior, or what? And isn't it reasonable even to consider P's behavior to be the cause of P's behavior? That is, P acts in such a way as to create the stimulus situation to which P then responds. A certain simplistic neatness is lost; as the concept of interdependence suggests, any behavior may be both cause and effect.

We examine this perspective on cause and effect in more detail in Chapter 2; it is an important part of the interactionist view.

Attitudes and Behavior: An Interactionist Lesson in Multiple Determination

In our earlier discussion of the person-centered perspective, we noted its general failure to predict actual behavior. An interactionist perspective would argue that the relationship between attitudes and behavior cannot properly be understood unless the joint effects of attitudes and situational factors are considered. Behavior is a joint function of several factors, one of which may well be P's attitudes. As an illustration, a study sought to uncover the complex of person- and situation-factors that accounted for the use of marijuana (Jessor, Jessor, & Finney, 1973). Relatively large samples of high school and college students were surveyed. Data indicated that person-factors accounted for some 21 percent of marijuana-use behavior: users were higher than nonusers on such attitudinal items as valuing achievement and independence; users were also more alienated, expressed greater criticism of American society, were more tolerant of deviation, and were less religious than nonusers. Situational factors accounted for 46 percent of marijuana-use behavior: users were more oriented towards peers than parents; more users friends used drugs; users were under greater peer pressure to use drugs than were nonusers. As the authors note, use of marijuana is a joint outcome of person-centered factors (i.e., personality and attitudinal factors) and environmental supports and opportunities. If one were to obtain a measure of attitudes alone and then relate this to marijuana use, the correspondence would be low until the environmental factors were introduced. But likewise, environmental opportunities without disposing attitudes cannot account for the behavior.

One of the major techniques employed by Jessor and his associates, *multiple-regression analysis,* permits the investigator to statistically separate the weighting of each of the multiple determinants of the behavior under study. Its use in attitude-behavior research permits the investigator to do statistically what might not be feasible to do experimentally. We will briefly examine both multiple-regression and experimental approaches that shed further light upon the interactionist view of the relationship between attitudes and behavior.

A MULTIPLE-REGRESSION APPROACH

Ajzen and Fishbein (1973) employed multiple-regression techniques in their efforts to relate attitudes with behavior. They present the theoretical position that behavior is a function of a personal-attitudinal factor and a social-normative factor. This latter factor involves the belief that group members who are important to a person expect the person to behave in a particular manner in a given situation. In other words, behavior is seen to be a joint function of attitude towards a specific act in a specific situation and beliefs about what one's group members consider appropriate and expected (i.e., normative) behavior in that situation. Ajzen and Fishbein maintain that the weighting of these two terms vary by person and by situation. For some behaviors, normative influences will be more important than attitudinal ones; likewise, for some persons normative factors may be more influential determinants of their behavior than their attitudes, and vice versa. For example, a fair-weather liberal is one who holds liberal political attitudes but who will act on these only in normatively supportive settings (Yinger, 1965). The normative factor—this liberal's desire to be accepted by his or her group—is a more important determinant of behavior than are the liberal attitudes. The all-weather liberal's behavior, by contrast, is guided more by attitudes than by normative considerations.

In their research program, Fishbein and his associates measure the attitudinal factor usually by having subjects make ratings of the specific behavior in question (e.g., sexual intercourse) on several evaluative scales (e.g., good versus bad). The normative factor is assessed by having subjects answer questions regarding their perception of other's expectations for their behavior. Note that similar to Endler and Hunt's approach (p. 34), this is a self-report measure of a situational effect. In summary Ajzen and Fishbein report an average multiple correlation between these two factors and intended behavior of .808. This very high correlation indicates that predictions about P's behavioral intentions (and thus presumably about P's actual behavior as well) are relatively accurate given knowledge of the attitudinal and the normative determinants.

Our interest, however, is not entirely in the improved predictability that derives by considering multiple factors; we are as concerned with understanding the differential weighting of each component as a function of the persons and of the situations involved. An interesting study of this was reported in 1966 by Fishbein; the research dealt with premarital sexual behavior. Data indicated that for females the attitudinal component had a weight of .757, while the normative component was .232; for males the weighting was reversed showing an attitudinal component of –.148, while the normative component was .947.

> *Thus it appears that attitudinal considerations of the consequences of premarital sexual behavior were more important than normative considerations for female students. Normative beliefs and motivation to comply, however, were the primary determinants of behavioral intentions for males* (Ajzen & Fishbein, 1973, p. 50).

In other words, the premarital sexual practices of females were more influenced by their personal-attitudinal concerns than by their concerns with what others would think or expect of them; males, however, were more concerned with others' expectations. Thus to understand the determinants of premarital sexual behavior, we can see the need for an interactionist view: behavior is a function of both person- and situation-factors, but as importantly, those factors relate differently to the behavior in question for males and females.

Further investigations revealed how situation-factors rather than person-factors (i.e., male versus female) influenced the relative weighting of each component. Fishbein suggested that in a cooperative setting, normative considerations should be relatively more important (e.g., being concerned with what one's partner expects), whereas in a competitive situation, attitudinal considerations should be relatively more important (e.g., an interest in maximizing one's own gain). Research was designed to experimentally create either a cooperative or a competitive situation; the normative and attitudinal components of P's behavior were measured in each setting. In support of the theory, Fishbein reports that under cooperative conditions, the normative component had a weight of .707 in accounting for behavioral intentions; the attitudinal component had a weight of only .229. By contrast, when the setting was competitive, the attitudinal component had a weight of .691 whereas the normative component had a weight of only .327. These data suggest how situation-factors (e.g., cooperation of competition) change the weight of the attitudinal and normative components in determining behavior. Although these data pertain to behavioral intentions rather than to observed behavior itself, there seems to be a sufficient correspondence between intentions and actual behavior to warrant our serious consideration of this approach (Ajzen & Fishbein, 1973).

Table 1.2 summarizes these findings so as to focus upon the interaction effects that are revealed:

Table 1.2. A Summary of Complex Interactions

	Situation Is		Person Is	
	Cooperative	Competitive	Male	Female
Relation between attitudes and behavior	.229	.691	–.148	.757
Relation between situational norms and behavior	.707	.327	.947	.232

Adapted from Ajzan and Fishbein (1973).

The interactionist perspective that is suggested in this approach is in many respects more complex than the initial model we employed to explain the statistical concept of interaction. In this present case behavior is not only seen to be a function of two factors, but also those two factors are differentially important in accounting for behavior as a function of still further person- and situation-factors. As we have just seen, the relation between attitude (as a person-factor) and behavior is dependent upon person-factors (e.g., sex of subject) and upon situation-factors (e.g., cooperative versus competitive situation). Similarly, the relation between the normative component (as a situation-factor) and behavior is a function of these same additional person- and situation-factors.

An Experimental Test of Multiple Determinants. The preceding approach examined the multiple determinants of the attitude-behavior relationship primarily by means of the statistical technique of multiple regression. A directly experimental approach to this issue was reported in 1969 by Warner and DeFleur. They hypothesized that two situational factors were important determinants of whether a person with a given racial attitude, either pro- or antiblack, would behaviorally express it. They referred to the first situational factor as *social constraint;* the idea is similar both to Fishbein's concept of the normative determinant of behavior and to Price and Boufford's analysis that we previously considered. Basically, constraint is high if behavioral expressions are open to scrutiny by group members who are important to the person; if these group members do not know what P's behavior is, low constraint operates. For example, if P is a member of a fraternity that preaches strong antiblack attitudes, he is under high social constraint to express a negative attitude (or not to express a positive one) whenever members of his fraternity are around to see him or to learn about what he's done; however, if they will never know, constraints are lower.

The second situational factor Warner and DeFleur identified is referred to as *social distance.* They suggested that specific behaviors may serve either to reduce or to maintain P's existing social distance from another person. For example, some behaviors would place P into a context with blacks in which the social distance between them is minimal (e.g., home to dinner, out dancing). Other behaviors retain whatever social distance presently exists.

The interactionist thesis proposes that these two situational factors interact with P's attitudes to determine P's behavior. Thus knowledge of P's attitude alone (i.e., a person-centered analysis) is not sufficient to make behavioral predictions; however, knowledge of these situational factors alone (i.e., a situation-centered analysis) likewise is not sufficient for making behavioral predictions: rather, behavior is a result of their joint functioning.

In experimentally examining this interactionist thesis, Warner and DeFleur asked their subjects to sign and mail in a pledge in response to a letter sent out by the experimenter who represented himself as being from a campus organization. The pledge was to involve P in one of a variety of actions with a black, ranging from having a date to making a contribution to an educational charity. It was assumed that signing the pledge and mailing it back was a behavioral commitment. The pledge form indicated either that participants would engage in the action outlined or that they disapproved of it entirely. All subjects had previously been measured for their general attitudes towards blacks.

Social constraint was experimentally manipulated by indicating to subjects either that their action would be anonymous (low constraint) or would be disclosed to the rest of the campus (high constraint). In the particular college setting of their research, the authors suggest that general attitudes were hostile towards integration; thus publicity about integrating behaviors would indeed define a condition of high constraint.

It will be helpful in understanding the results of this investigation to organize and discuss each one separately:

1. Regardless of P's pro- or antiblack attitude, social constraints reduced P's willingness to sign the pledge. Thus, when behavior was to be open to public scrutiny in a setting where that scrutiny would reveal a behavior in conflict with the general norms, most persons' behavior was inhibited.

2. Under low constraint, persons were more willing to act in accord with their attitudes; the low-prejudiced subjects were more willing to sign a pledge and the high-prejudiced were less willing. Under these situational circumstances, behavior was predictable from knowledge of general attitudes.

3. High constraint was more inhibiting to less prejudiced persons than to the highly prejudiced. Recall that the behaviors requested deviate from college norms; thus when these actions are made public the group most likely to engage in them by virtue of their pro-

black attitudes were the most constrained by publicity not to do so. Those who were attitudinally disposed not to engage in these behaviors did not mind publicity about their refusal.

4. Under low constraint, both the more and the less prejudiced felt freer to engage in problack actions. In another context, the social psychologist, Pettigrew (1961), introduced the concept of *latent liberal* to describe the person who is constrained by social norms from engaging in integrating behaviors. A change in those norms—or in the Warner and DeFleur case, a minimization of the publicity surrounding the behaviors—facilitates the latent liberalism's being behaviorally expressed. The point is an important one in that it suggests that some prejudiced attitudes were expressions of prevailing campus views. Thus some of the prejudiced persons are like the latent liberal who is ready to act inconsistently with a publically stated attitude provided that the resulting publicity is minimal so that no group member important to the person will be aware of a norm-deviating behavior.

5. Regardless of P's initial pro- or antiblack attitudes, behaviors that reduce social distance tended to inhibit all subjects. Less prejudiced persons were willing to sign the pledge to engage in behaviors that maintained social distance; more prejudiced persons refused to sign pledges for any activities, whether they implied reducing or maintaining social distance. A more recent study (Green, 1972) reports a similar main effect; his subjects, regardless of their pro- or antiblack attitude were less willing to be photographed with a black person as the degree of intimacy increased from minimal (e.g., photographed together in a public setting) to high (e.g., a close heterosexual relationship).

6. The most refined data analysis examined the interaction of all three factors—attitude, constraint, and distance—on behavior. This analysis suggested the following:
a. Unprejudiced persons under high constraint were willing to engage in behaviors that maintained social distance. Under these specific conditions, therefore, there was a correspondence between their general attitudes and their behavior. Note that in this setting, this means that these persons were willing to engage in distance-maintaining, approved behaviors when others would see what they had done.
b. The prejudiced persons were most eager to show their refusal to engage in distance-reducing behaviors under conditions of high constraint. They were willing for others to note that they were not going to engage in more integrative actions; thus, under these specific conditions, there was a consistency between their attitudes and their behavior.

Warner and DeFleur's work adds further to the interactionist perspective in suggesting how attitudes combine with situational factors to determine behavior. Person-centered, attitudinal dispositions are clearly important determinants of behavior; we have seen this affirmed in Fishbein's work and in the Warner and DeFleur work; it has been affirmed as well in the work of others (e.g., DeFleur and Westie, 1958; Green, 1972). But, we have also seen the need to consider the interactions with situational factors as well.

Interactionism: Fields and Systems

There are certain compelling parallels between the interactionist perspective we have presented as most fitting to social psychological inquiry and several other efforts to go beyond a separatist emphasis.

FIELD THEORY

Kurt Lewin's famous formulation of the determinants of behavior employs the same two elements that we have been considering: B = f (P,E), behavior is a function of person and environment (Lewin, 1951). It was Lewin's contention that the result of the encounter between person and environment was an interactive field (variously termed the total situation or field, the life space, the psychological environment) and that our search for the causes of behavior must be based upon an analysis of this interactive field as a whole. In his view, person and environment are interdependent parts of the total field; as he phrased it, "the state of any part of this field depends on every other part of the field" (1951, p. 25). Therefore, even as we noted in Raush's findings, the state of the environment depends upon characteristics of the person; the state of the person depends on characteristics of the environment.

Lewin's is a strong statement of the interactionist perspective; his field theoretical emphasis, searching for the causes of behavior in the field created as a resultant of the interaction between P and E, stresses the fundamental need to begin our analysis with the field as a whole rather than as is more typical, with an analysis of each part, person, or situation, separately.

> *What is important in field theory is the way the analysis proceeds. Instead of picking out one or another isolated element within a situation, the importance of which cannot be judged without consideration of the situation as a whole, field theory finds it advantageous ... to start with a characterization of the situation as a whole* (1951, p. 63).

Basically, if behavior is a resultant of the joint effects of P and E, then we will never be able to understand it adequately unless we deal with the field that is created by their interaction. To begin with the parts rather than the resultant interactive field is to go about our analysis in the wrong way. The field as a whole gives meaning to the parts of which it is composed. And because P depends upon E and E upon P, it is not reasonable to evaluate the state of any one without considering its interaction with the other. What we deal with then is the total field that results from the interaction between person-and-environmental factors; not only is this the world in which we live, but also the world that our social science must seek to understand. Lewin's approach will be examined in more detail in Chapter 2; it is a model for the interactionist perspective in social psychology.

SYSTEMS THEORY

The approach known as systems theory has many parallels with both the interactionist and the field theoretical perspectives (e.g., Bertalanffy, 1968; Kuhn, 1974; 1975; Miller, 1971). The term *system* literally means things that stand or fall together, an interdependence among elements and their unity is emphasized. Thus elements or parts related together such that one's falling, for example, affects the state of the other (Lewin's concept of interdependence) are said to form a system that is a resultant of the interaction among the parts. The interaction between person and other, for instance, is said to create a new phenomena, an interpersonal system, that functions in a manner that neither person nor other alone do. P and O jointly interact and create interpersonal conflict, for example; conflict is a property of their interpersonal system, a result of their joint interaction rather than of something that either alone possesses.

Systems theory examines all levels of phenomena, including for example, the cellular, the intrapersonal, the interpersonal, the organizational, and the societal. The systems view seeks to develop concepts and principles that apply to understanding phenomena at all of these levels, arguing that similar processes are involved. We do not seek here to develop a full systems analysis for social psychology; rather, as we noted and as we shall see in Chapter 2 and elsewhere, our interactionist emphasis shares much with the systems view in general.

Conclusion

Both in its history and in its contemporary versions, social psychology can be characterized in terms of three major perspectives or points of view: situationist, person-centered, or interactionist. In social psychology, all three examine the relationship between person and situation, where *situation* usually refers to other people both individually and collectively. The approaches differ in their emphasis: the situationist attributes the primary determinants of the behavioral events being studied to the eliciting and maintaining conditions of the situation; the person-centered view stresses the underlying dispositions of the person. The interactionist perspective argues that neither element alone, neither person nor situation, are adequate for explaining behavior; rather, behavioral events are jointly determined as a result of the interaction between person-factors and situation-factors.

Our own emphasis is interactionist. Strictly speaking, that means that we should always seek our understanding in the total field or system that results from person-situation interactions. Yet, in order to provide coverage of several important areas of concern to contemporary social psychology and to dig more deeply into relevant phenomena at the level of person or situation, we will at times abandon this emphasis; at those times, we will look at person or situation rather than their joint effects. We shall endeavor, however, to point out the role that the "missing person" surely must play when our particular focus at the moment seems to be overly situational or that the "missing situation" must play if for the moment we appear to have overemphasized the person.

In giving primacy to an interactionist perspective, we do not deny an important role to the person, the person's personality, learning history, needs, motives, particular style, or whatever. Neither do we deny an important role to the situation, including culturally-shared definitions of situations, roles, rules and norms regarding proper behavior in given settings, the behavior of other persons, or whatever. Nor does our perspective proclaim that all phenomena are determined in equal measure by person and situation. We fully recognize that person-factors may be more weighty in some situations for some behaviors for some persons and that situation-factors may be more weighty in some persons for some behaviors in some situations.

So what then is social psychology all about? As Gordon Allport noted some years ago (1954), it is *"an attempt to understand and explain how the thought, feeling, and behavior of individuals are influenced by the actual, imagined, or implied presence of other human beings"* (p. 5). Ideally, its perspective is interactionist, seeking that understanding of which Allport speaks in the total field that is generated from the interaction between person and situation, where situation typically but not exclusively includes Allport's "other human beings" and their social and cultural products. But as we have noted, this ideal is not always achieved.

We now approach Chapter 2 with this general context within which to better understand the several illustrative examples of the interactionist perspective in social psychology and the key concept of interdependence.

"THE CHAIN," MURAL DETAIL BY EDWARD BIBERMAN.

INTERDEPENDENCE AND THE COLLECTIVE REALITY

2

THE INTERRUPTED AND THE RECALLED

The early 1920s, Germany, a small cafe across the street from the Psychological Institute of the University of Berlin, where Kurt Lewin and his students would gather over coffee to discuss various psychological issues. A lunchtime observation leads to experimentation and the formulation of a psychological principle. Lewin's waiter apparently had an excellent memory, recalling in detail everyone's order. Lewin noted, however, that as soon as the bill had been paid, the waiter, when informally questioned, simply could not recall anything about the orders of just moments earlier (see Atkinson, 1964). For most of us this observation might pass by unnoticed or perhaps as something insignificant; for Lewin and his students, however, this formed the basis for a classic series of studies initially conducted by Bluma Zeigarnik (Lewin, 1951).

The observation involved the waiter's perfect memory before the bill had been paid and his apparent loss of memory immediately thereafter. What did the payment have to do with this loss of recall? Lewin reasoned that the waiter's intention to serve everyone and collect payment created a tension that was reduced only when the goal (i.e., serving and getting paid) had been accomplished. Much later, other researchers (e.g., Mandler, 1964; Mandler & Watson, 1966; Sher, 1971) demonstrated how the blockage or interruption of goal-directed activities results in tension that is measurable physiologically: for example, by changes in the dilation of the pupil or by changes in the skin's electrical conductance, somewhat as in lie detection work. To return to Lewin, he further argued that any intention to perform an activity set up a tension that persisted until that activity was completed and a state of equilibrium was restored. This view is similar to Freud's conception in which wishes create tension that persists until the wish is satisfied, either in reality or in fantasy. It is also similar to the idea that physical needs (e.g., hunger or thirst) create a tension that persists until the need is satisfied. In Lewin's view, the intention to do something was like a need (he termed such intentions, *quasi needs*) that disrupted the person's equilibrium until satisfied.

The Zeigarnik Effect. In her series of experiments, Zeigarnik presented subjects with several tasks, informally interrupting their completion of some tasks while permitting them to complete others. She reasoned that if tension persists until the activity that initiated it is accomplished, subjects should reveal a persisting tension for the incompleted activities but they should experience no tension over those tasks that had been completed. Zeigarnik further reasoned, using the waiter's memory as a clue, that one index of a persisting tension is a heightened ability to recall incompleted as compared with completed tasks. Zeigarnik formed a quotient to reflect this:

$$\text{Zeigarnik Quotient} = \frac{\text{Recall Incompleted}}{\text{Recall Completed}}$$

The prediction was that this quotient should be greater than 1.00; what Zeigarnik actually found was a ratio of approximately 1.9, thus substantiating her prediction that more incompleted than completed tasks were recalled.

Another of Lewin's students, Ovsiankina (see Lewin, 1951), reasoned further that a sign of the persistence of tension will be the subject's tendency to spontaneously return to complete the incompleted tasks if given a chance to do so. To test this, Ovsiankina permitted her subjects an opportunity to return to any activity they wished while she ostensibly was preparing a second set of materials for additional experimentation; not surprisingly, all subjects chose to complete the still uncompleted activities.

Additional questions were asked by these and other investigators. If a tension is initiated because one particular task has been interrupted, is it possible to reduce this tension by the completion of a different task, one that has *substitute value?* With a physiological need such as hunger, a hamburger or a hot dog might successfully reduce the tension; thus we could say that hot dogs and hamburgers have substitute value. A group of Lewinian students undertook a research program to discover the substitute value of various activities. Their research suggested that it was possible to rate this substitute value by noting the degree to which the completion of one activity reduced the person's tension that had been aroused by the noncompletion of a different activity; with such substitution, persons tended not to recall the uncompleted original activity. (Deutsch, 1968 provides a good summary of some of this research).

INTERDEPENDENCE

When we speak of a field, we are referring to a whole with parts that are interdependent such that a change in one part has consequences for other parts of the whole. One important idea to understand from these studies of psychological substitute value is that tension can be viewed as a property of a system or field as a whole, in this case an *intra*personal field—that is, within the person. In this case, a tension that arises because one activity is not completed can be reduced by the completion of another, interconnected and thus interdependent activity. That two activities have substitute value for one another tells us that they form part of an interdependent system or field. In our earlier discussion in Chapter 1, the parts of the total field we emphasized were person and situation; in the present case, we are referring to parts within the person. The overall interactionist view remains similar however, whether we are speaking of *intra* personal relations (e.g., between two activities of the person) or *in-ter*personal relations (e.g., between P and O).

Interdependence informs us that the parts of a total field are so related that the state of one affects the other; each one has consequences for the others. Interdependence is a major concept that captures the essence of the social psychological, interactionist perspective; it demands that we seek our understanding of behavior within a total field composed of interdependent parts rather than within any one part independent of the rest. This means that as social psychologists interested in person-situation interactions, we do not conceive of P as being isolated from the context within which P lives and within which P forms one part of a system of interdependencies.

This is an important point to keep in mind now that we ask a more complex question involving tension and substitute value at the level of interpersonal relations: can P's own tension be reduced by O's activities? In essence, we are asking whether O can be so related to P that O's activities have substitute value for P's own behavioral intentions. If the answer to this question is yes—that is, if O's completion of P's interrupted activities can substitute for P's own completion, and thereby reduce P's tension and P's recall of such activities—then we have revealed that O and P are parts of an interdependent system or field. Furthermore, in such circumstances, the tension we have been discussing would be a property of that interdependent field in which O's acts have consequences for P and vice versa—that is, P and O jointly affect the state of tension initiated by P's failure to complete activities that P intended to complete.

The ostensibly simple cafe observation and program of experimental research on the Zeigarnik effect took a distinctly social psychological turn as it moved away from a consideration of intrapersonal fields to interpersonal fields involving the interdependencies between P and O.

COOPERATION AND COMPETITION

The Zeigarnik format provides a valuable test of human interdependence and thus offers us a model for the interactionist perspective in social psychology. Let us suppose that we bring together pairs of individuals to work cooperatively on several tasks. Let us suppose further that my interrupted task is completed by my cooperating partner. Does my partner's completion of my incompleted task serve to reduce my tension and thereby result in my tendency, like the waiter's or Zeigarnik's original subjects, not to recall partner-completed tasks? Research evidence suggests that insofar as pairs of subjects are working together in a cooperative relationship, O's completion satisfies P's needs; however, when the pairs are not cooperatively connected, O's completion does not reduce P's tension (e.g., Lewis, 1944; Lewis & Franklin, 1944).

Morton Deutsch (1953; 1962), reflecting on the meaning of this work, argued that persons can be interdependent in two distinct ways. Under conditions of cooperation, or what he termed *promotive interdependence,* P's achievement of some goal has the meaning of simultaneously achieving that goal for all P's cooperating partners. In other words, P's activities have complete substitute value for O's: my success means your success; my failure means your failure. Thus, when partners cooperate, P's tension can be satisfied by O's task completion. Under conditions of competition, or *contrient interdependence,* one person's attainment of a goal means others cannot attain it. If P wins, O loses or vice versa. With contrient interdependence, P's activities cannot substitute for O's; P's task completion does not reduce O's tension. Deutsch recognized that these were two extremes of interdependence and that one could also speak of degrees of promotive or contrient interdependence.

To systematically study the effects of cooperation and competition, Deutsch created an experimental situation as part of a regular university course in industrial relations. Cooperation was induced by grading the group as a whole as to its effectiveness in handling several discussion problems; thus if a group received a high grade, all of its members would likewise receive the same high grade. Therefore, if one person made a significant contribution to the groups' high grade, all persons would benefit; one person's contribution was a substitute for another's goal attainment. The competitive groups, by contrast, were graded on an individual basis, such that each individual's contribution to the group's problem-solving effectiveness was ranked separately; thus one person's goal attainment could not substitute for another's, yet persons were still interdependent: if P scored highest, O could not. Deutsch's results are many and varied; we will consider them in some detail in a later context. For our present purposes, we note that his data generally support the thesis of interpersonal substitute value: P's actions did serve as a substitute for O's in the cooperative group, and thus persons could subdivide the task and trust one another to work together towards their common goal. The competitive form of interdependence did not allow one person's achievement to substitute for another's; thus there was less division of labor on the task and less harmony in the group.

In another group context, Horwitz (1954) used the original Zeigarnik quotient to further clarify and support the notion that cooperatively interdependent persons are so related that one person's goal attainment can satisfy another's tension. Horwitz formed teams that were asked to vote on whether or not they wanted to complete certain tasks. He found that if a group voted not to complete the task, then in general, individual members of that group were unlikely to recall these interrupted tasks. Even though we would expect tension to exist for interrupted tasks, and thus there should be greater recall for such tasks, when a person is a member of a group that decides not to complete those tasks, the person's own tension system is thereby satisfied: thus there is no recall of such uncompleted tasks. This work further demonstrates the nature and strength of interdependence in human relationships. Here, as before, an individual's own tension is satisfied by an agreement achieved among cooperating group members.

ON FORMING A UNIT RELATIONSHIP

A slightly different phrasing of the question refocuses our attention on another aspect of human interdependence. Our initial inquiry examined what happens to tension when P and O are interdependent. Another way of looking at this matter is to ask about the conditions that create a unit relationship between two individuals such that if P fails to reach P's goal, O's tension will be aroused thus leading O to help P reach the goal. Suppose, for example, that you find an envelope containing a contribution to a charity lying open on a street. The person who lost the envelope had the task of mailing it interrupted. But will you complete the job? In a series of fascinating, realistic studies, Hornstein and several of his colleagues (see Hornstein, 1972) suggested a tentative answer of yes, but only to the extent that P's and O's relationship had a quality best captured by the German term *Zusammengehorlichskeitgefühl* (a feeling of belonging together). For example, if the envelope with the contribution were dropped in a predominantly Jewish neighborhood in New York and if in addition to the contribution it contained the answer to a public opinion survey indicating a pro-Israeli stance on the Arab-Israeli situation, thereby establishing this *zusammen*-feeling or unit relationship, persons are likely to complete the other person's task by mailing the envelope. In general, we are more likely to complete another's interrupted activity if we like them or feel some togetherness or kinship with them, than if either we dislike them or if those *zusammen*-feelings are not aroused. We return to this theme of interdependence and helping again in Chapter 9.

We have come a long way from a Berlin cafe in the 1920s to the streets of New York in the 1970s. But the trip has focused our attention upon the concept of interdependence, wherein one person's motives, needs, and tensions are so related to another's that their actions have consequences for his and vice versa. This interactionist conception tells us that our understanding of human behavior cannot be satisfied with explanations that dwell entirely within the person; the essence of interdependence is that behavior is a result of many forces jointly operating, that we must seek our explanations in the field that involves P and E, person and situation including O.

Recall Lewin's statement from Chapter 1—B = f (P,E)—behavior is a function of the person and the environment. In this formulation, P and E form a system of relationships that has its own properties. The field that contains P and E has qualities, properties, or characteristics that emerge as a joint function of P and E; these are system or field properties, qualities of a collective reality, requiring both P and E for their presence. When O's behavior can substitute for P's, for example, then, as we have noted, even P's recall is a function of O's behavior. While it is indeed true that the individual person does the recalling, we have seen how when P and O are linked together into an interdependent field, P's recall is not a simple individual function; rather it is a joint function of P and of O. This is the essence of the interactionist perspective of social psychology introduced in Chapter 1; to understand behavioral events we must begin our analysis with the total field and its collective properties.

We have spent considerable time upon this point; its seeming simplicity conceals its major importance. Recall that an implication of a person-centered analysis is that explanations for behavior are located in the person; the situation-centered view locates explanations in the environment. The interactionist perspective (e.g., Lewin's field theory) locates its explanations in the interactive field jointly determined by P and O. While most of us recognize that individuals do have properties and characteristics and that even environments have properties, most of us are less readily able to recognize that interactive fields or systems also have properties and characteristics, a collective reality that cannot simply be located in the separate parts. Our examples from Lewin's initial work in Berlin up to the subsequent work of others in New York has focused upon recall and helping as collective outcomes; in other words, as events that are characteristics established by P and O jointly rather than by P or by O separately.

We introduced the interactionist perspective in order to avoid the error of overindividualizing our analyses of behavior by assuming that because only persons think, feel, and act, then surely they must be the sole explanatory source of all our behavioral understanding: if this were the case, all explanation would be attributed solely to the individual. As we embark on our examination of the collective reality created jointly by P and E, we must not err in the other extreme by speaking about a collective reality without specifying the network of interaction and mutual adjustment among the parties that are involved. This latter error is most apparent when we look at such collective realities as groups and social organizations forgetting that they are composed of persons and their intricate weave of relationships and joint activities (Allport, 1962; Blumer, 1966; Becker, 1974). As we progress through the remainder of this chapter, we will continue with this theme, presenting other examples and related analyses.

FROM SCHISMOGENESIS IN NEW GUINEA TO FAMILIES IN THE UNITED STATES

We journey this time to New Guinea in the mid-1930s where we join Gregory Bateson and the Iatmul tribe with its unique, fascinating, and instructive *naven* ceremony (Bateson, 1936). Bateson observed a frequent, recurring ritual among the Iatmul, termed the *naven,* that involved what seemed to be some peculiar interaction among the males of the tribe. *Naven* was usually celebrated whenever a young boy, the *laua,* achieved something for the first time (e.g., his first kill) and became boastful about this feat. At such moments, an older male relative, the *wau,* performed the *naven.*

The main characteristic of *naven* behavior was its transvestism and seemingly sex-inappropriate activities. When performing *naven,* the *wau* would typically put on very tattered and filthy women's clothing; often he would speak in a high-pitched cracking voice, mimicking the women of the village; at times, he would bind his belly with string as the pregnant women did; he was even called "mother" by others. In extreme form, the *wau* would turn his buttocks towards the *laua* and rub it fully along the *laua*'s leg in a gesture of sexual submission. Whenever the *wau* engaged the *laua* in *naven* behavior, the *laua* was expected to reciprocate with some offering, such as shells.

Bateson was aware that the Iatmul were a highly sex-typed society; he noted how important it was for males to be strong, assertive,
and at all costs to avoid any kind of female behavior, such as submissiveness. Against this background it was all the more strange, then,
to see the older male perform *naven* with its exaggeration of the
female. In his efforts to explain *naven* behavior, Bateson formulated several major concepts that he and others were later to apply
to family and group interaction in Western societies. These efforts
will be valuable for us to consider.

Bateson suggested that the ongoing pattern of interaction characteristic of *naven* behavior both expressed the Iatmul's concern with
male-female distinctiveness and of equal importance, was a major
factor in maintaining this sex-typing. The focus upon ongoing interaction between P and O as the location for explaining behavior
provides a major breakthrough for social psychological understanding. One way we typically attempt to understand behavior, is
to seek the purpose or end-state that the behavior presumably
serves. The purpose is then invoked to explain the behaviors that
precede it: e.g., the Iatmul do *naven* in order to achieve social harmony. In these terms, the purpose is the cause of the behavior that
we take to be the effect.

In another typical approach to behavioral analysis, we explain
behavior in terms of some prior historical conditions that presumably gave rise to it and of which it is an expression. We may turn to
historical circumstances in the life of the persons involved, locating
the cause of P's behavior in P's personal life history (e.g., some
problem in early childhood); or we may search in the history of the
established structure of the society, locating the cause of *naven*
behavior, for example, in the customs of the Iatmul culture. Thus
we see the participants simply to be playing out their role in a
personal or a societal drama; they are the medium through which
these personal or social forces are brought to their expression. While
this form of explanation might adequately explain a small class of
highly ritualized behaviors in which the presence of others makes
little difference (e.g., social roles that are followed precisely according to script and the other's behavior is ignored totally), it is not
sufficient to deal with the complex give-and-take of ongoing interaction. Whether we seek "purposes" or "history," we fail to focus our
attention on the actual behaviors of the persons who are present and
interacting, adjusting their behavior to the behavior of others (see
Allport, 1962; Blumer, 1966; or Jones & Gerard, 1967 for a parallel
analysis).

Developing this last point, it is Bateson's contention that the field
created by P's and O's ongoing *naven* interaction is not to be understood by reference to the purposes it serves or to historical condi-

tions underlying it, but rather requires an analysis of the ongoing pattern of interaction itself. The ongoing manner by which the *wau* and *laua* interact in the *naven* is the important event to examine if we wish to understand how the Iatmul's male-female distinctiveness is maintained through *naven* behavior.

SCHISMOGENESIS

On the basis of his observations, Bateson conducted a detailed analysis of *naven* interaction; the analysis suggested the operation of two opposing processes. One process, termed *complementary schismogenesis,* produces an increasing distinctiveness between the persons involved in an interaction. For example, when the *laua* is boastful and assertive, the *wau* responds by behaving submissively. If this sequence of interaction were to continue unchecked, then each time one was assertive, the other would react with the complementary behavior, submissiveness. In general terms, P's behavior triggers the complementary behavior from O, which in turn triggers more of its complement from P and so forth.

The second process, termed *symmetrical schismogenesis,* over a period of time leads to a pattern of increasing similarity in the behaviors of the persons involved in an interaction. For example, if P's assertiveness induces greater assertiveness in O, which in turn leads to a symmetrical behavior from P (i.e., more assertiveness), and so on, a competitive symmetrical spiral is established.

Dynamic Equilibrium. In examining these two processes, Bateson was confronted with the realization that either pattern alone, if unchecked, would result in a breakdown of the interaction between P and O. This led Bateson to assume that as either process moved towards an extreme, this served to trigger the opposing process; thereby the ongoing interaction between P and O was maintained in a state of equilibrium. The equilibrium was *dynamic* in that the stable state was preserved as a result of these ongoing but opposing processes. Thus, excessive symmetry triggered complementarity; excessive complementarity triggered symmetry. Extending this model, it seemed to Bateson that any enduring relationship must depend on similar dynamic processes.

Recall that Bateson's analysis of the ongoing patterns of interaction was undertaken in order to explain *naven* behavior in terms of the adjustments made between P and O as they interacted. He sought to understand the apparent stability of the *naven* behavior among the Iatmul in terms of these opposing processes *within* the field of interaction itself rather than by referring to historical, social, or personal factors which are somehow "imported" into and given expression through the interaction. In Bateson's view, stability is an outcome of processes that are here-and-now present.

Applying the concept of dynamic equilibrium to *naven* behavior suggests how a threat of excessive symmetry is checked by the introduction of a caricature of complementarity. In the presence of *laua's* excessive boasting, *wau* becomes a submissive female. This complementary behavior of submission in response to assertiveness serves to control the symmetrical rivalry that might otherwise occur if *wau* met boasting with his own masculine assertiveness.

NAVEN AND SOCIAL PSYCHOLOGY

Bateson's creative analysis of the Iatmul's *naven* behavior has several important implications for us to consider:

1. Parallel to Lewin's analysis, Bateson suggests the importance of analyzing the reciprocal adjustments involved in an ongoing, contemporaneous social situation. While this does not deny the need to examine historical or developmental factors, the clear emphasis is upon those factors that are here-and-now present. The question always to be asked, then, is how are the apparent constancies in the behavior patterns involving P and O maintained: our answers will be found by an analysis of their ongoing interaction.

2. Bateson's approach, again similar in many respects to Lewin's argues that to understand any given social phenomenon (e.g., the *wau's* transvestism) we must attend to the total behavioral field within which it occurs; we must adopt an interactionist perspective. In the case of the Iatmul's *naven* behavior, this means understanding the *wau's* seemingly bizarre behavior by examining the reciprocal activities of the *laua* and thus the interdependent field within which both occur. *Naven* behavior defines an interactive field, the parts being the actions of *wau* and *laua* that mesh together interdependently such that a change in *wau's* behavior triggers a corresponding change in *laua*, and so forth. More broadly speaking, any collective reality (e.g., a group or family) is considered to be a dynamic field in which the parts are the behaviors of the individual members so related to one another that the group or collective functions as a whole in the midst of variations in individual behavior. As we shall see, this kind of formulation has laid the groundwork for conjoint family therapy, in which the "illness" of a family member is understood to be a collective outcome, a result of the family's patterns of interaction rather than simply of something located within the individual.

3. The concept of a dynamic equilibrium informs us that a state of stability of a collective field (e.g., *wau-laua naven* behavior) is best understood as a resultant of opposing patterns, for example, complementary and symmetrical interaction; thus, even the status quo must be maintained as an ongoing accomplishment of interpersonal work. What this fundamentally means is that collective fields (e.g., social systems, small groups, families) are not static and unchanging, but in a constant state of flux; the apparent equilibrium and stability we may observe is an achievement that is dynamic, not static. Lewin made much this same point in noting how a particular social practice could best be conceptualized as a *quasi-stationary equilibrium*—that is, the outcome of opposing tendencies. The implication that Lewin drew from this, much like Bateson, is that a change in such a dynamic field can be achieved only by upsetting the balance, which Lewin termed *unfreezing.* We will have more to say about this in Chapter 7.

4. The maintenance of stability is understood by the concept of *feedback.* Bateson used this concept to account for the manner by which one interactive process provides the information that triggers the other process that in turn acts to control the operation of the former process, and so forth. A feedback network exists, for example, when A leads to B which in turn leads back to A. In this case, B, triggered by A, feeds back to modify the state of A, thereby maintaining the system in a state of dynamic equilibrium. Although the metaphor is by no means a perfect one, the manner by which a governor controls the speed of an engine offers a mechanical example of this self-corrective feedback. In this mechanism, the faster the piston moves around, the faster the governor is set into motion; its increment in motion, in turn, leads to a separation of its weighted extension arms; this separation, as it increases, reduces the power supply, which in turn reduces the speed with which the piston moves; this in turn decreases the separation of the governor's extension arms, increasing the power supply, increasing the speed of the piston, and around again. The mechanism corrects itself through such feedback (called negative feedback), and thereby remains around a steady state of dynamic equilibrium.

In the illustrative example, a *mechanical* structure exists and serves to keep the system functioning in a steady state. In social interaction however, we do not deal with mechanical structures, but rather collective structures that emerge as P and O adjust their own behavior in light of the action of the other. These collective structures can have as rigid and unvarying a stability as that involved in more mechanical linkages. As long as a cycle of interaction is initiated, for example, by *laua's* boasting, the response of *wau* and the subsequent chain of responses that each one emits, constitutes a structure or organization to their interaction that persists, in this case until the ritual is completed when *laua* gives a gift to *wau*.

In family interaction patterns, a high degree of structural stability can likewise be generated: for example, a given act of the husband is all that is needed to initiate an entire cycle of actions and reactions. Likewise, as we extend our analysis from P and O through the family into still larger collectivities within the society, stable patterns arise as persons fit their behaviors together into structures. Although these human structures are not as guaranteed as more mechanical ones to follow their course once initiated, there are sufficient redundant supports for their persistence to provide substantial security in our everyday lives. We do not have a mechanical guaranty that our behavior of asking a question of someone will be met with the response of their giving an answer, but probabilities for this cycle's being completed remain sufficiently high to suggest that a comfortable stable state will be achieved.

6. The concept of feedback leads to a further important point revealed both by Bateson's original works and the substantial amount of later analyses of family and group interaction. This involves the conception of *causality.* In a typical linear model of analysis, cause precedes effect and thereby we may readily indicate what is the cause and what is the effect. However, in an interactive field involving feedback, as with *naven* behavior and several examples discussed in Chapter 1 (e.g., from Raush), we have a situation of *circular causality.* When we ask what causes what, we are made aware of the degree to which the parts of the whole field are interdependent such that each is the cause of the state of the other. Thus, in a case of complementary schismogenesis, for example, P's assertiveness is both the cause and the effect of O's submissiveness; O's submissiveness, in turn, is both the cause of P's assertiveness and a response (effect) to P's assertiveness. In other words, P and O are linked in such a way that the behavior of each is both cause and effect. Rather than inquiring what causes what, it is more productive to seek an understanding of the patterned field that P and O have jointly created. Any change must take into consideration the circularity of cause and effect; to ignore this relation by attempting to change only one element without considering the entire field either will not be effective or will produce a variety of unintended consequences. For example, to try to change O's submissiveness by ignoring its responsivity to P's assertiveness might very well create the unintended effect of reversing their roles: O now becomes more assertive as P becomes more passive and submissive. The equilibrium of their interactive field remains intact, we have only managed to change the particular person that enacts a given role.

Or, to take another possibility, as O becomes more assertive, P becomes even more assertive (i.e., symmetry) and thus rather than staying in the relationship by changing roles, the relationship may break apart.

By now it should be clear that the interactionist perspective demands a widening of our typically individualistic point of view regarding human behavior. Reik (1948) argued that the therapist, in order to hear what the client is really saying and feeling must listen with a "third ear"; I think the same could be said of the requirements of the social psychologist who must come to see social events with a "third eye." This requires seeing the individual in perspective with the full network of relationships that form the total field in which that individual is a part.

HUSBAND, WIFE, AND HELL

Bateson's work with the Iatmul and the perspective he provided on ongoing patterns of interaction proves to be a useful tool for those involved in understanding healthful and pathological interaction patterns among families. Take the following examples as cases in point.

A husband and wife have established a definite pattern to their interaction, one that is complementary. The husband's behavior involves passive withdrawal, the wife's is more aggressive. To the observer, this husband-wife pair have established an equilibrium in their behavior together: every withdrawal from the husband is met with aggressive nagging from the wife; every nagging from the wife brings about a withdrawal from the husband. We might say that this complementary cycle is a major theme of their entire relationship. This is not to suggest that the purposes or conscious desires of either are to have created such a stable pattern; rather, we note simply that this is a repetitive pattern that recurs with a high degree of stability. The stability of the pattern is maintained, as we observe, by a feedback loop: the husband's behavior is both cause and effect of the wife's behavior and vice versa. A feedback loop is thereby completed and the interactive field thus perpetuates itself.

Another feature of this stable interactive pattern involves each participant's different sense of cause and effect. From the husband's point of view, his behavior is a response caused by the wife's nagging: "I withdraw as a defense against her constant nagging." From the wife's point of view, her nagging is in response to his withdrawal: "Without my nagging, he'd just sit back and do nothing all the time. I have to get at him to get anything done around here." Both husband and wife view themselves as the *victim* of the other's behavior; neither sees the interactive field (i.e., cycle) that they have jointly created, to which each contributes and thereby maintains. The question of who is the cause of this collective hell misses the major feature of this pair's interaction. Our interactionist perspective, focusing on the nature of the pair's interdependence, informs us and perhaps, with treatment, them as well, of the actual quality of their relationships (see Watzlawick, Beavin, and Jackson, 1967 for additional informative examples).

Interpersonal Knots.   R. D. Laing (1970) has captured the sense of paradox and dilemma that characterizes many of our collective realities wherein Jack and Jill are parts of an interactive field they have jointly created and which their joint actions maintain in a steady state. Note that in the cases that Laing describes, this stability is more pathological than health-inducing:*

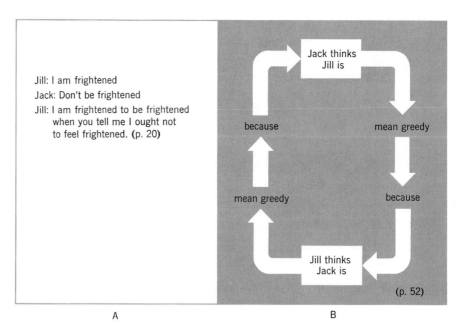

Jill: I am frightened
Jack: Don't be frightened
Jill: I am frightened to be frightened when you tell me I ought not to feel frightened. (p. 20)

Jack thinks Jill is

because   mean greedy

mean greedy   because

Jill thinks Jack is

(p. 52)

A   B

C.   Jill: I'm upset you are upset.
      Jack: I'm not upset.
      Jill: I'm upset that you're not upset that I'm upset you're upset.
      Jack: I'm upset that you're upset that I'm not upset that you're upset that I'm upset when I'm not. (p. 21)*

*From Knots, by R. D. Laing. Copyright (C) 1970 by the R. D. Laing Trust. Reprinted by permission of Pantheon Books, a Division of Random House, Inc., and Tavistock Publications, Ltd.

A WHOLE FAMILY PATTERN

Students of whole families viewed as social systems (e.g., Handel, 1965; 1972) as well as those who have sought to understand disturbed behavior as an outcome of collective systems of interaction (e.g., Sullivan, 1953), have emphasized the importance of viewing the pathology of the interaction system rather than of the sick person; and thus the importance of treating the collective system as a whole rather than the person in isolation. A helpful study of this model is provided in the research of Cohen, Freedman, Engelhardt, and Margolis (1958).

Subjects for their investigation were all psychiatric outpatients at a community clinic. Fifty-four males and seventy-two females were selected for the study. All subjects had been in treatment for three months or longer and had scored high on initial measures of aggressive behavior at home. They were randomly assigned to a drug treatment program; some received tranquilizers while others were given placebos. Measures were obtained about each person's home environment, specifically the degree of conflict and tension that was characteristic of the family living context. After a period of three months on the drug treatment program, measurements were made of each person's aggressive behavior. A change score was computed by comparing aggression before treatment with aggression after treatment; a negative number indicates a reduction in aggressiveness after treatment. Selected data are presented here:

	Tranquilizing Drug	Placebo
High-Conflict Family Setting	- 5.67	-6.50
Low-Conflict Family Setting	-15.13	-5.36

An examination of these data indicates a significant statistical interaction effect: the effectiveness of the drug varies as a function of the person's family setting. The drug is no better than a placebo when the setting is high in conflict; however, the drug is clearly beneficial for persons who live in low-conflict families. In explaining these results, the authors argue that to tranquilize someone whose family context reinforces aggressiveness is to create an added conflict within the family between its typical mode of relating to one another and the patient's drug-induced quietness. This conflict apparently provokes greater anger on the part of other family members, which in turn leads to more aggression on the part of the patient thereby undermining the medical treatment. Low-conflict settings, by contrast, provide an interpersonal context that supports the quieting direction of the drug treatment.

This study is a helpful addition to our understanding. It makes little sense to speak of the individual's health or illness without placing that person into those collective contexts that support or undermine a particular behavior pattern. It is an error to place the locus of causality for the problem solely within the person. In a total field, causality is part of a structure or pattern; the behavior of interest to us is an outcome of that pattern's maintenance and thus is a collective outcome of the whole field, not of any one of its parts.

Symbolic Interactionism

Although our last several cases were chosen from the exotic or the realm of the pathological, it would be unfortunate if the impression were given that the interactionist perspective in social psychology was suitable only to problems of abnormality or to the more exotic facets of interpersonal behavior. The perspective termed *symbolic interactionism,* as we shall see, suggests the importance of this same point of view for the more mundane aspects of life and behavior. The point is that social behavior, whether it is normal or pathological, whether it involves two persons, families, small groups, or larger collectivities, is best understood by examining the interactive field within which it is produced and maintained.

George Herbert Mead (1934), a social philosopher whose ideas have been influential in the formulation of the interactionist perspective in social psychology, offers us a helpful framework for viewing joint or collective action. We deal with Mead's analyses of "the self" in more detail in Chapter 6; for our present purposes, it is primarily important for us to review briefly Mead's argument that places the meaning of objects and events within the *social process* (i.e., his term for the interactive field) involving other persons.

The easiest way to grasp this matter is to take the simple case of P and O interacting. The question that Mead (1934; Blumer, 1966) addresses is how people fit their separate acts together, making the mutual give-and-take adjustments that results in a collective reality, their joint action. This is the same question that Allport (1954; 1962) asked and sought to answer in puzzling over the manner in which the recurrent structuring of behavioral events arises. Allport observed that each participant, although engaging in an individual line of action, nevertheless gears that behavior into the others, thus generating the characteristics of the whole: for example, the collective reality of their joint action. We need not concern ourselves here with comparisons between these two efforts to deal with the fundamental problem of the organization (i.e., structure and patterning) of behavior; it is sufficient to note that each stressed the same kinds of theme we have been dealing with in this present chapter:

1. the need to focus on the collective field jointly determined by the interacting, interdependent participants;
2. the need to understand the properties of that field by referring to actions here-and-now present that give the collective its pattern and shape rather than historical imports brought into the ongoing situation;
3. the need to adopt a dynamic focus on the processes involved in the mutual adjustments and alignments of actions rather than a more static view;
4. the need to understand how the properties of the collective affect the life of its parts

Mead's analysis of the fitting together of the separate lines of action to form joint action emphasizes the interpretative process that is involved. We first note that P makes certain gestures and O makes certain responses, ostensibly to P's gestures, which in turn serve as further gestures to which P now responds, and so forth. A gesture for most human interactions involves language. Thus, if P says to O, "Please pass the butter," we would refer to the verbal phrase as P's gesture. Gestures can also be nonverbal, for example, P's clenching a fist and waving it menacingly at O. In either case, P's gesture, which Mead terms the initial phase of the joint act involving P and O, indicates the later phase of that act. This is simply to note that gestures point out or indicate a direction for behavior, a later state of affairs that will come into being. For example, the clenched fist indicates a resultant hit in the head. The point is that a completed state of affairs can be envisioned before that state is reached; it is as though the completed state were already here-and-now present. Gestures indicate the completed state of action, even though that action has not yet occurred; O need not await its actual completion because the gesture carries with it (indicates) P's completed action.

Thus far joint action has two aspects: the initial phase that involves P's gesture, and the completed action or behavior that the gesture indicates. The third aspect of the full process according to Mead involves O's response to P's gesture. O's response is O's interpretation of P's gesture which makes it meaningful. For example,

O's response to P's clenched fist is to move backward and out of the way, or O's response to P's request for butter is to pass the butter. In both cases, the act that has been initiated by P's gesture is completed by O's response; this now becomes a gesture for P's responding and so forth.

We can see that in Mead's analysis, joint action refers to the interactive field or the collective reality of our earlier reference: the reference is to events that are constituted as a result of the interaction between P and O. Thus, to say that objects and their meanings (including the self as we will later see) arise in and are sustained by the joint action of P and O is to emphasize the extent to which events and outcomes are lodged within an interactive field. It is to emphasize as well our need to understand the ongoing actions within that field in order to grasp the nature of collective life:

> *A society is seen as people meeting the varieties of situations that are thrust upon them by their conditions of life. These situations are met by working out joint actions in which participants have to align their acts to one another. Each participant does so by interpreting the acts of others and, in turn, by making indications to others as to how they should act.* (Blumer, 1966, p. 541)

This view informs us that collective realities of whatever level (e.g., a family dinner, a war, a large scale organization) are composed of interlocked networks of joint actions. In other words, our understanding of something as large and complex as a society's educational system, for example, requires that we focus upon "the network of people, however large or extended, whose collective activity made it possible for the event to occur as it did" (Becker, 1974, p. 775). While a collective reality contains something more than or other than the individuals involved, that something more can be grasped by examining the mutual give-and-take adjustments of the participants who jointly constitute the collective event or outcome. This point becomes especially relevant when we consider collective events at the highest levels of the social system, where the tendency too often is to overlook the networks of interacting persons who compose the collectivity.

There is one further matter to consider before we move on; this involves the relationship between the whole (i.e., joint action) and its constituent parts. One of Mead's most ardent followers Blumer (1966) focuses upon this issue, in referring to the *career* of joint actions. Blumer notes how joint actions are built up over time and typically follow an orderly, recurrent career, yet remain open to modification. To speak of an orderly, recurrent career is to suggest how the parts remain in a relatively fixed relationship to one another such that once initiated the cycle of actions runs its course.

This is very much what occurs in the *naven* behavior in which once the *laua* begins to boast, the *wau's* behavior follows; it is also similar to the husband-wife example, in which once either party sets the cycle into motion, the behavior of the other party is highly predictable.

Blumer and Mead emphasize how the career of a joint action is built up as persons not only define their situation in common ways that supply "each participant with decisive guidance in directing his own act so as to fit into the acts of others" (Blumer, 1966, p. 541), but behave in ways that mutually *confirm* each other's common definition. For example, the wife's response of nagging to the husband's withdrawal confirms each party's interpretation (however implicit it may be) of their situation; if the wife did not respond by nagging or if the husband did not respond by withdrawing, the common interpretations would not have been confirmed by their behaviors and a new career thereby would be initiated.

In Allport's terms, as long as the wife's behavior leads the husband to return the cycle of their joint action back again to its starting region (e.g., NAG→WITHDRAW→NAG), the cycle will persist. However, if the cycle were broken, as the husband's response were to fight back directly (e.g. NAG→FIGHT→?), the old organization of their joint behavior would be transformed and perhaps a new pattern would in time emerge.

To have noted all of the preceding is to note as well how the parts are affected by the character of the whole. The structure and career of the joint action remains open to change; thus we are not speaking of mechanically fixed linkages. But, insofar as each participant acts to complete the cycle that has been initiated, each part is thereby shaped by the fact of its being located in that whole. Having noted that the links are not mechanical, or for that matter physical or biological, let me nevertheless choose as an illustrative example, something that is linked in that way, namely a wheel (see Sperry, 1970). The components of the wheel are many and varied, but for certain purposes we can think of them as atoms and molecules that are coupled together to form what we observe to be the collective reality, namely a wheel. Suppose, for whatever reason, that wheel is set into motion to roll down a hill. The fate of the atoms and molecules that jointly combine to form the wheel is determined by the properties of the whole wheel and the properties of the environment in which it is now rolling. Thus the character of the whole, its size and shape, for example, and its career in rolling down a steep rather than a shallow grade, over rocks and potholes rather than a smooth surface, all affect the atoms and molecules that are its parts.

To repeat, the linkages that join persons as the interdependent parts that form joint actions (e.g., the collective reality known as a small group or a social organization) are not the mechanical, physical, or biological forms of the example; thus these human links are open to change for any number of reasons, including the creation of new interpretations as existing definitions are not confirmed by the action that takes place. Nevertheless, patterns of the organization of behavior typically recur with sufficient regularity to warrant our accepting this view of the whole with its properties and career, as playing an important role in determining the life of its component parts. Remember, however, that the connections that join the parts together to form the whole (joint action) require nuturance, reinforcement, support, and confirmation. The recurrence of patterns of joint behavior motivates our search for the actual network of interactions that provides continued support; in the face of fixed and repeated links, we do not adopt a sense of absolute necessity as we would if we were concerned with mechanical linkages that relate parts together into wholes.

THE BENNINGTON STUDY

Another illustration will help further clarify the symbolic interactionist view. Many years ago, Theodore Newcomb (1943; 1958) undertook what has become a classic investigation of Bennington College and its impact upon its students. He was interested in studying the transformations in the students' values and attitudes that occurred as a function of their four-year encounter with Bennington. In general, Newcomb found that these women, originally from well-to-do conservative family backgrounds, emerged after their four years as more liberal. In his terms, Bennington College rather than their families had become the *reference group* by which they evaluated and judged their own worth and within which they acquired their liberalism. Naturally, not all were so transformed, nor all to an equal degree; but in general, the college setting created a climate conducive to becoming liberal and remaining liberal.

Popularity and general prestige tended to be correlated with liberal attitudes and behaviors; fitting into the Bennington culture involved acquiring new meanings for one's self and for the objects in one's everyday world. The Bennington setting was conducive to maintaining this new set of meanings; it provided a kind of reference group shield that helped insulate the women against backsliding when again introduced to their family setting. Up to this point, we have been speaking about the transformations in the individual's identity and in the meanings the individual finds for various objects (e.g., political issues) that cannot be understood without reference to the everyday interactions with others in the college; these interactions both facilitated and sustained these transformations. In the process of adjusting themselves to others in their daily environment, of fitting their lines of behavior together with others, of participating in the daily give-and-take of social interaction, transformations in the meanings of self and of issues were constituted and sustained.

As noted, not everyone at Bennington became liberalized in their outlook. Newcomb's study is also helpful in demonstrating how deviant attitudes were maintained while attending Bennington. To be deviant at Bennington meant to reject the dominant liberalism of the college culture; it meant to carry the onus of being rejected from positions of prestige and status within the college; to be isolated from the mainstream of events. Newcomb shows us that these deviant students insulated themselves from the main culture by forming into subgroups that acted in ways so as to affirm their beliefs. Countercultural beliefs at Bennington were maintained by creating a miniworld of interactions that reinforced the deviant rather than the dominant attitudes.

Twenty-five years after this first study of Bennington, Newcomb and several colleagues (Newcomb, Flacks, Koenig, & Warwick, 1967) did a follow-up study of those graduates of the original study. If these persons had become liberalized by their Bennington experience, what were they now? Politically liberal, thus showing some permanence in their change? Politically conservative, thus showing a return to their familial norm? In general, Newcomb and his associates found that even twenty-five years later, the Bennington graduates remained liberal in their attitudes, behavior, and concept of themselves.

In understanding their original transformation from conservative to liberal, we had to focus on the everyday life of the Bennington culture as the interactive field of relevance. But, to what can we now attribute this apparent permanence and stability in their liberal attitudes? Unlike approaches that seek such permanence entirely within the person as such, recall that our interactionist perspective requires that we seek the total field of which the person is a part; thus, we come to understand stability (as well as change) in terms of the processes within the total field that support or maintain apparent stability.

In the case of the Bennington follow-up study, Newcomb discovered that the liberalized graduates had married generally liberal husbands, thereby creating a new social field and circle of friends that in its parallel to the original Bennington experience itself, sustained their liberalism. Those points of connection and association with others, in this case, of one's own choosing, help us understand how attitudes and even self-concepts are lodged within and sustained through the interactive field that includes the individual and many others.

The Bennington example is instructive in yet another way; it informs us that far from being passive in this matter, the person quite actively seeks out social environments that help affirm and thereby sustain a given behavior pattern. To say that meanings are lodged within an interactive field in no way is to deny the role of the person in actively seeking out settings that give stability to meanings already negotiated and accomplished. People act to engender the environment that is their social field. Because we have adopted an interactionist perspective, we are sensitized to this issue; if we thought only in terms of structures within the person or within the situation rather than of processes within the field (i.e., P X S), we would have little reason to be concerned with how interactions of particular sorts are selected by the person.

COOPERATORS, COMPETITORS, AND THE PRISONER'S DILEMMA

Let us now turn to an example illustrating this last point. We are especially attuned to the ways in which persons interact so as to manage their social environment, creating meanings that help affirm aspects of themselves and thereby accomplish a sense of stability, of a recurrent and familiar social world. We return to this theme again in Chapter 6. While our first several examples began rather exotically in Berlin and New Guinea or somewhat more prosaically at Bennington College, our present example has its beginning in the social psychological research laboratory. The laboratory game is called the Prisoner's Dilemma (PD) because it involves a story of two prisoners who are being questioned separately by the district attorney. The prisoners are offered various deals depending on whether they confess to their joint crime or plead their innocence. If both confess, their sentence will be moderate; if both plead innocent, then the district attorney will nevertheless see them convicted on some minor charge; however, if one confesses and the other pleads innocent, then the former will be treated leniently for turning state's evidence while the latter will get the maximum penalty.

The dilemma facing the prisoners (or in the laboratory case, the experimental subjects), is basically what degree of trust can they place in their partner. Imagine yourself facing a dilemma that parallels that of the prisoners; you are paired with a partner and asked to indicate independently and without benefit of communication between you which of two choices, red or blue, you wish to make. You and your partner have been informed that various combinations of your choices produce different payoffs (e.g., money, points, etc.). A typical payoff matrix follows:

PLAYER P

		BLUE		RED	
	BLUE	P/5	O/5	P/10	O/−10
PLAYER O					
	RED	P/−10	O/10	P/−5	O/−5

In this matrix, the numbers represent points given or taken away; the first number indicates Player P's points for a given choice, the second number, Player O's points. For example, if P chooses blue and O chooses blue, then both win 5 points. However, if O were to choose red while P chooses blue, then P would lose 10 points while O would win 10. Although the blue-blue choice maximizes mutual gain and thus should be the preferred solution, it is not unusual to find persons often settling upon the red-red choice (see Rapoport & Chammah, 1965; Terhune, 1968, for a review of much research on the PD game).

The dilemma is that the red choice that would maximize either P's individual gain or O's individual gain brings them jointly a mutual loss; on the other hand, there is a risk for both in choosing blue and thereby maximizing their joint gain. In choosing blue, P must wonder if O will choose blue and thus benefit both of them, or if O will choose red and thus win 10 points at considerable cost to P; a similar dilemma exists for O.

While there are numerous variations on this basic PD game, including different payoff matrices, different subjects (e.g., varying age, sex, social class, personality, etc.) and different conditions of communication, what is of prime interest to our present concern is an interesting, provocative conclusion reached by Kelly and Stahekski (1970) based on their analyses of numerous PD studies. They suggest that:
1. there are two relatively stable person-types, a cooperator and a competitor;
2. these types are characterized by the view they have of others: the competitor sees others as competitive and out to maximize their own gain; the cooperator's view is more differentiated, seeing others as sometimes concerned with maximizing their own gain and sometimes concerned with achieving mutually satisfying benefits for themselves and others.

Of especial interest to our point is the behavior of competitive persons. Unaware of the impact of their behavior on others, they so structure their choices in the PD game, especially when paired with potential cooperators, that the latter become more competitive than they would normally have preferred; this affirms the competitors belief that everyone is out to get the most for themselves and that the only reasonable course of action to take is to do the same. By contrast, cooperators seem aware that their behavior has an effect on other's choices, and thus that their own cooperative or competitive choices will influence others' choices.

This work provides us with a clear demonstration of the manner by which an individual characteristic, in this case competitiveness, is maintained by means of an interactive process. This work further demonstrates that this stability is maintained by means that on the surface appear to be reasonable, even rational responses to other's behavior. That is, P's competitiveness is affirmed as a reasonable response to O's own competitiveness. As P sees it, P is competitive because O is and if P weren't, then O would win everything. The flaw in this kind of reasoning, however, is its failure to take into account the extent to which P's own behavior helps create the very conditions that P then responds to. It should be noted that the cooperator in this setting makes frequent cooperative overtures only to be rebuffed as the more competitive P exploits O's cooperativeness for P's own gain. So, in time, the cooperators becomes more competitive, even though they may wish it otherwise.

This example informs us that while P's competitive behavior is a result of the field containing P and O, P's behavior helps create an environment (i.e., behavior from O) that elicits a specific reciprocating behavior by P; and this typically occurs without much self-awareness that P is a party to this process. P is much like the husband who blames his wife for causing his withdrawal or the wife who blames the husband for causing her nagging; neither can readily see the recurring collective reality that their own behavior has helped to establish:

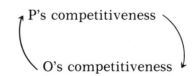

The Self-fulfilling Prophecy. A similar self-maintaining process has also been referred to as the *self-fulfilling prophecy* (Merton, 1957). In this formulation, P's expectations about the occurrence of some event (P's prophecy) leads P to act in such a manner so as to help bring the event about, thus fulfilling the prophecy, albeit without any necessary self-awareness. Indeed, as with the competitors' actions, people who fulfill their own prophecies may be quite indignant when their behavior is questioned. Afterall, not recognizing their contributions to the effect they experience, they are only responding as reasonable people would in similar circumstances. The self-fulfillers' experiences with others stand as self-testimonials of the sensibility of their own world view; and as importantly, that view is maintained by virtue of its being repeatedly affirmed within the interactive social field. In the PD context, as we have noted, a competitive prophecy is fulfilled by virtue of the way in which P's own behavior serves as a stimulus for O's symmetrical reply, which in turn serves as a stimulus for P's own symmetrical (i.e., competitive) response. In this case, P is aware of P's response to O but not of O's response to P's own choices.

From Micro to Macro: Traps, Fences, and the Commons

> *Every individual lives, from one generation to the next, in some society ... he lives out a biography ... within some historical sequence. By the fact of his living he contributes, however minutely, to the shaping of this society and to the course of its history, even as he is made by society and by its historical push and shove* (Mills, 1959, p. 6).

To this point, our examination of human interdependencies and of the collective realities created by P and O's joint interactions, has primarily been on one level of human behavior—the micro or interpersonal level. In speaking of the levels on which human actions may be considered, I am simply noting that what we refer to as an interactive field at one level can involve the parts for a field at some still higher, more complex level. For example, the schismogenic processes that form an interpersonal field linking *wau* and *laua* may also be seen as elements of the larger social system that links one family within Iatmul society to another. To take another example, a family can be examined from the perspective of the interactions between parents and among parents and children; for certain purposes, it can also be seen as a part of more complex systems.

Following Miller and Swanson (1958), we can view the family as an element in a society's economic system; the link between the family and the economy, in this case, is thought to occur in the person of the family's breadwinner. Different economic systems create different patterns of interaction, influence, and childrearing within a family as a function of the position of the breadwinner in the larger economic system. Miller and Swanson argue that there are two major types of family settings, one reflecting an entreprenurial economic situation, the other a bureaucratic situation.

The entrepreneur competes individually in the open marketplace; his or her success determines the family's status within the larger society. The bureaucrat succeeds in an organization either through seniority of position and accords stated in labor-management contracts (blue-collar workers) or by presenting a good front, demonstrating, at least partially through family relationships, a smooth and happy interpersonal pattern of living (white-collar workers). Miller and Swanson's argument is that the entreprenurial linkage places the breadwinner in a position of substantial influence and authority within the family; Family decisions are made by the breadwinner, whose tasks are seen as being more important than those of the other family members. The bureaucratic linkage, on the other hand, requires more collegiality and sharing of family tasks, functions, and authority, especially among the white-collar workers whose whole family may serve as an instrument of economic success. The Millen-Swanson model suggests how a family may be seen as an element in the larger social system; and how the organization of the family is influenced by factors within that larger system: that is, how macro-level issues of the economic system affect micro-level issues of the family and in turn of individual living.

As the opening quotation from C. Wright Mills suggests and as the Miller-Swanson thesis illustrates, although each person leads an individual life, he or she is part of an historical drama occurring as well on a macro level with its own patterns and career. Those macro-level patterns can be studied; they typically form the subject matter of sociology and several other social sciences (e.g., political science, economics, history).

PERSONAL TROUBLES AND PUBLIC ISSUES

Although as social psychologists we do not systematically study phenomena on the more macro level, we need to be sensitive to the ways in which these larger systems influence the character of the smaller systems within which the person lives; too, we must become aware of the way in which the conditions of larger system maintenance and change can affect the person. Recall the example of the rolling wheel. Mills distinguishes between what he calls the "personal troubles of milieu" and the "public issues of social structure." Troubles occur within each of our lives; we may face unemployment and experience all the consequences that being out of work entails, for us personally and for all of those dependent on our income. Personal trouble can be seen also as a property of a larger social system:

Issues *have to do with matters that transcend these local environments of the individual and the range of his inner life. They have to do with the organization of many such milieux into the institutions of an historical society as a whole, with the ways in which various milieux overlap and interpenetrate to form the larger structure of social and historical life.* (Mills, 1959, p. 8)

We are able to examine the unemployment figures for a nation, for example, as an issue of the public, a macro-level concern that transcends the troubles of any one unemployed person. On the macro level we can study the relationships between unemployment and other aspects of the larger social system, noting, for example, how there may be a trade-off between unemployment and inflation: an increment in unemployment is used to cool down an inflated economy; an increase in employment is used to heat up a recessed economy. The social psychologist is interested in these aspects of the larger social system primarily in terms of their affect upon the life circumstances of those persons who are involved as elements of the larger system. Just as not every atom is implicated in the rolling wheel, so too, not every person is a part of every larger system.

While the connections that link persons together into the network of relations that compose the family seem relatively clear and usually easy to identify (e.g., the daily interactions between family members and the mutual adjustments each makes to the others), linkages that establish interdependencies with others in the larger social system are often less readily identifiable, though necessary to our analysis. Before we can assert that occurrences at the macro level affect the life of a particular person or group of persons, we should inquire about which persons are joined together as interdependent parts of the larger system, and thus who is thereby affected by these system-wide, macro-factors. Although on the macro level a relationship may be discovered, for example, between unemployment and inflation, our concern is to identify those persons who are a part of the whole system that is affected by this macro-level relationship. A close examination of unemployment data demonstrates that not all persons are equally vulnerable to shifts in the economy that influence the availability of jobs—that is, not everyone is an interdependent part of the same larger system. Thus, blacks, women, youth, and blue-collar workers are more affected than others by an upswing in unemployment.

This is an important point for the social psychological investigator whose interest lies in the relationships between these events on the macro level and the lives of individuals. By zealously focusing on persons as elements of the larger system, the analyst may inappropriately think that everything is linked to everything else and that we are all parts of the same whole. To speak meaningfully of a collective reality at any level, but particularly at the larger level of the society, we must be able to indicate the interdependent elements that interact to form that system. Recall that the social field is constituted out of the mutual adjustments among the parts; not everything or everyone is necessarily an interdependent part of the whole. It is our goal to discover just what are the parts that mutually affect one another to create the collective reality. Yet, we must also be sensitive to the role of symbolic interdependencies that link some persons with others who are experienced as parts of the same total situation. The mass media have made this basis of human interdependency increasingly possible; we may indeed be linked into our global community, at least for certain purposes.

Two further points need to be made. For a public issue at the macro level to be a personal trouble (i.e., an event with consequences at the personal and interpersonal level), the person must be linked to the larger system. In the unemployment example, we have seen that not everyone is linked in the same way, thus not everyone is equally vulnerable to system-level effects. We must seek to identify the network that ties persons together into a whole before we readily assume that all public issues generate personal troubles (or joys). Looking at the matter from the other side, we must also recognize that not all personal troubles become public issues. For this to occur, some degree of *organization* must take place. As Katz has noted (1974; also Katz & Kahn, 1966); this requires both some common statistical frequency of the trouble or characteristic among the population and some degree of awareness among the persons troubled of their collective character (interdependencies). The media are often influential in this regard.

A Note on Art. Though not dealing with troubles *per se,* in his analysis of art, Becker (1974) provides us with another helpful example of how macro-level processes constrain behavior at the individual and interpersonal levels. We are all aware that while artistic expression may itself involve the act of a single individual, the entire artistic process is a collective enterprise. The symphony orchestra, for example, is dependent not only upon the acts of each musician and the director, but also upon the makers of instruments, the printers of sheet music, the acceptance and understanding of a notational system, composers who write within that system and for the existing set of instruments the musicians play, the schedulers of times and places for rehearsal, the availability of financial support, etc. The poet, though perhaps following personal creative inclinations, typically requires an entire collective network of other persons for her or his works to reach the public. It is reported, for example, that e.e. cummings had great difficulty in getting his first works published because printers did not want to set up his unconventional formats.

Becker (1974) reports the case of an artist who used lithographic roller marks as part of his works who could not find any printers willing to reproduce them because in the printing trade such roller marks were assumed to be the sign of poor printing workmanship. The sculpter whose media involves large constructions (e.g., movements of masses of earth) that cannot be accommodated within a museum may find no public acclaim or recognition; in this case, the museum is the larger institution that sets guidelines for defining what is art. It is noted, by way of further illustration, that the composer, Charles Ives found that orchestras would not play his music, claiming that their instruments could not make the sounds he required. Not getting a public hearing for his music, in this case, freed Ives from the constraints he would otherwise have experienced if his works were playable. "If no one could play his music, then he no longer had to write music that musicians could play ... since his music would not be played, he never needed to finish it" (Becker, 1974, p. 773).

These and many other cases could be cited to show how the links that make artists interdependent members of a larger system serve to constrain their creative behavior as a function of meeting the requirements of this larger network and adjusting themselves to these macro-system demands. As Becker notes for art, and Katz (1974) for social change in general, these macro-system constraints tend to be redundant, involving several complex interdependent systems. Thus change in any one part of the whole is very difficult in that the overlapping, redundant network pulls for a given mode of behavior:

> A system of conventions gets embodied in equipment, materials, training, available facilities and sites, systems of notation and the like, all of which must be changed if any one segment is (Becker, 1974, p. 772).

The resistance to change in any one segment, for example, cummings' attempts to use a different layout for his poetry, is thereby substantial, and serves to constrain the individual's behavior and to reinforce a recurrent cycle of behavior. These are constraints that are illustrative of the networks that tie persons together into more complex organizations, making individual behavior a part of a larger field, to be understood only when we can grasp the essential features of that total field.

THE COMMONS

The commons was pasture land open for all to use for grazing their herds. While this purpose is generally no longer served, many cities and small towns retain their commons or public parks, if not to graze their cattle, at least to enjoy themselves, or simply to rest awhile from a weary day. As open, free grazing land, the concept of the commons worked extremely well—that is, until one herdsman thought it reasonable to add one animal to his herd. He reasoned that one animal would net him greater income and furthermore the additonal pasture that would be depleted by one other animal's grazing would be minimal: thus, he would benefit and no one else would be harmed. It seemed to be a perfect arrangement.

Writing in *Science,* Garrett Hardin (1968) referred to the *tragedy* of the commons. Fundamentally, the tragedy lay in two related features of the situation: (1) individual decisions reached individually and (2) congestion of numbers or high population density. To put it succinctly, as the number of herdsmen wishing to use the commons became greater (point 2), and as each person individually reasoned that his addition of one animal would do little harm (point 1), the joint addition of all these animals soon rapidly depleted the public commons; in the end, all suffered, as the pasture land was grazed into extinction. Parallels between yesterday's commons and today's problems of congestion are clearly evident. And for similar reasons, individuals make decisions for themselves which, in combination with all those other individual decisions, creates crises for everyone.

Though he began from an analysis of a somewhat different social problem, panic in collective behavior, Mintz reported in 1952 the results of an experimental investigation that further illuminates the "maladaptive" quality of individual solutions to what basically are collective issues. In brief, Mintz provided his subjects with separate strings attached to small cones that were placed in a large glass bottle; bottlenecks were relatively easy given the size of the cones, the smallness of the neck of the bottle, and the fifteen to twenty-one subjects in each group. To induce "panic," Mintz introduced water to the bottom of the bottle in some versions of the experiment. Of special interst to Mintz, and to our own utilization of his results, was his introduction of rewards and fines in some of his conditions while other conditions were termed "no reward." His results suggested how the reward structure of the situation, providing incentives for individual self-interest over cooperative action, produced numerous traffic jams and essentially what he termed nonadaptive group behavior. Mintz reports that there were no jams in the no-reward condition. Whether in the laboratory or out on the commons, it would seem that individuals pursuing their own self-interest do so not only at the cost of others' interests, but also at considerable cost to themselves: no one comes out the winner. Recall as well the Prisoner's Dilemma.

TRAPS AND FENCES

John Platt (1973) formulated a way of conceptualizing several contemporary tragedies, including the commons, among others. His scheme calls our attention to the differentiation between short- versus long-term benefit or cost, and individual versus group benefit or cost. A *social trap* is said to exist when a short-term benefit leads to a long-term cost, or when an individual benefit leads to a collective cost. A *social fence* exists when a short-term cost prevents action that would achieve a long-term benefit, or when an individual cost prevents action that, if taken, would lead to a collective benefit. Briefly, a trap can be seen to involve an error of *commision,* in which acting in a particular way or for one's self-interest produces long-term or collective troubles. A fence, on the other hand, involves an error of *omission,* in which a failure to act because of the individual cost involved, prevents the achievement of a potential benefit. The tragedy of the commons and Mintz's experimental work are examples of social traps. The individual's pursuit of short-term benefits produces long-term collective costs—for example, the loss of the grazing land in the case of the commons.

An example of a social fence is taken from one of the writings of Thomas Schelling (1971) who describes a return drive from Cape Cod on a Sunday evening. The northbound lane of the two-lane highway is clogged with returning traffic; the southbound lane has some traffic but not nearly as much. A pickup truck heading along the northbound land and carrying a mattress jerks to a sudden halt and then takes off again; the mattress, however, falls off and blocks the northbound roadway. The heavy traffic piles up for miles. Those far back in line have no idea what has caused the delay and so cannot act in any way to remedy the problem. Those near the mattress, who could haul it to the side of the road and thereby free the traffic lanes, are too busy gauging the southbound traffic and waiting their chance to pull around the mattress and continue on their trip. Naturally, once they have passed the mattress, it is little to their own benefit to stop, return, and remove it. In this instance, a fence exists. The immediate cost to the individual involves getting out of the car and moving the mattress, and thereby perhaps missing a chance to pull out and pass the obstruction; or having already passed it, the cost involved is stopping the car, getting out, going back, and moving the mattress. Both kinds of costs operate as a fence, preventing persons from acting in ways that would in the long run benefit everyone. When we later consider altruistic behavior (Chapter 9), including instances of helping a person in trouble, we will have reason again to consider this same fence-like quality of many social situations.

To use the terms social trap or fence or to speak of the tragedy of the commons is to indicate a self-maintaining, in this case, destructive system of human interdependencies. It describes a locked-in pattern, a kind of vicious cycle of the sort we have seen in some family interaction examples: e.g., interpersonal knots. A trap is a trap because people catch themselves in it and usually cannot see that it is a trap until it is too late. Although the kind of human interdependency of the commons may be more anonymous than that involved in family and small group interaction, a trap-like quality exists for both. However, whereas the family system may exist in a state of dynamic equilibrium by means of countervailing forces, the social traps described here involve processes that function without such self-corrective feedback; thus they spiral into an increasingly costly, finally system-destructive state. Of course, much the same outcome may await the family or group whose equilibrium is achieved at the cost of maintaining one member in constant pathology. That person's death, flight into health, or departure from the family may break that system apart as well. Whereas our values might lead us to cheer the sick child's flight into health that brought about a dissolution of their family's equilibrium, few of us would cheer as loudly the dissolution of the larger social system— for example, the commons—that occurs as a trap- or fence-like process unwinds towards destruction.

SYNERGY

The fascinating, yet insidious quality of traps, fences, and the commons lies in their being a feature of our everyday landscape and not simply events called into question in moments of crisis. People may abandon short-term individual gains for long-term collective benefits in time of national or international emergency; likewise, a Battle-of-Britain mentality may lead persons to choose short-term individual costs in order to achieve a hoped-for long-term collective benefit. The real tragedy, however, is that these kinds of interdependency occur in our everyday world as part of the taken-for-granted background, something of which we are unaware often until the emergency is upon us, and then sometimes too late for anything but band-aid, remedial action. Thus, we pursue our own business, seeking our own individual benefits, oblivious to the implications of these individualized choices on the world around us. Or, we fail to take costly action now and in this failure ensnare ourselves in ways which, until the crisis arrives, we remain unaware. Until the food runs low, we overconsume and are unaware of the long-term collective (i.e., worldwide) costs that derive from our individual rate of consumption here-and-now.

In essence, the tragedy of the commons is that the kinds of individual actions that consider collective and individual goals, a cooperative orientation, to use Deutsch's (1953; 1962) term or one of high *synergy,* to use Ruth Benedict's (1970) concept, often do not occur until a crisis is experienced; and then it may be too late.

Benedict's concept of synergy is especially useful in directing our attention to the ways in which the individual's goal of self-interest are related to collective goals of mutual benefit. She speaks of societies of high synergy in which persons have learned from birth that personal rewards are intimately tied into collective rewards; one attains personal goals, thus, by means of mutual, joint action. In such societies, one person's gain is everyone's gain; one person's loss is likewise everyone's loss. By contrast, a low synergy society, by far more typical of our Western social forms, is one in which personal gain is something privately sought, separable from mutual benefit for all. Even in primitive societies of low synergy, one seeks control over supernatural powers, for example, in order to attain wealth or power for one's own benefit rather than for the benefit of everyone. We might say that in societies characterized by low synergy, individual self-interest is likely to produce the kinds of social traps and fences that work for long-term collective disaster.

The social psychological perspective on human interdependencies, on systems of benefit and cost that ensnare us in traps or surround us by fences, is by no means an idle, irrelevant concern. If our earth is thought of as a spaceship, a total system on which our collective survival depends, it becomes increasingly apparent that without this kind of perspective, we could not even define our problems or know what questions to ask, let alone seek solutions to the ever widening array of problems that population density and finite resources create. And the need for adopting such a perspective is ever more apparent when we realize that the commons of yesterday may well be the energy and food resources of today; that the road from Cape Cod is only a minor model for numerous, simple interdependencies that shape our lives in even more dramatic ways than being delayed on our trip home.

Conclusion

While the social psychologist may not have all the solutions to the major problems of the day, an interactionist perspective is helpful for those who would know even where to open their inquiry after such solutions. The idea of a perspective itself, a way of viewing phenomena, is the key. Without a point of view, one sees only chaos or at best snippets of material without apparent meaning or relation. The perspective of a discipline gives the practitioner a way to look and to see, a way to think, to understand, to know.

As we have seen, the interactionist perspective maintains that when social psychologists confront the individual they are in fact looking at a relationship, at a participant in a field or complex set of interdependent fields. To understand P's behavior or for that matter even to know what questions to ask about P requires seeing the lines of relationship that tie P to others. The functioning of social systems and fields affects the life of P, who in turn contributes to the whole itself.

The apparent simplicity of this perspective belies its actual power and complexity. The apparent reasonableness of seeing in the perspective's framework belies as well the actual degree to which our commonsense thinking does not in fact see, interpret, or understand in these terms. This point is important; the way in which we see and understand a particular event will influence the decisions we make regarding the betterment of troubles or the maintenance of benefits. While one person's troubles may perhaps be dealt with by individual therapy, to the extent that we are dealing with properties of social fields, our treatment must be focused upon the collective reality of the field. This is not to deny the importance of approaches that seek to provide individual relief for individual troubles; rather it is to point out the importance, for long-run solutions, to work on the level that is most relevant to the problem.

But, it is not only troubles we may wish to deal with; health, benefit, and goodness are also things we wish to maintain. Insofar as these too are aspects of social fields and not simply properties of individuals, then clearly the maintenance of benefit also must be dealt with at the proper level. Recall that to say that something is a characteristic of a social field is to note that in understanding a particular part we need to consider the interdependent whole in which it is embedded.

Whether seeking to create and maintain things of positive value or to eliminate things of negative value, the interactionist perspective of the social psychologist demands that both good and evil be seen as properties of systems of relationship. The evil dictator we may despise requires a supportive system for maintenance, even if such support only be the tacit approval that unquestioning silence brings; likewise, the saint cannot dwell on an island, but rather must rely on collective support for sustenance through moments that would otherwise cause doubt. The examples are numerous; we have already seen some and will see many more demonstrated in the text.

But lest we forget our concluding comments of Chapter 1, the interactionist ideal we have outlined and touted is not always followed by investigators in the discipline. Though field properties are called for, we often will find only events within the person or within the situation analyzed. Keep the goal in mind, however, as something to be sought and considered even when the approach we are dealing with seems not to have done so. An interactionist perspective as our goal can often serve as a healthful remedy for an otherwise too narrowed focus.

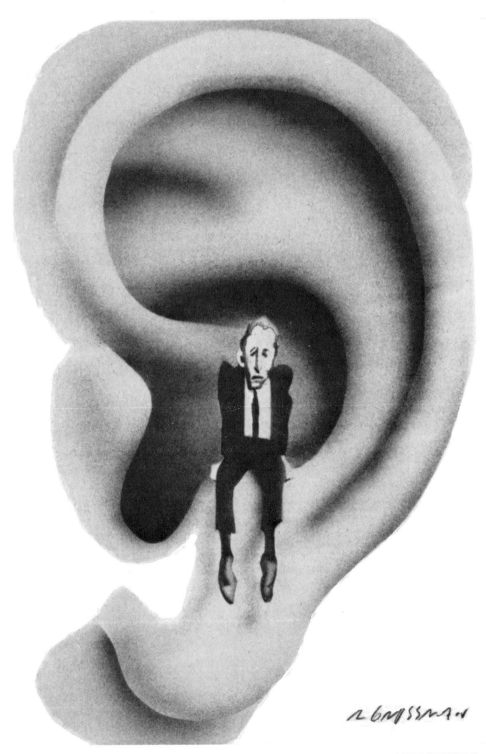

ROBERT GROSSMAN

THE COGNITIVE PROCESSES ON KNOWING AND UNDERSTANDING:

3

A basic proposition of social psychology notes that persons do not react immediately to objective stimuli in their physical or social environment; rather, people transform these outer events into an inner system typically termed a *life space* or psychological environment (Lewin, 1951; Neisser, 1967; Scheerer, 1954 among others). It is fundamental to the understanding of human behavior to recognize that persons act in situations as a function of their definitions and understandings of these situations (e.g., Thomas, see Volkhart, 1951). Alfred Schutz, a major figure in the philosophy of social science notes that:

All our knowledge of the world, in common-sense as well as in scientific thinking, involves constructs, i.e. a set of abstractions, generalizations, formalizations, idealizations specific to the respective level of thought organization. Strictly speaking, there are no such things as facts, pure and simple. All facts are from the outset facts selected from a universal context by the activities of our mind. They are, therefore, always interpreted facts (1970–1971, p. 5).

Nothing said thus far should be understood to deny the existence of an environment containing personal and impersonal stimulus objects (e.g., other persons, chairs, rooms, rocks, roads, etc.). The point is that between this world of situations (S) and our behavior in it, there exists an interpretive process that transforms S into a psychological environment, a life space. This is the world as it exists for us, as we define and understand it.

As an example of this issue, take a sensitivity group with which I am familiar, having worked with it some years ago. The group was composed primarily of young people between 18 and 30; however, one member, Larry, was in his mid-50s. The group spent much of its early time together trying to define what their task was, particularly what it meant to be a sensitivity group. Larry was adamant as he sought to get a firm definition. Repeatedly he would ask everyone and then answer his own question. "Why are we here? To have an encounter? But what is an encounter? It's when you skewer each person and pass them around for others to probe and pick at. It's when you use a crowbar and try to break through a person and pry into them, open them up wide. It's when you peel away barriers and try to get to the real person inside." No one challenged his definitions, yet everyone seemed to challenge Larry. They'd say, "OK, Larry, so you want an encounter, well, then, how do you feel about me right now"? Larry would invariably reply evasively, changing the subject or often just reminiscing about some past experience he recalled from his days as a kid in Chicago. Exasperated, others continued to question him, nearly yelling that if he really wanted an encounter, then he'd have to talk about himself and his feelings right here and now. Yet Larry persisted in being evasive and in frustrating everyone. But he also continued to inquire repeatedly about when were we going to have our encounter.

A grasp of Larry's behavior can be had simply from listening and hearing his definition of the situation. Read through his ideas again. What is an encounter? To be probed, picked at, skewered, pried into, peeled away. Is there any wonder then, given this definition of the situation, that he backed off, or that with each demand that he open up, his definition was thereby reaffirmed and his fears of participating only further increased? Paradoxically, the greater pressure brought to bear on Larry to join in, the more reticent he became; our understanding of his understanding makes this paradoxical behavior understandable. (See Kelly, 1955; 1963 for a similar analysis of what he calls personal constructs.)

The Cognitive Model: An Interactionist Perspective

An interest in cognition, those processes whereby persons define and give meaning to the environments in which they live, can have a person-centered, a situation-centered, or an interactionist emphasis. The person-centered approach places its primary emphasis upon those attributes within the person that determine the way in which stimulus situations are perceived and hence are responded to. It asks questions about how a person's needs, values, attitudes, momentary mood, internal organization of concepts, styles of thinking and perceiving and so forth, affect the way in which situations are defined and understood. The situation-centered approach to cognition, on the other hand, emphasizes the role that situational factors play in evoking particular kinds of cognitions within the person. It asks questions about what kinds of internal structures are built up from living in particular kinds of environments or what constructs develop in specific kinds of situations. The situation-centered perspective sees cognitive events within the person as responses to specifiable situational factors. These two approaches to cognition can be summarized in the following diagrams:

1. Cognitive factors ⟶ Constructions ⟶ Behavior
   and definitions   as a response
   of situations   to definitions

2. Situational stimuli ⟶ Evoke cognitive ⟶ Behavior
   responses

The interactionist approach to cognition makes a two-way street out of what the other views see primarily as a one-way flow. In this view, not only are situations defined in terms of the cognitive operations the person performs on them, but those cognitive operations are themselves affected by the out-thereness and reality of situations. Thus, situations both cause and are an effect of cognitions; cognitions, in turn, both cause and are an effect of situations. Behavior thereby is an outcome of the joint determination of person's cognition of situations and situation's transformation of person's cognition. Dual transformations are involved: by the person of the situation and by the situation of the person.

Of the several ways of formulating the nature of these dual transformations I find it most helpful to call upon the view offered by the developmental psychologist, Jean Piaget (1952; 1954; 1955; 1962; also see Flavell, 1963). Piaget's view of cognition stresses the interaction that is involved in the commerce between the person and the environment, whereby each is transformed by its encounter with the other. Piaget speaks of two basic processes, *assimilation* and *accommodation*. Basically, assimilation involves the transformation of the environment that occurs as it is assimilated to what Piaget refers to as the person's internal *schema* or existing cognitive organization (e.g., constructs). Accommodation focuses upon the transformation of those schema as the person interacts with the environment. Dual transformations are involved. In this view, the life space is created by assimilating features of the environment into its existing structures and patterns of organization, while in turn, those structures are transformed through accommodating themselves to variations in the environment. Stability is thereby an accomplishment of these two processes.

CONSTITUTING A STABLE WORLD

Gaze at some object across the room—perhaps a plate or ashtray on a table—now walk slowly towards that object. It remains psychologically an ashtray; that is, we continue to recognize it as an ashtray in spite of the many variations in the pattern on our sensory receptors that occur as we move towards the object. Its physical shape on these receptors is modified, yet we retain a psychological stability of reference for the object.

In a similar manner, in spite of the many variations in which, for example, a favor is sought, we recognize it as a favor: a smile, a direct request, a statement of please, a gesture of helping us in hopes of getting help in return (Heider, 1958). All of these different forms retain a stability of psychological impression. Likewise, in spite of the many variations possible in P's manner and appearance, we maintain a constancy in our recognition of P as the "same" person. As we saw in Chapter 2, stability of an interpersonal event can also be maintained. We have more to say about this in a moment. As we shall see in Chapter 5, language plays a major role in establishing these constancies.

Conservation.   Jean Piaget's studies of what he calls *conservation* in children provide us with a further demonstration of the transformation of environmental events into psychological events having a constancy beyond their mere physical forms. A child is presented with a small, squat container that is filled with water from a nearby tap. The water is then poured from that container into a tall slender one and the child is asked to indicate which container has "more." As adults, we know that the water in both is the same because the new container has been filled by emptying the original container into it. However, for the young child, seeing that the level of the water is in fact higher in the second container than in the first, it seems as though the second has more. Beyond a certain age, however, children function as adults do and psychologically *conserve quantity* in spite of the apparent physical feature of a higher level of water. For conservation to occur, the person must function at an abstract rather than concrete cognitive level. Conservation requires that the child not focus upon the concrete details of the situation one at a time (e.g., higher water level in one jar), but rather abstract simultaneously both water level and container size and shape.

Specifically, Piaget suggested that conservation in the water jar problem involves the person's being able to focus or *center* upon two aspects of the situation simultaneously. To focus only on the height of the water leads to a distortion in judgment; to focus only on the shape of the container likewise leads to a distortion in judgment in which quantity is not conserved. To shift back and forth in an *isolated sequential manner,* focusing now upon height and then upon shape would also produce an unstable conservation of quantity, one that oscillates back and forth between two opposite poles. True conservation requires *simultaneous decentering*, or focusing simultaneously upon all relevant aspects of the situation. And this requires a level of cognitive development that permits the person to take distance from the immediately given, concrete situation and to consider simultaneously, in mind, what is not present simultaneously in physical reality.

Interpersonal Conservation. An interpersonal illustration of Piaget's principle of conservation will be helpful in underlining the importance of grasping the cognitive processes in order to gain a better understanding of a person's behavior. This will also help clarify our discussion of symbolic interactionism in Chapter 2, in which we noted that recurrent, stable patterns of joint action require all participants to identify their common situation. Essentially, to speak of the conservation of an interpersonal event is to focus on the way in which each participant constructs a line of action and fits it into the other's developing line thereby creating a potentially stable organization to their joint endeavor. This conservation of an interpersonal event presumably involves the same decentering process that Piaget has outlined. That is, it involves the integration of separate events into a unified whole.

For two people to carry a log, for example, they must be able to coordinate their efforts, pulling together rather than at odds with one another (Asch, 1952). This kind of joint effort demands that each person not only be self-aware but as well and simultaneously be aware of the other person; one might say that P must be self-oriented in the situation and at the same time be able to conceive of the situation from O's perspective: that is, to take O's role (Mead, 1934).

Recent investigations of the structure of children's groups is informative on this point. Leinhardt (1972) examined the transitivity of liking relationships in groups of varying ages. A *transitive liking relationship* is one in which, for example, if P likes O and P likes Z, then O will also tend to like Z. In his research, Leinhardt studied the liking patterns of groups from junior nursery school (age 3) through the sixth grade (age 11), noting generally greater transitivity with increasing age. In fact, he reports that the age 3 liking patterns are almost random. He notes further that transitivity in liking relationships requires a perspectivist orientation in which P is able to be aware not only of personal liking preferences, but also of those of other persons with whom P interacts.

Another investigation (Smith, 1973) comparing interaction patterns in childrens groups and adult groups (i.e., groups composed of persons age 5, 6, 8, 10, 13, 16, or 20), noted that before the age of 4 children cannot interact in groups containing more than five persons, and that even after age 4, children's groups tend to break down into dyads more often than adult groups. In other words, young children do not yet have the capability of thinking about groups, presumably because to conceptualize beyond a dyad and thereby to interact with something larger than a twosome requires the developmental capability of abstracting simultaneously across numerous others and thus seeing self and many other perspectives at the same time.

In another program of research, this time specifically studying interpersonal conservation, Feffer (1967; 1970) became interested in assessing the individual's differential ability to engage in simultaneous decentering: that is, a focus upon both self and other. Feffer developed what he termed a role-taking test (RTT) which asked the individual first to make up a story to a picture that was presented and then to retell the story from the perspective of the other characters. For example, the picture might show two people standing close together and the subject might tell a story about one person attacking the other. Subjects were then to retell the story, this time from the victim's perspective. Feffer categorized the subject's stories according to the degree to which the retold version not only included a different perspective, but one which was coordinated with the initial version.

Feffer reports a developmental sequence of responses to the RTT. First level, similar to the nonconservation of quantity in the water jar problem, involved *uncorrected decentering;* the story was told without any continuity between the different versions. Thus, if in the first version, the mother was angry, in the second version there is no reference at all to mother's anger; rather some irrelevant matter, let us say, of clothing, is mentioned. The second level involved an isolated, sequential process; the retold version, while considering the original version, did so as though it were in a sequence rather than as a part of some more highly organized story containing both original and retold versions. The example Feffer offers is of a first story in which the characters proclaim that they are going for a ride and a retold version in which the characters exclaim, "That's great, where are we going"? The third level of cognitive functioning involved simultaneous decentering, whereby the interpersonal event was conserved and stabilized. In this form, the story tellers were able to synthesize the different versions into a more highly integrated whole. The example offered is a first story in which a tenant feels cheated because her landlady raised the rent after apparently agreeing that she wouldn't; the second version, told from the landlady's point of view, shows the landlady seeing that the woman was angry but feeling that she had no choice but to raise the rent, as her own expenses had gone up.

Feffer and his colleagues have used this RTT assessment technique in several experimental settings. In one, (Feffer & Suchotliff,

1966), subjects were chosen to reflect different levels of the cognitive ability measured by the test and paired in a task that required cooperation. Results showed that subjects who scored at the third level of interpersonal coordination were better able to work together than those who scored at the lower levels. The task required persons to provide clues that would lead their partners to guess the correct secret word. Those subjects who were only able to focus on their own perspective or who were unable to integrate their's with their partner's were less facile in suggesting clues that would satisfactorily communicate to their partner. "In focusing on the word to be communicated, they typically lost sight of the other's response to their previous clue." (p. 212). However, those subjects who were able to simultaneously take their own and their partner's perspective were able to offer the best clues and to benefit most from their partner's previous responses and clues.

What we have learned from this journey through Piaget's approach to cognition is that to interact with another in something other than parallel form—that is, in which P acts without reference to O and vice versa—requires a cognitive capability that itself develops as a result of interactions within a social environment. We have noted therefore that persons too young to have yet developed this level of cognitive organization (e.g., simultaneous decentering) have great difficulty in conceiving of collective entities, such as small groups. In other words, the concept of interactive field and other similar ideas developed in Chapters 1 and 2 are learned within a social environment as an outcome of the dual processes of assimilation and accommodation. Persons with different learning histories or incapacities, momentary or longer term, thereby even as adults will have greater difficulty in conceptualizing their part as a member of an interdependent field. They may function more like Feffer's level-one or level-two persons than the level-three individual.

Cognitive Structure

Thus far we have been concerned with the structural aspects of cognition. Specifically, Piaget's formulation and Feffer's extension of it into the interpersonal arena direct our attention to two key structural concepts: differentiation and integration (also referred to as organization). A metaphor may be helpful in explaining these structural factors. If we imagine that a person's cognitive system is like a filing drawer containing folders that classify material, then the degree of differentiation of this cognitive system refers to the number of different folders that exist. A highly differentiated system is one in which many ways exist for classifying stimulus material; a less differentiated system, by contrast, contains few ways, that is, few folders or schema by which such material may be classified. A highly differentiated cognitive system would allow the person to perceive many fine distinctions among elements; if you were to describe a friend and could only use two adjectives, whereas another person could use thirty separate terms, we would consider you to be cognitively undifferentiated relative to the other person's high degree of differentiation.

The degree to which a cognitive system is differentiated, however, is only part of the structural picture. Cognitive systems vary as well in the degree to which the differentiated elements are organized or integrated into some more complex unity. One person may see each tree but not the forest; the other may see both trees and forest. The former is highly differentiated but poorly integrated, the latter is both highly differentiated and integrated. A file drawer may contain many file folders and thus be highly differentiated; its integration, however, would require some manner of organizing these elements into more inclusive categories; these in turn could be organized into still more complex, highly integrated groupings. Basically, integration refers to the degree to which differentiated parts of a cognitive system are interdependent. The focus, thus, is upon the relationships that exist between the elements of P's intrapersonal system.

Both differentiation and integration are structural properties of cognitive systems. In our initial interpersonal example (e.g., P and O carrying a log), differentiation refers to P's viewing self, other, and task as three elements of a system; integration involves P joining into one unity P's and O's perspective on the task. As you will recall, the lack of integration hinders the creation of an interpersonally stable relationship.

Several authors (e.g., Crockett, 1965; Zajonc, 1960) have suggested that the combination of differentiation and integration creates a further structural attribute that they refer to as cognitive complexity-simplicity. A cognitively complex structure is one that is both highly differentiated and highly integrated; simplicity describes lesser differentiation and integration.

PERSON PERCEPTION

In addition to the relation between cognitive structure and interpersonal coordination (e.g., Feffer's RTT studies), several investigators (e.g., Crockett, 1965) have been concerned with the influence of cognitive complexity-simplicity on P's perception of O. Insofar as each of us can be seen in a variety of ways, a cognitively simple person will do us a disservice in their impression of us; their few concepts are likely to give them a somewhat distorted, even erroneous impression of us when compared with the richer impressions available to those who are cognitively complex. Furthermore, in that each of us gives off potentially conflicting or inconsistent images, a cognitively complex person's greater capacity to integrate differentiated elements into a larger, more coherent unity, should make it easier to deal with these interpersonal contradictions than would a cognitively simple person's lesser interpretive capacity.

The concept of *ambivalence,* involving conflicting impressions of a person or event, captures the sense of this matter. Presumably, a cognitively complex person, as compared with the cognitively simple individual, should be better able to deal with ambivalence; in other words, he or she should better be able to integrate the disparate views or feelings about another person. One effort to study this prediction (Nidorf, reported in Crockett, 1965) presented subjects with a set of traits that presumably described a single O: Pessimistic, Intelligent, Competitive, Sensitive, Kind, Self-centered. Subjects were to write their impressions of O. The researchers analyzed these impressions seeking to determine whether the subjects had integrated opposite traits into some broader framework, perhaps by calling upon the requirements of O's social role, or if they had simply retained them unintegrated. An unintegrated impression would occur if P either restated the opposing traits without trying to deal with them, or formed impressions by including only traits that had the same value and direction. The researchers independently assessed each person's degree of cognitive complexity-simplicity and correlated this score with their assessment of the degree to which P's impression of O integrated the disparate elements. A significant although admittedly low correlation of .36 supported the prediction that persons who were more cognitively complex would be better able to produce integrated impressions.

Other researchers using a slightly different experimental format report confirmative data. One of these (Scott, 1963) asked the subject to sort a listing of nations into several clusters, finding that the more cognitively complex subjects were able to group nations into the same cluster that had oppositely valued characteristics. Another researcher (Campbell, reported in Crockett, 1965) in parallel fashion, found that more cognitively complex subjects were better able than simple subjects to group their friends in ways that permitted two friends they liked not to like one another. Cognitively simply subjects tended to assume that any two of their friends would necessarily have to like one another. To state this in another way, cognitive complexity seemed to permit the person greater leeway in representing the tension that might derive from having friends who did not like one another.

Several researchers have been interested in examining additional factors that would appear to correlate with a cognitively simple or a cognitively complex cognitive structure. (Adams, Harvey & Heslin, 1966; Harvey, *et al,* 1961; Harvey, 1966; Harvey & Ware, 1967; White & Harvey, 1965. Also see Schroder, Driver & Streufert, 1967.) In general, this program of research undertaken by O. J. Harvey and his many associates has suggested that a cognitively simple structure is related to the following:

1. an extreme and highly polarized evaluation of objects, events, and persons: for example, an all-or-none view that does not take shades of grey into consideration;
2. a tendency to be intolerant of novel or ambiguous situations, and a tendency to form rather quick judgments in such situations;
3. the forming of impressions from relatively incomplete information;
4. a tendency towards rigidity in thinking which leads to a greater degree of stereotyping in judgment and creates difficulty in modifying behavior in response to new information;
5. a difficulty in taking the roles of others and gaining perspective in interpersonal situations.

Political Dogmatism.   The correspondence between cognitive complexity and political outlook has interested several social psychological investigators. Milton Rokeach (1956; 1960), for example, formulated a conception of the *dogmatic person* whose world was dichotomized into a simplistic good versus bad. Rokeach argued that dogmatism (cognitively simply structure) could be a characteristic of those of the political right or the political left, both of whom, independently of the actual content of their political ideology, structured their world into a two-category system: with me or against me. He developed a test to assess a person's dogmatism which provided empirical support for this contention about a dogmatic structure of thinking. His data suggest that dogmatism is a measurable characteristic of what he termed the *closed mind* (cognitive simplicity). In this view, the political ideologies of the right and the left share the same cognitive structure, while differing in the content of their beliefs; both constitute a similar psychological environment to which they then respond.

Further work and thinking on this matter (e.g., Harvey, Hunt, & Schroder, 1961), has suggested that persons with similar cognitive structuring are more alike than their ideological differences would initially lead us to believe; thus the movement from far right to far left politically or vice versa is easier than we might imagine. One shifts the content of beliefs in such a move, but does not shift the structure or style of thinking itself. The world thus remains the same, filled with enemies or supporters; the names of the characters simply are changed.

However, to avoid becoming overly simplistic, we should consider a few qualifications regarding the preceding analysis. In the first place, it has not yet been clearly demonstrated that simplicity-complexity are general characteristics of persons that cross all domains or areas of the person's life. A person may be complex in one domain of life and simplistic in another. Thus, for example, one may have a highly complex conception of human anatomy and physiology and yet be simplistic in political matters. In the second place, the issue regarding the cognitive similarity between the politically far right and left is itself a controversial matter, with critics of the concept of dogmatism noting how the political left has a much more complex view of the world than many on the political right; furthermore, that while indeed there have been instances of persons from the right adopting leftist ideologies, this may be more a matter of new and complex learnings than of a simple similarity of cognitive structures.

Prejudice. Another set of behaviors and thinking styles of particular interest to social psychologists involves attitudes of prejudice. The reasoning is that persons with a cognitively simplistic structure, characterized by their rigidity in thinking, their tendency to stereotype others, and their general intolerance of ambiguity, are primed to deal in prejudicial ways with members of what they easily consider to be outgroups. A fascinating nine-year follow-up study by Kutner and Gordon (1964) is instructive in demonstrating both how cognitive variables influence prejudicial attitudes and, as importantly, how a change in these cognitive variables over time is paralleled by a change in attitudes of prejudice.

In 1950, Kutner had studied a group of sixty seven-year old children, rating them as either high or low in prejudiced attitudes towards several minority groups. He found at that time that persons we would call cognitively simple tended to be the most highly prejudiced. Early in 1959, Kutner and Gordon had the opportunity to restudy about half of the original sample. They were able to ask and answer two important questions by comparing the first and second studies: (1) Were those who had been most prejudiced at age 7 still highly prejudiced at age 16? (2) Did changes in cognitive structure over the nine year period from complexity at age 7 to simplicity at age 16 or from simplicity at age 7 to complexity at age 16 relate to changes in prejudice over this same period? Their findings generally indicate *no* pattern of consistency in prejudiced attitudes over the nine-year period: Eighteen children were as prejudiced or as unprejudiced at age 16 as they were at age 7, while fifteen changed.

Perhaps the most important and interesting research finding demonstrated that shifts in cognitive structure over the nine-year period were related to shifts in prejudice. The two groups of primary interest are those who either became more or less prejudiced over the nine-year period. Kutner and Gordon report that persons who were highly prejudiced at age 7 but were low in prejudice at age 16 moved away from cognitive simplicity towards complexity, whereas those who were low in prejudice at age 7 but high at age 16 showed the reverse trend, moving towards greater simplicity over the nine-year period. See Chapters 7 and 8 for a further, relevant discussion of this and related matters.

The preceding review has been primarily a person-centered analysis of the role that cognitive structure plays in affecting the manner in which person's perceive and define situations. This emphasis has also been primarily on assimilative transformations, where the situation, including other persons, is transformed to better fit what is assumed to be the person's relatively stable, ongoing cognitive organization. If nothing else, common sense alone informs us that only part of the picture has been represented; our lives would indeed be peculiar and private were the entire picture composed of assimilations of the sort we have examined. The degree to which cognitive organization is transformed as we actively accommodate ourselves to the realities of the world around us has an equally obvious and important role.

Yet, person-factors, especially in the realm of cognitive processes, remain vital matters for us to consider. We interact with situations differently and experience them differently, in part, as a function of our different organizational capacities for dealing with environmental stimuli, in part as a function of other, both momentary and longer-term aspects of our person. It is to these functional aspects that we now turn our attention.

Functional Factors: Selectivity of Information Processing

Let us start with an experimental observation reported by Mischel and several of his associates (e.g., Mischel, Ebbesen & Zeiss, 1972). Preschool children are first asked to indicate which of two objects they would like, a pretzel or a marshmallow. They are then told by the experimenter that he has to leave the room for a period of time, but when he returns they can have the object they most want; however, if they prefer not to wait, they can ring a bell calling him back into the room at which time they can have the less preferred object. The investigators examined how waiting was influenced by various factors; as one example, they noted how being distracted from thinking about the preferred object facilitated waiting whereas activities that led the child to attend more closely to the object shortened their waiting time. Thus self-control was accomplished by a selectivity of attention, in this case by not attending to the objects.

In another study, the same investigators (Mischel *et al.,* 1972) demonstrated how if children could think to themselves about "fun things," they could increase their delay period more than if they thought about either "sad things" or about the objects themselves. In another investigation, Mischel and Baker (1975) found that children who were instructed to "transform the stimulus" from a pretzel into a little brown log or the marshmallow into a white cloud or cotton ball, could wait longer than those instructed to think of the pretzel's salty taste or the sweetness of the marshmallow. As Mischel (1973) comments: "The results clearly show that what is in the children's heads—not what is physically in front of them—determines their ability to delay" (p. 260).

More generally, peoples' abilities to transform stimulus situations, selectively attending to some aspects and not to others, affects their behavior in the situation. As the preceding research suggests, such selectivity can occur on the basis of instructions given to the person by others in the actual situation; on the other hand, instructions can be self-generated as a function of the momentary states of the person (e.g., hunger or other needs) or even long-term dispositions (e.g., attitudes, personality traits, etc.). In either case, behavior is jointly determined by factors within the person (e.g., attentional mechanisms) and within the situation (e.g., availability of objects, distractions, instructions, etc.).

Further research both illustrative of this issue and relevant to a concern with cognitive mechanisms of coping with environmental stress has emerged from several different sources. The extensive research program undertaken by Lazarus and his associates is instructive in this regard (e.g., Lazarus & Alfert, 1964; Lazarus, Opton, Nomikos, & Rankin, 1965; Lazarus, 1966; Lazarus, Averill, & Opton, 1970). One major method employed by the Lazarus group is to show subjects a stressful film, for example, a primitive subincision ritual in which the male is circumcised with a sharp stone instrument; the sound track of the film offers the subjects different ways of defining the situation, for example, as something of anthropological interest or as something truly painful. Physiological and psychological measures obtained from subjects viewing the film under these different instructional sets suggested how their experience of stress could be systematically reduced as a function of being able to cognitively define the situation.

Employing a somewhat different method, Monat, Averill, and

Lazarus (1972) were able to demonstrate how selectivity of attention could likewise be used by the subject in order to reduce the experience of stress. In this latter study, one group of subjects knew that they would receive a painful electric shock, but did not know when it would occur; a second group knew when a shock might occur, but did not know if they would actually receive one. Measures of subjects' level of arousal under these different conditions were obtained. The results are consistent with the following interpretation: knowing that a stressful shock will occur but not when it will, permitted the subjects time to deploy their attention, to think about other things, and thereby to reduce their arousal and overall experience of stress. On the other hand, those subjects who knew when a shock might be delivered became highly vigilent, awaiting the event's arrival and thereby experiencing greater stress.

A recent study provides further confirmation of the role that cognitive factors play in coping with stressful situations. In the Holmes and Houston study (1974), subjects who were expecting to receive a painful shock were given instructions designed to help them redefine the experience, for example, to think of the shock as a vibrating sensation rather than as an electric shock. Measures of physiological arousal indicated that while expecting to receive a shock did increase the subject's arousal level, redefining the shock and thinking of it as a vibrating sensation helped reduce what otherwise would have been a higher level of arousal. Once again we see how instructional sets, in this case provided by the experimenter, helped redefine a noxious situation and facilitate the person's coping with it.

A considerable interest was generated many years ago in the role of so-called functional functions (e.g., values, attitudes, beliefs, needs, etc.) in the selectivity of attention (what P attends to in the environment), of recall (what P stores and is later able to retrieve), and of exposure (what kinds of situations P selects to be exposed to). It will be helpful to our broader understanding of the role of cognitive factors as determinants of behavior to briefly examine several of these earlier efforts in the context of an information-processing model of thinking and cognition.

INFORMATION-PROCESSING MODEL

If we may speak metaphorically for the moment, it is helpful to think of cognition as an information-processing system, composed of elements and their interdependent relationships (e.g., Erdelyi, 1974; Neisser, 1967). In speaking of an information-processing system, we intend to convey the picture of the person's receiving input or information from the environment and then subjecting that information to a variety of transformations before generating some form of output or behavior. Although our emphasis in this model is on the transformation of the input as a function of the person's processing system, it is also clear, as we have noted elsewhere, that the system itself undergoes transformations as it accommodates itself to the environmental input.

The models available for representing information processing are varied and differ in their specifics. Our concern here is not to produce the definitive model, for that remains a distant ambition of investigators in the field, rather, we simply wish to share a sense of this approach within which the functional determinants of selectivity will become more readily understood and meaningful. In schematic form, with only some of the major elements and relationships filled in, Figure 2 provides a helpful summary of one information-processing model of cognition (adapted from Erdelyi, 1974):

Receptor systems refer to the actual physical receptors, for example, the eyes, the ears, and so forth, through which information enters the total cognitive system. Iconic storage is assumed to be a system in which the incoming stimulus event is very briefly retained, for a fraction of a second or so; the term icon is used to suggest that the information exists as some partial, rapidly fading replica of its original form. Short-term storage refers to a somewhat more stable, longer-term (e.g., 30 seconds) system where information selected from the raw or iconic system is encoded (i.e., selected for transfer); it is the world of our short-term memory. It is typically assumed that information at this level of processing is available for our conscious awareness. The encoding system refers to the various processes that transform information from one system to another; for example, examining input for its meaning may involve encoding for long-term storage only information that fits existing long-

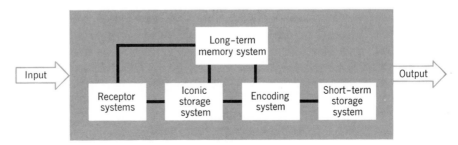

Figure 2

term memory or that is consistent with wishes or that does not trigger traumatic recollections.

The diagram indicates both the elements of this hypothetical information-processing system of human cognition as well as several possible lines of relationship between these elements. Note that a line connecting two systems, for example, between long-term memory and iconic storage represents an examination of the material in the iconic system by the contents of the long-term memory. Such an examination, however, does not necessarily mean that the material so scrutinized will be encoded into long-term memory. In fact, material examined may be selected out and thereby not be transfered from one system to the next.

Let us leave out of our discussion a more complete analysis of this hypothetical system; it would really take us too far afield. What is important for us to see are the various points at which some selectivity of processing can occur. For example, at the receptor level we can selectively attend to various aspects of a stimulus situation; in the simplest case, we can close our eyes and literally not look at those things we don't want to see. Likewise, as some research suggests (e.g., Hess, 1965), even pupil size can change as a function of our attitudes and needs, dilating when we confront interesting stimuli and constricting when not. As the diagram suggests, long-term memory is linked with the receptor system; this is intended to suggest how deeper facets of one's personality, such as traumatic memories from the past, may affect the openness of receptors to certain kinds of stimuli. Chronic long-term *sets* or directions for perceiving stimuli exist, as well as relatively less enduring sets induced by one's self or by others, as in the Mischel and the Lazarus studies. In either case, selectivity can occur as the receptor system is opened or closed to certain kinds of input.

Information in iconic storage is also selectively processed either by short- or long-term memory; thus, P could be said to have scanned input before awareness of its presence and to have selected out certain inputs for further processing, for example, for transfer from iconic to short-term storage, while rejecting other material. Material not so processed would rapidly disappear. This is an especially important point; it suggests that we may perceive input at one level (e.g., iconic storage) and selectively process out parts of that material before we perceive it at a level of awareness (e.g., short-term storage). In turn, processing at that level of the system may further transform the input so that what remains to be called upon later from long-term memory is only a highly selected and thoroughly processed survivor of this total information-processing system.

The importance of this model is that it directs our attention to the many levels on which cognitive processing occurs and thus within which selectivity of attention, recall, and even exposure are possible. The model also stresses two related points that we might otherwise have overlooked. Human survival in a world containing such a vast array of potential stimuli requires the operation of some selectivity of processing; the alternative would be chaos. But survival likewise demands that the selectivity that occurs be built upon a base of learned experience in negotiating situations in the world. We would be in sorry straits if we had to face each situation anew without benefit of experience built up through earlier learnings. Thus any model we examine must deal both with selectivity and memory.

If the particular version of the model we have diagrammed does not turn out in the long run to be a precise replica of what actually transpires, it matters less than it does to have noted the important role that selectivity plays in our everyday lives. None of this requires that we attribute great rationality to the processing system; indeed while adaptation clearly demands selectivity built upon experience, who is to say that experience has taught us how to select the best out from the array of our daily confrontations of what we should attend to and recall. The persistence of interaction cycles that seem more destructive than healthful (e.g., the nagging wife and withdrawing husband of Chapter 2) offer us but one of many cases in which we are guided to select a response that completes a cycle that, although it is familiar, is not necessarily the most productive alternative available. We can now turn to an examination of some early and more recent work dealing with human selectivity.

Set and Selectivity.   In 1904, Külpe presented subjects with groups of stimuli consisting of letters that varied in color, location, and the number and way in which they were clustered. Just before some presentations, he told his subjects to note only one of the several possible dimensions; for example, attend to the colors you will be shown. On other presentations subjects were not given any specific set. Subjects were asked to report the characteristics of the stimuli as best they could. Results indicated that they were more accurate in reporting stimulus qualities to which they had been set to pay attention. It was suggested by Külpe and later taken up by others, that set served to facilitate the clarity of the particular stimulus quality.

This idea implies a *perceptual tuning* or *perceptual enhancement* effect (Haber, 1966); what we are set to attend to stands out with greater clarity or greater vigor than nonset material. Although the sets that Külpe and other early workers dealt with involved explicit instructions (as even with Mischel's and other's more recent work), it seems likely that a person may establish implicit sets (from long-term memory, for example) to pay attention to certain parts of an otherwise complex stimulus situation. In more contemporary usage, aspects of the early notion of mental set persist in such notions as attitude, expectancy, value, need, motive, and so forth. A few examples of this work that employ the concept of need or motive will be helpful for us to consider.

SELECTIVITY: NEEDS AND MOTIVES

A substantial portion of the early work that sought to relate P's needs to perceptual selectivity employed physiological need, in particular, hunger. The research focused on the extent to which a hungry person was more sensitive to food or food-related objects than was a sated person. Presumably, if this question could be answered affirmatively for the psychological need of hunger, then it might apply as well to psychological states of need and attitude. One of the earliest and still classic investigations was conducted by Levine, Chein, and Murphy. They presented subjects with cards of ambiguous drawings, food objects, and general household articles all shown behind a ground glass screen. Those in the experimental group had been deprived of food for one, three, six, or nine hours, while those in the control group were tested immediately after lunch. Subjects were simply asked to view the cards and to associate verbally to each one. Results indicated a rise in food-type responses with one to three hours of deprivation, then a drop in food responses with six to nine hours of deprivation. The authors concluded that up to a point, food deprivation helped influence the subjects perception of the environment in a wish-fulfilling manner; thus, hungry subjects, wanting food, saw ambiguous figures as food objects.

Other researchers (e.g., Atkinson & McClelland, 1948; McClelland & Atkinson, 1948) offered general substantiation for this effect, particularly when the stimulus material was in some manner relevant to the need rather than being completely ambiguous. The point is that persons who are hungry are more likely than sated persons to perceive food in settings where such visions are relevant; however, the hungry person does not indiscriminately experience visions of food regardless of the nature of the situation and the information it provides.

The program of research undertaken by Atkinson and McClelland (1948) is relevant to consider. They employed the Thematic Apperception Test (TAT), consisting of pictures to which persons are asked to make up stories telling what is happening, who the persons are, what they are doing, feeling, and thinking, what they want, what will happen, and what the outcome will be. Atkinson, McClel-

land, and their associates developed a systematic procedure for analyzing these stories and for coding their content. Their initial
research used TAT pictures to assess hunger, noting, for example,
that stories from hungry subjects frequently referred to food-related
issues and that activities of the protagonists involved overcoming
obstacles in order to get more food. Their subsequent work focused
on the social psychological needs for achievement, for affiliation,
and for power (see Atkinson, 1958 for a useful summary). Their
research now dealt with whether people high in need for achievement—that is, having a need to excel according to some internal set
of standards of excellence—when that need was aroused, would
selectively structure their psychological life space in ways to reflect
achievement themes.

Vigilance and Defense. Preliminary work indicated that the TAT
could be scored to reflect individual differences in psychological
needs, such as achievement. It was then possible to present subjects
scored as having differential degrees of the need for achievement
with ambiguous stimuli and note to what extent the need influences
their perception. One way of doing this is to use a tachistoscope, a
slide projector that precisely times the exposure of a slide's presentation, to present subjects lists of words varying in their degree of
relatedness to achievement, success, and failure. With this device,
it is possible to assess the individual's threshold for given words, by
noting the speed with which the subject reports seeing the word. A
high threshold suggests a longer exposure required to see a particular word; a low threshold, the reverse. The argument, of course, is
that subjects high in the need for achievement should have a lower
threshold to achievement-related words than subjects low in
achievement. This effect, confirmed in several studies, (e.g., McClelland & Liberman, 1949; Moulton, *et al,* 1958) was termed *perceptual
vigilance;* it suggests how a psychological need selectively sensitizes
a person to certain environmental features.

In a related study, Postman, Bruner, and McGinnies (1948) employed a paper-and-pencil test—the Allport-Vernon scales—to assess an individual's religious, aesthetic, political, social, theoretical,
and economic values. They noted that there was a lower threshold
to value-relevant words; a person highest in the religious value, for
example, had a lower recognition threshold for words relevant to
religion than for those relevant, say, to political values. If we can be
highly sensitive to one class of stimuli, is it not also likely that we
will be blind to another class? The answer, framed in the terms of
a model of *perceptual defense* rather than vigilance, is generally
affirmative. One of the earliest and most controversial demonstrations of the defense effect was provided by McGinnies (1949) who

presented his subjects with a set of taboo, emotion-arousing words as well as the garden-variety nontaboo terms. He noted that his subjects took longer times to report seeing the taboo words than the neutral words; McGinnies saw this as the operation of perceptual defense.

Critics, however, were quick to note several serious questions about his research methodology, and after several years of additional research essentially laid his original efforts to final rest. Yet, as the information-processing model suggests, defensive or vigilant selectivity in perception can occur, especially if we think of perception as the entire process from input to output rather than only one facet of that process as the McGinnies and other related works originally suggested.

MEMORY AND RECALL

There has also been substantial interest over the years in studying the selectivity of P's memory and recall. The oft-repeated classic study, reported first in 1943 by Levine and Murphy, presented strongly pro-Communist and strongly anti-Communist subjects with pro- and anti-Communist material to read and then later to recall. They met with their subjects over a period of four weeks and were thereby able to study both the learning of the material as a function of their subjects attitude and its recall. Their results indicated that the pro-Communists learned the pro-passage better than the anti-Communists; in their turn, the antis learned the anti-passage better than the pros. The results for forgetting were as striking: the pros forgot less of the pro-passage than the antis, who forgot less of the anti-passage. These results suggest that the content of an individual's cognitive schema influences both learning and recall and thereby structures the person's life space.

While several other investigators (e.g., Alper & Korchin, 1952; Jones & Kohler, 1958) were able to replicate the selectivity effect of the Levine and Murphy study, others (Greenwald & Sakamura, 1967; Waly & Cook, 1966) using more controlled research designs, were unable to find this effect. Recently one set of investigators, Smith and Jamieson (1972) argued that *ego-involvement* was the crucial attribute that influenced P's learning and recall. The more personally involving the pro or anti attitude, the more likely it is to have the differential learning and recall effects of which Levine and Murphy originally spoke. Coming at the matter from another perspective, Greaves (1972) has argued and demonstrated experimentally that P's complexity of cognitive structure was related to P's differential learning and recall. Greaves' research design assessed the degree of cognitive complexity within his subjects, had a lecturer present them pro and anti material about the United States or Sweden, and then evaluated their recall of the details of the arguments presented to them. His findings suggest that subjects with a more cognitively simple structure function more selectively in their recall than subjects with greater complexity; the latter show more accuracy (i.e., less selectivity) in their recall. The point that Greaves makes is that he would find no selectivity effects if he had not examined the influence of cognitive complexity-simplicity; apparently, then, ego-involvement and cognitive complexity-simplicity are important factors to consider in tempering our analysis of the principle of selective learning and recall of controversial material.

On Cognitive Balance and Selectivity. Reasoning from yet another, though related perspective, one consistent with the information-processing model, Norman T. Feather (1969) has suggested that persons will selectively recall material as a function of its degree of congruence with their ongoing cognitive system. This is reminiscent of Herbart's early view which spoke of a person's *apperceptive mass* as that ongoing organization of the mind that provided the basis for selectively processing incoming material; things that fit with the state of the apperceptive mass were more welcomed than things that did not fit. Feather provided experimental support for this view.

His Australian University students were presented with pro and anti arguments concerning U.S. involvement in Vietnam; a week before the arguments were given all the subjects had their own attitudes on U.S. involvement assessed. Feather reasoned that a pro-U.S. attitude, for example, formed the basis for an ongoing cognitive system in which pro arguments with which P agreed or anti arguments with which P disagreed would be congruent, while pro arguments with which P disagreed or anti arguments with which P agreed would be incongruent. The reverse should hold for persons having an anti-U.S. attitude; the following table summarizes these expectations which were borne out by Feather's experiment.

	Arguments Congruent with Attitude System	Arguments Incongruent with Attitude System
Pro-U.S. Viet-Involvement Attitude	Pro-agree Anti-disagree	Pro-disagree Anti-agree
Anti-U.S. Viet-Involvement Attitude	Anti-agree Pro-disagree	Anti-disagree Pro-agree

Feather's theory and research is especially instructive in that it suggests the importance of taking P's ongoing cognitive system into account in evaluating the manner by which learning and recall will be selective. The point then is not if P will or will not selectively recall material, but rather under what conditions.

In a theoretically related investigation, McLaughlin (1971) suggested that if P likes O, then this forms the basis for an ongoing cognitive system with consequences for P's recall of O's personal characteristics. Essentially, attributes of O that fit this system (i.e., that are congruent with P's liking of O) will be better recalled than attributes that are incongruent. McLaughlin's experimental work generally confirms this finding, thus adding further to the theoretical model upon which both he and Feather base their work.

By way of previewing a discussion we shall shortly get into, Feather's study, and McLaughlin's, are based on a theory of cognitive balance: items in the table that are listed in the congruent column indicate a balanced cognitive structure; items listed in the incongruent column indicate an imbalanced cognitive structure. The argument has been that "balanced attitude structures ... will be more likely to survive in memory than unbalanced attitude structures, and that arguments keyed into these balanced attitude structures will therefore be more available for recall" (Feather, 1969, p. 317). Keep this formulation in mind as we will have reason to return to it soon.

ON RUMORS

The study of rumor formation and transmission, of early interest to social psychologists, provides another instance of the role of selectivity in organizing P's psychological environment. Research on rumor also gives us further insights into the active role that an ongoing cognitive structure plays in arranging and rearranging new information, to create a coherent, congruent unity, in this case, a rumor. The classic work in this genre was conducted years ago by Gordon Allport and Leo Postman (1947), building upon the ideas suggested earlier by Bartlett (1932). Allport and Postman presented a slide of a complex social scene and had the subject describe the scene to another subject (who had not seen it), who described it to still another subject, who in turn described it to another, and so on through six or seven persons. With this format, it is possible to evaluate the degree and nature of the changes that occur as the story moves from person to person. In this study, we are dealing with the influence of cognitive factors on P's selective attention to aspects of the scene or to the story being told, on P's immediate recall of this material, and on P's reorganization of the material seen and recalled as P transmits it to another person.

As the story traveled, Allport and Postman report several major processes occurring, each of which involved a manner of embedding the story into an ongoing cognitive organization. *Leveling* involved dropping out details as the story moved down the chain of persons. Elements were combined and recombined into a more concise form. *Sharpening* involved the selective perception, recall and reporting of certain details while ignoring others. But perhaps the most significant process involved *assimilation,* several forms of which were uncovered:

1. *Assimilation to principal theme.* As the story moved down the line of subjects, a leading theme emerged as the framework within which all other details were integrated, resulting in a more coherent story than originally existed. For example, one picture evoked a war theme in which successive storytellers introduced war-related elements to preserve the theme even though this distorted the facts in the original picture.

2. *Assimilation to closure.* The stories showed what in Gestalt Psychology is termed *closure, pregnänz,* or good figure, a tendency to modify events in the direction of simplification and good or complete form. For example, in one picture a sign read "Lowe's Pa ..." Subjects completed this in their stories as "Lowe's Palance."

3. *Assimilation by condensation.* This process parallels the process that Freud noted within dreams; it involves fusing several items into one. Instead of reporting several ads on a streetcar, subjects reported a "billboard" in the background. Instead of detailing the people present, subjects summarized the scene as "several people sitting and standing."

4. *Assimilation to expectation.* When arrangements and relationships that we expect do not actually occur our recollection often puts them back into their expected places. In one scene a drugstore was located in the middle of the block; in the stories it was moved towards its expected location (for 1947 at least), the corner. But perhaps the most startling assimilation of this type involved the streetcar scene. In the original picture, two men, one black, one white, were standing; the white man held a razor in his hand. Allport and Postman report that in more than half of their separate studies, the subjects moved the razor from the white man's hand to the black man's to fit their stereotyped expectation.

5. *Assimilation to linguistic habit.* The tendency noted in the study was for subjects to fit events to linguistic cliches. For example, a professor might be reported as a "long-haired professor" or an Oriental person as a "Japanese spy." Short-hand verbal cliches were employed instead of the full details of the scene.

Cognitive Tuning. The kinds of distortion that Allport and Post-man's work reveal can be said to occur in our everyday efforts to receive and transmit messages. Robert Zajonc (1960) offers us a useful way of thinking about the cognitive factors involved in what he calls *cognitive tuning.* Zajonc argues that a person who is tuned or set to receive a message has a more loosely structured cognitive system than one who is tuned to transmit a message. His research set subjects to be either receivers or transmitters; his findings showed that subjects who were set to transmit had a more highly differentiated and more organized cognitive system as compared with those who were set to receive. Follow-up work by another researcher, Cohen (1961), indicated that subjects who were set to transmit an impression of another person maintained a highly differentiated view of this person and therefore were less likely than receivers to integrate conflicting material contained in the impression.

These studies suggest that cognitive factors that could lead to selective recall occur more as the individual prepares to transmit a message, a rumor, or an impression than when one prepares to receive it; it is during the period preparatory to transmission that the person begins to select out material to differentiate, to reshape, to reorganize. During this phase, the individual may eliminate details that do not neatly fit into an existing, organized cognitive structure, or he or she may condense elements into a single thematically consistent focus.

SELECTIVE EXPOSURE

Up to this point, our emphasis has been on factors that influence the selectivity of P's attention, recall, and transmission of material. Observers of the social habits of persons suggested the existence of still another kind of selectivity, best termed *selective exposure.* It is likely, for example, that the majority of those in attendance at a political rally will have opinions similar to those of the candidate they have come to hear. They expose themselves to arguments supportive of opinions they already possess. Or as another example, examine your own and your friend's reading habits; it is likely that *The New Republic* will be found in the homes of those of a liberal political persuasion, while more politically conservative individuals will be reading *National Review.*

This kind of selectivity of exposure has been noted by those concerned with the effectiveness of political and advertising campaigns designed to influence public opinion. Some early work on political perception conducted by Berelson, Lazarsfeld, and McPhee (1954), focusing on the 1948 presidential election between Truman and Dewey, found that there were really two distinct kinds of political campaigns running simultaneously. The first is the objective campaign of information and advertising carried on by the candidate and his aides. The second, equally important campaign is carried on in the voter's mind and involves selectivity of perception, recall, and exposure. And there is no simple correspondence between the two campaigns. Berelson and his colleagues report, for example, that voters who were most strongly in favor of one candidate were likely to perceive his position on issues to be closer to their own than it really was, meanwhile misperceiving the opposition by distorting actual similarity between their stand and his. Work by other investigators provide corroborative evidence. Hyman and Sheatsley (1958) report results from a national survey showing that persons tend to expose themselves selectively to information that is supportive to their attitudes. They also report finding a hard core of "know nothings," a group that avoids exposure to any information, supportive or nonsupportive.

While few would argue that selectivity of exposure does occur, and that indeed there is a strong correspondence between our ongoing cognitive system (e.g., our attitudes, values, and beliefs) and the kinds of persons, places, and things we choose to attend, read, listen to, and so forth, understanding both the reasons why and the equally apparent contradictions to such selective exposure remains a complex and difficult matter to settle. Using the experimental research laboratory to conduct their studies, social psychologists have come to the realization that selectivity of exposure which is indeed helpful to us by supporting our existing belief systems, at the same time, can work to our disadvantage by limiting the range within which our opportunities for growth can occur.

Much of the laboratory work on selective exposure (see Freedman & Sears, 1965) has taken off from a consistency theory framework, similar to the notions argued by Feather for selective recall. Presumably, if given a choice to read material that supports or that challenges one's existing attitudes on important issues, the individual would prefer to read supportive materials: that is, because such material is congenial to the person's ongoing cognitive system. Repeated efforts to study this rather clear and simple expectation, however, have turned up an inconsistent set of findings; many persons do not function as this consistency model would predict, preferring to read the oppositional over the supportive material.

One especially valuable field study of this effect was undertaken by Janis and Rausch (1970). They interviewed Yale students, some of whom had signed a high commitment pledge not to serve in the military in Vietnam if drafted; others were nonsigners. These subjects were later interviewed, shown the titles of magazine articles, four of which were supportive of the "we won't go" pledge and four of which were antipledge, and asked to indicate their interest in reading these articles. A consistency model of selective exposure would argue that the pledge signers should prefer to expose themselves to reading the four supportive articles, while the nonsigners should prefer the antipledge material. Results, however, indicated no difference between the signers and nonsigners in their interest in reading the propledge material. More importantly, those who were pledge signers actually had a higher preference for the anti-articles than did the nonsigners, an apparent reversal of the model's prediction.

It would seem that the consistency argument for selectivity of exposure, while applicable under certain circumstances, is not sufficiently complex to handle the multitude of reasons why people would see benefit to themselves by being exposed to the opposition. In the Janis and Rausch study, for example, interviewing suggested that reading opposition arguments would help the pledge signers in their dealings with parents and friends who might try to dissuade them of their commitment not to go into the military. Vigilant concern about the other side may be especially useful to an individual who is facing a decision dilemma or who wants to rehearse in advance the answers to the kinds of questions he or she is likely to be challenged with from the opposition. In other words, becoming familiar with the opposition, rather than undermining one's own beliefs, might be seen as a reasoned tactic for enlarging and later supporting those beliefs.

It also seems clear that in many circumstances, people might selectively expose themselves to information primarily to gain some social rewards. For example, a businessman may attend a political speech or dinner and be counted among our selective exposure audience but not because he's there only to hear supportive arguments —which he may indeed enjoy—but because it is good for business to be in attendance. On the other hand, a person who highly values being reasonable and fair-minded might find it important to give the opposition a fair hearing, and thus be counted among our exceptions to selective exposure: that is, because they are exposing themselves to oppositional material.

What may seem to be exceptions to a principle of selective exposure, in fact, are really an outline of the complex array of factors involved in the organization of P's psychological environment. Indeed, we all expose ourselves to persons and material more supportive than questioning of our beliefs; yet we also tend to seek out apparently oppositional material, paradoxically at times to further bolster our arguments, or at times, for reasons that have less to do with cognitive support than with other functions (e.g., being fair-minded).

Our capacity of being selective in our attention, recall, and exposure provides individuals with one of the few shields by which they can maintain their integrity in an otherwise intrusive, attention-grabbing world. Without such selectivity, persons would be at the mercy of the winds and currents of opinion. Yet, with total selectivity, no one would ever grow or change, but would only spiral more deeply into narrow, private, tunnel-visioned burrows. Somewhere between these poles, persons may both grow and maintain their integrity.

Cognitive Balance

In our description of an information-processing model of selectivity, we spoke of a cognitive system with parts and their relationships. What we could also have said was that each part of that whole system (e.g., long-term memory system) may also be seen as a system in its own right, containing elements and relationships. For example, we can say that the elements are in the form of ideas or concepts about things and that these elements can exist in an interdependent relationship, functioning as a whole rather than as independent parts. To understand the part under such circumstances, we must understand the whole system of relationships in which it exists; its fate is a function of the fate of those parts with which it is related.

In our discussion of selective recall, we saw an analysis of this sort in Feather's research. The elements he presented were:
1. P's attitude towards U.S. intervention in Vietnam;
2. arguments about U.S. intervention;
3. P's attitude toward those arguments.
For each element, there could be either a positive (+) or a negative (–) position, where positive means agreement or approval, and negative connotes disagreement or disapproval. It is Feather's contention that these three elements are parts of an interdependent system that can be expressed in Figure 3.

It is Feather's further contention and empirical finding that recall will be better for arguments within congruent or, as we will now call them, *balanced cognitive systems,* than within incongruent or *imbalanced systems.* In the diagram, systems 1 through 4 are balanced, while systems 5 through 8 are imbalanced. To read the diagram and refer it back to Feather's study, simply note for system 1, for example, that P agrees with the arguments about U.S. inter-

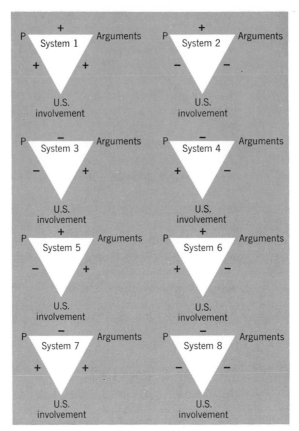

Figure 3 *An Example of Cognitive Balance and Imbalance.*

vention (P + Argument); that the arguments approve of U.S. intervention (Argument + U.S. Involvement); and that P likewise approves of U.S. involvement (P + U.S. Involvement). Let us take as another example system 6. Here we note that P agrees with the arguments (P + Argument); the arguments disapprove of U.S. Involvement (Argument – U.S. Involvement); and finally, that P approves of U.S. involvement (P + U.S. Involvement).

Following up the thesis of the Feather study that showed how *recall* of material that was embedded in a balanced configuration was better than recall of material that was part of an imbalanced configuration, several other investigators have demonstrated that persons *learn* balanced structures better than imbalanced ones. Zajonc and Burnstein (1965), for example, presented their subjects with hypothetical social structures and found that it was generally easier for them to learn a balanced than an imbalanced structure. Consistent with the contention that imbalance is evident when P likes O and when disagreements about X exist, Zajonc and Burnstein also found that positive relationships within social structures were easier to learn than negative relationships in which P disliked O.

To say that a cognitive system is balanced or imbalanced is to take note of an attribute of the system as a whole, of the interdependent relationships among the elements. A review of the diagram from Feather's Research informs us that a cognitive system is balanced when the algebraic multiplication of the signs of its elements yields a positive result; it is imbalanced whenever this result is negative (Cartwright & Harary, 1956). Thus four of the three-element systems of the diagram are balanced in that either all the signs are positive (e.g., system 1) or at least two signs are negative (e.g., systems 2, 3, and 4).

This mechanical manner of determining the balance of a cognitive system, of course, does not provide us with much information about the psychological meaning of cognitive balance or imbalance. Fritz Heider (1959), a pioneer in the study and analysis of cognitive systems, suggests that we all intuitively sense when a situation is disharmonious or imbalanced and thus when an unsteady cognitive state can be said to exist. He points out, for example, that we sense such imbalance in people who avoid others they like, or who dislike people with whom they agree but like persons with whom they disagree. Likewise, we sense imbalance and disharmony if the hero gets killed at the end of the film or if the person who does all of the hard work receives no rewards, while the lazy individual achieves fame and fortune. When our world is balanced and harmonious, all of the good, positive elements fall together on one side of our personal cognitive ledger and the bad, negative elements fall on the other side.

Recalling Newcomb's research on the attitudes of Bennington College students reported earlier will offer us another version of the theory of cognitive balance. Newcomb's argument essentially was that he could not understand the students' attitudes on major public issues of the day without at the same time considering their attitudes towards persons and groups within the college itself and the attitude of these latter persons towards those same issues. In other words, these sets of attitudes formed an interdependent system.

Let us use X to represent the public issues that Newcomb investigated; let P be the student we are studying and O in this case refers to persons and groups within Bennington College. Newcomb is suggesting that in order to understand P's attitudes towards X, we must realize that these attitudes are themselves one element of a dynamic system composed of P's attitudes towards O and O's attitudes towards X. This system is said to be balanced, for example, when P likes O, and P and O agree in their evaluation of X, both either favoring or disfavoring it.

Coorientation. In Newcomb's version of balance theory (see Newcomb, 1953; 1959), the stress is placed upon what he terms a process of *coorientation* in which P's orientation towards X-objects is always accompanied by an orientation towards other persons who are assumed also to have an orientation towards X. Coorientation also suggests that P's orientation towards O is always accompanied by P's orientation towards X-objects, towards which P assumes that both P and O are oriented. Coorientation informs us that from P's perspective, a psychological field is constituted to form a system in which other persons are seen in the context of their attitudes (i.e., orientation) towards important X-objects or in which X-objects are seen as they are related to the other person's attitudes. The state of any one element in the total field (e.g., P's attraction towards O) is said to be a function of the state of the total field. Thus, as noted, if P's orientation to X is similar to O's orientation, then the total system is balanced if the P–O relationship is positive: the state of P–O is a function therefore of this total field.

THE BASES OF BALANCE

Heider's conception of balance places its major emphasis on the idea that a cognitive strain exists when a set of relationships is imbalanced. The person whose cognitive system is imbalanced is said to experience tension that motivates a change towards the preferred state of balance. We will examine shortly both the nature of this tension and some of the ways in which balance may be restored within a system.

In his efforts to understand the bases for the preference for a balanced system, Newcomb turned to person's learning history. He noted that our own direct experiences with things, persons, and events is limited, much of what we know about our world is based on information that comes from others. Children may learn that the stove is hot by direct experimentation, but they may also learn this important lesson by listening to their parents. Children, however, and for that matter parents, cannot readily learn directly by their own experience that Hitler was an evil man or that Lincoln was virtuous; for this, they rely on the information that others provide. Newcomb notes further that we all learn to rely on trusted or liked others to provide us with such information while discounting the information from distrusted or disliked others. Thus insofar as a discrepancy is generated between P's assessment of some matter (i.e., X) and the assessment of a liked or trusted O, an unsteady, disharmonious state exists.

Essentially, then, coorientation (e.g., evaluating X against the background of O's evaluations of X) is a basic process of our learning; it is similar in many respects to Piaget's concept of decentering in which the person attends to different aspects of the whole. Cognitive balance, thus, is similar to the state of equilibrium that results when these differentiated parts are harmoniously integrated into one whole. Tension results when such balance or equilibrium cannot be accomplished.

Besides the sheer cognitive strain that can result, the disharmonious state of imbalance can also be seen in terms of what has been called *effectance* (Byrne & Clore, 1967; White, 1959). It is presumed that P is motivated to become competent in dealing with the environment and that a significant part of such competence requires that P learn to construct an ordered, meaningful, and trustworthy world. Effectance motivation refers to a drive to learn how to function competently; in this view, then, balance and imbalance refer to conditions that are either conducive to effectance and competence (balance) or troublesome for effectance and competence (imbalance).

There are two basic countereffectance meanings that occur when P realizes an imbalanced state with respect to O:
1. The accuracy of the assumptions upon which P's relation to O has been based is now open to doubt and question.
2. The correctness of P's own conceptions about the world is potentially undermined.

Picture a situation in which Jane, who for sometime has had a good and trusting relationship with Betty, discovers that in matters of war and peace Betty is a hawk while Jane is a deeply committed pacifist. The discovery of this disagreement over an important X-matter (war or peace), a discrepancy of which Jane was not aware, has built one aspect of their relationship upon a false assumption, requiring a reevaluation of the relationship itself. Furthermore, to discover that her trusted and liked friend disagrees with her may plant a seed of doubt in Jane's own mind about her own position on war and peace; perhaps she relied on Betty's support to reinforce her own position and on learning that she and Betty disagree, she loses this support and now questions the basis of her own views.

Not only is the relationship open to question, but as the example suggests, so too is Jane's assessment about X. For the most part, we are likely to assume that "What I see as correct, others see as correct," and to assume it about both the nature of our relationship with others and our conception of reality (see Schutz, 1970–1971 on this point). We are inclined to assume that persons we like, like us in return and the world we live in for the most part appears similar to the world O lives in, when O is trusted and liked. All of this informs us that:

1. Imbalance is an unsteady cognitive state within P, with implications for P's relationship to both O and to X.
2. A symptom of the unsteady state is the tension that P experiences and that may be communicated to O.
3. A preference exists for balanced over imbalanced states.
4. This preference will be revealed both by efforts to resist the transformation of a balanced state into an imbalanced one and vice versa.
5. Imbalance introduces doubt about relationships between persons as well as between persons' own conceptions of the nature of reality.
6. P's effectance and competence are undermined when striking imbalances are revealed.

An Expanded Conception

A theory of cognitive balance, as we have seen, emphasizes the relationship between the elements of P's cognitive system; the argument is that tension will be generated when the patterning of these relationships within P's intrapersonal cognitive system is imbalanced. Alternate views regarding the bases for such tension have also been posited. It will be helpful for us to review several of these contrasting and expanded perspectives.

For the most part, the alternate conceptions emphasize the importance of one element of the system rather than the patterning of elements to form a system. For example, one position suggests that tension occurs whenever P dislikes O regardless of P's and O's agreement or disagreement on X-issues. Basically, whenever dislike is present, P will feel uncomfortable and will endeavor to leave the relationship. In this view, therefore, we are not dealing with tension as a result of the interdependence among the elements of P's cognitive system; rather, one element, in this case P's liking for O, is posited as the main determinant.

Several investigations led to this conclusion (e.g., Jordan, 1953; 1966; 1968; Price, Harburg & Newcomb, 1966; Rodrigues, 1967). In the typical research design, subjects are presented with a set of hypothetical P–O–X configurations and asked to make pleasantness ratings: for example, is the following situation pleasant or unpleasant? P likes O, O likes X, and P dislikes X. Results have tended to support the balance theory but only when P likes O; when P dislikes O, the situation tended to be rated as unpleasant regardless of the overall configuration of other relationships within the system. In essence, it appeared that when P likes O a system of interdependent relationships is thereby created and tension can occur as a resultant of the relationships within that system; however, when P dislikes O, the elements do not form parts of an interdependent whole and so tension results from the one element (disliking) rather than the patterning of the relationships.

On the basis of these findings, Newcomb (1968) was led to formulate a modified version of his original theory, arguing that balance tendencies existed only when P likes O; when P dislikes O, then P is presumably not involved in the situation and thus such situations should be thought of as nonbalanced. In other words, Newcomb proposes that we speak of two kinds of cognitive systems and one nonsystem:

1. balanced systems, when P likes O and they share the same orientation towards X;
2. imbalanced systems, when P likes O and they differ in their orientation towards X;
3. nonsystems, when P dislikes O

In this last case, the elements do not function as parts of a system; they are not interdependent.

Additional data consistent with this reformulation have been reported by Crano and Cooper (1973), by Fuller (1974), and by Crockett (1974). Fuller's research, for example, provided subjects with hypothetical P–O–X configurations and had them make pleansantness ratings. Her data demonstrated that when given P likes O and P and O agree on X, subjects felt the situation to be more pleasant than when P likes O and P and O disagree on X; the latter was seen to be unpleasant. However, when P disliked O, subjects tended to provide somewhat neutral pleasantness ratings, as they might be expected to do if Newcomb's idea about disengagement or noninvolvement in the situation is correct.

Crano and Cooper also provided their subjects with sets of hypothetical P–O–X configurations to be rated for pleasantness; in addition, they asked their subjects to rate the situations according to their likely "involvingness": "An involving situation is an engaging situation, one in which the relationships between the various members of the group prove to be of real interest to you" (p. 350). Their data suggest that situations in which P likes O are rated as more involving than situations in which P dislikes O; it is as though the negative P–O relationship motivates persons to try to disengage themselves from the situation rather than to undergo the kinds of cognitive transformations that would be involved were they to try to restore balance: that is, a cognitive system is not constituted under such conditions.

Another approach to understanding the balance demands of cognitive systems focuses upon the P–X and O–X bond, rather than on either the P–O relationship or on the configurational aspects of the situation. In this version, the key feature involved in either creating or reducing tension is the degree to which P and O share a similar conception of X. Disagreements regarding X are assumed to be tension producing, whether P likes or dislikes O. This position has been termed the *affect-reinforcement version* (e.g., Byrne & Clore, 1967; Gormly, 1974). It emphasizes a nonsystem analysis of cognition.

One interesting test of this conception was reported in 1974 by John Gormly. Unlike the studies we have just examined that used hypothetical P–O–X situations, Gormly involved his subjects in an actual encounter with another person (actually an accomplice). The accomplice was trained to appear to the subjects as someone likeable, dislikeable, or relatively neutral. Subjects were all evaluated as to their own attitudes on twelve topics including birth control, the death penalty, legalization of marijuana, and such. Subjects answers were made available to the accomplice who could thereby answer in either a similar or dissimilar way. All subjects were attached to a physiological recording device that recorded their skin conductance which was taken to be a measure of their state of physiological arousal or tension. The study permitted the experimenter to evaluate the degree of arousal experienced when disagreements or agreements were generated by an accomplice that the subjects either liked, disliked, or felt neutral towards. The major research question that Gormly sought to examine was whether tension would be greater for disagreements regardless of the P–O relationship or if the entire configuration, including the P–O relationship had to be included in order to understand the measures of physiological tension. His data suggested a significant arousal effect from the disagreement factor, but no significant effect attributable to the overall configuration: that is, no interaction effect involving liking and level of agreement. Although their methods were different, similar support for the importance of agreement rather than balance was suggested by the research of Gerard and Fleisher (1967), Whitney (1971), and by Zajonc's (1968) review of a set of several studies within the general balance model.

The complexity of the matter is further revealed and some resolution suggested by the work and approach of several other investigators who emphasized the implications of given configurations for P's interaction with O (e.g., Brickman & Horn, 1973; Crockett, 1974; Touhey, 1974). Crockett speaks of the *hedonic implications* of given P–O–X configurations. He notes first of all that in the original formulation of the theory, the X-term in the P–O–X system may refer to anything from a third person to some general attitude, issue, or personal value. He reasoned that when X is a third person about which P and O have attitudes, it would be more congenial to interact together when P likes O and they agree about person-X than when they disagree. In other words, a balance effect should be involved when X is a third person. If P dislikes O, then regardless of their view about X, the situation would generally not be congenial for further interaction. Thus, when X is a person, Crockett reasons that Newcomb's reformulation of the balance model should hold. If X were an issue, however, P's and O's agreement becomes of major importance; agreement helps validate P's world view regardless of whether or not P likes O. Thus the balance of the system is not as relevant when X refers to issues rather than to persons. Crockett's research generally supports these contentions, showing how both balance and agreement effects are involved depending on whether X is a person or an issue. We see in this view how by focusing our attention on the interpersonal implications of the intrapersonal principle of balance, we gain a better understanding of the likely processes involved.

In a valuable addition to this same, interpersonal approach, Brickman and Horn (1973) reasoned that balance or imbalance involving a P–O–X triad, where all the elements are persons, contains some rather important implications for the smoothness of the interaction that is likely, in particular, for the possibility for P to form alliances and coalitions within the situation. They term theirs an *interpersonal coping theory.* To get a sense of this theory, let us take the following possibility: P is about to enter a situation in which O and X like each other. According to balance theory, the P–O–X configuration will be balanced if P either likes both O and X or dislikes both O and X. The interpersonal coping model, on the other hand, argues that in the situation in which P dislikes both O and X (who like one another), P is at a decided disadvantage; the other two can form an alliance in which P is left out in the cold. Thus, although that situation would be cognitively balanced, it would not be interpersonally satisfying for P as compared with the former situation. As Brickman and Horn note, their model argues that regardless of whether a situation is cognitively balanced or imbalanced, persons will prefer situations in which they can form alliances with others. To take another example, P is about to join a trio in which O likes X; according to balance theory, as noted, the situation will be balanced if P disliked both of them. We noted that this would leave P out in the cold, however, and thus that P would prefer the situation to be one in which P liked either O or X. In other words, P's preference would be either the cognitively imbalanced configuration, P likes O, O likes X, P dislikes X, or obviously, a P–O–X system that contained all liking. The point, however, is that to the extent that our analyses get caught up too much within P's cognitive system, forgetting perhaps the interpersonal implications of that system, we may lose sight of an important basis for preferring balance or imbalance, depending on those action-implications as they arise within that particular social context.

In their study, Brickman and Horn presented their subjects with hypothetical situations in which P was about to join two other persons they referred to as X and Y. The relationship between X and Y was varied in the situations as was the relationship between P and X, and P and Y. Subjects were asked to indicate how pleasant or unpleasant they would find each situation. Figure 4 indicates a selection of their results.

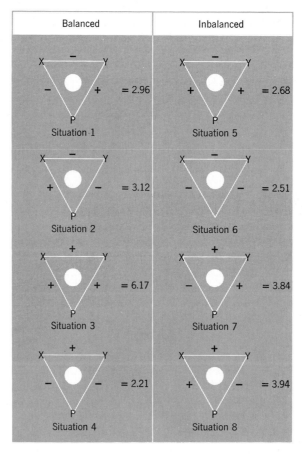

Figure 4. *Average pleasantness ratings. (Adapted from Brickman, P. & Horn, C. Balance theory and interpersonal coping in triads.* Journal of Personality and Social Psychology, *1973, 26, 347–355. Copyright 1973 by the American Psychological Association. Reprinted by permission.)*

As even a brief examination of the figure will indicate, the fact that a situation is cognitively imbalanced does not necessarily mean that it will be rated as unpleasant; nor does a cognitively balanced situation necessarily receive a rating of highly pleasant: the interpersonal implications of the situation must be taken into consideration. For example, situation 4 is cognitively balanced but is rated as less pleasant than situation 8 which is cognitively imbalanced but allows P the opportunity to form an alliance in the situation with X.

Another approach that emphasizes the interpersonal rather than the intrapersonal aspects of cognitive balance has been recently suggested by Touhey's research (1974). Building on some of the ideas of G. H. Mead who argues that the meanings of various objects, including one's self, arise within social interaction (recall our discussion in Chapter 2; see also Chapter 6 for further details), Touhey suggests that when P and O come together to interact, each is concerned with creating a socially desirable identity. To create such an identity requires that P and O act in ways that will lead each to think well of the other. Touhey next suggests that what is defined as a balanced cognitive configuration (e.g., P likes O with whom P shares a similar orientation) produces a more desirable identity than an imbalanced configuration. For example, if P likes O, P will act in ways to be similar to O so that P will be thought of well by O; P does this not because to do otherwise would be cognitively uncomfortable, but rather because to do so helps P create a positive identity.

Touhey's research is suggestive but by no means definitive on this point. What he did basically was to simulate a typical study of cognitive balance. He had his subjects read through the case of P and O; different subjects received different stories that varied P's similarity in attitude to O and P's attraction to O. Subjects were asked to make ratings describing the kind of person that P was, given these various combinations of P–O similarity and P–O attraction. Touhey compared the descriptions given to P for two relatively imbalanced configurations (points 1 and 2) and one relatively balanced one (point 3) as follows:

1. When P's attraction to O is greater than P's similarity to O would warrant, P is described as submissive, dependent, passive, naive, and trusting.
2. When P's attraction to O is less than P's similarity to O would warrant, P is described as cold, dominant, indifferent, and suspicious.
3. When P's attraction to O is balanced with P's similarity to O, P is described as fair, intelligent, and sensitive.

It is Touhey's contention that balance and imbalance in a relationship have interpersonal implications beyond whatever intraindividual properties they may possess. To act in ways that suggest imbalance (e.g., being different than someone P likes) creates different kinds of identity within the situation. To be more attracted than similarity would imply suggests someone who is almost seeking to ingratiate O; to be unattracted when similarity implies a good base for attraction suggests someone who is relatively aloof. The most socially desirable identity in many situations derives from a balanced configuration, being as attractive as the similarity implies.

While reviewing Touhey's study we should recognize that his research involves a simulation of a social situation rather than an actual situation (but in this regard is similar to the majority of balance studies that likewise use hypothetical situations). However, that fact in itself suggests that considerations about the interpersonal meanings ascribed to balance and imbalance in actual situations are known and shared among persons of the same general social and cultural background; thus, such meanings may function in actual situations and play a role as an interpersonal basis for preferring balanced to imbalanced social relationships.

The point, to repeat, is that balance in a relationship may have an important interpersonal meaning. People may not seek to establish and maintain balance in their relationships simply because it reduces internal tension and creates an internal sense of pleasantness and harmony; rather, they may seek to negotiate a relationship that is balanced so that they may be thought of as fair, sensitive, and intelligent persons. In this latter case, we are dealing with factors within the interpersonal setting that play a role in determining P's preferences for balance or imbalance rather than factors within the person's cognitive system. For example, in some settings, it may be advantageous to be seen as aloof and cold and so P may accept cognitive imbalance as a preferred state that accomplishes this identity.

It would be fair to conclude that the pressures that derive from the need for balance thought of as some internal desire for an internally harmonious cognitive system may be relatively weak when compared with the pressures that derive from a consideration of the implications of a given pattern of relationship for living and acting within a particular social setting. Unfortunately this point is often overlooked by those approaches in which P's cognitive system is examined without due consideration being given to the interactional events and processes that are involved. Indeed, while persons may prefer a balanced cognitive system to an imbalanced one, these pressures may be weak in actual interpersonal contexts involving long-term relationships. The use of hypothetical situations or relatively short-term experimental situations may lead us to overemphasize the intrapersonal basis of balance. We will now examine this matter more closely.

INTERPERSONAL IMPLICATIONS OF BALANCE

We have noted how cognitive balance can be seen as a process that affects the way in which intrapersonal systems function, influencing recall and learning of material (e.g., Feather and Zajonc & Burnstein) as well as P's feelings of comfort, at least under certain specifiable conditions. We have also seen how this intrapersonal process can play a role in affecting P's preferences for certain kinds of relationships over others. What we need is a feeling for the interpersonal dynamics that may be involved when P and O engage in an actual give-and-take relationship over a period of time. Though both the Brickman and Horn and Touhey research suggest these possibilities, they too involve hypothetical settings. While we might say that balance considerations are involved when P thinks about relationships and perceives some social situations, in what sense do such considerations play a role in the actual way in which P and O jointly structure their relationship? Specifically, does agreement between P and O regarding X-issues or X-persons actually produce a recognizable structure and patterning to ongoing social relationships? If this were so, of course, then surely O would have to act in ways to confirm P's internal preference for balance as even P would for O. The expectation from balance theory is that affective bonds linking P to O and perhaps to others as well arise on the basis of similar orientations to X-issues and X-persons; thus group structures evolve according to balance considerations.

The Acquaintance Process.   One of the most extensive, systematic studies of this aspect of the balance model was undertaken by Newcomb (1961) in his analysis of what he called the *acquaintance process,* tracing the development from strangers to friends on the basis of the balance theory prediction: that is, that agreement on X-values would facilitate the creation of P's liking O. Newcomb rented a house large enough for about seventeen college students. He mailed letters to entering students before the beginning of the term, offering them free room for the semester in exchange for a few hours commitment to social psychological research each week. From a pool of interested students, he selected a group who were total strangers and invited them to arrive at the house at roughly the same time. Lengthy questionnaires had previously been completed by these men assessing their attitudes and values on a wide variety of X-issues. On their arrival, they were asked to guess about their new roommate's attitudes on these same issues, in spite of their protests that it was not possible to do this for a total stranger. Throughout the semester, additional tests and measures were obtained on these seventeen students, giving Newcomb a fairly complete set of information on how a group of strangers weaves itself into a complex fabric of friendships. His findings are interesting and offer a valuable contribution not only to the study of cognitive balance, but importantly to its interpersonal consequences in the acquaintance process.

1. Newcomb reports that the early ratings that P made of his prospective roommate O were generally balanced. That is, although O was a total stranger, P tended to see him as feeling "much the same as I do" on issues of importance. What we have here is a demonstration of a cognitive process that assumes similarity and hence balance to social relationships. Without other information, we tend generally to assume that others like what we like, dislike what we dislike, and so forth.

2. Newcomb also found that in spite of this assumption of similarity early in their relationship, there was little actual similarity; thus the perception of balance was greater than was the actual balance. However, after having lived together in the house for a substantial period of time, actual balance was achieved. Its achievement was accomplished by means of changing friendships rather than changing attitudes or values. Whereas a group of friends who disagree might try to influence one another towards agreement and thereby preserve the balance in their relationship, a group of strangers accomplishes their friendship by a variation of assortive matings, in this case by forming attitudinally homogeneous subgroups based on a similarity of attitudes and values.

3. From Newcomb's theoretical perspective, cognitive balance offers us a clue as to how social structures evolve in groups. He has already shown how a dyad emerges on the basis of balance; he next sought to demonstrate how even larger subgroups were formed in a similar manner. Newcomb spoke of a perceived perfect triad when P likes O and X (where X is now another person, rather than an attitude or value), and when P perceives that O likes X and is liked by X in return. Newcomb found such triads both as perceived by P and as actually existing within the house; again, assortive mating occurred to achieve balance. When P liked O and X but discovered that in fact O did not like X, one of several things occurred: the initially positive P–O combination split; O changed his mind about X and began to like him; P changed his mind about X and began to dislike him. In any case, balanced conditions were actually achieved as the strangers became acquainted; in many cases, triads of friends evolved from an initial mixture of separate individuals. In much the same manner, Newcomb was able to outline how tetrads and larger groupings were formed within the house, such that this initially undifferentiated collection of strangers over time, became parts of minisocial systems; group structures emerged, cutting through the house with a predictable web of interconnections.

In reviewing Newcomb's research from the perspective of their own more recent investigation, Curry and Emerson (1970), suggested that although actual group structure within Newcomb's house was constituted in a manner consistent with the balance theory predictions, the process involved may not be the intrapsychic one of seeking balance but rather an interpersonal process in which P seeks to engender a rewarding environment. We saw a hint of this view in both Brickman and Horn and in Touhey's prespective in which the intrapersonal preference for balance was not always as potent as the interpersonal concerns with establishing a helpful and rewarding interpersonal situation. As Curry and Emerson note, the determinants of actual group formation may not entirely rest on the intrapersonal factors that balance theory suggests but rather upon these more interpersonal ones.

Curry and Emerson's research is instructive; like Newcomb's original work, theirs involves real groups in natural living situations studied over time. Their subjects came from dormitory clusters at the University of Washington where persons lived in sets of cluster arrangements, four twosomes composing each cluster. While all the precision of Newcomb's research design in selecting and assigning persons to rooms within clusters was not followed, the authors report sufficient mixing of strangers within these natural groups to reduce the likelihood of excessive predetermination of results.

Also, like Newcomb, Curry and Emerson were concerned with studying the determinants of attraction. They obtained measures of persons attitudes, values, and attraction to others at various times during an eight-week period. Several different variables were studied, including:

1. P's perception that P and O agreed in their attraction towards others in their group.
2. P's perception that P and O agreed in their general attitudes and values.
3. P's perception of O's feelings of attraction towards P.

An analysis of their overall results provided firm support for Newcomb's original findings. That is, attraction between P and O at both weeks 1 and 8 was a function of their perceived agreement in attraction to third persons (variable 1); likewise, if there was value agreement between P and O, they tended to be mutually attracted (variable 2). Finally, the measure of P's perception of whether or not O was attracted to P (variable 3) had a strong relationship with P's attraction to O: That is, P was more strongly attracted to O when P felt that O was attracted to P. This last variable, in fact, produced the strongest relations with P's attraction to O.

Although these overall results support the balance theory model and Newcomb's original findings, several additional analyses suggest that processes other than balance may be at work. For example, Curry and Emerson examined the balance theory predictions within each cluster of eight persons. They found a rather broad range of results all the way from one cluster of persons in which P's attraction to O was perfectly correlated with P's perception that P and O agreed in their attraction towards other members of their group (i.e., supporting the balance model of how group structures are formed), to near zero correspondence in another cluster. Thus, while average results across all the clusters of their sample support Newcomb's findings, within any given cluster there may or may not be comparable support. Clearly, if the sole basis for group structure was P's efforts to achieve cognitive balance, then such extensive variability across clusters of roommates within their sample should not be found. Something else must be happening.

Although the full array of data on which Curry and Emerson's conclusions are based would get us into needless and excessive detail, the main thrust of their argument and supporting data runs as follows. We assume that P is initially, and tentatively attracted to O and that this generates a perception of balanced relationships: that is, P perceives that P and O agree about X-issues and X-persons. In the course of P's interactions with O, P attempts to attract O. If P succeeds, then P becomes attracted to O; if P fails, then P does not feel attracted to O.

One way of examining this assumed process is to note patterns of attraction between P and O over time. In examining these patterns, Curry and Emerson conclude that P acts in such a way as to engender reciprocal attraction from O; if P perceives the attraction is reciprocated, P in turn becomes attracted to O. It is P's success in getting O to like P that generates the attraction to O; it is not simply in order to achieve cognitive balance that P is attracted to O. In actual living groups over an extended period of time, attraction is based on P's efforts to solidify a rewarding relationship with O, in which P is both attracted to O and in turn is attractive to O. In this view, social structures based on attraction are generated as P seeks to establish and to maintain an effective and rewarding relationship with O. Balancing concepts are important determinants of P's attitudes; but forming a long term, stable reationship with others depends on creating reciprocal exchanges with them.

BALANCE AND IMBALANCE

The key principle in the original theories of cognitive balance is the dual notion that forces exist either to maintain the steady state of balance or to change the unsteady state of imbalance into a balanced system. Whether these forces derive from an intrapersonal tendency for good form or a more interpersonal view that sees imbalance (especially when P likes and trusts O) to be interpersonally disharmonious, a threat to P's effectance and competence, the effect is similar. Just how is imbalance to be reduced or balance to be maintained? Although systematic research has not examined all the modes that have been formulated, a listing of the possibilities is nevertheless illuminating.

1. P may deal with an imbalanced condition by trying actively to stop thinking about it. The mechanism of repression can be viewed in these terms. While P's conscious role in repressing conflicting material may be minimal, the material nevertheless gets placed beyond reach, possibly later to roar back with a vengence. Ambivalence, in which P has a love-hate orientation towards another person, object, or even some aspects of self, represents a condition of imbalance, an unstable state that may be dealt with by a mechanism much like repression. *Leaving the field* is another variation on this same theme. This is a phrase coined by Lewin to provide a way of thinking about actual physical and psychological withdrawal from a difficult context. P may be physically present in a discussion with liked O's, when a potentially imbalance producing, tough X-issue is raised for discussion; at this moment, P may pick up a magazine and appear to be preoccupied with reading it, or in some other way actively leave the field in order to avoid having to deal with the disagreeable disagreements.

2. Newcomb emphasizes a second manner of dealing with imbalance by influence-oriented communication. Suppose, for example, that P likes O but they disagree about X. P may undo the disharmony of this situation by trying to convince O to see things P's way. Newcomb maintains that discrepancies of this sort, especially when the P–O bond is strongly positive, provide a primary instigation to communication towards reducing the discrepancy. In Chapter 6 our analysis of influence will build upon this idea.

3. In many circumstances of everyday life, P may deal with imbalance by distorting or modifying perceptions of key elements of the situation. Thus, for example, P may be able to attribute greater similarity between P's and O's attitude toward X than actually exists. Recall the previous political example in which persons saw favored candidate's views as more similar to their own than they actually were (i.e., an assimilative process). Especially when the matter involves some X-object or a P–O relationship that is both complex and ambiguous, P's ability to see things as P may wish them to be rather than as they actually are is maximized.

4. Given a liked O with whom there exists some clear disagreement over an important issue, P of course may restore balance by

experiencing a change in attitude. This is the other side of the influence-oriented coin, in which, given imbalance, P experiences self-pressure as well as pressure from O to alter P's views of X. After all, hearing the orientations towards X of someone we like and trust may lead us not only to form particular attitudes towards X, but also to alter those views we already have in the light of learning about O's views.

5. If the X-issue is of major importance for P, possibly embedded in a context of other core values and beliefs, P may alter a once positive relationship with O, coming to like O less on discovering their disagreement over X. Naturally, if the P–O bond was itself only slightly positive, then P may come to like O less for disagreements over even less major X-issues.

6. When confronted with imbalance, P may engage in a variety of selective tactics, ranging from choosing interactions with O to choosing those O's with whom P selects to interact. Selective conversation, in which P maintains a positive relationship with O by avoiding discussions on topics about which there exists substantial disagreement is one such example. Two persons in love may come to talk only about certain safe topics, leaving aside all discussions of religion, for example, for the sake of harmony in their relationship. This relative harmony, of course, is achieved at the cost of exploring a variety of topics and issues; thus the relationship is founded on a potentially narrow base.

7. As Newcomb has noted, persons may deal with imbalance by agreeing to disagree. In this manner, specific imbalance is reduced by embedding it within a larger, normative context that sets forth rules that permit disagreement on X-issues to occur without threatening the P–O bond itself. Two debators, for example, may continue to like, trust, and respect each other, while disagreeing vigorously and effectively over X-issues. Or two lawyers may accept the normative framework of the courtroom that helps reduce the disharmonious impact of the disagreements that occur. A variation of this form of dealing with imbalance is to place the one disagreement into a cognitive context of many agreements; the specific disagreement thus pales when compared in P's mind with the total picture. One swallow doesn't a summer make, nor one disagreement a relationship break. Likewise, as noted, P may prefer imbalance to balance in situations in which a more rewarding coalition is thought possible.

JOYFUL IMBALANCE

Several authors, including Heider (1958), have suggested that persons may enjoy or prefer imbalance, not always acting to do away with it. Heider argued that most people we consider interesting, in fact, are interesting by virtue of the kinds of cognitive disharmonies they create. We come to enjoy meeting and knowing someone who doesn't fit all together as neatly as the balance perspective suggests. On meeting such a person, we may wish to probe further, to explore, to learn more about rather than to dismiss or to withdraw from in haste. How dull, in fact, is the person whose whole life seems to hang together in a balanced manner as compared to the mysterious person who "dislikes everything he produces, who hates to own what he likes, and who always tries to live with people he dislikes" (Heider, 1958, p. 181).

Cognitive balance is only one dynamic property of cognitive systems; forces towards inconsistency and novelty can also be seen as properties of both intrapersonal and interpersonal systems. It may be that just as with the opposing schizmogenetic forces referred to in Chapter 2, the tendencies towards imbalance are offset in their extreme by tendencies towards balance, which in their extreme feedback to reintroduce a movement towards balance. We know that a tendency towards balance exists and is an important property of cognitive systems; we also know that the pursuit of novelty, paradox, puzzlement, imbalance, and inconsistency is likewise characteristic of cognitive systems. Effective functioning may well involve achieving an optimum level between these two extremes. If our entire learning histories were based on balance and harmony, we would not grow far beyond a sheltered infancy. For, even as we shall later examine in another context (Chapter 8), the motivation for growth involves the kinds of disconfirmations that imbalance provides.

Cognitive Dissonance

During the last decade and a half, an intrapersonal cognitive process that seems not only to have captured the imagination of the majority of social psychologists, but also to have generated myriad publications, has involved another consistency principle, termed by its founder, Leon Festinger, the theory of *cognitive dissonance* (1959; see also Brehm & Cohen, 1962). The notion is simplicity in itself. From P's perspective, two cognitions —that is, beliefs, attitudes, or knowledges about something—can be either in an interdependent relationship to one another or can be independent. If they are interdependently related, thus forming a cognitive system, that system can be either in a state of consonance or dissonance. Consonance occurs whenever the implications of one cognition are consistent with those of the other; dissonance exists, as Festinger formulates it, whenever the obverse of one cognition follows from the other. For example, if cognition A is my belief that "it is raining out" and cognition B is my belief that "while standing outside I am getting soaked to the skin," then A and B are said to be in a consonant relationship. However, if cognition B were "though standing outside, I am not getting wet," then the interdependent A–B system would be in a dissonant relationship.

It is important to realize that as this theory is formulated, the cognitive system need only contain two elements (two cognitions). As with balance theory, the presumed harmonious condition of the system is consonance; further, as with balance theory, but in this case even more strongly than a preference or a tendency, there are clear and definite forces towards consonance and away from dissonance.

There are two major ways in which dissonance, when present, can be reduced or eliminated. The first involves what is called *bolstering,* and is similar to the way in which imbalance is reduced by seeking cognitions that are consonant with one or the other element in the system. The second involves changing the nature of the existing cognitions themselves to bring them into a consonant relationship.

BOLSTERING

Bolstering is a major approach to dissonance reduction; it involves altering the ratio of consonant-to-dissonant elements of the cognitive system. For example, if I believe that it is raining (cognition A) and yet I am not getting wet (cognition B), I may reduce the dissonance experienced by finding other cognitions consonant with A or with B. Cognition C, that I am standing under an umbrella, is consonant with B and thus changes the overall ratio of consonance-to-dissonance within this mini- and hypothetical cognitive system.

One of the most obvious ways of finding elements that bolster one set of cognitions over their dissonant partner is to discover other persons who provide support through their own beliefs or behaviors. The founding study was undertaken by Festinger, Riecken, and Schachter (1956) several years before Festinger's publication of his work on cognitive dissonance. Their study is instructive on several counts, particularly in demonstrating how the act of proselytizing new members for a religious group served to bolster the beliefs of existing group members that had been shattered by the disconfirming realization that their doomsday prediction had failed to occur. The group had predicted that on a certain day the world would end and only those who were believers would be saved from certain destruction. As the day came and passed and the world remained intact, the group experienced cognitive dissonance. Bolstering took the form of getting additional members for their religious group; for if others were willing to join, their faith in their group's beliefs could be reinforced by burying this one, major dissonant event in a context of self-confirmation.

This study is instructive in showing us how a cognitive dynamic (dissonance reduction) structures the person's life space in such a way that leads to behavior designed to restore cognitive harmony and consonance. Here we have a case in which the restructuring motivated by cognitive dissonance leads to behaviors that will support a new mode of cognition. It is not simply that P comes to think differently in the face of dissonance (although this too may happen), but rather that P comes to behave differently so that P may come to think differently; and this is an important point. Cognition influences subsequent behavior that in turn reshapes the state of the cognitive system itself. We see in this example, then, the complex interweaving of the elements that form a cognitive and behavioral system that encompasses both intrapersonal and interpersonal restructurings.

Dana Bramel (1963) outlined another manner by which dissonance may be reduced by an interpersonal bolstering technique, which in this case is much like the psychoanalytic mechanism of *projection:* that is, ridding oneself of the dissonant thoughts by attributing them to others. While the ethics of this experimental design are open to question, Bramel's research nevertheless demonstrated how male subjects who were made to feel that they were homosexually aroused by photos they were shown reduced the dissonant experience of this information by rating their partners as equally aroused.

What Bramel did was to instruct his subjects on the physiological mechanisms of sexual arousal, attach each man to an electrical apparatus that presumably recorded his arousal, showed them pictures of naked males while providing them with visible dial readings indicative of arousal. Bramel reasoned that those subjects he had previously provided information designed to increase their self-esteem would find this arousal information more dissonant than those subjects who had previously been given information designed to decrease their self-esteem. Afterall, the low-esteem person would consider this bit of news about himself just another element consonant with the entire tragic picture of himself that was being developed. The high-esteem person, on the other hand, would surely find his homosexual attraction difficult to deal with.

Bramel paired males together, one opposite the other, looking at the same nude pictures and having physiological meter readings separate for each. His subjects were asked to report what they thought their partner's meter read. His findings confirmed the notion of reducing dissonance by bolstering by means of projection. He found his high-esteem subjects saw their partners as more similarly aroused sexually than did the low-esteem subjects. In other words, the most dissonant subjects sought to reduce their own dissonance by seeing that, afterall, they aren't that much different than other persons; they are all in the same boat together. Support, in this case, involved a kind of intrapsychic proselytizing, whereby the subject made the other person into one like himself; in the Festinger, Schachter, and Reicken study, we saw interpersonal proselytizing.

SOURCES OF DISSONANCE

The study of a doomsday prophecy that failed gives us one kind of event that produces dissonance; in this case, we can see that *disconfirmed expectations* provide a source of cognitive dissonance. Robert Zajonc's (1968) perspective on the theory of cognitive dissonance suggests several additional sources for dissonance.

1. Sensory dissonance occurs in the face of optical or other kinds of illusions, in which our sense receptors provide us with misleading or contradictory clues as to the reality of events in our world.

2. Social factors are a very common source of cognitive dissonance, as we receive contradictory demands for our behavior from different persons—for example, conflicting role demands—or the actual social rules and norms provide contradictory guidelines for our behavior.

3. Informational inconsistency, as in receiving discrepant reports from different persons ostensibly about the same event or person or even about ourselves offers another source for dissonance. The Bramel study is one example of this.

4. Choice behavior offers another opportunity for dissonance to operate, in that with each choice among options, we must come to terms with not only what we have chosen but with what we have thereby not selected. It should be dissonant having chosen object A, for example, to learn all the good things about B and the bad things about A. Postdecision situations, thus, provide us with another ready source of dissonance.

5. Insufficient justification, as we will soon come to see, provides one of the most interesting kinds of dissonance theory investigations. Presumably, when we engage in some activity, typically one not especially to our liking, yet one that we seem to have chosen more or less voluntarily, we can experience dissonance and thus are

motivated to search about for some way of sufficiently justifying what we are doing.

6. A rather fascinating source of dissonance derives from the logic, or perhaps better stated, the at-times illogic of our own cognitive systems. For example, when two beliefs we hold in separate cognitive systems are brought together, if they are inconsistent, we experience dissonance. Gunner Myrdal's (1944) analysis of what we termed the American dilemma is a potent example. The credal values speak of freedom and equality for all, yet many of our practices and our beliefs are discriminatory. When these values are joined with our contradictory beliefs, cognitive dissonance results.

INSUFFICIENT JUSTIFICATION

While numerous research findings have emerged that examine most of these sources of dissonance, some of the most interesting and intriguing work has been conducted around the theme of insufficient justification. This theme captures the dissonance theory sense of how persons can be influenced to alter their beliefs and preferences, and thus gives us some rather interesting insights into the cognitive aspects of the influence process. While we might intuitively reason that the best way to get someone to alter their beliefs is to place them under a situation of high pressure to change, for example, promise of high reward or threat of severe punishment, the dissonance theory logic of insufficient justification takes the opposite stance.

We can rather readily trace the dissonance theory logic of insufficient justification by using the following diagram:

P does X:
1. With sufficient external reasons $\longrightarrow$ no dissonance
2. Without sufficient external reasons $\longrightarrow$ dissonance $\longrightarrow$ development of internal reasons for having done X

The theory, as outlined in point 2, suggests that to the extent that we can minimize the external reasons for P's doing X, as for example, by getting P's compliance by using low reward or low punishment (because high reward or punishment would be external justification enough for doing X), we will create a state of dissonance that will lead P to seek some internal reason for having done X, for example, by changing P's evaluation of X.

If a gun is held to your head and you are threatened with death unless you help out in a robbery, becoming a robber for a night does not create dissonance in that your actions had sufficient external justification: "I had to be a robber." However, if you are induced to rob without sufficient external justification, dissonance is created between your sense of yourself as an honest person and as a robber; in that the action of robbery has already taken place and thus cannot be readily changed, the major avenue of reducing the dissonance is by changing one of the internal elements of the relevant cognitive system: for example, you can think less of your own honesty or you can increase your valuation of being a robber.

The classic laboratory study on this theoretical derivation was reported in 1959 by Festinger and his associate Carlsmith. Subjects were invited to the laboratory to participate in an experiment in which they were given a long, boring, repetitive task to perform. After their time was up, under the pretext of needing assistance, the experimenter then hired the subject as his assistant, paying him either $1 or $20, depending on which experimental condition he was in, to tell a waiting subject how interesting and enjoyable a task they would soon be doing. Festinger and Carlsmith compared the $1 and $20 groups with a control group (which simply worked on the dull task) as to their ratings of the enjoyableness of the task; these measures were obtained at a later time. Their results showed that as predicted, the $1 group found the task to be more exciting than the $20 group. The insufficient justification argument is that $20 provides sufficient external justification for telling a lie, whereas $1 does not. Thus, telling a lie for $1 creates greater dissonance that can be reduced by overvaluing the boring task. After all, if the subject can feel that he did not sell out for $1, but actually found the task exciting and thus was telling the truth to the waiting subject, then clearly, his cognitive world would once again be all harmonious.

Several critics of this original study argued that the $20 was so great an amount that it surely must have aroused the subject's suspicion about the entire experiment. In 1962, A. R. Cohen, heeding these criticisms, reported a replication in which his subjects were paid amounts varying from 50¢ to $10 to write an essay taking a position counter to their own. The insufficient justification argument maintains that a person who writes the essay for 50¢ should change his or her attitude more to fit the essay than a person paid $1, who in turn should change more than the person paid $5, and so on. Results from Cohen's replication strongly support this trend.

In a fascinating variant of this same time, E. E. Smith (1961) reports a study in which Army reservists were induced to eat grasshoppers by a leader who was either casual and likable or cooly official and distant. Can you guess which kind of leadership induced the reservists to like the grasshoppers the most? The theory of insufficient justification argues that doing X without external justification should create greater dissonance and thus greater valuation of the activity than doing X with external justification. Reasoning that doing something for a "good person" is sufficient justification (e.g., like the $20 payment) whereas doing something for a "bad person" is not (e.g., like the $1 payment), the prediction confirmed by Smith's actual findings is that the bad-guy leader should create more liking of grasshoppers than the good-guy leader. Presumably a subject's conversation with himself ran: "I've eaten these hoppers because that bastard asked me to. He's still a bastard, but damn it, I've eaten them, so maybe they aren't so bad after all." A reservist with a nice-guy leader, on the other hand, might have said to himself, "Hoppers ... ugh. But that nice guy asked me to eat them and I suppose I should ... he's a decent sort ... but I still don't like the critters."

Threats and Change. The dependent variable in the dissonance theory work on insufficient justification typically involves P's changing valuation of some activity or some object. What we have seen in general is that low or insufficient reward for doing X leads P to overvalue X. It would seem to follow from this reasoning that a mild threat of punishment would more effectively result in P's valuation of X changing, than a high threat of punishment. Again, as before, the high threat offers sufficient justification for doing X and thus requires less internal cognitive reorganization than is required when X is done without sufficient external reason.

In 1963, Aronson and Carlsmith reported what is now the classic dissonance study testing this derivation. They asked preschool children to indicate their liking of six toys, eliciting an actual ranking of the six in terms of the child's preferences. The experimenter then selected the child's second most liked toy, placed it on the table in the center of the room, while placing the remaining toys on the floor, told the child that he (the experimenter) would have to step out a few moments but that the child could play with several toys but not the one on the table. All of this was said either under mild threat (e.g., "I'll be annoyed if you play with X—the toy on the table"), or high threat (e.g., "I'll be very angry if you play with X; I would have to take all my toys back and go home and never return again"). On his return, the experimenter permitted the child to play with all six toys and then had them go through the ranking procedure again.

As predicted, Aronson and Carlsmith report that under mild threat the children changed their evaluation of the forbidden toy, derogating it in order to reduce the dissonance experience.

In the Severe Threat condition, an individual's cognition that he did not play with an attractive toy was consonant with his cognition that he would have been severely punished if he had played with the toy. There was no need for him to provide further justification for his abstinence. However, when he refrained from playing with the toy in the presence of a mild threat, he experienced dissonance. His cognition that he did not play with the toy was dissonant with his cognition that it was attractive. In order to reduce the dissonance, he derogated the toy. (Aronson & Carlsmith, 1963, p. 587).

Several other investigators have replicated this same striking effect in which insufficient justification for an action (or in this case inability to play with the toy) produced dissonance and a change in valuation of the action. A recent replication and extension of this powerful effect sought to pinpoint more closely the actual cognitive conditions that should be met if the effect is to be most pronounced. Zanna, Lepper, and Abelson (1973) reasoned that we can often avoid dissonance by not attending to or thinking about the opposing cognitions; thus bringing the child's attention to the presumably dissonant cognitions would create a stronger derogation effect than might usually occur. Their research developed a procedure whereby the child could be reminded during the period of the experimenter's absence from the room (in the Aronson and Carlsmith procedure), that he was not playing with the forbidden toy, and that he was under mild or severe threat to avoid playing with it. Making these cognitive elements salient to the child, under conditions of mild threat, did create a strong derogation effect. The authors suggest that by drawing the child's attention to the forbidden toy and the severe threat for playing with it, they created the sense of sufficient justification for avoiding it that would minimize dissonance and the consequent requirement for reducing dissonance by derogating the toy. On the other hand, this reminder to the child both of the forbidden toy and the mild threat for playing with it, if anything, simply reinstated the insufficient justification, thus the sense of dissonance and the need to reduce it by means of derogating the toy.

Suffering. Another variation of this same theme argues that psychologically we come to value things we have suffered for; to do otherwise would be dissonant with our suffering. That is, suffering for doing or believing something is akin to an insufficient justification for having done X. The way to justify having suffered is to reorganize our cognitive system, overvaluing X and thereby making X consonant with suffering. The classic study in this genre was reported in 1959 by Aronson and Mills, who invited female students to join a sex discussion group. As preparation for their entry into this group, the women were to meet individually with a male experimenter. In the mild initiation condition they read a list of sex-related words to the experimenter; in the severe initiation group, they read a list of obscene words. Each woman listened to what was supposedly an ongoing discussion by their group; in actuality, what they heard was a taped session of a group discussing sex in a decidedly scientific, even boring manner. Each woman then rated the discussion and how much she thought she would like the members of the group. As predicted, the results showed that women who had gone through the embarrassing, severe initiation were more favorable toward the group and the discussion than either a control group (which simply rated the group but had not undergone any kind of initiation) or the mild initiation condition.

As with all work in this area of theory, a cognitive reorganization occurred, producing a more consonant cognitive system. In this latter case, by increasing the woman's valuation of the group in order to make the group's worth consonant with the severity of her initiation into its membership. Reporting in 1965, Marlowe, Frager, and Nuttall reasoned that if P suffers for holding a certain set of beliefs, then P should value them more highly and be more willing thereby to take action congruent with those beliefs as a demonstration of this heightened importance than if P is not made to suffer for believing in X. Marlowe and his colleagues created an experimental situation in which P's belief in X (where X involved attitudes towards blacks) either led to negative or neutral consequences. They then provided their subjects with an opportunity to behave in a manner congruent with their beliefs, in this case by volunteering to guide a group of black students around Harvard. It is to be noted that this study is one of the few in which P's actual behavior (in this case volunteering of services) is measured as a consequence of cognitive reorganization; most of the research, as noted, deals with the cognitive reorganization itself (e.g., P's overvaluation or derogation of X). Marlowe and his associates' results fit the predictions from dissonance theory in that subjects who suffered for their beliefs were more inclined than those who did not suffer, to volunteer as guides and thereby in this manner presumably to justify the suffering experienced for believing as they did.

Conclusion

We opened this chapter on the cognitive processes by noting that persons act in situations as a function of how they define them. From this point of view, therefore, it is essential to inquire about the processes whereby input from the environment is transformed by the person. We also noted, however, that not only do persons transform situations but indeed are transformed in the process of coming to terms with those situations. Dual transformations are involved. Each aspect of this total process has formed a focal interest to several views we have examined. The total process itself emerged most explicitly perhaps in our consideration of a more interpersonal version of balance theory. The confrontation between a mode of cognitive organization (i.e., balance) and the realities of coping with the living presence of another person jointly determine P's social behavior. Our understanding is enriched once we can grasp the ways in which P's definitions are endowed with their meaning through the acts of others.

As we progress now to the next chapter, we will see these same themes again: a major emphasis upon cognitive-defining processes and their role in structuring P's behavior, and a continuing concern with how that behavior as others respond to it transforms P. Our theme of interdependence remains, whether we are searching within the intrapersonal level, noting how elements combine to form a cognitive system, or at the interpersonal level, noting how P's definitions and O's behaviors form part of the social field within which P and O dwell and from which their behavior emerges.

ROBERT NEUBECKER.

THE ATTRIBUTION OF CAUSE: ITS PSYCHOLOGICAL AND SOCIAL ASPECTS

4

As we have seen, a stable, predictable environment over which we can gain some mastery is an accomplishment, not a given. The work of creating whatever stability exists for our life space is jointly determined by the assimilative and accommodative processes that we have been considering.

Now that we are familiar with several concepts and processes, we have a basis for turning our attention to the processes of cognitive *inference,* which allow us to answer questions of "why" by attributing causes to events, and thereby transforming what is potentially chaotic into something more stable and meaningful. To ask a why-question is to seek a causal answer. Why did Ms. Jones hit the man? Because she was angry. Why did Mr. Smith laugh at the TV announcer? Because he was funny. The attribution of a cause to some event involves a process of inference.

We integrate a variety of information-bearing cues from an event to infer its cause. Our cognitive goal, so to speak, is to infer those stable features of the object, the situation, or both the object and situation, that give rise to the event; having accomplished this, we have thereby created a psychological world that has some continuity, predictability, and controlability. For example, when we can attribute Ms. Jones's hitting behavior to some relatively enduring disposition within Ms. Jones, which we conveniently call "anger," we have satisfied ourselves that we understand what happened and why. We have formulated a world of some predictability and mastery: Ms. Jones is an angry person; angry persons are likely to strike out at others; I'll be cautious when dealing with Ms. Jones (Heider, 1958).

THE "CAUSES" OF RIOTS

A few interesting case examples will be helpful at this point. During the summer of 1967, the United States experienced several major urban riots. A report published in 1972 by Charles Schmidt sought to systematically analyze the way in which persons understood the causes of these riots. From the period June through October 1967, Schmidt searched through the editorial pages of newspapers and magazines, selecting those articles that offered explanations for why the riots occurred. Sampling was done in such a way to include a broad political and geographical range. Schmidt's search produced a listing of some seventy-six causal statements which he then presented to a group of judges who were asked to categorize these explanations in terms of their similarity to one another. It was then possible for Schmidt to subject the judges' ratings of the riot explanations to a complex statistical analysis that permitted him to determine:

1. whether or not the statements actually were clustered or categorized according to a major explanatory theme;
2. the actual content of these explanatory themes;
3. the relationship between the explanatory themes

Consistent with a substantial body of theory and empirical research, Schmidt's study uncovered two major categories of explanation. The first attributed the riots to some internal or personal properties of the actors (e.g., the rioters were deviants, were criminal types, were racists, etc.). The second explanatory theme stressed external situational factors such as government mismanagement and an irresponsible Congress. Recall that we encountered these same two themes in Chapter 1. In that discussion we were referring primarily to the causal focus of social psychology; now we are referring to our everyday, commonsense modes of attributing causes and explaining events. As we will see shortly, the typical manner by which each of us makes sense out of events in our everyday life is to attribute the causes of these events to personal dispositions of the actors involved or to factors within the situation. Attribution theory in social psychology is concerned with uncovering the conditions under which we make personal or situational analyses; P takes a very different stance towards O if P attributes O's actions to something within O (e.g., a disposition) or to something within O's environment.

Relevant to this latter point is Schmidt's further finding that those explanations that stressed some disposition of the actors tended to evaluate the riots as illegitimate occurrences, whereas those explanations that stressed situational factors evaluated the riots as legitimate. This is a rather interesting point. It suggests that the same act has a different meaning as a function of P's attributing its cause to O or to O's circumstances.

Several investigators have suggested, and in some cases demonstrated (e.g., Kruglanski & Cohen, 1973, 1974; Steiner, 1970), that when P can infer that O's actions are an outcome of something within O—for example, O's motives and desires—then P tends to believe that O acted freely; presumably, such freedom confers responsibility. Attributing the riots to the actor's personal dispositions suggests that the persons, if they so choose, could have acted otherwise; thus having freely chosen to act in a negative way, leads P to the judgment that their actions were illegitimate. We will have much more to say on this important matter involving personal responsibility in Chapter 8. In attributing the riots to circumstances beyond the actor's own willful control, P not only makes the actor (O) less responsible for what has occurred, but also tends to evaluate both the actor and the action as more legitimate, even though P may still think that riots are not generally a good way to solve problems. It can be seen that the stance we have towards both the actor and the action will vary as a function of the nature of the attribution process: personal attributions lead us to see more choice and responsibility for the actor than situational attributions and thus to respond negatively if we think poorly of the act. The question, of course, is what conditions lead us to make personal or situational attributions? But before we seek an answer to this question, let us review a second case example that further illuminates the important behavioral consequences that follow from our attributions.

Reporting in March 1973, Caplan and Nelson find that approximately 82 percent of the research dealing with black Americans abstracted in *Psychological Abstracts* during a six-month period in 1970 interprets the difficulties and problems this group faces to person-centered causes. This kind of attribution held special interest for Caplan and Nelson who outline several major policy implications:

1. Attributing the problems of a group such as black Americans to some personal qualities of the group facilitates releasing governmental and other social agencies from blame for their plight.
2. If social institutions are not the cause of a group's problems, then such institutions cannot be held responsible for playing a major role in ameliorating the problems.
3. By attributing the causes of a group's difficulties to person-centered factors, treatment is legitimately focused on changing persons rather than on changing social institutions.
4. Well-intentioned nonproblem segments of the society can now be recruited into managerial or treatment roles designed to help the unfortunate persons rather than roles that are designed to help change the unfortunate social system.
5. By attributing the problems of a group to person-centered factors, one's sense of having control over one's own fate is thereby

reinforced; after all, those without such problems must have been sufficiently adept to make it on their own, while those who failed must have lacked something within themselves.

Basically, Caplan and Nelson focus our attention on some of the larger consequences that result from the attributional processes that characterize disciplines such as the social sciences. Much the same argument can be applied to the consequences that result from attributional processes made by an individual. The point is that the manner in which P defines a situation influences how P will behave in that situation. In the cases just examined, when P is inclined to attribute the causes of a group's problems to some personal quality of that group rather than to something within the social situation of that group, then the kinds of consequence that Caplan and Nelson outline are likely outcomes. As their analysis strongly suggests, we are not dealing here with a matter of esoteric concern only to social psychologists; the policy implications for a large group hinges on the manner in which the group's problems are defined. Thus the study of attribution of cause is fundamental and has far-reaching social and political implications. We can now turn our attention to the conditions that facilitate our making personal rather than situational or systemic attributions.

Person or System?

Several related approaches have been presented that deal with the issue of person-centered versus system-centered attributions. One of the most important schemes was proposed several years ago by Jones and Davis (1965). They outlined the process whereby P uses O's actions and their effects to arrive at a dispositional (i.e., person-centered) or a situational inference. One of their classic and important studies will provide us with a useful way of looking at their theoretical model. In this study conducted by Jones, Davis, and Gergen and reported in 1961, subjects heard a tape-recorded job interview in which the interviewee, actually an accomplice, was being interviewed either for the job of astronaut or submariner. Subjects had previously learned that the qualities requisite for being a good astronaut were self-sufficiency and inner-directedness, while the personal qualities requisite for being a good submariner involved being gregarious and other-directed. In half the sessions, the accomplice had been instructed to portray someone who fitted the job requirements; thus when interviewing for the astronaut job he was properly inner-directed; when interviewing for the submariner job, he was other-directed. In the other half of the sessions, his behavior deviated from the job-description, being other-directed when seeking the astronaut job and inner-directed when seeking the submariner position. Any one subject, naturally, only heard one taped interview, and thus was unaware of these experimental variations.

At the conclusion of the study, subjects were asked to rate the interviewee as they thought him to be really. The question of interest is under which of the four conditions of the study (outlined below) did the subjects attribute the accomplice's behavior to some personal disposition and under which conditions did they attribute his behavior to situational factors (e.g., trying to behave in a way to fit the job requirements in order to be hired)?

1. Astronaut interview: job requires being inner-directed
   a. accomplice is inner-directed
   b. accomplice is other-directed
2. Submariner interview: job requires being other-directed
   a. accomplice is other-directed
   b. accomplice is inner-directed.

Jones, Davis, and Gergen report that in general, conditions 1a and 2a led subjects to attribute the accomplice's behavior to the situation, whereas conditions 1b and 2b led subjects to attribute his behavior to some personal disposition. Note the major features that differentiate the "a" set from the "b" set. In set a, the accomplice's behavior fits the situational requirements; in set b, the behavior departs from situational requirements. Behavior done in compliance with known situational factors makes it more difficult to make personal attributions; the behavior could be explained as someone who was simply trying hard to get a job and performing in a way to help assure employment. However, behavior that departs from the situational factors strongly suggests that the accomplice must really be that way: that is, a dispositional attribution.

Harold Kelley (1967; 1972; 1973), one of the major contemporary social psychologists involved in the study of attribution processes, invokes what he calls a *discounting principle* to interpret the Jones et al. results. In Kelley's view, "the role of a given cause in producing a given effect is discounted if other plausible causes are also present," (1973, p. 113). Thus as long as a plausible external cause is present, an internal, dispositional cause is discounted; likewise, as long as a plausible dispositional cause is present, an external cause is discounted. Kelley suggests that the Jones et al. interview situation as such is not a reasonable cause of behavior that doesn't fit it (e.g., set b), and thus the situation is discounted, setting the observers to search for plausible internal causes for the interviewee's behavior.

Kelley offers us an interpretation of an earlier study by Thibaut and Riecken (1955) that, he suggests, further demonstrates the discounting principle at work in naïve observers' attribution processes. The study itself involved inducing a high-status and a low-status person to comply with the subject's requests. The attribution question asks us to discover the "cause" of the compliance-effect: is it attributed to a dispositional property of the person who complied or to a circumstance of the situation? Kelly suggests that the observer of this situation

> *assumes that the low-status person's compliance is caused either by his* internal *attitudes and dispositions (e.g. his helpfulness) or by the* external *pressure of the force applied to him by the subject's request for help, or by both. On the other hand, the latter factor (the external pressure) is not assumed to be a plausible cause for the high-status person's compliance, he presumably being more powerful than the subject. Accordingly, his compliance is attributed to his internal properties. And, as suggested by the discounting principle, appropriate internal properties of the low-status person are inferred less strongly from* his *compliance inasmuch as there are plausible external reasons for it* (1973, p. 113).

Some additional work conducted in actual face-to-face interaction situations lends additional support to the preceding framework. Steiner and Field (1960) report a study in which groups of subjects were convened to discuss the desegregation of public schools. An accomplice of the experimenter's was instructed to play the role of a segregationist. In half of the groups, the experimenter publicly assigned the accomplice this devil's advocate role; in the other half, no such assignment was made although subjects were urged to consider all positions on the issue, including that of a segregationist. The question here as before is to what did subjects attribute the accomplice's behavior? Did they see the accomplice as a true segregationist when the role was assigned or when it appeared to be freely chosen? That we can readily answer this question suggests that our commonsense attribution model works without our actual presence in the experimental situation. That is, if we know that P was asked to perform a role, we take this to be a plausible situational explanation for P's behavior and thus tend to discount dispositional explanations; however, in the absence of such situational information, our attributions are more inclined towards the personal. Experimental results confirm this prediction.

P's understanding of whether O's behavior is dispositional or situational in its cause can be based on other factors in addition to the role requirements of a given setting. Kruglanski and Cohen (1973) provided their subjects with background information about the personality and character of a fictitous O that led them to think of O as a generally cooperative kind of person. Half of the subjects were led to believe that O's behavior in a hypothetical situation was in-character (i.e., consistent with O's cooperativeness) or out of character (i.e., that O behaved competitively). Among several questions that were asked about O, two are of particular relevance. One sought the subjects' perception of the degree of personal freedom for O's behavior; the other sought P's perception of O's personal responsibility for O's behavior. Results indicated that when O's behavior was in character, P tended to rate O both as freer and as having greater responsibility. When O acted out of character, P attributed less freedom and responsibility to O, locating the causes of O's behavior in an external situation-factor. These data help us appreciate how dispositional attributions are seen as most plausible when O behaves consistently with P's prior knowledge regarding O's personality and character.

A further factor that plays a role in affecting whether it is plausible for P to make dispositional or situational attributions regarding O's behavior in situations of decision and choice, involves the degree to which the options confronting O seem to be of relatively equal or unequal worth. We might expect, for example, that if O is choosing between two equal alternatives, P will view O's choice as more a function of dispositions than if O's options involved choosing between two unequal alternatives (e.g., something of greater and something of lesser value). In this latter case, situational demands to choose the item of greater value would predominate, thus making a situational analysis of O's behavior plausible. Two separate investigations of this matter are relevant for us to consider briefly.

Steiner, Rotermund, and Talaber (1974) presented their subjects with several decision situations that presumably were faced by business school students. The subjects were asked which of two investment opportunities should student K. W. select: Option A, provides a 50 percent chance of getting $30 and a 50 percent chance of getting $10; Option B provides a 50 percent chance of getting $24 and a 50 percent chance of getting $16. Subjects were asked to read through sets of these and indicate how much real choice each student selector actually had. Employing items similar to this example as well as several others, Steiner and his colleagues' data indicate that generally greater choice is seen when O must decide between options with relatively equal net gains than when O's choice must be between options that are relatively unequal. Dispositional attributions are thus more likely when P sees O's choices to be between relatively equal than between relatively unequal alternatives. Clearly, if the options are relatively equal then P can more readily discount situational demands and seek a causal answer within O's person.

Kruglanski and Cohen (1974) report a study in which they too examined how the relative attractiveness of the options available to O in a decision situation influence P's attributions to O's behavior. They presented their subjects with the story of a person (O) who was completing materials required for admission to a boarding school. Among the materials was a listing of the school's clubs that O was asked to rate. Subjects were informed that O rated sailing and aviation very high, but did not enjoy archeology and drama. Subjects were also told that after O got to the school, O was faced with the choice of which clubs actually to join from a listing of those still available. By this device, the experimenters were able to vary the attractiveness of the decision alternatives facing O. In addition to this concern with attractiveness, they were also interested in evaluating the effects of other variables on P's attributions regarding O —one in particular involved the degree of hesitancy that O demonstrated in making the decision. Did O make the choice rapidly and without hesitation or did O decide with much uncertainty and hesitation?

After reading this complex story about O, all subjects were asked to make ratings of how freely O's choices had been made. Results indicated that in general subjects felt that O had low freedom when choosing between two equally unattractive alternatives (e.g., drama and archeology) as compared with choosing between two equally attractive options. Kruglanski and Cohen report no significant differences in attributed freedom to O when the options were either both attractive or when one was attractive and one unattractive. Additional research will be needed to further clarify this issue. The authors report further than when O made the decision without hesitation, P attributed greater freedom and presumably greater dispositonal causation to O's choices then when O acted with uncertainty and doubt. We might assume that when O acts rapidly in a decision situation of the sort employed in this research, P assumes that O is acting in concert with O's personal desires: that is, hesitation suggests lesser personal freedom and greater situational press.

The preceding work is instructive in suggesting that two distinguishable classes of attributions establish a meaningful, coherent, stable psychological environment: (1) situationally defined rules, norms, and choice and decision opportunities; and (2) personal, psychological dispositions. Each serves the function of stabilizing interpersonal events by pointing out their causes and their implications. The actions of persons in our environment have the quality of meaningfulness either because we attribute psychological motives, traits, and dispositions to them or because we see them as governed by a situational, rule-following requirement.

PERSONS AS EVERYDAY SCIENTISTS

In an effort to lend further precision to the analysis of the conditions under which a situational or dispositional explanation will be forthcoming, Harold Kelley (1967; 1973) proposed a model that views the average person as facing much the same problem that the scientist faces: namely, to make inferences from observations of events to some more stable causal network that satisfactorily explains these events. We recall from Kahneman and Tversky's work discussed in Chapter 1, that though the problem may be similar, the scientist employing proper techniques of statistical inference may reach conclusions that differ from those we intuitively reach. Kelley speaks of three major sources of information that the average person uses in inferring from events to more stable causes: distinctiveness information, consensus information, and consistency information.

To understand these three sources, picture a situation in which you see O laughing at a comedian on TV (from McArthur, 1972). Our interest is in discovering to what you attribute O's laughter. Let us suppose further that you have access to these three sources of information about O and the situation. First, you are aware that O does not laugh at any other comic. This would provide high distinctiveness information, indicating that O's response is unique to this particular comic and to none other. Low distinctiveness information would occur if we know that O laughed at almost every comic. Second, you note that not only O, but almost everyone else laughs at this particular comic. This provides you with high consensus information, indicating that O's response is shared by most other persons seeing this comic. Low consensus information would occur if hardly anyone else other than O laughed at this comic. Finally, you know that in the past, O has almost always laughed at this particular comic, and that O's response on this occasion is highly consistent with previous responses. Low consistency information would occur, on the other hand, if we know that O has never before laughed at this comic; thus O's behavior on this occasion is inconsistent with past behavior. Recall that this was a key variable in the Kruglanski and Cohen study we previously considered.

Kelley's argument is that we seek and utilize these sources of information in order to make our causal attributions of O's response. Specifically, Kelley suggests that high distinctiveness, high consensus, and high consistency lead us to make an external attribution. In the preceding example, this means that we would attribute the cause of O's laughter to something external to O (e.g., the comic) if we noted that this was almost the only comic that O laughed at (high distinctiveness), that almost everyone else laughed at this comic (high consensus), and that O's laughter now was highly consistent with past laughter at this same comic (high consistency). On the other hand, person attribution is more likely to occur when distinctiveness and consensus are low and consistency is high. In other words, we would tend to attribute O's laughter to some disposition within O if we noted that O laughs at almost every comic (low distinctiveness), that hardly anyone else laughed at this particular comic (low consensus), and that in the past O has almost always laughed at this comic (high consistency).

An experimental test of the preceding formulation, reported in 1972 by Leslie Ann McArthur and using situations similar to those in the preceding example, provided general confirmation. Subjects did tend to make dispositional attributions or external attributions in ways consistent with the theoretical expectations. McArthur's results are also enlightening in that they suggest which of the three sources seems to be most influential in "pulling for" dispositional attributions. Distinctiveness information had the greatest effect on dispositional attribution, while consensus information had the smallest effect. McArthur reports that external attributions to properties of the comic were most influenced by distinctiveness information, while external attributions to general circumstances of the situation were most influenced by consistency information. In other words, the fact that O laughs at all comics (e.g., low distinctiveness) was a vital piece of information leading P to attribute O's laughter to some property of O. The fact that O does not laugh at any comics other than this particular one (e.g., high distinctiveness) was the crucial piece of information that led P to attribute O's laughter to some attribute of the stimulus situation, namely the comic. Finally, the fact that in the past O has almost never laughed at this comic, but in the observed situation did laugh, was important in leading P to attribute O's laughter to some general feature of the situation.

SUBJECTIVE STATE VERSUS ACCOMPLISHMENT: TOWARDS CONSENSUAL VALIDATION

Following up on a suggestion made by Fritz Heider (1958) whose seminal writings provide the base for most contemporary attribution models within social psychology, McArthur further sought to determine how the nature of O's response influenced P's attribution to external or to internal causes. In particular, the question was raised as to whether there would be a difference in the attributed locus of causality for O's emotions and opinions on the one hand, as compared with O's actions and accomplishments on the other.

Heider had suggested earlier that emotions are more likely to be attributed to the environment than to personal dispositions, noting, for example, that we tend to believe that some stimulus in the environment served to trigger or elicit the emotion we see in O; it did not simply pop forth from some internal disposition. On the other hand, Heider suggested when O accomplishes something, for example, successfully passing an examination, there exists some degree of confusion in P's mind as to whether this accomplishment was caused by a disposition within O (e.g., O is a very intelligent person or someone who studied long and hard, being highly motivated to succeed) or by some property external to O (e.g., it was an easy examination). While some previous research suggests a tendency for P to attribute O's accomplishments to properties of O, McArthur sought to further examine this matter. By the way, note how this parallels the view reported by Caplan and Nelson who examined the policy implications of attributing failure to the person rather than to the system.

In her study, in addition to varying the factors of distinctiveness, consensus, and consistency that we have already examined, McArthur structured her vignettes so as to vary O's behavior, including these response categories: emotions (e.g., Sue is afraid of the dog.); accomplishments (e.g., George translated the sentence correctly.); opinions (e.g., Bill thinks his teacher is unfair.); actions (e.g., Jack contributed money to an auto safety fund drive.). By analyzing her subjects' attributions as a function of these four response categories, McArthur was able to demonstrate that in general, accomplishments and actions (e.g., directly observable states) result in personal attributions while emotions and opinions (e.g., subjective states) result in external attributions. In other words, in viewing O's behavior, P tends to attribute its cause to something in the situation that elicited it when the behavior is an emotion or an opinion, and to something within O when the behavior is an accomplishment or an action.

Let us think briefly about this finding and its interpretation as it will become a base for several of our later discussions of social influence processes as well as our discussion of the attribution of emotions. Kelley poses the question for us that he then answers and that McArthur's data on the external attribution of subjective states likewise suggest: How does a person know that his or her own perceptions, opinions, judgments, and beliefs about things in the world are valid? Kelley's answer: One's perceptions are valid to the extent that the person can make external attributions.

As we already know, external attributions are based on high distinctiveness (the response is made distinctively to that external stimulus), high consensus (the response is similar to the responses of other persons to the same stimulus), and high consistency (the response to that stimulus is similar over time). Consensual validation, consistency, and distinctiveness, the conditions for external attribution, provide us and others with a sense of living together in a shared social and physical world. In fact, this belief in external attribution is so strong that other analysts (e.g., Alfred Schutz, 1970–1971) have termed it one of the taken-for-granted rules of our everyday life. As a rule, it is compelling; and as something taken for granted, it is not open to doubt unless challenged by circumstances that suggest that the world as P experiences it and the world as O experiences it are somehow demonstrated to be noninterchangeable. As McArthur shows us, this taken-for-granted rule applies to the causal attribution of subjective states, where we come to assume that external conditions elicit these states and thus that persons in similar stimulus conditions will generally have the same subjective experience triggered in them. In the absence of other information, then, this is the kind of attribution our commonsense personal psychology will make.

McArthur presents us with a paradox: our subjective states—our emotions, opinions, beliefs, evaluations, judgments, and such—are known to be valid to the extent to which we and others can attribute their cause to some external set of conditions that elicit them commonly to all in that situation. "We firmly believe that consensual validation of our subjective responses should be the rule because we believe these responses to be caused by external stimuli" (p. 187). What is most fascinating about this paradoxical linkage between our subjective state, external consensual validation, and our sense of objectivity, is that it implies at least two things, each of which has become a topic of major concern in social psychology and elsewhere:

1. Because we believe that subjective states are caused by external stimuli, thus believing that persons should respond similarly to the same apparent conditions, discrepancies between persons in these subjective states threaten a person's own sense of having valid and stable conceptions of the world, and thus serve to elicit influence pressures towards gaining and maintaining uniformity of subjective states. We see a link here with our earlier discussion of the bases of balance (Chapter 3). In Chapter 6 we will again encounter this important theme.

2. In that we believe that emotions, as one kind of subjective state, are elicited by external conditions, the experiencing of an emotion should require that we uncover the proper external circumstances

that have elicited it in order to know what the experience actually is. Insofar as this is correct, then the subjective experience of an emotion will vary significantly as a function of the external conditions within which it can be seen to appear.

This latter point introduces us to some of the fascinating work of Stanley Schachter and his associates (e.g., Schachter & Singer, 1962) who have demonstrated, for example, that given the same degree of physiological arousal, persons report anger or euphoria as an inference from the external stimulus conditions in which they find themselves. But more on this in a later section of this chapter.

Attributional Biases

A valuable and interesting additional finding of McArthur's work leads us into still another facet of the attribution model. She reports that overall, her subjects were biased "in favor of attributing behavior to characteristics of the person rather than to the stimulus properties of his environment" (p. 177). To phrase this another way, in observing O's behavior, P tends to see its cause to lie within some property of O rather than within O's situation. Recall that McArthur's research shows instances when this general tendency is not maintained; yet, a general psychological bias does seem to exist. While the universality of this bias is in doubt, one team of investigators, Reisman and Schopler (1973), direct our attention to a feature of the English language that facilitates our tendency to attribute causes to persons rather than to situations. They note that in English we use the verb *to be* in order to describe an individual's states, for example "Tina *is* hungry"; this is contrasted with several other language systems in which, for example, we would have to say "Tina *has* hunger" (e.g., in Spanish, *Tina tiene hambre*). To *have* hunger suggests a separation between the state and the person that is not as clearly delineated when we say that a person *is* that state. Although we are not aware of systematic efforts to examine the influence of this linguistic difference on the attribution process, the point is really not that the linguistic feature determines whether attributions are made to persons, but rather that this language feature facilitates person-centered attributions.

This apparent tendency to attribute causes to persons even when a situational explanation exists and is plausible has been experimentally validated by several investigators. In 1969, Alexander and Epstein reported a study in which subjects as observers were to make causal attributions for O's behavior under conditions in which external explanations were also available. Did the subjects, however, go beyond these external explanations and seek something within O to fully explain O's behavior? Their answer is a definite yes; subjects tended to attribute trans-situational properties to O, seeing him to be the cause of his behavior. In Heider's terms, subjects tended to form a *unit* relationship bringing together into one percept the person and his or her acts, attributing a causal dynamism to the person.

I think we can get a relatively good sense of the meaning of this preceding point if we think of the issue from the perspective of the actor, O. O may be compelled by circumstances to engage in actions that O might not in fact have preferred. These compelling circumstances provide the plausible external explanation for O's behavior; thus presumably, both the observer and O can thereby discount internal reasons. However, while engaged in the behavior, O may have a variety of experiences that are self-informative about some internal disposition. For example, the soldier who kills in wartime might attribute the act to external causes (e.g., "I was following orders."), and indeed we might agree. (In Chapter 8 we consider this issue of personal causality and responsibility in more detail). However, the soldier might come to experience some pleasure in the act of killing, thus informing himself, and observers who may perceive this pleasure in his behavior, that some dispositional property is also present. One may engage in a required activity with a zeal beyond the call of duty, thereby revealing something internal to the actor in addition to the clear external causes.

Mark Zanna (1973) reports an investigation in which he placed experimental subjects into a situation in which certain aspects of the preceding possibility could occur. His results indicated that "how" a person engages in an activity is informative to that person about his or her personal dispositions (e.g., attitudes) even when plausible external reasons for the behavior are present. As we will have reason to return later to this study and some of its implications (p. 186), I will not present details here. Sufficient to note, however, that there seems to be several reasons and empirical confirmations of the tendency to attribute to persons, even in the face of compelling external causes. This latter point is of theoretical as well as practical interest.

THE STIMULUS PROPERTIES OF THE SELF-IN-INTERACTION

Caplan and Nelson, as previously noted, point out several major policy implications that derive from person-centered attributional biases. In a 1971 publication, Jones and Nisbett developed, tested, and confirmed an important related hypothesis that argued that observer's causal attribution of a person's behavior tends to be dispositional in nature, whereas the person's self-attribution tends to be situational. Thus, when P observes O's actions (as in the McArthur study, for example), the tendency is for P to see the cause of O's behavior to lie within O, whereas from O's perspective, the cause lies within the situation.

Jones and Nisbett offer several plausible reasons why this reversal in attribution could occur. First, the actor is primarily concerned with the situation and in trying to respond appropriately to the stimulus cues within that situation; as such, therefore, the actor is responding as a function of the situation. The observer, by contrast, is primarily concerned with the actor's behavior rather than with the stimulus cues that may have triggered it; as such, therefore, the observer is more likely to attribute behavior to something within the actor.

Second, the observer and the actor differ in terms of the amount and depth of information each possesses about the actor's past history. Place yourself in the role of actor: because you have more information about your own past behavior than an observer does, you can more readily see the uniqueness of your response in any present situation; or, in the context of an ongoing encounter, you may be aware of the previous history of that encounter and thus that your behavior at this moment, which may be the only one that the observer sees, is in response to an historical buildup rather than something within you. For example, let us suppose that Paula and Tom have been having a heated political discussion for about an hour. For most of that time, Tom has been provoking Paula, challenging her every point, pushing her towards an angry retort. And just as Janet arrives in their room, Paula angrily shouts at Tom. From Paula's perspective (and perhaps even Tom's, but not likely) her shouting is in response to an hour's provocation; to Janet, it may appear to be caused by Paula's short temper—in other words, an internal disposition of Paula's rather than of the situation.

I said parenthetically that Tom may also attribute Paula's behavior to an inner disposition; Tom might be unaware that his own behavior has causal properties, and thus he sees Paula's outburst as an unwarranted display of her bad temper. Recall the discussion of Chapter 2 in which "competitors" were oblivious to the causal properties of their own behavior; thus they attributed their partner's competitiveness to some personal disposition rather than to properties of the situation, but especially to themselves as a stimulus which causes others to respond in a particular manner. A similar over attribution to the person is likely in the Paula-and-Tom example, as Tom, the observer of Paula's behavior, discounts his contribution as a cause and makes a dispositional attribution to some property of Paula (her short temper).

Jones and Nisbett and several of their colleagues have conducted experimental investigations that examined the actor-observer differences in causal attribution.. An example of one study, conducted by Nisbett, Caputo, Legant, and Marecek and reported in 1973, will give us a better sense of the research method employed as well as of the results obtained. Nisbett and his associates asked a group of male college students to write a brief essay explaining why they liked the woman they dated and why they chose their major. The same subjects were also asked to write brief paragraphs explaining these for their best friend. These written explanations provided the source of data; coders determined whether the explanations were dispositional or external to the person. For example, a statement that said that the girlfriend-choice was based on the fact that "She's a relaxing person" would be coded as referring to some property of the stimulus situation, whereas the statement, "I need someone I can relax with" was taken as indicative of some internal property of the man. The results of this study, consistent both with the theoretical predictions and with other research conducted by the Jones and Nisbett team, demonstrated that subjects tended to attribute their choice of girlfriend and of major to properties of the situation, whereas they attributed their friend's choices to some quality in their friend. A similar follow-up study was made in which subjects were simply asked to rate the reasons that were uncovered in this first study. The subsequent research provided further confirmation of the original finding: subjects tended to make more external attributions when selecting reasons for their own choices and more internal attributions when selecting reasons for their best friend's choices. In other words, "actors attribute causality to the situation while observers attribute causality to the dispositions of the actor" (Nisbett et al., 1973, p. 163).

To See One's Self Acting.   As fascinating and provocative as the Jones and Nisbett hypothesis is, it leaves us wondering about this process as it occurs in an actual interactive encounter, which after all is what our concern is about. Examining the hypothesis further by developing its logic, Michael Storms reported in 1973 the results of a study using videotape of actual small group interactions. Storms reasoned that one of the fundamental reasons why actors and observers have a different perspective on the actor's behavior is quite simply that the actor cannot see himself or herself acting. Typically, while we are engaged in behaving, we cannot observe ourselves behaving; we have to stop behaving in order to reflect on what we have been doing. Indeed, we can anticipate what our behavior will be and we can see what the consequences of our behavior is, but the act itself escapes our attention. In fact, to attempt to focus on our own behaving proves to be disruptive to the behaving; we become too self-conscious as we try to see ourselves doing something. For example, typing is disrupted if we try to focus our attention on the very actions that are involved.

The observer, of course, has direct and immediate access to our behaving, a privileged access that we possess only by reflection once our behavior has stopped and we come to think about it. This important distinction that Storms makes was made some years ago in Alfred Schutz's (1970–1971) monumental three-volume analysis of the phenomenology of our everyday lives, and which other analysts of the phenomenology of the present have likewise made (e.g. Mead, 1932; 1934). Schutz and these others, however, formulated their conceptions prior to the development and increasingly widespread use of videotape. While we cannot simultaneously act and see ourselves acting, we can watch ourselves acting in a videotape replay. In this manner, we become observers of our own actions. The question to which Storms addresses himself is whether this videotaped opportunity to see ourselves from the observer's perspective will change the nature of our attributions. In particular, will we now report more dispositional causes for our behavior? Storms further explored, via videotape, the possibility that observers who were provided with the actor's perspective on a situation would likewise change their attributions, seeing the actor's behavior as being situationally determined.

To study these possibilities, Storms brought together four subjects to hold "a brief getting-acquainted conversation." Two subjects were instructed to be the actors actually involved in the conversation while the other two were instructed simply to be observers, watching but not participating. The conversations were all videotaped. In the experimental conditions of the study, Storms played back the videotape of the conversation, varying the perspective that was shown. For example, the tape that had focused on actor 1 was played back; actor 2 thereby saw the same situation in which he had just been in and from the same point of view. Actor 1 saw himself, but this time as an observer of his own behavior. Observer 2 (who had been observing actor 2), saw a tape of the actor that he had not been observing previously, while observer 1 had another opportunity to observe the actor that he had originally been observing. In the control condition of the study, no tapes were shown, but all subjects were given questionnaires to complete; experimental subjects completed the same questionnaires, but only after viewing the videotape. Questionnaires were designed specifically to determine the degree to which the subjects thought personal characteristics caused the behavior they observed (or engaged in) and the degree to which characteristics of the situation caused the behavior.

Storms' results are informative and provocative. First, fitting the original Jones and Nisbett hypothesis, Storms likewise found that under the appropriate conditions of his study (i.e., either when there was no videotape playback or when the playback simply presented the same perspective to the subjects), actors tended to attribute their behavior to situational factors while observers attributed the actor's behavior to personal characteristics. Second, and consistent with Storm's own hypothesis, the effect of the actor's seeing himself on tape and thus from the perspective of an observer led the actors to make more dispositional attributions for their own behavior, while observers now seeing the situation from the new perspective of the actor made fewer dispositional and more situational attributions. Finally, at least in the relatively short time of the interactive encounter he studied (e.g., 5-minute conversation), Storms reports that simply seeing the same perspective on tape did not influence a subject's attributions. In other words, a simple playback from the same point of view did not influence a subjects' understanding of the causes of behavior; only a playback from a different perspective, providing them with new information, especially about their own behavior, modified the subjects' attributions.

As Storms notes, and as I strongly second, the observation of one's own behaving can prove to be a major determinant to changing the attribution of one's behavior from situational to personal factors. To put this in still another way, the change in orientation brought home to the actors their own value as causal agents in an ongoing interaction setting. There are clear implications of this analysis for all change-oriented techniques, especially for therapy. Presumably, as people see their own causal contributions to their behavior, rather than seeing themselves as simply responding to situational requirements, they will be more inclined to assume more personal responsibility. We may assume that accepting responsibility as a causal agent is the first step towards behavioral change. In family settings, for example, in which the husband sees the wife as the cause and his behavior as the response, a new orientation of seeing himself as an observer does, could be influential in showing the husband his contribution to their marital conflict.

In this connection, it is important to note that videotape playback is only one means of reorienting the actor's perspective. Much of what goes on in individual and group therapy or even in sensitivity group training seeks to achieve a similar end but typically without videotape. The end, of course, is to help us see ourselves as others do, and from this new perspective gain a better sense of our own contributions to behavior. The worry, of course, is that in such a reorienting the actor might be lead to overvalue personal contributions at the expense of situational contributions. Switching the person from a naïve sociologist (i.e., placing the emphasis on situational causes for behavior) to a naïve psychologist (i.e., placing the emphasis on dispositional causes for behavior) may prove as detrimental to an accurate assessment of a complex situation as retaining the typical naïve psychological perspective alone. Perhaps, however, the first step towards adopting a more complex, social-psychological attributional framework is for us to be able to see ourselves from the observer's perspective and as Storms has demonstrated, as a causal entity. The next step is to integrate these two differing perspectives; while the integration clearly requires their differentiation as a first step, by itself, such integration has been little studied and only minimally practiced.

On Self-Attribution

While the argument has suggested that observers and actors, having different perspectives, make different attributions, the point we do not wish to lose is that the processes involved remain similar for both. Both actor and observer use information from the act, the consequences in particular situational contexts, and whatever biographical material about the actor they possess, to derive a causal attribution. Several recent analysts, including Kelley (1967; 1973) and Bem (1967; 1972) have used this notion to suggest a self-attribution model that parallels the other-attribution model we have been discussing. The model states simply that attributions we make regarding our own behavior follow the same process as attributions we make regarding another's behavior. In other words, we use our actions to make inferences about the causes of our behavior in much the way we use other's actions to make inferences about the causes of their behavior. As Bem and an associate Keith McConnell state it:

> *Individuals come to "know" their own attitudes and other internal states partially by inferring them from observations of their own overt behavior and the circumstances in which it occurs. Thus, to the extent that information from internal cues is weak, ambiguous, or uninterpretable, the individual is functionally in the same position as an outside observer of his behavior, an observer who, necessarily, must rely upon those same external cues to infer the individual's inner states* (1970, p. 23).

A similar analysis of self-awareness was made by G. H. Mead (1934) who, however, stressed the important role that other's behavior plays in shaping our self-attribution. In the Meadian formulation of self-attribution or self-perception, the question would be phrased "If I do X, what kind of person will O think me to be"? In other words, what are the dispositional implications of my actions? We will examine this more interactional perspective of self-attribution in the next section of this chapter. Note, however, that in all versions of the general model, actions or bodily states are used as sources of information for perceiving and knowing oneself. Behavior thereby becomes a primary shaper of cognition, both cognition about self and cognition about others.

SELF-ATTRIBUTION VERSUS COGNITIVE DISSONANCE

One of the initial applications of the self-attribution model that Bem (1967; 1972) presented was as a different, he claimed, simpler analysis of some of the cognitive dissonance work on behavior performance with insufficient justification. Recall the infamous $1–$20 study (p. 136) in which subjects presumably experienced greater dissonance when telling a lie about a boring task without sufficient justification (i.e., for $1), and reduced their dissonance by overvaluing the task about which they had told the lie. Bem's argument is that one need not turn to a notion of dissonance in order to explain these and related results. Rather, we assume that by seeing our own behavior as an observer does, we make an inference from this observation about our true attitudes. Thus, P is aware of taking $20 to tell a lie and readily infers that sufficient external justification exists to discount any internal causes; thus, P's attitude towards the task (the possible internal cause of the behavior) remains the same. On the other hand, by taking $1 to tell the lie, P might well ask, "What must my attitude be if I am willing to tell a lie in this situation"? Surely, the $1 was not sufficient cause, and therefore external reasons are discounted. That leaves internal reasons for the behavior—namely, "Because I behaved in this manner in this situation, I must really believe the task was interesting."

Bem's major methodology for testing this model is to conduct a series of *simulations* of several of the cognitive dissonance studies, including the $1–$20 study. He presents his subjects with all the information descriptive of the dissonance situation, but does not actually create any internal state of dissonance within them, as they are neither required to lie nor do they receive any special payment. The subjects, who now are like observers of the actual experiment, are asked to indicate how the "real experimental subject" would feel. Bem reports that simulated results conform to the dissonance-theory results, even though no apparent dissonance has been created. In other words, observers who know that a subject accepted $1 to tell a lie say that it would seem that the subject's true attitude must be more closely alligned to his or her behavior than for the subject receiving $20, who has a true attitude that is not revealed in this kind of situation.

Over the years a considerable debate has raged concerning the contrasting and competing dissonance versus self-attribution analyses of the insufficient justification effect. While nothing really has been settled, perhaps it is as Bem himself concludes after still another effort to demonstrate the validity of his analysis:

> *If the past history of controversies like this is any guide, it seems unlikely that a "crucial" experiment for discriminating between the two theories will ever be executed. At this juncture each theory appears capable of claiming some territory not claimed by the other and one's choice of theory in areas of overlap is diminishing to a matter of loyalty or aesthetics"* (Bem & McConnell, 1970, p. 30).

Perhaps because he was less involved than others in being loyal or disloyal to one theoretical formulation or another, John Wallace's investigation, reported in 1966, offers us some further insights into the role that behavior can play in informing P about P's beliefs. Wallace had subjects engage in a debate about capital punishment before an audience, adopting a position in the debate with which they privately disagreed. Subjects were given what was presumably audience feedback about their performance as debators. Wallace's results indicated that rewarding subjects with positive feedback for being good debators had the effect of influencing subjects to change their private attitudes to be more congruent with the publicly stated debate attitudes.

Wallace turns to what seems to be a self-attribution argument in order to more fully explain these results. He suggests that the rewarding audience feedback provided the subjects with information that allowed them to interpret their own behavior much as the audience did—namely, as a good example of a sincere person. By way of illustration, Wallace cites one subject who changed twenty-five points away from his original position in response to being rewarded by the audience as a good debator. This subject, who liked to think of himself as a sincere and honest person, on learning that the audience thought him to be a good debator, says: "I was somewhat baffled . . . actually, a little offended. The more I thought about it, the more I became convinced that what I had said in the debate was what I truly believed" (p. 311).

The important point to note is that P uses O's response to P's behavior as a cue to finding out what P's own internal attitude or state must be. In this case, O's rewarding of P's good debating performance combines with P's self-image as a sincere and honest person, to suggest that perhaps P's private and public attitudes are more similar than P originally had thought. This same point will arise again when we consider how it is that P makes attributions to other internal states, using O's behavior and responses as informative clues.

That P's behavior influences self-perception has received support in a variety of settings. In one simple yet important demonstration of this notion, John Schopler and John Compere (1971) report that subjects asked to be experimenters who behave positively towards another person come to believe that they must like that person, whereas those who were asked to behave negatively come to believe that they must dislike the other person. While this sounds both simple and perhaps even a bit too commonsensical, think about its meaning and implication. What is being said is that how P behaves towards O influences the internal attitude P has towards O.

We behave positively or negatively towards others for a variety of reasons, some of which may have little to do with our liking of O; the point is that the behavior itself is informative to us (and to others) about our attitudes, and in fact, may eventually shape those very attitudes. This latter point of view is dominant in role theory (which we will consider in the final section of this chapter), according to which behaving in accordance with a role's requirements can have rather striking effects on a person's internal attitudes and beliefs. Thus, if a change in laws can bring together persons of different races and sexes in schools and on the job, this behavioral contact can be a significant source of attitude change.

FOOT-IN-THE-DOOR: ON CHANGING SELF-CONCEPTS

What appears at first to be a wily salesman's approach, aptly called the "foot-in-the-door" technique, offers us yet another illustration of the self-attribution principle. In 1966, Freedman and Fraser published the results of a study they conducted in which they got persons to comply initially with a trivial request (hence, the foot-in-the-door) as a device for getting them later to make a commitment to a decidedly greater request. In their study, Freedman and Fraser initially asked suburban housewives called upon in their homes to put a small sign in their window or to sign a petition on issues of either safe driving or beautifying California. A few weeks later, these same housewives were approached by a different experimenter and this time asked if they would place a large billboard on their front lawns; the billboard promoted auto safety. Results indicated that getting one's foot in the door via an initial small request had striking influences on the willingness of these subjects to comply with the far larger request later. Early compliance produced significant later compliance.

The self-attribution view of this phenomenon suggests that having seen herself as an activist in a small way, the housewife's perception of herself changes. She now comes to think of herself as being more of an active citizen-participator, such that she is now ready to engage in behaviors to which before this change in her self-perception she would be resistant. Her perception of her own attitudes and beliefs, and in this case, her self-concept, were thereby changed by her initial behavior: "Well, I signed the petition, so I must be the kind of person who is really interested in and involved with community matters." Furthermore, as the attribution model suggests, because the housewife's first action was taken without apparent external cause, it must have been because of the internal cause of "being that kind of person who signs petitions, puts signs in windows, etc!"

More recently, Snyder and Cunningham (1975) replicated the original Freedman and Fraser findings, attempting to provide a more direct test of the self-perception interpretation. Snyder and Cunningham conducted a field experiment in which female and male subjects were approached by telephone and asked for either a small initial request designed to evoke compliance with it or a large initial request designed to evoke noncompliance. The small request was to answer eight telephone survey questions; the large initial request was to answer fifty questions. Subjects were then told they would be contacted later if they were needed. Two days later, another experimenter called all the subjects back and asked them a moderate request to answer thirty telephone survey questions; this ostensibly was for a different survey organization than the first. A control group of subjects was contacted only for this second request.

The self-attribution prediction would be that subjects who complied with the initial small request would now see themselves as the kind of person who answers telephone surveys and thus should agree to the moderate request. On the other hand, those who refused the initial large request should come to define themselves as noncompliers and thus should be more resistant to the moderate second request. Data generally support these expectations. Compared to the control group's agreement to the moderate request (one-third agree), slightly over one-half of the initial small compliers agree; the compliance rate for the initial noncompliers was significantly lower than the control group rate. Although, once again, no direct assessment of P's actual change in self-perception was obtained—

the act of obtaining such a measure in the present design, of course, might bias the results—the data are consistent with the self-perception analysis. They also suggest that not only compliance but also resistance can evolve from initial actions that affect P's self-perception.

Using much this same reasoning, Mark Lepper (1973) sought to replicate the classic Aronson and Carlsmith forbidden-toy study (see p. 137). Lepper argued that by forbidding children to play with a toy and using only a mild threat to do so, they come to see themselves as "good" children who follow adult suggestions. Again, take the observer's perspective on this situation. O sees P told not to play with a particular toy and also sees that there is little external pressure brought to bear on P. O is therefore likely to infer an inner disposition, that either P doesn't really like playing with that toy or that P is a "good and obedient kind of child." P has the self-knowledge of liking the toy, and attributes compliance to being a "good child." With strong threat, by contrast, there is no need to search for an inner disposition, as the external justification for compliance is great.

Lepper next argued that seeing one's self as a good child in the initial situation of the forbidden-toy experiment, comparable to the foot-in-the-door technique, sufficiently changes P's self-concept so that in a later context P will be more resistant to giving in to temptation. By contrast, the strong threat, by not influencing P's self-attribution (i.e., because circumstances alone can account for P's compliance), will lead the person later to be more likely to give in to temptation.

To study this, Lepper brought his subjects, most of whom were in the second grade, into two experimental sessions. In the first session, they experienced the forbidden-toy situation; approximately three weeks later in the second session, they were presented with a bowling game in which they could win prizes, but only by giving in to temptation and falsifying their scores.

Lepper's results are consistent with the self-attribution model. Subjects who complied initially under mild threat were more resistant than subjects who complied initially under strong threat to falsify their scores in the second situation. As an additional assessment, Lepper sought directly to measure a change in his subject's self-perceptions by a questionnaire administered after the first experimental session. Although his assessment questionnaire did not demonstrate the expected effect as strongly as one might have hoped, it did provide some interesting confirmatory evidence for the self-attribution model. He found, for example, a tendency for subjects under mild threat in session 1 to report themselves as being "more honest" than subjects under severe threat. Recall that the theoretical point is that to comply without substantial external cause to the experimenter's request in session 1 should produce a self-perception of "I must be an honest person;" this is presumed to make the person more resistant to temptation in session 2.

Self-Perception of Emotions and Internal States

William James (1884, 1890), a prominent figure in the early history of psychology whose ideas always seem contemporary, proposed a theory of emotion that shares much with the self-attribution model. Take a person confronting a wild bear. It was James' contention that bodily changes involved while escaping from the bear give us the subjective emotional experience of fear. In self-attribution theory terms, as we see ourselves escaping, we ask ourselves "What must my feeling be if under the circumstances of seeing a bear, I take off and run away rapidly"? Note that we presumably would ask the same question were we to see another person running: "What kind of person is that who runs away from bears"?

Some interesting research reported by Laird (1974) is instructive in this regard. Laird reasoned that in addition to the bodily changes of which James' spoke, referring primarily to the activity of the autonomic nervous system, changes in the skeletal muscles may also be sources of information to us about our internal, subjective states. For example, if you become aware of yourself smiling, you may come to think that you are feeling happy; or if you become aware of yourself frowning and clenching your fists, you may come to experience yourself as angry. In either case, the fundamental idea is that behavior (in this case a pattern of muscle activity) precedes and helps cause the subjective state that is experienced. The causal link in this model occurs, as we have noted, by means of the self-inferences that we make from those bodily sources of information.

For his study, Laird brought subjects to his laboratory where he told them that he was interested in the activity of their facial muscles while they perceived various pictures. Subjects' faces were carefully arranged by the experimenter to depict either a happy or an angry expression. Pictures were then shown and subjects asked to make ratings descriptive of their mood. Different kinds of pictures were shown in Laird's several studies; in some he employed cartoons, in others, children playing, or Ku Klux Klan members. In all cases, the data support Laird's self-attribution theory prediction that subjects would use information from their facial expression as a basis for rating their responses to the pictures. Cartoons were funnier and subjects reported themselves to be more elated when they were smiling than when they were frowning. KKK members were rated as more aggressive if the subjects were frowning while viewing the pictures than if they were smiling.

In some later work Laird and Crosby (*in press*) further suggested that some persons tend to emphasize these self-produced cues from their body (i.e., both states of physiological arousal and outwardly expressive behavior—for example, of the skeletal muscles), while others tend to emphasize situational cues. The former, seeing themselves smiling as in the previous studies, will use that as a source of information about what they must feel; the latter, noting that they are at a party rather than a funeral, for example, use that cultural distinction as a source of information about what their subjective internal states are likely to be. Some of Schachter's work which we will shortly examine is relevant in this connection. He suggests that normal weight people define themselves as hungry, using self-produced, internal bodily cues as a source of this inference; obese persons, on the other hand, tend to overemphasize situational cues that inform them that this might be an eating situation, and thereby eat even when not "hungry." Applying this distinction to his smile-frown work, Laird was able to separate out persons who were primarily oriented to self-produced cues from those who were primarily oriented to situationally-produced cues. The former groups were responsive to the fact that their faces were smiling or frowning, while the latter were not: for example, the former groups rated the cartoons as funnier when they were smiling, the latter groups were not similarly affected by these bodily cues. Recall that the essence of the self-attribution notion is that P uses personal behavior and the circumstances in which it occurs as an important source of self-information, in particular about P's own attitudes, beliefs, opinions, subjective states, and such.

One rather interesting derivation of the preceding model was reported in 1968 by Bandler, Madaras, and Bem. They created an experimental situation in which subjects observed themselves either escaping an electric shock by pressing a button if they so choose, or enduring the shock, (termed the no-escape condition) because they were informed by the experimenter that they were in the condition that was not to turn off the shock although they could if the pain became unbearable. The subjects in all experimental conditions were asked after each shock to rate its degree of discomfort and painfulness. The prediction from self-attribution theory argues that the subject's perception of pain (i.e., perception of one's own internal state) should vary as a function of the inference that the subject makes from personal behavior in the situation. Thus, subjects in the escape condition should rate the objectively same intensity of shock as more painful than subjects in the no-escape condition: "Since I tried to escape it, the shock must have been quite painful." Results confirm this expectation, suggesting that P's behavior is indeed informative to P about his or her internal experience.

Recall that P assumes the observer's perspective. Thus, an observer viewing P in the escape condition might conclude that the shock must be painful because P always tries to escape it; an observer viewing the no-escape condition, by contrast, might conclude that the shock can't be all that bad, because P is not trying to escape it. Self-attribution theory suggests that P takes the observer's perspective in coming to understand his or her own internal states.

The self-attribution model places its emphasis upon cognitive processes that give meaning to and help define P's or O's internal states. We might say that internal states have a degree of plasticity that permits them to be known differently as a function of the kind of attribution they are given. Laird's work demonstrated how the cues derived from facial expressions affect our feelings about things we see. Cues, of course, arise not only from the changing state of our skeletal muscles but also from the changing states of our autonomic and other physiological systems. For example, we may be physiologically aroused, our bodily state characterized by an increased heartbeat, a rise in blood pressure, and so on. We would be likely to describe ourselves as "emotional." But what emotion are we experiencing? We could turn to the situation around us for cues to help define this arousal. Of course, if this state were experienced while looking closely at a bear who stood menacingly before us, we might readily define our emotion as fear. In this case, the bodily arousal and its explanation correspond.

The preceding line of thought suggested to Schachter and Singer (1962) the possibility of experimentally separating what is typically correlated in nature, physiological bodily states from external cognitive information. Usually the same event that gives rise to a bodily condition also gives rise to a situational explanation adequate to understand the bodily condition. But this connection can be modified within the laboratory and the consequences studied.

Schachter and Singer brought a naïve subject and their hired accomplice together for an experimental session. Both received an injection of epinephrine (or a placebo in some conditions) that would produce a state of bodily arousal including increases in blood pressure and heart rate, usually a slight tremor and a feeling of flushing. (The accomplice, of course, never actually received any epinephrine.) The accomplice had been trained to engage in one of two routines. In one routine, the accomplice sought to behave as though he were euphoric by acting rather giddy, playful, and child-like, ending his routine by playing with a Hula-Hoop. In the other routine, the accomplice sought to convey anger by ripping up a questionnaire given by the experimenter, stomping about, and finally, in anger getting up and leaving the room.

What Schachter and Singer created experimentally, then, was a separation of the bodily arousal from situational cues that would also help explain it; their accomplice, in essence, provided the subject with these situational explanations. Thus, we would expect the aroused subjects who witnessed a presumably aroused fellow subject acting euphorically to attribute their own arousal to their feeling of euphoria, whereas those aroused subjects who are in a situation which suggests anger should attribute their arousal to being angry. In other words, the actual emotion experienced by the subject should be a joint function of arousal and external information that offers an explanation for it. And indeed, this is precisely what Schachter and Singer found. It is important to realize that without the ambiguous bodily state to explain, for example, when the subject received a placebo rather than the epinephrine, there was little influence of the accomplice's behavior on the subject.

To summarize their theory and relevant findings, Schachter and Singer suggest that:

1. When P is physiologically aroused and has no appropriate explanation for this arousal, P will search for explanatory cues from the situation: for example, the accomplices' behavior provided these cues.
2. When P is aroused and at the same time there exists a relatively clear explanation for the arousal, there will not be any evaluative needs triggered in P, so there will be no need to search for something to explain what P is experiencing.
3. Finally, cognitive factors alone will not influence P's self-perception (e.g., as happy or angry) unless a state of physiological arousal is also present.

THE FAT AND THE LEAN

While the initial program of both theory and research undertaken by Schachter and his colleagues sought to separate experimentally bodily states from cognitive factors of attribution, several of his investigations of eating behavior among normal and obese subjects, suggested that even in its natural state, a comparable separation is found. In particular, research evidence suggests that normal weight persons have a learned coincidence of the bodily states of hunger (e.g., gastric motility) and the cognitive labeling or attribution of those states to hunger. Obese persons, on the other hand, seem to have a learned separation between physiological states appropriate to eating and the cognitive cues that mean hunger. Thus, it would appear:

that the obese have not learned to discriminate between the physiological symptoms accompanying food deprivation and the condition of arousal characteristic of emotional states such as fear, anger, and anxiety (Schachter, Goldman, Gordon, 1968, p. 91).

Thus, while the normal individuals will attribute gastric arousal to hunger, the obese do not seem to connect gastric arousal with hunger and seem to misattribute other states of arousal to hunger. The obese subject may feel hungry and want to eat under circumstances that have very little to do with the actual physiological arousal appropriate to hunger: hence the obesity.

Schachter's and his colleagues' research has consistently demonstrated the preceding (e.g. Schachter, 1967; Schachter & Gross, 1968). In one of several efforts (Schachter, Goldman, & Gordon, 1968) they experimentally created a bodily state appropriate either to increased or decreased hunger, noting that whereas normal weight subjects tended to eat in a manner corresponding to their bodily states, the obese were relatively uninfluenced. For example, fear arousal tends to inhibit gastric motility and thus decrease hunger. Normal subjects do eat more when calm than when fearful; obese subjects, however, seem uninfluenced by these conditions, eating about the same regardless of the manipulated experimental conditions.

It seemed to Schachter and his associates (see Schachter, 1967 for a summary) that the obese subjects' lack of sensitivity to internal states led them to utilize external cues as a source of their information about their hunger. For example, seeing others eating, knowing that it was dinner time, smelling or seeing food or food-related objects are external cues that could lead obese persons to attribute hunger to themselves and thus lead them to eat. Normal weight persons, on the other hand, are less likely to attribute hunger to themselves when external cues suggest food unless appropriate internal cues such as gastric motility are also present. Recall Laird's parallel results to which I referred previously, involving two types of persons, the one stimulus or situationally oriented, the other, more oriented to self-produced bodily cues.

This tendency to be externally oriented for the obese has been reported as a conclusion of a variety of investigations, including one reported in 1969 by Nisbett and Kanouse relating to supermarket shopping behavior. The typical experience for normal weight subjects, validated in this study as well, is for them to buy more when hungry than when shopping after having recently eaten. The obese subjects, however, being unresponsive to these internal cues of hunger, but being highly sensitized to external food-related information did not show a simple relationship between eating and shopping.

More recently, Rodin and Slochower (1974) report further confirmation for this difference in responsivity to internal as opposed to external sources of information. In her work, Rodin reasoned that if obese persons were more sensitive to the situation around them than normal weight persons, they should be more readily distracted by extraneous environmental cues and thereby should have greater difficulty in perceptual and learning tasks. Her experimental data generally substantiate this expectation. Why these differences between the obese and the normally weighted person or for that matter why the same kinds of differences that Laird uncovered occur, is by no means clear; we might speculate that we are dealing here with an important person-factor that affects the sources of cues that the person processes.

Similar analyses have been proposed by others in what on the surface may seem to be quite another behavioral realm. Witkin and his associates (Witkin, Dyk, Faterson, Goodenough, & Karp, 1962) for instance, discuss different styles of cognitive organization, referring to a *field dependent* person, who like the obese in Schachter's and Rodin's work and some of Laird's subjects, seem situationally oriented for cues regarding their internal states. Others, termed *field independent* seem more oriented towards internal, self-produced cues. While to pursue this matter here would take us too far afield, perhaps we can at least better appreciate some of the complex interactions involved in understanding how P deals with self-information as well as information about others. Would a person who seems especially sensitive to externally based cues in order to assess his or her own states of feeling be likewise inclined to apply similar criteria in judging others? And would those who use internal cues to understand themselves likewise try to employ similar cues for evaluating others? And might these difference hold for more complex matters involving the determination of responsibility and causality? These are but some interesting questions that remain to be answered.

That these are realistic possibilities is suggested by the related research of Sosis (1974) employing a person-centered variable termed *internal versus external locus of control* (further details of which we will consider in Chapter 11). For our present purposes, it is sufficient to note that "externals" believe that the factors that determine their behavior lie outside themselves and beyond their control, whereas "internals" believe themselves able to exercise control over their behavior. Strictly speaking, externality in this sense is not precisely the same as being field dependent or situation bound; yet we might very well assume that people who see themselves controlled by external forces are not as concerned as the internals with self-produced cues.

What Sosis did in her research is to present subjects who were premeasured on their degree of internality-externality with a hypothetical accident case; subjects were asked to rate the defendant as to his degree of responsibility and to indicate what penalty he should receive. Results indicated that as compared with externals, internals tended to attribute greater responsibility to the defendent and to think he should be dealt with more harsly. In other words, P perceived O in much the same way he perceived himself: thus if he felt that his life were internally controlled he felt that O's likewise was and thus that O was responsible for the accident and should be dealt with harshly.

Before we leave this matter, we should recognize as well that though our focus has been on self-attribution of emotions and other internal states, we have not really left behind the Chapter 1 issues involving person, situation and person-situation interaction. There has been a long-term interest in understanding the degree to which "consistency" or "inconsistency" of behavior across situations may be conceptualized as a typical characteristic of persons (e.g., Bem & Allen, 1974; Campus, 1974). Even if our conceptualization is interactionist, are there some persons who behave more consistently in different situations than others? In turn, are these others more sensitive to situational demands? Evidence reported by Bem and Allen and by Campus illustrates the relevance of speaking about behavioral consistency as a characteristic of some persons. It would seem that these persons are more internally oriented, taking their cues from self-produced states. Those persons who seem more inconsistent and responsive to situational demands are more situationally bound in their preceptions of themselves and others.

By Way of Summary

The important point to keep in mind from the preceding work is the suggestion that cognitive factors can significantly influence the kind of attribution that is made by the person to explain a given internal state. The research on self-attribution theory that we have considered suggests that the cognitive factors that are informative to P include: the self-observation of P's behavior; P's observation of another's behavior; the circumstances in which P and the other persons are involved; the response of others towards P's behavior; a learned connection between an internal state of bodily arousal and external circumstances that adequately explain it. Likewise, the internal states that we have considered include P's attitudes and beliefs, P's self concept, P's experience of emotions, including pain, anger, euphoria among others, and P's experience of physiological states including hunger.

Misattribution

The possibility of separating the internal state from the information that P employs to attribute a stable meaning to it introduces us to what has been termed *a misattribution model.* The point is that P will attribute the cause of some internal state that he or she is experiencing to those plausible sources of information that are present and seem relevant to explaining and interpreting it. As we previously noted, internal states of arousal are explained by reference to the stimulus conditions that evoke it (e.g., the bear).

Misattribution is simply a special case of attribution; in this case, however, the investigator manipulates the information that P has available for attributing meaning to P's internal state. Thus, Schachter and Singer can be said to have led P to misattribute P's physiological arousal and understand it as anger or euphoria as a function of the accomplice's performance. The argument that misattribution is simply an unnatural device of social psychological experimentation is weakened, recall, by Schachter's work on obesity in which it seems that obese persons have learned to misattribute the basis of their hunger; they report hunger under a wide variety of circumstances.

The argument is further weakened as we realize that each of us may have a learning history of misattribution, linking our internal states of arousal to what we misattribute to be plausible causes, but which, in fact, though plausible, need not be inevitable. Phobias offer us a good case in point. P may misattribute an internal state of anxiety to closed places, high places, snakes, and what have you. Thus P comes to believe that it is high places that both arouse anxiety and explain it; this is a misattribution insofar as some inner conflict may actually trigger P's anxiety; however, P believes it to be explained by heights. This is also an example of how such misattribution can form a self-reinforcing cycle: being in high places explains the inner tension that, in being attributed to high places, becomes even greater as long as P remains in the high place. We can thereby hypothesize that the intentional use of a misattribution approach could break this cycle: if P no longer explains inner tension by attributing it to high places, then presumably when in a high place, P will experience less internal arousal.

Using this misattributional model, Storms and Nisbett (1970) report an approach to curing insomnia by leading their insomniac subjects to attribute their condition to a pill given to them by the experimenter. Specifically, Storms and Nisbett provided one group of insomniac subjects with a pill (actually a placebo) that presumably would produce a heightened state of physiological arousal; a second group of insomniacs were given a pill that purportedly would relax them. The theory argues, paradoxically in this case, that the arousal pill should actually be more facilitative of an insomniac's going to sleep than the relaxation pill.

The derivation from the theoretical model is actually rather straightforward. If P, the insomniac, is given a pill that can explain the probable emotional arousal that is preventing sleep, then P will be more likely to attribute any arousal experienced to the pill, thereby no longer having to view the sleep disturbance as symptomatic of something pathological about self. The arousal pill thus permits P to misattribute the source of interfering internal tension and allows P to break a vicious cycle in which worrying about not being able to get to sleep actually exacerbates the difficulty involved in getting to sleep.

Receiving the relaxation pills, on the other hand, that cognitively should reduce the symptoms and facilitate P's getting to sleep, actually compels P to attribute any continuing sleep difficulties to self; actually, because P should be relaxed by the pill but is not yet relaxed, P might even worry more about the severity of the insomnia, thus feeding the vicious cycle rather than breaking it. Storms and Nisbett's research findings provided support for the hypotheses; although this internal conversation that presumably went on within P's mind was not studied, the experimental results are consistent with it and, as we have seen, with other similar kinds of research work.

The implications of the preceding line of investigation are of value. An obvious therapeutic suggestion is that by providing P with alternative sources to explain the internal states, P's experience can be significantly modified. In another clinical context involving a person's fear of snakes, Valins and Ray (1967) report that a false feedback of heartbeat to the subject, increasing the beat to shock but decreasing it to seeing the snake, helps the person to learn to believe that the arousal is not caused by a fear of snakes, and thus the subject is more willing to have direct contact with a real snake. In this case, the internal state of arousal itself is not changed, rather the person's attribution of its source is modified: thus, the person's understanding of its cause is different, the emotional experience is thereby modified, and the behavioral consequences altered.

We would expect there to be limitations to the possibilities that a misattribution technique allows. The plasticity of our internal emotional states is by no means unlimited; cognitive misinformation apparently cannot override strong internal physiological responses as readily as weaker ones, as Goldstein, Fink, and Metee (1972) report from their research conducted within the Valins false feedback model (Valins, 1966). Their data suggest that when subjects are weakly aroused and provided with false information about their heartbeat, they tend to use that information as a guide to their probable emotional reaction. Thus, a male subject reports being excited about female nudes when hearing his heartbeat increase. As the actual physiological arousal, however, increases (i.e., as his real heart rate goes up), false information about his arousal cannot readily override his awareness of his actual internal state. Thus, if real heartbeat increases, but the false feedback suggests a normal beat, Goldstein and his colleague's findings suggest that the actual rate will be more influential in leading P to attribute emotionality than will the contradictory feedback that P is receiving. This, of course, is consistent with the Valins and Ray finding in which the internal arousal state is not altered by P's receiving false feedback; rather P's behaviors are altered. In turn, a change in behavior should feedback self-information that P may be less frightened of snakes than P initially thought, for P is now approaching and touching one.

A More Complex Picture.   In much of the preceding work we have examined, P reports a change in the experience or the label P applies to it as a result of the misattribution technique that has been employed. Other critical questions remain to be answered; we shall now examine a few studies that provide further clarity to the misattribution model. In the first, Ross, Rodin, and Zimbardo (1969) demonstrate how subjects can be made to misattribute their fear arousal and change their actual behavior while working on tasks presented to them. In the second, Loftis and Ross (1974a) provide a most powerful demonstration of how misattribution techniques can actually influence P's physiological state itself; in this case, unlike the previous examples, self-report and physiological arousal mutually support one another.

Ross, Rodin, and Zimbardo (1969) used the misattribution approach to demonstrate how an aroused internal state of fear could be attributed to different sources with strikingly different behavioral consequences for their subjects. Fear was aroused by the possibility of receiving electric shock. The source to which the subjects could attribute the bodily symptoms of fear was systematically varied. Some subjects were led to believe that noise, introduced as part of an experiment studying the effects of noise, was the cause of the symptoms of arousal; others were led to believe that the threat of shock was the cause of the symptoms they experienced.

All subjects were given two puzzles on which they could work for the remainder of the experiment. Although both were actually insoluble, one was introduced as a way of earning a monetary reward if it were solved, while the other was introduced as a way of avoiding the shock if it could be solved. The authors' summary of their results indicates the manner by which fear can be controlled by the person by attributing it to (or misattributing it in this case) to a benign source:

> *Subjects made fearful by the possibility of receiving electric shock attributed their physiologically aroused state to the threat of shock. Consistent with this attribution, they characteristically persisted in attempts to solve the simple but insoluble puzzle that they believed would spare them from shock. In contrast, subjects provided with an emotionally irrelevant cognitive explanation for their arousal formed a nonemotional attribution regarding this state and manifested less fear by turning their attention from the shock-avoidance puzzle to one that might gain them monetary reward* (p. 286).

In terms of the self-attribution model, the preceding study can be diagrammed as follows:

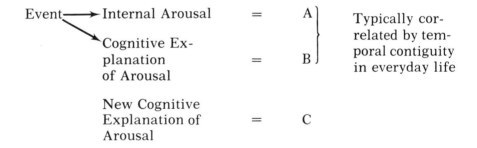

Under typical circumstances, the same event—in this case the threat of receiving an electric shock—leads to both an internal set of bodily symptoms (A) and to a plausible explanation for this state (B). Thus, P attributes internal arousal to the threat of shock and experiences the emotion of fear. Under conditions of misattribution, A occurs in conjunction with C, permitting persons to attribute their internal state to a different, unrelated cognitive explanation. In the Ross, Rodin, and Zimbardo study, this new cognitive explanation involves a loud noise and the fearful experience was thereby attenuated.

Loftis and Ross (1974a) also employed shock and noise in their investigation. Unlike the preceding study and much of the previous work, Loftis and Ross sought to determine whether P's misattributing bodily arousal to a benign source (e.g., noise rather than shock) would have an effect on P's actual state of physiological arousal in addition to whatever effects it would have on the label that P attached to the experience: that is, would misattribution reduce P's real arousal? An answer to this question is obviously important; if misattribution can effect P's actual arousal state, then the self-maintaining cycle that we mentioned earlier (p. 174) can be broken. We will examine their research in some detail in order to clarify these important points.

The research design Loftis and Ross employed involved classical conditioning, in which P learned to respond emotionally to a once neutral, nonemotional event (a light) by having it paired with a naturally arousing event (electric shock). In this learning model, a light (termed the *conditioned stimulus* or CS) is paired over a series of trials with an electric shock (termed the *unconditioned stimulus* or UCS) and P's physiological response is recorded: (i.e., P's physiological arousal in response to the CS–UCS pairing). If the UCS alone is introduced, P will show a demonstrable arousal response that can be recorded on an appropriate apparatus. This response is termed the Galvanic Skin Response (GSR); it is a measure of P's state of physiological arousal and is often associated with work involving lie detection. By pairing the CS and UCS, in time, P will become aroused to the CS (light) alone. In the classical conditioning model, P learns to respond to the once neutral event, the light, as though it had the same noxious qualities as the naturally arousing event, the shock.

Once P has learned this habit of responding emotionally (as recorded by the GSR) to the light, it is then possible to introduce a series of what are called *extinction trials* designed to extinguish or get rid of the learned habit. In extinction trials, the light (CS) is presented without being paired with shock (UCS). In a short time, P learns that the light no longer signifies shock and thus extinguishes the learned habit; the light can be turned on and P will not evidence any heightened GSR.

Loftis and Ross used the preceding design to show how those persons who could be made to misattribute the source of their arousal to something other than the light, would thereby extinguish their learning; and this would show up as a low level of GSR arousal during the extinction trials. Now for the details of this part of their procedure. First, subjects learn to connect the onset of a light with a shock; in time, they respond with high GSR arousal whenever the light itself is turned on. Second, subjects are now introduced to an extinction series in which the light is put on but no shock is delivered. Third, all subjects are told that during this extinction series, they will hear a continuously sounding loud noise, presumably because the experimentor is interested in studying the effects of noise upon learned behaviors. Fourth, before they are put through the extinction series, subjects are divided into two different groups as a function of the specific instructions they are given. The *misattribution group* is told that some typical responses to extreme noise are palpitations, rapid breathing, hand tremor, and butterflies in the stomach. The control group is told that some typical responses to extreme noise are dull headaches, weariness, dizziness, and ringing in the ears. Before we go on, let us look more closely at these instructions and their meaning.

The listing of bodily symptoms given to the misattribution group are actually those that are most likely when a person is fearful; the symptoms given to the control group, on the other hand, are not likely to occur when one is fearful. Therefore, when a subject in the control group begins to experience fear responses when the light is turned on (recall, they have learned to associate light with shock and have actual fear responses to shock), they will suppose that it is the light that explains their symptoms rather than the loud noise they are also hearing. After all, their fear symptoms are not those associated with loud noises. On the other hand, when subjects in the misattribution group try to explain the symptoms of their fear arousal, they can more readily explain them as a response to the loud noise rather than to the light. After all, their fear symptoms are just the ones that are supposed to occur when a loud noise is presented.

Misattribution theory maintains that if persons can attribute their heightened arousal to a relatively benign source such as the noise, then they should more readily extinguish the learned fear reaction to the light, when compared with persons who continue to explain their heightened arousal by attributing it to the light. For this latter group, each time the light comes on and they experience fear symptoms, they attribute those symptoms to the light and so they continue to react fearfully until they unlearn this connection. The cycle is thereby maintained for a longer period of time. For the former group, each time the light comes on and they experience fear symptoms, they attribute those symptoms not to the light but to the noise, and so they begin to react less fearfully to the light. The cycle is thereby disrupted; they no longer respond with fear to the light and in fact now tolerate the once feared object.

The data that Loftis and Ross report supports this theoretical expectation. What they find is that the actual physiological arousal in response to the light during extinction trials is much higher for subjects in the control group than in the misattribution group. The misattribution group is less physiologically aroused (i.e., fewer GSR responses to the light) when they can attribute their fear to the noise as compared with the control group who continues to attribute their fear to the light and thereby take longer to unlearn this habit. In fact, misattribution group subjects extinguish as rapidly as those subjects who were unable to learn the conditioned fear response in the first place. That is, they act physiologically in seeing the light in a manner similar to those who never did develop a fear reaction to the light. The point is important; we have a powerful demonstration here of an actual attenuation in physiological arousal as a function of misattribution instructions. It is not simply that P reports experiencing less fear or labels emotions as nonfearful or misperceives the experience; but that P's actual bodily state of fear arousal is lowered through this technique!

As Loftis and Ross note, we have a demonstration of how physiological states interact with cognitive states in a mutually supportive way. The physiological change helps sustain the subjective experience; P can experience himself or herself accurately to be less aroused and fearful. Unlike the Valins work we spoke of previously, in the present work, the persons are actually less aroused, and thus their perception of themselves as less aroused corresponds to their bodily reality.

In this connection, it is valuable to recall our discussion in Chapter 3 of attentional mechanisms that helped P better cope with stress. That research suggested how certain kinds of instructions (either self-induced or given by others) actually reduced P's physiological stress response to what is otherwise a stressful event. Much the same thing has occurred here; in this case, the instructions permit P to misattribute the source of P's response to something benign. In the earlier work, we noted how instructions (e.g., the movie sound track) likewise helped redefine P's experience and thereby reduce P's actual arousal. Both involve instructional sets given by others to P. If we think of the same possibility with misattribution that we examined with perceptial selectivity, we can also see how *self-induced sets* can play an equally important role in reducing the consequences of learned stressful responses. We can learn to instruct ourselves to reattribute our fears and thereby to reduce their effects.

Their research technique permitted Loftis and Ross to examine several other features of the misattribution model and its effects. We will only briefly note some of these; the interested reader can refer to the original sources for exact details. Of particular interest to the practitioner, however, who might wish systematically to employ some version of misattribution theory as a therapeutic approach, Loftis and Ross report two additional, important findings. First, in recognition that individuals differ in the degree to which the shock is actually physiologically arousing, data indicate that persons in the misattribution group who were most aroused during learning were least aroused during the extinction phase. That is, the misattribution technique seemed to work best on those persons who were originally most fearful. In applying this to therapy, these findings suggest that persons who have the most pronounced fear symptoms might be the most readily treatable by a misattribution approach. Second, data from their original study (Loftis & Ross, 1974a) and from a follow-up study (Loftis & Ross, 1974b) suggest that persons who have already experienced an emotional reaction who are then given misattribution instructions can use those instructions retrospectively to reinterpret their past arousal. The therapeutic implication of this finding is its importance in showing that misattribution efforts do not only apply to future events (as in the first study), but can also apply to help the patient reattribute past-arousing events.

A BRIDGE TO THE INTERPERSONAL WORLD

In the next section we examine some broader social aspects of causal attribution. To move us in that direction, it will be helpful if we examine briefly the misattribution framework from the perspective of P and O interacting. In this interpersonal context, we realize that P's misattributing internal states is not only a private matter of relevance to P, but can also be seen as something important to the P–O relationship. Presumably, if P misattributes internal states, whether on instructions from O as in the experimental research or from some other source (including self), a change will result in P's behavior and thus in the P–O interaction. Loftis and Ross's subjects not only report feeling less fearful but their bodily arousal confirms that; presumably, not only P but also O could be made aware of this change in P. It is not difficult to imagine, therefore, that misattribution can play an important role in interpersonal relationships; it may well be to P's or to O's advantage, for example, for P to misattribute arousal sufficiently both to appear and to be calm.

Let us suppose that P experiences anger in response to O's actions; for whatever reason, somewhere in P's learning history, the kind of behavior that O produces is like the CS that triggers an angry emotional response. Let us further suppose that P becomes aware of an altered bodily state; P could maintain that what he or she is experiencing is anger and that O's behavior explains it, even though P might not understand why that act of O elicits P's angry response.

O, somewhat like the experimenter who introduces a misattribution technique, may likewise wish to induce P to misattribute feelings so that O and P can continue their relationship. P, in turn, may also like their relationship to continue. Therefore, both O and P might wish this potentially disruptive cycle to be broken. In this case, unlike the typical experimental approach we have examined, we might see both P and O colluding, perhaps quite implicitly, to misattribute P's emotional arousal to something benign: that is, to something other than O's behavior. They may agree that it's the hard day P has had or something else that could as plausibly explain P's feelings as the stimulus, O. Or, in a therapy setting, they might agree that it is not O's act and thus O that explains P's angry state, but rather something back in P's life that is triggered by O and that explains P's present feelings. Thus P's anger towards O should be attenuated as an alternate source is located.

What I have described is a hypothetical exchange in which P and O wish to preserve their relationship and so seek alternative sources than O's acts to attribute (or misattribute) P's feelings. Of course, they may not wish to maintain the relationship and so misattributive efforts fall upon deaf ears. Many of our own everyday experiences suggest the relevance of the kind of interpersonal misattribution that has been described. P and O search about for a parallel to the loud noise of Loftis and Ross's research, something that helps P and O continue together without a disruptive arousal; or they do not search for this noise, but let the feelings be directly attributed and expressed.

As we also know, O may be the misattributed source of P's arousal that may be due to another person or to some other stimulus event, even something in P's past that is now made salient. Displacement of aggression is often of this sort: for example, the real source of P's anger is her boss, but at home her son does something that becomes for P the source of her angry feelings. In this case, misattribution serves to increase tension between P and O rather than to decrease it, but it deflects the tension away from its actual source, P's boss, perhaps thereby sparing P from a worse fate than a family argument brings.

From the interpersonal persepctive we examined in our discussion of balance theory, we can see another use of the misattribution concept. P wishes to establish and have confirmed a particular identity in P's interactions with O. Let us suppose that P wishes to be seen as a calm, easy-going person, but that O tends to be provocative enough to get P's angry feelings aroused. P becomes aware of these feelings and indeed may even attribute their source to O; but P's image would be tarnished were these feelings to explode into an angry outburst as a result of interacting with O. Loftis and Ross's research suggests how by misattributing the source of internal arousal to something plausible but benign, the actual physiological base for the arousal can be transformed. In this case, P can maintain a desired self-image by remaining calm and misattributing the angry feelings to something more benign than O. Misattribution thus may be one way of exercising self-control; we noted in Chapter 3 how changing one's attention or redefining the stimulus object was also helpful in this regard. As we suggested previously, misattribution may be akin to those processes of induced or self-imposed set that redefine the nature of the stimulus situation in a way that helps P better cope with it; in this case, better coping means exercising sufficient self-control to lead O to validate P's desired self-image as a calm, unflappable person.

As the preceding has been described, it tends to sound overly conscious and even manipulative. While indeed certain instances may be, the same kinds of processes can and do operate on a much more implicit level. P does not always need O's instructions to misattribute the source of an annoying event; nor does P always need to be aware of any self-imposed instructions. In either case, P may exercise control over physiological reactions either with or without awareness by changing the focus of the causal analysis. During actual interaction between P and O, there may be much negotiation as each seeks the upper hand in defining what each is responding to and thereby experiencing, as well as the kind of person each wishes to be taken for, given their apparent affective responses. We are not aware of systematic research that has sought to apply this kind of misattributional analysis to interpersonal situations; such work, however, would be of obvious value.

The Social Aspects of Attribution

The preceding work on self-attribution and misattribution will help us bridge the gap between a cognitive psychology of knowledge and a sociological analysis of motivation and causal labeling. We have already noted the degree to which external conditions can and do influence the label we attribute to internal states, the experience we subsequently have, and the level of our actual physiological states of arousal. In essence, the point of the preceding research and theory is that the label (i.e., cognitive explanation) that is attached to an internal event influences the way that event is experienced and actually transpires. Whereas the experimenter in the laboratory can vary the availability of labels, in our everyday lives, these labeled connections already exist in the form of *typifications* (Kelley 1972; 1973 calls them *causal schema*), which we take for granted as objective, unalterable givens.

Basically, a typification (see Berger & Luckman, 1966; Schutz, 1967; 1970–1971) involves a standard definition of a situation that links an actor's observed behavior to some underlying conditions that are presumed to have caused it. A typification (for example, motives and roles) is a property of organized social systems, and as such, is a culturally shared attributive framework that informs the observer, P, that O's behavior is a specific instance of some general category; too, it is a way of categorizing behaviors and their causes. The important point is that the kinds of attributions with which we have been dealing, when viewed as typifications, focus our attention on their socially and historically shared quality rather than upon their individual, idiosyncratic quality. When P observes O do X, therefore, the attribution that P makes, whether it is to some disposition or motive within O or to some circumstance external to O's person (e.g., O's role), represents a social typification that others of P's general society would also make. But this is something we have already touched on in examining Caplan and Nelson's and McArthur's analysis of our own culture's individualisitc attributive bias and some of its implications. The tendency to make person-centered attributions is a culturally shared typifying perspective.

The psychology of attribution is thus informative about its sociology as well; when we understand how 150 subjects at UCLA make their attributions, we are also obtaining a view of typifying schemes that persons of this social system employ. These typifications or causal schemes are attributes of social systems, not simply attributes of individuals. Our membership in a given culture constrains us to make the kinds of attributions that we make. This is in no way to deny unique individual differences, but rather to stress what is too often lost in such analyses—that is, the culturally shared constraints to label and to experience phenomena in a given way.

There is another sense in which our attributions are sociological, public, and shared procedures for making behaviors and events understandable. Let us take an action of O and our attribution of its cause; for example, O leaves a party early and we attribute that behavior to boredom. Is this disposition, boredom, a property of O or is it perhaps better conceived of as "a rule which depicts the social character of the act itself" (Blum & McHugh, 1971, p. 100) clarifying those circumstances that make O's actions socially recognizable? To make O's behavior intelligible by attributing it to boredom is to place the act into a social context that we understand and accept as a plausible way of characterizing and explaining O's behavior (Gerth & Mills, 1953). Thus although attributions may indeed be acts of P's cognitive system that may even refer to private states within O (e.g., boredom), they are fundamentally socially learned, public procedures for understanding events and behaviors.

The intelligibility of an attribution is given by virtue of the fact that both we and O have knowledge about rules and norms governing behavior in our social system and about actions that are reasonable ways for attaining certain goals. The plausibility of the explanation and the intelligibility it provides us for the behavior, are all attributes of the social system.

LEVELS OF ATTRIBUTION

The preceding discussion indicates that our focus on the psychological nature of attributions may have obscured what is as vital a concern—namely, the everyday typifications that we employ without much attentiveness to the processes of their origin; that is, unless something forces us to reconsider what we have heretofore been taking for granted. I think it useful if we view things in terms of levels of attribution. On level 1, we have the processes that we have spent most of our time in examining, whereby the connections between a behavior and its meaning are established: (e.g., as person-centered dispositions or as statements of external cause). On level 2, we have attributional typifications, the already constituted connections between behavior and meaning, that we employ in our everyday dealings with others. On level 3 and upwards, we find even higher order typifications, that come to have the appearance of a "theory" about human behavior.

In their analysis of this overall process, Berger and Luckman suggest that once typifications (i.e., on level 2) have become firmly rooted within a social system, presenting standardized and historical analyses of both *types of actors* and *types of action*, we have what they term *institutionalization,* a higher level organization of attributional schemes. Institutionalization is said to exist when behaviors are classified according to types and attributed to actors who are also classified according to types (e.g., role analyses). For example, marriage is a social institution in which actors are typed or classified into roles, such as husband, wife, child, mother, father, and so forth; in which certain types of action are expected from each role-player; and in which the connection between type of actor and type of action explains the behavior of individuals as though they were specific representatives of the general, institutionalized arrangement. Thus, when John does act X, an observer understands John's behavior by attributing it to his being a "father."

Most institutionalized typifications involve something similar to the preceding role-analysis: P explains O's behavior by attributing it to O's role and thereby sees the behavior as a specific instance of a more generally intelligible class of behaviors. However, even per-

son-centered dispositional attributions are institutionalized typifications. The language of motives, in other words, is also a property
of the social system. And this, of course, is precisely the point of the
preceding paragraphs. In attributing a motive to O's behavior in
order to explain it, P provides a description that, similar to a role
description, makes the behavior intelligible and thus provides a
sense of a stable world. Both person-centered and situation-centered
attributions involve institutional typifications based upon a shared
language of motives for the former and a shared language of roles
for the latter.

Role Enactments as Attributional Phenomena

To return to the model proposed to account for the attribution of
emotional states, we can now say that typifications (e.g., social roles)
lead to a particular set of behaviors, and at the same time offer an
explanation for those behaviors and induce and explain the person's
internal states. For example, the role of professor establishes a
guideline for the behavior of the role occupant and at the same time
explains that person's behavior by labeling it an instance of profes-
sorial behavior. Furthermore, the internal states of the role occupant are induced and explained by reference to role typification: for
example, as a professor, O is thought to be wise, intelligent, critical,
etc.

Because the same processes that P applies to understanding O are
assumed to apply to P's self-perception and self-understanding, it
can be seen that insofar as P enacts a role, P thereby learns something about self. The role provides the cognitive label that helps P
explain to himself or herself the meaning of the behavior and indeed even the internal states that may be experienced. It is this very
point that has been so intriguing and important to those interested
in the influence of role behavior on individual attitude formation
and change (e.g., Backman & Secord, 1968; Lieberman, 1956). The
thesis, quite simply, is that by engaging in a particular role behavior, P thereby induces a modification in own attitudes, beliefs, and
other internal states. To put this more concretely, by taking on the
role of professor, P comes to feel wise, intelligent, and so forth.

The laboratory experiment cited previously (p. 756) conducted by
Mark Zanna reaches a similar conclusion. His argument, recall, is
that even in a forced-compliance setting, in which P has little choice
about performing a role, the performance itself still proves self-
informative about P's internal states (e.g., P's beliefs and attitudes).
Zanna stresses that the manner in which one enacts the role—for

example, enthusiastically—leads P to say, "I guess that I am the kind of person who does things that way."

Zanna's method involved placing his experimental subjects into a task situation in which their attitudes towards the experimenter could be varied: some subjects were led to view him negatively and others positively. Subjects were then required by the experimenter to work on his behalf, preparing materials that he would use in some of his later research; some of these subjects were informed that their level of motivation while performing this task was exceptionally high; others were told that their motivation was quite low. Subjects finally were asked to evaluate both the experimenter and the task.

In the context of Zanna's study, subjects performed a required activity not one of their own choosing. Yet, would their manner of having performed it—that is, with high as opposed to low motivation—influence their judgments of how well they liked the activity or the person who required it of them? Zanna's data suggest an affirmative answer. We will look at those subjects whose performance was consistent with their initial positive or negative attitudes towards the experimenter— that is, they performed well when they liked him and poorly when he was disliked—who, however, were reported to have performed in an exceptional manner. These persons attributed their exceptional performance to their attitude towards the experimenter. Thus if they did this required task with exceptionally high motivation, then they must really have liked the person for whom they did it. Or if they had done it with extremely low motivation, then they must really have disliked the person who required this of them. In either case, persons used their own behavior in a required situation as a source of information about some disposition within them, in this case, their attitudes towards the experimenter.

Social psychologists, especially of the dissonance-theory persuasion or those attempting to disprove the dissonance model, have likewise emphasized the importance of role behavior in influencing P's attitudes and beliefs. In most cases, usually laboratory investigations, P is asked to perform a role in a debate or discussion or some other similar forum in which P takes a position on an issue contrary to the one initially professed (recall our earlier discussion). The hypotheses maintain that in arguing the role's attitude, P comes to alter a former position. The dissonance prediction is straightforward in emphasizing that P's role-performance is dissonant with an initial attitude and that this dissonance can be reduced if P comes to believe more in the attitude for which P just argued.

Non- or antidissonance analysts, such as Janis and Gilmore (1965) have stressed a process they term *biased scanning* to explain attitude changes after role playing. In their view, it is not dissonance that motivates any change, but rather, while P prepares role-related arguments and is motivated to perform well, P actually selects good arguments for the role position, coming even to convince himself or herself of their validity. Still others, for example, Sarbin and Allen (1968) have emphasized how the process of taking on a new role, improvising arguments consistent with it, elaborating points relevant to it, and so forth, all serve to increase and intensify P's commitment to the role and its various attributes.

THE INTERPERSONAL SIDE OF ROLE ENACTMENTS

From a more social psychological perspective, in taking on a role, P is only one actor in a complex drama. There is more involved in taking the role of professor and thereby coming to feel wise and intelligent, for example, than biased scanning, reduction of dissoance, or increased commitment, although aspects of all of these primarily intrapersonal processes may be taking place. As importantly, however, professors are what they are and do what they do by virtue of there being a set of role partners with whom they interact and who jointly determine each other's actual role: that is, the outcome of interpersonal processes. The wisdom of a professor derives in great measure from the wisdom that students and at times colleagues and the entire institutional context attribute to the role's occupant and which therefore the occupant comes to use in his or her self-perception as well. In other words, typifications (e.g., roles) are either sustained or modified within an interpersonal system of interaction. An implication of this view of role taking has proved important to those concerned with the long term fundamental influences of role performances and role change upon the individual.

Role Enactment and Personal Change. Let us examine a classic investigation of the influence of role changes on changes in P's attitudes and self-concept in a natural rather than in a laboratory setting. The study was reported in 1956 by Lieberman who was fortunately given the opportunity to study a group of workers both before and after they had been promoted to shop foreman or had become union stewards. Some time after these role changes had taken place, Lieberman remeasured the attitudes of twenty-three men who had become foreman and thirty-four who had become union stewards. He was also able to obtain comparable attitude measures on persons who had not changed roles over this same period of time.

Lieberman's data indicate that these role changes altered individual's attitudes: men who had similar attitudes as general workers before their role change now showed divergent attitudes after the change. Specifically, those who became foremen, with responsibilities to management, took on attitudes congruent with that role, becoming more supportive of management; those who became union stewards, with responsibilities to the workers and their working conditions, changed their attitudes towards a congruence with that role, becoming more critical of management.

Several years later, Lieberman was able to reinterview a small subgroup of his sample who were transferred back from foreman to their original roles as factory workers. He reports that their attitudes also reverted to their original positions apparently as a function of the role change. As workers they had been moderately critical of management; as foremen they became supportive; when demoted they again became moderately critical.

A Labeling Perspective

The plasticity of which Schachter and his colleagues spoke in discussing how internal states can be defined and experienced differently as a function of cognitive conditions of their labeling would seem from Lieberman's study to apply as well to the influence of roles (as cognitive labels or typifications) upon P's internal states—in this case P's attitudes. Yet, from an interpersonal and institutional perspective, this plasticity is not as passive or as automated as it may first appear to be. Enacting a role or being given a role label (e.g., P is a delinquent), involves an active interpersonal process, a *negotiation,* between P and O, where P might be an individual or a collective of like-labeled individuals and O might be another person or an entire institutional context that seeks to define and regulate the labeling processes.

Although the data are not provided by Lieberman's research, the interpersonal process that is involved requires us to examine several interrelated matters:

1. How does P act in ways that would lead O to attribute to P dispositions appropriate to P's new role?
2. How do other persons placed into similar new roles collectively organize themselves in ways that help support and sustain a new set of attitudes and self-perceptions?
3. How does O individually in interactions with P or collectively as a body of workers help to sustain or undermine P in P's new role?
4. How does the entire institutional structure in general help to establish and sustain P in P's new role with its consequent attitudes and behaviors?

The point of these inquiries is to call our attention to the kinds of system interdependencies discussed in Chapter 2 that place a larger context around P's role performances and that thereby view changes within P (or for that matter, the absence of any changes) as the outcome of social rather than purely individual processes.

ON DEVIANCE

What has been called the "labeling perspective" (e.g., Becker, 1963; 1964; Lemert, 1967; Scheff, 1966; Schur, 1971) especially as applied to understanding deviant behavior, provides us with a major example of these several points. The important first step in the process of becoming a deviant is to have one's behavior labeled as deviant by an agency whose task is to identify and control deviants. That is, deviancy is not to be understood as the outcome of some inherent internal disorder (e.g., a criminal mind), but rather as a result of an entire social process that gets underway once P is given the role of "deviant." Once this role label has been applied, often without P's self-consciously having chosen that particular role, the proper agency, whether it be the police and the criminal justice system, the psychiatric and the mental health system, the social welfare system, the school system, or whatever begins to relate to P in ways that help sustain the role and thereby help transform P into a better characterization of the role than P may have been upon initial entry into this deviance-becoming-and-maintaining network.

The labeling theory argument is that the very process of giving P a role and providing a context that both induces P to play it and reinforces P only to extent that P sustains the performance, not only changes P's attitudes and self-perception, but in the case of agencies whose purported goal is to bring health or relief to persons such as P may actually create conditions more conducive to P's continued deviancy. One of the major examples cited for this effect involves the psychiatric and mental health system, but in particular, mental hospitals.

Erving Goffman (1961) is one analyst in this tradition whose writings on becoming a mental hospital patient vividly portray the institutional and interpersonal processes that follow the person from labeling through rituals that result in the full assimilation of the role of mental patient. Depriving persons of their rights as human beings, humiliating them, removing their sense of personal worth and dignity, denying them privacy, treating them as a unit in a large and impersonal bureaucratic institution are all parts of an initiation in the role of mental hospital patients that may reinforce illness rather than help patients regain health.

Brainwashing (e.g., Lifton, 1961; Schein, 1958) offers us another instructive example of how a role change, in this case becoming a POW, can transform a person's attitudes and self-concept. The POW camp is an institution having almost total control over the person's daily life, doling out rewards and punishments according to its rules. A prisoner in the camp can be drained of his physical strength by a minimal diet. He can be kept awake or standing for endless hours. He can be interrogated and punished. He can be cut off from his buddies so as to face these treatments alone. He can be placed with those who urge him to reform his beliefs. He can be humiliated; he can be compelled to recite his sins, to prostrate himself and undergo a daily round of self-criticism. In this structured and controlled environment, his captors can relate to him as a helpless, dependent child or as an incompetent who cannot even urinate without asking permission. Soon, the person may come to think of himself in these terms; he may cry out for the aid that his dependency requires and that his captors are willing to provide if he will only confess once again.

We need not always deal with such large and complex agencies as mental hospitals, prisons, and schools to note similar effects. The parent who continuously refers to their teenage child as a lazy, irresponsible, good-for-nothing bum, a real failure, in spite of all reality to the contrary, may help thereby to create a child who may readily come to believe that "If I've got the name, I might just as well play the game". Thus, the label and the interpersonal processes which the parent uses to sustain it may turn the role occupant to behaving in ways that fit the label: i.e., they become a failure.

ACTIVE OR PASSIVE?

The degree to which people are passive agents in their own transformation is open to serious question. Indeed to the extent that the labeling perspective has tended to focus upon relatively coercive social institutions, we are led to believe that P is a passive victim without recourse to escape or resist; P's only choice seems to be no choice at all: complying and yielding. Two issues must be considered. In the first place, P may indeed collude (albeit without much awareness) to role performance in ways consistent with the role's characterization, soliciting the very feedback that P may wish to receive. In this, P is an active party to the interpersonal processes whereby this transformation is achieved.

From the theoretical perspective of G. H. Mead (see Chapters 2 and 6), to the extent that P is able to see his or her own behavior from O's perspective, P can attempt to manage the impressions that are received from O about the kind of person that P is. For example, a psychiatric patient may actually find it attractive to be considered passive and dependent, one who is unable to accept responsibility for successfully dealing with everyday life. The patient, therefore, may actively seek to maintain that role by managing the impressions received from the audience of relevant O's with whom he or she interacts. None of this should be taken to imply that such a person is consciously manipulative or malingering; rather that the role of patient (both medical and psychiatric) offers various benefits that the person may seek to retain by behaving in ways that ensure receiving feedback from O of the sort that supports dependency ("You are a dependent person"), thereby sustaining P's sense of self as a dependent person. Again, I think that we can see here how P and O orchestrate their interpersonal system to create and sustain a role and the various dispositional properties that are a part of it.

There is a second sense, however, in which P can be said to be an active participant in the role labeling and taking process. The person labeled—for example, the hospital patient—may appear to follow the role while actively and secretly resisting it; or, in what is a likely alternative, the patient and institution negotiate a compromise role that each finds mutual satisfying. Even in the case of a compromise, the role label and the process involved with it has influenced the person's attitudes and view of self. Recall that when O applies a label to P, gives P a role, or in terms of our earlier analysis, attributes P's behavior to being mentally ill or delinquent (or whatever typification is employed), this is both the outcome of a social process and the induction of P and O into a social process. Thus, when I speak of P's and O's negotiating about the label and its full meaning, I am stressing the process that is involved in their interaction together. While the laboratory metaphorically freezes an attributional event on a microscope slide to examine its structure at that moment, the analysis we are now examining is more akin to a film that follows the process as it emerges, develops, and changes; and it is within this interpersonal process that such negotiations occur.

The Politics of Labeling

The process of negotiating and renegotiating role labels can be seen to involve a collective politics of labeling. Within hospital settings it may indeed be the exception rather than the rule to encounter collective patient action designed to involve them in the formulation of their roles; within many other settings, including prisons, in fact, substantial client involvement in the labeling process may occur. Since the mid-1960s, we have seen an increasing number of instances in which populations of labelees have sought collectively to resist the implications of their label, by negotiating a new label, by rejecting the original label, by seeking self-determination of the entire labeling process. Women's groups, homosexual groups, radical groups, and especially ethnic groups have been actively involved in seeking to transform themselves and their collective identity by various political means, importantly including the whole role labeling and taking process. In 1973, for example, after much collective protest and lobbying by several homosexual groups, the American Psychiatric Association relabeled homosexuality by removing it from its official list of mental disorders. This issue obviously involves much more than labeling per se, but includes the entire social process that is brought into play once the label has been applied by those agencies and institutions (e.g., psychiatric associations) granted a legitimacy for determining such matters. A change in label in this case involves a change in behavioral attribution by P and O and a change in the manner with which P is now dealt. Similarly, when several states, in conjunction with national medical groups, concluded that alcoholism was a disease, the implication was that rather than routinely throwing drunks into jail, they should now be accorded out-patient medical treatment.

MASTERS AND SLAVES

Some of the most striking analyses of the politics of labeling is to be found in what I term the master-slave relationship. The historian Kenneth Stampp (1964) referred to pre-Civil War slavery as America's "peculiar institution." Gunner Myrdal's (1944) classic analysis documents this American dilemma wherein the credal values intoning "equality for all" conflicts with the post-Civil War maintenance of minority groups in low social positions. While there obviously is more involved in these matters than the analyses this chapter focuses on, the case of slavery in America, colonialism as it was practiced world-wide, and the maintenance of ethnic minorities in their "down" position, offers us a glimpse into the manner in which an attribution process to explain this state of the "slave" becomes a societal ideology that was held by the "masters," taken on as true by role-playing "slaves," while directly and more often, indirectly resisted by some of the "slaves."

In the history of the United States, we need only refer to Thomas Jefferson to get a sense of his and others' understanding of why slaves were in their subservient position and why Jefferson, a firm believer in democracy and equality, was in his position (see Jordan, 1968). Some of Jefferson's writings attribute to blacks a lesser need for sleep, a courage based on an inability to anticipate dangers that might lie ahead, a passion that made them both more ardent while giving them the blessing of only transient, passing sorrows, an inferior power of reason, and a dull, uncreative imagination. Blacks were in lowly positions, therefore, because their psychological and intellectual characteristics inclined them towards subservience. And what is more, given these attributes, they were naturally contented with their lot.

Jefferson was not alone in this kind of analysis; a helpful analyst, Rush, attributed the blacks' position to a disease, basing his analysis on skin color that Rush maintained was indicative of a malady akin to leprosy. Because they were diseased, he reasoned, they should be treated with compassion. Given these analyses of slave personalities and their happy contentment, slave rebellion could best be explained by seeking the outside agitator who put evil thoughts into their childlike minds. After all, the master was seen to be a kindly, stern, paternal figure, dealing with his slaves as he would deal with backward children or prize livestock; he even called them "boy" or at times "uncle" or "aunt," in turn receiving a happy childlike countenance turned up in obedience to this, their paternal and caring master. Obviously, only someone out to stir up trouble could upset this otherwise happy scene. As one history text discusses the impact of the Nat Turner slave uprising of 1831, "the incident served to unsettle the good relations between many southern masters and their slaves for years to come" (Hicks, 1943, pp. 292–293). This passage indicates rather clearly from whose perspective the attributional analysis is being made. From the master's point of view, things indeed were unsettled; the harmony he had sought and found so useful for his economic gain was shattered. One does wonder, however, what analysis exists from the slave's perspective: was this rebellious moment perhaps an act of resistance that is appropriate to those oppressed yet thought to be contented?

In his analysis of colonialism, Memmi (1967) draws several striking parallels to the slave situation in pre-Civil War United States. The European colonizer creates an economic colony out of the labors of the resident colonized peoples, developing a view of the colonized that explains the propriety of his superior role. For as Memmi notes, the key trait which all colonizers attribute to their colonized is "laziness":

> *It is easy to see to what extent this description is useful ...*
> *Nothing could better justify the colonizer's privileged*
> *position than his industry, and nothing could better justify*
> *the colonized's destitution than his indolence. The mythical*

*portrait of the colonized therefore includes an unbelievable
laziness, and that of the colonizer, a virtuous taste for
action. At the same time, the colonizer suggests that
employing the colonized is not very profitable, thereby
authorizing his unreasonable wages* (p. 79).

Thus, "laziness" explains why the colonized are in their positions
while simultaneously explaining why they should receive poor
wages; afterall, they do little work when they do work. To explain
the colonizer's need to use repressive tactics to keep order, the colonizer attributes weakness, childlike impulsivity, and irresponsibil-
ity to those colonized. Thus, in order to be defended against the
colonized's foolish acts (e.g., thievery) while really protecting them
from themselves, the colonizer employs a firm police force.

Even the squalor in which the colonized live fits neatly within the
colonizer's attribution theory; they live in dirt yet seem happy, so
naturally they must not care about how they live—and if they don't
care, why should I? Further explanations justify low pay and improper treatment. This is not to say that the colonizer's belief system
is totally consistent; its logic, however, follows the economic needs
of the colonizer who, for example, sees the colonized "as frugal,
sober, without many desires, and, at the same time, he consumes
disgusting quantities of meat, fat, alcohol, anything; as a coward
who is afraid of suffering and as a brute who is not checked by any
inhibitions of civilization, etc" (Memmi, 1967, p. 83).

In a relationship there are always at least two parties involved. If
the persons on top, whether called master, colonizer, oppressor, or
whatever set the definitions for the entire system, the persons on the
bottom, the colonized, the oppressed, the victim create their own
world of response. From the perspective of the victim, two kinds of
reactions are likely: the first involves an actual change as a function
of "being down so long." Growing up as a victim of oppression can
produce a person with a lesser amount of creativity, curiosity, initiative and achievement, one who may become childlike in many ways,
needing prodding to be productive, lacking vision and imagination.
The oppressed are also changed by their profound desire to reach
the top if only vicariously by emulating their masters. The colonized
adopts the colonizer as their model and reject their own models in
pursuit of this emulation.

*A blond woman, be she dull or anything else, appears
superior to any brunette. A product manufactured by the
colonizer is accepted with confidence. His habits, clothing,
food, architecture are closely copied, even if inappropriate. A
mixed marriage is the extreme expression of this audacious
leap* (Memmi, p. 21).

Identification with the Aggressor. In 1938–1939, Bruno Bettelheim (1958) was imprisoned in a German concentration camp. His observations during that period document a pattern of prisoner adjustment that he termed *identification with the aggressor* that parallels this consequence of playing the oppressed role.

> *From copying the verbal aggressions of the Gestapo to copying their form of bodily aggressions was one more step ... Old prisoners, when in charge of others, often behaved worse than the Gestapo ... Old prisoners tended to identify with the Gestapo not only in respect to aggressive behavior. They tried to arrogate to themselves old pieces of Gestapo uniforms. If that was not possible, they tried to sew and mend their uniforms so that they would resemble those of the guards ...* (p. 309).

These and other related examples offer us evidence of the transformation that the victims experience once they accept the master's label and theory for understanding their own behavior. That label and theory, as we have seen, justifies the manner in which victims are treated by masters. Thus, when the victims accept this, internalizing the role as though it were actually themselves, they accept as well the treatment they are given, eventually coming to hate who and what they are, while adoring from afar all that the master's way and style appear to be.

Resistance. But resistance to adopting the role, the label, the theory, the justification, can and does occur. While open resistance and revolt are rarely readily available, especially in extreme master-slave contexts, avenues of passive resistance remain. To the master, slaves were by their very nature stupid, indolent, dependent, childlike, and lazy. For the slave, however, being stupid and lazy meant getting away with much less hard work; slaves were given fewer responsibilities and had fewer demands made on them. In fact, one of the keenest tactics of passive resistance involves wrapping one's self fully in the role and thereby putting-on the master through one's excessively childlike, lazy, and subservient qualities. (Brachman, 1967, p. 57):

MASTER: Are you trying to make fun of me nigger?
SLAVE: Oh *no, suh.* No *suh,* Boss.

Goffman's (1959) analysis of self-presentations offers still another view on how it is that some persons, in this instance those stigmatized by the abnormalities of body and blemishes of character (e.g., addicts, homosexuals, etc.) are expected to perform their assigned roles in ways that fit the audience's stigma theories.

> *I learned that the cripple must be careful not to act differently from what people expect him to do. Above all they expect the cripple to be crippled; to be disabled and helpless; to be inferior to themselves, and they will become suspicious and insecure if the cripple falls short of these expectations. It is rather strange, but the cripple has to play the part of the cripple, just as many women have to be what the men expect them to be, just women; and the Negroes often have to act like clowns in front of the "superior" white race* (Goffman, 1936, p. 110; Carling, 1962, pp. 54–55).

In these and other cases, the role player does portray the character as expected, but does so somewhat defiantly as a gesture of passive resistance. When the oppressed manage to organize themselves into collective, self-conscious groups, control over the politics of the attribution process can begin to change. When, for example, history is rewritten from the "down" rather than from the "up" perspective, then the military victories of the U.S. Cavalry against the Indians may be seen as massacres, while the Indian attacks against invading white settlers may be viewed as victories (Carmichael & Hamilton, 1967).

While our chapter focus clearly is not on social movements, I think it helpful to understand the important part that such movements play in negotiating for control over the labeling and theory that will be attributed to it and hence the social process that follows from that label. When we realize that the attribution of a cause to an event is a *social act* that typifies that event, labels it, provides a minitheory about it, and hence justifies a social process (e.g., a treatment program) surrounding those who are so labeled, then such negotiations take on the major proportions that they must. It is no idle matter, then, when those in the "down" position, long suffering another's attribution theory about them and their kind, seek to reattribute their behaviors and thereby gain some measure of control over their own lives and identities.

The psychological analysis of the cognitive processes involved in attribution gives us an approach to mapping the everyday social world in which we all live; once the map is drawn, however, and its contours more clearly seen, there will be those who will endeavor to negotiate a change.

ALICE BRICKNER. REPRINTED FROM
"AMERICAN WAY," INFLIGHT MAGAZINE
OF AMERICAN AIRLINES.

LANGUAGE, COMMUNICATION, INTERACTION

5

The private world that we each experience alone, dreaming our dreams of tomorrow, recalling a past that we left behind; the public world that ties us to each other, that makes the interpersonal network of human life possible—these are the worlds of human language. Its rich texture of verbal and nonverbal formulations create and sustain this moment, the last, and allow us to ponder one yet to come.

Objects, events, ideas, persons all come packaged in symbolic, linguistic bundles. Language itself offers us new views and perspectives; it reveals possibilities unavailable to the infant, literally, one who does not speak. With language we can create worlds that have neither an objective nor a physical reality: dreams, fantasies, ghosts, monsters, hopes. We can manipulate in thought rather than in deed; we can bend symbols to our whim while the physical world resists our efforts to change it. With language, we can touch another who is not directly present; we can convey information; we can request, question, deny, command; indeed, we can pray (Church, 1961).

Before the Word

The Bible tells us that in the beginning there was the word. A more likely developmental scenario, however, did not begin with the word, but rather with something more fluid and vague, "expressive experience which lives in the moment and spends itself in the moment" (Cassirer, 1957, p. 115). Language marked the beginning of civilization, of control over nature, self and others. The preverbal beginning lies in a world beyond language and symbolic forms, a world of fleeting experiences that continuously flow like a well-fed stream. This is a world undifferentiated into parts, relationships, and unities; a world characterized by a dynamic totality; everything is fused with everything; the boundaries that verbal organisms place around themselves and objects do not yet exist.

Preverbal organisms participate with their entire being in everything; they do not feel or respond in piecemeal fashion, but rather seem "to be pregnant with and activated by some generalized 'energy' that links together all objects and events" (Church, 1961, p. 17). Joseph Church terms this kind of total organismic involvement, *participation:* persons respond directly and immediately, participating in every event, not yet taking distance from the world, separating themselves from the ongoing flow. This latter capability awaits the development of the symbol and of representational function.

FROM SENSORIMOTOR TO REPRESENTATIONAL KNOWING

Jean Piaget speaks of the preverbal child's primary, nonrepresentational state of experiencing as the *sensorimotor* (1954; 1955; See also Flavell, 1963). In this early phase of development, there is no differentiation between doing and thinking—early thought *is* sensorimotor. Sensorimotor experiencing, characteristic of the first year to year-and-one-half of our lives, lacks awareness either of a self as such or of action. There is no experience of an actor who acts; no experience of a self that has experienced. This world is a nonpermanent moment, a here-and-now world of things now-present, then-gone; objects do not retain permanence when *not-here* and *not-now.*

In time this participative or sensorimotor form of preverbal experiencing gradually yields to representational or symbolic thinking, where language becomes dominant. A new beginning comes with language and the world it now makes possible. Language breaks up the fleeting flux of primary experiencing, gives us concepts, provides our experiences of stability as well as of change; permits us to note similarities and speak of differences; allows us to know identities, to find again the experience that would otherwise be only a passing moment. Representation permits us to retain in thought a world that is not here, not now. With language, we can step twice into the same river in spite of the flux that flows past (Cassirer, 1957). "What has been culled from the total sphere of consciousness, does not fade away again when the spoken word has set its seal upon it and given it definite form" (Cassirer, 1946, p. 38). In the act of naming every living creature, Adam thereby took "possession of the world both physically and intellectually" and subjected "it to his knowledge and his rule" (Cassirer, 1946, p. 83).

These several ideas direct us to the foundation of the importance of language. We see revealed the roots from which our civilization springs and on which our interpersonal world is built. In the preverbal, sensorimotor mode, objects that are not directly and immediately before us do not exist. To know objects that are not immediately present requires an internal schema that permits us to re-present those things not here and not now. Language permits us literally to create a world that has permanence in time: for example, we can think of the chair in the room upstairs while we are sitting downstairs by the fire; we can think of the mother who is not before us.

As language functions develop, our horizons extend as far as our imaginations will allow; we are not restricted to the immediate present. We can manipulate things in our minds, using symbols that re-present these things to us. With words we can experience ourselves experiencing; we can differentiate ourselves from others, and develop a view of the viewer. Language permits us to retain an internal representation of what is past—namely our own actions—and allows us to reflect on those actions (e.g., Strauss, 1969).

Language permits us to defer responding directly and immediately to specific occurrances. We can replace action with contemplation. The capacity to reflect on action already taken or action yet to be taken, to delay responding until we assess alternatives, to anticipate consequences of acting prior to having acted: all are derivatives of our linguistic and symbolic behavior. The representation of persons, objects, and events gives us the kind of distance that permits us to respond internally and symbolically rather than being required always to respond overtly and immediately through our actions. While action developmentally precedes representational thinking as our primary basis of knowing the world around us, thinking later comes to play an increasingly central role in influencing the knowledge that we have about that world.

TO REFLECT AND TO SHAPE

The argument that the linguistic system transforms human experience and re-presents the world to us suggests that there must exist an important relationship between language and communication on the one hand, and social structure and the interpersonal system on the other. Specifically, it would seem reasonable to expect language both to reflect a particular interpersonal system and to be a major vehicle for shaping, defining, and sustaining that interpersonal system. Insofar as language is a dependent variable reflecting social structure, the study of language would offer us insights into the nature of interpersonal relationships. For example, the study of the language forms persons use in addressing other people, whether P addresses O by title and last name (e.g., Mr. Jones; Dr. Smith; Ms. Adams); by last name only (e.g., Jones); by first name (e.g., Ed); by title only (e.g., Your Holiness); and so forth informs us about the kind of social relationship that exists between P and O.

Insofar as language is an independent variable serving to shape, define, and sustain a particular system of interpersonal relationships and social structure, the study of language offers us insights into the ways in which a wide variety of human relationships are created, maintained, or modified. For example, Basil Bernstein's work to which we will shortly refer, notes ways in which parents use different kinds of linguistic appeals to exercise control over their children. His work and that of others informs us of the complex form of the language-social system relationship in which the language of social control varies as a function of the parent's position in the social structure of a particular society. Thus, language both reflects those structural differences and simultaneously influences the maintenance of parental control over children.

To take another example, as P and O interact, they manage to coordinate their behavior so that figuratively P's message does not constantly bump into O's and vice versa: they manage to take turns. The role of language, both verbal and nonverbal, in creating and sustaining this basic capability for turn-taking is important for us to understand; it suggests a system of signals and rules that govern our behavior. Clearly, the serious student of social psychology must be concerned with language behavior.

Linguistic Relativity

One of the best-known perspectives on the relationship between language and society has been termed the *principle of linguistic relativity.* The development of this principle is usually attributed to several authors and thus is also called the von Humbolt, Sapir, Whorf, Cassirer hypothesis, with Whorf often winning out in this naming contest. The basic notion is that because the kaleidoscopic flux of sense impressions is transformed by linguistic concepts into ordered and intelligible arrangements, persons socialized into different linguistic systems should literally live in different worlds. *John, Juan,* and *Giovanni,* in other words, dwell in different psychological environments as a function of their different languages. In English we say *horse,* in Spanish, *caballo,* in German *pferd,* and so on. In the Whorfian view, a horse is not a horse is not a horse. Our conceptions of reality are in their very essence relative to the language system in which we were brought up and which we speak.

Lexicon and Codifiability. In 1960, Fishman sought to provide some coherent organization to the linguistic relativity hypothesis by presenting a four-fold analytic scheme (See Table 5.1). His scheme

Table 5.1. An Analysis of the Whorfian Hypothesis*

		Data from Speaker's Behavior	
		Language Data	Nonlinguistic Data
Data about Language	Lexicon	I	II
	Grammar	III	IV

*Adapted from Fishman (1960).

distinguishes between two kinds of language characteristics, the lexical and the grammatical. Lexical characteristics consist primarily of the words in a given language. One language may have several words for a given phenomenon, while another language might have only one or perhaps none. *Codifiability* describes the lexical differences between languages; while in general it is possible to say anything in one language that can be said in any other, the ease with which certain things can be said reflects a difference in codifiability. Thus, if we can refer to something by one term in English but require five in Hopi, we say that the thing is more easily codified in English.

Grammar.   Grammatical characteristics of language refer primarily to syntactical arrangements, or how words are formed into sentences, sentences into paragraphs, and so forth. For example, in English we say "the red house" rather than "the house red," which is a construction found in several other languages. In his studies of the Hopi language in comparison to English and other Standard Average European (SAE) languages, Whorf (1956) stressed the differing grammatical treatment for time forms (e.g., hours, days, weeks, years, seasons, etc.). In English, time forms are *nouns* that are treated grammatically in the same way that all nontemporal nouns are treated. Thus we treat "ten days" grammatically the same way that we treat "ten apples," as though both were countable realities possessing physical properties.

The Hopi, by contrast, have different grammatical forms for nontemporal and temporal terms. Nontemporal terms in Hopi are nouns, whereas temporal terms are like adverbs. Recall that adverbial forms qualify or modify verbs. If time is grammatically treated as an adverb, it is not something real, but rather, something that qualifies the action that is taking place. In English we say that "John is 40 years old"; in Spanish, that *"Juan tienne quarenta años."* But in Hopi, John does not *have* 40 years, nor *is* he 40 years old; rather, *he is old fortyishly* or *is acting fortyishly.*

Fishman's four-fold scheme differentiates between two kinds of data: language behavior itself and nonlinguistic behavior—for example, sorting objects or some other similar behavior that in and of itself does not require the person to speak.

Of the four resulting distinctions that Fishman's scheme outlines, the third is one of the most tantalizing but least well validated. The first level involves the relationship between the lexicon of a given language and the speaker's ease of formulating particular ideas. Eskimo has many individual words to indicate kinds of snow whereas English has one basic word; thus varieties of snow can more readily be noticed, remembered and talked about among the Eskimo as compared with speakers of English.

Level two phenomena involve the relationship between a language's lexicon and the nonlinguistic behavior of those who are speakers of the language. In 1954, Brown and Lenneberg reported what is now the classic investigation of this relationship. They presented subjects with a series of color discs, finding that colors that were most highly codified in a given language were responded to more rapidly than those colors that were the least codified. Thus, a red disc was responded to, recognized, and recalled more readily than a greenish-yellow disc: the former is more easily codified in English (i.e., by the single term, red) as compared with the latter.

WELTANSCHAUUNG: OUR WORLD VIEW

As noted, level three relationships, while most tantalizing, have been the most resistant to proof. Whorf's work comparing Hopi with SAE languages and Hoijer's (1951) with the Navajo, however, contend that fundamental differences in the Indian grammars create basic differences in the speaker's *Weltanschauung* (i.e., world view). In particular, Whorf argued that the SAE treatment of temporal forms as nouns disposed its speakers to a world view in which time could be saved, spent, lost, gained, and such. The Hopi, by contrast, were disposed to think of a world of recurring activities; time was only an adverb that qualified how the activity was done. In English, Whorf claimed, we are grammatically set to focus on the time taken to run the race: one minute, five minutes, ten minutes. The Hopi are grammatically attuned to experience how the race was run: rapidly, slowly, or whatever.

Research conducted by Ervin-Tripp (1967) on bilinguals offers us another insight into level three relationships between language and world view. Her work involved bilingual Japanese women who had married American servicemen during World War II. The women were given a variety of tests that asked them to make up a story to pictures, associate to words, and complete incomplete sentences. Ervin-Tripp was able to compare the content of her bilingual subjects' responses with those of monolingual American and monolingual Japanese. Her bilinguals, when asked to respond to the tests in English produced content that was similar to monolingual speakers of English; and when asked to take the tests in Japanese, produced content similar to monolingual Japanese speakers. For example:

> *Japanese women more often say "what I want most in life ... is peace." Americans say ... "happiness." "When I am with men ..." Japanese women [say that they] are uncomfortable, American women [say] contented. "When a husband finds fault with his wife, the wife ..." in Japan, [says she] "is defensive," in America, [she says that she] "tries to improve"* (p. 84).

Apparently, therefore, shifts in language create major shifts in content, indicating an important correspondence between a language system and imaginative thought.

The classic investigation of a level four relationship between a language's grammatical system and a speaker's nonlinguistic behavior was reported in 1958 by Carroll and Casagrande, who presented groups of children with an object-classification task. Children were given a pair of objects that differed from each other in two qualities—for example, in color and shape—and were asked to class a third object with one member of the original pair. Subjects were Navaho-dominant Navaho children, English-speaking Navaho children, and a sample of white middle-class Bostonian children of about the same age as the two Navaho groups.

Navaho verb forms change grammatically as a function of the nature of the object being dealt with. Long, flat objects, for example, receive one verb form while round and squat objects receive a different form. The Carroll and Casagrande study was so arranged that when a child's behavior was governed by the Navaho grammar she would select a specific one of the original pair of objects with which to match the third. For example, if Navaho grammar demanded the same verb form for all long, flat objects, she would classify the long and flat *red* third object with the long and flat *green* original object, rather than with the round and squat *red* object of the original pair.

Carroll and Casagrande's findings not only demonstrated an important correspondence between language and behavior, but also showed the importance of nonlinguistic factors. Results showed that Navaho-dominant Navaho children made object choices predicted from their grammatical verb forms more frequently than did the English-dominant Navahos. However, the Bostonian school children made even more Navaho-like responses than the Navahos! It would seem, therefore, that nonlinguistic cultural factors, possibly experience in playing with particular kinds of objects, also importantly influence a person's behavior in any given situation.

Language and Interpersonal Relationships

The functions of language in both reflecting and influencing (e.g., defining and maintaining) interpersonal relationships, which the Whorfians emphasize between different linguistic systems exist as well within the same general linguistic system. The hypothesis of linguistic relativity, recall, argues that language systems provide a filter between the person and the continuous flux of experiences, thereby creating different psychocultural environments for learners and speakers of different languages. If it can be demonstrated that the notion "different languages" can be applied to classifications of language codes within a general language, then the range of applicability of the linguistic relativity hypothesis is thereby widened. This latter demonstration, of course, would require the investigator to answer the question: do persons in different positions within a social structure have different patterns of language behavior? Taking English as our example, the question asks if there is a correspondence between different patterns of English usage and categories of social structure or interpersonal relationship. Even more explicitly, in what way can we see English language codes both reflecting and influencing interpersonal behavior?

BERNSTEIN'S APPROACH

According to several influential investigators in the growing field of sociolinguistics (e.g., Bernstein, 1958; 1971; 1973; Labov, 1966; 1972a, b; Ervin-Tripp, 1969; Gumperz and Hymes, 1972, and others), there is indeed a correspondence between linguistic code and social structure. The work of Basil Bernstein, which is especially enlightening in this regard, concentrates on different language codes as reflected primarily in different social classes in England. A linguistic code fundamentally acts as a set of rules for representing and regulating forms of social relationships. Bernstein's and his colleague's research has led them to formulate the existence of two separate language codes: a restricted code and an elaborated code. A restricted code provides the individual with a limited range of alternate ways of representing intentions, motivations, clarifications, and analyses of events and ideas. An elaborated code, on the other hand, provides the person with a relatively extensive range of ways of formulating ideas, clarifying, expanding, and interpreting meaning and intentions. The two codes establish different ways of exercising control and engaging in verbal planning.

For example, when the child who is told "No!" in response to a request to stay up asks "why," the restricted code answer may take the form, "Because I told you so"; the elaborated form, by contrast, may expand on the reasons suggesting that "tomorrow is a school day, and you need your sleep so that you won't be irritated and so that you'll be better able to pay attention." Bernstein's point is that the use of these two different code systems results in different forms of self-regulation on the part of the child. The child whose mother says, "I'd rather you made less noise, darling," uses the words "less" and "rather" to convey a sense of her intention and the consequences of not obeying that are substantially different from the more direct "shut up" that, while likewise seeking to quiet the child, does not orient the child to linguistically rich or subtle analyses of behavior.

From Bernstein's perspective: "The form of the social relationship acts selectively on the type of code which then becomes a symbolic expression of the relationship *and* proceeds to regulate the nature of the interaction" (In Hymes, 1964, p. 259). And this is a point of major importance. His argument is that linguistic codes, whether restricted or elaborated: reflect a given social relationship; transform the relationship into a symbolic expression; shape the relationship by regulating the interaction that then follows. In essence, the linguistic code reflects and sustains a particular social relationship.

Take the following interchange reported by Ervin-Tripp (1969):

"What's your name, boy?" the policeman asked.
"Dr. Poussaint. I'm a physician."
"What's your first name, boy?"
"Alvin."

This linguistic exchange contains within it the entire history of black-white race relations; it reflects much more than a policeman's inquiry after someone's name. It establishes a hierarchy of authority and control; it symbolically represents this relationship by the use of the term "boy" to address an adult and by the demand for a first name rather than accepting the title-last-name that Dr. Poussaint uses in his own effort to transform the relationship which the policeman has linguistically instituted. In this example, we can readily see the three aspects that Bernstein suggests: the relationship is reflected, symbolically expressed, and sustained.

Restricted versus Elaborated Codes. It is Bernstein's contention that the restricted linguistic code constructs a different kind of social reality for its users than the reality available to those employing an elaborated code. In particular, he notes several key aspects of restricted code use. First, descriptions of persons and events tend to focus on more concrete than abstract matters. An early interview study by Schatzman and Strauss (1955) further illuminates this matter. They interviewed persons of different class backgrounds, as assessed by income and educational differences, asking their subjects about a tornado disaster that had hit their community. They report differences between upper-middle-class and lower-class persons in the number and kinds of perspectives used to describe the event. Lower-class persons gave descriptions entirely through their own eyes, rarely qualifying anything they stated. Upper-middle-class individuals, on the other hand, offered descriptions from different, more general points of view, also qualifying and enriching their descriptions by providing the context within which their observation had been made. Schatzman and Strauss report a general lack of coherence in lower-class descriptions; they had difficulty in creating a straight story.

A second aspect of restricted code use that Bernstein notes is the role that nonverbal information plays in signaling a change in the speaker's meaning. In elaborated code usage, the speaker and listener both are attuned to subtle nuances of verbal information in order to detect the meaning of something that is said. Children learn to look for clues in what their parents say, for example, in order to detect a change in mood or to understand more fully the meaning of what is being expressed. The restricted code allows fewer opportunities for subtlety to be verbally expressed; thus nonverbal information is sought.

The Schatzman and Strauss study revealed what Bernstein argues is a third important aspect of restricted code usage—namely, the narrowed range of others' points of view that it allows the individual to adopt. The elaborated code permits the individual to view a situation from numerous perspectives; the person, so to speak, can use language as a vehicle for traveling into other's minds and seeing things as they might. A restriced code, however, is more narrowly rooted to one perspective. Bernstein suggests that because of this restrictiveness, the social ties to those whose views can be adopted are more powerful among restricted code users while social separation from those with differing views is likewise enhanced. In other words, one would expect bonds that tie similar users and separate dissimilar users to be stronger for those of restricted code than for those of elaborated code. The social group thus should be tighter and stronger for the former than for the latter, as should be the separation between groups.

This is an interesting point to think about; it suggests that an interviewer with elaborated code usage at his disposal might find it difficult to penetrate a group with restricted code usage as they are unable to take his perspective even if he may be able to understand theirs. He remains an alien to them; a linguistic code barrier of a substantial sort separates them. Some of Labov's (1972b) analyses of what in black English vernacular are called *lames* is revealing in this regard. A *lame* is an isolated nonmember of a particular peer group. Labov's data indicate that *lames* differ from group members in several linguistic ways, including their lack of proficiency in using members' verbal skills which can only be achieved and then maintained in the kind of daily group interaction that only members can have. As Alan Grimshaw (1973), a sociologist interested in language phenomenon, points out, most social researchers are *lames* vis-a-vis their subjects, and thus remain linguistically and in other ways outsiders to many groups they might wish to study. Belonging to a group involves participation in its linguistic community as well.

A fourth aspect of code usage that Bernstein suggests is a derivative of the difficulty in abstract thinking that the restricted code implies. If problems to be solved become more abstract, those with restricted code usage will become increasingly unable to deal appropriately with them.

Finally, Bernstein suggests that the time perspective differs between the two codes. The restricted code is more rooted in the immediacy of the here and now; thus withholding responses and delaying action until all aspects of an issue have been examined is attenuated among restricted code users. Elaborated code users, however, have an expanded time perspective and can better tolerate delay. There is a greater time separation between a stimulus and its response.

It is clear from Bernstein's research on linguistic codes that there is a correspondence between social class and code availability. It is also apparent, however, that these correspondences, even in class-dominated England, are not as clear-cut as one might imagine. And in fact, it would appear that as his research has progressed over the years, factors of social class become less important as determinants of code selectivity than matters of family socialization. In other words, whereas there does exist a general correspondence between class and code, lower-class families can and do socialize children in elaborated code usage with its resulting influence over their cognitive abilities and forms of social interaction.

One of the research dilemmas in studying the relationship between social class and language codes involves the tendency for researchers to be of a different class than the persons studied, thus constraining their subjects speech and thereby helping to create the very class differences that they presume exist independently of such circumstances. Thus, one may uncover a restricted code among lower-class respondents in response to a middle-class interviewer, but note in less restrained contexts, a rich language usage. Some of William Labov's (1972b) analyses of black speech patterns has suggested how rich and subtle it is in free situations in contrast to its restrictiveness under more controlled laboratory conditions.

Furthermore, family or class or regional differences in code usage only refer to a different linguistic mechanism of social control and not to a ranking of inferior to superior. It may well be, for example, that the reliance of the restricted code on authority relationships to handle issues of social control (e.g., Do it, because I say so) results in a more secure world than the confusing and anxious world that results from the elaborated code use of so many verbal qualifiers. Furthermore, the verbal nuances that the elaborated code allows may impede direct communication between persons, and especially direct expression of feeling. Elaborated code users can reformulate their emotions into verbal statements that may eventually work to their disadvantage as pent up feelings pass unrecognized until a final burst. Restricted code users are more direct in their emotional expressions and thus may suffer less from the problems that are associated with such expressive difficulties.

Emotion and Language.　The relation between emotional experience, social class, and language code has been put to a more systematic analysis in some of the recent work of Bourque and Back (1971). In particular, they have been concerned with the role which language code plays in persons' interpretation of strong emotional experiences that they may have. Bourque and Back argue in a manner that joins Schachter's and other's work on the labeling of emotion that we considered in Chapter 4 with Bernstein's and Whorf's work on sociolinguistics. Specifically, Bourque and Back's position is that differential availability of language codes within a society influence the way in which intense emotional experiences are given meaning by the person having such experiences and thereby influence the way in which ostensibly similar emotions are actually experienced. The intense emotions that their research examined involved transcendental experiences including those with a religious quality (e.g., feeling one's self to be in the presence of God) and those with an aesthetic quality (e.g., seeing or hearing something so beautiful that it made one indescribably happy or sad).

Their thesis was that persons who had a religious, fundamentalist linguistic code available, primarily as a function of their social class background, would be able to use that language to give meaning to these transcendental experiences; on the other hand, persons of differing class background who did not having a religiously based linguistic code, would find it more difficult to describe any states of ecstatic emotional experience. Much as Schachter's labeling approach to emotions suggests (Chapter 4), the existence of a religious language code facilitates the person's labeling these ineffable experiences, placing them into a context of definite meaning.

Take two persons, P and O, where P is a religious fundamentalist and O is not. Each has an intense emotional experience, but only P has a ready linguistic basis for labeling and interpreting it: it is a religious experience. For O, that intense emotion may be a sign of deviance or even of mental disturbance. In that O does not have a clear-cut language code for describing it, the nature of the subjective experience is itself different from P's. Bourque and Back present results from a national public opinion survey that permitted them to examine these intense emotional experiences, the social class background of these persons, and the actual meaning that they attributed to the experiences. Whether one is able to understand a transcendental subjective experience as religious, then, depends on the availability of an appropriate linguistic code, which in turn is a function of one's social background.

MORE ON SOCIAL STRUCTURE AND LANGUAGE.

While many of the preceding ideas of Bernstein and others involve fascinating material on which to weave our more speculative thoughts, the point nevertheless remains that differences can be uncovered in code usage within a society, that these differences both reflect and sustain a different social structure and set of interpersonal relationships. How definitively such differences are linked to social class is an empirical question; in particular, we would expect that where social mobility exists within a society, distinctions between code usage based on class factors should be less than where such mobility is either nonexistent or minimal.

In this regard, Labov's (1966; 1972a) work is instructive in demonstrating systematic class differences in English usage in New York City. His techniques of data gathering are themselves a fascinating outline of sociolinguistic research methodology. In one such effort, for example, he went to department stores that had a known class difference in sales personnel, checked in the store's directory for departments located on the fourth floor, and then asked sales persons where that department was, thereby getting their pronunciation of the word "four." In still other work, he asked persons what channels on their TV gave them the best reception, thereby getting an opportunity to hear how "four," "thirteen," "nine," and "five" were pronounced.

His data suggest some striking social class differences in speech usage, with the "r" sound revealing both class and context differences. As Labov states it, the language of the streets is basically r-less; "r" enters increasingly with the formality of speech and with the social class of the respondents. When a speaker takes great care in speaking—a language behavior pattern less likely on the streets than when being interviewed, for example—a process termed *hypercorrection* is noted. Hypercorrection involves the spread of an aspect of linguistic usage towards higher prestige. Thus, because retaining the "r" in one's speech is more typical of higher-class usage, when using care in speaking, persons who in the streets would not use "r," can and do use it.

Language and Impression Formation.   The process of hypercorrection suggests not only a class-and-context linked usage of speech, but also the existence of linguistic stereotypes and prejudices. There exists a politics of language that involves conflicts between social categories over which usage should prevail. Several of these political-linguistic conflicts have been well documented for such countries and cultural areas as Norway, India, the Caribbean, and recently by means of experimental techniques, for Canada.

W. E. Lambert (1967) and his associates employ what is termed a *matched-guise* technique to measure subjects' impressions of a speaker based on the language that the speaker uses. The procedure is to have judges react to a taped passage that is read by perfectly bilingual speakers, first in one language and then in the other. These are the matched guises. Several of Lambert's investigations were conducted in Montreal, where there is a long history of rivalry and tension between French and English speaking Canadians.

In one study, a group of English-speaking Canadians (EC) was asked to evaluate matched guises speaking French Canadian (FC) and English. Results indicated that EC judges rated the English speaking guise more favorably. Surprisingly, a group of French Canadians also favored the English-speaking guise. Other investigations conducted by Lambert and his associates using male and female raters and guises, demonstrated that EC judges rated FC female guises more favorably than EC female guises; paralleling the previous findings, however, EC male guises were more favorably rated than male FC guises. It would seem from these data that when the speaker is a woman, French creates a more favorable impression; for a man, English gives the better impression. It is to be noted that FC judges also generally evaluated EC guises more favorably as with Lambert's initial study.

We form stereotypes and create impressions of persons on the basis of their speech patterns; at times, as the Lambert results indicate, displaying linguistic disloyalty to our own forms as we prefer the speech of others. Triandis, Loh, and Levin (1966) conducted a laboratory study in which they varied the race (white or black), status (working or middle-class), quality of spoken English (excellent or grammatically poor English), and attitudes towards integrated housing (pro or con) of an actor about whom the study's subjects were to form an impression. Their data indicate that the quality of the actor's spoken English was one of the most important characteristics that influenced the subjects' attitudes towards him! As Ervin-Tripp suggests, "A new test for liberals might be this: 'Would you want your daughter to marry a man who says ain't'?" (1969, p. 155).

Code Selection and Switching

Most persons have several linguistic code and speech possibilities from which to choose in their interaction with others. Hymes (1964) has suggested, as one example, that most languages have three levels of style: *formal, colloquial,* and *slang* or *vulgar.* We also have choices that involve the linguistic forms we use in addressing others. Supplementing the use of titles and such, some languages differentiate between a *vous*-form and a *tu*-form; the former is used in more formal interactions while the latter is employed with intimates and small children (e.g., Brown, 1965). Choices also exist as a function of situations, topics, roles, power, identity, and such. In other words, when P and O interact, their selection of language codes and speech forms from among an array of alternatives serves the functions outlined previously: selection reflects their social relationship, expresses it symbolically, and serves either to sustain or transform the relationship. Our linguistic choices convey information to us and to others about our relationships; shifts in choice are likewise informative. Thus switching from a *vous*- to a *tu*-form suggests a shift in relationship from distant to intimate. This does not mean to imply, however, that these choices and shifts are always made with full awareness. Surprisingly, although we intimately know the language we speak, we are hardly aware of our language behavior unless or until it is pointed out to us.

ADDRESS FORMS

You are invited to your friend's house; she answers the door: "Hi, Jerry," she says; "Hi, Brenda," you reply. You move from the entry into the living room to meet Brenda's parents. "I'd like you to meet my mother. Mother, here's my friend Jerry Robinson." "Hello

Jerry." "How do you do, Dr. Morgan." "And my father." "Hi Jerry." "Hello Mr. Morgan." This small exchange of introductions contains several selections of address forms that most of us use everyday without much awareness or for that matter concern. Substantial research, however, has been done to uncover the underlying rules of such forms of address.

We have learned to use one address form with children, another with adults; one form with peers and intimates, another with superiors and strangers. The brief encounter with Brenda and Jerry and the Morgans includes an instance of the address rule between friends, a mutual exchange of first names (FN). The dialog also includes the address form employed by those older to those younger, a nonreciprocated use of FN: the older calls the younger by FN and recieves a last name (LN) or a title-last name (TLN) in return. The use of LN or TLN is another aspect of the American address system. In formal settings, such as business meetings, or in encounters in which impersonality governs, persons exchange LN or TLN: "How do you do, Mr. Jones." "Pleased to meet you, Professor Smith." In settings of greater intimacy or equality, a FN exchange is more common.

In the previous example, another address rule involving a shortened greeting form, is demonstrated. The "hi" communicates intimacy, friendship, and informality; in contrast, the use of "How do you do" suggests greater distance, formality, or impersonality in the relationship. In the example involving the policeman and Dr. Poussaint, we have an instance in which the American address rule is violated by the policeman's calling a doctor by his first name. As Ervin-Tripp notes,

> *Under no circumstances should a stranger address a physician by his first name. Indeed, the prestige of physicians even exempts them from first-naming ... by used-car salesmen, and physicians wives can be heard so identifying themselves in public in order to claim more deference than "Mrs." brings. Thus, the policeman's message is quite precise: "Blacks are wrong to claim adult status or occupational rank. You are children." Dr. Poussaint was stripped of all deference due his age and rank* (1969, p. 98).

Roger Brown and several of his colleagues have done extensive investigations of two-choice systems of address, involving the *tu-* or the *vous*-form (Brown, 1958; 1965; Brown & Ford, 1961; Brown & Gilman, 1960). Their research data suggest that a mutual exchange of the *tu*-form communicates solidarity and intimacy, whereas a nonreciprocated exchange indicates a status differential. The French Revolution, in which equality and fraternity were stressed, placed a major emphasis on the mutual exchange of *tu*-forms and the elimination of the status-based rule involving *vous.* Interestingly enough, however, the Russian revolutionaries demanded that *vous* forms be used rather than *tu,* suggesting thereby an insistance upon respect rather than solidarity. Contemporary forms tend to follow a mutual exchange of *tu* among kin and a nonreciprocal exchange among nonkin in status relationships: that is, superiors give *tu* and expect to receive *vous* in return from their subordinates. It should be noted that in situations involving equals in age and rank, the use of the *vous*-form may indicate distance and impersonality rather than deference and respect.

The choice among alternative forms of address both reflects and influences social interaction. A shift in the form chosen likewise informs the participants of some change in their relationships. Brown reports, for example, a shift from *vous* to *tu* among mountain climbers after they have reached a certain height together and their lives hang literally by a slender rope. Ervin-Tripp reports temporary shifts from *tu* to *vous* among intimates in public who wish to disguise their intimacy, or who shift back and forth, using *tu* when discussing personal matters and *vous* when the topic is impersonal.

Ervin-Tripp (1969) also reports work by Kantorovich who suggests a change from *tu* to *vous* when a worker needs a bawling out. She notes further that many individuals who normally use *tu* in addressing others switch to the *vous* form when cursing. Although English no longer has a *tu-vous* differentiation, the manner by which FN, LN, or TLN are employed communicates much the same information. If students, for example, are asked to role-play being a guest in their own home (see Garfinkel, 1967), part of that portrayal would involve using TLN to address one's parents. When this was tried, the students reported that their parents thought them to be sick or hostile or both. In other words, calling one's parents by TLN, which would be appropriate for use with someone else's parents, changes the meaning of the relationship for one's own.

Observant students taking relatively small classes may note the forms of address that are employed among students, between students and professor, and professor and students, noting as well any changes as the relationships are transformed.

FACTORS INFLUENCING CODE CHOICE

As the investigation of address forms suggests, our choice of linguistic code or speech form is a function of a variety of separate matters. Status relationships and those involving deference and respect provide one occasion for selecting speech form, including both forms of address and language choice itself. Ervin-Tripp reports results of work by Rubin which indicated how Paraguayans will use Spanish in relationships involving deference and respect, switching their language to Guarani when the relationship involves greater intimacy and status-equality.

Roles within interaction also may call for different linguistic selection. Blom and Gumperz (1972) for example, report an observation in which the local residents of a Norwegian town use standard Norwegian when enacting their roles as buyer and seller, but change to the local dialect if they wish to initiate a private conversation on more personal matters. In this case, the choice of the form serves as a cue for a change in the nature of the relationship, and simultaneously serves to sustain the new form of the relationship.

Familiarity itself influences the choice of form and the meaning embodied in switching from one form to another. Elliptical phraseology not only marks informal speech, but also forms employed between familiars, including friends as well as persons who work together; this is in contrast to the greater elaboration and specification that is involved in formal speech and among strangers. Thus, for example, restaurant workers communicate orders in a manner rather unlike the form in which the order is given by the customer. The customer asks for a bacon and tomato sandwich without mayonaise to take out; the waitress translates the order to the cook as a "B & T to go, hold the mayo." Or a family may communicate wanting more cake that is being served by a variety of elliptical forms including "me," "I would," "sure," and so forth, while a guest might use the more complete and formal form, "Yes, please, I would like some more cake."

Age is another factor that plays a role in the choice of language and speech forms. Adults are often familiar with the transformation in their own speech forms when addressing a young child or infant; lexicon shifts (e.g., potty, weewee, night-night) as do a variety of tonal and syntactical arrangements. Adults addressing infants and young children tend to use higher-pitched voices and engage in a sing-song pattern of intonation.

Age also influences linguistic choice as the growing child is urged to stop talking baby talk. For example, a twelve-year-old child might resort to baby talk as a vehicle for communicating dependency or a desire to be treated again as a little baby. Adult lovers and married couples likewise revert to such linguistic forms. Labov's (1966) research on the use of "r" among New Yorkers indicated another kind of age-related variation in linguistic-form. Among the higher class groups, the younger respondents used "r" more than did older respondents, even though "r" was more prevalent among upper classes as a group.

Rules of Code Consistency.   Ervin-Tripp (1969) speaks of *co-occurrence* rules to refer to the consistency of linguistic forms within utterances. It is possible, for example, to select an informal form of interaction that is appropriate to the situation and then switch midstream to a more formal code, thus breaking the consistency of form: that is, violating the co-occurrence rule that basically allows one to predict to later linguistic forms of an utterance from knowledge of the initial forms. The graduation speaker who begins with a formal address and then lets more colloquial forms leak in provides an example of breaking a co-occurrence rule.

Breaking this kind of linguistic rule informs the listener of a shift in the social relationship between the listener and the speaker, or of some previously hidden quality of the speaker. Thus, when Eliza Doolittle is being trained to use proper English, part of that training is geared to keep her from letting a slang form slip into her otherwise formal speech; the ever suspicious language Professor who meets her at the ball, however, is watchful, waiting for that telltale breaking of co-occurrence that would give her away. The break, of course, can be a very minor one, as when the upwardly mobile New Yorkers, so careful about their speech, drop the "ing" and say "in" as in the phrase, "It is goin' well"; or drop one "r" in an otherwise perfect linguistic performance.

Taking Turns.   If you pause to think about it, a fascinating aspect of human interaction involves the general tendency for persons to take turns in conversing with one another. This is fascinating not only because we seem generally to be able to manage this fundamental coordination in our interaction with others, but as importantly, that for the most part we are not aware of just how we accomplish this feat. In suggesting that turn-taking is a fundamental accomplishment, I do not mean to also suggest that we always are successful in such joint coordination; we are all aware of those times when our messages seem to step on those of others and vice versa. It would seem, however, that much of the time we manage to coordinate our turns and thereby engage in a relatively smooth exchange. But how is this accomplished? Are there signals we use to indicate that "My turn is up, start yours" or that "It's still my turn, don't interrupt me"? Are there rules we follow indicating when the signals apply and what the appropriate response to them is?

The answer to these questions seems to be "yes," but the methods employed to obtain a systematic answer are extremely complex. Let us look in some detail at one effort, reported in 1972 by Duncan, who obtained his data from two interviews lasting about 19 minutes each. The interviews were videotaped and careful transcripts prepared. As Duncan notes, 19 minutes is hardly a large slice of interaction time; interestingly, the full analysis of these two 19-minute segments of interaction took him approximately two full years!

The basic research question to which Duncan's efforts were directed was to determine if there were definite signals that P, the speaker, gave to O, the auditor (i.e., the person not speaking at the moment), that P's turn is up or that P's turn is not yet completed. If there were definite signals, what were they and what form did they take? When such signals were used, did O respond appropriately by taking a turn? When such signals were absent or ambiguous, did P and O begin to engage in simultaneous interaction rather than taking turns?

A close examination of the transcriptions of these interviews revealed several kinds of signals that P and O employed to take turns:

1. A rising or falling in intonation at the end of a clause was a signal for turn-taking. It was noted that as long as P remained within the same general intonational range, no signal for turn-taking was thereby communicated; it was a definite change in intonation that signaled P's turn is up, O's can now begin.

2. Body language, in particular the termination of a hand gesture or the relaxation of a tensed hand signaled the termination of P's turn and the beginning of O's.

3. What Bernstein (1962) has referred to as *sociocentric* sequences were also signals for turn-taking: for example, "but uh"; "or something"; "you know."—expressions that do not add additional content to the message being communicated.

4. A drop in pitch or in loudness usually signalled a turn was over and that a new turn was permissible. As with intonation, it was the change in pitch or loudness that signaled a turn, rather than any particular level of either.

5. Content-related signals, including the syntax that completes a clause, also provided cues that P's turn was over and O's could begin.

This listing is not exhaustive but rather only illustrative of turn-taking signals. While other signaling cues were also determined, this listing will give the reader a sense of both the nature of the processes involved and its complexity. As Duncan's examination of the interview interactions suggested, persons were readily able to read these signals and coordinate their interactions successfully. He notes that, in fact, the more "yielding cues" presented by P, the greater the likelihood that O will attempt to take a turn; fewer signals increase the ambiguity of the situation leading more often to simultaneous speaking rather than a coordinated flow. This kind of research gives living meaning to the phrase, "give-and-take" that we employed previously to discuss the joint actions between P and O. It suggests how a combination of verbal and nonverbal signals provide the interactants with information that they need to coordinate even something as fundamental as taking turns when communicating.

Interaction Content and Interpersonal Behavior

We now know that information is conveyed by means of choosing among linguistic codes and forms; in the concluding section of this chapter we will examine the role of nonverbal material in conveying information and sustaining or transforming interpersonal relationships. We are also concerned, however, with the role that the content of verbal messages plays in defining and influencing interpersonal behavior. Our search is for certain recurring patterns in the relationship between various behaviors. If we can discover regularities between certain verbal events as stimuli and others as responses, then we can uncover a basic structure for social behavior. For example, if P's behavior is to speak and act positively towards O, is this more likely to elicit a positive response from O or a negative response? Insofar as we can construct analyses that show these connections and others, we can map out the structure of social behavior (e.g., Benjamin, 1974). Several efforts to analyze interaction content have been developed; the system employed by Robert Bales (1950a; b; 1955a; b; 1958) is perhaps the best known and most often employed, having a strong basis in both theory and fact.

BALES'S APPROACH

It was Bales's theoretical view that any social system, including a dyad, and even society as a whole, has two major classes of problems to be dealt with. He referred to these as task-related or instrumental problems on the one hand, and internal, socioemotional or maintenance problems on the other. A group of persons has come together for some particular purpose; that purpose helps define their task problems. In addition, every group faces problems of maintaining itself, its sense of comraderie, purpose, morale, cohesiveness, and so forth, while it is working on its task.

From Bales's perspective, successful handling of the task poses demands on group structure that work to the detriment of socioemotional needs and vice versa. In other words, the more a group seeks to efficiently solve its task-related concerns, the more it must abandon its maintenance functions; the more it seeks to solve its maintenance functions, the more it must sacrifice efficiency in getting the task accomplished. Put most simply, Bales argues that for a group to get a job done, it usually requires that someone take charge and dole out some unpleasant, but necessary jobs; this, in turn may create dissension within the group. But a group that seeks to keep everyone happy and equal may indeed succeed at that, but soon no one will be willing to take the responsibility for doling out the dirty work that still has to be done. To keep itself happy, the group may sacrifice the task; to get the task done efficiently, it may sacrifice people. A successful group, in Bales's view, must seek an equilibrium between these two extremes, achieving a sufficient amount of role differentiation and hierarchical authority to deal adequately with task issues, while retaining sufficient equality and harmony to maintain itself.

We note some parallels between this analysis and Bateson's perspective discussed in Chapter 2. Bales's concern with task issues focuses on those processes that produce differentiation among the members of a group; these are similar to Bateson's description of complementary interaction. Socioemotional processes on the other hand, like the symmetrical interaction of which Bateson speaks, lead toward a greater similarity (i.e., equality) among the members of an interacting group. Both Bales's and Bateson's formulations emphasize that the stable state for a group lies in a balancing between these two opposing tendencies; as either process becomes extreme, the opposing process is triggered, thereby providing a self-maintaining feedback system that keeps the group at a stable level. Bateson derived these processes from his analysis of the institutionalized *naven* ritual; Bales's data were obtained by observing the patterns of interaction among persons working together on tasks that were assigned to them.

In order to assess the theory, Bales developed a coding scheme for analyzing the content of specific acts during group interaction. He trained observers to use a 12-category system noting over time who interacted with whom and what the content of each interaction was. The scheme of categories follows his theory in that six of his categories (1, 2, 3, 10, 11, 12) apply to the groups' socioemotional system and involve the nature of relationships among members; the remaining six apply to the task system:

1. shows solidarity
2. shows tension release
3. agrees
4. gives suggestions
5. gives opinion
6. gives orientation
7. asks for orientation
8. asks for opinion
9. asks for suggestion
10. disagrees

11. shows tension
12. shows antagonism

A closer examination of these twelve categories will indicate that Bales's asks his observers to make a distinction between messages that apply to positive socioemotional factors (1, 2, 3) and those that involve negative socioemotional factors (10, 11, 12).

Bales's empirical work using this system has provided some interesting and important validation for these theoretical hypotheses regarding group processes and tendencies towards equilibrium between task and socioemotional concerns. In particular, his work has uncovered a tendency for successful groups to form two separate structures (i.e. recurring patterns) of interaction: one structure focuses on task matters and contains one set of persons (he calls them task specialists); one focuses on socioemotional matters and contains a different set of persons (social specialists). Bales reports it rare to find a great person-leader, one who ranks high in both task and socioemotional kinds of interactive behaviors.

In his efforts to understand why there exist few great person-leaders, Bales examined what he termed the *feedback ratio* of each interactant. This is the ratio of communications sent out to communications received. Persons with a high ratio are those who are very active in their own participation and who also allow much interaction to be directed back to them; persons with a low ratio give out a great deal but accept back very little. By examining his data with this ratio in mind, Bales discovered that task specialists who had a high feedback ratio were higher on socioemotional behavior than those with a low ratio. The point is that combined task and socioemotional contributors within a group have to establish a high degree of equality between their own communications out to others and those that they get back from others; the successful task specialists who only send out and receive little, may indeed contribute to task solutions, but are not helpful in dealing with the groups' interpersonal dilemmas; in fact, they may exacerbate these problems through their own one-sided behavior.

Bales's work has informed us that interaction within small groups reflects two fundamental patterns (task and socioemotional), each of which is basic to sustaining the group as a viable social system. Thus, from analyses of the content of social interaction, we see the importance of linguistic forms in defining a social structure or social relationship that it maintains. The behavior of the task or the socioemotional specialists defines the role and manner of relating to other group members; their continued interaction around task or socioemotional issues, in turn not only sustains their particular role within the group, but simultaneously serves to maintain the group itself.

We can interpret a change of the task specialist's verbal behavior from categories 4, 5, 6, to 7, 8, 9, for example, as analogous to a code switching. This content change signals a change in the person's relationship to others in the group. The leader no longer leads, but now seeks guidance from others. For example, the classroom instructor who is usually the task specialist who directs and organizes group interaction may stop performing this role; this sometimes occurs within sensitivity groups or often in nondirective, participative teaching approaches. In not giving suggestions, for example, the secure foundations of the entire class can be undermined until another specialist is found or until the groups' members share the functions that the specialist serves. The teacher's refusal to direct creates a change in his or her relationship to the group, and simultaneously causes a change in others' relationship to the group. As soon as another person emerges to take on those interactive functions of task leadership, they will have thereby transformed their identity in the group by having differentiated themselves from the rest of the members. A typical observation in sensitivity groups, for example, is the way hostility is directed towards other group members who take on the directive functions that the group's "official" leader does not carry out.

INTERACTION PHASES AND GROUP DEVELOPMENT

In his theorizing, if not always as clearly in his research data, Bales examined changes that occur as a discussion within a group continues over time. In particular, he sought to determine stable patterns of interaction, in which, for example, if P emits one category of behavior, O will respond with a specific category of behavior. At the level of the group as a whole, Bales and his colleagues were able to demonstrate three phases of group problem solving, each phase being marked by a particular interactive exchange: orientation, evaluation, and control. Orientation asks "what is the problem," evaluation poses the question "how do we feel about it"?, and control answers "what should we do about it"? What is important for us to note about this kind of analysis is that it suggests constraints on interaction that might otherwise appear to the participants to be freely chosen. When a group of persons tries to solve some collective problem, they initially face the issue of orienting themsevles to one another and to the various aspects of their problem. Interactions during this early phase of their encounter are thereby constrained to deal with matters of orientation (both task and socioemotional); and these constraints can be observed by using the Bales's coding system and noting the predominance of orientation interactions in early phases of a group's life together.

In Bales's analysis, evaluation involves the group's efforts to develop a common frame of reference of values and interests relevant to their task at hand; control, the final phase, emphasizes ways in which the group works to arrive at the solution to their task or socioemotional problems. In addition to the constraints that are coordinated to these phases of group interaction, Bales was also interested in empirically determining for each kind of interaction the probability that another specific category of interaction would be given in response. We shall have more to say about this kind of interactional constraint in the section on proaction and reaction.

Group Development. Other analyses of the development of interaction within small, face-to-face groups suggest similar patterns of constraint on the content of members' interaction as a function of the particular developmental phase in which a group finds itself. One summarizing scheme was proposed by Bruce Tuckman (1965), based on his review and interpretation of the relevant literature in the field. He outlined four major developmental issues that all small interacting groups face, these being reflected in both task and socioemotional areas:

1. Forming: Similar to Bales's notion of orientation, all groups must define their joint situation with respect to who they are, what their member resources are, what the task is, how best to proceed working on it, and so on.
2. Storming: Tuckman uses this term to describe the formation of subgroups that produce conflict, disagreement, polarization, and such over issues involving the task and how it should be done, as well as over member relationships, including over group leadership and authority. This is similar to Bales's phase of evaluation.
3. Norming: Once the conflicts have been settled the group now begins to develop norms or rules governing their internal relationships and their approaches to solving the task. In this phase, we can see the beginnings of a sense of the group as a cohesive entity facing a common set of problems that require joint effort to solve.
4. Performing: This phase is essentially the equilibrated outcome of which Bales speaks; it involves sufficiently integrating task and socioemotional themes so that the group may function together more effectively in doing the work for which it was initially formed and in developing stronger internal bonds of membership. Bales's phase of control involves aspects of both norming and performing.

While not all groups will pass through all of these phases, nor can we state with certainty just how much time will be required in any one phase, Tuckman has provided a reasonable summary statement of the kinds of interactive issues that small groups face and that can be assessed by examining the patterns of interaction that emerge. That we can meaningfully and reliably identify patterns of interaction, and in fact outline a developmental sequence for such patterns, itself indicates the nature of the constraints that exist that lead interactants to select from a large array of possible contents of verbal behaving, a smaller and identifiable subset.

We might stretch the point in order to reemphasize it; these phases of group interaction outline different sets of linguistic codes: for example, a code that involves task issues of forming; a code that involves socioemotional issues of storming, and so forth. And as with all linguistic codes, they not only reflect or express a particular kind and phase of social relationship, but serve as well to shape the very relationship (i.e., phase) that they reflect. Thus, the group member who "gives orientation" when a group is first formed, is reflecting a phase of group development and through the verbal behavior of giving information, clarifying issues, and so forth, is simultaneously helping to maintain the relationship as one of "orientation or forming."

PROACTION AND REACTION

In examining patterns of group interaction, Bales focused not only on the general phases of orientation, evaluation, and control, but also on what he termed *proactive* and *reactive* tendencies. Both refer to the frequency with which a given interaction tends to be followed by another identifiable type of interaction. In proaction, the person speaking continues with the same general theme. Bales's data suggest several proactive tendencies:

1. After having given an act of orientation, opinion, or suggestion, the likelihood is high that P will continue with the same kind of interaction.
2. If P's interaction involved showing antagonism, P's next likely action will be either more antagonism or a change to tension release rather than a return to task issues.
3. Tension release tends to induce more tension release as the next interaction.

Reactive tendencies refer to tendencies for P to respond in a particular manner to O's interaction which serves as the stimulus. Bales indicates several kinds of reactive tendencies:

1. Rather than continuing to interact in the task area, when O's act has been an attempt to answer a question, P's reaction is likely to be a positive response of agreement.

2.   When O's act is more directive, P's likely response is negative.
3.   An antagonistic act from O is likely to produce an antagonistic reaction from P, while a positive solidarity-producing act of O is likely to produce a similar positive response from P.
4.   As Bales notes, laughter is contagious; if O laughs, so too does P.

Recall again the discussion in Chapter 2 of complementary and symmetrical patterns of interaction; we can see similarities with Bales's analyses of proactive and reactive tendencies. That antagonism serves as a stimulus for antagonism as a response is an example of a symmetrical interaction pattern. Complementarity was found by Bales who noted how P's efforts to get orientation produced a response from O to provide P with orientation. We can see in these examples of interactive tendencies within small groups the systems focus of our earlier concern. In particular, we note how the group forms a social system in which the specific actions of a given element (i.e., individual) both reflect the state of the system and contribute to sustaining or transforming that state.

Insofar as individual interactions are nonrandom but follow particular patterns of proaction and reaction, individuals are constrained in their manner of interacting as a function of the state of the group as a whole. As Bales notes, the group must attain a state of equilibrium or otherwise disperse and no longer remain a group. The problem of equilibrium is that disturbances that are created in one phase of interaction must be dealt with in some later phase, thus constraining the patterns of interaction that are likely to occur. It is not so much a matter then of separate individuals simply talking together, but rather of an interdependent group of persons whose talking together in patterned ways serves to maintain the group as a functioning whole.

Interpersonal Reflexes.   A related approach to examining the content of verbal behavior during interaction was proposed by Freedman, Leary, Ossorio, and Coffey (1951; also Leary, 1957) who suggest the presence of what might be termed *interpersonal reflexes.* This perspective offers us an analysis of how an interpersonal structure can be maintained or transformed through the observable exchanges between interacting persons. We know that by shining a light in the eyes, the pupil will retract; or by hitting the patella, the knee will jerk upwards; what the Leary group proposes is that by asking for help, for example, P elicits a particular kind of response from O. This, of course, is Bales's analysis of reactive tendencies.

P and O are linked by observable bonds of interaction in which P's behavior calls forth a response from O. Thus it should be possible to map out rules of interactive exchanges in a manner analogous to the way in which it is possible to map the rules of address in the

English language. With these rules in hand, we could then observe the content of verbal interaction and come to a better understanding of how interpersonal relationships are sustained or transformed.

The Leary group proposed a 16-category scheme for analyzing interpersonal behavior. Observers using this scheme are to ask themselves "What is P's behavior doing to O"? The answer is located in one of the sixteen categories. The categories are arranged on a circle that reflects two major axes: dominance-submission and love-hate. These are the same kinds of interpersonal dimensions that numerous other investigators have revealed to be basic in any human encounter: that is, a dimension that deals with power and authority (e.g., Bales's concern with task functions); a dimension that deals with bonds of intimacy (e.g., Bales's concern with socioemotional functions). Other categories around the circle are seen to reflect variations on and combinations of these basic interpersonal qualities.

A recent effort to study the kinds of interpersonal reflex that the Leary group suggested was undertaken by Shannon and Guerney (1973; see also Benjamin, 1974). They divided some eighty-four un-

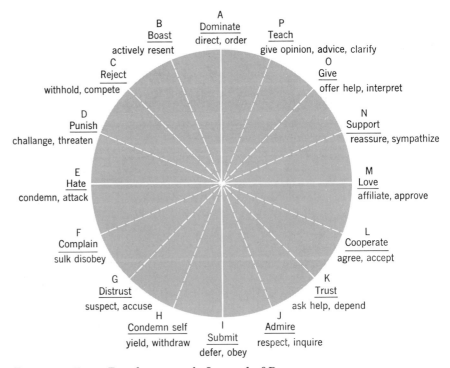

Figure 5. *From Freedman et al.,* Journal of Personality, *Vol. 20. Copyright 1951 by Duke University Press.*

dergraduates into groups of six persons each, giving them topics to discuss for about one hour. The discussions were recorded and coded using the sixteen interpersonal dimensions outlined in Figure 5. They coded behavior into octants (combinations of two related categories) rather than into sixteenths. Thus, for example, a behavior was coded as AP if it involved some combination of directing, ordering, giving opinion, clarifying, and so forth. A summary of their major findings appears below; using letters from the figure to indicate the interpersonal response connections they found:

P's Stimulus Behavior	O's Response Behavior*
1. AP (dominate-teach)	JK (admire-trust)
	LM (cooperate-love)
2. BC (boast-reject)	BC (boast-reject)
	DE (punish-hate)
3. DE (punish-hate)	BC (boast-reject)
	DE (punish-hate)
4. JK (admire-trust)	AP (dominate-teach)
	JK (admire-trust)
5. LM (cooperate-love)	AP (dominate-teach)
	LM (cooperate-love)

*Adapted from Shannon, J. & Guerney, B., Jr. Interpersonal effects of interpersonal behavior. *Journal of Personality and Social Psychology,* 1973, **26,** 142–150. Copyright 1973 by the American Psychological Association. Reprinted by permission.

Shannon and Guerney's overall results support the concept of an interpersonal reflex; their data indicate strong connections between the nature of P's behavior and the kind of response it evokes from O. As the summary data presented above indicates, there are combinations of both symmetrical and complementary interactive patterns. For example, P's boasting brings forth boasting from O, a symmetrical cycle; on the other hand, P's tendency to be more docile (admire-trust) brings forth dominance from O, a complementary cycle as well as the symmetrical docile response. It is also interesting and important to note that symmetrical patterns of interaction do not necessarily lead a group towards disintegration: in fact, the strong response of returning trust with trust and cooperation-love with cooperation-love, suggests that there is truth in the Golden Rule. As Shannon and Guerney note, at least for the college students who were their subjects, the more negative responses (BC and DE) are elicited primarily in a symmetrical manner as a reaction to receiving boasting or rejection. Thus, once again, we have a homeopathic rule of interpersonal behavior: like elicits like.

The Politics of Language: A Note on Language and the Sociology of Knowledge

The point has been made and demonstrated that languages, linguistic codes, and speech forms reflect, symbolize, and influence social relationsips. On the level of two-person or small-group interaction, as we have seen, language forms are the vehicle whereby the interaction system is sustained or transformed. Where choice among alternative codes is possible, the person who controls the selection can control the way in which the relationship is formulated and maintained.

Our analysis, however, need not always focus on individuals or small groups. Where choice among code-learning is possible, institutions of socialization (e.g., schools) may create differences among persons or classes of persons in their access to different code systems, thereby exercising control over the manner in which social change can occur. For example, access to learning an elaborated code may be restricted to certain social groups. To the extent that high economic gain within a particular society necessitates obtaining jobs that require the use of an elaborated code, denying one group access to such codes serves to maintain the existing economic class structure.

If we can understand language control as a vehicle for controlling the symbolic order of a society, then we can see how powerful a force language can be in both exercising control and in wresting control from those in power. This process of influence and counterinfluence is especially noted when two separate linguistic communities are brought into contact. When colonial powers take over another land, the language differences, in particular, the development and maintenance of pidgin languages, can often be seen in terms of a struggle for power between unequal groups. It has been noted (e.g., Hall, 1955), for example, that several efforts to eliminate pidgin languages have "heightened the use of such languages as vehicles in nationalist struggles for independence." (Grimshaw, 1969, p. 316).

Linguists studying the use of Creole and standard forms in the Caribbean (e.g., Hymes, 1971; Stewart, 1962) have likewise stressed the importance of taking social power arrangements into consideration in attempting to understand shifts and changes in the Creole forms. To the extent that group identities are entwined within a particular linguistic system, efforts to introduce a new system can be seen as a threat to long standing cultural ties. Yet, to the extent that upward mobility within a society is dependent on learning new linguistic habits, resistance to such learning can impede mobility until alternate channels for mobility are possible that do not require abandoning loyalty to one language system. This is usually the outcome of a political struggle.

THE SOCIOLOGY OF KNOWLEDGE

It is important to keep in mind that language is an active agent that influences the manner in which we experience and understand events, persons, and even ourselves. It is that agent that sustains a system or motivates its transformation. The subspecialty of sociology, known as the sociology of knowledge, has been especially interested in analyzing the correspondence between social structure and symbolic forms, including language and ideology. The perspective of the sociology of knowledge argues that our forms and modes of thinking can never be fully understood without taking their social origins into consideration (e.g., Berger & Luckman, 1966; Mannheim, 1936; Marx, 1956). Thinking and all such symbolic activity is a social act in which individuals participate; as a social act, thinking has historical and sociological roots.

It is the aim of the sociologist of knowledge to uncover these roots and thereby link our thoughts to the historical era in which they emerged and to the sociological position that we occupy in a particular society. It is the thesis of a sociology of knowledge, for example, that when society was agrarian, people's knowledges about life and the world were different from that now possessed in modern, industrialized society. Likewise, it is a thesis of the sociology of knowledge that persons of differing occupational or educational location within a society will thereby come to formulate different conceptions about the nature of reality.

It can be seen that Bernstein's research on elaborated and restricted codes is a contribution to the sociology of knowledge. Karl Mannheim, most of whose writings fall within the field of the sociology of knowledge, adds the historical dimension to the social-structural analysis of thought that Bernstein and other similar linguists provide. Mannheim suggested that "Every epoch has its fundamentally new approach and its characteristic point of view, and consequently sees the 'same' object from a new perspective" (1936, p. 271). He further emphasized that just as we date art forms according to their style, so we can date knowledge styles according to their historical origins.

Both Bernstein and Mannheim inform us of an important relationship between social structure, historical epoch, and the manner by which particular forms of knowledge are experienced and sustained. Furthermore, from their individual perspectives both argue that control over the linguistic and symbolic order is a major means whereby dominant groups attempt to maintain their dominance over subordinate groups.

An example will be illustrative of this latter point. Liston Pope (1958) conducted an investigation of life in a small southern mill-town during the 1920s and 1930s. Like so many similar towns, this town was almost entirely owned and operated by the mill owners. In addition, the town's churches survived as a function of the donations provided by the mill owners. A gift of money from the mill could make or break a church, revealing an interesting symbiosis between economics (the mill) and symbolic order (the churches).

In a symbiotic relationship each member gives and gets, and each needs for survival what the other gives. In this mill town, the churches espoused a doctrine of morality that kept the mill hands thinking and acting in ways essential to their being effective workers. The preachers urged the workers to adopt a morality stressing the virtues of hard work while decrying the evils of excessive drinking and laziness. In turn, the churches received sufficient capital from the mill owners to maintain themselves. A national union movement sought to come to town and organize the workers; the mill owners were opposed to unionization that would threaten their profits in an already competitive national market. The battle to keep the union out was not waged, however, solely within the mills, but in the churches as well. The preachers spent many Sunday sermons arguing against unionization, pointing out the dangers of being taken in by these outsiders, these Communists, these evil persons.

Control over the symbolic order of the community was in the hands of the preachers; they created values and ideas that workers came to believe in as their own. These keepers of the symbolic order, however, were thereby also keepers of the community's social order in which the workers were in their place and the mill owners and managerial personnel in theirs. Acceptance of this social arrangement was maintained through the preachers; their control, in turn was a matter of economics, and this was in the control of the mill owners.

The situation here is much as Karl Marx and others have noted: dominant classes feel that the specific conditions requisite for their own economic well-being are the general conditions necessary for the survival and betterment of everyone. In the mill town, the dominant ideology of the mill owners, conveyed through the churches, created a belief and value system that helped the dominant group maintain its own specific advantages.

BY WAY OF SUMMARY

The point, while simple to state, has many ramifications as we have already seen. Control over the manner in which experience is symbolized, which is itself a reflection of dominance arrangements within a society or social group, functions to help sustain the very system from which it derived. In submitting to "boy" and "Alvin," Dr. Poussaint was yielding, albeit with much personal anguish and shame, to the policeman's authority and right to dictate the linguistic forms that governed their encounter. In accepting the ideas of the preachers about the proper beliefs and behavior for workers and the evils of national labor unions, the mill workers were formulating their personal situation in ways put forth by the dominant group in their community, the mill owners. In learning the restricted code that the family employs and that peer groups and educational experience reinforces, the individual is experiencing self and life in ways that may hinder upward movement into more dominant and controlling positions in society. For anyone interested in understanding how interpersonal as well as larger, social systems are created, sustained, or transformed, the understanding of language and symbolic systems is imperative.

Nonverbal Interaction

The same general framework that we have employed in examining verbal interaction can be applied as well to the functions of nonverbal interaction. Our interest, then, is in the ways in which a social relationship is defined (i.e., produced and created), expressed by means of, and influenced (i.e., shaped, sustained, or transformed) by varieties of nonverbal communication.

In general, students of nonverbal behavior have grouped such behavior into four major types: tactile; proxemic; kinesic; paralinguistic. Briefly, tactile communication, as the word suggests, involves a language of touch. While touching is more prevalent among animal species—for example, the grooming behavior that takes place between monkeys and between gorillas—human beings are not without their own use of tactile sources of information. One person's weak handshake may prove very informative to another.

Proxemics involves the study of how space is used, with examinations of territoriality and its defense in animals providing a basis for somewhat similar analyses of the human use of space. Kinesics calls our attention primarily to bodily movements including gestures, motions of the limbs, the face, and especially the eyes and the direction of one's gaze. Paralinguistics focuses on vocal qualities that can convey information beyond that contained in the actual content of a verbal message. The cracking or high pitch of the anxious person is informative even when the person verbally claims to be calm. We noted several such paralinguistic as well as kinesic cues in our previous discussion of turn-taking signals. It will be helpful to our own understanding of the nonverbal aspects of interaction and communication to outline three related areas that have been of primary interest to social psychology:

1. Verbal and nonverbal channels of communication or different nonverbal channels themselves may at times be congruent, providing the same information, and at times incongruent, providing discrepant messages; many investigators have been interested in studying the meaning and the implications of such discrepancies. What does it imply for a relationship, for example, if P verbally says to O, "I love you," while his head nods negatively? Or what does it imply when P's face brightens in a smile, but her fists clench tightly at her side and her body leans away from O?

2. One of the major focal interests in nonverbal behavior has been concerned with identifying the lexicon of the nonverbal. Research strategies have usually involved providing persons with a particular nonverbal stimulus (e.g., photos of faces with varying expressions) and asking them to indicate what it means. This has been called a *decoding method.* An alternate approach, the *encoding method,* as one major research example indicates, has individuals role play a particular idea, mood, or personality; their nonverbal behavior is studied during this role playing. For example, subjects in an experiment may be instructed to try to win someone's approval, and their nonverbal behavior during this role-playing endeavor provides the investigator with information about the way in which such behavior is encoded and transmitted during social interaction. Both decoding and encoding strategies try to arrive at the meaning of particular nonverbal actions, and thus to eventually map out the lexicon of the nonverbal language system.

3. The first two areas of interest emphasize distinctions between verbal and nonverbal communication; a third perspective stresses the interdependence between the verbal and the nonverbal in the process of symbolizing experience. In this view, the assumption is made that nonverbal and verbal are elements of a total representational and expressive system. Thus, for example, persons' gestures while talking are understood to be part of the overall effort to represent their experiences and to communicate these experiences to themselves and to others. We will now examine these three topics in more detail.

Communication and Metacommunication

Several years ago, Gregory Bateson (recall *naven* from Chapter 2) suggested that all communication contains at least two aspects, the report and the command (Ruesch & Bateson, 1951). A report refers to the content of a communication; the command aspect refers to how the message is to be taken, or more fundamentally, the relationship implied between P and O: for example, "This is how I see myself . . . this is how I see you . . . this is how I see you seeing me . . ." (Watzlawick et al., 1967, p. 52). Another way of looking at this distinction is to speak about a communication between P and O (the report) and a communication about that communication (the command), also called a metacommunication. An example will be helpful (from Watzlawick et al., 1967).

A husband and wife get into an argument, but it is over something about which they both agree. The husband had received a call from a mutual friend who was passing through town for a few days, and invited the friend to stay with them. Both husband and wife like the friend and agreed that the friend should have been invited to stay with them. However, they have a bitter quarrel. The argument is not over the content or report aspects of the situation but rather about their relationship, specifically which one of them can take the independent action of inviting someone over without consulting the other. In other words, their argument is over the metacommunicational or command aspects of the husband's statement to his wife: "Fred is in town and so I invited him over."

As an interesting aside, the situation described would called "balanced" in the terms we employed in Chapter 3. That is, P and O like each other and agree about X. Yet, as described, the situation is also imbalanced, if we do not consider the communication content involving X but rather the metacommunication that is involved. This suggests that situations may be balanced with respect to communication about issues or persons but imbalanced with respect to metacommunication about those issues or persons. Indeed, this possibility suggests how intrapersonal and interpersonal tension may result even from a situation that, like the one described, ostensibly is filled with harmony based on both liking and agreement.

In the preceding example, the relationship between P and O is conveyed through a combination of verbal and nonverbal means. The husband's facial expression while informing his wife of the invitation may have joined with the implications of the message to communicate "I'm in charge around here." In many cases, however, the nonverbal channels carry the burden of the metacommunication while the verbal carries the message content. For example, P may say to O, "Thanks a lot for your help," conveying many different meanings as a function of nonverbal cues that inform O just how to interpret the content of that message: for example, as a joke, as sarcasm, as a sincere comment, as a hostile remark, as teasing, and so forth. The relationship between P and O is thereby both defined and reinforced by means of the metacommunicational aspects of their exchange: for example, "you and I have the kind of relationship in which we can joke with each other" or "you and I have a hostile relationship," and the like.

Some experimental investigations conducted by Mehrabian (e.g., 1971) are consistent with these preceding notions. His subjects were presented messages in two channels: verbal and vocal or paralinguistic. Messages were consistent when both verbal and vocal communicated the same impression and inconsistent when the verbal message communicated one impression and the nonverbal message sent a different impression. His data indicated that when verbal and vocal were inconsistent, subjects tended to use the verbal to make inferences about content and the nonverbal to make inferences about the person, (i.e., relationship inferences). It was also found that inconsistency led P generally to discount the content in favor of believing the message's tone. Thus a positive content paired with a negative tone (e.g., the word "love" said as though the speaker disliked the listener) led to a judgment that the message was negative (e.g., Mehrabian & Weiner, 1967).

THE DOUBLE BIND

The fascination with discrepancies between verbal and nonverbal or between content and relational aspects of communication stems in great part from the double-bind hypothesis proposed some years ago by Bateson, Jackson, Haley, and Weakland (1956). A double bind is a communication that imposes a contradiction between the content and the metacommunicational aspects of a message:

a message is given which is so structured that (a) it asserts something, (b) it asserts something about its own assertion, and (c) these two assertions are mutually exclusive. Thus, if the message is an injunction, it must be disobeyed to be obeyed; if it is a definition of self or the other, the person thereby defined is this kind of person only if he is not, and is not if he is. The meaning of the message is, therefore, undecidable (Watzlawick, et al., p. 212).

A double bind places the person into a paradoxical situation in which there is no proper way to respond. Bateson and his colleagues argued that double-bind communications within families were a crucial factor in producing and sustaining schizophrenia in some family members. In somewhat humorous form, one example of a double-bind is the mother who gives her son two ties for a birthday gift, and, as he comes into the room wearing one of them, she comments, "O.K., so you don't like the other one, I'll take it back and exchange it."

The double-bind hypothesis suggests that inconsistent messages are confusing because they do not permit the person to infer the actual meaning of the message's content or of the relationship between themselves and the other person. Thus it is not possible to determine either the behavior expected of them or the definition of themselves and the other person. Several systematic efforts to study the effects of inconsistent communications are informative, even though not all demonstrate a link between pathology and inconsistency. And, as we have noted, persons do resolve inconsistent messages and thus are not inevitably caught up in an impossible dilemma.

Bugental, Kaswan, and Love (1970) have made an important contribution to understanding the consequences of verbal-nonverbal discrepancies. Prior research from this same team of investigators suggested a link between pathology in children and incongruent verbal-nonverbal communication of mothers. The basic format of their research involves using actors on videotape to systematically present varying combinations of voice, picture, and verbal messages. Scripts (i.e., verbal content) included such statements as "You really did a fine job"; "Thanks a lot for your help"; "I give up on you. You're impossible"; "You're going to drive me out of my mind," among others. The subjects for their study were eighty children and their parents.

Two major sets of results were uncovered. The first pertains to differences between adults and children in their response to incongruent messages. As the authors summarize this difference, "children, when confronted with a conflicting message, resolve the incongruity by assuming the worst." When an adult experiences a message that is critical but offered with a smile, the tendency was to assume that the person was joking somewhat and didn't really mean the criticism as much as the verbal content alone would suggest. On the other hand, children tended to see the same kind of joking (i.e., being critical with a smile) more negatively. This is apparently consistent with other research that suggests that children tended to experience joking criticism as ridicule and thus as more negative than the smiling critical adult may intend. Likewise, when vocal and verbal channels convey criticism, but the videotape is of a smiling female, adults report a somewhat neutral interpretation of the message's meaning whereas children experience it negatively. The woman's smile, which triggers a softening of the critical or unfriendly blow for the adult, does not do so for the child.

The second set of findings from their research is relevant to the issue of how the several channels interact to create the interpretation of the message that the subjects make. Their data suggest the presence of what they term a *discounting process,* in which if either the content of the message or its vocal rendering was unfriendly, for example, then the overall impression was unfriendly, even if the other channel was friendly. For instance, if the message content were negative, then a positive style of delivery was discounted: the interpretation was negative. Likewise, if the vocal style were negative but the content positive, the content was discounted and hence the interpretation was negative.

A related result is the finding that visual cues were especially important in the interpretation of conflicting information. We have seen how a smile for adults can lessen the negative impact of criticism. Combining this with the discounting process, it would seem that one auditory channel can lead the person to discount the implications of the other, but a visual message carries even stronger weighting, at least for adults.

A recent follow-up investigation (Bugenthal, 1974) sought to specify in more detail the nature of the resolution process that occurs when persons confront inconsistency between channels of communication. Bugenthal reasoned that communications that occur in natural rather than in the acted settings of much of the previous research, allow for greater variability in the *credibility cues* that are contained in either the verbal or the nonverbal channel; and that the nature of these cues will influence how P resolves any apparent inconsistency. An example of a nonverbal credibility cue is a message whose intonation is congruent with or fits the facial expression of the person giving it. When tone and face are congruent, the credibility of the nonverbal information is said to be high; when tone and facial gestures are noncongruent, then the credibility of the nonverbal channel is said to be low. It was Bugenthal's hypothesis that inconsistent messages that provided greater credibility cues for one channel (i.e., verbal or nonverbal) than the other would lead P to discount the information from the less credible channel and thereby resolve the potentially binding inconsistency.

To study this in a natural setting, Bugenthal recorded the spontaneous communications made by mothers to their children while in a waiting room. She selected sets of these messages to present later to a group of judges who rated the messages in terms of their approving and friendly quality. The sets varied systematically in content, intonation, and in particular, in their credibility weighting for a given verbal or nonverbal channel. Findings suggested the value of conceptualizing the resolution of double-bind communications in terms of the relative credibility weighting of a particular channel.

For example, a message given with a sincere tone in which nonverbal credibility cues are high (e.g. tone and face are congruent), leads to a sense of approval or disapproval as a function of the tone of voice regardless of the actual content of the message. In this case, the sincere tone carried high credibility thereby leading P to discount the content of the message. This is similar to other findings in which a convincing nonverbal message is believed whatever the content. However, if the message seemed to be given in a slow, deliberate way, as though P were weighing her words (i.e., low nonverbal credibility), then the judges tended to discredit the voice as informative about P's real attitudes. Under these circumstances of an uncredible voice, judges tended to rate P's message as unfriendly and disapproving if its content was extremely evaluative (e.g., "that is great"), and as friendly and approving if its content was more moderate (e.g., "all right, fine").

Affirming the earlier work (Bugenthal et al., 1970), the present data suggest that the kinds of message most likely to yield negative evaluations are extreme evaluative statements generated by an inconsistency between verbal and nonverbal channels with an incredible voice (e.g., a neutral face and a positive tone). As Bugenthal notes, this is the most likely combination that parents of disturbed children as compared with parents of normal children use.

Other efforts to assess the relative importance of different channels in resolving conflicting communications as we have seen have been reported by Mehrabian (1971) and his associates; their research data suggest that when an inconsistency exists between a verbal and a nonverbal communication, the nonverbal will usually carry more weight in interpreting the meaning of the communication. The data also suggested that people generally prefer consistency rather than inconsistency in communications.

Strictly speaking, the double-bind hypothesis suggests that it is not possible to resolve the inconsistency that is involved in the communication; thus persons are trapped in a paradoxical situation in which they are damned if they do and damned if they don't. While the clinical literature suggests the trap-like quality of strict double binds, it would seem from the work we have examined that persons can and do in fact resolve most inconsistencies. The important point, however, as regards pathology, especially among children, is the tendency to resolve inconsistencies in ways that are self-rejecting and that communicate to them "you are no good," "You are not loved," "you are not liked," and such. Even for adults the tendency to give strong weight to nonverbal information (i.e., metacommunication) in resolving apparent inconsistencies in communication can lead to similar self-rejecting implications, especially when the metacommunicational aspect of the message is negative, rejecting, or hostile. Thus, one may be able to resolve double binds, but nevertheless be trapped by the negative implications they suggest about one's self as a person.

The Lexicon of the Nonverbal

Most efforts to develop a lexicon of nonverbal communication have focused on proxemic and kinesic sources of information. Hall (1959; 1963) coined the term *proxemic communication* to suggest the important role that spatial cues play in conveying a message. Under the heading of territoriality, ethologists have examined proxemic patterns in animal species, noting how species mark out their territory and defend it usually through colorfully symbolic displays of aggression when another animal or another species invades.

TERRITORIAL MARKERS

Animal species mark their territories in a variety of ways: songs of birds, secretions of deer, bears' claw marks on trees are all spatial markers that communicate territorial ownership within the animal kingdom. It has been suggested that humans mark their territories by a variety of visual markers and body placement. Robert Sommer (1966; 1967; 1969) has noted territorial defense in settings involving sociofugal space: that is, areas or arrangements in which persons try to avoid interacting. Sommer observed the actual seating arrangements selected by students studying in the library; in addition, he used a questionnaire to elicit the approaches the students might employ to mark out a private territory in the library, one created to discourage interaction. Sommer's results indicated that persons who want to sit alone choose the end chairs of a rectangular table, while those who wish to discourage others from sitting at the same table select the middle chair, and thereby "hog" the table to themselves. In other words, some students marked territories to gain privacy through a defensive movement away from others (by choosing end positions), while others did so more aggressively by occupying a position designed to discourage others from sitting near them.

In some of his other investigations, Sommer (Sommer & Becker, 1969) had accomplices use literal markers to attempt to reserve their territory in a popular soda fountain on the university campus. For example, the accomplice might drape a sweater over a chair or stack up books on a table. While these investigations are only a beginning, their results are suggestive of the role that such markers play in keeping others away from one's own, even temporary, territory; they seem to serve as a warning device signalling others to keep away and thereby avoid any needless confrontations (Becker, 1973). Sommer reports that with light population pressure, markers are more effective than with a rush of persons to use the soda fountain, and that personal markers are more effective than less personal ones; even with a rush a people, however, markers delay the inevitable territorial invasion.

Another aspect of territorial markers emerges from some research conducted by Knowles (1973). His research was concerned with the degree to which an interacting group of persons implicitly marks out a territory with boundaries. He was especially interested in determining how such factors as group size and group status influenced the boundaries' permeability: i.e., the degree to which a group territorial boundary could readily be breached. Knowles's method involved placing groups in the main hallway connecting two buildings of a university. He varied the size by placing a group of two persons or a group of four persons; status was varied by the age and the dress of the group members. Older and more formally dressed persons were used to indicate high status; younger and more casually dressed, to indicate lower status. For a comparative control condition, Knowles placed wastebaskets in the same hallway. An observer noted the behavior of passersby under these several different conditions. Did they penetrate the groups' boundary by walking through the interaction or did they seek to avoid it by walking around the group?

Data analyses provide some interesting results. For example, while 75 percent of the passersby penetrated the space when wastebaskets were present, only 25 percent did so when a group of persons was interacting: an implicit territorial boundary seemed to have been created by the presence of an interacting group of persons. Size and status were also found to be of some importance. More passersby walked through the two person as compared with the four-person group (30 percent compared with 19 percent); and more walked through the low as compared with the high status groups (30 percent compared with 18 percent). While no formal territorial markers were involved, Knowles's research like Sommer's parallel research on sociofugal space is instructive in suggesting the potency of implicit boundaries that exist around groups and indeed mark out their territory that one enters with some caution.

That invading a group's territory can be a potentially costly or painful undertaking was demonstrated in work reported by Efran and Cheyne (1974). Observations and physiological recordings were obtained on subjects who in going from one experimental room to another had to walk down a corridor and either (1) walk through two conversing persons, (2) walk past them but not between them, or (3) walk past two inanimate objects. It was expected that having to penetrate the space of the two conversing persons would be costly and that this would show up in subjects nonverbal expressions while walking down the corridor, in their mood ratings obtained after their jaunt, and in measures of their physiological arousal.

Data suggested support for the nonverbal and mood ratings, but not for the measures of physiological arousal. Subjects who had to penetrate the groups' territory as compared with those in conditions (2) and (3) showed a higher frequency of gazing downwards, of closing their eyes, and of showing pained or negative mouth gestures, including for example, "tongue out, lips in, tight lips, mouth corners back, pursed mouth, and twist" (p. 222). Mood ratings likewise indicated that those who had to violate group territory reported feeling the least positive. As noted, physiological recordings of arousal (measured by heart rate) did not show any significant effect as a function of the particular experimental group that the subject was in.

CONVERSATIONAL DISTANCE

Hall (1959; 1963) noted that the most frequent proxemic cue was the distance maintained for comfortable conversation. Many investigations have tried to determine this distance under varying conditions of person, culture, and situation. The point of much of this work has been to identify the standard distance under these varying conditions so that violations of that standard can be interpreted as a proxemic message that structures a change in the social relationship that is involved. For example, if under casual everyday circumstances, standard distance for U.S. males interacting with other males is 3 to 5 feet, then P's movement to an 8-foot distance might be a proxemic signal for P's leave-taking; or P's movement to a 2-foot distance might signal an aggressive or intimate meaning.

Although exact measures of distance are not always clearly obtained, there remains some provocative material concerning interaction space. A study by Argyle and Dean (1965; also see Argyle, 1969) placed subjects at 2, 6, and 10 feet from one another. At 2 feet, subjects tended to lean backwards or avert their gaze; at 10 feet, there was a tendency to lean forward and to establish greater eye contact, as though to maintain the standard distance that had been experimentally violated. Sommer's work (1962) has indicated preferences for side-by-side sitting when the distance for sitting across and facing one another exceeds about 3½ feet.

Several investigators have followed up Hall's original view that cultures vary in their standards of comfortable conversation. Little (1968) used a doll placement technique to determine differences in interaction preferences among five cultural groups: Americans,

Swedes, Greeks, Southern Italians, and Scots. Two male and two female plastic dolls were used; however, subjects were given only dolls of their own sex to place. Subjects were provided with descriptions of nineteen situations: for example, two good friends talking about a pleasant topic; an employer reprimanding an employee for some error in the employee's work; two people talking about the best place to shop. Their task was to place the two dolls on a piece of paper "so that they looked natural" in the particular situation described. Little's results confirm some of our hunches; the Mediterranean cultures (Greeks and Italians) and the Americans had the closest interaction distances while Swedes and Scots had significantly greater distances. Little was also able to examine several other determinants of interactive distance. His results indicate that friends interact more closely than acquaintances who in turn interact more closely than strangers; that the distance is somewhat closer when pleasant rather than either neutral or unpleasant topics are being discussed; that females placed interactions with authority figures at a greater distance than did males.

Jones and Aiello (1973) observed the proxemic behavior of pairs of school children in actual classroom settings in lower-class black and in middle-class white schools. Distance provided one proxemic source of information; the directness of orientation provided the second (i.e., face-to-face; side-by-side; back-to-back). Their results suggest that at least in the first grade, blacks stood closer than whites; this difference, however, disappeared by the third and fifth grades. They also found that males, both black and white, stood less directly than females, suggesting a proxemic sex-role pattern which is already learned by early elementary school years.

Immediacy Cues and Compensation. Jones and Aiello's inclusion of "directness of orientation" into their study and the Argyle and Dean findings of postural and eye gaze changes as a function of interaction distance both suggest that interaction distance is not simply a matter of physical proximity but rather some combination of what Mehrabian (1971) has termed *immediacy cues,* including distance, body orientation, and other kinesic cues, such as eye gaze. Based on data, Mehrabian reasoned that immediacy cues reflect the social relationship of liking-disliking, help establish that relationship among strangers, and help maintain the relationship among friends. That is, persons use interaction distance and related immediacy cues as nonverbal vehicles for informing one another about their relationship as well as for establishing and maintaining a relationship.

An assumption either of unwarranted intimacy or unwarranted aversion is part and parcel of violating distance and immediacy norms; whereas operating within the standard range keeps a relationship at an equilibrium point. Recall Argyle and Dean's findings that with distances too close, thereby suggesting unwarranted intimacy, subjects tended to lean backwards and avert their gaze as though these actions would serve to reestablish the proper balance point in the relationship. Likewise, with distance too great, thereby suggesting unwarranted aversion, equilibrium was reestablished by leaning forward and by maintaining eye contact. This is what Argyle and Dean call the *process of compensation* whereby an equilibrium of intimacy-aversion is maintained nonverbally by compensating in one mode (e.g., kinesic) when another is excessive (e.g., distance too close or too far).

Patterson (1968) reviews much of the relevant literature on this point and concludes that the compensation process appears to function as indicated in social interaction. Once again we see the role of interdependence in social interaction: upsetting a dynamic equilibrium triggers processes to reestablish that balance and thereby to conserve the relationship. In this case, the proper amount of intimacy is conserved by compensating with one set of immediacy cues for an overadjustment in another set. The point is particularly applicable to everyday public lives where interaction contexts cross the boundaries of intimacy that we may feel comfortable with: the person who leans too closely in talking with us; the conversation held in the crowded elevator, and so forth.

KINESICS

Efforts to establish a lexicon of kinesics have involved searching for those motions of body, limb, face, and eye that are informative about our moods, intentions, and feelings. One of the most extensive research programs in this regard has been undertaken by Paul Ekman and his associates (Ekman & Friesen, 1969; 1971; 1974; Ekman, Friesen, & Ellsworth, 1972). Through the use of motion pictures, videotape, and still photos, the Ekman team has sought to demonstrate both the meaning of movements and their universality. Ekman and Friesen (1971) contend that there are cross-cultural universals in the facial expression of emotions. Their research strategy has been to identify in one culture the emotional meaning that is conveyed by various facial gestures. Although their method varies in different studies, in general, they have their subjects match photos of faces with emotions, checking the results in a variety of different cultural contexts.

Preliminary investigations indicated the existence of several universals in the emotions that facial gestures communicated. That work, however, had been open to the criticism that the several cultures studied had all been exposed either to mass media or Western civilization in sufficient doses to possibly create the homogenization of reporting that the investigators discovered. For purposes of establishing a lexicon of facial gestures, universality even of this sort would still be important. However, Ekman and his colleagues were intent in demonstrating that the universality was more innate than learned; thus they sought out cultural groups that had only minimal contact with Western or Eastern civilization.

They selected two isolated groups in New Guinea for study. Their results for both children and adults in the cultures studied indicate sufficient uniformity with results from the other cultures studied to warrant their proposition "that particular facial behaviors are universally associated with particular emotions" (Ekman & Friesen, 1971, p. 128).

For this research, they asked their subjects (members of the Fore linguistic-cultural group of New Guinea) to point out the picture that contained the emotion conveyed in various stories that they were told. Stories covered such emotions as happiness (e.g., his friends have come and he is happy), sadness (e.g., her child has died and she feels very sad), anger, surprise, disgust, fear. The data are based on the degree to which subjects identify the correct picture, that is, the one that depicts the emotion conveyed in the story. Results show that with the exception of discriminating fear from surprise (which they could not readily do), correct pictures were chosen by both the adults and the children of the Fore group. These results compare almost exactly with those obtained from more Westernized groups. It is on this basis that Ekman and Friesen were led to conclude that there must exist some universality in the connection between specific emotions and particular facial behaviors.

Microexpressions. Ekman's (1968) investigations of micromomentary facial expressions (MME) is an especially exciting development in the study of kinesic communication. If an interview is filmed and then the film is run very slowly, certain components of the gestural act will become visible. These components are MMEs. Some of Ekman's work has demonstrated a striking and informative discrepancy between a person's verbal message and the MMEs that are generated. For example, a patient is filmed stating several times in succession, "I don't hate him any more." When the film is slowed down considerably and played back, the patient's gestures and MMEs now become strikingly apparent. The patient's hand movements appear to be like a clenched fist or claw moving backwards along the arm of her chair; and her face, especially her mouth moves up in a hateful sneer, belying the statement, "I don't hate him anymore."

Nonverbal Leakage. Ekman and his colleagues have also been interested in what they term *nonverbal leakage*—nonverbal cues that inform us, for example, that P is telling a lie. The person may have good control over verbal behavior, proclaiming "I am not a crook," yet, the sense we observers have is of someone not quite telling the truth; the person nonverbally leaks the message. Ekman suggested that body information is under less conscious control than head information; thus under circumstances of telling a lie, the body will be more informative of the lie than will head messages. An experiment was created in which O was instructed to withhold information about her emotional upset. Subjects were asked to rate O's affective state after some had seen a film of O's head or O's body. The prediction was that subjects who had seen only head cues would not be able to detect O's actual emotional upset as well as those who saw body cues. Subjects made their ratings on an adjective checklist. Those who had seen O's head described her as sensitive, friendly, cooperative, and self-punishing. Those who had seen O's body, described her more accurately as tense, excitable, high-strung, fearful, and restless.

Some follow-up work (Ekman & Friesen, 1974) further suggested that subjects felt that one who wished intentionally to deceive another should exercise greatest control over their facial gestures. This is supportive of the Ekman thesis that leakage is therefore more likely in the body than in the face which O is attempting to control. The same follow-up study provided further support to the contention that observers will be better able to detect another's deception from body than from facial cues. This was true, however, only when the observers could compare O's being honest with O's being deceptive.

MORE ON EMOTION: SOME COMMUNICATE MORE ACCURATELY THAN OTHERS

As we noted, Ekman's approach focuses on nonverbal information that inadvertently gives P (the receiver or decoder) information about O's (the sender's or encoder's) actual feelings. His concern with the accuracy of these inadvertent nonverbal messages is based primarily on the bodily source of this information: that is, body cues are more informative than head cues. Others who have also been interested in the nonverbal communication of emotion (e.g., Buck, Savin, Miller, & Caul, 1972; Buck, Miller & Caul, 1974; Lanzetta & Kleck, 1970) have employed a variation of an encoder-decoder research technique in order to determine other factors involved in communication accuracy, in particular, characteristics of the sender and of the receiver. In this work that we will examine, bodily source is restricted to the face and upper body.

Although the method of study has varied in its detail across several different investigations, the outlines for this approach to the study of emotional communication remain essentially the same. A sender undergoes an emotionally arousing experience; a receiver sees the sender on videotape or by means of closed-circuit TV. The task of the receiver is to indicate the emotional experience of the sender. One of the initial uses of this approach used animals as subjects (e.g., Miller, 1967 Miller et al, 1967). The sending animal is initially trained to press a bar in response to a visual stimulus in order to avoid an electric shock. After this learning, the sender is paired with a receiver who can see the sender's face. In these paired sessions, if the receiver can accurately read the emotions being expressed by the sender in response to the visual stimulus, then the receiver can press the bar to avoid the shock for both of them. The research suggests that the sender's facial gestures in response to the visual stimulus that indicates that a shock is forthcoming does accurately communicate to the receiver so that the receiver can press the bar and spare them both the shock.

Lanzetta and Kleck (1970) adapted this method for use with human subjects. Their senders first underwent a training session in which they learned that the onset of a red light would be followed by a shock 12 seconds later, while the onset of a green light indicated a nonshock learning trial. During this learning period, and unknown to them, they were videotaped from the waist up. In later sessions, receivers were shown the tapes and asked to indicate, before they could see whether the sender received a shock or not, whether a given trial they viewed was shock or nonshock. When they were incorrect, they received a mildly irritating shock. In addition, the experimenters obtained measures of the sender's physiological arousal, obtained by attaching them to an apparatus that measured their skin conductance.

Several interesting findings emerged from the Lanzetta and Kleck research:

1. Senders communicated nonverbally whether they were in a shock or nonshock setting in that receivers were able to read the situation better than a chance guess would have provided.
2. Not only did receivers make judgments about others; but in addition, all receivers got a chance to see their own videotapes when they were senders. Analyses of these data suggested that persons were no better in receiving from themselves than in receiving from others. In other words, subjects were not especially more sensitive to their own nonverbal than to other's nonverbal behaviors. Recall, of course, that our own nonverbal behavior tends to be beyond our own awareness.
3. Data also suggested an inverse relationship between physiological arousal and judgmental accuracy. Those who were the most

physiologically responsive to the threatened shock were the least good senders of their emotional state; others made more judgmental errors when evaluating those who were most physiologically responsive to the stimuli than when evaluating stimuli from persons whose physiological responsiveness was low.

We shall follow up this last finding as it suggests a connection between responsiveness at one level of functionoing (e.g., the physiological) and nonresponsiveness at another (e.g., the behavioral).

Employing another variant of the same general methodological approach, Buck, Miller, and Caul (1974) further illuminate the nonverbal communication of affect and its physiological correlates. In their design, senders were presented with slides in five different content categories: sexual, scenic, pleasant people, unpleasant, and unusual. They were asked to verbally describe their emotional response to each slide. A receiver watched on closed-circuit TV in an adjoining room but did not hear the sender's behavior during this description period. Senders were also asked to rate the degree of pleasantness of each slide. Receivers were asked to indicate which of the five categories was being viewed by the sender; they were also asked to make their judgments regarding the pleasantness ratings for the sender. Note that these are all judgments that the receiver is to make based on viewing the sender's nonverbal behavior while the sender is viewing the slides. Physiological measures of the sender's skin conductance (as in Lanzetta and Kleck's work) and heart rate were obtained throughout the experiment.

Paralleling the Lanzetta and Kleck study, the present investigators report nonverbal communication of affect between sender and receiver at a level significantly better than chance. The receivers were able to make reasonably accurate judgments both of the category of the slide that the sender was viewing and of the sender's ratings of pleasantness.

Perhaps even more interesting and important than the preceding finding were the data involving individual and group differences. Buck and his colleagues report an overall group difference: female sender-receiver pairs produced more accuracy of communication than the all-male pairs. An analysis comparing sex with position of sender or of receiver suggests the source of this difference lies in the greater nonverbal responsiveness of female senders as compared with that of male senders. Thus, while male and female receivers did not produce differential amounts of accuracy, when females were senders there was greater accuracy than when males were senders.

Related to this sex difference in communication accuracy, Buck and colleagues also report the same kind of physiological finding that Lanzetta and Kleck uncovered. The more physiologically responsive the person, the less successful the nonverbal communication of affect; the less physiologically responsive the person, the more successful the nonverbal communication of affect. Female senders tended to be less physiologically responsive than male senders. In analyzing these last findings, Buck, Miller, and Caul turned to earlier literature on physiology and emotion, calling on two person-concepts introduced in 1935 by Jones: *externalizers* and *internalizers.*

Externalizers are persons generally characterized by their high level of overt emotional expressiveness (e.g., many facial gestures when experiencing emotional arousal) but a low level of physiological responsiveness (e.g., as measured by skin conductance and heart rate fluctuations under emotional arousal). Internalizers are persons characterized by the opposite pattern: low levels of overt expressiveness but high levels of physiological arousal. A sender who is not overtly expressive when confronted with emotionally arousing material cannot as accurately communicate the state of his or her feelings as a sender who is more openly expressive; the internal, physiological expressiveness does not get communicated. Thus, internalizers were less accurate senders. Buck and associates also found that even in describing their emotional state, internalizers used more impersonal verbal descriptions. Note that physiologically, internalizers were emotionally aroused; it is primarily in terms of their verbal and nonverbal modes that this arousal is not communicated.

Several interpretations have been put forward in an effort to understand the bases for this internalizer-externalizer difference. In one view of the apparent sex differences found, males in U.S. society are taught to inhibit their overt emotional expressiveness while females are given permission to more openly display their emotions. This view assumes that when one channel of expression is thwarted, in this case by cultural learnings and continuing sanctions, another channel for expression will emerge; physiological activity and overt behavior are assumed to be substitutable modes for reducing tension. Another approach to understanding this relationship argues that when persons are punished by overtly expressing an emotion, they learn to inhibit its expression; but at the same time, the punishment is physiologically arousing. If males are punished for being overtly emotional, this view reasons, they will thereby learn to inhibit the overt expression but remain physiologically aroused. Females, on the other hand, are less punished for overt expressions and thus do not inhibit the overt response nor develop any necessary physiological correlate in the absence of punishment.

Mehrabian's Approach. Mehrabian's program of research on non-verbal communication has provided further specification of the meaning of various patterns of postural and gestural cues (see Mehrabian, 1971, for a summary). The lexicon of the nonverbal that Mehrabian suggests has three meaning referents: liking or evaluation; power or status; and general responsiveness to another. These three referents, in turn, are related to nonverbal immediacy cues, postural relaxation, and overall nonverbal activity.

Immediacy cues, as we have already seen indicate the degree to which the relationship is evaluated positively or negatively; high immediacy communicates greater liking and sustains that relationship: for example, physical proximity, eye contact, body orientations towards rather than away or at a sharp angle to the other person.

Postural relaxation has been found to provide meanings about status relationships. In general, one is nonverbally more relaxed with someone of inferior status and less relaxed with someone of superior status. Nonverbal postural cues of such relaxation include the asymmetrical placement of arms and legs, body leaning to the side or reclining if seated, and specific relaxation of limbs and neck, as well as rocking movements and leg and foot movements.

Finally, overall nonverbal activity has been found to have the meaning of being responsive to the other person. Some research has found, as one example, that P's intention to persuade O of something will increase P's overall level of nonverbal activity; and furthermore, that P's nonverbal activity level itself contributes to P's degree of persuasiveness.

For these three meaning referents, the same point that we have previously made can and should be made once again. In each instance, a relationship is nonverbally defined, expressed, and maintained or transformed. This silent language, then, provides us with an ample source and amount of information that we routinely, usually unconsciously employ in understanding and in sustaining our interpersonal lives.

THE EYES HAVE IT

In most human encounters, as we have already noted, the face is one of the most important senders of kinesic cues. And on the face, the eyes take on a special importance. As the sociologist Simmel stated:

Of the special sense organs, the eye has a uniquely sociological function. The union and interaction of individuals is based upon mutual glances ... So tenacious and subtle is this union that ... the smallest deviation from it, the slightest glance aside, completely destroys the unique

*character ... By the same act in which the observer seeks to
know the observed, he surrenders himself to be understood
by the observer. The eye cannot take unless at the same time
it gives* (1921, p. 358).

Ralph Exline (1963; 1971; Exline, Gray and Schuette, 1965; Exline
& Winters, 1965) has made the eyes, and in particular the gazes of
power and of affiliation, a central area of his investigation. He
sought to determine, for example, what degree of eye contact was
experienced as being most comfortable under conditions of speaking, of listening, and of mutual silence. His preliminary results indicated that contact 50 percent of the time (rather than 0 percent or
100 percent) was reported to be the most comfortable; that although
it is desirable to have eye contact while either speaking or listening,
silence should be accompanied by no contact.

As we would expect, the content of a discussion influences the
kind of eye contact that is sought and is experienced as comfortable.
Exline reports little eye contact during task-oriented discussions but
more contact when listening than when speaking. However, when
the other person is presumably an interviewer and the content of the
interview tends to be personally derogatory, there is less mutual
glancing than when the content tends to be more complementary.
Additional work on a related point reported by Ellsworth and Carlsmith (1968) suggests that when interaction content is positive, eye
contact results in subjects liking the interviewer, but when the content is negative, less eye contact is felt to be most desirable. In other
words, when discussing things that are not favorable, P prefers to do
so with someone who does not establish eye contact. Some more
recent work (Scherwitz & Helmreich, 1973) has opened these
findings to question.

Central to Exline's concern is the relationship between eye contact and power. His data suggest that those with less power look
more at those with high power than vice versa. Further investigations indicated that subjects who were concerned about having
power and control over others but who could not capture the gaze
of the other person, tended to interpret their failure in terms of the
other person's being more powerful than they. If the formula is "low
looks to high," then looking but not receiving must mean that one
is thereby "low."

Some rather fascinating human-monkey eye contact studies reported by Exline and relevant to the meaning of eye contact and
power suggest that the mutual exchange of glances between humans and the rhesus macaque is a dominance challenge; and that
this challenge can be reduced by the human averting eye contact.
Without aversion of gaze, threat display will be triggered; thus gaze
aversion inhibits this triggering mechanism. While generalizations

across species or between humans and animals are usually fraught with difficulties and error, one cannot help but see parallels in human interaction. Goffman's (1963a) analyses of behavior in public places, for example, suggests that to gaze at another person for a period of some few seconds is to violate a rule of *civil inattention,* sending any one of several messages to the other person. The results of the human-monkey research suggest that one of these messages might be a dominance challenge; thus agression either as a display or in fact may be the result of staring too long at another person. Of course, there are other possibilities, including creating such discomfort that the other persons think something must be wrong with them, or perhaps with you.

The Nonverbal and the Symbolization of Experience

It has long been recognized that bodily movements play an important role in what Ekman has called "accenting" speech, dramatizing and emphasizing a particular point that is being made. It has also been known that there is a motor spill over of the buildup of tension connected with verbally formulating an idea. For example, if the person has some difficulty in expressing something, this difficulty is itself communicated not only by hesitations in speech itself, but also in a variety of accompanying kinesic body movements. As a simple exercise demonstrative of this point, try to explain the word "twist" to someone; it is likely that your verbal explanation will have a considerable kinesic component, as your body helps convey the notion of "twist."

The relationship between speech and such body movements has been of growing interest to a variety of investigators. Several have sought to determine if there is a definite correspondence between the rhythmic patterning of speech and the movements of the body. Some of the research of Dittmann and Llewellyn (1969), has suggested, for example, that body movements appear early in the formulation of speaking and in addition follow hesitations in speech. This has led Dittmann and Llewellyn to argue that movements must play a role in the process of encoding speech, whereby thoughts and feelings are transformed into words.

Building on this same notion, Freedman, Blass, Rifkin, and Quitkin reported in 1973 the results of a careful investigation of the relationship between body movements and the verbal expressions of aggression. Freedman and his associates differentiated between movements that were object-focused and those that were bodily-focused. What they term *speech-primacy gestures* are an example of the former and include "movements that punctuate and qualify what is said but do not represent the content of the thought itself." The body-focused movement of special interest to their investigation involves hand-to-hand motions: "a continuous rubbing and stroking of the hands onto each other repetitively without any effort to depict what is being said."

The question to which their research directed itself concerned the relationship between these two kinds of kinesic gestures and the verbal expression of either overt or covert aggression. They hypothesized that there would be a correspondence between overt aggression and object-focused movements and a correspondence between covert aggression and bodily-focused movements. Their reasoning for this prediction was based on two things: the results of prior research that suggested that object-focused movements accompanied more complex and highly differentiated speaking; and the theoretical view that a direct expression of aggression demanded substantial differentiation between the speaker and the object or person who is the target of one's aggression.

Subjects for their study were twenty-four female college students brought in to be interviewed by a research psychiatrist and asked to talk without interruption about something that was personally meaningful and significant to them. These interviews were all videotaped and later the content was analyzed for both the two major types of kinesic movements and the degree of overt or covert hostility that was expressed. An example of a statement that was coded as being overtly hostile is, "I felt an aversion to him from the very first"; a statement of covert hostility, "The police handcuffed her boyfriend before carrying him into emergency." In these two examples, hostility is scored as overt in that it is an expression of the speaker about someone else; it is scored as covert if the hostility is attributed to someone else, or if hostility is denied (e.g., "but he didn't mind it at all").

The results provided support for the predictions in that those subjects who scored high in object-focused movements expressed more overt verbal aggressiveness than those low in such movements, while subjects high in body-focused movements expressed more covert hostility than those low in such movements. A further analysis of the actual rhythmic correspondence between movement type and the type of aggression also indicated that during peaks of speech-primacy movements (i.e., object-focus), there was more overt hostility expressed than during valleys; during peaks of hand-to-hand kinesic activity (i.e., body-focus), there was more covert hostility expressed than during valleys.

In addition to uncovering the correspondence between emotional expression and type of bodily movement, Freedman and his colleagues were able to further demonstrate that when hostility was being openly expressed in an intensive manner, bodily movements tended to diminish at that moment, but to rise in frequency either before the verbal expression or afterwards. The authors reasoned from this and the other data they presented, that body movements participated in the process of symbolizing aggressive experience; the movements that preceded overt and intense verbal expression helped pave the way for such expression. In other words, the movements actually facilitated the symbolization of the experience.

Although their actual evidence is not direct, their data nevertheless are suggestive of what they term "an envelope of kinetic behavior" that surrounds the symbolization and expression of feeling states such as hostility and aggression. There is a kind of kinesic buildup preceding the symbolization that may function to anticipate what will be verbalized and facilitate its expression. These nonverbal gestures, then are not a separate language system, a kind of nonverbal lexicon of hostility, but rather are one phase of a total process whereby the persons symbolize their experiences. If we recall that in the beginning was not the word but the body movement, we can better understand the continuing role that such movements play in the formulation of our experiences.

RHYTHM: VERBAL AND NONVERBAL

Some of the most interesting work that has focused on the relationship between speech rhythm and nonverbal behavior has been reported by Condon and Ogston (1966) who have demonstrated that "the body of the speaker dances in time with his speech. Further, the body of the listener dances in rhythm with that of the speaker" (p. 338). That simple summary of their research reveals a fascinating relationship between the individual's speech rhythm and body movements, and between interacting individuals in which the other's body dances to P's speech.

> Thus, a person speaks, blending elements of sound into wider syntactic patterns, "while" the arms and fingers move —and these body parts move in ordered configurations of change in relation to these segments of sound (pp. 341–342).

And, as O listens to P, O shows patterns of changing body movements that are synchronized with those of the speaker. Yet, perhaps even more fascinating to ponder are Condon's results for schizophrenics that showed both a self-dyssynchrony and a self-other or interactional dyssynchrony: that is, the body movement was out of synch to one's own speech as well as to another's speech.

One can readily see in Condon's work the same kind of conclusion that Freedman and his colleagues, and Dittmann and Llewyllan have suggested:

> *Human expression appears to be a function of both speech and body motion inextricably locked together within the flow of behavior, reinforcing and counterpointing one another* (p. 345).

All of these perspectives suggest that there must exist some underlying organizational principles that unify these diverse forms of behavior into the patterns that we observe, in which we participate, and through which we become part of an interpersonal system.

The threads that tie P and O together while they are interacting have perhaps never become more visible than with these investigations of Condon and his associates. If Lewin has given us a view of interdependence as a tie based on tension systems, this present formulation gives us a sense of interdependence as a tie of synchrony between P's speech and O's body movements.

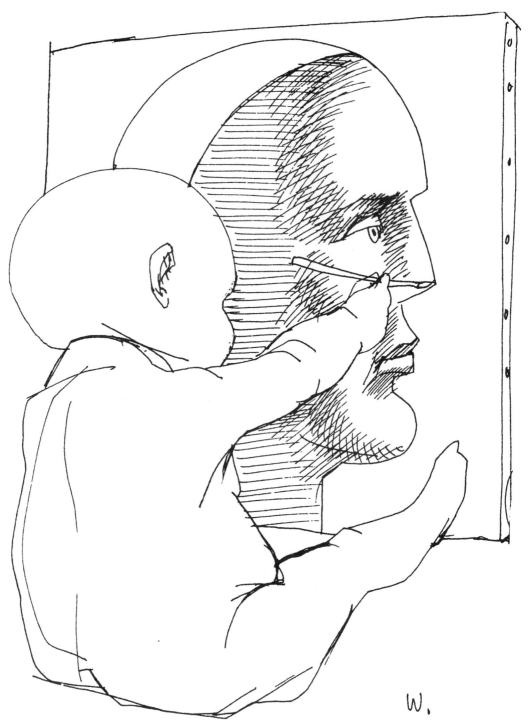

HOWARD WARSHAW, "THE CENTER MAGAZINE."

IDENTITY AND SELF

6

"Each to each a looking-glass Reflects the other that doth pass"

With this Emersonian couplet, C. H. Cooley (1902) introduces us to the social self as a looking-glass or mirrored view of who we are. And thus are we introduced to a concept and a perspective that lies at the heart of much social psychological inquiry. For Cooley, this mirrored self consists of three elements: how we think we appear to others; how we think they evaluate that appearance; the feeling of shame or pride that results. It is paradoxical yet true that our very selves, this something that is seemingly so unique and so personal a possession, has its roots and its continuing existence in an interpersonal process in which others play a vital role. The concept of self, therefore is truly social psychological, the key juncture between person and society.

William James (1910), who had much to say about the self, differentiates between a material self (e.g., the body, clothing, home), a spiritual self (e.g., a core sense of *me*), and a social self, similar to Cooley's looking-glass notion. Along with Cooley, James recognizes that there are as many kinds of social selves as there "are distinct *groups* of persons about whose opinion" (in Gordon & Gergen, 1968, p. 42) we care. Our "me" is reflected differently in different human mirrors.

So vital is this social self that in James's view, there could be "no more fiendish punishment" than to "be turned loose in society and remain unnoticed by all" (in Gordon & Gergen, p. 42); to speak but not be heard; to enter a room and not be seen; to have our very existence nullified as though we were invisible. Ralph Ellison (1952) describes this "fiendish" state:

> I am an invisible man ... I am invisible, understand, simply
> because people refuse to see me ... it is as though I have been
> surrounded by mirrors of hard, distorting glass ... That
> invisibility to which I refer occurs because of a peculiar
> disposition of the eyes of those with whom I come in contact ... I
> am not complaining ... It is sometimes advantageous to be

A version of some material in this Chapter originally appeared in E. E. Sampson, "Studies of Status Congruence", in L. Berkowitz (Ed.), Advances in Experimental Social Psychology, Vol. 4. New York: Academic Press, 1969.

> *unseen, although it is most often rather wearing on the nerves. Then too, you're constantly being bumped against ... Or again, you doubt if you really exist ... It's when you feel like this that, out of resentment, you begin to bump people back ... You ache with the need to convince yourself that you do exist in the real world, that you're part of all the sound and anguish, and you strike out with your fists, you curse and you swear to make them recognize you. And, alas, it's seldom successful* (pp. 7–8).

If our sense of who we are, our self, is defined by others, when those others do not take notice of us, their act of nullification can lead us, as with Ellison's invisible man, to doubt even our own existence. Ellison's invisible man sought to create his existence as a self in society by bumping people, by striking out at them, and in this manner hoping to receive the notice that is requisite to knowing who one is or that one is.

An Interactionist Perspective on Self and Identity

The interactionist perspective to understanding the development and the maintenance of a person's self or identity (and we shall use these terms interchangeably) derives from the important writings of G. H. Mead (1934), C. H. Cooley and others of the Chicago School of Sociology, as well as the analyses of H. S. Sullivan (1953) and the Washington School of Psychiatry, among others. This perspective can be summarized in the form of three major propositions:

1. The self is lodged or situated in an interpersonal, social process;
2. The self is to be understood as a process or activity rather than as something thing-like;
3. The stability of the self, so fundamental to individual and to collective well being, requires achieving and maintaining a stability of the interpersonal, social process.

It will be helpful to our understanding of the concept of self, if we examine the preceding propositions and their several implications.

THE SITUATED SELF

The self is lodged or situated in an interpersonal, social process. Recall the discussion in Chapter 2 of G. H. Mead's symbolic interactionist model in which the key idea about human interaction was the role that symbols, especially language, played in calling out in P what was called out in O, thereby permitting P and O to interact rather than simply to react. The point that Mead makes is that P's symbolic gesture (e.g., what P says in talking with O) indicates a behavior to which O responds; it is O's response that completes the social act that P's gesture initiated; it is O's response that endows P's gesture with meaning. Insofar as P can take O's position and thereby relate to P's own gestures as O might, engaging in what Mead calls a "conversation of gestures" (i.e., thinking), P is able to modify behavior in anticipation of O's probable response—that is, in terms of their meaning for O; thereby P and O are able to interact and to coordinate their behaviors. In taking O's role, P sees himself or herself as a "me," as an object from O's standpoint.

Mead's formulation of the complete social act and the emergence of meaning within social interaction, is very similar to Sullivan's conception. For both theorists, the meaning of a gesture does not inhere in the words used but rather in the response evoked. Sullivan, a psychiatrist who was especially concerned with faulty communication, suggested that,

> communicative behavior miscarries because words do not carry meaning, but evoke meaning. And if a word evokes in the hearer something quite different from that which it was expected to evoke, communication is not a success (p. 184)

The key notion for our present purposes is that words evoke meanings rather than carry meanings. That is, P's gestures (e.g., words) are meaningful insofar as they evoke a response from O. It is O's response that completes the social act and gives P's gestures their meaning.

A helpful example that Sullivan offers is of the crying infant. It is the parent's interpretation that the crying represents something that the infant needs rather than the crying per se that provides meaning to the gesture of crying. The parent's response completes the social act initiated by the infant's crying and provides the meaning for that gesture. In time, children learn that crying means parents will help by virtue of having learned to see their own gestures from the parent's perspective. In similar manner, because we are able to represent others' responses to our own gestures, we are able to interact meaningfully. Mead termed this process taking the role of the other; the process permits P to view self as an object seen from the standpoint of that other, O.

Meanings as Emergents.   The role that others play in the process whereby gestures and objects take on meaning by now should be clear. The next point stressed by Mead, by those who followed his theoretical line, and by Sullivan and others of his persuasion, is that meanings are not properties that inhere either in gestures or in objects as such, but rather are emergent properties of the interpersonal process of social interaction. To phrase this another way, the meanings of gestures and of objects are situated in social interaction. Thus, for example, crying is meaningful because of the response it evokes in the parent (or others); a chair is a meaningful object as a piece of furniture because of the response made of sitting in it. Introducing a chair to someone who had never before seen anything like it, whose response was to jump on it, break it into pieces, and toss it into the fire, would provide another meaning for chair. The point is that meanings are constituted within social interaction rather than being contained within the object or the gesture itself.

Significant and Generalized Others.   The meaning that the self has is likewise constituted within social interaction; and thus it is said that the self is situated within the social process. Indeed, as we recall from our discussion in Chapter 2, it is the individual who thinks, feels, and acts and who has a self or an identity. But the meaning for that self emerges through the interaction between person and others, and in this sense we may say that the self is situated in social interaction. In taking the role of the other and seeing self as a me from O's perspective, P becomes an object whose meaning emerges on the basis of O's response. In Mead's developmental analysis, P's self is initially constituted on the basis of seeing self from the perspective of a set of specific, significant others, such as mother, father, siblings, playmates and such. Over time, Mead posits the capacity to see one's self from a more abstract community or societal standpoint that he terms the *generalized other.*

In order to convey a sense of self that is constituted in terms of this generalized other, Mead asks us to focus on a distinction he draws between *play* and *the game.* Children and even adults may engage in play behavior, putting on this role or that, playing at being a doctor, a lawyer, a mother, a father. In a game, however, the person must not only take on the role of each of the participants and define self from their different points of view, but in addition, must so organize the participants' different perspectives that they interpenetrate and relate one to the other.

In examining Mead's analysis, Swanson (1974) suggests that while play-like situations permeate all of our social relationships, requiring primarily that we take account of the views and acts of others, game-like situations require that we do something more: we must integrate these different points of view "under a whole of which they are but aspects" (p. 463). Returning again to our discussion of Chapter 2, we can say that the game is organized in the same manner as an interactive field; it is a whole with parts that are interdependent such that a change in one affects the others and hence the whole. In the game, the person is aware of these field properties and thus of the relationship not only between the person's own behavior and that of the separate others who are likewise involved in the game, but of their joint relationship to the whole game of which they are each parts.

Mead uses several examples to communicate this important distinction between play and the game. In hide-and-seek, one is either hunter or hunted; thus it is possible to play at being hunted by hiding from the hunter, trying to guage one's own hiding from the perspective of the hunter (e.g., if I were the hunter would I think of looking for me here?). But in such a game, there is really little need to integrate one's own behavior with those of multiple others. Thus hide-and-seek is more play-like than game-like. In baseball, however, the organization of these multiple perspectives becomes vital.

> *He must know what everyone else is going to do in order to carry out his own play ... at some moments he has to have three or four individuals present in his own attitude, such as the one who is going to throw the ball, the one who is going to catch it, and so on* (1934, p. 228).

The point Mead makes is that the separate perspectives that one takes in the game are organized "into a sort of unit, and it is that organization which controls the responses of the individual" (p. 231). In the baseball example, each of P's own actions is controlled

> *by his being everyone else on that team, at least insofar as those attitudes affect his own particular response. We get then an "other" which is an organization of the attitudes of those involved in the same process.*

> *The organized community or social group which gives to the individual his unity of self may be called "the generalized other." The attitude of the generalized other is the attitude of the whole community* (p. 233).

Thinking involves an internal conversation of gestures in which P takes the perspective of the generalized other; in essence, language and abstract concepts evoke this generalized standpoint. We can note here the similarity between Mead and our earlier discussion in Chapter 4 of both Kelley and Schutz on attribution theory. Their notion of causal schema or typifications basically involves thinking in terms of meanings evoked by generalized others: that is, in terms of what anyone knows.

By Way of Summary.   To repeat, the point is that the person's self or identity is situated within the social process. When we think of ourselves, make evaluative judgments about ourselves, comment on ourselves, learn about ourselves from our behavior, and so forth, we do so by engaging the social process, by seeing ourselves and attributing meaning to ourselves, from the perspective of a generalized other. In an ongoing encounter, we engage the social process and see ourselves from the perspective of the specific others who are involved, whose roles we take and whose attitudes we adopt for defining and giving meaning to ourselves as "me's." The importance of this framework for viewing the self as situationally and socially lodged will become more apparent as we examine the issue of stability of self. But before we can do that, we must deal with the notion of the self as a process rather than as a thing-like structure.

THE SELF AS PROCESS

Both Mead and Sullivan are clear in their emphasis on the self as a process—and as we have seen as an *interpersonal* process—rather than as a psychological structure with thing-like qualities. Sullivan most strongly states the case in his description of personality as *"the most enduring pattern of recurrent interpersonal situations which characterize a human life"* (pp. 110–111). While the concept of personality extends beyond the concept of self, Sullivan's process-definition nevertheless makes it clear that the personality (and self) is an interpersonal process, rather than a thing. Indeed, Sullivan chose to refer to the self as a "self-system," seeing it as a major dynamism (his process term for mechanism) for securing satisfaction and avoiding anxiety in our interpersonal relationships.

Our language uses noun or pronoun forms to talk about the person, personality, the self, I, me, and so on; it thereby conveys a thing-like quality for what is better understood in verb-like process terms. This distinction was ably captured by Alan Watts (1961) in his effort to relate Eastern and Western thought. Watts noted how Western language forms compel us to focus on the actor who is engaging in some activity, rather than focusing on the activity or process. This is just the point made in the Whorfian analysis of linguistic relativity (Chapter 5). Whorf noted, for example, that the favorite type of English sentence is actor-action; so strong is this tendency that we insert an actor into certain sentences even when it is not clear that any actor is involved: for example, "It's raining." We might say that to view the self as a process is to place our stress upon the interactivities that are involved rather than upon the thing that acts.

Self as a System.   Basically, to view the self as a process is to focus upon the self as a system. The following diagram summarizes several different though related conceptions that parallel this view of the self in process terms as a system.

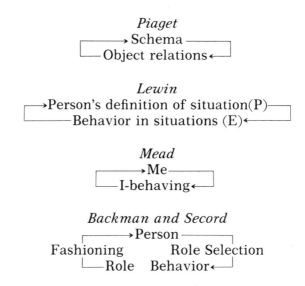

Recall that all systems have elements and relationships between those elements. In the case of the self-system, the elements are the two major aspects or phases of the interactive process that constitute the self. In the examples presented, one phase of the total process refers to some preliminary formulation of behavior (e.g., schema, definition of the situation, me, person); the other phase refers to ongoing behavior itself (e.g., object relations, behavior in situation, I-behaving, role behavior). The self emerges within this total process: that is, from the interaction between organizing principle and ongoing behavior.

In Piaget's analysis (Chapter 3), a cognitive schema transforms the objects with which the person relates (called assimilation) and in turn is transformed by the manner of the person's utilization of those objects (called accommodation). We would be totally egocentric selves if assimilative processes were the total picture: that is, if we related to the world entirely in terms of our internal schema. It is the interaction with things in our world (especially other people) that frees us from this egocentrism as we are forced to accommodate our points of view in the light of those of others.

In Lewin's analysis, the person defines the situations in which his or her behavior occurs; in turn, those situations in which the behaving occurs define the person. In Mead's analysis, the organization of other's standpoints, the self as a *me,* both influences P's emerging behavior (i.e., the I), and is influenced by that behavior. Finally, Backman and Secord (1968) see person-factors influencing the situational roles one selects which in turn fashion the person. In each instance, an interactional relationship—that is, a process—exists where elements both define and are defined by the total process. Therefore, one cannot readily locate the self in any one part of the total—neither in P nor in E; nor can one say that the self is a thing as such. We use nouns to describe what is fundamentally a verb (or perhaps a gerund) in form.

The outcome of these interactions between P and E is what we call the self or the person's identity; it is not a thing, but a process that involves various phases. These are phases in a social process, recall, not simply things located within the person. While this formulation may be complex, requiring the student to recognize that we are dealing with an interactive process rather than a static entity, it is nevertheless an important and necessary way of conceptualizing self and identity.

Perhaps the best way to provide greater clarity to both of the preceding propositions is to move directly into an examination of the implications of this formulation for the stability or change of self.

STABILITY AND CHANGE IN SELF OR IDENTITY

There are three preliminary points to be made:
1. The self plays a major role in personal and societal well-being. It is especially implicated in what are best termed mastery functions, whereby the person becomes competent in handling the manifold issues required for organized social living and human survival. (Our previous discussion of effectance and consistency in Chapter 3 is relevant in this context.)
2. Stability of the self is more likely to facilitate the achievement and maintenance of such mastery than instability.
3. In that the self is lodged within an interpersonal process, stability of the self is in great part a function of achieving or managing a stability of the interpersonal process.

In Sullivan's view, the self-system is the major dynamism whereby we learn to control our interpersonal experiences. The self-system emerges as we learn how to live with significant others (e.g., mother, father, etc.), to secure from them the kinds of satisfactions that meet our needs, and to minimize the disruptive quality of excessive anxiety. Mead's analysis emphasizes the interpersonal coordination and social control that is requisite for the maintenance of the social order, and thus the individual as well. The development of the self makes it possible for persons to engage in cooperative ventures that establish and maintain the social order. Simply put, there could be neither a game of baseball nor hide-and-seek, neither society nor individual, were it not possible for persons to engage in role taking and anchor their own behaviors in the interpersonal process. Society would not exist; thus neither would the individual. In Mead's view, the social order makes it possible for individual selves to emerge, just as these selves make it possible for the social order to continue.

If we think of the self as instrumental in these mastery functions, it seems reasonable that a stable sense of self is more likely to facilitate such mastery than an unstable identity. Much as object constancy is an accomplishment that permits the person to live within a world having continuity, permitting an experience of not here and not now (see Chapter 3), a constancy of self likewise can be seen as an accomplishment that permits continuity between experiences within the general flux of all things, a semblence of order in what would otherwise prove chaotic and anxiety-producing. Stability of self-definition then becomes instrumental to a person's individual and society's collective well-being. A great deal of human social behavior can be understood in these terms as an effort to achieve and to maintain a stable identity.

Our trust in others is founded on an implicit assumption "that a person will not contradict that which he seems to be" (Gergen, 1968, p. 300). We behave towards others and in turn are responded to by others in terms of the conceptions we have of them and they of us. When their behavior and ours is consistent with such conceptions, interaction can flow smoothly and a trusting relationship can be established. Stability of our percept of others and theirs of us, therefore, helps to constitute a world that is sufficiently trustworthy to be predictable and not in a state of capricious flux. As Piaget (1950) has noted, we all operate under an obligation not to contradict ourselves so that both interaction and cooperation may proceed and that a sense of verifiable objectivity can emerge.

Ralph Turner (1968) calls our attention to another, related perspective regarding the important personal, interpersonal, and societal mastery function that a stable self-concept allows. To paraphrase his idea, Turner maintains that as social beings we need to have a concept of self as part of the human equation in order to deal with issues of responsibility—that is, of credit and of blame. The self is that social object "that warrants the assignment of credit and responsibility" (p. 105); it is "the basis for social control" (p. 105) in that its stability over an extended period of time permits a determination to be made (by the individual of self and by others of that individual) of responsibility, of credit for positive things accomplished and of blame for negative activities. In other words, a stable concept of self is a requisite to issues of social control and thus to the establishment and the maintenance of the social order itself.

Paradoxically, but understandably, given the knowledge that the self is lodged within an interpersonal process, its stability usually requires a stability of that process. Constancies of self, therefore, are accomplishments of interpersonal work. In the view we have taken, a constancy in P's sense of self, the sense of being an enduring personality, the "perception of . . . selfsameness and continuity in time; and the simulataneous perception . . . that others recognize [his or her] sameness and continuity" (Erikson, 1959, p. 23), is to be understood in terms of an "enduring pattern of recurrent interpersonal situations" (Sullivan, 1953, p. 111), rather than the carrying forward of some enduring, internal, psychological structure. This major point bears repeating. That individual security and societal order require a relatively enduring concept of self does not mean that we must seek the roots of that stability entirely within the person; rather, our search requires that we uncover stable modes of interpersonal interaction whereby the object constancy of self is established and maintained.

The person is by no means a passive party to the achievement of a stable self-conception. Admittedly, the view of the self as in part a mirrored image (i.e., the "me") seems to suggest passivity. We will come to see, however, how active we are in seeking out those who will mirror the image we wish to achieve, in behaving in ways that induce our fellow mirrors to confirm the self-conception that we seem dedicated to preserving.

Modes of Self Maintenance

In the discussion that follows we will examine five modes whereby self or identity is sustained in our interpersonal behaviors:
1. selectivity and consistency processes;
2. comparison processes;
3. influence processes;
4. nullification processes;
5. solicitation processes.

SELECTIVITY AND CONSISTENCY PROCESSES

Let us begin with cognitive processes of selectivity and consistency (see Chapter 3). One manner in which P seeks both to establish and to maintain a relatively stable image of self involves a selectivity of attention, of memory and recall, where selectivity may also involve misperception. In the instructive case history of a transsexual, Agnes, who lived her first 17 years as a male, the sociologist Harold Garfinkel (1967) suggests how important it was to Agnes's new identity ("I am a woman") to selectively recall her past history. Most of us cannot readily appreciate the difficulty that must be involved in reconstructing a past in such a way as to highlight events supportive of the present self, while playing down instances that undermine that present. Agnes's problem was to recall a past that did not contain her life as a male. A not too dissimilar problem faces the adolescent who is beginning to take on the identity of an adult and who seeks to redo his or her own history in ways that do not recall infantile or immature past behavior. The problem occurs when teenager, friends, and teenager's parents all convene for casual conversation, recalling past memories, many of which contradict this "idealized biography" that the teenager has recalled, his or her redoing of the past in ways that help sustain the present or desired self image.

As Garfinkel notes:

> *Not only did Agnes directly express the claim, "I have always been a girl," but it was advanced by the device of a remarkably idealized biography in which evidences of her original feminity were exaggerated, while evidences of a mixture of characteristics, let alone clear-cut evidences of a male upbringing, were rigorously suppressed. The child Agnes of Agnes's accounts did not like to play rough games like baseball* (p. 128).

It is important to keep in mind that this redoing of one's past in ways that help affirm a contemporary concept of self need not be nor typically is a conscious or deceitful act. To recall history is not simply to replay a tape; rather, it is the selective reconstruction of a past.

While our emphasis in this discussion has been on individual identities, much the same kind of analysis can be applied to the identities of persons who comprise nations or specific collectivities of persons (e.g., blacks, women, Indians, etc.). In each case, individuals selectively reconstruct their groups history in order to prove consistent with a desired contemporary image. As previously noted (Chapter 4), the victors or master's version of both the past and the present may differ radically from the victim's or slave's version; each version of history, however, redoes the past in the service of some contemporary picture that is desired.

A helpful study of national self-images is provided by White's analysis (1966) of the variety of perceptions and misperceptions involved during the U.S. military involvement in Vietnam. White noted several kinds of self-serving processes that functioned to maintain desired national self-images. White outlines several major types of distortions:

1. *The diabolical-enemy image.* The enemy is viewed as diabolical; he fights dirty and is out to capture the world.

2. *The virile self-image.* The United States is seen as a country that is courageous, firm, and indomitable; those who wish to harm us are seen to be traitors, weaklings, and cowards.
3. *The moral self-image.* The United States is seen as the defender of truth, goodness, and freedom, having committed itself to be the guardian of world-wide freedom.
4. *Blindness of involvement.* This is White's summary concept for the tendency of each side to ignore everything on the other side that if noted might force a change in national self-image. It is a kind of tunnel vision that is produced as a nation becomes caught up in war.

It is important to note that while these processes of self-serving selectivity are focused on the national image of the United States, the same kinds of processes were found among the North Vietnamese and their allies as well. National self-images are sustained by means of these and other perceptual-cognitive processes that not only idealize the past, but also rewrite and idealize the present.

Consistency theory (Chapter 3) has taught us that persons tend to operate in ways that promote a degree of consistency between the several elements of their cognitive system. The interpersonal applications of consistency theory—for example, Newcomb's and other related versions of cognitive balance—suggest how cognitive consistency helps accomplish a stable self and identity for P. By liking those who agree with us and thereby associating more with persons who provide affirmation for our views rather than with persons whose disagreement does not offer such affirmation, our pursuit of cognitive balance helps establish an interpersonal world and a concept of self that is relatively stable.

The Bennington coeds that Newcomb and his associates studied offer us a helpful case in point. First, recall how those who had been transformed by their Bennington experience from conservative to liberal accomplished this feat by associating with those persons at the college whose views on the major issues of the day were consistent and thereby confirmatory of their own. Next, note that transformation was sustained on graduation by marrying a liberal whose views would continue to provide a supportive context for the person's own self image.

Using this same notion, Backman and Secord (1968) sought to demonstrate how persons select roles that are congruent with their self image. In a series of several investigations, they examined women's preferences for types of marital roles, occupational role preferences for both males and females, and the selection of college major. In each instance, Backman and Secord sought to determine a correspondence between the person's rating of self on a series of adjective descriptions (e.g., hostile, imaginative, withdrawn, rational, etc.), and characteristics attributed to the roles. In general, their research suggested that people tend to select roles that are affirmatory of self image. Thereby, persons' actively take part in creating conditions that sustain their self images in interpersonal behavior. As Backman and Secord note, their investigations reveal the other side of a two-sided process: the first side involves the influence that roles have upon persons' definition of themselves; this second side indicates how people select roles that reinforce a particular self-definition.

Achievement and Ascription. Some years ago a distinction was made between achieved roles and ascribed roles (Linton, 1936). Occupational roles are an example of achieved roles: that is, those positions within a society that are generally open to individual choice and selection. Ascribed roles, including age and sex roles, for example, are not really open to significant choice, although as with the case of Agnes, even in the realm of sex roles, some degree of choice does exist. This distinction between achieved and ascribed is clearly relevant to the preceding work of Backman and Secord. Generally, we do not expect persons to be able to select ascribed roles that are congruent with their self; selectivity thus applies primarily to achieved roles. With ascription, we could expect a greater shaping effect of the role on the self. Yet we are aware of how age roles, even though ascriptive, can be selected in ways that affirm a person's desired self. The young person who "acts" older or the older person who "acts" younger are examples of persons who are trying to shape their ascribed role in a manner to fit their self-image. At some point in all of our lives, no matter how we may wish to distort ascribed reality, we must yield our selves to the influences of the role —that is, we must recognize that selectivity can only go so far.

Self and Role Congruence. As we might expect, issues involving self and role congruence have been of interest to social psychologists. The research laboratory permits the investigator systematically to examine the effects of incongruence on interpersonal behavior. What happens, for example, if a person is asked to perform a role within a group that is not congruent with that person's self-characteristics? Everyday examples come readily to mind: the shy person who is asked to take charge of a group, the dominant person who is involved in an activity that places him or her into a more submissive role within the group, and so on.

In Chapter 1 (pp. 19–20), we presented two communication networks as descriptions of small group structures that influenced behavior. We indicated that measures of individual satisfaction were a function of the person's position in the network: those with more

central and powerful positions were more satisfied than persons in
positions without power. This was an example of a situation-centered analysis. Relative to our present discussion and its more interactionist view, Hrycenko and Minton (1974) suggest a more
complex view of this matter. They created positions of high and low
power in a communication network, where high power permitted
the person a wide range of control over a group's success in solving
the problem presented to them and low power placed the person in
a position of great dependency on others. They used the internal
versus external locus of control measure (see pp. 492–495 for details)
to differentiate types of individuals. They find that for their male
subjects, those whose personality is not consistent with being in a
position of high power in a communication network (i.e., external
orientation) report being less satisfied when in that position than in
the low power position; and someone whose personality is more
congruent with a high power position (i.e., internal orientation),
prefer that to the low power position. In other words, as we have
noted, when people who do not see themselves as having qualities
compatible with positions of leadership are assigned such positions,
they feel uncomfortable when compared with those for whom leadership positions better fit their personal characteristics.

In another context, Bunker (see Sampson, 1969a) offers us a particularly helpful study of self-role incongruence and its effects on interpersonal behavior. Bunker selected as his experimental task the
electric train board originated by Ghiselli and Lodahl (1958) and
used in several other studies (e.g., Smelser, 1961). In this task, subjects are asked to push buttons and levers that control the movements of two trains and two sidings, to maneuver one train from
position A on the board to position B, while moving the second train
from its home at B to A. The task is one that demands considerable
coordination between the experimental subjects in order to avoid
accidents. Bunker created two job roles in this situation, one involving a high degree of responsibility and decision making (the dispatcher), and one involving lesser responsibility and minimal
decision making (the freight train operator or FTO).

All prospective experimental subjects were given a short form of
a test known as the California Psychological Inventory, which was
used to measure the characteristics of dominance and submission
that were thought to be of relevance to this task situation. To assign
a dominant person to the dominant dispatcher role and a submissive
person to the more submissive FTO-role would provide a case of
self-role congruence; to assign a dominant person to the FTO-role
and the submissive person to the dispatcher role, on the other hand,
would provide a case of self-role incongruence. Bunker composed
his subjects into dyads that were either congruent or incongruent as

indicated above, noting their performance skills in this experimental task. The prediction that incongruence between self and role would prove detrimental to effective group performance was upheld by his results on the number of successful train trips a particular group made.

By assigning roles to his subjects, Bunker essentially created a condition of role ascription rather than role achievement. However, in a very instructive analysis of the incongruent conditions, Bunker suggests how subjects actually sought to change their assigned roles to make them more congruent with their self-characteristics: that is, examples of role selection. Even though the dominant person was assigned the submissive FTO-role and the submissive person the dominant dispatcher role, Bunker reports job changes occurring in some groups. For example, dominant persons transformed the FTO-role into one that was more in accord with their self-characteristics by taking charge of the situation, while the submissive dispatcher let the other person take charge by taking on the dispatcher role in a more submissive way. Self-concepts thus were affirmed in this particular investigation not by P's selecting roles that were congruent with self (because roles were assigned, this couldn't be done), but rather by P's transforming their role performances to fit their self-concept.

COMPARISON PROCESSES

As we have just seen, one way to achieve and maintain a relatively stable identity occurs through the selectivity of interaction choices; we seek interpersonal settings that are consistent with our self-image, thereby affirming it. Recall that the development of our self concept involves a social comparison process in which we learn to see ourselves as significant others see us; others become central sources of information that we turn to in order to evaluate ourselves. In other words we stablize our identity by comparing our ideas, beliefs, attitudes, abilities, personal characteristics, and so forth with those of significant others. A consistency of this social comparison helps provide stability: for example, similarity with liked others and dissimilarity with disliked others serves to affirm and thereby stabilize our identity.

The Asch Study. We know from numerous social psychological investigations that values, attitudes, and judgments are influenced by the viewpoints of those with whom we interact. Two classic investigations deserve to be mentioned in this context. The one study, conducted by Asch (1952), presented groups composed of one naïve subject and up to fifteen accomplices with a perceptual judgment task. All persons enter the experimental room and are seated before a screen on which the experimenter displays a standard-length line and three comparison lines; the task is to indicate by stating out loud which of the comparison lines is closest in size to the standard. The naïve subject is seated in the last position of the line of subjects; the accomplices have been instructed to give an incorrect answer on several critical judgment trails. For example, in the first critical trial each accomplice, in turn, states his or her choice out loud, selecting what is clearly the incorrect comparison line. Suppose the standard line is about 8 inches and the comparison lines are 6 inches, 8 inches, and 6 ½ inches; on a critical trial, the accomplices announce their choice to be the 6 inch line. Being in the last position, the naïve subject experiences considerable pressure either to report what others have apparently seen (the incorrect line), or to begin to doubt his or her visual ability. Asch reports that more than one-third of the naïve subjects gave erroneous judgments; control subjects, not facing this false majority, achieved more than 90 percent accuracy compared to the 67 percent accuracy of subjects in the experimental conditions.

To examine even more extreme deviations from objective reality, Asch used comparison lines that were radically different from the standard: for a standard line of 10 inches, comparison lines of 3, 10, and 2 inches were presented. Again, while a control group achieved almost perfect accuracy, the experimental groups' accuracy was only about 72 percent. These rather striking results suggest how important O's perceptions are for P's own sense of reality. In comparing P's perceptions with those of others, P notes a discrepancy. Is P correct and the fifteen of them incorrect? Are they correct and P simply not seeing well? Asch reports that many subjects actually saw the lines correctly, but in order to avoid the embarrassment of being seen by others as wrong, they publicly yielded to the majority position.

Of those who did not yield to the incorrect majority, many experienced doubt regarding the accuracy of their own judgments. In other words, we are so dependent on others to validate our conceptions of reality (including the reality of our identity), that a comparison that produces differences threatens our sense of stability. Thus we experience pressures to fit into ongoing confirmations of reality, and thus is that reality sustained.

In a valuable variation of this study, Asch had one of the accomplices become a "deviant partner." Instead of facing a unanimous majority, the naïve subject now had a partner who saw as he or she did. Under these conditions, Asch found that subjects were able to stand up in opposition to the majority and utter the correct answer.

Sherif and Autokinesis. Another classic investigation was conducted by Sherif (1935) and involved the *autokinetic effect.* A pinpoint of light in an otherwise totally darkened room appears to be in motion, even though it is in fact stationary: this self-movement is called autokinesis. The situation of a totally darkened room is very ambiguous; one cannot readily judge depth and distance and thus a stationary pinpoint of light could be seen to move. Sherif had subjects estimate how far the light moved during a specified period of time. In some of his experimental conditions, subjects judged the light's movement for several trials alone before they were brought together with others. In the group condition, subjects were asked to announce their judgments out loud. Sherif noted the development of convergences in judgment towards a common judgmental frame, or in his terms, a judgmental norm. Persons who if alone may have diverged in their judgments achieved a judgmental norm after being together in the group. This was especially true of those who had experienced the group situation first. Those who had first established a judgmental norm alone, although affected by the group, were more resistant than those who came into the group without such norms.

Much as with the Asch situation, Sherif's work reveals the social comparison process and its role in the achievement of a stable conception of reality. The important point to consider is that pressures towards uniformity in judgments regarding reality arise within persons who, without this uniformity, would be confused and doubtful about their own capabilities, even about their own identity. Leon Festinger (1954a; b) developed the details of a theory of social comparison, stressing the important function that others play in providing validation and hence stability for our own world views. Am I correct in my view of the world? Do I see what you see? Do we live in the same world? Am I really who I think myself to be? These and related questions are answered *socially:* we turn to others who think as we think, see and know as we see and know, in order to validate our own perspectives. We are who we are because others we know think as we think.

Self and Social Comparison. While the Festinger model and the Asch and Sherif investigations involve perceptual judgments and evaluations of one's abilities, a more direct examination of the role that social comparison processes play with respect to personal identity was reported in 1970 by Morse and Gergen. Subjects who had been recruited in response to an advertisement for a part-time job were placed in a room to complete several application forms and questionnaires. A second job applicant, actually an accomplice of the experimenter, was brought into the same waiting room and presented as another job applicant. For half of the subjects, the accomplice presented a highly desirable personal appearance, which the authors termed Mr. Clean. He was dressed in a dark suit and seemed highly confident of himself; he carried an attache case, several books including statistics and philosophy texts, and so forth. The other half of the subjects were introduced to Mr. Dirty. "He wore a smelly sweatshirt, ripped trousers, no socks, and seemed somewhat dazed by the whole procedure" (p. 150). His reading material consisted of a worn copy of *The Carpetbaggers.*

Morse and Gergen investigated the influence on P's self-concept of being in a comparison situation with a Mr. Clean versus a Mr. Dirty. Their results confirm the prediction that people who compared themselves with Mr. Dirty would increase their evaluations of themselves (i.e., their self-esteem) while those who compared themselves to Mr. Clean would decrease their self-esteem. These results were confirmed. In other words, how the subjects felt about themselves was influenced by the comparison they made between themselves and the other person; they felt good about themselves in comparison to Mr. Dirty and less good about themselves in comparison to Mr. Clean.

A further analysis of their data is even more relevant regarding the role of comparison processes as an interpersonal mode for stabilizing one's identity. Morse and Gergen had independent ratings before the experiment of the degree of similarity between their subjects and Mr. Clean and Mr. Dirty. This made it possible to examine the joint influence of O's characteristics (i.e., Clean versus Dirty) and P's and O's similarity on P's self-esteem. The results indicate that

> the mere presence of another person who is like oneself may be sufficient to boost one's self esteem, while a person who is dissimilar may tend to reduce one's self-estimate. When another is seen to be similar to self, he places a stamp of legitimacy on one's conduct or appearance ... Encountering an individual whose characteristics differ from one's own may initiate a process of self-questioning and doubt (p. 154).

This is very much like Asch's finding involving the deviant partner. In both cases, a stability of self is achieved by virtue of having one's own perspective validated by the presence of another, similar person. Instability is introduced and doubt increased when such allies are either not present or cannot be conjured up. Let us briefly pursue this last point, as it provides a helpful perspective on how P may face up to comparison pressures and not appear to yield.

In suggesting that P may conjure up a comparison O to become a psychological ally, I am not referring to a magical process as the term *conjure* might suggest. Rather I am stressing the point that stability through comparison is so fundamental that persons actively seek and create relevant comparison persons or groups that affirm and sustain themselves, often when actual persons or groups are not present.

Marie Jahoda's (1959) instructive analyses of conformity and independence is directly to this point. Jahoda examines conditions under which P's comparison of self with O leads P to change in order to be more like O (e.g., yielding in an Asch-type situation) or to maintain an independent stance. She concludes her lengthy analysis by noting the importance of P's time perspective in facilitating independence. In particular, she suggests that

only to the extent that the scope of the life space extends beyond the physically given present situation can past experiences, absent reference groups, anticipations of consequences of one's actions, shifts in frame of reference, and other such factors support [P's independent] position (In Sampson, 1964, p. 110).

To the extent that P is dominated by the immediately given situation, yielding rather than independence is more likely. However, to the extent that P is able to place the present situation into a larger context, to bring into play those absent reference groups, P's position and identity can be validated. In so doing, P minimizes the impact of present comparison pressures by perceiving comparison persons who are absent (i.e., and thus conjured up). Recall that the significant others from whose perspective our "me" is constituted, need not be here-and-now present. What Jahoda's analysis informs us is that absent reference persons remain an influential source for maintaining our sense of identity even under present strong comparison pressures.

Reinstating the comparison reference group as a means of increasing P's resistance to yield to immediate pressures has been the focus of several investigations, one of these being Kelley's (1955) replication and extension of an earlier investigation of Charters and Newcomb (1952) Kelley experimentally tested and confirmed the following hypothesis:

When group-anchored attitudes are exposed to counter-pressures, their resistance to change at the particular time will be greater with high salience of the relevant group than with low (p. 277).

Kelley's procedure involved presenting high school and college students of differing religions with material that advocated attitudes divergent from an acceptable Catholic point of view. This material was designed to influence the students' initial attitude on a variety of issues. Some students were given preliminary material to read that was designed to heighten the salience of their Catholic group membership. Others received neutral material to read. Kelley computed the differences between the students' initial attitudes and their attitudes after receiving the influence attempt. He examined this difference by comparing those Catholics whose group membership had been made salient with those whose reference group membership was of low salience. Results confirmed the hypothesis in that Catholics made aware of their religion were less influenced by the material than were Catholics whose group membership was not relevant to them at that particular moment.

Relative Deprivation.   The potency of comparison processes in establishing and sustaining self-identity is perhaps most keenly demonstrated in work involving the concept of *relative deprivation.* Samuel Stouffer (1949a, 1949b) and his colleagues' monumental study of the American soldier demonstrate the impact that others' positions have on our judgments of our own well-being. Here are several findings from that study:

1.   A married soldier, comparing himself to his married civilian friends, felt that his induction into the army was a great sacrifice.
2.   A black soldier comparing himself to black civilians in the South felt that he was relatively well off.
3.   More highly educated soliders who were not promoted felt a greater sense of personal failure than less educated soldiers who were not promoted.
4.   A man in the Air Corps who did not get promoted felt more failure than an MP who was not promoted.

In these last two cases, the soldier felt himself a failure because his nonpromotion occurred within a context of relatively high promotion, or not a failure because his nonpromotion occurred within a context of relatively high nonpromotion. In other words, the soldier's sense of self-esteem and his sense of deprivation is relative to the comparison context. In the Air Corps where promotions were generally high, a person who was not promoted would experience a greater sense of failure; indeed, the black in the army felt himself relatively better off than the black civilian.

A broadly instructive point to be extracted from these investigations suggests that as P's expectations for upward mobility increase, not moving upward should produce greater feelings of deprivation and failure than in someone who has minimal hope for upward movement. This frustration of rising expectations occurs in many contemporary social contexts. It refers especially to a sense of dissatisfaction among persons in developing nations and among minorities in the United States, when hopes for upward mobility are high but when actual movement is low.

But upward is not the only direction in which one can move. According to the comparison process notion, the person who has been riding high and suddenly fails will experience greater frustration than the person who has never been up in the first place. In fact, we would expect that persons on the bottom would experience a relative rise in status and sense of well being when they noted a former stockbroker standing next to them in the breadlines. Henry and Short (1954) used this comparative concept of relative deprivation to understand data linking suicide and homocide as responses to economic prosperity and economic depression.

In times of depression, persons who lose most relative to others are those who have most to lose. Because they usually have been in control of their lives, they tend to blame themselves for their failure. Thus, one response to loss is the intrapunitive, angry act of suicide; during economic depression, those of higher status are more prone to suicide. On the other end of the status scale, it is in times of economic prosperity that persons on the bottom feel most frustrated. They are likely to have been pawns and they tend to blame others for their lack of success; their response to this frustration is turned outward and becomes homocide. Historical lynching data indicates that lower-status whites have lynched more blacks during economic depression than during periods of propserity. During depression, the barely discernible distinction between lower-status white and black breaks down. Whites feel that they have lost more relative to blacks and may take out their frustration on those to whose status they are now too threateningly close. We will return again later to some of these same themes of social comparison.

INFLUENCE PROCESSES

The other side of this social comparison coin introduces us to influence processes. If the first side emphasizes pressures that we bring to bear upon ourselves to formulate our perspective in concert with others, the other side stresses the pressures that we bring to bear on others to see and think as we do. In other words, social comparison directs our attention to how P attempts to become like O, to use O as a frame of reference for self-validation; influence processes direct our attention to how P attempts to transform O into a P. The root of influence processes is found in P's efforts to constitute and maintain a stable interpersonal environment, including a world in which P's perspectives are validated. The presence of someone who is different can be understood as posing a threat to P's sense of security regarding self-identity. As we have noted in our earlier discussion of balance theory (Chapter 3), one way that we can deal with a discrepancy between our views and the views of others on an important issue, is to try to influence those others to change their views and to see things as we do: in so doing, we validate our conceptions of social reality.

A classic and, in my estimation, very instructive study on these matters was published by Schachter in 1951. Schachter employed three accomplices, each of whom played a particular role in a discussion group. The case history of a juvenile delinquent, Johnny Rocco, was presented to groups of subjects (each group included all three accomplices) for their discussion. They were given a 7-point rating scale to help focus their discussion around the question: What should be done with Johnny? Point 1 on the scale urged extreme compassion and care; point 7 emphasized punishment as being the only way to treat Johnny. Schachter reasoned correctly that his college-educated subjects were likely to adopt a position somewhere between points 2 and 4 on the scale, balancing love with a little discipline. This permitted him to instruct each accomplice to adopt a position that in various ways related to the dominant group opinion.

The *deviate* was instructed to take a position of extreme punishment—position 7—and to stick with it throughout the entire group discussion. The *slider* was instructed to take position 7 at the beginning of the discussion and, about half-way through, to slide toward the modal position. The third accomplice, the *mode,* was to adopt the dominant group position and retain it throughout the discussion. Observers noted the nature of the interaction within the group and towards whom it was directed; in addition, all subjects completed several questionnaires, some of which asked them to rank the attractiveness of group members and to nominate persons for membership on committees that had varying degrees of desirability.

Schachter's data indicated that the deviate and slider received more communication than the mode, with the communication to the slider dropping off as the slider began to "see the light" and move towards consensus with the rest of the group. In general, communication to the deviate began to drop off slightly when it appeared that the deviate could not be swayed by the group's efforts. Questionnaire data indicated clearly that the deviate was not liked by the other group members, and in fact, when choices for continuing group members were made, the deviate was the one most rejected.

A replication and extension of this important study was conducted by Sampson and Brandon (1964). In their research, they used only one accomplice, and changed the name and implied race but not the description of the delinquency case. Groups of five females (four subjects plus the accomplice) were to discuss the case of James

Johnson, a black delinquent, again using the 7-point rating scale to guide their discussion. Half of the groups had the accomplice play a deviating position 7, while the other half had the accomplice play a modal position. The results here confirmed Schachter's original findings in that much communication was directed towards the deviate and relatively less towards the mode; and as with Schachter's original findings, communication to the deviate decreased when it became apparent that the deviate's position would not be altered.

The important extension in the Sampson and Brandon study involved creating another kind of group deviate: if the first deviation could be said to involve opinions on the delinquency case, the second could be said to involve the accomplice's entire character. Through careful instructions, manner of dress, and self-presentation, the accomplice for half of the groups appeared to be what was privately termed a "bigot"; for the other half, the accomplice was a "liberal." It is important to note that the liberal's character was more similar to the subjects used in the experiment than was the bigot's. Observers examined the amount and nature of communications directed towards the accomplice. Unlike their attempt to influence the opinion deviate into changing, the group's response to the character deviate (i.e., the bigot) was active avoidance. The character deviate received increasingly less amounts of communication; it was as though subjects were actively seeking to avoid any confrontation. Physically, group members even turned their chairs at an angle to avoid any contact with the deviate. Their reaction was similar to one many of us have on seeing badly crippled persons on the street; we may actively try to avoid looking at them (e.g. Goffman, 1963b), even as they may be made uncomfortable by our presense (e.g. Comer & Piliavin, 1972).

The Schachter and the Sampson and Brandon experimental studies are among many studies that confirm the importance of influence processes in achieving and maintaining a validation for our sense of identity. The deviate threatens the consensual validation of social reality; members attempt to influence the deviate to adopt their position. They are correct because others agree with them; the deviate is wrong, and wrongs must be dealt with, even eliminated if need be. When it appears that the deviate cannot be swayed, the response is to cease comparing one's self with him or her; essentially, the group redefines its boundaries and excludes the one who threatens its consensual validation.

Schachter's research is further instructive in demonstrating two additional conditions that increase these pressures on the deviate to change into a proper group member. Schachter experimentally varied both the cohesiveness of each group and the relevance of the case discussion for the group's reason for being formed in the first place. A highly cohesive group is one in which, among other factors, members are very attracted to one another; a group low in cohesiveness is one in which members expect minimal positive attraction. Thus, the deviates in half of Schachter's groups were expected initially to be liked by other group members, whereas in the other half, there was minimal expectation of liking the deviate. In theory, one would expect greater pressure on the deviate when others expected him or her to be liked and similar to them than when the group expected indifference (i.e., low cohesiveness).

Schachter experimentally made the discussion of Johnny Rocco relevant to half the groups by having them form initially to discuss just such material; the case was of low relevance to the other half of the groups because they were formed for other purposes. Again, in theory, one would expect greater pressures towards uniformity and thus towards consensual validation when the deviation involved relevant issues. In general, Schachter's findings support both theoretical expectations. Greatest pressure on the deviating accomplice occurred under the combination of high cohesiveness and high relevance; least pressure, under low cohesiveness and low relevance.

It is important for us to keep these two factors in mind. They suggest that influence processes to validate our identity occur most intensively when the persons and issues involved are most central to the kind of person we think we are or would like to be. That is, doubt and personal insecurity are more likely when we disagree with significant others on issues central to our self-definition or our purposes at hand, than when the disagreement involves casual others or issues less central to our identity. Indeed, one can gain a fair sense of where a person's or even a group's collective identity is centered by noting the degree of outrage and upset that occurs from varying kinds of deviations. During the late 1960s, for example, when long hair on males began to be popular, there was considerable protest and outrage from the short-haired citizenry, including school principals, coaches, politicians, and others. It was as though long hair meant protest and rejection of a particular way of life, a challenge to the validity of the identity, sexual and social, of many persons.

NULLIFICATION PROCESSES

Recall that it was William James who suggested that the worst possible punishment that could befall a person was to pass by unnoticed and unrecognized, to be an invisible person, a nullified being.

Recall further that precisely this response occurred on the part of the Sampson and Brandon subjects who faced the bigot character. In essence, they nullified the bigot's existence. We turn now to a discussion of nullification processes as a mode of self-maintenance.

For some time, clinical psychologists and psychiatrists have dealt with a defensive process variously termed *depersonalization* or *dehumanization* (e.g., Bernard, Ottenberg & Redl, 1968); it involves the use of denial, repression, and the isolation of affect. As a defense, dehumanization helps us cope with extremely stressful interpersonal situations by denying person-status to those with whom we must deal. During an extreme crisis—for example, a violent accident or community disaster—an individual who is able to depersonalize those who are involved, who can thereby relate to them without pity or disgust, is often better able to be of help. Certain occupations require a degree of depersonalization. Surgeons, for example, would do poorly if they were not able to maintain some distance from their patients. Likewise, many activities required of the police and the military are best accomplished by means of a depersonalized relationship to the target persons who are involved. It is more difficult indeed to see one's self as a murderer of mothers, fathers, and children than as a soldier simply killing the enemy, the gooks, or whatever.

Robert Lifton (1969) interviewed many survivors of the Hiroshima atomic bombing and noted several depersonalized-type reactions. For one, his subjects (a dehumanizing term in itself) reported how after the initial horror they experienced they soon became devoid of all feeling; they felt nothing, even when confronted by the writhing and blistered bodies of their fellows cut down and burning alive in the streets. Second, Lifton noted a change in himself. Initially he experienced nearly overwhelming emotions during these interviews; later, when he came to view himself as a scientist engaged in data collection and the people as "his research subjects," he was not so deeply affected.

Although the previous examples were taken from occupational roles, similar nullification processes do occur in our everyday dealings with those whose presence might be threatening to our own sense of a stable identity; thus, they are neutralized, nullified, dehumanized. When we turn our back or deny legitimacy to the existence of another person, another way, another perspective, basically, we are nullifying that person's reality. When we suggest that O should not be taken seriously, we are nullifying O's reality. When we note a deviant perspective and argue its existence away, maintaining that O really can't be that way, but really would prefer our way if O only could manage it, we again are involved in nullifying O's reality as such. And we pursue these nullifications all in the name of preserving our own version of reality. In essence, the potentially threatening other is taken as a basis for affirming the rightness of our own identity by nullifying the reality of the other.

Berger and Luckman (1966) offer us a useful example of nullification or in their terms nihilation. In their framework, persons, ideas, events, and things that do not fit into P's own sense of the universe and his or her proper place within it, are neutralized, often in such a way so as to reaffirm P's sense of self and reality. Berger and Luckman ask us to suppose that we are dealing with a society in which homosexuality is the proper way of life and heterosexuality is improper. In such a society, they reason, the heterosexual individual is a deviant whose mere presence is a threat to the integrity of each homosexual self in that society. By supposing, however, that the heterosexual really would prefer to be a homosexual—that is, he or she really wants to be like the rest of society—the actuality of the heterosexual's existence is denied (nullified) and the heterosexual's potential as a threat is used to affirm the rightness of the society's way.

Berger and Luckman obviously selected the example they did in order to highlight an everyday process that might otherwise get lost were they to take our society as it is presently constituted. The point remains, nevertheless, that threats to the self are nullified in ways that seek to preserve and even bolster the identity we presently have.

That nullification is an active process is shown clearly in the research reported by Geller and his colleagues (Geller, Goodstein, Silver, & Sternberg, 1974). They sought to systematically study the phenomenon of "being ignored"; they reasoned that to be ignored is to be excluded from social interaction even though physically present, and hence to be left powerless to affect others. As they trained their accomplices (P) to ignore their experimental subjects (O), they noted that the endeavor was most successful when P recognized O's presence but paid minimal attention to O; and importantly, that P never showed any interest in O's comments or ideas and often changed the topic of discussion that O may have initiated or have been participating in. To nullify others by ignoring them in social interaction, therefore, may not involve total exclusion, but rather just enough inclusion to actively communicate to the persons that they and their ideas do not count for much of anything. As expected, Geller's research demonstrated that when P actively ignored O in this manner, O's self-description revolved around such terms as alone, withdrawn, and shy.

INDIVIDUATION AND DEINDIVIDUATION

P may not only nullify O in order to provide a manner of stabilizing P's own identity, but under certain conditions, may also seek to nullify his or her own identity. Two related concepts are of value for viewing this aspect of nullification: individuation and deindividuation. In general, individuation refers to P's efforts to present a self that is unique from others; deindividuation involves P's efforts to minimize the differences between self and everyone else: that is, to nullify P's individuated, unique identity. There is a similarity between these two processes and the earlier discussion of two forms of schismogenesis (Chapter 2). Symmetrical schismogenesis, like deindividuation, results in a greater similarity between P and O. Complimentary schismogenesis, like individuation, results in a greater differentation between P and O.

Our everyday lives are filled with examples of both individuation and deindividuation. When we buy the latest fashions so that we will not stand out from "our crowd", we are deindividuating ourselves; when we buy an unusual outfit that will let us stand apart from others, we are individuating ourselves. Recall as well the Asch study that suggests efforts on the part of some subjects to avoid individuating themselves, so they gave judgments that were similar to those of others in their groups. Researchers within social psychology have become increasingly interested in these dual processes, examining the conditions under which individuation and deindividuation will occur, and the presumed consequences that follow from deindividuation rather than individuation.

One experimental investigation (Maslach, 1974) of the conditions that provoke individuation or deindividuation argued that when people expect something beneficial to happen to them, they seek to individuate themselves from the crowd; however, when something negative is likely, then they seek to deindividuate themselves, becoming part of the invisible background. Maslach reports an investigation designed to test this hypothesis. Subjects were convened in groups of four for a city planning game. One subject was to be chosen as the designer; half of the subjects expected the chosen designer would receive extra money, while half expected the designer would receive punishing electric shocks. A variety of measures was obtained in an effort to determine whether the designers who were expecting a monetary reward would seek to individuate themselves, as though to say, "Me, me, choose me from this group of four"; while the designers who were anticipating electric shocks would seek to deindividuate themselves, as though to say, "Not me, I'm no different than anyone else around here."

Maslach's results provided strong support for her predictions. Of special interest, however, were the ways in which subjects expecting rewards sought to individuate themselves. They tended to give more unusual (i.e., individuating) self-descriptions and more unusual answers to questions; they engaged in more expansive and expressive arm gestures; they tended to look more at the experimenter. In the rather stringent confines of the laboratory experiment, the options for deindividuating one's self are not very great; one could not readily become invisible and anonymous by means of putting on a disguise, changing one's manner of clothing, and such. Subjects in this research, however, could and did tend to deindividuate themselves by conforming more than the individuating subjects (who sought to be unusual and different), by looking away from others, and when talking, by making short, personally uninformative and unrevealing comments. In other words, when facing a negative consequence for being identified from out of the crowd, persons sought whatever means was at their disposal to nullify themselves, to deindividuate, and thereby make themselves anonymous. We might say that P sought to preserve a self-identity by concealing that identity. One thinks readily of the concentration camp internee who seeks to avoid being chosen for execution by fading into the woodwork; or the shy, retiring child, whose insistent pursuit of anonymity is done in the service of self-maintenance.

The consequences of deindividuation have been of special interest to many social psychologists interested in what they have taken to be the contemporary American cultural scene, where anonymity means nonresponsibility and thus "everything is permitted." Philip Zimbardo (1969) has been especially concerned with the links between individuation, reason, and social order on the one hand and deindividuation, impulsivity, and chaos on the other. Through both laboratory and field experiments, his research has demonstrated how the deindividuated person who is anonymous as to personal identity and thus personal responsibility for his or her actions, is thereby freed to engage in socially harmful and destructive behavior.

In one series of laboratory investigations, for example, Zimbardo used hoods to create deindividuation in one experimental condition and name tags and introductions by name to create individuation in another condition. Subjects were to provide an electric shock to another subject. Results indicated that deindividuated subjects administered shocks for a significantly greater duration than individuated subjects. Interestingly enough, the use of hoods for natural rather than ad hoc laboratory groups of subjects actually had the reverse effect by isolating persons from their typical network of social support and thereby inhibiting rather than facilitating their aggressive use of shock.

Zimbardo's field investigations are perhaps more striking than his laboratory work in suggesting the cover that anonymity can play in releasing persons from the normal bases of social control over their behavior. In one field demonstration, Zimbardo and an associate purchased an automobile that they left unattended on a street across from New York University; for 64 hours, they observed the car being systematically stripped. In fact, the first strippers arrived after about 10 minutes and were a father, mother, and their eight-year old son. After three days and twenty-three destructive incidents, "what remained was a battered, useless hulk of metal." A similar effort across from Stanford University, a less populated, presumably less deindividuated setting produced no vandalism, and indeed even one act of apparent altrusim as the vehicle's hood was closed by a passerby when it began to rain.

Additional investigations of the effects of deindividuation on group behavior lend further confirmation to this developing theme: where P is able to nullify self, P is freer to engage in less inhibited behaviors. In some investigations (Festinger Pepitone, & Newcomb, 1952; Cannavale, Scarr, & Pepitone, 1970) for example, deindividuation increased the degree to which persons were able to make negative comments about their parents; in another (Singer, Brush, & Lublin, 1965), the anonymity seemed to increase the freedom of subjects to use abrasive and obscene language.

The general point, for our purposes, is to note that nullification processes when applied to one's self, such as deindividuation, can and do serve an identity-stabilizing function. To nullify or make anonymous one's own existence can permit P to engage in actions that may be dissonant with a desired self-image; under deindividuated conditions, such actions can be expressed without the kind of personal responsibility and identifiability that would force a change in P's self-image. That is, with deindividuation, P need not own up to his or her own feelings and actions. Deindividuating or nullifying one's self may be used to avoid challenges to one's identity. Aspects of this same theme occur in our discussion of authority and responsibility (Chapters 7 and 8).

SOLICITATION PROCESSES

Solicitation processes, whether as conscious manipulative ploys or more typically as unconscious patterns of interacting with others, involve P's gaining affirmation for self-identity by actively soliciting such affirmation from O. There are two major interpersonal strategies for negotiating or soliciting an identity: self-presentation and altercasting.

Erving Goffman (1959) is perhaps the best known analyst of self-presentations, those processes whereby P creates and projects an identity in order to oblige O to respond to P as someone with that identity has every right to expect. In essence, P enacts a performance before O, seeking to manage the impression O receives. Goffman suggests that because of this prevalent feature of interaction, we should undertake a *dramaturgic analysis* of interpersonal encounters, seeking to locate the cast of players, the performances, the audience, the props, and all those elements that P employs in presenting the self that he or she wishes to have. The student who wants to appear "intellectual," for example, may carry, exposed for public view, a copy of Kant's *Critique of Pure Reason;* or one who wishes to be taken as someone of lesser means than he or she actually is, may dress down before heading off to classes.

Altercasting is a bit more complex than self-presentation; it too involves P's efforts (conscious and unconscious) to solicit an identity and thereby to stabilize a self-concept in social interaction. In altercasting, P creates and projects an identity for O (recall that in self-presentation, P creates and projects an identity for P); specifically, P seeks to cast O (alter = O) in a role that will confirm the image that P wants for himself or herself.

A few simple examples will help clarify this process (Weinstein & Deutschberger, 1963): P says to O, "As a good friend of mine, I know you will give me proper advice"; Parent says to child, "Big boys don't behave that way." In the first example, P altercasts O into the role of friend in order to get the kind of advice that only a friend could provide. By invoking friendship, P may in fact be asking O to provide support rather than give actual advice. Thus, P may have blown up in anger at a subordinate and while feeling somewhat guilty about it and a bit worried that such an outburst doesn't coincide with P's desired self-image as a compassionate person, P may seek out O and invoke friendship in order to receive support from O: i.e., to get O to agree that "yes you are really a compassionate person." In the second example, the parent casts O in the role of "big boy," a more responsible kind of position, one that presumably helps affirm P's own parental identity as a parent with mature, responsible children.

In Chapter 2, we were introduced to a form of altercasting in the review of Kelley and Stahelski's study of cooperators and competitors. Recall that the competitive person acted in such a way so as to cast O (potential cooperator) into a competitive stance, thus justifying O's own competitive behavior in response to a competitive alter. P was competitive because, in P's view, it was the only sensible response to a competitive O; of course, P was unable to see how this behavior towards O helped create the situation. Thus, P was engaged in altercasting, yet was unaware of the use of this process. As Kelley and his colleague noted, by acting in this manner, P could stabilize a self-identity as a competitive person, never or rarely noting disconfirming instances in which P could have been cooperative.

The clinical literature abounds in similar cases. Eric Berne (1961; 1964) reports numerous case histories in which persons employ altercasting to solicit and thereby affirm a particular identity for themselves, oblivious, however, of their own contributions to this identity outcome. In the clinical cases, it is not unusual to see persons stabilizing an identity that they claim they don't really like. Thus, altercasting can establish and sustain a self that, while consciously not desired, nevertheless remains continuously confirmed; some kind of therapeutic intervention is required to break the cycle.

Berne reports the case of Camellia who is continually being hurt by others. From her perspective, no one ever understood her, but rather always criticized and hurt her. What actually occurred in Camellia's interaction with others, however, was that she continually misunderstood and criticized others, leading them to respond with some anger, her to respond with weeping which brought forth an apology and comfort from them, thereby completing the circle and confirming for Camellia her identity as a "person to be pitied."

Clinical cases are not always met in the clinic, however. The concept of altercasting has much in common with that of self-fulfilling prophecy (see Chapter 2). In both, the person acts in such a way as to create the very conditions that fulfill expectancies, in particular those central to the person's concept of self. In an interesting experimental effort to study altercasting in a nonclinical context, Blumstein (1973) got male subjects to engage in role playing with female accomplices. The instructions asked the male to get a date with the female while she was instructed to get to know the male further to see if he was the kind of person she would like to go out with. In private, the females were asked to try to altercast the males, to get them to accept a particular kind of identity as a condition for getting the date.

Measures were obtained to assess the degree to which the male subjects accepted or resisted their altercast identity. The authors report both kinds of responses, but particularly note that when P altercasts O (e.g., the female altercasts the male), O may willingly comply in order to gain some concessions from P. In other words, altercasting is an interpersonal process in which P's efforts to altercast O may be reciprocated by O's agreement, often implicit, to accept that identity in order to get something from P. In the specific case of their study, the males were often willing to be the kind of person that the females wanted in order to get the date with the woman.

While the experimental setting makes the process openly conscious and manipulative, altercasting and the agreement to accept it are an important and often unconscious part of many interpersonal relationships. For example, a wife may implicitly agree to be the kind of wife her husband needs to confirm his own identity in exchange for certain concessions from him, and vice versa. Or, an employee may agree to be the "yes" man his boss wants in exchange for certain privileges that the boss will grant those who confirm his identity.

Concessions need not always be tangible as the preceding examples suggest. Those interacting with Camellia implicitly agree to pity her in exchange for being released from the guilt that they may experience over responding too critically to her manner of misunderstanding them. In this latter instance, the following complex but implicit sequence is likely:

1. Camellia is critical of O.
2. O gets angry and critical of Camellia.
3. Camellia begins to cry and says that she is always misunderstood by others, that all she wanted to do was to be of help to O.
4. O accepts the crying and apologizes to Camellia which Camellia accepts thus relieving O of the guilt: that is, as a concession for being relieved of feeling guilty, O accepts the role that Camellia has cast him into, namely one who pities Camellia, one who is apologetic, thereby reinforcing Camellia's image of herself as someone who is always misunderstood and towards whom people are always overly criticial.

As Berne has noted, the cycle is broken only when someone comes forth and rejects the crying and the identity into which its acceptance would cast them.

Development and Transformations of Identity

Intrapersonal and interpersonal processes whereby a constancy of identity, a selfsameness, is accomplished, thus far, have been our major concern. In contrast to some points of view that see a person's identity as something formed and crystallized early in life, the approach we have taken stresses how the person's identity continuously develops throughout life. This does not mean, however, that early childhood patterns are irrelevant. Rather, we can see development as a process in which the manner by which age 5 is accomplished influences the way in which age 6 is handled, which in turn influences age 7 and so on. Early patterns can be and are sustained and thereby help shape later patterns which in turn affect still later patterns.

Take a simple example. Two children are born separated in age by about 14 months. The one child at age 13½ is gregarious and sociable and seems happiest when everyone is around and together; the other child, age 12, is much more of a loner, quieter, seemingly happiest when off reading alone. This same pattern also characterized the children in their first year of life. The gregarious child tended to cry and fuss a great deal as a baby whenever left alone, so the mother would carry him around with her as she did her chores around the house. The other child, rarely fussing as an infant, was left more to herself. The point is that the interpersonal context provided by the mother's reaction to these early differences in the children's temperment reinforced those initial differences. Behavior at age 6 months may thus be correlated with behavior at age 13 because a pattern of interpersonal relationships helps sustain that behavior. In like manner, the now gregarious adolescent sustains his sociability and thus participates actively in maintaining his own identity.

To suggest that one's identity is a lifelong development is to recognize that socialization processes are never over until death. Although this does not mean that early developments are unimportant, it does emphasize "the potency of the environment in which the organism is functioning" (Kagen & Klein, 1973, p. 960). This perspective is the conclusion of a cross-cultural investigation conducted by Kagan and Klein:

> *There is no question that early experience seriously affects kittens, monkeys, and children. If the first environment does not permit the full actualization of psychological competences, the child will function below his ability as long as he remains in that context. But if he is transferred to an environment that presents greater variety and requires more accommodations, he seems . . . capable of exploiting that experience and repairing the damage wrought by the first environment . . . (p. 960).*

Although the Kagan and Klein focus was on cognitive and intellectual functioning, this same point of view applies with equal vigor to other aspects of the person's functioning, none perhaps as emphatically as the person's identity.

STAGES OF DEVELOPMENT: ERIKSON'S VIEW*

The issue for the serious investigator of identity is to determine the critical developmental phases that the individual experiences from

*Material quoted from Erikson has been reprinted from "Identity and the Life Cycle" by Erik H. Erikson. Psychological Issues, Vol. 1, No. 1. By permission of W. W. Norton and Company, Inc. and the author. Copyright 1959 by International Universities Press, Inc.

birth through the many stages and challenges of life within a particular culture. It is to the writings of Erik Erikson (1959), that we must
turn for one of the most extensive and informative statements regarding these lifelong developmental processes. In Erikson's view,
all human growth follows a general plan out of which specific parts
arise at special times "until all parts have arisen to form a functioning whole" (1959, p. 52). The eight stages of human growth and
development that he outlines represent decisive encounters between the person's unfolding developmental ground plan and the
interpersonal and historical settings of the person's sociocultural
environment. Each stage, as Erikson envisions it, represents a crisis,
the resolution of which is fundamental to the individual's total
growth; and each stage, in turn, is a crisis, because it represents a
"radical *change in perspective*" (1959, p. 55).

> *There is, at the beginning of life, the most radical change of*
> *all: from intrauterine to extrauterine life. But in postnatal*
> *existence, too, such radical adjustments of perspective as*
> *lying relaxed, sitting firmly, and running fast must all be*
> *accomplished in their own good time. With them, the*
> *interpersonal perspective, too, changes rapidly and often*
> *radically, as is testified by the proximity in time of such*
> *opposites as "not letting mother out of sight" and "wanting*
> *to be independent."* Thus, different capacities use different
> opportunities *to become full-grown components of the*
> *ever-new configurations that is the growing personality* (p.
> 55).

Erikson's view of human development gives us an outline of eight
psychosocial crises with two distinctly opposed modes of resolution;
hence, the eight stages are represented by a listing of eight opposite
terms, the first representing what Erikson takes to be normal and
healthful resolution, the second, psychosocial ill-health.

Psychosocial Crises of Development

Stage 1:   basic trust versus mistrust
Stage 2:   autonomy versus shame and doubt
Stage 3:   initiative versus guilt
Stage 4:   industry versus inferiority
Stage 5:   identity versus identity diffusion
Stage 6:   intimacy versus isolation
Stage 7:   generativity versus self-absorption
Stage 8:   integrity versus disgust and despair

Before we examine each stage specifically, it is important to note
that although only stage 5 mentions the issue of identity, Erikson's
point is that the crisis over identity reaches its peak during this

phase of adolescence: "identity *formation* neither begins nor ends with adolescence: it is a lifelong development" (p. 113). All eight stages, then concern vital matters of identity as new psychosocial challenges are encountered. Stage 5 represents a crucial period during which time, as we shall see, "who one is" and "who one will be" takes over as a dominant theme.

Basic Trust versus Mistrust.   The first year of life is most important to the development of either a sense of trust in ourselves and in our world or a sense of living in a dangerous and unpredictable psychosocial environment. It is during the early interpersonal experiences of feeding that Erikson sees the foundation laid for trust or mistrust. The stress here is on the preliminary development of a sense, however vague, of mutuality and reciprocity between feeder and the one who is fed; on the quality of the relationship between the provider (e.g., the mother) and the infant. So important is this early foundation that some analysts (e.g., Ekstein, 1972) have argued that all reason and rational behavior are built on faith, namely this early and primitive development of a trusting relationship with another human being.

Autonomy versus Shame and Doubt.   This crucial issue with which the child and family must deal involves developing a sense of *"self-control* [i.e., autonomy] *without loss of self-esteem"* (p. 68). Erikson emphasizes the importance of toilet training during this phase of the individual's growth; the interpersonal resolution develops in the young child either the sense of autonomous control and a feeling of pride or the sense of having yielded to others' control, with a consequent feeling of impotence, of shame and of doubt in one's own capabilities.

Initative versus Guilt.   Erikson now brings us into the world of the child of age 4 or 5 (at least in Western cultures) who meets still another psychosocial crisis. "Being firmly convinced that he *is* a person, the child must now find out *what kind* of person he is going to be" (p. 74). The child's increased range of free movement, his or her developing use of language, and the expansion of imagination that is thereby facilitated, help the child begin to form identifications with parents. It is during this period that the "child . . . develops the prerequisites for *masculine* and *feminine initiative,* that is, for the selection of social goals and perseverance in approaching them" (p. 78). Competition and rivalry emerge; yet the child must learn to forgo the immediate satisfaction of these developing urges in the name of youth, inexperience, and further growth. The outcome of this period of early crisis can be one that leaves the child with a strong and continuing sense of initiative and goal-striving or a deeply etched sense of guilt, for ever having imagined himself or herself to have achieved full adulthood sexually as well as in other ways. As Erikson phrases the nature of the dilemma, using father and son as a case in point, there is a need to develop "an experience of essential *equality in worth,* in spite of the *inequality in time schedules*" (p. 82).

Industry versus Inferiority
> One might say that personality at the first stage crystallizes around the conviction "I am what I am given," and that of the second, "I am what I will." The third can be characterized by "I am what I can imagine I will be." We must now approach the fourth: "I am what I learn." The child now wants to be shown how to get busy with something and how to be busy with others (p. 82).

The psychosocial focus of this stage involves working and playing and developing a sense of personal talents and skills: that is, a sense of mastery over things, over self, over persons—not manipulation or control, but a sense of being competent in mastering the tasks of one's later childhood. A failure here involves developing a sense of personal inadequacy and inferiority. It is during this period that the child begins to develop strong identifications with those who are able to do things well or who know things—for example, teachers and parents. It is here that the child develops a sense of working together with others.

Identity versus Identity Diffusion.   Childhood is now at an end and adolescence begins. With this beginning there comes a combination of the physiological changes of puberty and the social changes of new and different roles and possibilities. Identity as Erikson sees it involves an integration or a synthesis of the various "me's" of the individual; it is not a mere summation of all that has gone before, but rather a new Gestalt, a new configuration of the variegated others and their reflections of "me." Its opposite, identity diffusion, reflects a loss of any integrated sense of self, any synthesis of one's significant identifications. A premature grasping for one identification often occurs as a defense against this sense of diffusion. The period of adolescence, where issues of identity reign supreme:
> can be viewed as a psychosocial moratorium during which the individual through free role experimentation may find a niche in some section of his society, a niche which is firmly defined and yet seems to be uniquely made for him. In finding it the young adult gains an assured sense of inner continuity and social sameness which will bridge what he

was *as a child and what he is* about to become, *and will reconcile his* conception *of himself and his* community's recognition *of him* (p. 111).

Intimacy versus Isolation.   At the end of adolescence, the person moves increasingly towards a world in which career and marriage-like choices begin. The intimacy of which Erikson speaks involves more than a sexual intimacy; rather, the emphasis is on the person's ability to establish a strong and close relationship with another person. Without first establishing a firm sense of one's identity, it is difficult if not impossible to risk the kind of merging and blending with another that true intimacy requires. Failure to form an intimate bond with another results in isolation, a distancing of one's self from others, a superficiality of relationships or perhaps a more combative form of competitive linkage without genuine intimacy. Freud's view of the normal person was one who could love and work; as Erikson recognizes, love means being a loving being.

Generativity versus Stagnation.   The issue at this stage involves parenting: "Generativity is primarily the interest in establishing and guiding the next generation" (p. 97). Generativity need not involve actually becoming a parent, but rather involves a general altruistic concern with the next generation. The opposite pole, stagnation, conveys both Erikson's evaluation and description of the nonhealthful resolution of this psychosocial issue. "Individuals who do not develop generativity often begin to indulge themselves as if they were their own one and only child" (p. 97). Having children, however, does not in itself mean that the generative resolution has won out; many have children yet due to a "lack of some faith, some 'belief in the species' " they do not experience "a child ... to be a welcome trust of the community" (p. 97).

Integrity versus Despair and Disgust.   In later years, as one looks back on life, the combined joys and sorrows, triumphs and disappointments, there emerges a sense of integrity or of despair. Integrity represents an "acceptance of one's own and only life cycle and of the people who have become significant to it as something that had to be and that, by necessity, permitted of no substitutions" (p. 98). It is an acceptance of parents, rather than wishing they had been different; an acceptance of one's friends and comrades, of one's self. The alternative is a loss of this final integration that permits further growth; it is a sense of despair and of disgust with one's life; wishing things could have been different. This despair is often hidden behind a general contempt for all people and all institutions, basically, a contempt of self.

A LIFELONG PROCESS

Processes of socialization, of growth and development, even as they pertain to so central a matter as our identity, are rarely static or settled once and for all. Life within society and with others provides ample opportunities, as Erikson's scheme suggests, for new events and relationships to reopen issues that we may have thought had long ago been settled in adolescence. The woman whose life had centered around being a mother to her children faces a new challenge of identity when that inevitable time arrives (at least in the American family pattern) for the grown children to leave home and strike out on their own. Middle-aged persons, a shortened future time-span before them, triggering the awareness that the many tasks they set for themselves must necessarily go unfulfilled, likewise may experience in their mid-40s a crisis of identity every bit as intense as presumably faces the adolescent. Aging persons, whose bodily well-being now plays a central part in self-definition, face issues that again challenge their sense of identity.

Transformations: The POW.   In addition to the preceding "normal" cultural occurrences, normal in that they are an aspect of the everyday lives of most persons living within Western civilization, some persons face special circumstances that provide opportunities for transformations or reformulations of their identities. An Olympic skiier who breaks her neck in a bad fall and is paralyzed for life must come to terms with a dramatically changed self-image; our judgments of others' courage are often founded on how well they come back after such an occurrence and lead productive albeit different lives. Systematic investigations of prisoners of war, centering especially around the concept of brainwashing, stand as stark testimony to the potential for dramatic change in identity as a function of becoming a prisoner. The results of several investigations of POW's in Chinese and Korean camps are informative on this matter. Schein's (1958) follow-up examination of Western prisoners in Chinese prison camps, uncovered several who on returning home never fully understood why their extreme attitude change within the camp had occured; others showed conflicting loyalties, seeing a midpoint between the Communist position and their older points of view; still others, however, had undergone extensive, even dramatic personality changes, adopting a new set of attitudes and values, a new sense of self as an outcome of this extreme experience.

Anecdotal reports of the several hundred returned POW's from North Vietnam indicates still another consequence of this imprisonment. Wives left alone and on their own for four, five, six, and more years, had to develop a resourcefulness in family decision-making that transformed them from a docile and dependent traditional female to a dominant organizer and director of the family. Husbands, now returned home, sought to take up their former roles only to find resistant wives. The wife's transformation triggered a transformation in the husband; or in several cases, saw the family as a unit break apart through divorce.

Continuities and Discontinuities

What is normal within one culture or one segment of a culture, of course, may not be typical for another. Several years ago, Ruth Benedict (1938) applied her anthropological insights to an examination of some fundamental discontinuities within Western cultures that were central to making adolescence in the West a period of *Sturm und Drang:* that is, a period of turmoil over issues of identity. Continuities and discontinuties exist in several areas of major importance for the person's identity: for example, age, generation, and sex role. Benedict focused her analyses upon age-graded discontinuities where the values, knowledges, and behaviors appropriate to the younger members of the society contrast with those appropriate to adult members of the society.

In Benedict's view, in cultures such as the United States and most Western societies in which an age-graded discontinuity exists, we can expect to encounter the kinds of identity crises of adolescence that Erikson and others have posited; however, in cultures in which continuity between various age grades is emphasized or those in which transformations between different age-graded expectations are marked by major ceremonials, adolescence is not marked by such crises over issues of identity.

> *From a comparative point of view, our culture goes to great extremes in emphasizing contrasts between the child and the adult. The child is sexless, the adult estimates his virility by his sexual activities; the child must be protected from the ugly facts of life, the adult must meet them without psychic catastrophe; the child must obey, the adult must command this obedience* (in Kluckhohn, Murray, & Schneider, 1956, p. 523).

Benedict's analysis focuses specifically on three major discontinuities between child and adult. The first calls our attention to the nonresponsibility that acrues to the child and the responsibility that acrues to adult roles. This age-graded difference in Western societies contrasts with other groups (e.g., the Papago of Arizona) who expect children to take on adult-like responsibilities tailored to their smaller size and capacities. A story is cited of a group of Papago elders, one of whom asks his three-year-old granddaughter to close a heavy door. She struggles with its weight and no one comes to her aid; no one took the responsibility away from her. Finally, after much effort and time, during which the elders sat gravely waiting for her to close the door, the youngster managed to shut it. The point that Benedict stresses is that in some cultures children from an early age onward are trained to take active, participatory, and thus responsible roles within the community, unlike the Western way in which children's participation in responsible ways is discouraged or at times denied entirely.

The second age-graded discontinuity that Benedict examines concerns the pattern of submission that characterizes the child's role versus the dominance of the adult role. This Western pattern of discontinuity is contrasted with other cultural groups that give to persons of differing age-gradings "reciprocal privileges and obligations which in our society can develop only between age mates." Reciprocity is founded more on an equality of statuses within culturally defined areas rather than the kinds of inequality that Western cultures stress and that we have noted, Erikson emphasizes in his analysis of initiative versus guilt.

Benedict's third area of age-graded discontinuity examines the continuities and discontinuities of sexual activity. Her argument is that while all cultures must deal with the physiological fact that children are sexually immature until a certain age, continuity nevertheless exists in some cultures (e.g., the Zuni, Melanesian cultures of Southeast New Guinea, the Marquesans) in which what the children are taught need not be unlearned when they become adults. It is Benedict's contention that in cultures such as the United States, a discontinuity exists when children must unlearn all the myths about sexual wickedness, for example, in order to engage in appropriate adult sexual behavior.

Discontinuities: The Golden Years. While Benedict's age-graded analysis of cultural discontinuities compares childhood with adult behavior, it is possible to witness similar discontinuities, again especially in the United States and other technological and industrial societies, between adult roles before and after reaching the age of "retirement." Talcott Parsons (1942) provides us with a statement descriptive of this particular discontinuity: retirement from work places persons into a functionless role, removes them from primary avenues of identity that have come from work, loosens ties to community and even to kinship groups and in any number of ways creates a relatively meaningless, isolated role, discontinuous with their previous experiences. It is no wonder that there may indeed be a return to a second childhood, a return of the various aspects of childhood roles especially of nonresponsibility and relative submission to those younger, still occupationally active and in dominant positions. When the calendar strikes 65, one must come suddenly to unlearn previous learnings; and few are prepared to face this dramatic transformation in identity. Culture's time clock conquers nature's. Thus, not surprisingly, death, illness, and despair come earlier than need be.

GENERATIONAL AND HISTORICAL CONTINUITIES AND DISCONTINUITIES IN IDENTITY

The student of identity must be historian as well as social psychologist: "personal identity is meshed with group identity, which itself rests upon an historical past" (Strauss, 1969, p. 173). There can be no full understanding of the person's identity without placing that person within the historical context, "his conception of the past as it impinges on himself" (Strauss, p. 164). In outlining the influence of history on the person's sense of identity, Anselm Strauss asks us to examine the autobiography of an English aristocrat, Sir Osbert Sitwell, concluding that "Sir Osbert knows his many ancestors as others know their immediate relatives" (p. 166). As Strauss emphasizes, Sir Osbert's aristocratic class membership stresses matters of kinship; but this stress should not lead us to overlook historical material that "one ought to look for [as well] in men whose lives are not so obviously enmeshed in long group histories" (p. 175).

The cultural heritage of the United States seems to betray us here, though never completely. The American nation of immigrants leaves many of its citizens cut off from their cultural pasts and their kin who remained "behind." Yet even in contemporary America, those who have inherited lengthy historical genealogies carry with them a log of inherited prestige and status that no moneyed new immigrant's son or daughter can easily match. For those cut off, however, thoughts of history and the past, especially as terms for persent self-definition, may seem alien.

Yet, the point, to repeat, is that although not all of us, nor even many of us may exist with such sensitivity to our cultural past as Sir Osbert, we nevertheless can see a connection to our past. Erikson, following up on a remark by Freud about his own inner identity based upon his link to the Jewish people, likewise stresses the importance of historical and generational continuity for the individual's sense of identity. For Erikson, identity "connotes both a persistent sameness within oneself (selfsameness) and a persistent sharing of some kind of essential character with others . . . an inner *solidarity* with a group's ideals and identity" (Erikson, 1959, p. 102).

If we grant the importance of historical and generational matters to the ongoing formation of the person's identity, what then is meant by a generational continuity or discontinuity? I think that the answer will be easiest if we think of two generations, that of P, and that of P's parents, O. Continuity exists insofar as there is a convergence between the ideas, values, and identifications of O and those of P; discontinuity is descriptive of a divergence, even a rejection by P of his or her own past as represented by P's parents. Just as the cultural discontinuities of which Benedict wrote were seen to provide disturbance for the individual who had to unlearn the past in order to function in the present, it is clearly noted by Erikson, for example, that a generational discontinuity would likewise prove disruptive for the individual's sense of identity. In particular, a generational continuity not only provides the person with roots, but also a foundation on which to build new learnings and new identities. We might then expect to find signs of stress and disturbance in persons who were discontinuous with their own generational past.

Examining this issue in 1972, Jeanne Block reported research on a group of college students and their parents. Her methods permitted Block to extract a continuity group from her sample, defined in terms of a general correspondence between student and parent values and political ideals; and a discontinuity group, defined in terms of the students' rejection of parental values and ideals. These two groups were then compared on several measures of self-concept. Block's findings tend to support the contention that generational discontinuity proves to be disruptive to the formation of identity. Continuity females describe themselves as having vitality and confidence, as being independent, assertive, talkative, informed, perceptive and responsible; compared to this continuity group, female discontinuity students describe themselves as rebellious, doubting, shy, self-denying, stubborn, and worrying. Continuity males when compared with discontinuity males describe themselves as less unconventional, more responsible, masculine, orderly, and practical.

Block obtained additional data regarding both the students' perceptions of their parent's child-rearing practices, and for another sample of parents, parent's perceptions of their own rearing practices. From both sets of information, conclusions were reached regarding the kinds of parental practice which seem conducive to creating continuity or discontinuity. In general, continuity seems to be the outcome of training for independence and autonomy, of encouragement for confronting problems and arriving at one's own resolutions, of reasoning and rationality. Discontinuity appears to be the outcome of parents who are themselves tense about relationships with children, concerned with issues of control, emphasizing appearances and impressions, tending to be suppressive and unresponsive to the needs of the child.

Cut off from their immediate, generational past, young adults seek to form an identity that is more rejecting than accepting of their own cultural heritage, tending as some of Block's data also suggest, to reject the present as well. The outcome appears as a strong sense of alienation, a theme and a topic that will concern us more in Chapter 11. The person without history, rejecting even the present, is a profile of early despair. This is by no means to suggest that generational continuities are the assured road to inner peace and harmony; but surely building on a firm foundation makes the trials of the present that much more approachable.

We hasten to add, however, that the efforts in the People's Republic of China to eliminate specific aspects of the past in order to create a nationally unifying identity for all its citizens, suggests a political and social circumstance under which discontinuity is positively valued. Where identities rooted to past traditions thwart efforts to solidify a people and transform the present into a picture of greater equality, breaking apart those roots may be a necessary step to establishing a firmer foothold for present identities.

Continuities and Discontinuities in Sex-role Identities

Of all the cultural roles through which one passes from birth to death, none is either more primary nor more important in self-definition and identity than that of sex. And, as has already been suggested, (see the case of Agnes), although the physiological differences between males and females play an important role in sexual identification, cultural conceptions regarding the "proper" male and the "proper" female are as or even more definitive. A discontinuity of sex role other than in a few instances of actual physiological sexual change, refers primarily to aspects of sex-role learning that either must be unlearned as the person comes to take on new roles within his or her life cycle, or that serve less to facilitate than to hinder the persons' realization of their full potentialities. For example, the idealized, soft, frilly, and passive U.S. female sex-role training for the little girl stands in the way of the young woman's taking on the more active and aggressive behaviors that may be required to achieve occupational success and independence; or the demands for highly competitive and aggressive masculinity may thwart the young man's accepting roles that require succorance, humane caring, or passivity and receptiveness.

Important discontinuities in sex-role socialization also involve the primary persons of one's sexual identification. The basic outlines of the argument begin with the assumption that separation of self from early figures of identification is necessary for the self to emerge as an independent, well-defined entity. That is, the initial lack of differentiation between self and other must be replaced by a differentiation if one is ever to emerge with a separate, individuated identity. The argument next notes that in general, the mother is the primary figure for both males' and females' early identifications and attachments. The typical course of later development however is one in which the boy is encouraged to identify with male figures, thereby facilitating his separation from his primary attachment to his mother; the girl, on the other hand, is encouraged to maintain her early identifications, and thus, presumably is:

> *not likely to establish an early and independent sense of self. If the early experiences of coping with the environment independently are crucial in the development of competence and self-confidence ... the delayed and possibly incomplete emergence of the self should mitigate against this development* (Hoffman, 1972, p. 144).

The preceding line of thinking has led to the hypothesis that females who develop more masculine identifications—that is, a discontinuity with their primary object of identification—are more likely to develop higher achievement in occupation and career than females who do not similarly break away from these early identifications. While some evidence in support of this hypothesis does exist (see Hoffman, 1972 and Maccoby, 1966), it would seem that a more plausible interpretation of such findings and a better statement of the hypothesis would focus less on discontinuity than on the nature of the mother with whom the female identifies. A girl who identifies with a mother who is "traditionally feminine" may indeed not evidence as great achievement as one who under these circumstances forms a more masculine identification. On the other hand, a girl who identifies with a mother involved in occupational roles and who maintains this identification, may herself develop a strong nontraditionally feminine identity. Research reported by Tangri in 1972 supports this latter point of view.

Tangri divided her sample of women respondents into three groups on the basis of their occupational choices made during their senior year in college: *role-innovators* were women who indicated occupations in which in general there are 30 percent or fewer women involved; *moderates* were women whose occupational choice involved occupations with 30 percent to 50 percent women;

traditionals chose occupations with more than 50 percent women. It is to be noted that over 70 percent of American women are in only four occupations: teaching, nursing, secretarial work, and social work. Thus a choice of these occupations would be considered traditional.

From her overall questionnaire data, Tangri was able to determine some characteristics differentiating these three groups. Relevant to the hypothesis indicated above, Tangri reports a strong relationship between mother's role innovation and daughter's selection of a male-dominated occupation. Furthermore, Tangri reports evidence suggesting that role-innovating daughters have generally strong identifications with their mothers (i.e., continuity rather than discontinuity), adopting some of their career values, but if anything even exceeding mother's own aspirations and careerist orientations. Tangri stresses that even though some evidence for role-modeling exists (i.e., daughter maintaining an identification with a nontraditional mother), the evidence also suggests a strong sense of autonomy and even some distance from both mother and father. Tangri concludes about her role-innovating subjects that:

> *They do not show evidence of having identified with their fathers in preference to their mothers. In fact, more educated working mothers, particularly those who are themselves in male dominated occupations, are taken as role models by such daughters ... As compared to women going into feminine professions, innovators are more autonomous, individualistic, and motivated by internally imposed demands to perform to capacity* (pp. 196–197).

It would seem that establishing an individual identity requires a balancing between breaking away from parental identifications and building on or modeling such identifications. It has been argued that males have an easier time breaking away than females in that males more often than females are placed into conflicts with their parents. In part, this is said to stem from innate differences in temperament which sees the male child generally more active motorically than the female and thus requiring more parental intervention and control. Boys tend to be disciplined more than girls, presumably facilitating their break from parents. Some investigators have indicated that girls who have a degree of maternal rejection have a better chance to develop autonomy and independence than girls who rarely come into conflict with their mothers. As Hoffman notes, rejection does not really mean a hostile withdrawal of love, but rather "the absence of 'smother love'":

> *Many girls experience too much maternal rapport and protection during their early years ... they find themselves as adults unwilling (or unable) to face stress and with*

> *inadequate motivation for autonomous achievement . . . She continues to be dependent upon adults for solving her problems and because of this she needs her affective ties with adults* (Hoffman, 1972, pp. 146–147).

SEX-ROLE STEREOTYPES

By now it should be apparent that continuities and discontinuities in sex-role identification proceed differently for males and for females and have different consquences for the sexual identification of the individual. At another, though related, level the issue of continuity and discontinuity is equally important to the individual's sexual identity. Male and female stereotypes and idealizations exist both as an outcome of the social process whereby sex roles are culturally determined and as an ideology that serves to reinforce and maintain existing sexual identifications. As an analysis of male and female characters in prize-winning children's picture books reveals, not only are female characters minimally present (e.g., 261 pictures of males and 23 pictures of female characters, a ratio of 11 to 1), but in addition, the representation of each sex creates and reinforces sex-role stereotypes for the preschool reader. Weitzman, Eifler, Hokade, and Ross who published this investigation in 1972 report that:

> *boys are active while girls are passive; boys lead and rescue others while girls follow and serve others . . . men engage in a wide variety of occupations while women are presented only as wives and mothers* (p. 1125).

As the authors note, even the girl's clothing suggests that she is not to be an active person; she is dressed too fragiley and fancily to engage in life's active endeavors. Likewise, picture books combining persons with animals invariably show the little boy in clear control over the animal, while the little girl is helplessly being controlled by her pet. "The picture of the little girl . . . makes us seriously doubt any grown-up self-confidence and authority" (p. 1138).

Given these characteristics of the female, "It is easy to see why many little girls prefer to identify with the male role . . . Girls who wish to be more than placid and pretty are left without an acceptable role alternative" (p. 1138). To be what the role portrays, then, may require the little girl to alienate herself from herself; yet rejection of the role also creates alienation. This kind of sex-role idealization, of course, is not only potentially harmful to young girls, but likewise places strong, rigid constraints on the little boy who must be "fearless, brave, and clever at all times" (p. 1138).

Some valuable research conducted by Inge Broverman and her colleagues (Broverman et al., 1972) gives us a further sense of how intense social pressures and consequent self-alienation can be. Broverman and her group have developed a sex-role questionnaire designed to assess the existence of sexual stereotyping. Of the several findings this research group reports, none perhaps is more disturbing for the development of the female's or the male's identity, than the higher evaluation that both men and women place upon sterotyped male traits (e.g., competence, rationality, and assertion) as compared with stereotyped female traits (e.g., warmth, expressiveness). Because of this differential evaluation of traits,

> *women tend to have more negative self-concepts than do men. The tendency for women to denigrate themselves in this manner can be seen as evidence of the powerful social pressures to conform to the sex-role standards of the society* (p. 75).

Matina Horner's (1972) investigations on the fear of success in females is also informative on much this same point. The point that Horner's research makes is simply that if competence and achievement are felt to be masculine ideals, then the female who treads on such territory is thereby introducing a threat to her female identity. Thus, a fear of success is generated in achievement situations in which to succeed conveys the meaning "I am not a woman." The other side of the coin exists for the male for whom not-competing or not-winning comes to mean "I am not a man." Horner concludes that for females:

> *the anticipation of success is anxiety provoking and as such inhibits otherwise positive achievement-directed motivation and behavior. In order to feel or appear more feminine, women, especially those high in fear of success, disguise their abilities and withdraw from the mainstream of thought, activism, and achievement in our society* (p. 173).

AGENCY VERSUS COMMUNION

Building on ideas proposed by David Bakan (1966), Jeanne Block (1973) offers us both a useful formulation of several of the preceding issues and some empirical data revelant to their examination. Bakan presented the concepts of *agency* and *communion* to distinguish between two basic modes of orientation towards life. Agency is a more individualistic, self-protective, self-enhancing, even competitive modality; communion emphasizes the union of self with the whole, a mutuality and harmony between self and the group or society. The agentic orientation basically stresses the stereotyped

masculine principle of competition and individualistic achievement; the communal orientation stresses the feminine principle of
interpersonal harmony and submersion of self for the good of all. I
think it is possible now to see the parallels between these two concepts and several ideas discussed in Chapter 2, in particular Bene-
dit's concepts of high synergy (communion) versus low synergy
(agency) and Deutsch's perspective on promotive interdependence
(communion) versus contrient interdependence (agency).

It is both Bakan's original view and Block's expanded interpretation that the healthful social character is one who has achieved a
balance between these two principles. Either extreme agency or
extreme communion, as such, proves detrimental to the individual
or the collective. Unfortunately, however, as Block notes, the sex-
role stereotypes are such that males are pressured towards agency
and females towards communion, thereby constraining each to sacrifice achieving a maximization of their human potential.

> The present American cultural emphasis on masculine
> machismo and feminine docility appears to impede the
> development of mature ego functioning. Because children
> are socialized early into culturally defined sex-appropriate
> roles, introspection and self evaluation, which appears to be
> essential catalysts for psychological growth, are discouraged.
> Further, there appear to be significant personal costs paid by
> both sexes when the socialization of sex-appropriate
> behaviors, defined in such narrow terms, is "successful" (p.
> 522).

Block's research suggests the theme of discontinuity in sex-role
socialization for the woman who aspires to achieve her fullest po-
tentials as a person in a society that requires such achievement to
be accomplished at the cost of retaining early role-learnings. The
young girl is socialized into a communal-type role and is discouraged from agentic-forms of behavior. If all roles that are creative,
autonomous, and such are defined in terms of the culturally masculine principle of agency, then the female's early training must be
unlearned in order for the woman to accomplish things for herself:
that is, discontinuity is required by the structure of societal socialization and its ideologies regarding proper sex-role behavior. Block
concludes:

> For women, the socialization process tends to reinforce the
> nurturant, docile, submissive, and conservative aspects of
> the traditionally defined female role and discourages
> personal qualities conventionally defined as masculine:
> self-assertiveness, achievement orientation, and
> independence. The sex role definitions and behavioral
> options for women, then, are narrowed by the socialization

*process, whereas, for men, the sex role definitions and
behavioral options are broadened by socialization. The
achievement of higher levels of ego functioning for women is
more difficult because individuation involves conflict with
our prevailing cultural norms . . . it [is] simply too difficult
and too lonely to oppose the cultural tide* (pp. 525–526).

While substantial costs accrue to women, the total social system
suffers whenever one part, and in this case, a majority at that, is
required to abandon so much in order to achieve status and personal
growth within the social system. The politics of sex-role socialization is characterized by efforts to uncover and demystify sexual
biases within the fabric of society, especially its economic system.
Policies and ideologies regarding sex-role socialization have less to
do in fact with biological necessities than with culturally based
perspectives. From the point of view of the social psychological
study of self and identity, sex-role socialization, in particular the
kinds of issues that we have touched upon, form a critical and continuing source of individual and collective tension within the social
system. This once neglected aspect of identity is increasingly taking
its proper place at the center of the social psychological inquiry
about identity, not surprisingly as more women enter the profession;
and not surprisingly, more women enter the profession as a result
of a growing sensitivity on their part and others of the grave personal and social implications that have derived from being female
in a male world.

AUTHORITY AND THE TASKS OF FREEDOM

7

The themes of this chapter and the next are intertwined and must be considered together, as the following classic investigation clearly indicates. The investigator, Stanley Milgram (1963; 1965a; b), was concerned with a crucial behavioral aspect of the cement that holds together all social systems: obedience to authority. Our everyday lives are replete with instances of such obedience: we could not readily navigate the expressways of our daily commutes or engage in the trade that buys our daily bread were it not for our and other's obedience to rules, conventions, commands, and requests.

There are various kinds of authority to which we may yield in obedience or perhaps confront with rebellion, including those based on O's ability to reward or to punish us (see French & Raven, 1959 for a helpful analysis). However, no basis for authority is more central to our contemporary form of social organization than that which involves *legitimate authority*. The crux of legitimacy is its sense of moral rightness that extends beyond the authority's (i.e., O's) potential to reward or coerce us, and even beyond any liking or disliking we may personally feel towards O. We obey because it is right and proper to do so, "quite apart from questions of coercion or utility" (McIntosh, 1970, p. 901). This sense of legitimacy can be illuminated by several brief examples with which most of us are familiar.

A democratically held election for a leader confers on the winner certain legitimate rights to command, within the range defined as appropriate by the office to which he or she has been elected. Government represents one of the major locations from which legitimacy emanates; and stable governments, regardless of what coercion and naked force might have been employed in their origins (or lay in their contemporary background), could not long rule without the consent of the governed: that is, without gaining and sustaining legitimacy.

In a military context, those of superior rank have a legitimate right to command others to obey. A judge is granted legitimacy within the legal justice system to use prescribed procedures for levying fines and passing sentences on those found guilty of violating laws. A doctor is given legitimacy to engage in a variety of medical practices which, were others to engage in them, would be considered violations of our person. In some religions, the clergy are granted legitimacy to demand and to expect obedience from their flock in matters of their religious and behavioral practices (e.g., drinking, marriage, dancing, birth control, etc.). Science and scientists in contemporary society are granted legitimate authority to pass judgments that have major consequences for our lives. Much as the physician's pronouncement "you are sick, spend the next seven days in bed; drink plenty of fluids," makes our illness legitimate so that we are thereby absolved of our daily work responsibilities, scientists, in general, can similarly legitimate a wide range of behaviors for us to follow: "eat this, don't eat that; this is a healthy form of behavior, that is a pathological way."

SOURCES OF LEGITIMACY

The great sociologist, Max Weber (1947; Gerth & Mills, 1946) outlined several systems whereby authority may receive its touch of legitimacy: traditional, charismatic, rational-legal. Traditional authority is based on shared cultural beliefs that the traditions of a society have a sanctity and moral rightness that demands they be followed. One does not follow the traditional authority, the king, or the chieftain, because of the reason or rationality inherent in the authority's demands, but rather because one accepts the ancient, traditional roots out of which that authority has emerged. Charisma as a basis for legitimacy rests on the devotion of persons to the exceptional and infectious qualities of another. The charismatic authority rules because others attribute to them some kind of supernatural, uncanny powers. Rational-legal bases for legitimacy, seen by Weber to be the essence of our modern forms of social organization (e.g., bureaucracies) is based on an acceptance of the idea that persons in positions of authority have a right to issue commands in their efforts to provide a rational approach to accomplishing certain common goals. Rules that are applied according to a system of principles by the person in the position of authority, equally to all members of the society: this is the key quality of rational-legal bases of legitimacy.

It can be readily noted that each basis for legitimating authority calls on a different sense of why one should be obedient. One is obedient to tradition for that is the way things have always been done; one is obedient to charisma because of the exceptional powers of the person giving the orders; one is obedient to rational-legal authority because one accepts the power of the office or position which the authority inhabits, and the reasonableness of the procedures that they follow in issuing their commands.

It was Weber's contention that our modern era, in its pursuit of rationality and of egalitarianism under the law, has moved from traditional and charismatic to rational-legal bases for legitimating authority (we examine this theme further in Chapter 11). Thus the office holder in the institution follows impersonal rules applied to everyone, minimizing the influences of kinship and family ties, for example, that were so prevalent when legitimacy was based on tradition. Reason and rationality, a kind of natural law, are seen to inhere in the bureaucratic form of social organization: we are obedient because we have faith in such reason and rationality; we believe that the commands are issued within a context of reason and that in being obedient we are thereby acting most wisely and intelligently; we accept the network of relationships that tie persons together into a social structure and view our commitment to behave in ways that conform to the designated relationships of power and authority necessary for the structure itself to be maintained. To behave otherwise, to be disobedient to the legitimately designated authority, to become a deviant, would not only prove embarrassing and unpleasant (Gamson, 1968), but would also imply acting in a manner that threatens to disrupt the very structure of relationships that we have learned to value and respect (e.g., Allport, 1962; Berger & Luckman, 1966). Being obedient to the legitimate authority is requisite to maintaining the structure of relationships that tie both together and which each values.

None of this, by the way, should be construed as seeing Weber favoring this kind of rationalization and bureaucratization of legitimate authority; for indeed, in Weber's view, and as we shall next see, in Milgram's and related investigations, the willing obedience to such authority may be a most insidious form of modern evil, outdistancing even the ruthless monarchs of tradition or the potential demagogues of charisma. But let us now turn to Milgram's classic investigation for a closer view of this complex but vital matter.

The Milgram Study of Obedience*

Two experimental subjects arrive at the laboratory and each is paid $4.50 for his or her time. The experimenter informs both subjects that because little is known about the influence of punishment on memory, the experiment in which they are to participate will study

*From S. Milgram, Human Relations, Vol. 18, 1965, Plenum Publishing Corporation, New York and S. Milgram, Obedience to Authority, Harper & Row, 1974.

this effect, that on the basis of a random drawing, one of them will be the teacher and one the learner. After the drawing is held, the learner is taken to the next room and strapped into an "electric chair." The teacher is shown an electric shocking apparatus and is informed that whenever the learner makes an error in learning a list of paired words, the learner is to be given a shock; furthermore, each shock is to be progressively more severe than the preceding one: thus as errors increase so will the intensity of the shock. The electric shocking apparatus that the teacher uses has thirty voltage levels ranging from 15 to 450 volts. Various levels are marked as follows: slight shock, moderate shock, strong shock, very strong shock, intense shock, extreme intensity shock, DANGER: SEVERE SHOCK, and after 420 volts, the markings are simply XXX. So that the teacher may experience a sample of the shock that will be delivered to the learner, the teacher is given a test shock of 45 volts.

In the typical experimental session, the following occurs. The learner makes several errors and the teacher delivers shocks, each time of increasingly high voltage.

> *Starting with 75 volts the learner begins to grunt and moan. At 150 volts he demands to be let out of the experiment. At 180 volts he cries out that he can no longer stand the pain. At 300 volts he refuses to provide any more answers to the memory test, insisting that he is no longer a participant in the experiment and must be freed* (1965b, p. 60).

The typical teacher, in response to these complaints of the learner, might turn to the experimenter for assistance. The experimenter simply indicates that "You have no choice, you must go on. Disregard the learner's protests." In some cases, especially when the learner ceases responding at 300 volts and the teacher is asked to continue increasing the shock intensity, counting no-response as an error, the teacher refuses to take responsibility for "whatever might happen to him"; in these cases, the experimenter indicates that he will accept the responsibility but that the teacher must continue administering electric shocks.

I have now described most of the essentials of Milgram's procedure plus some typical teacher and learner behavior. What would be your prediction about the teacher's obedience to the experimenter's requests to continue shocking the learner, essentially up to the 450 volt level? And what about your own likely behavior in a similar situation? Would you be obedient and administer a shock of 450 volts? Milgram asked forty psychiatrists to predict the results. They predicted that most teachers would not go beyond 150 volts, that by the time 300 volts was reached and learners ceased responding, only 4 percent of the teachers would still be obedient, and that "only a little over one-tenth of one percent . . . would administer the highest shock on the board."

Milgram also described these procedures to a group of forty subjects asking them to indicate what they think they would have done if they were the teacher. Three of the forty indicated that they would refuse to administer even the slightest shock value (15 volts); by the time 150 volts was reached, 70 percent of these subjects said that they would refuse to continue; and fully 100 percent said they would have stopped at the 300-volt level. Similar results have been reported by other investigators (e.g., Larsen et al. 1972).

Other subjects who had the situation described to them were asked to indicate the proper moral stance to take; the consensus was that the moral position if one were the teacher in such a situation would be to defy the experimenter and follow one's conscience. Thus, it seems clear that for persons outside Milgram's situation, including psychiatrists, other adults, and college undergraduates, conditional obedience (i.e., following the experimenter's requests but only up to a point) is the predicted behavior for the teacher.

In numerous variations of this basic design we described, Milgram reports that approximately 65 percent of the nearly 1000 subjects studied continued administering shocks up to the final, 450-volt level.

> *With numbing regularity good people were seen to knuckle under the demands of authority and perform actions that were callous and severe. Men who are in everyday life responsible and decent were seduced by the trappings of authority, by the control of their perceptions, and by the uncritical acceptance of the experimenter's definition of the situation into performing harsh acts.*
>
> *What is the limit of such obedience? At many points we attempted to establish a boundary. Cries from the victim were inserted; not good enough. The victim claimed heart trouble; subjects still shocked him on command. The victim pleaded to be let free, and his answers no longer registered on the signal box; subjects continued to shock him. At the outset we had not conceived that such drastic procedures would be needed to generate disobedience, and each step was added only as the ineffectiveness of the earlier techniques became clear. The final effort to establish a limit was the Touch-Proximity condition [where the teacher had to physically keep the learner's hand on the shock plate after 150 volts for the learner to receive the shock]. But the very first subject in this condition subdued the victim on command, and proceeded to the highest shock level. A*

quarter of the subjects in this condition performed similarly ... A substantial proportion of people do what they are told to do, irrespective of the content of the act and without limitations of conscience, so long as they perceive that the command comes from a legitimate authority. If in this study an anonymous experimenter could successfully command adults to subdue a fifty-year old man, and force on him painful electric shocks against his protests, one can only wonder what government, with its vastly greater authority and prestige can command of its subjects (1965b, pp. 74–75).

In considering Milgram's research and findings, it is important to realize that the subjects who administered the shocks did not enact their obedience without protest or without symptoms of pain and tension. Milgram reports numerous instances of subjects who broke out in a sweat, who trembled, who stuttered, who bit their lips, who groaned as they became more and more caught up in the experimental situation. Subjects, in fact, loudly protested and indicated their desire to quit; yet 65 percent continued in spite of their own tension and distaste for the entire matter. As Milgram notes, there was a dissociation between word and act; words of protest were accompanied by acts of obedience. What is this power that commands such obedience? The experimenter did not threaten his subjects with punishment for their disobedience, nor did he promise them great riches for their obedience. The payment of $4.50 was given at the beginning and was theirs no matter what they chose to do. Rather, it is the legitimacy of the scientists' role in our contemporary society, the assumption that they must know what they are doing and thus in the name of scientific research it must be legitimate to follow their commands.

VARIATIONS IN MILGRAM'S DESIGN

Several variations of Milgram's research design did decrease obedience. Thus, when compelled to physically hold down the learner, obedience dropped from 65 percent to 25 percent; likewise, the farther away the experimenter was from the subjects, the greater their disobedience. In fact, when the experimenter was actually absent from the room but giving orders nevertheless, many subjects cheated by giving shocks at a lower level rather than the higher levels required. But perhaps the most significant approach used to induce resistance rather than obedience to authority involved the social comparison model we previously discussed (Chapter 6).

In this variation of his basic design, Milgram (1965a) used three teachers and one learner. As usual, the learner was a paid accomplice; however, so were two of the teachers. In this way, it was possible to program his teacher-accomplices to be disobedient in order to study the effects of this kind of group pressure in liberating the naïve subjects from the legitimacy of the experimenter. The first teacher-accomplice refuses to continue with the experiment at the 150-volt level because of the learner's complaints. In spite of the experimenter's insistence, the teacher-accomplice is adamant about refusing to continue and so gets up and moves away from the shock apparatus. The experimenter now informs the remaining two teachers that they will have to continue. At 210 volts, the second teacher-accomplice refuses to continue and moves away from the shock apparatus, leaving the naïve subject alone to obey the experimenter's requests that the error-prone learner be shocked.

Under these conditions, Milgram reports that 90 percent of the subjects were disobedient, compared with the 35 percent in the typical experimental condition. In other words, social support for disobedience helps us disobey even what we consider to be a legitimate order from the experimenter. Recall our Chapter 6 discussion of the Asch study in which the presence of a deviant-partner facilitated the naïve subject's refusing to accept the majority judgments of line lengths; in the present case, it is not majority group pressure that the subject is helped to defy, but rather the unseen but potent hand of legitimacy. But where in our everyday lives is this accomplice?

The role of models in the acceptance or rejection of authority that this version of Milgram's research suggested to be of importance, has been studied by others employing variations of Milgram's teacher-learner research design. It seems reasonable to think of the model (i.e., other subjects in the same situation) as providing several kinds of information to P:

1. The model's behavior informs P of action possibilities that might otherwise not have been thought of.
2. The model's behavior informs P about what the consequences of certain actions are—for example, whether disobedience to authority is punished. In Milgram's disobedient group variation, the accomplice's refusal to continue went unpunished by the experimenter; thus P could note that P's defiance might also be carried out without punishment.
3. As a variation on this theme, the model's compliance with the experimenter's requests to act aggressively when not punished, might facilitate the subject to act aggressively. Of course, by not punishing the subject's own aggression in the first place, the experimenter is thereby approving and legitimating such behavior; models who act similarly should only further reinforce and legitimate such approval.

In a variation of his design, Milgram (1965a) employed accomplices who complied with the experimenter's requests. Subjects' level of obedience under these circumstances was no greater than when they responded only to the experimenter. More recently, Larsen, Coleman, Forbes, and Johnson (1972) provide further confirmation for this effect. As we will see shortly, Larsen and his colleagues also studied the effects of P's watching an obedient model in facilitating P's own later obedience.

4.   The model's behavior helps P define the intensity of the situation; for example, a model who appears unconcerned about the learner's fate helps P define the situation as less dangerous than P might otherwise have thought.

5.   The model's behavior, as we already noted, gives P an ally such that their joint power may be used to overthrow the power of the authority.

6.   The model's behavior helps reinforce or undermine the legitimacy of the authority; an obedient model helps further legitimate the authority, whereas a disobedient model may help delegitimate the authority.

Mantell's research (1971) conducted in Germany with German citizens and employing much the same kind of situation and apparatus as Milgram is informative about the effects of modeling designed to undermine the authority's legitimacy. Recall that in Milgram's group design, the naïve subject was in a face-to-face setting with other persons who acted defiantly. In Mantell's design, subjects arrived and were asked to observe the experiment that was in progress in order to familiarize themselves with the setting that they would soon enter. What they observed was another subject (actually an accomplice) not only refuse to continue with the experiment after administering a few shocks and hearing cries of complaint from the learner, but openly attack the experimenter's basis for legitimacy. The naïve subjects witnessed the challenge to the experimenter's credentials and status; they noted that the experimenter, under this challenge, revealed himself to be a student doing unsupervised research without any institutional backing or affiliation. Finally, they watched the challenger leave the room. Mantell's model goes well beyond Milgram's in seeking to undermine the legitimacy of the authority and in successfully (i.e., without apparent punishment) breaking off the entire experiment.

But what would these subjects do when placed into the same situation a few moments later with the same experimenter? Mantell compared his baseline condition (similar in most respects to Milgram's comparable condition) with this delegitimating model condition. Whereas 85 percent of the baseline subjects pressed the full range of shock buttons, 52 percent of those with the delegitimating model did so. Recall that Milgram's baseline rate was about 65 percent and that his disobedient group rate was 10 percent; with Mantell's subjects, even with a model who cast grave doubts on the legitimacy of the experimenter, 52 percent were totally obedient, a figure not that discrepant from Milgram's baseline!

While the use of such different subject populations makes it difficult to offer any unequivocal understanding of these differences, it appears that the direct attack on the authority's legitimacy that Mantell's model portrayed, may have both helped lower the model's legitimacy for some subjects while leading others to discount anyone who would so upset a proper experiment. We would need to know more about what the subject's interpretations were of the model's behavior. Participating with disobedient others may also be a rather different experience than witnessing a defiant model and then having to enter the situation alone. Again, it would be helpful to get a better sense of the subjects' conceptions of the situation. It is likely, however, that a defiant model not only provides P with information about successful defiance, but can also provide an example of the kind of person that P would not like to be.

In reflecting on his results and subjects' comments made during the experiment, Mantell expressed continuing puzzlement about why such results occur. He noted that even without models, the context of the experiment delegitimates itself: how absurd it must seem to try to teach someone by using punishment when all you notice as the teacher is that the more punishment you administer the more pain you elicit. And yet, persons continue inflicting the pain. Mantell implies that perhaps what we assume to be a socially undesirable act—administering electric shocks to another human being—may not be that undesirable to some people.

Returning to the United States, Larsen and his colleagues (1972) employed a technique similar to Milgram's, though not an exact replication. They introduced a modeling group in which, similar to Mantell's, the naïve subject was asked to learn the procedures he would soon participate in by observing a session in progress. Unlike Mantell's, however, these subjects observed an obedient accomplice run through the final series of shocks, ending with the maximum level. Their results suggest that the legitimating model increases the subject's obedience as compared with a control condition in which subjects choose their own shock levels. For example, the average maximum voltage used in the control group was 199 volts; the model's condition maximum was 244 volts: 390 was the maximum voltage possible. Larsen reasoned that the model provided information for the naïve subject that acting aggressively in this situation would not be punished and that obedience to the experimenter's authority was right and proper (our previous point 3). Efforts to relate selected personality measures to subjects' behavior were not successful, leading Larsen and his associates to conclude that situational factors undoubtedly are more potent under these kinds of experimental conditions.

Though not precisely concerned with modeling as such, the research reported by Kilham and Mann (1974) lends itself, in part, to a modeling interpretation. Their primary interest was in examining the degree to which roles within a network of authority affected the degree of obedience or disobedience that resulted. In particular, would the person pressing the actual button to deliver the shock (called the *executant*) be more resistant than the person who simply *transmits* the order from above from the experimenter, and thus is not as directly involved in the actual delivery of the shock. The question is especially important when we realize that in most everyday, organizational contexts, few persons actually carry out the orders by directly punishing others; more are involved at earlier points in the chain of command. Does this distance from actual harm-doing facilitate their obedience to commands?

To study this possibility, Kilham and Mann created executant and transmitter roles in a Milgram-like situation. The executant actually pushed the buttons that administered the shock, while the transmitter simply conveyed the request from the experimenter. Their subjects were male and female students from Australia. Results indicated that overall, transmitters were, as expected, more obedient than executants. Among males, for example, the obedience rates (i.e., shocking all the way to the maximum level) for transmitters was 68 percent, while it was 40 percent for executants. Among females, 40 percent of the transmitters and only 16 percent of the executants went all the way in shocking the learner.

These results not only show a role difference, but also a sex difference; women tended to be less obedient in all conditions than men. Just why this difference or what it means is by no means clear, though it obviously does warrant further work. Perhaps male aggression is more permitted than female aggression. Sex differences were not very pronounced in the data reported by the Larsen group: out of the many comparisons made, only two were statistically significant; in both, as compared with females, males both administered shocks for a longer time and at a higher level in the modeling condition than in the control condition. It may be that the unpunished aggression of the model helped free the more predisposed males as compared with the females to likewise express their own aggression. These findings are consistent with the Kilham and Mann data.

Modeling is involved in the Kilhman and Mann research in that role occupants had the behavior of the other subject (an accomplice) as a model for their own. In particular, the authors note that the model's behavior may have different meanings depending on P's own role as executant or transmitter: when the naïve subject was a transmitter, seeing an unconcerned executant may have facilitated a willingness to obey; after all, if the button-pusher doesn't care, then perhaps nothing serious is happening. On the other hand, the executant who sees an unconcerned transmitter may feel that it is he or she who is on the front lines and that is why the transmitter seems so blasé about the entire matter.

We have seen the potency of situational factors in affecting P's behavior; in particular, the ways in which the authority structure of a situation have a potency that in these several cases seem to carry us beyond reason and sensibility. But, as our analyses have suggested, it is not simply the legitimacy of the authority that elicits P's obedience, but also the actions of others likewise involved with P in the same situation. The sense of rightness about a given authority situation can be enhanced or undermined by the actions of others; yet even here, as we have seen (e.g., Mantell's striking findings), the aura of legitimacy may hang heavy in spite of other's defiance. Perhaps defiance is easier when one's comrades are here-and-now present rather than models no longer around; or perhaps, as noted, authority-defiant models represent something socially undesirable to P, namely those who would challenge rightful authority, and thus rather than P's identifying with resistance, P seeks to dissociate from such defiant models.

To respond with obedience to legitimate authority, though it may appear at times to be reflex-like, involves a more complex evaluative process. While much effort has gone into studying the situational components of such obedience, fewer efforts have been invested in determining the definitional and decision processes within P that result in obedient or defiant behavior. As Mantell suggests, just what must people be thinking when they shock someone to silence in the name of teaching!

The issues that Milgram's and the other's investigations examine and into which we will delve further in this and the next chapter and again in our final chapter show us the frightening element in Weber's idea of the legitimacy of rational-legal authority. We wonder, along with C. Wright Mills (1959) and others, if we are but "Cheerful Robots," robbed of our reason and hence our freedom by great systems of rational authority to which we yield ourselves, following orders and performing our technical skills without the intervention of that power of reason that lets us freely see and freely choose among alternatives. We, like the hypothetical subjects and the psychiatrists of Milgram's research, sit back and perceive choices and options that were we in the situation, we are less likely to have noted.

But, let us not get seduced by the term Cheerful Robot into believing that either cheer or mechanical obedience is involved. Few if any of Milgram's or the other researcher's subjects could be described as cheerful; they went about their work, but without much pleasure. And, indeed, as we have emphasized, their behavior was not mechanical in the way a clock or machine works, but rather flowed from the way in which they defined their situation. The definition of self as a good subject seemed more important in general than self as a moral being, although a conflict did exist between these two possibilities.

Accepting the experimenter's role as legitimate helped persons to accept as well the experimenter's definitions of their choices and options; to yield their responsibility to the authority; to define themselves in terms of their compliance. These several laboratory studies, along with the Nazi atrocities, Vietnam, Watergate and such all illustrate the extremes to which persons have gone in the name of obedience to legitimate authority. It is no wonder then that Mills sees freedom to be the fundamental issue of our time, the basic issue to which all social scientists should direct their efforts.

Participation and Decision Making

Our daily lives are filled with occasions in which one person seeks to direct or channel our behavior in specific directions: O tries to get P to do X. And much of this occurs within interpersonal (i.e., small groups) and organizational contexts. Milgram's focus on obedience to legitimate authority in which O gets P to act in a potentially harmful way to another offers us one dramatic and instructive example. But not all authorities seek to engage us in harmful acts. Often, they may wish to change the direction of our behavior in other ways, including some that we might consider beneficial to ourselves and others. However, in what ways can authorities influence our behaviors so as to engage our critical reason in the process? Are some arrangements of authority more likely to facilitate this intrusion of reason whereas other arrangements, perhaps like the context Milgram and the others created, are more likely to thwart its presence? It is to these and other related questions that Kurt Lewin and his associates directed many of their efforts.

Kurt Lewin said it well in 1947:

> The social scientists, perhaps more than the natural scientists, have to learn to be unafraid and at the same time fair-minded. To my mind, fair-mindedness is the essence of scientific objectivity. The scientist has to learn to look facts

*straight in the face, even if they do not agree with his
prejudices. He must learn this without giving up his belief
in values ... He has to learn to understand how the scientific
and moral aspects are frequently interlocked in problems,
and how the scientific aspects may still be approached. He
has to see realistically the problems of power, which are
interwoven with many of the questions he is to study,
without his becoming a servant to vested interests. His
realism should be akin to courage in the sense of Plato, who
defines courage as wisdom in the face of danger* (1947b, p.
153).

And, as importantly, Lewin and the students and colleagues he in-
spired did it well. We first met Lewin in this book in Berlin in the
1920s (Chapter 2). In 1932, he left Germany for the United States.
Perhaps it was his background in Germany with fascism's challenge to freedom; perhaps it was his deep commitment to research
and to social action; regardless of why, Lewin carried with him a
passion for democracy, for freedom and self-determination. His
work at Iowa with Lippitt and White and his later efforts both as
part of a social scientists' contribution to the U.S. war effort in the
1940s and as part of a person's passionate concern with social issues,
all reflect this deep conviction.

Democracy Versus Autocracy: Lewinian Views of the Person and Authority

Milgram and others inform us of how readily we can become like
robots, cheerful or anxious, obediently following orders of those in
positions of legitimate authority. While the authority of O over P
may be legitimate, O may nevertheless exercise that authority in
various ways. An elected official, for example, may manifest authority in ways that increase or decrease P's own freedom of choice.
Lewin's concern was to explore ways in which legitimate authority
establishes conditions that are either conducive to self-determination or that constrain people, inclining them towards obedience.
The classic investigation was reported in 1939 by Lewin, Lippitt and
White. The leadership style of the adult leaders of children's groups
was systematically varied in one of three ways: democratic, authoritarian, and laissez-faire.

The democratic leader was to engage his groups in discussion and
involve them in group decisions over matters of concern to the
group. He was to help keep the group's overall goals in mind and to
aid them in clarifying the relationship between their specific activi-

ties and these overall goals. In other words, he was to facilitate the group member's formulation of various options open to them and to facilitate their choice among these options: that is, to help increase member's freedom. In manner, he was to be a regular group member; but he was instructed not to do much of the actual work of the group.

The authoritarian leader was to establish the general policies of his groups, to formulate their options for them, and then to make specific decisions regarding which options they would choose. He was to keep the group in the dark, to a certain degree, concerning its long-range goals and how its present activity fitted into this larger picture. He was instructed to remain fairly aloof from any participation in group work. Note how this description of the authoritarian leader is consistent with the manner in which the experimenter in Milgram's investigation operated and with the manner in which many persons in positions of legitimate authority also operate. This is descriptive of a style of leadership in which members are not permitted to formulate the choices available to them nor to actively decide, but rather are passively to receive the leader's definition of their situation.

The laissez-faire leader was to play a passive role, responding primarily when asked, never taking any initiative to facilitate group activity or to help members clarify their goals and options unless asked. He was to be more friendly than aloof, yet not to participate much in group work.

The groups studied were several clubs of 11-year-old boys. They were put through a program in which the adult leader was changed every seven weeks; some began with a democratic leader and shifted to an autocratic one while others reversed this procedure. Measures were obtained through observational records and interviews with the participants, their parents, and their classroom teachers.

In addition to its normal routine, each club experienced three rigged events. In the first, the leader arrived late for a meeting. The second required that he be called away during one of the sessions. Finally, a stranger—either a "janitor" or an "electrician"—came into the room while the leader was gone and began to criticize the work that the group was doing.

Lippitt and White (1958) report several findings of importance. They noted two distinct responses to the authoritarian leadership style. Most of the groups reacted passively and dependently, showing low levels of either tension or frustration; but one club was more actively aggressive, demonstrating both frustration and aggression towards the adult leader. We will return to this shortly. But for now, the dominant response of passivity and dependence to the authoritarian leadership style parallels the kind of passivity and dependence that Milgram reports in his investigation. In both cases, the leader's orders are obeyed and open resistance is minimal.

In the authoritarian group there were greater feelings of general dissatisfaction than in the democratic groups; there were more efforts to gain the adult's attention; there was less personal, friendly, or intimate conversation between members; there was greater intragroup irritability and hostility. This last finding also differentiated the democratic from the laissez-faire style; these latter groups were more like the authoritarian than the democratic in that there were general expressions of irritability towards fellow group members.

The groups responded differently to the three rigged events as a function of the style of leadership they experienced. The democratic groups were able to work well on their own, being minimally disrupted either when the leader arrived late or was called out during a meeting. The authoritarian groups did not take any initiative to start without their leader's presence. The laissez-faire groups were reported to be more active but not productive without the leader present. The arrival of the critical stranger in the authoritarian-led groups was met with greater hostility toward the intruder and higher intermember tension and scapegoating than in the democratic or laissez-faire groups. It was as though the autocratically led groups were fearful of directly rebelling against their leader and so reacted angrily towards the outsider; the more self-directed and self-governing democratic groups, not having similar frustration, tended not to overreact in this way to the outsider.

Lewin noted how the transfer of autocratically-led groups to a democratic leader was met with a kind of all-hell-breaking-loose freedom, as though the original leader had served primarily to keep the lid on their bubbling caldron of anger and frustration. Sadly, he noted as well, how readily those who had initially been under democratic leadership yielded when transferred to an authoritarian leader.

> There have been few experiences for me as impressive as seeing the expression in children's faces change during the first day of autocracy. The friendly, open, and cooperative group, full of life, became within a short half-hour a rather apathetic-looking gathering without initiative. The change from autocracy to democracy seemed to take somewhat more time than from democracy to autocracy (1948, p. 82).

We hear echoed in Lewin's personal sadness over the ease with which the children gave up their freedoms, Milgram's own concern over the apparent ease with which average citizens complied with the experimenter's requests. One senses that it was this sadness that continued to motivate Lewin's efforts to create more democratic, participatory techniques for bringing about necessary change. It was indeed all too easy but all too costly for O to induce compliance from P (see Kelman's discussion on pp. 351–352); it took more effort apparently to bring about the active involvement and concern of persons in self-determination in the face of a legitimate authority figure (e.g., the adult group leader). Lewin's commitment, however, was to the latter, more difficult task.

Group Processes and Change: The Lewinian Perspective

During and after World War II, Kurt Lewin and others were engaged in research on the problem of inducing relatively permanent and stable changes in others' behavior. In the now classic study, the behavior to be changed involved a person's eating habits. The question was how to produce a change in eating behavior such that the choice meat necessary to serve the fighting men was replaced on the home tables by more esoteric cuts, such as beef hearts, sweetbreads, and kidneys.

First of all, Lewin (1951; 1958) conceptualized the problem, noting that it is the housewife who is the *gatekeeper* to the kitchen table, occupying a critical link in the chain of events that brings food from market to table. To induce change, therefore, one heads for those key figures (i.e., gatekeepers) whose behavior must be changed in order to effect a new level of activity in the family system as a whole.

Once you find that key to the system's structure, the next problem is to figure out why she does what she is already doing. Lewin recognized that most eating behavior involved social habits that served as rather strong obstacles to inducing change. A social habit does not exist in isolation, but rather is a habit within a social context that supports and maintains it. That the housewife serves the particular food she does is a behavior that is maintained and reinforced within a social context. This understanding led Lewin to make the following statement:

> *Perhaps one might expect single individuals to be more pliable than groups of like-minded individuals. However, experience in leadership training, in changing food habits, work production, criminality, alcoholism, prejudices, all seem to indicate that it is usually easier to change individuals formed into a group than to change any one of them separately. As long as the group values are unchanged the individual will resist changes more strongly the farther he is to depart from group standards. If the group standard*

itself is changed, the resistance which is due to the relation between individual and group standard is eliminated (1947a, p. 34).

The essential point is simple and often overlooked:

1. Our habits, attitudes, and so forth, all exist within a social context.
2. That context, usually a group or groups to which we belong, supports our continuation of the habit or our belief in the attitude.
3. Deviating from the group's level of habit or opinion is usually cause for the application of sanctions.
4. Any process of individual change must overcome the group's standards that support a particular level of behavior.
5. If one can work to change the standards of a group, he or she can thereby effect a change in the behavior of individual members of that group.

In a later updating of Lewin's views, more differentiated than the original, Dorwin Cartwright (1951) indicated three ways in which a group enters the process of change. He argues that a group may be a *medium* of change, a *target* of change, or an *agent* of change.

As a medium of change, the group has the ability to exercise power over its members either to conform to or resist efforts towards change. Recall the influence the resisting accomplices had in facilitating the naïve subject's resistance to the experimenter's legitimate authority in the Milgram study. Furthermore, presumably, the more strongly an individual is attracted to membership in the group and the more cohesive the group itself is, the stronger those influence forces. Several studies lend support to this argument. Recall the Schachter study in which cohesiveness was experimentally varied (p. 276). The more highly cohesive groups placed greater pressures on their members to conform to their standards. Studies by Festinger and by others have likewise demonstrated that the more cohesive the group or the more strongly the member wishes to remain a member, the greater power the group has.

The notion of the group as a target of change is one we have previously mentioned. The standards of the group become the target of the change agent's efforts. The change agent assumes that if he or she can change the group's standards, and if the group has power over its members, then, the agent will have successfully altered individual behavior.

Finally, the group as an agent of change exists whenever the group as a whole becomes the change agent working to alter some other group. For example, a neighborhood group might form to achieve change in city government policies involving recreation facilities in their neighborhood.

For Lewin, the group's standards were to be changed in order that the individual member of that group whose own behavior was anchored by those standards could be changed. Furthermore, the method chosen for changing the group's standards was to be both effective and as importantly, ideologically democratic. Lewin was vitally concerned that change agents be self-conscious and moral.

As his work with children's groups had previously suggested, a democratic style of leadership was effective in gaining the intelligent participation of all members in the decisions affecting their club. In addition, the decisions that were made by the group, once made, appeared to be independent of the adult leader. By contrast, recall that the adult leader in the authoritarian-run groups was an essential cog that kept the entire affair in motion. Group members were so dependent on him for guidance that they could not work when he was absent. In the democratic groups, however, work went on with or without the adult leader. For one who wanted to induce rather permanent change, change that was arrived at by an agreement among equals rather than forced from above, and a change that did not require continued surveillance of the authority in order to be maintained, the democratically led group decision method seemed preferable on almost all counts.

UNFREEZING AND REFREEZING

In his food-habits research, Lewin conceptualized the change process as involving three stages: *unfreezing, movement, refreezing.*

Unfreezing, as the term suggests, conceptualizes the behavior to be changed as frozen in a social context requiring rapid thawing or unfreezing. As Lewin notes, this unfreezing might involve breaking "open the shell of complacency" or sometimes deliberately bringing about an "emotional stirrup." Movement involves actual change in the group's behavior from its former position to a new level. Finally, refreezing requires firming up the group's standards so that the change will be more permanent.

In the 1940s, Lewin and his coworkers undertook a series of investigations in which they tested this conceptualization of change, contrasting group decision with lecture techniques. In one food-habit study, for example, groups of Red Cross volunteers ranging in size from thirteen to seventeen members were to be targets of efforts to get them to serve beef hearts, sweetbreads, and kidneys. Some of the groups were given lectures:

> *which linked the problem of nutrition with the war effort, emphasized the vitamin and mineral value of the three meats, giving detailed explanations with the aid of charts.*

Both the health and economic aspects were stressed (Lewin, 1958, p. 202).

In addition, these lectured groups were given recipes for preparing the foods in a most tasty manner.

The group decision conditions, by contrast, met with a democratically oriented leader who engaged the Red Cross volunteers in a discussion, covering most of the same topics dealt with in the lectures that the other groups had experienced. Towards the end of their discussion, a show of hands indicated how many of the women were now willing to try these new foods.

A follow-up examination of these women showed that whereas 3 percent of the lecture group served at least one of the new meats, 32 percent involved with group decision served them. Thus, although the lecture was an interesting and well-conducted one, it was relatively ineffective in producing any behavior change.

As part of that same research program, Lewin reports several further studies, all of which indicate the relative effectiveness of the group decision over the lecture method for producing behavior change. Dana Klisurich, for one, attempted to get housewives to increase home consumption of milk. Follow-up at intervals of two weeks and four weeks after either the lecture or the group decision method had been employed indicated that the group method was more effective after both time periods than the lecture approach. In yet another study (see Lewin, 1958), group discussion methods were more effective than lecture approaches in getting mothers to use orange juice and cod liver oil with their newborn children.

Decision or Discussion?

In 1955, Edith Bennett Pelz (see Bennett, 1955) brought the complexity of Lewin's group versus lecture methods under careful scrutiny. She was concerned, as others had been, with the precise distinction between these apparently contrasting methods. In order to tease out the differences, she isolated four factors that seemed at play in the group decision approach:

1. Group discussion in order to convey information. For example, in Lewin's group methods, the discussion itself was a means of getting the same kinds of information before the group that the lecturer had presented.
2. Decision making. In the group approach, the housewives typically are asked to make a decision to do something, for example, to try out the new meats.
3. Commitment, or the degree to which the decision is made publicly for all to see.

4. Degree of consensus refers to the extensity of agreement in the group about trying out the new behavior.

As her change goal, Pelz sought to get University of Michigan introductory psychology students to become more willing to volunteer for psychology experiments. She experimentally varied both the type of influence attempted—that is, discussion versus lecture—and the level of commitment required: (1) no decision made; (2) decision made anonymously; (3) partial anonymity about the decision—that is, subjects briefly raised their hands; (4) public commitment—that is, subjects both raised their hands and publicly gave their names as being willing to volunteer for psychological research if asked.

An analysis of her data led Pelz to conclude that of the four factors initially thought to be crucial, only two turned out to be critical elements of the group method as compared with the lecture approach. These were the actual process of making a decision and the degree of perceived consensus concerning that decision. Neither group discussion alone nor public commitment were essential in producing behavior change. As Pelz herself suggests: "In the light of the findings here reported, therefore, 'group decision' might profitably be redefined as 'decision about individual goals in a setting of shared norms regarding such goals'" (1955, p. 219). These two factors shed further light on the meaning not only of group decision as a technique of change, but also of the actual dynamics of behavior and opinion change. It appears that the anchoring of opinion and action within a social context, in which norms of enforcement are present and sanctions for deviation are taken, serves as a strong resistance force against individual change. The techniques of group dynamics call on this reality of group factors and seek to induce a change by working on the very group that supports the behavior in question.

In a real sense, then, the application of democratic or participatory methods as Lewin suggested is one that engages the individuals of a group in an active reexamination of their present position. It places the individual and the group in the position of coming to a decision about a new level of behavior. This is a decision that they reach about their own group; it is a decision made from within rather than one dictated from without. From Lewin's value bias as a change agent, this latter point is critical. The democratic leader as a change agent is a guide, a resource person, a procedural expert who assists persons in discovering whether or not change is needed, the implications or consequences of that change, and how best to accomplish the change if it is decided upon. Notice that while the lecture method could allow for both individual decision and perceived consensus—the two factors that Pelz finds to be significant—

it cannot as readily allow for group participation in the discussion, in the formulation of alternatives, and in reaching a decision, as compared with the group method. Thus, the lecture approach typically is less democratic, more of a one-to-many than a one-to-one form of communication.

INDIVIDUAL AUTONOMY AND GROUP PRESSURE

The theme that runs through these several studies concerns the role of individuals in directly affecting decisions that have some consequence for them and for their lives: that is, freedom and self-determination. Lewin, Lippitt, and White created a situation in which the democratic leader helped group members play an active role in determining their group's policies. Similarly, the food-habit studies created situations in which persons varied their degree of active involvement in the process of their change. Even Pelz's study picks up on this theme. One of the strongest effects in her study involved comparing those subjects who were asked to make some decision concerning their future behavior (i.e., I will or will not volunteer for future studies) with those who were dismissed after the influence was attempted but before any decision was required of them. The personal activity of making this decision was more effective in producing a behavioral change than was the degree of publicity concerning the decision. It seems plausible to suggest that democratic or participatory techniques allow the individual a greater leaway in making this personal decision to change than does an authoritarian leadership style. In a real sense, then, as a passive member of a lectured audience one need not take steps to make a decision; likewise, as a passive member of an autocratically led group in which someone else makes all the decisions, one is a nonparticipant.

To pull this together in yet another way, I suggest that Lewin's program of planned change argues for both an individual autonomy effect and a group pressure or consensus effect. The individual autonomy effect derives from active participation that allows the individual to be an actor who affects the environment. He or she is an active, causal agent, rather than a passive pawn whose fate is determined by others. And for Lewin, autonomy of this sort is both ethically appropriate and effective in producing change.

In addition, the change that eventually comes about as a function of individual autonomy and participation tends to be less dependent on the change agent than change that is induced with minimal individual involvement. Recall that those who worked with a democratic leader worked independently and on their own when he was no longer present; by contrast those with the authoritarian leader were sufficiently dependent on him that they ceased effective working when he was absent or late. Finally, involving individuals in the process of decision making gives them a greater sense of personal responsibility for the decision that was made or for the new actions taken. Remember the apathetic response of those under the autocratic leader and contrast this reaction with the stronger sense of comraderie and group responsibility that the democratic participatory leadership style created. It makes good sense that the less the individual's involvement in the process of change, the less sense of personal responsibility he or she will feel about the change. While we will have more to say about this in the next chapter, keep this point in mind. Milgram's subjects, not participating in the decisions made by the experimenter, could more readily perceive him to be the responsible party for the actions which in his name they carried out.

We often hear the complaint about a silent majority or a do-nothing, apathetic citizenry. Too often we hear stories of persons just standing by and watching some horrible fate befall another, proclaiming calmly after the knifing in the street that, "I just didn't want to get involved" (see Chapter 9). The attitude of active involvement in the affairs of one's nation, one's organization, or one's group often seems to be at a low ebb: "Let George do it, don't bother me." Likewise, the attitude of social responsibility seems to have been lost, as people look out for themselves and their own, leaving others to get by as best they can. But before we throw stones at these seemingly uncaring ones, let us speculate that they are all victims of a relationship to societal authority in which they feel themselves effectively cut off from significant participation in the processes of change. Decisions are made somewhere out there in the blue and handed down. Letter-writing to one's congressional representative, placing complaint slips into the organization's suggestion box, and, unfortunately, often even voting itself, seem to make little impression on those who bring about change. If this is the way we view our relationship to our government, our organizations, our universities —a view of ourselves as powerless—then it comes as no surprise that there is a societal response of apathy, silence, and minimal responsibility for whatever happens (see Chapter 11). The opposing perspective, to which Lewin and his associates have directed their own efforts as potential change agents, is one which involves individuals sufficiently in the process of change so that they feel themselves to be active agents responsible for whatever comes about, not passive and irresponsible pawns, victims of someone else's decision. In Chapter 9 we also examine this theme in the context of altruism.

Group Pressure. The second factor involved, group pressure or consensus, is based on the fact that opinions and behaviors are all rooted in social contexts. Change occurs when an individual participates in the group's redefinition of social reality. To the extent that the individual is strongly attracted to membership in this group, as its norms change, as it comes to see the world through different lenses, pressures are brought to bear on that individual to view things in a different way, or take actions that formerly were difficult, unlikely, or taboo. The effects of group pressure, however, need not be seen either as an all-or-none matter, or as a newer, more insidious form of dictatorship. As a member of the group, the individual participates in redefining its boundaries and its perspectives and thus is actively involved in the process of change.

GROUPTHINK

Not all, however, have been quite as sanguine about the effects and implications of group processes in behavior change; misgivings about the potentially nondemocratic, constraining qualities of even seemingly participative and democratic group approaches have been raised. Several bodies of research and theory stand out in particular as warnings to those who would adopt participative group techniques in the name of freedom and self-determination.

Irving Janis's (1973) analysis of what he termed *groupthink* gives us some critical light on this matter. Janis studied several important decisions made by government leaders in the United States and Europe, including the decisions that led to Neville Chamberlain's appeasement policy in the late 1930s, the Bay of Pigs invasion of the Kennedy Administration, the Korean involvement of the Truman Administration, and the Vietnam escalation decisions of the Johnson Administration. Janis sought to understand the group dynamics involved in reaching these decisions, noting that although historians may attribute a decision (e.g., Bay of Pigs) to one person, such decisions are really generated out of a series of meetings of small high-level policy groups. Analyses of the dynamics of such decision-making groups led Janis to conclude that a process of groupthink is involved:

> *a mode of thinking that people engage in when they are deeply involved in a cohesive in-group, when concurrence-seeking becomes so dominant that it tends to override critical thinking ... Most of the main symptoms of groupthink arise because the members of decision-making groups avoid being too harsh in their judgments of their*

leader's or their colleagues' ideas. They adopt a soft line of criticism, even in their own thinking. At their meetings, all the members are amiable and seek complete concurrence on every important issue, with no bickering or conflict to spoil the cozy atmosphere ... In a sense, loyalty to the policy-making group becomes the highest form of morality for the members (p. 78).

We see in groupthink that an illusion of invulnerability exists; members may thereby be inclined to take chances. Group pressures towards unanimity also prevail, leading members to fear expressing contrary views as though dissent is a manifestation of disloyalty.

Janis recognizes that groupthink is not an inevitable consequence of all group decision making; rather, it is a pattern that is likely to occur among highly cohesive groups unless certain critical steps are taken towards its prevention. He notes in particular the importance of breaking the group's isolation from others who are not in the group, and thus not under its narrowing focus and uniformity pressures. In other words, one manner of removing an in-group's blinders involves setting up procedures whereby other perspectives are brought into the group. Lewin's democratic group leader presumably serves this function through his or her efforts to bring forth for group examination all points of view (for more on this point, see the next section on human resources). Janis would argue that an even more broadening procedure must be built into group decision making in that the democratic leader as a part of the group and thus subject to its narrowness and pressures, might not serve this function well.

Consistent with the preceding idea, Janis further suggests that outside consultants, especially those sensitive to moral issues and informed by differing points of view should actively be brought into the group. In the hope of minimizing group pressures towards uniformity of opinion in agreement with the leader's own opinion, Janis suggests that leaders act truly democratically in the Lewinian sense and do not state their own views initially. By acting in this manner, the democratic leaders do not set the norm that brings about conformity prior to adequate discussion of the issues involved. In summary, Janis concludes that:

the most corrosive symptoms of groupthink are preventable by eliminating group insulation, overdirective leadership practices, and other conditions that foster premature concurrence-seeking ... awareness of shared illusions, rationalizations, and other symptoms fostered by small-group interaction may curtail the influence of groupthink (pp. 87–88).

AUTONOMY OR MANIPULATION?

With the preceding issues in mind, and a recollection of Milgram's original work, let us now look at a classic study conducted by Coch and French (1948), in order to examine another ideological underpinning of the participatory approach.

With technological advances in business and industry, workers are required to unlearn old and relearn new ways of working. Even when the change has less to do with technology than it does with time-study efficiency, workers nevertheless are expected to undergo a change in their behavior. In the usual circumstance, management, being apprised of the needed change, directs the working force to institute the new procedure. However, when management is more psychologically sophisticated, they may take a somewhat different approach to this matter.

For the psychological sophisticate, the issue is one of planned change, or how to introduce a change procedure in such a way as to minimize the expected resistance. Lester Coch and John French sought to use the Lewinian participation approach in a pajama factory in Virginia. The Harwood factory that they studied used an individual incentive system, paying employees according to piece-rates determined by time-study. Whenever an employee was changed from one type of work to another, a transfer bonus was paid. The bonus was computed such that the transfer would not produce a loss in pay during the period of relearning. However, the employees' attitudes towards any job change were negative. Coch and French report that some employees preferred to quit rather than change.

Coch and French selected subgroups from within the factory to undergo separate change treatments in which the employees amount of involvement with the decision to change varied. They used three procedures:
1. No participation. In this group, the employees were informed in the usual manner about their job change. The production department involved in time-study matters set a new piece-rate. A meeting was called in which the group was informed about the need for a new rate in order to keep up with the competition. Questions were answered and then the meeting was dismissed.
2. Participation through representation. In this group, management met with the workers and, to quote Coch and French, presented the need for change "as dramatically as possible." Management then presented a change plan for the workers to discuss. This plan involved having the workers select several of their number to undergo new training. Importantly, it was indicated that the new piece-rates would be set on the basis of this representative group's experiences. After the training period

with these representatives, another meeting was held with all the workers in which the new rates were presented and the representatives were assigned to train the other workers.

3. Total participation. These groups were smaller in size and more intimate in member association. As with the preceding groups, a dramatic presentation of the need for change was offered. This time, however, rather than selecting a few persons as representative trainees, all members of the group served in this role. Thus, everyone participated in designing the new job.

Coch and French studied these groups over a substantially long period, tracing their production rates for over thirty days after the transfer to the new job. Their results are rather striking. While all groups show an initial drop in productivity when the transfer is first instituted, the two participation groups return to their former level and even beyond, whereas the nonparticipation group retains a low level.

In one further experimental variation, Coch and French selected those members of the nonparticipation groups who were still working at Harwood (17 percent had quit) and used a total participation technique before transferring them to still another kind of job. Whereas this group under a nonparticipation procedure had transferred poorly, under total participation they transferred with ease and recovered their former levels of efficiency or even went beyond. Furthermore, there were fewer expressions of aggression after using the participation technique as compared with the higher level of hostility expressed when the transfer was made without employee participation.

This evidence suggests that the participation approach to planned change is more effective both in terms of productivity factors and morale factors as compared with methods that call on less individual responsibility and initiative in the change process. An important point, however, concerns the distinction between real participation in decision making and psychological (perhaps illusory) participation. That is, are we discussing situations in which the members actually can affect a change in their environment? Or is it only that they believe that they are producing a change? Could the total participation group, for example, decide that they did not wish their jobs to be transferred and thus force management to choose another group of workers? Or was it really more a matter that management had decided what was the best policy and that the workers were simply to feel themselves participating in making this decision?

In the Coch and French study it is likely that both real and illusory participation occurred. The participation was illusory in that it is unlikely that the workers could have decided to refuse any job change. It was real, however, in that the workers did determine for themselves the new piece-rate they would be earning after transfer. The distinction, nevertheless, is an important one. Often someone at the top makes a decision and then introduces illusory group participation as a technique to convince the group members that they in fact are playing a part in determining their own fate. This kind of participation, even though it may work—that is, make the change more effective—is quite unlike the participation that Lewin's value bias urges.

The issue, however, is a complex one. One could argue for instance that in this age of specialization and expertise, there are certain persons who possess knowledge that the lay citizen lacks. A dental expert, for example, may know that fluoridation in the water supply helps prevent tooth decay in children. Or a medical expert may have strong evidence that links cigarette smoking with cancer and heart disease. If these experts are brought in as change agents, should they be concerned with community participation in these health decisions as a technique to overcome anticipated resistance or as a genuine democratic process in which persons might reject the expert's presumably health-giving advice? The ideology of a democracy argues that experts should be concerned with genuine community involvement and participation in decision making. Presumably, the experts advise the elected lawmakers who are the representatives of the people. Yet, as a society becomes increasingly complex in its organization, as voters become further removed from the centers of decision-making power, their voices as collaborators in the process of planned change tend to become whisper thin. Voters may be led to feel that through their elected representatives they are participating; yet this is often more illusory than real participation.

To what extent should the public be involved in these health decisions and other similar matters of specialized expertise? Why shouldn't the team of experts and lawmakers, or perhaps just the experts themselves, make judgments and approve changes that are then handed down? After all, unlike the factory situation in which a decision may help the owners more than the workers, a health decision helps all the people. If this is the position taken, then a participation approach is useful mainly as a public-relations ploy, a technique to induce change without resistance. On the other hand, a full commitment to real participation would demand that efforts be directed towards creating opportunities for an informed citizenry to have a vote on matters affecting them. The experts, then, are resources rather than decision makers. When the unit is a small group or relatively small organization, this latter approach seems possible; but even then, clearly not for every decision that is to be made. Perhaps let the group vote only on important decisions and let a committee of elected representatives determine trivial matters. But who decides what is important and what is trivial?

If I may recapture the spirit of the participation approach, especially as Lewin envisioned it, the change agent, who may in fact be more expert or more experienced than his or her clients, does not try to put something over on them for the agent's benefit, but rather tries to work together with them in a collaborative adventure of change. In this endeavor, participation becomes essential especially as it allows those who will be affected by any change to join in its determination, to see and evaluate the need for change, to formulate and to discuss options and alternatives, to understand consequences for them and their lives, to assess the relationship between this change and other changes and thereby to evaluate the connection between the change and the values and priorities they feel are important. At the same time, and as a direct consequence of this collaboration, resistance to change is itself diminished, any change that finally occurs is better stabilized, and as importantly, those who have changed are autonomous and independent rather than continually dependent on the change agent. Though Lewin worked with participation approaches primarily on the scale of the small group, I believe that he felt these techniques to be applicable to larger organizations and to the community itself. The mechanics of participation in a large and complex society, though extraordinarily more difficult to achieve than with a small group, nevertheless are not unfeasible. Public opinion polls can more rapidly link elected representatives with their constituents today than ever in the past. Decentralization or overlapping social organizations offer yet another way of bringing more persons into the arenas of decision making.

An Organizational Example. An effort to apply the participation approach within an organization was undertaken by Nancy Morse and Everett Reimer (1956). Although Coch and French's work took place within an organization, their efforts concentrated on small groups within that organization. Morse and Reimer, on the other hand, actually sought to restructure the organization in order to allow greater or lesser amounts of worker participation in decision making. Essentially what they did was to restructure the divisions within an organization such that two divisions increased their rank-and-file participation in decision making and two other divisions increased upper-level decision making. These they called the autonomy program and the hierarchically-controlled program, respectively. Whereas authority in decision making was delegated to lower levels of the organization in the autonomy program, upper-level authority was increased in the hierarchy program. Morse and Reimer followed the organization for a period of one and one-half years. This included a before measurement of employee satisfaction and productivity, a training period required to produce the two kinds of experimental condition, followed by one year's functioning under the new organizational structure before final measures were obtained.

Morse and Reimer expected to find that both satisfaction and productivity measures would be higher in the autonomy program as compared with the hierarchy program. True to their expectation, they found much greater satisfaction with self and with organization in the autonomy program; in fact, satisfaction actually decreased under the conditions of hierarchy. On the other hand, however, both programs resulted in greater productivity. If anything, the hierarchy condition showed a greater increment in productivity than did the autonomy condition. In essence, however, introducing significant decision-making participation to lower levels of the organization increased both satisfaction and productivity —a manager's and an employee's dream come true.

Though not concerned with productivity, a study by George A. Miller (1967), offers further confirmation of the relationship between personal autonomy within an organization and the level of general satisfaction. Miller studied professional scientists and engineers in two divisions of a large aerospace company. He correlated measures of alienation from their work (e.g., "I really do not feel a sense of pride as a result of my work") with the type of organizational control structure encountered. Here, he differentiated between a directive structure—unilateral decision making and low interaction rates—and a participatory structure—joint decision making and high interaction. His data showed a positive correlation between structure and alienation; the most alienated scientists worked in the most directive structures. We pick up on this theme again in Chapter 11.

One would expect, however, that not every flat organizational structure (i.e., shared decision making) would produce an equally salutary effect. While workers (including scientific professionals) might enjoy their increased autonomy, management personnel who have lost some of their organizational power and privilege might feel less joyful about the entire matter. Recall the field perspective of Chapters 1 and 2. Giving joy to one part of interdependent relationship while simultaneously giving sorrow to another can produce an unstable situation that will not long endure.

Participation and Human Resources

In examining the nature of the relationship between person and authority, my emphasis has been on the degree to which opportunities exist, especially from leadership style or institutional structure, for a decision process to take place in which the person is actively involved. The emphasis has been on the role of critical reason as mediating between the authority's inductions and the person's response. As we have seen (e.g., groupthink), insofar as persons are members of groups whose approval they desire and thus whose pressure they are responsive to, it appears that reason may not intervene even when group discussion and participation are involved. We know from the Asch and Sherif investigations among others, how persons are willing and able to modify their judgments in order to structure their world view in concert with the ways of their group members. It would seem reasonable then, that the tyranny of the group might be as constraining as any tyranny of authority, and thus that the efforts of Lewin and his associates to use participatory techniques of decision making never fully create opportunities for reason to play its part. The democratic form of person-authority relationship of which Lewin spoke, however, is a self-conscious effort to overcome both sources of potential tyranny (i.e., authority and group) by using the leader as a vehicle to open up the human resources that exist in all groups.

To speak of a group as containing human resources is to note that each member brings with him or her a range of values, interests, opinions, experiences, skills and so forth that may lay dormant unless tapped by an appropriate style of group leadership. The role of the democratic leader is to facilitate opening up this potential diversity for one or more of the following reasons: First, the more people there are involved in a process, the more ideas and points of view that can be generated and combined. Second, the more people actively involved offers the possibility for a system of checks and balances, a screening of ideas. If the first point suggests that a democratic group process should seek to open the floodgates to new information, this second point suggests that group members can function as egos-superegos to provide some checks on the ensuing flood. And third, the introduction of more diverse perspectives creates the opportunity for a creative conflict, a clash of disparate points of view out of which more innovative alternatives and decisions can emerge. To open up a group's resources, then, is to create opportunities for a process of creative conflict and resolution to emerge; it is to facilitate the emergence of decision alternatives; to increase the role of reason, intellect, and passion; to diminish mechanical obedience to either the authority or the group. In other words, it is the Lewinian antidote to groupthink.

The role of the leader or institutional structure is vital in facilitating the emergence and utilization of these human resources. There are two kinds of investigation of this issue that we will examine.

The first notes the important function of the leader in creating a climate within which minority opinions can emerge in a group and have an opportunity to influence group decision making. The second focuses on the role of conflict as a human resource in decision making.

The Minority Perspective.   N. R. F. Maier and Allen R. Solem (1952) presented discussion groups with the following problem: "A man bought a horse for $60 and sold it for $70. Then he bought it back for $80 and again sold it for $90. How much money did he make in the horse business?" Maier and Solem experimentally structured the situation so that about half of the discussion groups had leaders whose only function was to be an observer, simply listening to the discussion but not contributing any views of their own. The other half were given discussion leaders who were to encourage everyone to participate; they too were urged to refrain from expressing their own views, but rather were to be more democratic in their style.

All group members recorded their estimates of the correct answer to the problem both before any discussion occurred and after. Examination of the correctness of the answers indicated that both types of groups (i.e., observer and leader) began with about the same level of correct answers; but whereas both increased in their correctness after the discussion, the leader groups increased significantly more than the observer groups.

Of particular interest to Maier and Solem, however, was to test the proposition that the positive benefit of democratic leaders is that they allow minority opinion, which may in fact be correct, to be expressed. That is, by encouraging everyone to participate, democratic leaders make maximal use of the resources within the group and thereby increase the quality of the group's problem solving ability; they permit correct minority views, which may be unpopular and normally inhibited, an arena for expression. A careful analysis of their data was conducted by dividing the groups not only by leadership type (observer or democratic leader), but also in terms of minority with correct answer before discussion versus majority with correct answer before discussion. In this manner it is possible to see if the leader, in fact, is helpful in permitting the correct minority view to eventually sway the group in its final decision. The general trend of their data suggest this to be the case. When the majority holds the correct view at the beginning, then the presence of a democratic leader does little; however, when it is the minority who have the correct answer at the onset, then a democratic discussion leader helps by guaranteeing them a hearing and by reducing the normal social pressure exerted against minority or deviant views. The conclusion, then is that a democratic discussion leader employing the true participation approach can effectively bring out opinions that might otherwise be omitted and thus make maximal use of the group's resources.

Oh yes, the answer to the horse-trading problem: a frequent answer is $10. But that's incorrect. But if you thought the answer was $20 . . .

A conclusion similar to that proposed by Maier and Solem was put forth by E. P. Torrance (1954). During his investigations of bomber crews given survival problems to solve, he found that crews with a rigid structure prevented those lower down in the command hierarchy to use their full talents in dealing with the problem, while the more flexible crews facilitated communication between members and called on a wider range of crew resources and member skills.

In yet another study, Maier and L. R. Hoffman (1961) found that foreman in a simulated work situation who thought of their workers as idea people had groups that produced more innovative solutions to the issue they faced than foremen who defined their subordinates as problem people. In essence, the way a leader views workers, either as resources with potentially good ideas or as problem persons to be dealt with, influences the overall quality of good performance.

In each of these cases, the leader who viewed the group in terms of a resources conception or acted in such a way (usually democratically) so as to increase the likelihood that various opinions, skills, and ideas would come forth, contributed to a better overall group performance.

THE RESOURCE OF CONFLICT

We commonly view conflict within a group or between groups as something negative and to be avoided. Several sociologists in particular, but others as well, have called attention to the positive functions that conflict can serve. The absence of intragroup conflict in the name of loyalty was already noted as a prime symptom of groupthink. Georg Simmel (1957) and Lewis Coser (1956) talk about conflicts that help growth and development or that serve as a positive force of cohesion:

> *An absolutely centripetal and harmonious group, a pure "unification," not only is empirically unreal, it could show no real life process. The society of saints which Dante sees in the Rose of Paradise may be like such a group, but it is without any change and development; whereas the holy assembly of Church Fathers in Raphael's Disputa shows if not actual conflict, at least a considerable differentiation of*

*moods and directions of thought, whence flow all the vitality
and the really organic structure of that group* (Simmel, 1957,
p. 195).

The relationship between conflict and participation is straightforward in theory if somewhat troublesome in practice. A structure of communication that maximizes individual involvement and participation should allow for greater conflict of ideas to emerge within the group when compared with a more autocratic structure that tends to inhibit diversity or to view conflicting ideas as a negative rather than as a potentially positive force for growth. An autocratic teacher, for example, may resist intrusions of student ideas that might disrupt the classroom. Peace and order are maintained at the expense of potential growth that a conflict of ideas within the classroom could offer.

The point of balance between conflict that produces growth and conflict that forces retreat or disastrous disruption and incapacitation is a most delicate one. Often with the benefit of hindsight, we are able to turn to history in order to point out where, when, and how the point of balance has been exceeded in either direction. I emphasize either direction, in that either too much or too little conflict within a social system (e.g., a group) can lead to destruction of the system on the one hand or to its stagnation on the other.

Although the balance point is as difficult to specify as to systematically study, a glimpse of it may be had by looking at a classic study in group dynamics conducted by John French (1941). French brought two differently structured groups into his laboratory for study. The one, which he termed *unorganized,* consisted of a group of unacquainted college students. The *organized* groups, by contrast, were members of intramural sports teams, many of whom had known one another for some period of time. French presented both types of groups (he actually used sixteen total groups, eight of each kind) with either a puzzle that could not be solved or a fear-arousing experience. Both observational and questionnaire data revealed that the organized groups expressed more aggression and hostility when faced with the frustrating situation presented to them; in addition, they tended to experience greater minor disruptions. On the other hand, however, the organized groups did not tend to split themselves into subgroups as the unorganized groups did. Though French did not have any measures of group productivity, the descriptions he presents of the two kinds of groups strongly suggest that the organized groups kept together, used fuller member participation, and took pride in their group: in other words, they acted more like an effective group than did the more splintered and divided unorganized groups.

In seeking to understand these findings, French turned to what most of us intuitively sense—namely, the stronger the forces that initially hold a group together, the more frustration, hostility, and conflict it can tolerate without splitting apart. With little positive to tie them together and the negative qualities of frustration driving them apart, the unorganized groups tended to split into factions and subgroups. The organized groups, though clearly annoyed by their failure, kept together and continued trying to deal as a group with the troublesome situation presented to them. In this case, then, conflict did not create division, but rather seemed to bind the group together.

How true this also seems for an intimate relationship—as in marriage—and the relationships that exist in the larger society. Marriage partners who have little in common to hold them together can barely afford even the minor conflicts that a more strongly united pair could withstand. On the national scene, a society with little cohesiveness or sense of community and shared purpose will find most kinds of conflicts troublesome and potentially disruptive. Such a society would have to resort to naked force in order to maintain a semblance of togetherness in the face of conflict. Totalitarian states spin out their lives in this manner. Democracies, presumably, call on each person's goodwill and mutual respect to keep the democracy together when conflicts develop. When goodwill is lacking, when people face each other as though they lived in a jungle rather than in a cooperative community where trust and love are shared and justice for all is a valued principle, then force comes into use to fend off conflicts that break out within.

An interesting approach to the study of naturally occurring conflicts within real groups demonstrates some of the complexities of the issue. Guetzkow and Gyr (1954) studied a series of conference groups, dividing them on the basis of observer ratings into high and low conflict. The groups were further divided in terms of the type of conflict expressed. Groups expressed interpersonal conflicts or task-oriented conflicts. The aim of the study was to come to some understanding of the processes by which groups in conflict still achieved decision-making agreement. Some findings of particular importance indicate how groups in which there were many expressions of self-oriented needs hindered the achievement of consensus. On the other hand, whether the conflict was interpersonal or substantive (i.e., task related), a pleasant atmosphere within the group facilitated the achievement of final agreement. Likewise, even when conflict was present, if group members examined one issue at a time in an orderly fashion, they were likely to be able to come to some final decision.

Whereas substantive conflicts, when present, could be effectively reduced and consensus achieved by a leader directing the group towards factual matters, interpersonal conflict was best handled by withdrawing from the problem or one another.

In the preceding, achievement of consensus is assumed to be the reasonable end to which a decision-making group should strive. Groups that are set up merely to generate ideas, of course, need not be concerned with final consensus. On the other hand, most groups have somewhere they are trying to go; they need a degree of consensus within the group, therefore, in order to move. As this work indicates, conflict within a group does not necessarily prevent consensus, although the findings also clearly indicate how much higher consensus is reached in low conflict groups as compared with high-conflict groups. However, conflict can still be usefully overcome. Much depends on the atmosphere created within the group, the minimization of self-oriented or personal need expression, the approach to facts, and the withdrawal from personal conflict. This latter point may strike many as annoying, for it suggests retreating in the face of interpersonal conflicts. Sensitivity training seems to make its living off of the confrontation side of interpersonal conflict rather than withdrawal. However, sensitivity training or encounter groups rarely have a decision-making agenda to get through; they can afford the luxury of infighting. Conference groups may often have to put personal battles aside in order to make any progress at all.

Conflict in Ideas. The notion of actively inducing conflicts within a group in order to broaden its resource base is a rather interesting one to contemplate. Theoretically, the view is that by bringing potentially disparate perspectives together in a setting in which they can be freely expressed, one could increase the resources out of which problems are solved and thus come up with a better, more innovative solution. This requires that both disparate perspectives be brought together and that they be allowed to gain expression. This latter point, as we have noted previously, argues for a group structure or leadership style that is democratic and participative.

L. Richard Hoffman, Ernest Harburg, and N. R. F. Maier (1962) sought to experimentally produce the conditions that would result in conflict and creative group problem solving. They reasoned that one of the problems that a potentially creative group faces is overcoming the dominance of its leadership. If divergent ideas are present in a group but a strong leader keeps them unexpressed, the group will not be able to use them effectively in problem solving. So, how to reduce the leader's importance? One technique that we have already seen is to instruct the leaders in participatory or democratic techniques. This allows minority perspectives to be drawn forth and used. Another approach, however, is to strengthen the commitment of subordinate group members to their own opinion. It is felt that the more committed a person is to a particular point of view, the more likely he or she is to express it, even though the leader may try to dominate. Hoffman and his colleagues created a role-playing work situation in which instructions were used to increase or decrease a member's commitment to a particular opinion. They also used role-playing instructions to vary the dominance of the group's leader. The prediction is that greater conflict will exist in those groups in which the role players are strongly committed to divergent points of view. Furthermore, where the leader's role is less dominant, and thereby the conflict is allowed to gain expression, high-quality problem solutions will be offered. In essence, therefore, the prediction requires both divergent points of view to produce conflict and a style of leadership that will allow the conflict to be expressed in order to achieve creative solutions.

The task given to these role-playing groups consisted of a meeting in which the foreman was to discuss a change in work procedure with several of his workers. Hoffman, Harburg, and Maier differentiate between three kinds of solutions to this work change problem:

1. the foreman wins by convincing the groups to change;
2. the workers resist his efforts and wish to retain the old method;
3. the integrative solution in which both individual demands and company requirements are met in a unique manner.

The integrative solution is rare in most of the studies in which this kind of problem has been employed. It is considered to be the more innovative or creative of the possible solutions.

Results from this study indicate that integrative (i.e., creative) solutions were produced in about 48 percent of those groups in which workers were strongly committed to a particular point of view concerning the job change, whereas only 18 percent produced the integrative solution in the presumably low-conflict (i.e., low-commitment) groups. An analysis that combined both type of foreman with commitment of worker indicated that the highest percentage of integrative solutions was offered in those groups in which there were strongly committed workers and a less dominant foreman. The figure here is 54 percent integrative solutions. However, when the workers were only minimally committed to a particular position, the foreman dominated the group's solutions even when he was minimally dominant. Thus 66 percent of the solutions were in line with the foreman's request when he was dominant and the subjects were low in their commitment; likewise, when the foreman was less dominant, the same percentage chose his solution.

Two important points emerge from this study. First, persons in a group discussion who are strongly committed to a particular point of view produce greater conflict and in turn more creative problem solving. Second, the preceding holds primarily in a setting in which the style of leadership is hospitable to emergent conflict: that is, where others' viewpoints are tolerated and used rather than suppressed.

Conflict in Personality and Cognitive Style.   In the realm of the human few things are simple. In the preceding study, conflict referred to divergent perspectives between role-playing workers and the role-playing foreman. Thus there was conflict when the workers were committed to a position that the foreman wanted to change. Conflict, however, can also exist between the members of a group. Furthermore, as Guetzkow and Gyr note, conflict can exist both in terms of specific ideas or opinions as well as in personality or cognitive development.

If one examines the group dynamics literature as it relates to homogeneity versus heterogeneity of personality and its effects on creative group problem solving, a somewhat mixed picture emerges. Haythorn (1958), for example, composed groups that were homogeneous or heterogeneous with respect to the degree of authoritarianism between their appointed leader and his followers (see Chapter 8 for more on authoritarianism). A group was homogeneous if both the leader and the followers were comparably high or low in authoritarianism. Heterogeneous groups were those in which the leader was high and the members low or vice versa. Haythorn reports that leaders in the homogeneous groups were more aggressive and autocratic when compared with their counterparts in the heterogeneous groups. Followers in these homogeneous groups, in turn, were described as seeking group approval and withdrawing more than followers in the heterogeneous groups. Finally, Haythorn's observers report more conflict within the heterogeneous groups. Although there is no measure of group problem solving, Haythorn's results for the homogeneous or low-conflict groups indicate some of the qualities that other work we have examined suggests might produce less innovative solutions. For instance, the greater autocratic leader behavior and the greater withdrawal of the members in the homogeneous groups would undoubtedly reduce the effective use of the group's human resources. On the other hand, the clashes between member and leader personality in the heterogeneous groups could be of sufficient magnitude to incapacitate the group as an effective problem solving force. The work of William Schutz (1960) likewise suggests how homogeneity of interpersonal

orientation allows for compatibility and consequently for performance efficiency.

An investigation by Pollock (1967) using nonstructured, sensitivity groups, argued that heterogeneity of members' orientations
to authority would be more conducive to personal change than
homogeneity. He reasoned, using a confrontation-support model
proposed by Harrison, that the heterogeneity would provide the kind
of conflict needed to unfreeze individuals from their present points
of view, but that such confrontation, to provide positive change
rather than retrenchment, would have to occur within a generally
supportive context. Pollock created sensitivity groups composed of
members who were similar to one another in their orientation to
authority (e.g., all highly wanting to be controlled by someone in
authority or all wanting not to be controlled), and groups composed
of members differing in this orientation. His results indicated that
heterogeneity allowed for greater conflict between members and
also resulted in greater positive change in individuals; by contrast,
homogeneous groups were less effective in producing individual
change.

An effort that I for one find hopeful in that it combines a plausible
theory with some interesting data, involves a study conducted by
Paul Stager (1967). Stager argues that we each can be characterized
according to our particular level of cognitive development. This
level affects the manner in which we structure and process information from our environment. Persons at a high conceptual level tend
to make many alternative differentiations of their environment,
while those of a lower conceptual level differentiate minimally and
in terms of a few, fixed categories.

Stager next argues that a group composed primarily of persons
who are high in conceptual development should:
1.   make few demands that the group structure itself into carefully
     defined roles and thereby form a hierarchical arrangement;
2.   generate diversity and conflict;
3.   synthesize and evaluate alternatives that are generated;
4.   conduct a search for novel information.

The general notion is that persons who are conceptually high in
their development see the world in many alternative ways. Such
individuals can tolerate the uncertainty that an absence of rigid
group structure provides and will generate more conflict because of
the variety of alternatives they create; at the same time, they can
better synthesize these divergent views. Overall, people who have a
high conceptual level should be better able to produce innovative
solutions when compared with persons low in conceptual level. A
group that is composed of many individuals of high conceptual level
—a homogeneous group—should be able to generate many alterna-

tives to a problem and evaluate and integrate these in a better fashion than a low group or one that is composed of more low than high conceptualizers.

To test these notions, Stager obtained measures of individual's levels of conceptual development and then composed four-man groups so that they had greater or fewer numbers of high conceptualizers. The 100 percent groups consisted of all four members who were high conceptualizers; the 75 percent had three high, the 50 percent group had two, and finally the 25 percent had only one high conceptualizer; the other group members were low. Notice that in this case the homogeneous group is theoretically expected to be the most conflicted in that it should produce the greatest diversity of ideas. Clearly, one cannot simply speak about the effects of homogeneity or heterogeneity, but must of necessity specify both the characteristics being considered and the situational context that is involved.

Stager presented these variously composed groups with a rather complex decision-making problem involving a tactical military situation. He recorded individual and group behavior and in addition assessed the group structure that emerged. Uncertainty of group structure as a dependent variable exists when the members play a variety of decision-making roles throughout the duration of the study. High uncertainty therefore suggests lack of specific group structure, while low uncertainty indicates a more highly structured arrangement. True to the theoretical expectation, as the composition of high conceptualizers increased from 25 percent to 100 percent, uncertainty likewise increased. That is, the greater the number of high conceptualizers within the group, the more open and flexible was its structure. Groups with many low conceptualizers tended to structure themselves into definite roles rather quickly and thereby to reduce any uncertainty that a flexible structure might produce.

An analysis of conflicts that were generated offers further support for the theoretical predictions. The 100 percent or all-high conceptualizer groups produced more conflict than any of the other conditions. In terms of a group's ability to utilize the divergent material that was generated in forming a new synthesis, the 100 percent groups, once again, rank significantly higher than the other conditions. Other expectations were similarly borne out by the data.

Although Stager could not employ any measures of productivity with respect to some external criterion, his concern with relating level of conceptual development as a variable of group composition to the groups' subsequent information processing and decision making is quite relevant to our concern with the human resources approach to participation. Most importantly, his data indicate the kind of group in which conflicting persepctives are both generated and effectively utilized in decision making. This is a group in which hierarchical structuring in terms of specific roles is low and member participation is equal. Furthermore, both equality of participation and conflict generation and utilization seem to occur in this situation, at least, as a function of a particular composition of conceptual development. Although in practice one cannot easily control compositional factors, these data indicate a condition in which conflict within a group of a particular composition seems to offer a potentially creative utilization of the group's human resources. In addition, of course, this study suggests a condition of composition in which too much conflict might be more detrimental than helpful. That is, it seems to be a plausible implication of these data to suggest that the conflict within a group composed primarily of low conceptualizers would prove disruptive in that they would be relatively incapable of using divergent ideas in a helpful manner.

Cooperative Orientation and Conflict

Morton Deutsch, cut straight from the cloth of Kurt Lewin, is our guide on this trip. In the late 1940s, Deutsch published a classic study of cooperation and competition (see 1953). In the early 1960s with a colleague, Robert M. Krause, Deutsch published the outcomes of a series of experimental studies of bargaining and conflict (1960; 1962). And in the late 1960s, he combined these several works and themes into an analysis of conflict reduction within a context of cooperation (1969).

Recall our earlier discussion of Deutsch's work on cooperation and competition (Chapter 2); this research indicated several important advantages that accrued to cooperative group behavior:

(a) more coordination of efforts; (b) more diversity in amount of contributions per member; (c) more subdivision of activity; (d) more achievement pressure; (e) more communication to one another; (f) more attentiveness to fellow members; (g) more mutual comprehension of communication; (h) more common appraisals of communication; (i) greater orientation and orderliness; (j) greater productivity per unit time; (k) better quality of product and discussions; (l) more friendliness during discussions; (m) more favorable evaluation of the group and its products; (n) more behavior directed toward helping the group improve its functioning; (o) greater feeling of being liked by fellow members; and (p) greater feeling of obligation and desire to win the respect of others (Deutsch, 1962, pp. 284–285).

Of special importance are those findings that involve open communication, the development of trust, friendliness, and confidence, and the sharing and evaluation of ideas in a relatively nonthreatening context. Rather than vying competitively in a jungle of I-win, you-lose, persons within the cooperative context could actually work together towards common, shared ends.

The Game.   The kind of interdependencies that Deutsch discussed in his analysis of cooperation and competition can be represented in game-theory terms as well. One can speak of a zero-sum game in which one side's winning means the other side's losing. Or, one may speak of a nonzero sum game in which both parties can profit jointly if they manage to work well together. These latter types of games are of particular interest to the social psychologist in that they allow for psychological processes to intervene either to facilitate or to hinder the game player's achievement of the most satisfying solution. Furthermore, the nonzero sum relationship is one that characterizes *in fact* a great many human bargaining and decision situations. I say, *in fact,* in that the parties may not psychologically see themselves as standing to gain by cooperative bargaining even when such mutual gain is possible. Thus, they may face-off in a zero-sum battle whereas a nonzero sum venture would benefit all. The change agent's role, in this case, is to help the participants psychologically view their possibilities for nonzero sum cooperation

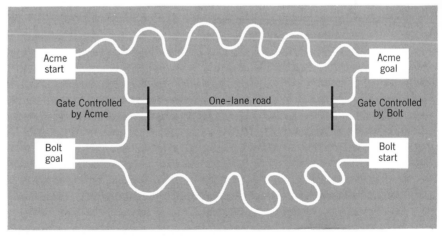

Figure 6. *The map is from Deutsch, M. and Krauss, R. M. The effect of threat upon interpersonal bargaining.* Journal of Abnormal and Social Psychology, *1960,* **61,** *181–189. Copyright 1960 by the American Psychological Association. Reprinted by permission.*

rather than the inevitable, usually escalating destruction that the competitive context produces.

The classic investigation of Deutsch and Krauss is instructive. They constructed a fairly elaborate game board, and asked their subjects to imagine that they were in charge of a trucking company, one called Acme, the other Bolt. Each company had a route over which it could travel as it moved its trucks from their point of origin to their destination. The map in Figure 6 roughly indicates this situation. Note that each company had two routes available to them, one considerably longer than the other. However, the most direct route consists of a one-lane road on which both trucks cannot pass at the same time. Furthermore, each company controls a gate that offers or prohibits access to this road. Deutsch and Krause see the presence of this gate as a *threat potential.*

The object of the game was simple: to get the trucks efficiently from their origin to their destination. Payment was given for each successful trip with operating costs deducted. These costs were computed in terms of time. A player could earn $.60 for each trip; costs were figured at the rate of $.01 per 1 second's run. If it took 30 seconds to complete a trip, the profits for that trip would be $.30. Clearly, as the situation is rigged, players can cooperatively help or competitively hinder each other's attainment of a maximally satisfying resolution. Recall the similar PD game of Chapter 2.

Deutsch and Krause studied several variations in the basic design. For example, they systematically varied the threat potential, having a condition of bilateral threats (both controlled the gates), unilateral threats (only one gate was controlled), and no threats (neither gate could be closed). In another variation, they ran a bilateral communication condition (both sides could talk) and a unilateral communication condition (only one side could talk). In still a third variation, they introduced a compulsory communication on every trial.

Results indicated that there was the greatest difficulty in coordinated activity, and consequently in monetary loss, in the bilateral threat condition; the unilateral threat was second worst. In fact, only in the no threat condition did players make a profit. It appears, then, that the potential to use threat against another in order to accomplish one's ends produces a mutually destructive, competitive relationship rather than a potentially constructive cooperative one. It is as if one player says, "You think your threats are going to intimidate me! Hell, I'll show you!" And into mortal combat they plunge forgetting in their passion to get even with the other, that a better solution based on cooperation could be possible.

The communication variable produced some interesting findings. In the first place, there was no essential difference in task performance between the bilateral and the unilateral communication conditions. For the most part, this seemed to be based on the tendency of the players not to communicate even when the possibility existed. It was for this reason that Deutsch and Krause introduced the compulsory communication condition. Forced communication was effective, but only under conditions of unilateral threat. If anything, forcing persons to communicate under conditions of bilateral threat resulted in each only repeating verbally the threats they had made in their action. Thus, when people communicate and have the potential to threaten another in a competitive context, the communication may work primarily to facilitate threat-oriented messages. And this only intensifies the conflict, helping little to attain the kind of cooperative efforts that are seen as essential.

On examination, it seemed to Deutsch, that the kind of orientation that exists is a significant determinant of the manner in which conflicts between groups can be resolved. An orientation that fosters trust, that shows the potential for shared interests, that minimizes threats—in other words, a cooperative rather than a competitive orientation—should facilitate the achievement of mutually satisfying solutions to conflict dilemmas. Deutsch continued with his experimentation on these themes, introducing a cooperative or a competitive orientation into a two-person nonzero sum game situation. His results indicated that joint gains occur when persons are given a cooperative orientation whereas mutual loss results from a competitive orientation. Communication was helpful primarily when it focused on the better outcomes likely when each side acted cooperatively. Communication under these conditions increased the establishment of mutual trust between the game players. Not one to be shy in generalizing the broader social implications of his work, Deutsch states:

> *We live in a time when international cooperation is required to avert nuclear catastrophe. Yet, cooperation founders because of the inability of one side to trust the other and the inability to resolve bargaining deadlocks ... We must each develop a genuine stake in the other's security and welfare, in the other's doing well rather than poorly, and we must promote cooperative endeavors which will foster the development of an interest in the other's successes rather than failures* (1962, p. 316).

In that quoted passage are the guiding directives for the change agent. Unlike the experimenter, change agents cannot simply give instructions to be cooperative and to look for mutual points of gain and joint benefit; they cannot simply insist that each person take a concern in the other's winning rather than taking pleasure only in the other's losing; they cannot demand that communications be directed only towards outlining a cooperative venture rather than a saber-rattling use of threats and tactics of intimidation. Yet, change agents can be aware that the democratic, participative approach is more likely than autocratic ones to produce mutual friendliness and trust, to allow for legitimate influence-sharing rather than illegitimate or inappropriate influence giving, to aid the weaker partner to gain the confidence that is basic to true cooperation, and indeed to create an atmosphere in which awareness of the benefits of exchange and a commitment to maximizing everyone's gain far outweigh insensitivity or the passion to be a winner at another's expense.

The fascinating field study by Sherif and Sherif (1953) conducted on groups at a summer camp, further demonstrated the validity of these cooperative notions. After systematically creating tension between two groups within the camp, they facilitated harmony by forcing the groups to cooperate. In this real setting, rather than telling the groups that cooperation was the best way, the Sherifs created a camp emergency that compelled the one-time warriors to work together in order to solve their joint problem. Out of distrust and tension this need to cooperate produced a harmonious camp.

As Deutsch has so aptly noted, a competitive context favors the escalation of conflict rather than its reduction. It sets people off against one another, blinding them to anything but their zero-sum goals. Competition in this case feeds off of faulty and decimated communication; it induces suspicion and distrust; it magnifies small disagreements into major wars; it calls out agression and hostility; it legitimizes differential judgment and differential sanctions.

Conflicts between persons, between groups, or between nations are not simply going to fade away. Deutsch's position is rather compelling. When viewed from the perspective of cooperative problem solving, conflicts become an exciting adventure and challenge, a vital force for growth and change. The contrasting perspective of competitive conflicts that escalate cancerously, however, destroys rather than affirms life.

Social Influence, Conformity, and Resistance

If the social psychologist's task is to understand the conditions of freedom, then it may rightly be said that by sheer number count alone, conformity and independence have been a major and continuing concern of the discipline. Major programs of experimental research have been conducted for the most part in an effort to determine those aspects of the person, the influence agent, or the situation that affect the degree of conformity observed. Yet, even to define conformity is itself a complex matter.

In general, the concept of conformity refers to a change in P that is a function of an act of O, where P or O may be a person, group, or some part of a larger social context (e.g., a role). O's acts may involve defining a situation, as in the Asch study; acts may involve P's knowledge of what O expects, as in most role relationships in which O's presence reminds P of P's obligations; acts may involve direct or indirect influence attempts, as when Milgram's experimenter tells P that P must continue with the experiment. In turn, P's behavior may involve a change in perception or behavior, including changes towards the position advocated by O (conformity), away from the advocated position (active resistance), or no change, as in passive resistance. Likewise, even though behaviorally P may not appear to change in response to O's actions, as noted in the Asch situation, P's self-confidence may have been undermined, making P ripe for change on another occasion.

The complexity of conformity and independence is heightened further when we realize that P's resistance to O may be the result of P's conformity to Y. This, of course, is what occurred in the version of Milgram's study in which P resisted the experimenter (O) by conforming to the model provided by the resisting teacher-accomplices (Y). Thus, resistance to one group or in one setting may be conformity to the norms of another. Freedom, self-determination, and independence in no way imply acting in total separation from others; such behavior is better reserved to describe alienation, the opposite of real freedom and real independence. Rather, as has already been suggested earlier in this chapter, independent action is done in concert with others on the basis of all having the opportunity "to formulate the available choices, to argue over them—and then, the opportunity to choose" (Mills, 1959, p. 174).

PUBLIC VERSUS PRIVATE CHANGE

One of the major issues involving conformity and independence concerns the extent to which the change that occurs in P as a function of the act of O is public or private. A public change is one that depends on O's continued surveillance of P; a private change is one that, although initiated by O, in time becomes independent of O's continuing presence. This distinction illustrates how the same apparent behavior can have different underlying psychological properties. For example, we note that both Peter and Barbara, in response to their teacher's urging, express an opinion that is congruent with the teacher's own opinion. On closer examination, we may determine that Peter has changed both his publicly stated view and his private belief as well, while Barbara has complied publicly, but has not accepted the teacher's influence on the private level. If we treat these two instances of conformity in the same way we will miss an important difference in their psychological meaning and the implications that flow from this difference. Thus, for example, Peter's new opinion is likely to endure when the teacher is no longer present, whereas Barbara's is likely to revert to its original position once the teacher is removed from the scene.

Several combinations of public versus private conformity are possible: public conformity with private acceptance; public conformity without private acceptance; public resistance with private resistance; public resistance with private acceptance. The first and third demonstrate consistency; the second and fourth indicate discrepancy. Note how the first defines the basic conditions of legitimate authority in which P privately accepts the system that calls for P to publicly following O's inductions. The second is easy to understand. Like Barbara, such persons may be under a direct or an implied threat of punishment for resistance, so they conform publicly in view of the threatening O while retaining their own freedom on the private level. Analysts of the behavior of inmates in prisons and mental hospitals (e.g., Goffman, 1961) cite numerous instances of how persons manage their affairs so as to behave publicly in conformity or even in overconforming obsequiousness to the authority's demands, while resisting privately and thereby retaining what "may be seen as the most elementary form of resistance—the refusal to have one's self totally defined by the authority structure" (Flacks, 1973, p. 193). It is this same form of freedom to which Viktor Frankl (1959) referred in discussing his and other's imprisonment in Nazi Germany, noting how the total authority of the camp, controlling all aspects of the person's life and death, still could not govern the person's fundamental attitudes towards this experience: public conformity to autocratic control, without private acceptance.

The fourth situation, public resistance with private acceptance, may at first appear unlikely: why would a person publicly resist another's influence while privately accepting it? One reason might be that P wishes to appear as someone who is rebellious or independent. Children, seeking to separate themselves from parental authority and dominance, for example, may publicly resist their parents' requests and beliefs, while privately entertaining considerable congruence with them. The role of devil's advocate provides still another illustration of this fourth type of situation. Here the person may publicly adopt a contrary viewpoint in order to stimulate discussion or force others to tighten their own thinking, while privately believing as these very others do. Janis recommends this role as one helpful antidote to the excesses of groupthink.

KELMAN'S MODEL

Kelman (1958; 1961) presents one of the best discussions of public versus private change. He differentiates three processes by which social influence can be accepted by P: compliance, identification, and internalization.

Compliance occurs when P is influenced by O in order to obtain rewards for conformity or to avoid punishment for nonconformity. P does not privately accept O's influence because of its intrinsic merit, but rather because acceptance is instrumental to attaining or avoiding something. Clearly, if conformity is instrumental to gaining rewards or avoiding punishments, P will conform only to the extent to which O has some knowledge about P's conformity or resistance; compliance thus depends on O's surveillance.

Identification is the acceptance of O's influence in order to maintain an important relationship with O. Kelman calls this a self-defining relationship; if P identifies with O, P adopts O as the model for self-definition. In this case, we would expect P to conform under conditions in which the relationship is most salient. Changes mediated by identification, unlike those of compliance, involve both a public and a private shift. The change is not dependent on continued surveillance by O; it does require, however, that the relationship between P and O be active and remain inportant for P if P is to express the new position under different circumstances. Thus, although O's presence is not required, P must reproduce the relationship in a new context in order to maintain a changed perspective. To this extent, the change remains dependent on O, although clearly less so than with compliant change. Kelman's discussion of identification is similar in many respects to Weber's concept of charismatic authority—one who gains obedience because of uncanny powers over an audience of followers.

Internalization occurs when P accepts O's influence because the content of the influence is congruent with P's value system. Unlike compliance, P does not conform for instrumental reasons, to gain something external; unlike identification, P does not conform in the service of P's relationship with O. Rather, P conforms because O's induction is congruent with P's value system. The change, therefore becomes a part of P, independent of O's continued presence. Kelman warns us, however, not to assume that internalization is always grounded in rationality.

> *... I would also characterize as internalization the adoption of beliefs because of their congruence with a value system that is basically irrational. Thus, an authoritarian individual may adopt certain racist attitudes because they fit into his paranoid, irrational view of the world* (1961, pp.

65–66). Weber's concept of the rational-legal basis of legitimate authority shares much with Kelman's analysis of the psychological process of internalization. In both, P is obedient to O's inductions insofar as they are congruent with P's value system, including P's sense that it is a proper value to follow the orders of specific O's, such as government officials, elected leaders and scientists.

An Empirical Test. Although Kelman suggested that these three processes rarely occur in isolation, that all are present in some degree in most social influence situations, in 1961 he reported the results of one effort to put this model to an experimental test. Kelman varied O's source of power and examined its consequences for P's behavior. Black college students heard a recording of an interview on a school desegregation case before the Supreme Court. Four different versions were presented: the content was always the same, but O's introduction was systematically varied. Kelman created O's who had high power to reward or punish—that is, to promote compliance; high attractiveness—that is, to promote identification; high credibility—that is, to promote internalization; low power, attractiveness, and credibility—that is, to minimize all three processes.

In one condition students filled out questionnaires under conditions in which O was relevant to and had surveillance over P; in another, relevance but no surveillance; in a third, neither relevance nor surveillance. The predictions were:
1. Social influence from a powerful O should be expressed only under O's surveillance. This is compliance.
2. Social influence from an attractive O should be expressed when P's relationship with O is salient. This is identification.
3. Social influence from a credible O should be expressed when the content is relevant, regardless of surveillance or salience of the relationship. This is internalization.

Kelman's data were consistent with these three predictions lending encouraging support to the model.

An Anthropological Note: Issues of Societal Control

One provocative application of Kelman's scheme extends beyond the individual to the entire society. The survival of any organized social unit demands that certain basic functions be served. The anthropologist, David Aberle (1950) and several associates proposed a listing of the functional prerequisites of any new society, including for example, such basic issues as reproduction, division of labor, communication, socialization of new members, and the means disruptive behavior can be controlled. Obviously, many key functions involve issues of socialization and social control.

Picture now each of Kelman's three processes of social influence in this context of socialization and social control. A society presumably could provide for both socialization and social control through each of these three mediators. That is, we could have a society founded on compliance, on identification, or on internalization. Naturally, every society builds on all three in a mix that varies in its emphasis through time. But for the sake of argument, let us suppose we have a pure case of each type.

The society founded on compliance is one that cares little for its members' development of internally based guidelines for their behavior. Social control is exercised entirely from without. This external basis of control could take the form of threats of punishment for getting out of line or even promises of reward for remaining in line. Recalling that such compliance techniques demand surveillance, a society of this sort would require a means to continually monitor its citizens' behavior. In this manner, all transgressions could be noted and immediately punished, while all compliant persons could be given their daily dole of societal rewards. This indeed would be Orwell's *1984.* It is not too far removed from any totalitarian regime in which socialization and social control are carefully regulated by compliance-based techniques. Personal freedoms in such a society rapidly diminish. Of course, as we have seen, compliance can also be based on rewards. Surveillance and observability must still be high in such a society so that the benevolent leader can see who should receive rewards. Police officers in this case would not carry clubs to punish transgressors, but perhaps a bag of hero medals to be handed out as reinforcements for proper actions. In either case, however, the citizenry of such a society become dependent on the controlling agents; they are guided not by internal direction but rather by the external power of the agents.

The society founded on identification would gain its requisite level of social control by means of the attraction between the citizenry and the controlling agents. People would want to do what is necessary in order to maintain their loving relationship with what is probably a benevolent, kindly societal leader. In fact, if we could talk about a pure case, a society founded on identification would undoubtedly be ruled by a *charismatic leader.* The electric quality of that charisma—a characteristic sensed in such people as Gandhi, Eva Peron, Chairman Mao, Martin Luther King, Jr., and to a certain extent John Kennedy—provides leadership through love, respect, admiration, or in Kelman's terms, through identification. Although surveillance is of lesser importance in such a society, and although changes within P are less dependent on O than is the case with compliance, the control that exists demands that the salience of the leader's relationship be evident. One might think of the teachings of another charismatic leader, Jesus, in this regard. The presence of Jesus in each person essentially means that one controls one's own behavior by reference to a continually salient relationship with the beloved "leader." If we are dealing with a truly charismatic leader, it is likely that the leader's salience will be assured in most situations. Gandhi's teachings of nonviolence and the devotion of his followers allowed him to exercise a high degree of control over their everyday lives, even when he was not present nor their behavior under any special surveillance. His aura, however, was so pervasive that one might say that the salience of his followers' relationship to Gandhi was a covering shelter like the sky, always present, always guiding.

If the society founded on compliance stresses relationships of power and the society of identification, relationships of attraction, the society founded on internalization emphasizes the knowledgeability and credibility of its leadership. This is indeed the knowledgeable society where behavioral control is achieved by relating specific behaviors to basic values that have been internalized. In such a society, one would expect to find an emphasis on facts and on specific details in order for O to induce behavior from P. Efforts would be directed towards pointing out the relationship between the new behaviors desired and the values that each person holds. A society founded on internalization techniques would continuously stress the degree to which new efforts fit into existing value systems. For example, one manner of approaching the racial issue in the United States has been to call up values of equal opportunity and equal treatment under the law that presumably have been internalized by most citizens. The idea is to induce improved white attitudes towards minority groups by activating these values.

Change then becomes incorporated into an ongoing system of values and thus has a substantial degree of permanence. Such change, if accomplished, does not require surveillance, and thus seems distinctly more suitable to a democracy than power-oriented techniques. Social control is achieved in an internalized society through each person's internalized values. For example, one does not kill or steal, not in order to avoid punishment, not in order to continue a relationship with the charismatic leader, but rather because killing and stealing have been internalized as violations of one's moral values.

FEAR, SHAME, AND GUILT

Roughly paralleling Kelman's triad, cross-cultural investigations have found it helpful to differentiate between fear, shame, and guilt as separate mechanisms that different cultures use in order to gain conformity from individual members. A fear culture emphasizes conforming in order to avoid being punished. A shame culture stresses conforming in order to avoid being ridiculed or rejected in the presence of real or imagined others. Benedict (1946) has described Japan as a shame culture. By contrast, guilt cultures emphasize conformity in order to avoid violation of internal standards; the ever watchful conscience (superego) remains witness to these kinds of transgressions.

Sorcery, Sin, and the Superego.   A fascinating cross-cultural investigation undertaken by John Whiting (1959) examined these three bases whereby conformity is obtained. He examined the institution of sorcery (fear), sin (shame), and the superego (guilt). Sorcery is the belief that societal members have mystical powers that can be used to destroy or injure another. In such societies there exists a fear that others may retaliate for any misdeeds; this fear serves to deter actions that are deviant from societal norms. Thus, one complies out of fear of retaliation. The concept of sin within a society focuses on the belief that transgressions against societal norms (i.e., deviant, nonconforming behavior) will be noted by the gods or ghosts of departed spirits who will then proceed to punish the offender. One is shamed in the eyes of the gods for transgressions. Superego cultures base their control on an internalized mechanism of guilt induction. One who even thinks of disobeying a societal norm experiences a sense of guilt and thereby is motivated not to engage in such actions or even to entertain such thoughts.

The Contemporary Scene.   As noted, this trio of fear, shame, and guilt have a parallel to the three mechanisms that Kelman discussed: fear and compliance; shame and identification; guilt and internalization. The relationship between these psychological and cultural mechanisms suggests the importance that cultural circumstances play in providing the fundamental conditions within which psychological mechanisms can and do work effectively. Thus, as Weber and others have noted, the demand of Western technological and democratic societies is for rationality and independence in the relationship between the person and authority. Independence, in this context, portrays P's behavior as something that is self-generated and therefore independent of O. Thus, approaches to control that appear to be based on fear (i.e., compliance) or identification are seen as less appropriate. This is not to deny that such approaches can be and are utilized, rather it is to note that the contemporary cultural emphasis is on rationality and independence. Thus O's efforts to win obedience through punishment or through appeals to something so irrational as charisma do not have as much legitimacy as the seemingly more rational means.

Of course, guilt is not commonly thought to be rational; yet it refers to an internalized standard against which one's acts are evaluated. Guilt thus parallels Kelman's concept of internalization and Weber's view of the rational-legal basis of legitimacy, whether the experience itself is guilt or a general sense of having violated a compelling moral norm, as Weber suggests. The point is that relationships between person and authority are mediated by cultural and historical conditions; if ours is an era of rational-legal, internalized controls, we would expect to find the appeals to this basis for legitimacy to be prevalent and to be relatively successful. And, of course, this indeed is what Milgram's investigations determined.

Inducing Resistance

Much of the social psychological tradition has examined the basic issue of the person's relationship to authority in terms of the conditions under which persons will accept social influence. One work, entitled *Anatomy of Conformity* (Walker & Heyns, 1967), boldly states how to do it:

> *If one wishes to produce Conformity for good or evil, the formula is clear. Manage to arouse a need or needs that are important to the individual or the group. Offer a goal which is appropriate to the need or needs. Make sure that Conformity is instrumental to the achievement of the goal and that the goal is as large and as certain as possible. Apply the goal or reward at every opportunity. Try to prevent the object of your efforts from obtaining an uncontrolled education. Choose a setting that is ambiguous. Do everything possible to see that the individual has little or no confidence in his position. Do everything possible to make the norm which you set appear highly valued and attractive. Set it at a level not too far initially from the starting point of the individual or group and move it gradually toward the behavior you wish to produce. Be absolutely certain you know what you want and that you are willing to pay an enormous price in human quality, for whether the individual or the group is aware of it or not, the result will be CONFORMITY* (p. 98).

On the other hand, a developing tradition within social psychology, based both on theoretical and value grounds, has focused on those conditions that induce resistance to influence rather than conformity. Social influence and power are relational concepts, dealing with an aspect of O's relationship with P. Lewin (1951) recognized this quality when he defined O's power over P in terms of two sets of forces: those that O induces and those that P offers in resistance; the outcome of these forces gives us P's conformity or resistance to O.

In an approach outlined by William Gamson (1968), the relationship between P and O—he calls P the potential partisan and O the authority—as regards social influence and control is one of opposites. As Gamson views this relationship, authorities initiate social control, while being the targets of partisans' influence efforts; in turn, partisans initiate influence and are the targets of social control. In other words, O attempts to get P to do something. P would like to have something to say about O's exercise of this control, so P tries to influence O. From O's perspective, O is giving control-oriented messages while receiving messages from P that seek to influence what O does. Thus O seeks to induce forces that will effectively control P's behavior. P in turn offers resistance that can take the form of trying to influence O's decisions concerning P. Thus O initiates controlling forces while receiving influence forces in the form of resistance from P.

Looking at P's resistance as an effort to influence O's decision making lends a meaningful social dimension to the concept of resistance. We can see that P's resistance is not necessarily a passion for rebellion, but rather can have an important rational basis in P's efforts to be effective. Realize that in many situations in which O exercises power, O is not entirely self-motivated but rather is influenced by those forces seeking O's attention who are trying to influence how O's power is used. College administrators, for example, have many audiences who seek to affect the decisions they make and the ways in which they control those under their jurisdiction. These form their circle of influence. There is the faculty to think of, the trustees, the public, and others. That the students may wish to be taken into consideration when decisions are made seems quite reasonable. They too want to have some influence over their own adminsitration. However, unlike those who presently have access to the administrator—that is, those who already form part of the circle of influence—the students may have to start from scratch. They must gain power in order to have hopes of joining that circle. From their perspective, then, just as the administrator is trying to control their behavior, they are trying to gain entry to the influence circle. In exchange terms, the students may be willing to work an exchange: they'll give the administration some control if, in return, the administration will receive some influence.

The administration, hesitant to add yet another member to the influence circle, may prefer to exercise control without receiving influence in return. Or the administrator may be willing to grant some influence provided that techniques of control can be used that are consistent with the aims of the administration: for example, persuasion or inducements of reward rather than threats of punishment. To the extent to which the students remain outside the system in which such techniques can be used, the administration may be forced to deal in punishment and constraint. However, it may be possible to bring the students into the system by allowing them some influence—for example, by permitting student participation in some aspects of university decision making. Through a process of *cooptation*—a term Philip Selznick (1948) introduced to describe the absorption of new elements into the leadership of a system—the authority gains an advantage of being able to exercise control by using persuasion and inducements. Thus, there are benefits to be gained by the administration permitting the potentially disruptive students entry to the circle of influence.

Although it may look as though through cooptation P has sold out, P too experiences certain advantages from the inside that were not available when P remained outside the system. As Gamson notes, cooptation gives the partisans access to resources and potential influence that were lacking before. It gives them a certain legitimacy that may in turn swell their ranks.

INNOCULATIONS FOR RESISTANCE

The laboratory tradition in social psychology has also been concerned with exploring additional circumstances under which P's resistance can be effected. Thinking in terms of a quasi-medical model, William McGuire (McGuire & Papageoris, 1961; McGuire, 1961; 1962; Papageoris & McGuire, 1961) wondered if you could *innoculate* persons against persuasive arguments by giving them an attenuated dosage of the counterarguments, just enough to stimulate their defensive system. The medical notion argues that you provide individuals with a sufficient amount of the disease for them to develop the proper antibodies to fight off the real thing when it arrives. Suppose that P believes X to be true; but we know that P will shortly undergo a massive propaganda campaign designed to change P's belief in X. We present P with small dosages of that campaign, just enough to arouse P's defenses against changing X but not enough to effectively persuade P to change; we have thus innoculated P and made P resistant to change.

McGuire undertook a series of experimental studies to test this general notion. In its basic format, the attitudes that he sought to innoculate against change were "cultural truisms": for example, everyone should visit a doctor once a year; people should brush their teeth after each meal if it's possible to do so, and so forth. It is assumed that these are beliefs that live an insulated life. They rarely, if ever come under attack or scrutiny. It is assumed, therefore, that the individual is not likely to have developed defenses against changing them. In order to help innoculate the individual, break the insulation and present small doses of the arguments that challenge these truisms; then see if the person resists changing them when later presented with the big campaign.

In one such study, Papageorgis and McGuire (1961) demonstrated that using immunizing arguments that seek to refute beliefs innoculate better than arguments that seek to support them. This would be expected if the function of the innoculation is to stimulate P's defenses. They should be more stimulated by challenging counterarguments in small doses than by providing P with even further supportive material.

In yet another study (Anderson & McGuire, 1965), it was demonstrated that threatening persons about the validity of their beliefs provided greater resistance to change than offering them reassurance that their beliefs were correct. Once again, this fits the innoculation model. Threats stimulate defenses that can be activated later when the big push for change arrives. Offering reassurance, however, does not help build defenses, as pleasantly unchallenging as such support may be at the moment. In a further examination of this matter, McGuire (1962) expanded the time interval, noting that refutational methods that threatened rather than supported P's beliefs conferred resistance to change immediately after receiving the "shot," as well as two days or even one week later.

The concept on which McGuire based his approach to increasing P's resistance to change is a rather interesting one. Recall that McGuire's efforts have been directed primarily towards beliefs that are cultural truisms. Recall also that the assumption is made that these beliefs typically are insulated and thus not well defended; presenting refutational arguments thus stimulates P's defenses. This same effect may not hold for beliefs that are more adequately defended or that are challenged almost daily, and thereby relatively resistant to easy change.

The Resistance of Power. Several other avenues for inducing resistance have also been examined. For example, the greater P's self-esteem and self-confidence, the more resistant P is likely to be. In group level terms, a community that feels itself weakened and incompetent is not likely to be able to resist intrusions from the outside. Nor is such a community likely to view itself as being capable of exercising counterinfluence over O. Aiding that community and its inhabitants to gain a sense of confidence and self-esteem becomes an essential part of creating a community that is resistant to social influence.

Though the preceding point is simple it is often overlooked, especially by the academic consultant who fails to recognize that not everyone is as self-confident as he or she might be. One problem in helping others to develop resistance is that the historically downtrodden too often have given up all efforts to be effective in modifying their environment. They have experienced the victim's position so long that they cannot think of themselves as being capable of mounting a countermovement. Even the simple notion that authority can be questioned or challenged is something that has escaped them as a possibility. One of the first steps in creating resistance, therefore, is to help persons realize the real possibilities that exist for them to flex their muscles. They can be encouraged to go to City Hall, to complain to the Police Department, to bring their arguments before government officials. Even a small success at muscle flexing can have wondrous effects in stimulating a group to think that they may in fact be able to exercise some control over their lives.

The several recent power movements have this quality, whether their focus be on blacks, students, Chicanos, women, or whatever. Such movements help to give people a sense of personal worth and self-esteem; these are essential in any power relationship. P must approach O not as a humble victim but as a person who counts, who has the potential to effect influence over O. Black power inestimably aids in providing a sense of dignity from out of a historical scene that deprived the black of that sense. In addition, these power movements offer people a chance to take an active rather than a passive role in shaping the affairs that affect them. Through the exercise of their organized power, they come to occupy a negotiating stance vis-a-vis O: in other words, they become a part of O's circle of influence, another factor that O must consider during decision making.

The essence of the preceding argument is that resistance originates in a position of power. The persons who can be the most resistant to influence are those who stand in positions of power; it is they who can enter into the social exchange with O and bargain in terms of a truer reciprocity. To reverse the formulation of the *Anatomy of Conformity,* this time looking at it from P's perspective, we note that when P has the power to satisfy O's needs, P has a better chance of resisting O's efforts to control P. For those in a powerless position, often the only needs of O over which they have some control are O's needs for peace and order. Thus, their power often lies in their ability to disrupt. They can exchange this with O, giving O assurances of minimal disruption in exchange for certain benefits. O gets peace and order and some compliance from P; P gets benefits from O.

If power allows for resistance, the other side is also true: resistance confers power. Not only does P's possession of some power allow P to resist O's inductions, but also P's resistance provides a basis for power over O. Short of using physical force, O must work to get P's compliance through less coercive means. To the extent that P can refuse to give O compliance, P has power to influence O. Thus, P's resistance forms a basis for pressuring O into an exchange position. If I refuse to comply with you, and if you need my compliance and are hesitant to get it by the use of brute force, then I have gained an ability to influence you. If you want my compliance, you had better come sit down and talk. I think we can make a deal. It is in this sense that resistance confers power that in turn allows for more resistance, and so on.

In dealings between the very powerful and the less powerful—including persons as well as nations—we have come to realize the limitations of power. The application of brute coercion to gain compliance usually brings about so many other negative consequences that the powerful resist the temptation to exercise force and thereby be done with the entire affair. This limitation of power (especially coercive power), helps the less powerful to gain a better bargaining position; in a sense, their lack of power works to their advantage, just as the powerfuls' possession of great power works to their disadvantage. A powerful nation or a powerful person, then, may receive counterinfluence from the weaker party that is out of proportion to their factual power differential. But weak parties who wish to resist the influence of the powerful must come to realize that there exists great strength in their apparent weakness; just as there is weakness in what passes for coercive strength.

For the person in authority, O, there is a lesson to be learned as well. Because O wants P's compliance, and because as we can assume, O does not want continual disruption, O's goals will be furthered by providing means other than disruptive ones for P to have influence over O. That is, if P's only source of influence over O is P's ability to withhold compliance and to disrupt, then neither P nor O will make much joint progress. However, if O provides a way for P to influence O in nondisruptive ways, O can use authority more effectively. By taking P into O's circle of influence, O brings P into the system and allows P to exercise influence in more constructive ways. To paraphrase something that John F. Kennedy said, a nation that does not allow for peaceful change will find itself beset by violent change. In other words, until P is permitted access to O, until lines of communication are opened and participation assured, the streets rather than the council chambers are likely to be the loci of change.

In Conclusion

Before we move forward into a continuing discussion and analysis of the issues involved with freedom and responsibility, let us briefly review some of the territory that we have just covered. We began with a striking series of laboratory demonstrations that show that persons placed into a context of legitimate authority tended to follow orders even when it involved doing harm to another person; apparently, persons followed such orders even when the meaningfulness of the entire situation seemed absent: that is, when they were teaching someone who was stunned into silence! Perhaps they assumed that the experimenter as the legitimate authority, a representative of science, surely must know what it is all about; they never seriously inquired about the ends that their rational though meaningless behavior served. In this regard, they were like Martin Orne's (1962) subjects who carried out equally meaningless though more benign activities simply because the experimenter had asked them to. They added columns of numbers, 224 per page, from a stack of some 2000 pages. Some continued this activity for over 5½ hours, waiting for the experimenter to tell them to stop! They are like most of us who simply go about out business, doing our piece of work, not seriously probing its purpose beyond making a living.

To refer to such activities as rational is to note several features of the activity and of the authority relationship that is involved. The activity is one part of a larger whole; and though the persons engaging in that part may have little sense of the larger whole and thus of the purposes which their specific activity serves, they have accepted the overall legitimacy of the structure within which they are functioning and hence believe that in some manner their activity is sensible. For example, the subject who does 5½ hours of addition may wonder what it is all about; but at some level of awareness, he or she believes that a rational explanation for the activity can be offered and that on learning of this larger purpose, the activity will be rendered sensible.

The activity is likewise rational in that the authority who requested the behavior of P occupies a position within a structure that gives the authority the legitimate right to expect certain things of

P. P, in turn, has learned that this kind of rational-legal legitimacy, is based neither on tradition (e.g., kinship) or charisma (e.g., attraction), but rather on the expertise and credibility of the role's occupant. P has learned that the commands do not issue from emotion or personal feeling but from an impersonal application of accepted procedures for accomplishing certain ends. P has learned to value rational behavior.

To speak of rationality in this sense is not necessarily to speak of reason. One may act rationally without seriously evaluating the actions taken or the purposes they serve. The subjects in Milgram's and others' research engaged in rational behavior. Within the context of psychological science, it makes sense to study how punishment can affect learning. It is reasonable to try to be a good subject, one who helps the experimenters with their research program. It makes sense to believe that they are not likely to cause harm or damage to others. It makes sense to believe that they must have some important purpose in mind that will render the whole matter sensible and quell one's own uncomfortable feelings and intruding doubts. Indeed, subjects were pleased to learn at the end, during the experimenter's debriefing session that they had really not harmed anyone, that it was just an accomplice playing a part.

As disturbing as some of these findings are, they are not really that surprising; the banality of evil, as we will see in the next chapter, makes us sensitive to the unfortunate truth that most of us are capable of behaving like Milgram's subjects. Perhaps if persons had behaved helpfully but for the same reason—that is, because they were asked to—we would feel better. But would we still wonder what happened to their critical reason?

We have seen that the ideological roots for legitimacy of authority in our present society lay neither in tradition nor in charisma, but rather in a rational-legal form epitomized by the large organization within whose network of roles and relationships we locate ourselves. To gain our conformity, authorities need not claim kinship or kingship, nor threaten punishments, nor offer any greater inducements than support for the structure of relationships that includes us with them.

Ideally, obedience to authority that is legitimated in terms of its rationality should give greater room for individual freedom and self-determination than that based on either tradition or charisma. The Watergate trials offer us a mixed case, demonstrating both that no one is above the law, yet crimes committed by important persons are not punished as severely as those committed by persons of lesser status. In the rational-legal system, indeed, no one should be above the law or beyond its reach; the essence of such a system is that rules are applied equally to all citizens, both chief and commoner. The reasonableness of such a system is the degree to which, unlike the traditional or charismatic forms, it frees persons from more personal bases of governance, putting all on a more equal footing. Of course, the ideal is not always achieved, as in the Watergate sentencing.

We have also seen in this chapter and will see again at other points in this book questions raised concerning just how far, in whose name, and to what end, freedom and equality exist under a rational-legal system of authority. We have raised questions concerning the rationality of acting in conformity to legitimated authority without asking some serious questions: not about who the authority is or what right the authority has to make claims upon our behavior, but rather about what are we doing and why and whose purposes are being served.

What may have begun historically as freeing of humankind has also produced some of the greatest onslaughts against human welfare and life that the civilized world has seen. Organized rationality grinds on without engaging persons in its process as anything other than agreeing cogs. We have raised questions about what we are when we abdicate our status as agents and become pawns.

To intrude reason into these great systems of rationality became the valued goal of Lewin and his associates. Perhaps Lewin wondered if persons can actively participate in the decision-making apparatus of their lives, then their collective wisdom can force reason and humanity on otherwise potentially dangerous decisions. At least it could hurt nothing but the smooth running of the organization to have people join together to discuss, to debate, and to decide the course of their action and lives. Lewin was not puzzled nor much surprised by the fact that persons could and would knuckle under to autocratic leadership, even if it had been legitimately constituted. Could small groups, however, working cooperatively within larger settings (e.g., organizations and communities) bring persons back in as real decision makers, as agents rather than as pawns?

But even here, as we noted, questions were raised concerning the degree to which group processes simply became another source of authority, as insidious as the others. In the name of groupthink or managerial technique, persons can and do act unwisely. Indeed a committee might sit down to discuss and agree upon Milgram-like research, everyone participating in the decision.

We next sought a more complex view of person-authority relationships. We noted how strong and deeply the roots of human resistance can go, even when the authority is legitimate. We also noted how the creation of resistance and its systematic analysis may provide an avenue by which to reintroduce reason into the system.

We recognize the vital and necessary role that authority relationships play in human survival; but we continue to ask about the extent to which the exercise of such authority calls on the reasoning of persons as active agents. This indeed has been a theme of this chapter. It will continue as a theme in several of the remaining chapters. Though we do not pretend to have *the* answer (or even *an* answer), we agree with C. Wright Mills earlier concern that these issues of freedom and of reason are vital and central to our lives today.

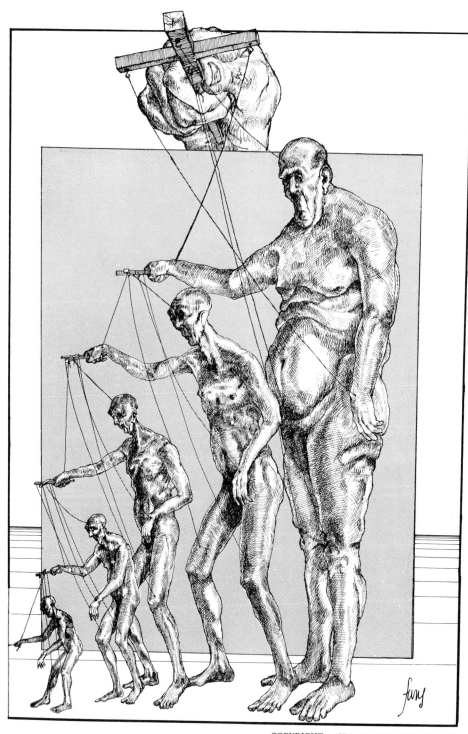

RESPONSIBILITY AND MORALITY

8

Let us begin with a commonsense formulation, consistent as well with attribution theory (see Chapter 4) and its empirical underpinnings: to the extent that we can attribute personal causation to P, we can hold P responsible for the consequences of P's acts. Insofar as P makes self-attributions using this same formulation, then P too is likely to accept responsibility for those acts that P has personally caused. Another way of stating the preceding is to note that our sense of P as a free agent, as well as P's sense of personal freedom, is based on the degree to which attributions to personal causation are made.

On the basis of attribution theory and research, we know some of the circumstances under which personal causation and responsibility are likely:

1. When P's acts are accidental or unintended or without awareness of their consequences, our tendency is to discount personal causation.
2. When P's behavior appears to deviate from role or situational expectations, we tend to attribute this deviation to some characteristics within P.
3. When P's behavior conforms to situational requirements, when P does what "anyone in such circumstances would do," we tend to discount personal causation.
4. However, if we have information that the behavior is typical of P in many situations, then we might very well find P responsible for acts committed even while under situational pressure.

What about acts carried out in response to an authority's inductions? We see P engage in actions that are neither accidental nor unintended. P may know some or all of their consequences; thus we cannot readily discount personal causation. However, we are aware of a strong external source—the authority—and thus we might feel that P's behavior fits what anyone would do in comparable circumstances and so relieve P of personal responsibility. If the authority threatened grave punishment or promised great rewards, we would find P's actions of compliance readily understandable, though even here we might feel P to be greedy or cowardly, especially if the act were one we felt to be immoral or bad. In general, however, acting under duress helps relieve P of personal responsibility. But what about acts done neither for love, nor money, nor fear, but rather in response to the legitimacy of authority? A certain ambiguity exists for this case. We know from the simulated and hypothetical versions of Milgram's situation (as reported by Milgram, 1965 and by Larsen *et al.,* 1972) that observers generally feel it is socially undesirable to administer electric shocks to another person. Presumably, therefore, O might think badly of P if P went ahead and administered shocks to the learner. Milgram tells us that psychiatric observers felt that anyone who applied the maximum shock level would have to be sick. In other words, observers seemed to find behavior in response to legitimate authority informative about the person, and thus presumably they would hold the person responsible for his or her actions. Yet, following the orders of a legitimately constituted authority seems to be what most persons would do (and indeed do); this should thereby attenuate the tendency to hold P personally responsible for P's actions. The subjects who actually were involved in Milgram's investigations minimized their sense of personal causation and responsibility, rationalizing their behavior: I was only following orders, being a good subject, meeting the requirements of the research, and so forth.

We also saw in the related research of Kilham and Mann (1974) that those in the role of transmitter apparently felt less responsibility than those in the role of executant. Thus, even while acting in compliance with the requests of a legitimate authority, persons may occupy different positions that convey different degrees of personal responsibility: the clerk who transmits the orders may feel less responsible and be held less responsible than the person carrying out the orders. Yet, even this latter person can see herself at the end of a chain of command, part of a structure in which her behavior is simply one element of the total, and in which responsibility inheres in the total rather than in any one of its parts.

Though the legitimacy of the authority and the placement of P in the chain of command may attenuate personal responsibility, it is not necessarily reduced to a zero point. For example, Larsen et al. (see Chapter 7), asked their subjects to estimate the actual shock levels that they were giving. Although the subjects could see the actual level on the apparatus they were using, there was a tendency to underestimate the level, believing themselves to be giving lower levels than they actually were. Is it perhaps their sense of guilt and their efforts to diminish its impact that led them to this kind of self-serving distortion? If so, then subjects, though they rationalized away their personal responsibility, must nevertheless have experienced some responsibility for their actions.

In Chapter 4 we noted an attributional bias in which person attributions seemed more prevalent than situation attributions (especially in judging the causes of others' behaviors). In Chapter 6, we suggested the important function that is served once we can identify another person as the cause of some action and thereby locate responsibility for the act within the person. As we have noted at several points in our present discussion, even in the face of a legitimate authority, both actor and observer do not seem to have reduced the actor's personal responsibility to zero. That we are sensitive to the important functions served by locating the causes of actions within the person should not blind us, however, to those situations involving legitimate authority in which personal causation is minimized. The claim of personal nonresponsibility when following legitimate orders is also a culturally learned and often reinforced perspective that serves useful social functions as well.

The individual citizen implicitly agrees to have a degree of personal freedom of choice and personal preference diminished when agreeing to follow the dictates of someone in authority; in exchange for this obedience, the individual expects to be relieved of much of the personal responsibility for such actions. A police officer who kills someone in the line of duty is acting as an agent of society rather than as a personal agent; as such, responsibility for the officer's actions are not entirely his or her own. In this manner, persons become agents of social institutions, vehicles with the capability of taking actions for which the vehicle itself is not held personally responsible. One does not blame the vehicle for the act; it is the passive form in this human cultural equation. One does not blame the soldier for killing in wartime; he was simply the vehicle with which his society functioned in its behalf. The responsibility was not his.

A theatrical metaphor will be helpful in illuminating the importance of this cultural pattern. When we in the audience view actors performing, we typically can separate them from their roles. The villain in the play, therefore, may be engaging in villainous acts, just as the hero may be engaging in great feats of daring do, but in typical circumstances, we attribute these actions to the role rather than to the person. And likewise, actors who enact the villainous parts are not likely to think themselves bad, nor are the heroes likely to have their esteem raised. Each was simply following orders, playing a role in a larger drama.

Similarly, societal definitions that differentiate between a role and the person performing it, permit us to play roles without necessarily feeling that we really are that way. Without this differentiation, it would be difficult for social systems to function. A differentiation between person and role permits persons to be recruited to socially essential roles without necessarily engaging themselves personally. Thus control over a performance may be obtained without necessarily having to change persons' desires to think well of themselves and to be thought well of by others. In these instances, the person becomes the vehicle through which the role performance is portrayed; the role is held accountable for what transpires, not the vehicle conveying it. The role essentially removes personal factors from the equation and thereby helps ensure predictability, stability, and control.

The important social function served by this differentiation is apparent, for example, when police are called into their own community to quell a disturbance involving their friends and neighbors. If personal preferences governed police behavior, they would not perform their duty to the larger society; but if, when they put on that uniform, they shed all personal preferences and personal responsibility, they can fulfill their obligations to the larger social system without necessarily engaging themselves. The situation as described is by no means an unusual one. During the 1974 school busing issue in Boston, for example, police and national guardsmen were called in to police areas of the city, often including their own neighborhoods in order to guarantee that the court ordered integration would proceed. When interviewed, several police and guardsmen indicated that while they personally disagreed with the integration policy, once they put on their uniforms, their personal feelings were no longer relevant. In uniform, they were the vehicle for carrying out the society's orders. The judiciary was the causal agent; responsibility was not theirs personally, but lay in the hands of the court. So the guardsman could return home at night and feel that once out of uniform he could let his own views be aired; his neighbors could appreciate his dilemma and recognize that he was simply doing his job.

War Crimes: A Case Example

To this point, we have suggested that when P acts in response to a legitimate authority, a certain ambiguity exists as to P's degree of personal responsibility for the action. Important social and personal functions are served when P can be identified as the cause and held responsible, or when responsibility can be lodged elsewhere. It would seem reasonable to suggest that persons might differ in their inclination to locate responsibility under such circumstances. It is to this matter that we turn our attention, using the valuable investigation of the Lieutenant Calley case conducted by Kelman and Lawrence (1972) as the basis for our discussion. Calley was tried and convicted of war crimes during what came to be referred to as the

My Lai Massacre during the Vietnam War. Kelman and Lawrence report the results of a national public opinion survey of attitudes toward Calley's trial and conviction and other related issues (e.g., the Nurenberg War Crimes Tribunal). The sample for their survey consisted of 989 persons, 18 and older, chosen to be a cross-section of the U.S. population. Kelman and Lawrence were particularly concerned with uncovering, if possible, different perspectives on this issue of authority and responsibility and to examine several correlates of these differences.

In their review of their data, Kelman and his colleague report two different attitudes towards the trial and towards Calley's responsibility for the killings:

1. One group of persons surveyed disapproved of the trial and felt it unfair to hold Calley responsible for carrying out his proper combat role; they were referred to as the DR group—disapprove responsibility.

2. The other group approved of the trial and felt that individuals, even soldiers in combat, must bear responsibility for their behavior; they were referred to as the AR Group—approve responsibility.

These two attitudes were then used by Kelman and Lawrence to examine further aspects of issues involving responsibility and authority. In particular, they were concerned to note the other attitudes that differentiated the AR and DR groups, some background characteristics of these two groups, and finally the broader implications of this distinction.

In examining AR versus DR attitudes towards convicting German officers for war crimes at the Nurenberg trials, for example, a similar pattern of responses is noted. Of the DR group, 57 percent felt it wrong to convict the German officers, whereas 67 percent of the AR group felt it was right to do so. In other comparisons, Kelman and Lawrence report that 68 percent of the DR group felt that they would have acted as Calley had done (i.e., follow orders and shoot), while 65 percent of the AR group indicated that if it had been them, they would have refused to carry out the orders. Likewise, whereas 67 percent of the DR group felt that "Calley's actions [were] justified because [it is] better to kill some South Vietnamese civilians than risk [the] lives of American soldiers," 70 percent of the AR group disagreed with this statement. What begins to emerge from these and several further analyses of their data are two rather distinct patterns of relationship to authority and to responsibility.

The DR group appears to feel that the moral imperative in the Calley situation and in most other situations involving legitimate authority, is to follow orders: that is, one's obligation is to be obedient to the authority; individual wishes and preferences do not play a role in such contexts. As Kelman and Lawrence note, from the DR perspective, it is a betrayal for the government, as the legitimate authority, first to give the orders that one is morally obliged to obey and then to bring the person to trial for having followed those orders. In their view, Calley gave his unquestioning obedience in exchange for the government's acceptance of the responsibility for the consequences of the actions undertaken. It is important for us to note that the DR perspective is one in which the legitimacy of authority makes personal values irrelevant, compliance morally proper, and individual responsibility nonexistent. Indeed, the person is merely the vehicle; the authority is the responsible agent. Thus DR persons can be and in fact often were opposed to the U.S. involvement in Vietnam, yet felt this personal opposition was irrelevant to the issue of complying with legitimate orders: personal beliefs and values are of lesser importance than doing one's duty by supporting the policies set by legitimate authorities. This echoes the view of the police and guardsmen involved in the integration example previously cited.

A not too dissimilar pattern has been noted by investigators who have studied other instances of what Dicks (1972) refers to as "licensed mass murder."* Dicks's own investigation of several convicted Nazi SS murders suggests the importance of loyalty and group membership as the overriding value in many cases. The concept *Kadavergehorsam* (cadaver obedience) captures a sense of this intense commitment to loyal obedience without question to the policies of one's superiors:

> *We must ... be prepared to face the full horror that some of these murderers were not superaggressive villains, but morally defective children who surrendered their decisions to objects for attachment. If there is a fanaticism ... it is in the quality of subordination, need to belong, not to question what the reference object of attachment wants. This is the* "Kadavergehorsam"* (p. 108).

The Soviet writer, Solzhenitsyn (1974), has also noted a similar pattern of unquestioning acceptance of the rightness of one's superiors among internment camp guards and interrogators. By stark contrast, the AR perspective is one in which personal values and beliefs must intrude upon judgments, "even in a situation of legitimate authority." The moral imperative is not simply that one's primary duty is to follow orders, but rather to evaluate the relationship between legitimate authority and moral principles, and to choose principle over authority because persons hold themselves to be

---

*The material quoted here and elsewhere is from Licensed Mass Murder: A Socio-Psychological Study of Some SS Killers by Henry V. Dicks, © 1972 by Henry V. Dicks, Basic Books, Inc., Publishers, New York. Chatto, Windus & Heinemann Educational Books for Sussex University Press (1972), London.

responsible for the consequences of their actions. From this perspective the legitimacy of an authority cannot relieve personal responsibility for people's actions, thus their actions must be the outcome of their own deliberation and the engagement of their values and principles.

What is clear is that the DR and AR persons have defined the same situation rather differently. For the DR person, the Calley situation is one of obedience to authority and personal nonresponsibility; for the AR person, the situation is one of obedience to principle and personal responsibility. It would appear that the DR Group feels itself to be pawns or vehicles of a social system, whereas the AR group feels itself more to be active agents or owners of the social system and thereby personally implicated in its policy decisions.

Dicks's work is again instructive on this point. He reports many instances of Nazi war criminals whose relationship to their society was that of "the little man," simply following orders and carrying out a routine job. The sense is conveyed of persons who view themselves passively being drawn into roles set for them by others. As Dicks notes, the Nazi movement not only called on such "little men" (the DR perspective in essence), but elevated them to positions of power and importance they would otherwise never have. This sense of being impotent in a setting of national omnipotence, expressed by a range of persons and military ranks from the lowest up to field-marshalls, is captured in the stark plea: *"Ja was könnte ich denn, war ja nur ein kleinen mann?* (What could I do, I was only a little man?)" (p. 37).

But again, lest we sit back securely in our beliefs that it is always the other person who is the "little man," the writings of Solzhenitsyn (1974) confirm the suspicions raised by Milgram's work: many are susceptible when the situation is right. Reflecting on his guards and interrogators, Solzhenitsyn wondered whether he could have become one himself. Answering affirmatively, he noted the pleasures of life that would have been simplified if he had accepted another's authority and granted them his personal responsibility; thinking would no longer be needed; decisions would be made elsewhere and he would merely carry them out. Importantly, he would be doing what everyone else was also doing; thus he would fit in and belong; he would be accepted and experience a sense of fellowship rather than isolation and rejection.

CADETS AND RESISTERS

While the context was somewhat different, the results of an investigation (Sampson et al., 1969) of senior ROTC cadet officers and indicted draft resisters lends further support to the twofold typology that the AR and DR perspectives reveal. A more recent investigation (Mantell, 1974) of green berets and war resisters provides additional confirmatory evidence. The national sample surveyed by Kelman and Lawrence responded to an incident not directly involving themselves; though as we have seen, the AR perspective envisions personal responsibility for all governmental policies. During the early phases of the Vietnam War, draft resisters personally implicated themselves in their refusal to serve in the military; ROTC cadets, on the other hand, had decided to pursue a career in the military, making this decision while their nation was actively engaged in the war.

The samples for this study were small in number; the methodology required rather intensive interviews (often up to 7 hours) with each person. There were twenty cadets and eleven resisters interviewed. While the investigation revealed many facets of human decision making during times of national mobilization both for and against the war, for our present purposes, it is most important to note the kinds of response to issues of responsibility and morality. The resister pattern reveals what we have noted to be a characteristic of the AR perspective—the cadets provide confirmation for the DR position. A few excerpts from the actual interviews will clarify this point. First the cadets.

> *I believe that the moral responsibility for my actions falls upon the government. I can't condemn the Germans ... If I were a German and they told me to go out and shoot that man, I would do it. If you disobey, you will be killed.*

> *... The U.S. Government has decided the moral issue and has chosen to fight. I disagree with this. But I don't think resisting the draft is the answer. As a citizen of the U.S. I must go. ... As for me, I will do what the Army tells me to do.*

Perhaps the strongest statement denying personal responsibility is seen in the following cadet's comment:

> *I am not, in that uniform, an agent of myself ... If I went to Vietnam, I would not think of myself as killing the people. If one walked into my sights and I pulled the trigger, I would have no moral conscience about it, because I was sent there by the government.*

Apropos of this quotation, Fritz Redl (1973) presents an insightful analysis of the role of tribal masks and uniforms in relieving the person from responsibility for his or her deeds. Redl notes that the mask-uniform makes the actor a faceless member of a collectivity and simultaneously makes "sure that everybody knows [his or her] behavior is acceptable only under temporary conditions and needs to be terminated when the show is over" (p. 95). In uniform, one need not feel the typical claims of conscience nor be held responsible for one's acts: "the collective superego ... replaces the personal one" (p. 96). Recall as well the Boston guardsmen whose uniform was their shield against personal involvement.

The cadets' conception of the situation is one in which their personal values are not relevant and following orders is primary. The government has made the decision and thus the responsibility for the cadets' behavior is no longer theirs (i.e., collective conscience replaces personal conscience); they are merely its vehicle and agents. This perspective stands in sharp contrast to the resister's oft-noted and demanding sense of personal responsibility, especially in the context of legitimate governmental authority.

> *My responsibility to the people I care about in this country is to provide them with the benefit of life ... I couldn't feel any integrity inside of myself with that draft card burning a hole in my pocket knowing that I was cooperating with that whole system ... I feel that I have some responsibility towards all the people my age who are now in the army and who are in Vietnam being killed because no one spoke out before them. I feel responsibility especially to the people who will come after, for whom the Resistance might really do some good.*

Another resister, whose comments clearly show the sense of personal responsibility he feels and the system-ownership role he envisions himself playing, puts it this way:

> *When I went to Africa in 1964–1965, Africans were asking how come you do this [put down peasant uprisings]? How come you hate the Congolese? How come you hate the Vietnamese? They literally hold you responsible. In one sense that isn't right, for you are not responsible for what your government does to them. But yet, you are in some sense if you live there [in the United States] and allow your country to be called democratic. If you allow yourself to take benefit of what your country offers, then you also have to take responsibility for what your country does. ... The most satisfying thing you can do for yourself is to face squarely your own complicity.*

The resisters, like the AR respondents of Kelman's investigation, define themselves as causal agents; they emphasize person-causes in contexts of legitimate authority in which we typically make external causal attributions, denying both personal freedom as well as individual responsibility. Before examining some background correlates of these contrasting perspectives on authority, responsibility, and morality, it will be helpful to add one additional theoretical approach to the issues involved. To this, we turn to the ideas of Lawrence Kohlberg.

Kohlberg's Theory of Moral Reasoning

Kohlberg (1958; 1968; 1969) sought to uncover a universal sequence of cognitive reasoning about morality. His approach was based on Piaget's pioneering ideas; it is similar as well to both Kelman and Lawrence's and the resister-cadet approaches to understanding how persons define situations involving moral choices. Kohlberg's cognitive developmental theory posits certain stages of development in human reasoning; each stage defines the world in a different manner. Stages are qualitatively different periods in the transaction between our tendencies towards structure and the input received from our environment. Unique transformations of the environment are made as we represent this external world to ourselves. And this representation varies qualitatively as we progressively pass through the stages of development. Persons make differentiations at later stages that they could not make at earlier stages. They structure the outside world differently at age three than at age ten, for example. Their manner of thinking at the earlier age does not permit them to see things in the same way as they are capable of seeing later when they have progressed far enough to make new differentiations and higher order integrations. In essence, each stage represents a different kind of moral philosophy and moral reasoning, a different manner of differentiating and integrating encounters with the environment. Kohlberg distinguishes between three major levels of moral reasoning and two stages at each level:

    I. the preconventional

        1. physical power

        2. instrumental relativism

   II. the conventional

        3. interpersonal concordance

        4. law and order

  III. the postconventional

        5. social contract

        6. universal ethic.

The Preconventional. At this level the individual does not differentiate between moral value and external sanctions. At the first stage in this level, "might makes right"; at the second stage, personal needs and desires make right. There is minimal differentiation between property or material objects and human values. Likewise, the power to enforce rules makes rules morally correct. There is great concern with avoiding punishment or getting rewarded by those in power: that is, with the instrumentality of one's acts. In the second stage of this level, the individual does not differentiate between his or her own desires and moral value. Things are right and proper if they satisfy one's own needs. There is a simplistic relativism in which the individual recognizes that others also have needs that they want to satisfy: let us each do our own thing. As Kohlberg notes, at this stage, life is like the economic marketplace with a minimal conception of reciprocity. However, there is no sense of justice or fairness in the exchange, rather just a base realization that we each have needs and for me to get mine satisfied, I'll sometimes have to help you get yours met.

The Conventional. At this level, moral judgment is rooted in a social order and in the fulfillment of the obligations and responsibilities of one's roles. Reciprocity is involved, but unlike the preconventional conception, there is a recognition that each person must conform to conventional social roles and expectations so that all may live harmoniously. Conformity to and justification of the social role is an end in itself. In stage 3 (i.e., interpersonal concordance), the individual equates moral value with being a good person who is approved by others while helping them. There is an emphasis on being nice and proper. At stage 4, the individual makes a definite commitment to convention and to the existing social order. Morality is defined in terms of the existing social order. Doing one's duty, respecting authority, supporting the system as it exists are all high moral ends in their own right.

Postconventional. At this highest level of moral development, the individual has carved out general and universal principles of morality or ideals of human conduct which are part of his or her personal system of values and are independent of any specific authority, society, or group. The individual differentiates between social customs and social norms on the one hand, and moral principles on the other. These latter conform to a higher authority than the society or the group, and pertain to general conceptions of human justice and equality. Stage 5 involves a social contract notion in which the individual is able to understand the arbitrary nature of specific rules and feels that they can be changed to better exemplify human values. A contract of a legalistic sort exists between persons and defines general rights for all; the contract, however, is not inflexible as with stage 4 thinking, but can be modified as greater social needs demand. Stage 6 morality—often seen as an alternative to stage 5, rather than as a separate stage in its own right —involves adherence to conscience and to general, universal, and abstract principles and ideals that cross historical eras and cultural or social customs.

As Kohlberg notes, a key distinction between the conventional and the postconventional level is that whereas the former defines morality and social justice in terms of the existing social order, the latter uses the principles of justice and equality to define the proper form of the social order. That is, the conventionally moral person does not differentiate between what his or her social order defines as just and a general concept of social justice. The postconventional person, on the other hand, differentiates between the general principles, and their application in any given society. His or her actions are guided by the principle not the customs or norms of a particular society. Thus, where the social order does not offer justice, the postconventional person opts for justice over the order. By contrast, individuals of conventional morality, not differentiating social norms and conventions from general principles, opt for the conventional order that they feel necessarily defines morality.

As Turiel (1969) has noted, the transition from stage 4 conventionality to stage 5 or 6 morality is difficult to make. He argues that this transition involves both an increasing degree of relativism as the individual recognizes the arbitrariness of the conventions and norms of each social order; and yet a decreasing relativism as the individual recognizes the validity of universalistic principles of morality. Since progression through these stages requires increasingly higher levels of both differentiation and integration, movement to the postconventional is especially complicated by its requirement of both stances towards relativism. The person must see things at once in a more complex light and also be able to integrate this complicated differentiation into a higher order stage before progress can be made. Perhaps for this reason research has shown that there are so few persons at the postconventional level.

The parallels between Kohlberg's analysis of moral reasoning and the Kelman and Lawrence analysis of differential orientations to authority and responsibility as well as the cadet-resister reasoning are quite apparent. The DR pattern and the cadet tend towards Kohlberg's conventional stages, although in some cadet responses aspects of preconventional reasoning were noted: for example, the concern with being punished for not complying with orders. On the other hand, the AR pattern and the resisters share much with Kohlberg's postconventional stages of moral reasoning. These parallels are all the more interesting and important when we realize the diversity of the samples on which these analyses have been made and the variety of research techniques employed. The AR–DR patterns were culled from an analysis of a national sample responding to items concerning the Calley trial and conviction; the resister-cadet data were based on lengthy interviews with relatively small samples of persons committed to resisting the draft or serving in the military during the Vietnam War; finally, both Kohlberg's samples and his research technique vary extensively. It is to this that we now turn our attention.

THE RESEARCH PROGRAM

In order to test his ideas, Kohlberg developed a measuring instrument consisting of a series of stories that contain classic moral dilemmas. For example:

In Europe, a woman was near death from a special kind of cancer. There was one drug that the doctors thought might save her. It was a form of radium that a druggist in the same town had recently discovered. The drug was expensive to make, but the druggist was charging ten times what the drug cost him to make. He paid $200 for the radium and charged $2,000 for a small dose of the drug. The sick woman's husband, Heinz, went to everyone he knew to borrow the money, but he could only get together about $1,000, which is half of what it cost. He told the druggist that his wife was dying and asked him to sell it cheaper or let him pay later. But the druggist said, "No, I discovered the drug and I'm going to make money from it." So Heinz got desperate and broke into the man's store to steal the drug for his wife.

The subject is asked several questions about this incident: "Should Heinz have done that?" "Was it wrong or right?" "Would a good husband do that?" "Did the druggist have the right to charge that much?" "Heinz was caught; should the judge send him to jail for stealing or should he be let go?" "Why?"

In the typical session, the subject is presented with ten such moral dilemmas and interviewed carefully about each incident. It should be obvious that the theoretical perspective that Kohlberg has adopted requires that one get deeply into the reasons and reasoning of the individual in each case; it is not sufficient to have the person state "no, he shouldn't have stolen it" or "yes, he should have." All interview material is carefully coded according to a system developed by Kohlberg; subjects are then assigned to a dominant stage.

What happens, in fact, is that individuals yield profiles that include the dominant stage that they are presently thinking at, the stage that they are just leaving but still think in terms of, and the beginnings of the stage that they are just beginning to move into. Kohlberg reports that about 50 percent of an individual's moral thinking will fall at one of the stages (see Kurtines & Greif, 1974, for a recent critique of Kohlberg's methods).

Several important empirical questions need to be answered. First, if these are thought to be universal structures of moral development, it should be possible to uncover the same stages and the same ordering in a variety of cultural settings. Studies undertaken in Taiwan, Mexico, and Turkey generally find results that are comparable to those undertaken in the United States. Although the rates of stage development by age vary from culture to culture, the existence of the stages and their order as posited has been supported by Kohlberg's empirical data.

Second, a documentation of the sequence of stages is best demonstrated by a longitudinal study that follows the same persons over time to see if they do change their moral judgments in accordance with the sequence that has been posited. Kramer (see Kohlberg & Kramer, 1969) administered the moral dilemmas at three-year intervals to a group of subjects during a period of thirteen years, as they progressed from age 14 to age 27. Although there is some doubt whether or not persons must pass through stage 5 before reaching stage 6, Kohlberg reports these data from Kramer as confirming the stage sequence that was posited.

Another aspect to the longitudinal data reported by Kohlberg concerns the correlations between moral maturity scores at various points in an individual's life history. Some data indicate generally high correlations, upwards of .76 between scores earned at age 13 and scores achieved in the mid-twenties. In other words, advanced development at an early age predicts to advanced development at later ages. Correlations of this magnitude are not typically obtained in psychological research; thus, though preliminary, they are suggestive of the value of the approach that Kohlberg has taken.

Thirdly, an implication of the stage model of moral development concerns the impact of training procedures in facilitating progressive development. Turiel (1966) in particular has been concerned with this matter. If persons pass through an invariant sequence of stages, then efforts to push them ahead should work best when people are introduced to a stage slightly beyond their present level. Presentations that are too advanced for the individual will not facilitate progress. To test this, Turiel experimentally presented groups of 7th grade boys from public schools in New Haven moral reasoning that was one stage below their own or one or two stages higher than their own. Remeasures of their moral reasoning after these presentations indicated that exposure to the stage one higher than their own level was the most effective in producing progression in their moral development. Presenting moral reasoning two stages removed from their initial level was found to be the least effective. In a related endeavor, Rest, Turiel, and Kohlberg (1969) found that children expressed a preference for the reasoning of stages somewhat above their own level. A study by Le Furgay and Woloshin (1969) further confirms these data.

A fourth line of research has taken Kohlberg's conception of moral development and applied it to groups with known characteristics. Three studies in particular are relevant to consider. One of the first was conducted by Norma Haan, M. Brewster Smith, and Jeanne Block (1968). They examined the level of moral development of several classes of students, in particular those who had been active in the 1964 Free Speech Movement at Berkeley. In general, their data indicate that the politically active students as compared with a random sample of nonactives, were generally of postconventional rather than of conventional morality. Their protest activity required them to define moral values that were beyond those of their institution; their allegiance was to general human values rather than to the form of justice they experienced in their university. Their action, then, was to protest the authority of the institution in support of these general ideals of social justice. This action was more consistent with the level of development of those of postconventional than those of conventional morality, in which maintenance of the institutional order was not differentiated from moral value.

Another investigation within this same genre was reported in 1973 by Fishkin, Keniston, and MacKinnon. They sought to relate a person's moral reasoning as assessed on the Kohlberg test to their political ideology. (Recall that Haan and her associates related moral reasoning to political behavior.) Subjects were selected from eight major university campuses located in different parts of the country. On the basis of their responses to the Kohlberg moral dilemmas, subjects were classified as preconventional (12 persons) conventional (36 persons) or postconventional (27 persons). All subjects were given a list of thirty-one political slogans (e.g., I fight poverty—I work, etc.) which they rated; the investigators subjected these ratings to a factor analysis that provided them with empirical clusters of slogans representing different aspects of political ideology: for example, violent radicalism (Kill the Pigs, Bring the War Home); peaceful radicalism (Give Peace a Chance, Ban the Bomb); conservatism (America, Love It or Leave It; Better Dead than Red).

Fishkin and his colleagues report results for the relationship between ideology and moral reasoning that are in many respects similar to those reported by Haan and her colleagues for the relationship between behavior and moral reasoning. Conservative ideology was found to be correlated with conventional moral reasoning; violent radicalism appeared correlated with preconventional morality; while postconventional moral reasoning appeared more correlated with rejection of conservative ideology than adoption of radical ideology. As the authors conclude:

> *Moral reasoning is thus tied to political ideology in that it partly determines the terms in which politics is understood ... Preconventional and postconventional subjects have in common the fact that they have experienced and rejected Stage 4 reasoning ... The psychodynamics of anticonservatism today seem to parallel the quest for moral structures more adequate than law-and-order reasoning"* (p. 118).

A further study (see Kohlberg, 1969) employing Kohlberg's framework examined those who had participated in Milgram's obedience study (see Chapter 7). Recall that this study puts the subject in a position of either defying authority in the name of higher principles or yielding to the authority of scientific legitimacy and administering presumably painful shocks to another person. Kohlberg reports that 75 percent of stage 6 subjects quit the study as compared with only 13 percent of those at lower moral stages. Once again, we see behavior following from the level of moral development. Going against authority, in this case, required allegience to a system of values that transcended both social contract ("the other subject and I made a deal to participate voluntarily") and conventionality ("this is what is expected of subjects in experiments and thus it is legitimate").

A WARNING

Neither the acts of P nor P's self-conception develop in isolation nor are they sustained in a vacuum. That Kohlberg and others assess a person-factor, moral development or orientation towards authority and responsibility, should not lead us to locate the sole cause of good or evil within the person. Remember that our ideal perspective is interactionist. We are concerned with the patterns of interaction and relationships within a society that facilitate or thwart the development of particular kinds of person-characteristics; we are concerned with the ideologies that proclaim certain kinds of person to be ideal and valued. The person who typically defines himself or herself as a nonresponsible pawn who simply follows the orders of others cannot long sustain that view without supportive contexts. A societal ideology that affirms unquestioning loyalty as a high ideal, that defines acts taken in its name as good, provides one kind of support. However, that ideology by itself is not sufficient if people's daily interactions do not likewise provide an affirmation of their being right and proper citizens by living and acting as they do.

Although morality and responsibility appear as personal characteristics, they are better understood as outcomes of the interactive field involving persons with others. We may long to find the good person, the moral person, or the evil and immoral person, someone on whom to pin the blame, Mills's Cheerful Robot; but our search will only reveal the network of relationships that nurtures good or evil. This warning is especially relevant as we next consider some early efforts to uncover the person who harbors what is potentially a dangerous set of characteristics—the authoritarian personality.

The Authoritarian Personality and the Holocaust

The sanctioned massacres (to use Kelman's term) that characterized the Nazi regime in Germany, in which millions of innocent men, women, and children were systematically slaughtered in the name of the *fatherland's* final solution to the "Jewish problem" motivated a social psychological inquiry in search of a personality type, the authoritarian, who might be disposed to such atrocities against humanity. In particular, the concern was whether such a personality existed in the United States as well. In 1950, a group of researchers, Adorno, Frenkel-Brunswick, Levinson, and Sanford, published the results of their massive investigation on the authoritarian personality. Their methods of research included both clinical case history approaches and social psychological measurements of attitudes and opinions.

The investigators argued that a person's political, economic, and social views formed a broad and integrated ideological pattern that reflected underlying personality trends. The anti-Semitism that characterized the Nazi regime, they argued, was not an isolated belief, but rather was part of a fascistic ideological system. To reveal this underlying ideological system, Adorno and his colleagues developed several questionnaire scales assessing different components of what they felt to be an antidemocratic ideology. One scale assessed attitudes of ethnocentrism (E), a tendency to see things and evaluate them in terms of in-groups, which are good, versus out-groups, which are rejected. Another scale dealt with political-economic conservatism. A direct measure of anti-Semitism was also included as was an F or fascism scale developed to measure attitudes towards self, family, sex, people in general, and so on.

The portrait of the authoritarian personality that emerged from these investigators' work was of a person with what Adorno (1951) called a bicyclist's personality: "above they bow, below they kick." This conveys the authoritarian's concern with the power aspects of relationships, readily acquiescing to those in superior positions while domineering, often ruthlessly, those who have less power. The authoritarian is further described as tending towards a rigidity in thinking, a tendency to stereotype. His or her sexual views are puritanical; conventional sexual values are sacred; deviation from sexual norms is to be severely punished. The authoritarian male is preoccupied with virility and manliness, with being rough, tough, and aggressive; the female is to be petite, soft, feminine, in the traditional housewife and mother role. The authoritarian's views on life, the world, and human nature tend to be pessimistic. People are self-centered and are not to be trusted; it is a dog-eat-dog world. People are evil, dirty, and dangerous. The authoritarian thrives on order and is intolerant of ambiguity; everything has a place and everything must remain in its place, neat and well ordered.

The clinical case history methods uncovered certain fundamental psychodynamics of the authoritarian personality. Authoritarians dislike introspection and do not want to examine motives and feelings. They tend to use such defense mechanisms as denial, repression, and projection: they deny their own impulses, especially those concerned with hostility and sexuality; they repress feelings to such an extent that they have little contact with their own emotions; through projection they cast on others the unwanted and denied impulses that they possess. The world is a hostile projection of their own burning hostility.

Let us put aside the numerous critical comments and analyses that followed the publication of this monumental work, ranging from various methodological critiques (e.g., Christie & Jahoda, 1954) to those based on issues of value bias (e.g., Shils, 1954: is there a politically left authoritarianism as well as a right authoritarianism?). Rather, let us recognize that this search and uncovering of the authoritarian personality was founded on the assumption that only a sick mind could have been responsible for the horrors of Nazi Germany. This pursuit of an evil or a sick personality type tends to play down social conditions that bring out the beast in all people. Likewise, it obscures the pressures that make people comply out of fear, and the pressures of social reality that lead people to yield because everyone else, including those in political and moral power, have defined a new base of legitimacy. It leads us to ignore as well real conflicts of interest that can characterize groups within certain societies, setting one against the other. In other words, while not dismissing the usefulness of person-centered concepts, we must concentrate on "the conditions under which normal people become capable of planning, ordering, committing, or condoning acts of mass violence of this kind" (Kelman, 1973, p. 31).

We would do better to conceptualize person-factors such as authoritarianism or level of moral development as providing a ready cadre of potential recruits to violence against humanity; ready to participate when the opportunities arise. As Kelman argues, we need to examine "the conditions under which the usual moral inhibitions against violence become weakened." Our concern, therefore, must focus on what Solzhenitsyn sees to be a slender line in all of us between good and evil, or what Dicks's in his study of the SS killers of Nazi Germany has also noted and what Hannah Arendt's own investigations have revealed, namely, "the banality of evil." Dicks's description of one of his subjects excellently communicates this basic point:

> *This average man could have lived his life in quieter days unnoticed, a respectable craftsman and probably harming nobody. But for the times in which he lived, and the way his weaknesses made him respond to the blandishments of group power and his own self-aggrandisement, his regression to living out his insecurely repressed hate would most likely have been confined to petty occasions. He seemed, at any rate, to have readily mastered his sadism when the sanction for it fell away, and returned to his deferential, bland facade* (p. 141).

Solzhenitsyn weaves a parallel tale of the young man who had little hope for future success until he became a guard. If he would agree to carry out orders and do his job well, a life of power, prestige, and even modest wealth would open up for him. He could rise from impotence to omnipotence, where others trembled even on hearing his name. But was he an evil person, this average man who seized an opportunity to become something in a system in which few opportunities for such rapid mobility existed?

Dicks's "average man" was convicted of war crimes including such horrible methods as drenching concentration camp prisoners in the winter and letting them freeze to death; using a powerful water jet on the neck and heart causing heart failure; forcing prisoners to run around a pole until they collapsed from fatigue at which time they were stomped to death with hob-nailed boots; crowding prisoners into a water closet like sardines, letting them suffocate.

The banality of such evil (i.e., behaving against humanity without regard for matters of morality and without accepting personal responsibility), carried on by average persons rather than raving maniacs—recall Milgram's subjects—argues for our examining the conditions that sanction evil:

1. conditions that facilitate the development and the maintenance of a ready cadre of obedient recruits;

2. conditions that develop and promulgate policies that provide opportunities for this cadre to act;

3. conditions that reduce the normal restraints against inhumane action by:

   a. freeing those ready to act from responsibility for their actions;

   b. routinizing national policies and structures of social organization so that persons may act out of habit and in piecemeal fashion without the need for self-conscious decision making;

   c. dehumanizing the victims, so that one does not destroy fellow human beings, but only cleanses the world of vermin, while simultaneously,

   d. engaging the actors in a process of brutalization that helps steel them against the intrusion of their own humanity.

MECHANISMS AND ANTECEDENTS

One of the major critiques of the research on authoritarianism, which is of particular importance to our present concerns with the social distribution of responsibility and morality, has been the emergence of what has been termed *working class authoritarianism.* Distinct from the more psychiatric pattern of authoritarianism implied by the Adorno group, working class authoritarianism is best conceived as a cluster of attitudes that derives from the stunted opportunities for learning that realistically confront the poorer, less powerful and less well educated members of a society. Kelman and Barclay (1963) used the term *breadth of perspective* to speak of the width or narrowness of a person's range of experiences. The person who has had little life opportunities to confront and deal with differences of value and of life style might very well measure as someone who is intolerant and authoritarian because of this narrowed breadth of perspective, rather than anything more deeply rooted in psychopathology. Kelman and Barclay provided a means whereby they could assess whether a high F (i.e., fascism) score was attributable to breadth of perspective or to psychological incapacity. Their data suggest that the usual measure of authoritarianism mixes these two distinct factors, and that having few social opportunities to gain a wide breadth of perspective can be as constitutive of authoritarianism as is a strong psychological incapacity.

This recurrent connection between social class variables and authoritarianism is made even more interesting by the findings from Kelman and Lawrence's investigation of DR and AR responses to Lieutenant Calley's trial. The AR respondents tended to be both more highly educated and of a generally higher social class than the DR respondents. It would seem that the DR's feelings of being a pawn may be a more factual than fanciful description of their situation. Again, the concept of breadth of perspective seems relevant, especially insofar as one's class position and educational level function collusively to thwart the individual's gaining variable perspectives on the world:

> *Pluralized perspectives foster an appreciation of social,*
> *cultural, and historical relativity. The increased recognition*
> *of the normalcy of human variability weakens the*
> *conception that the normative patterns of one's own group*
> *are supramundane. The broader one's outlooks on the social*
> *world, the more likely he is to perceive the imperfections*
> *and immorality which can characterize institutions and*
> *their human representatives. As the "sacred canopy" of*
> *cultural axioms begins to be regarded with a more skeptical*
> *eye, the locus of moral decisions tends to become less*
> *extrinsic to human actors* (Gabennesch, 1972, p. 867).

Role-Taking Opportunities.   Not surprisingly, Kohlberg's analysis of those conditions conducive to progressive moral development focuses on the notion of empathy that he conceptualizes in terms of *role-taking opportunities.* Kohlberg notes that role taking provides the person with a chance to see things from variant perspectives, and that participatory and conflict-resolving experiences offer the person such role-taking opportunities:

> *experiences of conflict and participation extend the human's*
> *capacity to differentiate and integrate and to contemplate*
> *different points of view, in other words, to develop principles*
> *for evaluating "right" and "wrong" and perfecting a sense of*

responsibility, obligation, law, and justice (Tapp & Kohlberg, 1971, pp. 86–87).

Love and Punishment.   The psychological literature on child rearing has typically distinguished between love-oriented or psychological forms of disciplining children, and punishment-oriented approaches. In the former, the child is disciplined by withholding love, while in the latter, actual punishment is applied. Morality taught by punishment and based on fear of external authority does not foster progressive moral development or a sense of one's self as a causal agent rather than as a pawn.

Two investigators, Hoffman and Saltzstein (1967) have further differentiated the category of psychological discipline, speaking of *induction* versus love-withdrawal. Induction is said to arouse empathy as the parent indicates the consequences of the child's action; love withdrawal, on the other hand, tends to arouse guilt. Hoffman and Saltzstein's research indicates a direct relationship between the use of induction techniques and moral development. Love withdrawal is barely related to moral development, while physical punishment is associated with weak moral development.

Although the preceding analysis emphasizes the relationship between family disciplinary practices, the development of empathy, and of a personal sense of responsibility, Kohlberg's focus on role-taking opportunities as the key ingredient to moral development implies that the family need not be the major locus of this development.

Kohlberg notes, for example, that children reared on an Israeli kibbutz evidence progressive stages of moral development even though they have only minimal contact with their parents or other adults. However, they do have a sufficiently stimulating and varied environment that provides ample opportunities to try on a variety of different roles. In this view, the important aspect of any relationship is the degree to which the relationship offers the individual sufficient freedom to participate in a variety of different role contexts. The more restrictive any of these settings are, the less the opportunities for role taking and thus the lower the level of moral development. Again we see the emphasis on breadth of perspective.

The basic idea is that role-taking opportunities offer the individual a chance to take others' roles and thereby have multiple views and perspectives. This varied role taking provides the stimulus to moral development both by casting the person's present position in a critical light and by showing the individual one or more new possibilities. Kohlberg suggests that any context has the potential to provide adequate or inadequate opportunities for role taking. As such, moral development carries on through many years of the individual's life, including the adult years, and is stimulated or thwarted by encounters within the family, the peer group, the school system, the community, and society in general. In each setting, approaches that open the doors to experimentation, facilitate moral development; approaches that are restrictive, punitive, nonparticipatory, or even so permissive so as to produce apathy and withdrawal, work against moral development.

Investigators of family interaction patterns (e.g., Levi, Stierlin, & Savard, 1972), have coined the phrase "loving battle" to suggest the kind of context within which conflicts between parents and children are permitted, thereby facilitating the child's progressive development. When parents, either out of their own confusion over values or out of some distorted need to maintain an illusion of familial harmony avoid such loving battles, they deny their children the chance to experience alternate points of view and to participate in both conflict and its resolution. Erikson (1969) has made much this same point in his discussion of the childhood of Gandhi:

> *the mere avoidance of physical cruelty as such is not enough
> ... We also do "violence" to children and arouse inner rage
> in them wherever we withhold from them a guidance
> without which they cannot develop fully* (1969, p. 248).

Kohlberg argues that participatory techniques provide the elemental groundwork for progressive moral development. He notes, as I have previously suggested, that the more the individual is responsible for group decision making, the more involvement he or she is given in the roles of others, the more social stimulation the person experiences, and thus the higher the level of moral development likely. Stunted moral growth derives from settings that deprive the individual of participatory rights and responsibilities. These may occur in any context—a restrictive family, an autocratic school system, a society that deprives people of a role in determining its affairs—these can all reduce role-taking opportunities, stunt moral development, and a sense of personal responsibility and thereby help recruit persons to the cadre of "average citizens" ready to be obedient for good or evil. Was Lewin (Chapter 7) then trying to create a climate within which moral and responsible behavior could be exercised?

CADETS AND RESISTERS REVISITED

The study of the resisters and the cadets offers us an informative look at these mechanisms. In several ways, the cadet's life, both in terms of family experiences and peer group preferences, suggests a relatively sheltered and restrictive style of living, one that does not seem likely to produce moral development beyond the conventional levels. As a group, the cadets preferred a well-structured life style as compared with the more loosely-structured, adventuresome approach of the resisters. The cadet was more likely to live in a fraternity where he could continue relating to others in terms of power and status, rather than in terms of equality. His life in the ROTC plus his life in the fraternity involved contexts in which he was less likely to gain the diverse role-taking opportunities that are essential to progressive moral development. The resister, by contrast, lived in an apartment often with a woman or a small group of men. He was more independent.

As compared with the resisters, the cadets still favored the traditional, institutionalized church, another ordered structure that provides few opportunities for the kinds of stimulating encounters so essential to progressive moral development. The resisters, by contrast, tended to have a personal religion, a moral ethic that they carved out for themselves. In terms of their family structure, we note the generally stern and restrictive quality of the cadet's home in comparison with the more open and participatory style that the resister experienced. This latter finding is consistent with several others' data that relates student activism to more participatory family structure (e.g., Block, Haan, & Smith, 1969; Flacks, 1967; Keniston, 1965; 1967).

Perhaps the most striking indication of the relatively impoverished encounters with their overly well-structured environments that marked the lives of the cadets in contrast to the lives of the resisters, was the entire impact of their college experience. One always hopes that the university is an institution that facilitates moral development and responsibility by opening up vistas and challenging old ways. The cadet showed an especially insulated pattern. Test scores on intellectual disposition obtained on these cadets—all of whom were college juniors and seniors—compared with normative data for college freshmen. In other words, as they neared graduation, they remained as intellectually open as entering freshmen. Apparently their well-routinized and sheltered existence on the campus prevented them from the kinds of encounters that would facilitate moral development as well as intellectual growth.

The resisters' reaction to college was twofold and complex. On the positive side, they often reported encountering a new book in philosophy or history or some new idea in a class that set them to thinking and that helped them crystallize some of their ideas. At times, however, college had a negative impact; their experience with this institution threatened to stifle their curiosity unless they dropped out or sought stimulation elsewhere.

One aspect of role-taking most relevant to moral development involves empathy, including the ability to anticipate the consequences of one's actions before taking them. The quality that best characterizes the cadets is a pattern I call "sorry-too-late." What happened is that they managed to blunder into situations with other people and do things that they later felt sorry about. But the regret was always too late and only after they handled the matter rather poorly. One cadet, for example, talked about persons as being like a rope whose strength is unknown until it breaks. This means essentially that he has no way of anticipating the consequences of his actions on others until they break down; then he knows, too late, that he has gone too far. He has a reputation for driving his men too hard. The resisters, by contrast, seemed very sensitive to others' needs; they were much better able to anticipate the consequences of their actions before acting and thereby to moderate their behavior in light of these consequences.

These data paint a portrait of a variety of conditions that operate to stunt moral development in the cadet and to facilitate its development in the resister. Stunting experiences begin in the restrictive home and move out from there to a variety of other settings; these remain so well structured and generally autocratic that the kinds of disconfirming encounters needed to broaden persons' perspectives and to open them up to critical self-examination rarely occur. Thus, when the cadet arrives at a level of conventional morality, he feels that the answers to all dilemmas lie in the hands of the society in which he lives and to which he feels he owes his major allegiance. Resisters, however, undergo a series of encounters with people, books, ideas, things, institutions, and what have you. They have opened themselves up to a variety of role-taking experiences. When their society calls them to a war that defies the general human values to which they owe their allegiance, they have no real choice other than to resist. At that point, it becomes only a matter of how best to resist. Most of this sample chose jail over leaving the country.

From Eligibility to Activity

The cadre of potential recruits for service in the name of authority, abdicating personal responsibility and acting in ways in which moral choices are not likely to be considered, exists in all social systems. It is probable, as Kohlberg suggests, that the majority of persons achieve a level of conventional morality and thus remain ready to answer the institutional or governmental call when the bugle is sounded. Yet, it is just as apparent that regardless of this potential, its realization in action requires the presence of societal conditions that transform potential energy into its kinetic forms. It was Kelman's thesis (1973), consistent with the writings of others as well, that this kind of transformation is best understood by examining those conditions that reduce the typical restraints to action. He suggested three such conditions: authorization, routinization, and dehumanization. We will join these three observations with others' analyses in our own examination of these societal triggers that ignite human behavior.

AUTHORIZATION AND REIFICATION

We have already noted the impact that authorization in the form of legitimacy has in freeing individuals from a sense of personal responsibility for their actions and thus making actions in which they might otherwise not engage more likely. And, using one part of Redl's (1973) model, we have also noted how authorization in the form of masks or uniforms likewise frees individuals to behave in ways that their "civilian superego" might otherwise find improper. Redl notes further how the *initiatory act* provides a similar authorization for those acts that follow it. He cites the example of a schoolboy who engages in some prank and when caught pleads innocently that "I didn't start it; he did it first." Following another's lead can serve to authorize one's own actions and free one from accepting full responsibility for what follows.

Kelman is quick to note that not only those lower on the societal hierarchies of authority yield to authorization, but so too may those even in the highest echelons of the social structure. The process can be similar in both cases, especially when in the name of some "transcendent mission" (e.g., national security, or the preservation of the state), even the leadership can see itself to be in the position of pawn rather than origin. Thus, even the President of the United States can claim that he is simply the vehicle whereby national policies are carried out and thus is a functionary to the state and its purposes and so not a responsible agent with origin-like properties.

Dicks's research with the Nazi SS is informative on this matter. SS leaders and followers alike believed themselves to have a transcendent mission as the "chosen instrument of the saviours and cleansers of the world." In essence, they were vehicles for achieving this important goal, and no sacrifice was too great for them to make in their efforts towards its attainment. They viewed themselves as the ones to be pitied, given the horrible tasks they had to undertake in fulfilling their mission. Dicks suggests that gas chambers rather than mass shootings were preferred by the Nazi's more to minimize their own squeamishness than to provide a humane manner of systematically destroying millions. Thus, the killers ask us to reserve our pity for them rather than those they must kill. This sense of a transcendent mission permitted all ranks, from high to low, to feel that their acts were authorized by something beyond themselves and their personal desires; thus, in claiming they were simply following orders, it must be understood that even many of those who gave the orders had deluded themselves into believing that their orders derived from this great mission of theirs.

Although we have not undertaken systematic examination of the Watergate situation, an informal examination of newspaper accounts of many of those accused of wrongdoing suggests a similar appeal to a transcendent mission (e.g., national security or loyalty to the President) as the authorization for their own legally questionable acts. As Solzhenitsyn notes, in Russia the guard's loyalty was the shield protecting them from the accusations of those who would hold them personally responsible for their acts. They exchanged loyalty and obedience for protection. Some of the Watergate participants seem to have claimed that there were many vehicles and no driver other than the state in whose name crimes were committed; and we are to excuse or feel sorrow for those who acted in its name without question or doubt. Their loyalty, they believed, should grant them protection.

Reification. In this connection it is relevant to consider a point raised by Howard Gabennesch (1972) in his analysis of what he termed the process of *reification.* To reify a social institution or a social practice (e.g., marriage, the nuclear family, etc.) is to view it "as if it were fixed instead of in process, absolute instead of relative, natural instead of conventional, and in general, as a product of forces which are more than human" (p. 863). By contrast:

> *When social reality is viewed in dereified terms, that is, as an ongoing human product, it is seen as legitimately subject to human efforts to participate in its construction and reconstruction. Reification, in contrast, discourages or obviates any activity which would tamper with a social world that is superordinate and infused with transcendental authority ... Being morally and ontologically superior to men [a reified world] demands that men strive to adjust themselves to it* (p. 864).

Where institutions have been reified, people take their places as pawns rather than the origin of institutional arrangements; they become subordinate to this superordinate, transcendent world that is not of their creation; obedience and loyalty to the reified institutional reality is deemed an end in its own right, rather than a means towards some still-human ends.

As Gabennesch notes, reification of social institutions is not simply a psychological process captured within the life history of the individual, but is to be understood as well as a sociohistorical process. Calling on the writings of Berger and Luckman (1966), Gabennesch indicates two important sociohistorical conditions that are conducive to dereification and thus to the reinstatement of the individual as the measure: dramatic transformations in existing forms of social organization brought about by natural or man-made catastrophes; and culture contact. We would expect that during periods of dramatic and rapid social change, processes of reification would begin to weaken. However, it is important to recognize that during these very periods, pressures toward reifying social institutions can actually gain in strength as a defense against the institutions crumbling and the consequent insecurity that would ensue. In other words, even as rapid and dramatic societal changes threaten the existing fabric of the social order, expanding individuals' perspectives, the demands for security can serve to reinforce processes of reification, leading persons thus to demean their own status even further.

Conditions that promote contact between different cultures, that permit persons with different life styles and ways of viewing the world to meet in a friendly confrontation, likewise can promote a dereification of one's own institutions by introducing relativising alternatives. Yet, what once might have proved relativising proves less so as technological and economic processes create a more homogeneous Western culture in which similarities rather than differences are in evidence.

The point of importance for our analysis of responsibility and moral development is to note that sociohistorical conditions that are conducive to the reification of social institutions place persons in the position of pawns to a transcendent order and thereby reduce the constraints against acting without personal responsibility in the name of that order's survival. Under such conditions, actions carried out in the name of the state may come to take on a transcendent meaning, with the leaders of the state also believing that they are acting in its name as vehicles for realizing its sanctified, moral goals: that is, they too are not to be held responsible.

Rationality or Charisma?   Two further analyses are important for us to consider, if only briefly, before we leave this important point. Recall our earlier discussion of Weber's conception of legitimacy, in particular his thesis that traditional and charismatic bases for legitimacy have given way in modern social organization to rational-legal forms. In summarizing this view, we can say that Weber saw the modern age as one in which reason (i.e., rational-legal bases of legitimacy) would override the exceptional passions that the charismatic basis entails. And yet, in reviewing the several previous conceptions of responsibility and morality, the point has been made that our modern forms of social organization (e.g., bureaucracies) often have lost much of their rational basis and have taken on some of the exceptional, even sacred qualities that Weber presumed to vest primarily in charisma. In other words, to refer to the state or to other reified social institutions as entities that transcend the individual's own world, placing each person in a pawn-like position, sounds very much like the survival of charisma even in this seemingly rational modern world. As Edward Shils (1965) noted, Weber

> *did not consider the more widely dispersed, unintense operation of the charismatic element in corporate bodies governed by the rational-legal type of authority* (1965, p. 202).

Shils attempts to understand why there is this apparent persistence of charismatic elements, suggesting a notion already familiar to us under the concept of mastery: Shils speaks of people's need for order and pattern in society and their reverence for those things that generate such order. Thus, insofar as organizations, corporate bodies, social institutions, and such help create and sustain an orderly universe (Berger and Luckman refer to institutions as providing a shield against terror), they take on charismatic qualities.

> *The attribution of charismatic qualities occurs in the presence of order-creating, order-disclosing, order-discovering power as such; it is a response to great ordering power* (p. 204).

Arguing further, Shils suggests that "Every legitimation of effective large-scale power contains a charismatic element" (p. 204). His point is that whenever we find great power, in particular in our modern forms of governance, we see significant elements of charisma; we sense that the roots of such power and thus its legitimacy lie in ultimate values and ideals that transcend the ruler as an individual. Our response to charisma is awe, respect, and deference in the face of the sacred.

> *Today, almost all the rulers of state-bound societies claim legitimation from the charismatically endowed citizens who form the electorate—although they do so with different degrees of reluctance* (p. 205).

Our awe and even reverence for the government and for persons occupying positions of great power within it (or within other such institutions) does not necessarily involve the charismatic quality of the person, but rather of the entire order-giving apparatus of which the individual is a representative.

In a real sense, therefore, reason pales before the awesome, charismatic qualities that the state and its great power calls forth. The roots of the impulse to obey, to be a pawn to the conventional order of society, are deep and profound; in resistance and questioning, one is challenging a rational-legal system whose very claim to legitimacy is less rational than sacred. The phenomena we have been discussing and analyzing deal with typical, normal persons and social systems; thus the ready cadre is large and self-reinforcing. Even in times of apparent governmental breakdown—as for example, the Watergate situation—the reverence for the system is maintained insofar as it is the system that functions to redo the wrongs that in its name have been committed.

Loyalty, a virtue that most of us would heartily applaud, as we have seen, can also be a disturbing survival of traditional forms of legitimacy when the basis for legitimation is rational-legal. To be loyal to the officeholder, to endow him or her with the uncanny powers of charisma, can blind the person to the true nature of the situation. It means one thing to be loyal to one's family; quite another to be equally loyal to the officeholder in the organization. The virtue of the rational-legal basis of legitimate authority is violated when either charisma or something such as intense personal loyalty intrudes; these forms call for an emotional response when the basis for the authority is presumed to be more rational. To respond emotionally in such a context is to yield one's power of critical thinking. Of course, those in positions of authority within a rational system of organization often seek to legitimate their authority by calling on more emotional matters such as attraction or loyalty. Legitimacy of the rational-legal form, however, seeks to insure that these excesses of tradition or charisma will not occur. The rational-legal forms help guarantee the impersonal application of stated procedures in the governance of all persons. To claim another base for legitimacy within such a context, even if successful, as it often is, robs persons of whatever reason and freedom they might have otherwise enjoyed.

It is important to distinguish between this argument and the one suggested previously. Both express a concern with the rational-legal basis of legitimacy. Our original argument, similar to Weber's among others, suggests that what began as a freeing, reason-giving form of human domination (rational-legal authority) threatens to become reason-destroying as persons follow their orders and do their work without seriously questioning the ends they are serving (we will pick up on this theme again in Chapter 11). Our present argument, building on Shils analysis among others, is that the potential advantages of the rational-legal form of domination are thwarted to the extent that persons in positions of authority collude (often implicitly) with those dominated to believe that the true basis of their legitimacy lies in some more traditional or charismatic concept.

A Freudian View. Arguing from a different perspective, but arriving at a conclusion not too dissimilar from those we have been considering thus far, Donald McIntosh (1970) builds his analysis around Freudian, psychoanalytic theory. His fundamental argument is that a truly rational system of authority requires post-Oedipal psychological development for its realization, and in that:

> *the vast bulk of mankind in their main psychic constellations either remain fixed at the Oedipal phase or regress to a pre-Oedipal level ... people have not achieved a sufficient degree or moral autonomy to enable [rationality] to be an effective legitimator of a system of domination* (pp. 906–907).

McIntosh next argues that because most persons are at the pre-Oedipal level, rational-legal systems must gain their legitimacy through appeals to charismatic elements. Institutions thus become personifications of superego identifications, invested with qualities that like the father in the primal group, are more godlike than human. To state this view in yet another way, the individual identifies with the institution as an entity that, as Shils has noted, gives order and meaning to one's own personal life and being. Thus, to defy the institution, like defying "the father," is to challenge one's own existence.

Using a related psychoanalytic framework for his examination of the Nazi SS, Dicks reaches conclusions that are compatible with those of McIntosh. In discussing one of his subjects, Dicks notes how the man "identifies with his orders," as though to bring them into question would bring the foundations of his own identity into question. Many of Dicks's subjects likewise could be characterized as relating to the Nazi party, its leadership, and its institutions as personifications of parental figures who could provide them with "security in return for unquestioning service." It is an identification with the all-wise and the all-powerful as a vehicle for giving one's feeble and passive self needed power and safety. Although there is little if any actual evidence for McIntosh's claim that people are fundamentally pre-Oedipal and thus prone to nonrational identifications, the Kohlberg thesis and data would seem to be consistent with this viewpoint.

These processes of authorization and reification are more usual than unusual. Our surprise therefore is less with those who abandon their personal responsibility and accept pawnship than with those who seem insistently to claim responsibility and self-authorship.

ROUTINIZATION

Kelman argues that a second condition that reduces the constraints to nonresponsible action involves the habitual, routinized quality of much of our everyday activities. The more habitual an activity becomes, the less we think about it before doing it. Analysts (e.g., Kimble & Perlmuter, 1970) of the processes whereby simple motoric activities (e.g., tying a shoelace) become routinized speak of two processes that seem to be involved: attention and motivation. As we begin to learn a habit, our attention is glued on each and every step involved; we pay close attention to details and to feedback that informs us of how our performance is running. On the other hand, once a habit is learned to the point of becoming routinized, our behavior runs its course without the intervention of our attention. Indeed, we pay attention only when something intervenes to block the otherwise habitual pattern. For example, as we drive to work for the first time, we attend to many details of our location, where to turn, and such. After a while, however, our driving becomes sufficiently habitual that we pay attention only when our routine path is blocked. In like manner, whereas in the learning of a habit, much effort and motivation may have been involved, once it is learned and routinized, we perform it without motivational preconditions. It simply occurs and runs it course.

The routinization of simple habits applies as well to the parallel routinization of our more complex behavior patterns. Functional fixity was a concept suggested years ago by Duncker (1935) in his analysis of the persistence of a person's mode of problem solving long after the nature of the problem had changed and an easier method of solution was possible. Persons, however, had become fixated on a particular routine method of solving the problem and thereby were oblivious to alternatives that were now possible. As personal habits and modes of problem solving become routinized, we fail to engage in decision making prior to taking action; rather, we simply carry out actions. Without this conscious intervention, we are unlikely to probe through our routines to issues of morality and personal responsibility. Furthermore, as Kelman notes, insofar as organizations routinize their activities, members pay more attention to how well they are doing their routine than to the consequences of their routines. The Nazi guards thus were more concerned with doing their job well than with what that job was.

Dicks's research on the Nazi SS is again informative on this matter. The focus on technique rather than on ends was evident in numerous instances that Dicks studied, including one in which five SS generals and one civilian met to discuss how best to dispose of several hundred captured Soviet army prisoners. The group spent most of the time examining ingenious ways of killing the prisoners, "only ways and means were debated, no one expressed any misgivings on the principle of preparing this slaughter" (p. 102). A reading of the White House transcripts of recorded Presidential conversations in connection with the Watergate reveals a similar focus on the details of technique rather than on the principles of morality. Dicks further reports one of his subjects complaining that the technical pressures and routines of his work gave him little time to think about what he was doing; as Dicks notes, "faithful routine becomes the defense against painful questioning of the values of what we are doing" (p. 218).

Routinization was likewise facilitated by the detailed division of labor involved in the entire process of mass murder. Recall Kilham and Mann's study of this in the laboratory in Chapter 7. Each person's job dealt with only a small part of the total; thus, individuals could readily get lost in their job and not experience themselves as contributing to the killing of millions. Some were armchair administrators pushing papers and keeping records; others drove trains or trucks carrying the prisoners; many were technicians responsible for the equipment of mass murder; others were medical personnel; still others were simply clerks: "... terror operations became 'normal' jobs ... like a factory routine that 'happens' to be connected with ... a crematorium" (p. 89).

One of Dicks's subjects was a captain at Auschwitz in charge of supervising the selection of in-coming prisoners, of keeping order on the way to the gassings, and of seeing to it that corpses from the gas chambers were disposed of properly. When asked if he was responsible for the gassings, his reply that "We did also help shove" (p. 118), led Dicks to conclude that this captain saw himself as only doing his little bit to help!

DEHUMANIZATION AND BRUTALIZATION

Although we have already briefly considered dehumanizing processes in our examination of some issues of self-concept (Chapter 6), Kelman's use of the term in this present context warrants our reconsideration. He notes how the processes whereby we collectively learn to dehumanize our opponents facilitates our behaving inhumanely and without normal considerations towards those persons. Specifically, Kelman argues that dehumanization requires that we deny the other person both identity and community.

To accord a person identity is to perceive him as an individual, independent and distinguishable from others, capable of making choices, and entitled to live his own life on the basis of his own goals and values. To accord a person community is to perceive him—along with one's self—as part of an interconnected network of individuals who care for each other, who recognize each other's individuality, and who respect each other's rights (1973, pp. 48–49).

I trust that it is understood that although our case examples of these several processes derive mainly from the Nazi years and crimes, this is primarily because of the excellent documentation that exists; the processes and outcomes can and do apply much more broadly. Recall Milgram's investigation. It can, has, and continues to happen here.

Dehumanization of the opponent and brutalization of the self are dual social processes whereby normally quiet and reasonable citizens, can participate even willingly in acts of evil towards others without feeling themselves responsible or their actions immoral. Dicks's interviews with convicted Nazi SS killers provides more than ample testimony to these two related processes. The dehumanization process begins early and partly involves the socially sanctioned labels that are used to describe not only the enemy but also one's behaviors towards them. Euphemisms abound: it is called the "final solution" rather then genocide or mass murder of an entire group of people; prisoners are chosen for "special treatment" rather than calling it gassing; prisoners and inmates of mental institutions had to be killed as the Soviets or Americans advanced in order to "secure the army's rear." Dehumanized prisoners are seen simply as "mouths to feed" or as numbers to be processed. One interviewee said of his prisoners, " 'those aren't people—they have to be handled quite differently' " (Dicks, p. 163). He then would mercilessly beat the sick and injured, often until they died.

Dicks summarizes what might well be the process involved as people of "averagely humane conscience" see some of the early acts of terrorism of the then emerging Nazi regime and see themselves carried along in the parades of "we-feeling" that also took place. At first, those citizens might chastise themselves, perhaps as many of us have done, for not having the moral courage to speak out in protest. Yet, to feel so badly about one's own self is not a pleasant thing to live with; better to be denied; better still to entertain the thought that perhaps there is some truth in the Nazi beliefs and that perhaps "I am not a hypocrite after all." The next stage emerges as those passive supporters see someone who is a known anti-Nazi or a Jew suddenly disappear one day from their place of work: " 'Surely I am not supporting criminals—these methods cannot be crimes—they arise from tragic necessities of fate—I am witnessing a great happening in history' " (p. 255). The stage is now set for these people to replace their memory and view of those who are taken away with a dehumanized stereotype: better to get rid of those dirty Jews now than let them remain here to infest our country with their kind.

Those more directly concerned with the "handling" of the prisoners, the SS group that Dicks studied, for example, further dehumanized their victims in ways that students of cognitive dissonance (see Chapter 3) are well aware: that is, derrogating the victims and seeing them as getting what they deserve. People are able to justify their own actions against these victims if they are not seen to be victims ("I am the real victim") but rather disobedient or vicious things "who only have themselves to blame." A stock phrase used when someone was to be killed was to note that "he was killed trying to escape" or was "killed while being unruly and disobedient." The extreme of this process was noted when the British marched a group of German civilians around the Belsen concentration camp and some Germans reacted to the horrible sights they saw by stating, " 'What terrible criminals these prisoners must have been to get such punishment' " (p. 262).

One cannot participate in dehumanizing another without brutalizing one's self as well. One begins in a small way to participate in a brutalizing group ethos, one that emphasizes the virtues of aggressiveness and unflinching loyalty to one's superiors and one's group. The SS leadership under the direction of Himmler sought to indoctrinate persons into their killer roles by innoculating them from their normal humane feelings:

> The newly enrolled "volunteers" of the SS . . . were then systematically introduced and inured to sights and sounds and methods of "punishment" of these "enemies." First, the whole company paraded to watch a flogging—without moving a muscle, and next an execution . . . demonstrations of what happened to SS men who transgressed . . . by being too soft . . . were included (p. 99).

Philip Zimbardo (Zimbardo, Haney, Banks, & Jaffe, 1973) and his colleagues' investigation of a simulated prison has also demonstrated the brutalization of the guards that occurs as an outcome of their treatment of the prisoners. Essentially, role enactments, as we have seen, are potent forces that shape the person's self-concept; thus, undertaking dehumanizing and brutalizing roles as a routine part of one's job produces grave transformations in the person, thereby increasing one's potential for continued action without moral intervention or a sense of personal responsibility. One's psychological definition of the situation is altered as a function of such enactments; prisoners are no longer human and one is no longer acting with personal responsibility as a moral agent.

Alienation, Responsibility, and Courage

A key theme that has bound together much of our preceding discussion involves the link between responsibility and power. The argument and evidence adduced in its support have suggested that low power within a social system is related to a denial of personal responsibility, while high power is related to an acceptance of personal responsibility. We have further noted that the self-perception of origin or pawn is not simply a matter of individual psychology, but rather is intimately linked to sociohistorical conditions that may actually limit a person's self-determining power, creating more pawns than origins.

Hannah Arendt's (1969) concise analysis of contemporary social organizations captures the sense of impotency that such forms of organization provide. She describes the various forms of government:

> as the rule of man over man—of one or the few in monarchy and oligarchy, of the best or the many in aristocracy and democracy, to which today we ought to add the latest and perhaps most formidable form of such domination, bureaucracy, or the rule by an intricate system of bureaux in which no men, neither one nor the best, neither the few nor the many, can be held responsible, and which could be properly called the rule by Nobody (p. 23).

This "rule by Nobody" is an alienating form of social organization that appears to give each person a voice in decision making but in fact sees decisions cranked out by an impersonal bureaucracy. While we will leave aside the analyses that describe the real interests that are served by such forms of social organization, the point remains that as persons become powerless to influence the course of their own lives, as decision processes are farther removed from the people, their accurate sense of powerlessness emerges and with it an abdication of personal responsibility for what may happen.

While powerlessness may breed rebellion, as the protests of the late 1960s suggest and even Lewin's early investigations with children's play groups revealed, it is also more likely to breed acceptance and withdrawal into passivity or the various forms of passive resistance to which we referred earlier (Chapter 4). I am reminded of a fable that Rollo May (1967) writes describing a king who had one of his subjects put into a cage in the palace courtyard so that he could be studied. We witness the man's transformation from puzzlement over his caged life, to a moment's flash of anger, through burning resentment, to final acceptance, accompanied by justifications about why he is enjoying his captured state: after all, even as the king himself notes, why should the man complain: all of his needs are being cared for.

Courage. Paul Tillich (1952) informs us that courage involves acting in spite of the threats to security that exist. While this may indeed be an accurate characterization, it forces us to overemphasize characteristics within individuals that may or may not lead them to intervene morally in the name of principles even when the cost is great. Yet, insofar as our analysis of conventionality in morality and responsibility has focused on many of the sociohistorical factors that are involved, surely our sense of postconventional reasoning and action should likewise extend beyond individual courage into the social realm as well.

For, indeed, if engaging in brutalizing roles can brutalize the individuals involved, so too can engaging in humane and responsible roles humanize individuals. Likewise, if conditions diminish participatory roles and thereby facilitate progression only to conventionality, conditions that increase participatory roles should facilitate progression beyond conventionality. To put it succinctly, our admittedly value-laden quest need not be in search of the courageous person who would stand up *in spite of;* rather our quest is for those sociohistorical and institutional conditions that will facilitate more persons standing up *because of.* The lone person of courage in Nazi Germany might have succeeded in some small way, and this is not to be demeaned. The more fundamental issue, however, is to establish those universal conditions where that lone person is many.

To recall our Chapter 1 focus on the social psychological perspective, morality and responsibility are not to be conceived simply as properties of individuals, but also as properties of systems of which persons are parts. We have made significant progress in understanding those system-wide conditions that are conducive to progressive moral development and the acceptance of personal responsibility. We are now in a better position to evaluate their likely attainment in given social systems and to work on their behalf.

ROBERT NEUBECKER.

ALTRUISM AND PROSOCIAL BEHAVIORS

9

The preceding chapter has focused on the apparent evil that is often a normal, routine part of our everyday lives; our concern in this chapter is on the other side of that coin. We search for those conditions that prompt persons to act altruistically. Some critics of the social sciences have suggested that the disciplines are not relevant, by which they presumably mean that major social issues have not received the proper attention of the field. Yet we have seen how the atrocities of the Nazis and other manifestations of human aggression have motivated a disciplinary concern with antisocial behaviors. The social psychological concern with issues of human caring, especially sympathy and empathy, have a relatively lengthy history in the field.

In his historical review of social psychology, G. W. Allport (1954) noted the role that sympathy has played as a fundamental principle of human nature, competing with hedonism and egoism for a key place in the conceptual lexicon of the discipline. The biblical story of the Good Samaritan who helped another at some cost to himself without apparent thought of reward, offers us a firm if perhaps somewhat idealized example of the intervention of human compassion into the affairs of everyday life. Yet perhaps it was the more recent fate of Kitty Genovese in New York that most forcefully reconstituted the discipline's concern with the more positive, prosocial aspects of human behavior.

In 1964 Kitty Genovese was attacked and stabbed to death by a knife wielding assailant. For nearly one-half hour, she was repeatedly and brutally stabbed, her cries of fright and pleas for help ringing through the streets. Although it was 3 A.M., some thirty-eight of her neighbors watched the entire episode, hearing her struggle and viewing the man stab her repeatedly. And yet not one sought to intervene, not even by so seemingly simple an act as calling the police. After Genovese was dead, one of the thirty-eight finally called in the police. News accounts reported that the witnesses claimed that they did not intervene because they didn't want to get involved, and anyway, they were frightened or embarassed or not really sure of what to do to be helpful (Milgram & Hollander, 1964; Rosenthal, 1964). If altruism involves stepping in to help another human in need, its absence in the Genovese case motivated much speculation and then finally systematic investigation of the circumstances under which persons will or will not be altruistic. We will shortly examine this literature.

The Law and Altruism. The legal establishment responded both to the Genovese case and to another case in a New York subway in 1965 when the young father of a 15-month-old daughter intervened to evict a drunken and abusive youth from the train, only to be murdered by the youth. The New York City Council established a good samaritan law to compensate those injured while attempting to prevent the commission of a crime.

In Massachusetts, the negligence law argues that a property owner has a duty to help someone in distress on his or her property, even though that someone is a trespasser. Judges' interpretations of this law go far beyond the New York legislation's economic view of samaritanism in emphasizing "the duty of one human not to walk away from another"; in the court's view, "a person has an affirmative duty to help not only a stranger but some one who illegally trespasses on his property" (Doherty, 1974).

Many states have instituted good samaritan laws pertaining primarily to physicians but often also including nurses and other health professionals, shielding them from liability for negligence if they stop to help in an emergency. As John Kaplan (1972) has noted in his brief review of the legal status of good samaritanism, legal motivation for helping others partakes primarily of the stick rather than the carrot approach. The stick is exemplified by laws that relieve physicians from liability for negligence if they decide to render aid. There is little use of positive incentives for behaving prosocially within the laws of our land. You are not guilty of a crime in most states in the United States if you do not intervene to help another in distress, such as Kitty Genovese; or as in an example Kaplan offers, if you sit idly on a pier finishing your sandwich while watching a fisherman who fell off his boat a few yards in front, bob under for the third time and drown.

BLOOD AND THE STRANGER

Thus far our examples of altruism have involved P's intervening to help O; the literature on prosocial behavior, however, includes in addition to helping or rescuing, such actions and sentiments as donating, sharing, cooperating, giving, caring, facilitating the well-being of the other, and so on. One of the most fascinating and informative investigations of prosocial activity has been reported by Richard M. Titmuss (1971), whose study of blood donating was formulated in terms of "creative altruism": social gifts to anonymous others, "carrying no explicit or implicit individual right to a return gift" (p. 212). In Titmuss's view, the free giving of one's own blood to a stranger is creative "in the sense that the self is realized with the help of anonymous others" (p. 212); the love of self derives from the need to love strangers.

Titmuss's study focuses on a societal spirit of altruism, a "caring community" that in fostering the gift of giving to anonmyous others fosters a sense of social integration and thwarts societal tendencies towards alienation. In this latter respect, Titmuss's concern parallels the concern of the social psychologists and others who saw uncaring alienation and apathy on the part of the thirty-eight passive bystanders to the Genovese murder.

Specifically, Titmuss felt that a careful comparative study of national policies and practices regarding blood donation would reveal the caring or the alienating character of different societies; it would be informative about the societies "moral, social, psychological, religious, legal and aesthetic ideas" (p. 71). He was especially keen to understand why persons would donate to strangers in a world more generally characterized, as he put it, by its emphasis on immediate advantage and the hedonistic calculus of an economic gain. The donating behavior of a member of such a society would be motivated by the knowledge of receiving some specific economic gain or advantage in return. For example, if a society must pay for the blood it needs from donors who sell it, we have a prime instance of a commercialized system of giving; although persons as such are not traded (as with slavery) human tissue is: blood is a marketable commodity to be bought and sold and is subject to the laws, practices, and economics of the marketplace. Under these conditions, giving is not based on the creatively altruistic concept of "a caring community."

Titmuss's study examined blood donating systems in several nations including Great Britain, the United States, the U.S.S.R., Japan, and South Africa among others. Although several national comparisons were made, the United States stands out as a prime example of a commercialized donating system, whereas Great Britain serves as a model of a noncommercialized, truly altruistic system of giving. Titmuss categorizes donors into various types, including those who receive some direct payment for giving, those who receive a family credit, those who are responsible either to pay or replace blood they have used, and those Titmuss refers to as "voluntary community donors" who give without tangible reward or threat of penalty to unnamed strangers. He reports that whereas the great American myth is that voluntary donations are most typical, the facts suggest that approximately 50 percent of all blood is bought and sold; only

7 percent of the population are voluntary community donors. In Great Britain, by contrast, the voluntary figure is nearly 100 percent. The United States, however, does not lead the world in the commercialization of blood gifts; paid donations in Japan are approximately 98 percent and while the Soviet paid-donor figure is 50 percent, the remainder is heavily composed of the nonvoluntary donations from captive donors, especially the military; and even the 50 percent nonpaid donors receive some fringe benefits (e.g., a day off work) for their giving.

Sweden offers another case that highlights the major theme of Titmuss's work. All of the donations in Sweden are paid, though the recipients, as part of the national health service, do not pay for the blood they get. Yet there is a blood shortage in Sweden as there is in most countries with a commercialized giving system. Should the shortage be made up by shifting to a fully voluntary system as in Great Britain or should the payment to donors be increased? The former might prove disasterous to patients if volunteers did not come forth to give blood; the latter, on the other hand, would lead to a rise in medical costs and also increase the risk of receiving poor blood. As we will see, one of the effects of a market in blood is to decrease the quality of the blood received; it seems that as with most things marketable, those in search of quick money are willing to pass on a bad product. Titmuss's comment on the dilemma facing Sweden and other similarly commercialized national systems of giving, notes that once economic principles have been instituted, they are less likely to be abandoned than are principles of altruism in giving; thus solutions are not likely to turn towards a voluntary system.

Let Titmuss's own words state the overall conclusion he reached from his research on the gift of blood:

> we have concluded that the commercialization of blood and donor relationships represses the expression of altruism, erodes the sense of community, lowers scientific standards, limits both personal and professional freedoms, sanctions the making of profits in hospitals and clinical laboratories, legalizes hostility between doctor and patient, subjects critical areas of medicine to the laws of the marketplace, places immense social costs on those least able to bear them —the poor, the sick and the inept—increases the danger of unethical behavior in various sectors of medical science and practice, and results in situations in which proportionately more and more blood is supplied by the poor, the unskilled, the unemployed, Negroes and other low income groups and categories of exploited human populations of high blood yielders (pp. 245–246).

Beyond these moral aspects of a commercialized blood donating system, Titmuss's investigation suggests other reasons why such a system does not work well nor provide good blood:

1. the system is "highly wasteful of blood," creating many shortages;
2. it becomes a bureaucratic nightmare, increasing both costs and inefficiency of operation;
3. the cost per unit of blood is from 5 to 15 times greater than the voluntary, noncommercial systems as characterize Great Britain;
4. a marketplace for blood is more likely than a voluntary system to distribute "contaminated blood," thus increasing the risks of disease.

The major theme of Titmuss's work and the reason for its being undertaken is captured in the first sentences of the previously quoted passage: an economic marketplace answer to the question, "why give to a stranger?" represses altruism and erodes the sense of community. He expands on this point noting how different institutional arrangements can either encourage an individual's freedom to make altruistic choices or discourage such choices through the coerciveness of marketplace interests. Titmuss suggests that the freedom to give altruistically to a stranger is dictated by the manner in which a society has organized its social institutions, particularly those involving health and welfare; this is one of the fundamental issues of freedom now facing modern society. It is Titmuss's view that national social policy can either reduce or enhance the "forces of market coercions" (p. 242); and that insofar as such policies enhance market forces, they restrict individual freedom to act altruistically; insofar as such policies reduce market forces, they increase individual freedom to behave altruistically:

> In not asking for or expecting any payment of money these donors [from Britain's National Health Service] signified their belief in the willingness of other men to act altruistically in the future ... By expressing confidence in the behaviour of future unknown strangers they were thus denying the Hobbesian thesis that men are devoid of any distinctively moral sense (p. 239).

The freedom of these National Health Service donors derives from the fact that by virtue of the voluntary nature of the system of giving, they can give or not give; their decisions thus can be creatively altruistic and devoid of any economic and thereby alienating factors.

The point that Titmuss makes is an important one. Basically, it is his contention that a private market system of giving, while appearing on its surface to offer individuals freedom to decide to give or not to give or to designate who will receive their gift, is not freeing of all persons in that system, nor does it provide the donor the freedom to behave altruistically without the intrusion of market forces. The private, market system of giving establishes an economic relationship between donor and recipient rather than a gift relationship. Payment for gifts robs persons of the choice to give freely; it thereby contributes to the alienation of fellowship that would otherwise be possible. If I can only give in exchange for commercial gain, then indeed I might give but never confront the fundamental human issue that involves giving freely to an anonymous stranger. In this view, an economic altruism thwarts creative altruism and thus erodes the foundation for building a caring community. What is built, rather, is an individualistic network in which one helps another or gives to another only insofar as the economics of the situation are in one's favor.

If we may return to one of the major points made in our discussion of morality and responsibility (Chapter 8), I think we can now see the significant parallel view. Social arrangements can bring out the best or the beast in persons; what it will be, it seems, depends less on the person's fundamental nature, which is capable of either good or evil, than upon the arrangements that encourage the expression of what is good.

Bystander Intervention: Uncaring Community or What?

Titmuss has argued and sought to demonstrate that a system that commercially trades in altruism fosters an uncaring community, and establishes primarily economic bonds between strangers. Was it this uncaring community that simply watched while Kitty Genovese was brutally stabbed to death or were other factors involved? We have already noted in our brief review of some of the laws pertaining to bystander intervention in rescue and emergency situations how an economic perspective dominates. To increase P's likelihood of acting altruistically to help another, the law endeavors to compensate P for damages P receives, or, as with physicians, to eliminate their liability to being sued for damages. At least as far as official policy views the situation, only by working on the economic bonds that tie persons together can altruism be increased. But what about the other motivations of the persons involved and specific situational circumstances that might facilitate or inhibit their acting altruistically in Genovese-like situations? Fortunately, social psychological laboratory and field studies have taken a systematic look at this issue.

A typical experimental paradigm for studying bystander response to emergencies is modeled after the work of Darley and Latané (1968). Subjects arrive in the laboratory to participate in an experiment. They are placed in a room and shown some communication equipment that will let them talk with other subjects. All presumably will discuss a personal problem; subjects are told that the intercom is used in order to minimize the embarassment that might otherwise occur were such a discussion to be held face to face. During this discussion, subjects hear an emergency take place: for example, another subject appears to be having an epileptic seizure. In other similar studies, emergencies involve a female who appears to be injured after a fall (Latané & Rodin, 1969) or the room begins to fill with smoke (Latané & Darley, 1968). Darley and Latané measured the speed with which subjects reported the emergency to the experimenter. The major independent variable involved the size of the group that experienced the emergency. Subjects were led to believe that they were alone with the other subject (who was the victim) or that they were a member of a three-person group (subject, victim, and one other subject) or a six-person group (subject, victim, and four other subjects). In fact, the "other subjects" and the victim were accomplices.

In their early investigation, Darley and Latané reported that subjects alone were more likely to respond and do so rapidly to someone's having an apparent epileptic seizure (85 percent offer help within 52 seconds) than were subjects in groups of three (62 percent offer help within 93 seconds) or six (31 percent offer help within 166 seconds). These results were interpreted as suggesting a "diffusion of responsibility" that can occur in group settings. Subjects, unsure about what to do and not wanting to make fools of themselves, hesitate, hoping that perhaps someone else will act. Thus no one accepts personal responsibility for acting nor accepts the blame for not having intervened. Perhaps this is what happened in the Genovese situation.

A second investigation (Latané & Darley, 1968) placed subjects in a room that began to fill with smoke, either alone, in a small group with two nonresponsive O's (actually confederates), or a small group with two other naïve subjects. Much the same effect was found: persons alone were more likely to report the emergency (75 percent) than those in the room with passive others (10 percent) or in groups of three (38 percent). In interpreting these data, Latané and Darley turned towards a group process effect, arguing that the passivity of others lends a nonemergency definition to the situation thereby inhibiting the intervention of the subjects. It is easier to dismiss the emergency as real if others seem to be denying it through their own inaction than either if others take action or if one is alone and thus without this group effect.

Staub (1970) has employed a similar research format and examined the matter from a developmental perspective. His subjects, ranging from kindergarten to sixth grade, were tested either individually or in pairs. They were brought to an experimental room where the experimenter told them she was interested in the kinds of pictures that children of different ages like to draw. She gave them some drawing paper but then, on "realizing" that she forgot to bring the crayons, had to leave the room. She left the subject or subject pairs with a game to play, noting that she would first check on the girl in the adjoining room. She did this, then returned before leaving to get the crayons. The girl in the other room was actually a tape recording of a girl playing, falling off a chair, then crying and moaning. The experimenter, presumably in search of crayons actually was observing the subject's behavior on hearing the girl's crying: did they seek to go directly to her aid, did they seek to find the experimenter, or did they do neither?

Staub's data suggest that in general, pairs are more likely to offer help (61 percent) than individuals alone (32 percent), but that both the degree of helping and the pattern vary across age levels. Thus, overall, helping first increases then decreases with age. Presumably, it is very difficult for very young children to empathize with the victim or to sense any personal responsibility for intervening. In children beyond the kindergarten age, the presence of a partner seemed to provide a sense of reassurance about hearing another in distress in what was a novel and perhaps fearful situation. However, in still older children (e.g., sixth grade), the presence of a partner seemed to inhibit helping behavior as the children feared being disapproved of or being criticized by the experimenter. In other words, whereas pairing facilitates helping in young children, it inhibits helping behavior as children get older and fear violating experimental norms or appearing foolish.

Lending some support to this kind of interpretation are some other data of Staub's (1971; 1972) that indicate that the experimenter's explicit granting of permission for the children to enter an adjoining room and help someone whose distress calls they could hear facilitated their entering; either prohibiting their doing this or giving no information at all had the same inhibiting effect. This latter finding suggests that in the absence of information, children tend to assume the experimenter does not wish them to leave the room and enter an adjoining room to offer their help.

Although the Darley and Latané investigations and those of Staub and others suggest that groups generally seem to inhibit bystander intervention—thus providing laboratory validation for one interpretation of the Genovese situation—this effect has not invariably been demonstrated nor is the entire theoretical explanation adequately covered in terms of responsibility diffusion or group influence processes, as important as these two are. Darley and two other colleagues, Teger and Lewis (1973), argued that the inhibiting effect of the group could be ameliorated if persons were in a more direct face-to-face setting, rather than absorbed in the tasks or physically separated as in Darley and Latané's and some others initial efforts. Specifically, the argument was that subjects who could witness another person's startled reaction to an emergency would thereby not be inhibited by the group; rather, the shared startle response would help redefine the situation as an emergency. In other words, the cool passivity that thwarted intervention in the typical setting could be shattered, leading to a redefinition of the situation, once the other's startled responses could be mutually observed. A test of this confirms the analysis. Darley, Teger, and Lewis report that 90 percent of subjects alone, 80% of those in face-to-face groups, but only 20 percent in non-face-to-face groups responded to the apparent emergency of a screaming and groaning workman who had a heavy screen fall on him.

Arguing from still another theoretical perspective, Clark and Word (1974) suggest that the actual degree of ambiguity of the emergency situation needs to be considered in evaluating whether groups will inhibit altruistic responses. Presumably, the more ambiguous an emergency is, the more group defining and influencing processes will intervene to formulate the situation either as an emergency or as something benign. Clark and Word suggest that the kinds of emergencies chosen by Darley and Latané are relatively ambiguous and thus should more readily demonstrate the group effect than a situation of lesser ambiguity. In their own investigation of this factor, Clark and Word created emergency situations of varying degrees of ambiguity, presenting these to subjects alone or in two-person groups. Situations were nonambiguous, moderately ambiguous, or highly ambiguous. For example, in a nonambiguous situation, subjects saw and heard the victim "sustain what appeared to be a serious shock" (p. 281); moderate ambiguity involved only hearing the victims cries of pain; high ambiguity was created by further reducing the cues pertaining to the emergency. Results indicated the importance of ambiguity as a variable affecting the relationship between intervention alone or in a group.

Specifically, Clark and Word report that regardless of whether alone or in a two-person group, P helps O more under conditions of low than under conditions of high ambiguity. With an unambiguous emergency situation, 91 percent of those alone and 100 percent of those in dyads intervened to offer aid; with a highly ambiguous situation, however, 18 percent of those alone and 33 percent of those in dyads intervened.

Moving their studies into the field, Piliavin, Rodin, and Piliavin (1969) and Piliavin and Piliavin (1972) created an emergency in a subway car and observed rates of bystander intervention under varying conditions. For example, a person collapses in a moving subway car; in some versions of this field experiment, the person is an invalid with a cane while in other versions, he appears to be a drunk. In the later variation (Piliavin & Piliavin, 1972), the person begins to trickle blood from the corner of his mouth as he falls. In general, the data indicate that the invalid receives help more often and more rapidly than the drunk; help is slower for the bleeding invalid than for the nonbleeding invalid, presumably because the blood signifies a more severe emergency that both may increase the bystanders sense of revulsion and their feelings of incompetence: conflict, indecision, and apathy thus may result.

Other aspects of their results are informative. First, overall, 78 percent of the time someone came to the aid of the victim, whether he was apparently drunk (where 50 percent rendered aid) or ill (where 95 percent rendered aid). Apathetic bystanders thus were not the norm. Second, and in apparent opposition to the Darley and Latané effect, the size of the group did not influence bystander intervention; small groups intervened as did larger groups. Finally, and perhaps more importantly than it might initially seem, the Piliavins report that once one person came to the victim's aid, whatever reservations others might have had were thereby reduced, and thus others also offered their assistance. Just as passive bystanders can help P define the situation as a nonemergency, so can actively intervening bystanders help P define the situation not only as an emergency but also as one in which P too can intervene.

Although, as noted, these results contradict the initial findings of Darley and Latané, they nevertheless illuminate the face-to-face and ambiguity factors that as we have seen can attenuate the presumably inhibiting effect of group processes. The subway emergency is nonambiguous and thereby less subject to variant group definitions; similarly, the close face-to-face proximity permits us to see the startled and emotional responsivity of others, thereby further minimizing the chances of defining the situation as a nonemergency. Likewise, one person's intervention facilitates others also taking altruistic action.

MODELING ALTRUISM

We have seen that group processes (i.e., social comparison and social influence) do not invariably inhibit altruism but can increase bystander intervention. Investigations of the modeling of altruism offer us a further sense of the positive influence of others actions on

P's behavior. Simply stated, the question is to what extent will P's observation of O's behaving altruistically lead P to behave altruistically? In several investigations, it has been demonstrated that setting a good example (by deeds more than by words alone) can lead P to behave to help another in need, donate to a charitable cause, be more generous towards others, and so forth.

One investigation, reported in 1967 by Bryan and Test and conducted in a field-setting, suggests that motorists are more likely to stop and render aid to a woman in distress (with a flat tire) if they previously saw another motorist (the experimenter's confederate) stop to render aid to someone else in distress. The same investigators also report that shoppers are more likely to contribute to the Salvation Army after they see someone else drop money into the waiting kettle. Research using children as subjects (Bryan, 1972) reveals a similar influence of the model's behavior on the child's own subsequent behavior. Importantly, much of this research suggests that verbal exhortations to be good or to be helpful and generous are not effective in eliciting altruistic behavior; it takes the model's acting altruistically to facilitate the child's behaving altruistically.

Although their research used neither helping models nor another's verbal exhortation to be helpful, Darley and Bateson's (1973) investigation is nevertheless highly informative about the difficulty of verbal set in transcending situational demands. Their subjects were seminary students who were asked to record a brief talk, either on the parable of the Good Samaritan or on the vocation of the ministry. Subjects were informed that the recording would take place in a nearby building and were either told that they were late already and should hurry or that they had plenty of time to get to their recording session. As the subjects went between buildings, they encountered a poorly dressed victim slumped in the alleyway. Measures were taken of whether and how the subject stopped to render aid. Results indicated that subjects in a hurry, even to speak on the parable, did not stop to render aid! Being in a hurry seemed to so narrow the person's focus that he did not think to articulate the connection between the parable and the parallel living situation that he had just encountered. The authors note that in several instances a seminary student hurrying to deliver the sermon on the Good Samaritan actually stepped over the victim. The situational demand of rushing seemed to overwhelm the meaning of the message; no wonder then that verbal exhortations to children (and to adults?) fall on deaf or otherwise distracted ears.

If we consider volunteering as well as donating and helping behavior to be part of the altruistic complex of behaviors, then the research suggests how a model's actions can influence P's actions. Several investigators (e.g. Blake et al., 1956; Rosenbaum & Blake,

1955; Schachter & Hall, 1952) report that seeing others volunteer for an experiment, for example, increases the subjects' likelihood of volunteering; in fact, seeing others not volunteer has the effect of reinforcing the subjects' unwillingness to volunteer, an effect similar to the Darley and Latané findings regarding the role that a group's passivity in the face of an emergency plays in leading P likewise to define the situation as a nonemergency.

As we saw in our discussion in Chapter 7, a model's effect on P's behavior involves many different factors, any or all of which operate in a specific situation. P can observe the model's behavior and note its consequences, thereby deciding whether the cost of rendering aid is too great or is appropriate to P's own situation. The model's behavior functions as an initiatory act, helping redefine the situation and releasing whatever hesitations P might have had. Much as in the Asch situation (Chapter 6) in which a deviating stooge facilitated P's suffering the embarassment of being wrong in the face of an overwhelming majority, a model's initiatory act can likewise serve to reduce P's worry about being different or embarassed. The model, whether it be another person or a group, plays a significant part in P's process of defining the situation and P's role in it; a passive model helps P to define the situation as passive whereas an active model can define the situation as one requiring action. The prestige and authoritativeness of the model play an important role in influencing whether or not P will follow suit; a more prestigious model's behavior will have a greater impact on P than will the actions of a model of lesser prestige. The model's behavior can create an alternative for action that P might otherwise not have thought of and thereby facilitate P's making a choice that prior to the model's action was not available for P. Thus P may not even have thought that stopping to render aid was a possibility until P sees O stop and help.

In these and other ways, group influence effects can serve to increase or, as we have seen, to decrease the likelihood of P's engaging in altruistic, prosocial actions. Perhaps, then, we can now understand Titmuss's sense of dismay over the long-range, extensive effects of a commercialized gift system in inhibiting person's tendencies to help others. For indeed, if our institutions serve as models for our own altruism, then surely we will give only insofar as the economics of the situation are to our advantage. But enough of this now; we will have more to say on this version of altruism in a later section of this chapter.

REACTANCE AND THE RESISTANCE TO ALTRUISM

In 1966, Brehm introduced the concept of *psychological reactance* to describe the negative motivational state that results in response to things that threaten freedom of behavior. In that same year, Brehm and Cole reported the results of an experiment that linked reactance to altruism. They reasoned that if O does a favor for P, then this obligates P to return the favor, thereby limiting P's freedom, for example, to be hostile towards O or not to return the favor. React- ance derives from this limitation to P's behavioral freedom. In their investigation, Brehm and Cole had their male subjects arrive for an experiment involving first-impression ratings of another subject, actually the experimenter's accomplice. Prior to making their rat- ings, half of the subjects were given a soft drink by the person they were to rate. In addition, half of the subjects were led to believe that the ratings they were making were highly important, and thus pre- sumably would feel that O's friendly gesture would interfere with their freedom to judge accurately; the other half of the subjects were led to believe that the ratings were simply part of someone's class project and thus presumably of much lesser im- portance.

After making their ratings, all subjects were given an opportunity to help the accomplice on another task. The data that Brehm and Cole report indicate that while subjects who received the soft drink did feel obliged to do something nice for the giver, under conditions of high importance, there is substantial resistance to returning the favor by helping the accomplice on the second task. These data are taken to be supportive of the reactance prediction; subjects felt obliged to return a favor, but refused to do so. It was as though the soft drink threatened to limit their freedom to rate the accomplice negatively and their response to this limitation was to refuse to offer him help.

A later investigation, reported in 1974 by Worchel and Andreoli, both confirms and at the same time extends the Brehm and Cole analysis. Worchel and his colleague demonstrate that subjects whose freedom is limited by both friendly and hostile behaviors of others will react to this limitation by rejecting the person involved. In both cases of friendly or hostile actions, the reciprocity assumed —namely, returning a favor for a favor or a hostile action in return for a hostile action—limits P's freedom to behave otherwise. P's response, therefore, is to reject the person who has thus limited P's behavioral freedom.

Berkowitz (1973) has argued much as Brehm has, that reactance serves to inhibit P's altruism, especially when acting to help another places a restrictive burden on P's own behavioral freedom. P may not wish to get involved in helping O because to do so emeshes P in a web of further obligations that restricts P's freedom. One deriva- tion from this perspective argues that the more O pressures P to be helpful, the more psychological reactance can be aroused, thus the greater P's resentment and the lesser P's helpfulness.

An illuminating examination of this possibility was reported in 1972 by Langer and Abelson whose research basically examined what they termed "the semantics of asking a favor." They suggested that O can ask P for a favor using two major kinds of appeal: victim-oriented or target-oriented. A victim-oriented request focuses on the needy condition of the victim, seeking to arouse P's pity or sympathy for the victim: for example, "What a mess I'm in"; "I'm suffering." A target-oriented request does not ask that P feel sympathy for the victim, but rather stresses the duty of the target person (P) to render aid: for example, "Can you give me a hand?"; "Would you do me a favor?" Langer and Abelson also distinguish between varying degrees of legitimacy for a given request. Thus some favors are illegitimate in that they seem to take advantage of P, the potential benefactor; these requests most clearly induce reactance as they make presumptuous demands on P.

Langer and Abelson reason that there should be an interaction between the form of the appeal and the legitimacy of the request in influencing how P defines the situation vis-a-vis O and thus whether or not P will render aid. In other words, reactance can be reduced and help increased by the manner of O's appeal. Specifically, Langer and Abelson suggest that when the request is illegitimate, O's chances of receiving help from P will increase if O's appeal does not seek to induce empathy but rather focuses on P's duty and responsibility. Thus, a victim-oriented appeal should produce less help than a target-oriented appeal. On the other hand, when the request is legitimate, an appeal that focuses on O's personal plight should be more influential in gaining P's help than one that stresses P's duty.

Two field experiments were conducted in order to examine this formulation. A female confederate either feigned a knee injury and asked the first lone female that came by to make a phone call for her (experiment 1), or asked someone to mail a letter for her (experiment 2). Legitimacy was varied as was the kind of appeal employed. For example, in experiment 2, the request to mail the letter was legitimate when O said she was rushing to catch a train; it was illegitimate when she said she simply intended to go shopping and would like P to mail the letter for her.

Results from the study demonstrate that victim-oriented appeals motivate differing degrees of helping as a function of whether or not the request is legitimate. Thus 75 percent offer help when the request is legitimate but only about 28 percent when it is not; that is, when it appears to be taking advantage of P. On the other hand, when the appeal is target-oriented, the legitimacy of the request has little affect on whether or not P helps: about 48 percent help when the request is legitimate and about 42 percent when it is illegitimate.

We might speculate that P experiences greatest psychological react-ance and thus the greatest reluctance to behave altruistically when an illegitimate request is made by someone who makes personal claims of being in distress and wants P's sympathetic response.

This latter finding is congruent with Berkowitz's own interpreta-tion that reactance can be induced when O appears to be dependent on P, claiming dependency as the reason for needing help (i.e., simi-lar to a victim-oriented appeal). Some of Berkowitz's and others' research provides confirmatory data showing how subjects become even less helpful when O's dependency appears to be generated by O's own deficiency rather than by circumstances beyond O's control. Other data similarly suggest that the more P feels pressured by O's dependency to render aid and the more that aid given now implies a continuing need for aid, thereby threatening P's freedom even more, the greater reactance is aroused and the less help P gives to O. In one effort examining this very point, Russel Jones (1970) dis-covered that when people felt that O was minimally dependent on them for help and that any help given now did not imply a continu-ing need for giving help, then they gave the greatest amount of help to O. We can see a parallel between these data and the Langer and Abelson perspective on an illegitimate request that seeks to make claims on P's sympathy but in so doing actually boomerangs.

An interesting examination of persons who were asked to volun-teer to be bone marrow donors provides further material that links illegitimacy, psychological reactance, and the refusal to act altruis-tically. Shalom Schwartz (1970) was interested specifically in the way in which persons could neutralize the moral norm to help a needy stranger by denying that their action would really be helpful; by denying that they have any personal responsibility; or even that they are capable of taking action that might be helpful. It is Schwartz's view that the manner in which an appeal for donors is formulated can either enhance or minimize these neutralizing fac-tors and thereby decrease or increase the rate of altruism.

His subjects were recruited while relaxing in the Red Cross blood center after having donated blood. An interviewer approached sub-jects and asked them if they would agree to have special tests taken on their blood to see if it could be used in bone marrow transplant work that was taking place in the nearby Medical Center. Subjects were informed that a specific patient, a young mother, was presently in the hospital and in need of a transplant. Data from the study consisted of the degree of P's commitment to serve as a donor, vary-ing according to stages of commitment: for example, agreeing sim-ply to allow further tests to be conducted on the blood already donated; agreeing to undergo further, more complicated tests; agreeing to be on call to be a donor for a future patient.

Schwartz's findings are informative regarding both altruism in general and the specific manner in which "giving" can be neutralized as reactance pressures increase. On the positive side, 59 percent of the persons interviewed agreed to the highest level of commitment measured, indicating their willingness to be tested now and to be on call for future work if needed; only 5 percent refused to participate in any way whatsoever. As Schwartz notes, it is possible that this relatively high rate of apparent altruism is due to the fact that most of the subjects (80 percent) were regular blood donors; but he notes that even thirteen of the 15 first-time donors volunteered for the bone marrow pool.

He notes further that the increased willingness to be a donor was probably a function of the momentum of compliance. Similar to the foot-in-the-door technique we discussed in Chapter 4, agreeing to a small initial request helps pave the way for later agreement to a larger request. Thus agreeing initially to donate blood helps pave the way to agreeing to having that blood undergo one further specific test; this in turn helps pave the way for still further, higher levels of personal commitment. Essentially, if we can imagine four degrees of commitment, the step between level two and level three is much less than between level one and three; having agreed to one makes two less distant, and having agreed to two, in turn, makes three less distant a commitment.

The data relevant to our present concern with psychological reactance involves the curvilinear relationship that Schwartz found between volunteering and the intensity of harm that would befall O if a donor were not found. When it was very likely that a compatible donor could be found (because subjects were led to believe that one in twenty-five persons could provide a likely match), then increasing the emotionality of the appeal by describing the dire consequences to O and to O's family (e.g., mother would die and her children would suffer from growing up without a mother, etc.) that would follow should no donor be found, had a boomerang-type effect: volunteering was significantly less under these circumstances than when the appeal described more moderate consequences. Though the difference was not statistically significant, the volunteering score was even lower under these high consequence conditions than when the appeal spelled out only minimal consequences to O if no donor were found.

In seeking an explanation for this curvilinear relationship—greatest volunteering with moderate appeal and least with either low or high consequence appeal—Schwartz turned to the reactance concept. He suggested that a highly emotional appeal under circumstances in which a likely donor will be found (1 in 25 odds) appear to make an illegitimate demand on P:

If the appeal was viewed as illegitimate, the sense of moral obligation could have been neutralized and negative self-attributions avoided by denying that refusal had serious consequences for others because anothor donor would have been found . . . (p. 292).

Schwartz notes that when the same high consequence appeal is used but subjects are led to believe that the likelihood of finding a compatible donor is very low, (because only one in 1000 are likely to have a compatible match with the patient), then the legitimacy of the request seems proper, reactance is thereby neutralized and the volunteering rate becomes very high.

The point is an important one. While persons will be helpful to others even at some cost to themselves in terms of time, risk, embarrassment, commitment, and loss of personal freedom, they will also seek to define a potentially "prosocial situation" in ways that will not require their action or commitment. The balance point between helpfulness and inaction can be tipped either way as a function of many things, including, as we have just noted, the degree to which the request seems legitimate. We will now briefly examine another, related quality of situations that, while clearly restrictive of P's personal freedom, nevertheless demand P's being helpful, neutralizing reactance and other bases for resisting altruism.

Beyond Reactance.   In what is perhaps one of the clearest statements of the preceding point, Staub and Baer reported in 1974 the results of a field investigation of helping behavior conducted in the streets and sidewalks of Cambridge, Massachusetts. In their study, an accomplice collapses in front of the subject. In the difficult escape condition, he falls to the sidewalk laying in the subject's path; in the easy escape condition, the accomplice collapses on the sidewalk across the street from the subject. If the subject approaches the fallen accomplice, he is reassured that the problem is relatively minor, but that he would appreciate the subject calling the accomplice's roommate to come pick him up. Results indicate that "when the victim was not in the path of the would-be helper, he was helped less. In fact, a number of subjects looked away, after a first glance, when the victim was on the other side of the street" (p. 283). A further finding indicates that nearly half of those who stop to help the accomplice do not make the telephone call, possibly because the accomplice informed them that he could manage on his own, thus freeing the subject from a more intense commitment than was demonstrated by their approaching him in the first place. It would seem that when P is "forced" to help O because O literally falls in P's path, then resistance to helping is reduced; but when escape from such a commitment is readily available, P is likely to seek such escape. Recall as well the hurried seminary students.

Another approach to forcing the scales in favor of P's behaving prosocially was reported in 1970 in Harvey Tilker's version of Milgram's obedience study (see Chapter 7 for a detailed discussion of the Milgram study). Paralleling Staub and Baer's own research question, Tilker asked whether or not subjects who were compelled by circumstances to be involved and take responsibility for another's welfare actually would do so. The Milgram obedience format was employed, using two accomplices and one naive subject for each experimental session. The situation was rigged so that the naïve subject would always draw the role of observer, while one accomplice was the teacher assigned to administer electric shocks to the other accomplice who was the learner. Tilker experimentally varied both the degree to which P as the observer was responsible for O's (i.e., the learner's) well-being and the kind of feedback about O's condition that P received. By means of instruction, in some conditions P was made totally responsible for O's well-being, with P's decisions about experimental procedures being the final word; in other conditions, P's responsibility was left ambiguous (e.g., you and the teacher discuss matters and resolve procedural difficulties between yourselves), or P was made totally nonresponsible (e.g., the teacher's decisions are the final word). Feedback was varied; it was near zero in the condition in which P only noted the learner's responses on the paired-associates learning task; it was greater when P had auditory information (e.g., P could hear O's cries of pain and pleading to stop); it was total with combined auditory and visual feedback in which P both saw and heard O's complaints and pains. Measures were obtained on the degree to which P sought to intervene to stop the experiment. P had a number of options: to get the experimenter who was waiting in an adjoining room; to physically assault the teacher; to disable the apparatus; even to refuse to begin the experiment, and so forth.

Tilker's results show, in the first place, that of the forty-five subjects only thirteen (29 percent) stopped the experiment. His results further inform us of the vital role that feedback plays in providing P either with information that "demands" intervention or that permits P to decline to intervene even verbally: twelve out of twelve subjects in the zero feedback condition made no protest about the procedures even when some were totally responsible for O's well-being.

A closer examination of the thirteen who intervened to stop the experiment shows the combined importance of both feedback and responsibility; eight of the thirteen received both auditory and visual feedback about O's condition; and of those eight, five were in the experimental condition that gave them total responsibility for O's well-being. In fact, those five represented all the subjects who were in the total responsibility-maximum feedback condition. As Tilker notes in reviewing his own findings,

> ... *at the point at which most subjects in the other conditions were just beginning to verbally protest, or were still protesting, the maximum feedback and total responsibility subjects were stopping the experiment...* " (p. 100)

Without much feedback about O's condition, P can more readily interpret the situation as one not demanding intervention; likewise, without direct responsibility for the situation, P can deny an active role in helping. When alternate interpretations are made less operable, as with Tilker's procedures, P will intervene to aid O even though in so doing, P is making a commitment that can be restrictive of P's own behavioral freedom. Of course, Tilker "forced" P to be involved and to be responsible; most everyday situations, as we have noted, are not so coercive, permitting P many alternative interpretations that can reduce prosocial activity: "Nothing major is happening, and besides there is nothing I can do about it, and besides I'm too busy to get involved anyway."

Altruism and the Marketplace of the Economic Person

If we pick up again on an earlier theme suggested by Titmuss's examination of the commercialization of "the gift of blood," we find it understandable that an economically oriented model has become one of the major perspectives in the social psychology of altruism. In order to grasp this economic or reward-cost analysis of prosocial behavior, we first need to define a few terms and introduce a few basic ideas that will facilitate our discussion. Relationships between persons can be said to have a reward and a cost component. In prosocial behaviors, potential rewards include feeling competent, being praised, receiving fame and fortune, and such; potential costs for helping include restriction of freedom (i.e., reactance), loss of time, personal risk and danger, embarrassment, and so forth, while potential costs for not helping include censure, guilt, loss of self-esteem, and such.

Let us think of P as the potential benefactor or help-giver and O as the potential recipient or victim needing help. In behaving altruistically towards O, P must weigh the rewards and costs that are involved. Basically, when the balance tips in favor of greater costs than rewards, P is less likely to behave in a helpful manner than when the rewards for helping outweigh the costs. Needless to say, we are speaking here about rewards and costs as they appear to P: that is, as a part of P's psychological environment or life space. Furthermore, circumstances that increase costs or decrease rewards for helping have the effect of decreasing P's altruism. We have already noted several of these circumstances.

When O's request is highly restrictive of P's freedom, the costs for helping can outweigh the rewards and lead P not to help. The Piliavin and Piliavin study of bystander intervention in a subway car suggested how the introduction of blood into the situation increased the personal costs involved in rendering aid and thereby decreased the likely intervention. In similar manner, Piliavin, Rodin, and Piliavin (1969), in a parallel study, argued that offering aid to a drunk was more costly than giving aid to an invalid in that the drunk's unpredictable behavior might prove embarrassing or harmful and thus costly to P. As we noted previously, the manner in which O's request and appeal are made can tip the balance, making P's intervention more or less likely; an illegitimate request is more costly and thus receives less help than a legitimate request.

But this economic perspective on altruism is somewhat more complex than we have thus far noted. In a version, termed *equity theory,* it is suggested that persons in a relationship seek to establish and to maintain an equitable balance between the reward-cost outcomes that exist; that when this equitable balance does not exist, persons will experience distress; and that persons will attempt to eliminate this distress by restoring equity in the relationship. However, when does an equitable relationship exist between P and O?

To understand this, we must introduce another term and clarify one with which we are already familiar. Relationships can be viewed in terms of the inputs or investments that are involved and the outcomes that emerge. Inputs or investments involve P's and O's contributions to an exchange that entitles each to certain rewards or costs. For example, in a work setting, putting in an 8-hour day is an investment that entitles P to certain rewards. Or in a friendship, if P devotes a great deal of time and energy to doing things for O, then we can refer to this time and energy as P's input or investment in the relationship. Outcomes, the second term we need, we are already familiar with. An outcome, simply, is the reward-cost differential that derives from a relationship. Thus if we could scale rewards and costs in grams, a reward of 8 grams and a cost of 5 grams would yield an outcome of 3 grams.

Equity in a relationship generally is defined as a proportionality between P and O in their outcomes relative to their investments or inputs:

$$\frac{\text{Outcomes for P}}{\text{Inputs for P}} = \frac{\text{Outcomes for O}}{\text{Inputs for O}}$$

In other words, if P's outcomes relative to P's investments equals O's outcomes relative to O's investments, the relationship between P and O is said to be equitable and thus nonstressful. The relationship is said to be nonequitable and thus stressful, if this proportionality is violated. Therefore, for example, if both P and O work at the same job for the same amount of time, thereby having similar investments, but P receives $20 pay while O receives only $15, the relationship is nonequitable: for similar investments, the outcomes are not similar. However, if P were to receive more pay for doing more work or if P's greater pay were based on seniority (seen as an investment of time in the work system), then equity could exist. We refer again to this equity model in Chapter 10.

The important link between this equity analysis of relationships and prosocial behavior is based on the dual ideas of "deserving" and "a just world" (e.g., Lerner, 1971; 1974; Long & Lerner, 1974). Imagine living in a world in which positive outcomes were given to persons who made minimal investments and thus were not deserving; this would be an unjust world. In a just world, equity is said to prevail; and it is in the service of maintaining or restoring a just world, that persons act in ways to benefit those deserving benefit or to withhold help from those who are not deserving.

Melvin Lerner and several of his associates have provided ample experimental evidence congruent with this just-world perspective on altruism. In an investigation by Lerner and Simmons (1966; Also see Aderman et al., 1974; Simmons & Lerner, 1968) it was shown that when a subject cannot help a victim escape a harmful situation, they derogate the victim, seeing them as bad persons deserving the fate that they received. Equity was maintained by seeing the outcome as appropriate to the inputs of a bad person. In similar fashion subjects restored equity in another investigation (Lerner & Mathews, 1967) by construing a situation in which someone receives positive outcomes by chance as one in which the person actually deserves those outcomes.

Think for a moment about these findings and their implications. P maintains equity by reconstruing a situation so that O is seen to be getting a just reward. As Jones and Aronson (1973) have demonstrated, a woman who is raped may be seen as being at fault and thus as getting what she deserved, especially if she is socially respectable! The respectable victim of rape does not deserve this negative outcome unless P can somehow reconstruct the situation as one in which she acted in some manner to deserve it. Thus she is judged to be more at fault than a rape victim whose social respectability is rated lower and who thereby already has outcomes deserved by her lower status.

On the brighter side, P may not invariably act to justify O's fate as a means of restoring equity, but rather may seek to act altruistically in order to help O or to compensate O. Equity can be restored by providing the victim with relief for his or her fate. Research has suggested that P will seek to compensate O in proportion to the degree of need; to do otherwise, would simply exchange one inequity for another. That is, if P's helping would provide too little or too much for O, then P is less likely to intervene to provide help than if P is able to provide help that just balances O's need. Berscheid and Walster (1967) provide some confirmation by showing how women who cheated others out of trading stamps and could compensate their victims by restoring exactly the number that had been "lost" were more likely to do so than women who could provide either too little or an excessive compensation.

I think that we can readily see in these works the interactionist perspective of Chapters 1 and 2. In this formulation of altruism, P and O are seen as interdependent elements of a total field; a stable equilibrium is maintained for that field and their relationship when P gives help to O that is proportional to O's deserved need. Disequilibrium in the field (i.e., inequity) creates tension that leads to action to restore the stable state of giving and receiving.

To create inequity in a relationship is costly and thus will be avoided; therefore if P's efforts to behave prosocially towards O would create more inequity than they would relieve, P is not likely to behave altruistically. Insofar as helping beyond a compensatory point places a burden on O to reciprocate in kind and in degree, thereby creating more inequity than equity, such benefits will neither be given nor sought. Walster, Berscheid, and Walster (1973) summarize several investigations that demonstrate that "Undeserved gifts produce inequity in a relationship" (p. 168). Most of the research demonstrates that the benefactor, O, is hesitant to accept benefits that cannot be repaid and thus that establish inequity in the O–P relationship; O actually likes P less for being helpful if O cannot repay in kind at some later time. It seems reasonable to suggest that in knowing this, P is less likely to give help to O unless P can believe that equity will be restored later.

As Titmuss noted, a key aspect of the commercialized blood donor system is its reliance on persons giving now so that they may draw on the bank for a similar number of units later, if they are in need. P's gift of blood in a commercialized system is indeed based on the equity perspective we have outlined. When the gift or the altruistic act threatens to upset an equitable exchange, it may either not be given or given with a clear understanding of proper repayment at a proper time.

Although there will be those who may find an economic view of altruism unappealing in its characterization of the human condition or for that matter even contradictory to the sense of true altruism as benefiting another without strings attached, I think it important to realize that an exchange model of human behavior may indeed be the most proper in a social system in which exchange and economic concepts so dominante most facets of life. Thus, if equity considerations are a vital and dominant theme in many spheres of everyday life, it should come as no surprise that even prosocial, altruistic efforts are governed by similar considerations. But, as with most things, the picture is even more complex.

Norms and Altruism

Basically, a *norm* is a shared set of expectations among a group of people indicating the proper behavior expected of group members under specifiable conditions. Norms are somewhat like rules governing social behavior. In our earlier discussion of Sherif's work with the autokinetic effect, we encountered the concept of a judgmental norm or standard arrived at by a group of interacting persons that defined a proper range within which judgments of the light's movement were made. In their analyses of prosocial behaviors, social psychologists have turned to the analysis of two norms that are thought to be implicated in P's behaving altruistically towards O: a norm of reciprocity and a norm of social responsibility.

NORM OF RECIPROCITY

The sociologist, Alvin Gouldner (1960) defined a norm of reciprocity as making two interrelated, minimal demands on all human relationships: "... (1) people should help those who have helped them, and (2) people should not injure those who have helped them" (p. 171). His argument is that this norm is at the root of all cultures' moral principles and value systems. It establishes a set of reciprocal demands and obligations that provide stability to a social system. That such a norm exists does not guarantee that it will always be followed without violation. The implication, however, is that when violation occurs strains are created within the system that motivate behavior directed towards its restoration. The analyses we just completed of the economic exchange theories of altruism build on Gouldner's concept of reciprocity; persons who receive a favor are presumed to be obligated to return a favor: reciprocity is the normative vehicle whereby equity in human relationships is maintained. The relationship between reactance and altruism, as we have seen, is based on this normative obligation.

We can see how reciprocity functions as a system-maintaining rule, restoring equilibrium to the system of relationships between P and O (and others) by establishing an obligation to return a favor with a favor. We can again see that in this formulation, P and O are interdependent elements of an interactive field, joined in this case by means of a regulating norm of reciprocity. As P, for example, makes increasing demands on O's helping, P thereby incurs a growing debt; their relationship is disequilibrated until such time as P reciprocates sufficiently to restore their relationship to a reasonable level of exchange. P and O are tied to one another by means of this normative obligation; as Gouldner suggests, larger units within the society are likewise similarly linked. The behavior of each interdependent part of the whole relationship is thereby affected by this regulating principle of reciprocity.

The kind of altruism that reciprocity deals with is not simply based on persons' good will towards others; but as Gouldner notes, "... if you want to be helped by others you must help them; hence it is not only proper but also expedient to conform with the specific status rights of others and with the general norm" (p. 173). A similar point was made by Long and Lerner's analysis (1974) of the "personal contract" that children learn as they develop the capacity to withhold immediate gratification for themselves and to incur some costs in order to achieve long-term benefits. Egoism gives ground to altruism as a sometimes costly investment that will bring better returns later. Long and Lerner's investigation used fourth-graders who were tested for their ability to delay immediate gratification and then placed into a situation in which they could either behave in their self-interest (e.g., egoism) or donate to others. Their results indicate that when children with the capacity to delay gratification received more than they felt they deserved, they were more likely to donate "this extra" to others as compared with children who were less able to delay gratification who thus kept the overpayment for themselves. Research reported by Durkin (1961) further showed that some children who were not the recipients of sharing, nevertheless shared with others in the hopes of reciprocation later on.

The norm of reciprocity obliges one who receives a favor from another to return a favor. As Gouldner notes, the norm

*thus provides some realistic grounds for confidence, in the
one who first parts with his valuables, that he will be repaid.
Consequently, there may be less hesitancy in being the first
... (p. 177).*

A norm of reciprocity not only helps stabilize an already existing
social relationship, but increases the likelihood that an nonexploita-
tive, prosocial relationship will be generated. If persons know that
in acting beneficially towards others, even at some cost to themselves, they are likely to receive some return benefit, then presumably, they will more readily take that first positive step. As we
previously noted in our discussion of equity theory, a norm of reciprocity complicates any simplistic reward-cost analysis of prosocial
behavior by suggesting how P will undergo the costs of helping O in
conformity with a norm that implies a debt with some appropriate
form of future repayment.

Gouldner's analysis of reciprocity describes a situation in which
P provides benefits for O which now oblige O to repay the debt O
incurs in accepting such benefits. The intensity of this debt varies,
according to Gouldner, with each of the following:

1. O's need when P initially gave to O. Giving to a person in need
    incurs a greater return debt than giving to someone not in great
    need.
2. P's resources at the time P gave to O. Giving even though one can
    hardly afford it incurs a greater debt of return than giving, even
    generously, when one can well afford to give.
3. P's motives and intentions. Giving without thought of gain in-
    curs a greater debt than giving clearly in the service of getting
    a substantial gain for one's self.
4. The constraints on P to give. Giving freely incurs a greater debt
    for O to repay than giving because P is constrained to do so.

Each of these factors has received some form of empirical support
from a variety of different though related social psychological investigations. Tesser, Gatewood, and Driver reported in 1968 a study
of some of the determinants of gratitude. They provided their subjects with stories in which one person helps or gives something to
another under varying conditions of intentionality (Gouldner's
point 3), cost (point 2), and value (point 1). For example, intentionality was varied by describing the gift as being given in order to
benefit O or in order to enhance P's reputation. Subjects were asked
to indicate how grateful they would be towards the benefactor, P,
and how indebted they would feel. Results confirmed Gouldner's
contention that each of these three factors affects the degree of
gratitude and debt O is under given P's altruistic act. Thus, giving
to benefit O rather than self, giving at more rather than less cost to
self, and giving something of greater than lesser value for O's needs
all resulted in ratings both of greater gratitude and greater indebt-

edness, thereby supporting Gouldner's perspective on the norm of reciprocity and its role in altruism.

Gouldner's fourth factor, involving the constraints acting on P at the time the gift or the help was provided, was studied by Goranson and Berkowitz (1966) and found to be an important determinant of altruism based on reciprocity. In their study, subjects had the opportunity to return the help given to them by another subject (called the supervisor), under several different conditions: for example, when the other person voluntarily helped versus when the help was compulsory. Results indicated that subjects returned more help to P when P's initial help to them was given voluntarily. Research reported by Pruitt (1968) offers further confirmation for several of Gouldner's hypotheses. For example, Pruitt reports that a subject's returning help to P was a function of the degree of prior help they received from P; furthermore, even when two different subjects previously received the same amount of benefit from P, their reciprocation of benefit to P was a function of the percentage of P's resources involved in the initial giving. As Gouldner has noted, the greater the cost of P's aid (i.e., the greater the percentage of P's total resources), the greater O's indebtedness to reciprocate, and as Pruitt's work demonstrates, the greater the benefit actually returned.

As Gouldner notes and as the Tesser group's research demonstrates, P's motives for altruism play an important role in the sense of debt that O will experience. Another investigation reported in 1968 by Schopler and Thompson provides further confirmation of this effect. In their research subjects were the recipients of a favor that they could reciprocate. As Schopler and his colleague note, however, whether or not reciprocation will occur is a function of O's attribution of motives to P's original giving. In a setting in which receiving a favor from P seems inappropriate, leading O to feel suspicious about P's actual generosity, O reciprocates less than either when receiving no favor from P or when the context within which the favor is given leads O to attribute true generosity to P. It would seem then that the old adage about not looking a gift horse in the mouth is not clearly supported by much social behavior, especially as one comes to wonder about the motivations behind the gift and the indebtedness that is implied.

Further Restrictions in Reciprocity.   In addition to those factors that Gouldner says contribute to increasing or decreasing the debt of reciprocity, several other investigations have suggested the role of other social factors, especially social class variables, in reducing O's adherence to the norm. Berkowitz and Friedman (1967), using the Miller-Swanson distinction between entrepreneurial and bureaucratic family settings, provide some valuable insights into the relationship between a family's niche in the economic system of a society and its tendency to follow the norm of reciprocity. Recall that an entrepreneurial family setting is one in which the family's status is determined by the breadwinner's efforts to compete successfully in the open marketplace. The bureaucratic setting, by contrast, is one in which the family's status is determined by the breadwinner's position in the bureaucracy; this in turn is established by rules of seniority or success in playing the role of a good organizational person (see Chapter 2).

Berkowitz and his associate reasoned that persons from entrepreneurial settings, being more involved with a money economy and its emphasis on proportional giving and receiving, should follow the reciprocity norm more than those from a bureaucratic context who "should be more willing than midde-class entrepreneurs to assist other persons in need of aid regardless of the benefits he can derive or has obtained from the situation" (p. 219). An experimental situation was created in which high school students received varying degrees of help from a partner and later had the opportunity to reciprocate or not. The prediction was that those from entrepreneurial backgrounds should reciprocate more when they initially received high-help than when they received low-help, but that the bureaucratic-background subjects would not be as greatly influenced by the level of help they received, returning help under both initial high- and low-help circumstances: that is, they should be less influenced by the demands of reciprocity. Results generally confirmed this expectation, as did the results of another study by Berkowitz undertaken in England.

A study of upper-middle class as compared with working-class women, reported in 1962 by Muir and Weinstein, suggests a tendency among the upper-middle-class women to operate by a reciprocity norm whereas the working-class women seem more concerned with issues of "mutual aid," giving when they are able to. In other words, the upper-middle-class women seemed to function more according to an economic view of human relationships, much like the middle-class entrepreneurs that Berkowitz and Friedman studied; the working-class women were more governed by mutual interest than issues of reciprocity as such.

Friendship seems also to play a role in restricting at least immediate reciprocity in response to being helped. Staub and Sherk (1970) report an investigation among children who could share candy with one another and then later share one crayon for making a drawing. Paralleling the general reciprocity norm, Staub and Sherk report that children shared the crayon the longest time with those who had shared the most candies with them. However, nonfriends tended to behave more according to this norm than friends. As Staub notes

(1972), "Perhaps the existence of friendship means that benefits can be balanced over a longer period of time" (p. 137), thereby not demanding immediate reciprocity. In this particular investigation, reciprocity involved not only sharing helpfully but also retaliating by not sharing. Once again, friends tended not to retaliate for their partner's initial selfishness, whereas nonfriends tended to behave in a tit-for-tat manner; if they were treated selfishly, they responed in kind by not sharing the crayon.

The Third Party.   In what may be a transition point between the specific norm of reciprocity as it applies to specific individual relationships and a more generalized norm of social responsibility—giving to others in need without expecting reciprocal benefits—some analysts and their research have suggested how the act of being helped may generate more general helpfulness in the recipient. For example, Berkowitz and Daniels (1963; 1964. Also Berkowitz, 1972) have demonstrated that when O receives help from P, but cannot reciprocate to P (who may have left the area), O is more likely to help a third party. Strictly speaking, this third-party help is not reciprocity in that O is not returning a favor to P; however, it may indeed be an altruistic derivative of the norm of reciprocity. Gouldner hints at this more generalized function of the norm in noting how the maintenance of social indebtedness joins with an ambiguity over who is actually in debt to whom to help cement a social system together:

> rough *equivalence of repayment . . . induces a certain*
> *amount of ambiguity as to whether indebtedness has been*
> *repaid and, over time, generates uncertainty about who is in*
> *whose debt . . . The norm, in this respect, is a kind of plastic*
> *filter, capable of being poured into the shifting crevices of*
> *social structures, and serving as a kind of all-purpose moral*
> *cement* (p. 175).

The previous research on modeling and altruism is relevant in this present context. Recall that in general, P's viewing a model behave altruistically has positive effects on P's own altruism. The third-party effect may work in a similar manner; that is, seeing or directly experiencing a favor may increase the salience of a norm of giving or a generalized norm of reciprocity. Thus P has a more heightened sensitivity to prosocial issues and is more likely to behave helpfully. It is also possible, of course, that a prosocial experience, again direct or observed, may produce a positive or even empathic mood within P. Aderman and Berkowitz (1970) report the results of a study in which P observed a helping situation and then later could provide help to the experimenter. Data suggest the important role that empathy played in P's helping after this observation.

Some work initially reported in 1970 by Alice Isen suggests another kind of intervening mood or affective state that may be implicated in P's reciprocating help under third-party conditions. (Also see Isen & Levin, 1972; Isen, et al., 1973). Isen demonstrated what she termed the "warm glow of success" in motivating P's helping O even though not receiving nor expecting any help in return. Success experiences motivate greater helping than failure experiences; after having a positive, self-enhancing experience, P becomes more generous towards a stranger than after a failure experience. Aderman (1972) provides further confirmation for this effect, finding after that providing his subjects with either an elating or a depressing experience, those in a good mood were more helpful than those in the depressed mood.

Although these mood effects did not involve issues of reciprocity, it seems reasonable that being the recipient of a favor is likely to increase P's "warm glow" which in turn may generalize, as these studies have suggested, into helping a stranger when direct reciprocation is not possible.

A further possibility relevant to the third-party effect (i.e., generalized reciprocity) involves a guilt-expiation notion. Research generally has shown that if P harms O, then P is likely to behave prosocially towards another person; presumably, the generalized altruistic deed serves to rid P of the guilt experienced over doing harm. Regan, Williams, and Sparling (1972; Also see Regan, 1971) report the results of a field investigation in which female subjects at a shopping center are first asked to help the experimenter (by taking his picture), are then led to believe that the camera they are using is broken because of something they did (to induce guilt), and then later are given the opportunity to help a fellow shopper (actually an accomplice) pick up her fallen bag of groceries. Results indicate that 55 percent of those in the guilt condition acted helpfully compared to only 15 percent in the control group in which no guilt was induced. This concept of guilt expiation may be useful as well in understanding the mediation of third-party reciprocity when direct reciprocation is not possible. That is, although no harm-doing has been involved, when P benefits O and O cannot repay directly, the normative obligation to repay may create a sense of guilt that can only be relieved by O's behaving altruistically to another. The argument is that guilt, whether caused by O's harm-doing or O's indebtedness to P, may be an important mediator of third-party altruism: that is, altruism towards a stranger.

NORM OF SOCIAL RESPONSIBILITY

The second general norm that has been posited to account for altruistic behavior has been variously termed the *norm of giving* (by Leeds, 1963) or the *norm of social responsibility* (by Berkowitz and Daniels). Unlike specific reciprocity but more similar to its generalized, third-party form, this norm presumably requires our being good samaritans and providing help to needy and dependent others without expectation of reciprocity. Reciprocity is thereby not required when O is highly dependent on P—for example, a child, or a person who is very ill or very old. That giving is a positive cultural value has been demonstrated with children by the research of Bryan and Walbeck (1970a; b) among others. Even in the primary school grades, children report that it is good to donate to needy people; likewise, they evaluate their peers according to their verbal endorsement of this value. On the other hand, the broad-scale investigation of Almond and Verba (1963) suggests that the virtues of being generous increase with educational level, implying that the norm of social responsibility may be differently distributed by social class.

The key circumstances that trigger the norm of social responsibility is presumed to be a situation in which O is in some way dependent on P's assistance. The extensive program of research undertaken by Berkowitz and his several associates provides substantial data in support of this view. The basic research design involves a worker and a supervisor performing a simple task; dependency is varied by having the supervisor's success be a function of the help provided by the worker. In general, Berkowitz reports more help provided when the supervisor is dependent on the worker than when dependency is low. However, as Schaps (1972) among others has demonstrated, when the cost of helping a dependent other is high, help is less likely than when costs are low. Schaps investigated the extent to which shoe salesmen in exclusive shoe stores in the Chicago area would help a female customer with a broken heel, thus needing a new pair of shoes, under naturally occurring conditions of high cost (when the store was crowded) or low cost (when the store was less crowded). The female customer (the experimenter's accomplice) was instructed to be a difficult customer. Measures were taken of the extent to which the salesman provided good service to the customer under these varying conditions. Results indicated that under conditions of high cost, dependent customers (i.e., with the broken heels) received poor service; that helpful service was given to the dependent customer only when costs were low.

Likewise, as previously noted when O's dependency seems to be internally caused rather than by forces beyond O's control, O's dependency does not motivate greater helping from P. It is as though O's causing himself or herself to be dependent attentuates P's sense of social responsibility. A related point has been made by Lerner who notes that P's need to dwell in a just world where people who deserve help get it and those undeserving do not, influences whether or not the responsibility norm will influence P's behavior towards a dependent O. Research reported by Simmons and Lerner in 1968 indicates how considerations of justice and deserving limit the degree to which social responsibility influences P's altruism towards O. In a situation that paralleled Berkowitz's use of a supervisor dependent on a worker, Simmons and Lerner found that workers did less for a dependent supervisor who seemed to have already been unjustly rewarded than for a supervisor whose performance had not been properly rewarded. Simmons and Lerner contend that while indeed a norm of social responsibility exists, as Berkowitz and Daniels among others have argued:

> that the norms which compel people to provide aid are much more specific in terms of how much aid and to whom . . . aid should be given to those who deserve help and withheld from the undeserving. These norms seem to support the person's desire to believe he lives in a just world where people merit their fate, and the providing or withholding of aid is one way of reestablishing justice (p. 224).

Interdependence and Atomism: The Roots of Altruism

As is unfortunately too often the case, our pursuit of empirical findings and systematic analyses of the bits and pieces of altruism may have deflected our attention from fundamental questions concerning the roots of altruism. The importance of understanding who helps who and under what specifiable conditions cannot be overstressed. Thus we remain indebted to those who have labored and continue to labor within their laboratory or controlled field settings in the service of providing us such information. Yet, it is equally vital for us to gain a sense of a fundamental principle of altruism, if only to speculate on its place in human affairs. We are all aware of the importance that hedonism and egoism play in human life; where the pursuit of an enlightened self-interest seems sensible from the perspective of the survival of the individual. But surely, if we are not atomistic islands but interdependent souls, then the concern for the welfare of others must run deeply within the human strain as well.

The paradox of human altruism reflects our apparently dualistic nature: we are separated from our neighbors and work in behalf of our own self-interests, yet we are joined interdependently with our neighbors and need to cooperate and share. In an important analysis, Donald Campbell (1965; 1972) argues that a self-serving egoism (i.e., hedonism) would more likely produce genetic survival than a self-sacrificing altruism. In Campbell's view, people are basically hedonistic creatures; genetic tendencies that reinforce this self-centeredness are selected for in biological evolution, while those favoring self-sacrifice are systematically eliminated:

> *modern evolutionary genetics points to something closer to Freudian narcissism: self-serving aggressiveness in competition with coworkers for food, space, and mates; self-serving cowardice in war; self-serving dishonesty to fellow ingroup members; cheating, greed, disobedience, etc. . . . The survival value of complex social coordination [i.e., altruism] . . . has been achieved in man as a* social-evolutionary *product which has had to inculcate behavioral dispositions directly counter to the selfish tendencies being produced by genetic selection* (1972, p. 22).

The point is an important one. Campbell's argument is that group survival demands altruistic, self-sacrificing behavior; it demands that we recognize our fundamental interdependence and join together in cooperative, mutually beneficial ventures. But this very survival is not guaranteed by genetic selection, which indeed, may only guarantee the survival of the self-serving, hedonistic individual. Rather, "culturally evolved indoctrination . . . has had to counter self-serving genetic tendencies" (p. 35). That cultural arrangements motivate our altruism, holding our individual hedonism in check creates a basic ambivalence in humankind between individual dispositions and social demands. Not unlike Freud's own analysis of this issue, Campbell sees each cultural commandment as endeavoring to keep the genetically selected hedonism in check in the service of "some social-systemic optimum" (p. 32).

A similar analysis is also put forth by Ronald Cohen (1972) who maintains that "altruism is composed of three elements—giving or its desire, empathy, and no motives of reward from the object of the altruistic behavior" (p. 41). Seeing person's heritage as basically self-serving and hedonistic, Cohen argues that the various components of altruism are derived from specifiable cultural arrangements. Further, group survival demands that aspects of altruism be part of a cultural heritage, passed on and learned by each generation and sustained by norms and cultural practices: "there is no innate origin of altruism in human nature" (p. 52). Cohen's resolution of the egoism-altruism paradox in human nature is based on his attributing human egoism to the basic, genetically endowed individual make-up, and human altruism to the learned cultural heritage. For Cohen, therefore, culturally sanctioned acts of giving may appear on the individual level to entail personal gain and thus carry the taint of egoism.

In his analysis of the several components of altruism, Cohen notes how the Western form, involving empathy with the victim, requires a particularly intense early emotional bonding as occurs between parents and their children. He sees a relatively stable, monogamous family arrangement to be an important determinant of the emotional components of altruism (i.e., empathy and sympathy):

> *Our family system and our socialization procedures have created a cathection for affect which is not common cross-culturally—just as the combination of our family, isolated household, and socialization procedures are not common* (p. 48).

Essentially, altruism as giving (e.g., the norm of reciprocity) without any especially intense affective involvement is a universal cultural arrangement. The emotional components of altruism, however, which are cultural in their origins, require a kind of nuclear family relationship that itself is neither universal nor widespread; thus the affective aspects of altruism may not be found everywhere.

This intense emotional bonding forms a major aspect of the psychoanalytic perspective on human development and on the cultural evolution of altruism as well. The sense of basic trust that Erikson describes (see Chapter 6), based on a dependable parent-child relationship, provides an early basis for the child's later sense of giving and sharing:

> *this first struggle between waiting and satisfying one's self, are the external organizers of later empathic understanding, of sympathy, and of altruism* (Ekstein, 1972, p. 75).

But, as Cohen informs us, not all cultures create or later reinforce this kind of affective involvement. He cites his own work with the Kanuri in Nigeria as an example of a group in whom any "deep emotional involvement in any other person is very uncommon" (p. 47). The Kanuri's early environment is characterized by its rather high turnover in people; divorce rates range from 58 percent to 99 percent of all marriages; in addition, children are likely to live in many different households containing many different and changing "fathers" and "mothers":

> *To become emotionally involved with people is ... to weaken or lessen one's capacity to cathect roles, norms, and rules rather than the individual who is filling any particular slot ... So the lack of emotional content of relationships taught by early experiences is adaptive* (p. 50).

A point of view that Joseph Katz (1972) calls self-realization theory contrasts with the essential message of both Campbell's and Cohen's analyses of the roots of human altruism. Unlike theories that pit the individual's pursuit of egoism against cultural arrangements that demand altruism, the self-realization perspective emphasizes the basic unity between person and other such that in satisfying self one simultaneously satisfies the other. Basically, one's self is completed only by the other; the emphasis is on mutuality rather than self-interest, on harmonization rather than atomism and isolation. Although this perspective does not even attempt to come to grips with the genetic-evolutionary issues that motivate both Campbell's and Cohen's analyses, it nevertheless achieves a different emphasis in its view of the altruistic paradox. To call on the terms used in Chapter 6, we might say that the *thesis* of total agency and the *antithesis* of total communion is transcended by the *synthesis* of self-realized mutuality and interdependence. In contrast, both Campbell and Cohen emphasize an individual genetic endowment of agency that is ameliorated but never fully transcended by a culturally learned heritage of communion. Thus, there forever remains an ambivalence between egoism and altruism rather than a synthesized realization of self through acts done in the service of others.

Whatever disagreements there may exist regarding the genetic or cultural sources of altruistic behaviors, their need for human survival is seen by all to be a fundamental and deeply rooted characteristic of all social and psychological systems. Cultural arrangements, from the highest levels of generality (e.g., synergy, reciprocity norms) to the more specific facets of a given situation, join with personal learning histories to influence the form that prosocial acts will take: whether it be giving freely as Titmuss describes and as the Berkowitz and Daniels norm of social responsibility suggests; or giving reciprocally with a return anticipated as Gouldner notes; or, for that matter, self-sacrificing as an investment in greater future personal gain and then only insofar as principles of equity are applicable.

There also seems to be substantial agreement among the several analysts of our prosocial life concerning the vital role that social learning plays in emphasizing and in reinforcing altruistic or egoistic tendencies. For most, this learned aspect of altruism holds out hope for transforming what may appear to be an uncaring community of self-seeking egoists into a more caring community. People can learn to be empathic, to care, to act in altruistic ways; cultural values represented by institutions of socialization (including home, school, and the media) can prove instrumental in this regard. Of course, those same institutions can inculcate values that are atomizing, glorifying the individualistic pursuit of personal benefit without concern for the well-being of others.

Yet, the altruistic paradox remains rooted perhaps firmly and beyond ready transformation in the very fabric of the existing Western tradition of individualism. In his review of research on the helping behavior of children, James Bryan (1972) directly but perhaps unintentionally expresses this issue as he notes some of the costs that may be involved in attempting to create "the concerned citizen":

> *A helpful person may well be intrusive (e.g., invade our privacy), moralistic (e.g., prevent us from "doing our thing"), or simply conforming to the status quo of proprieties ... a helpful person with all of his "good" intentions may well violate a variety of personal freedoms that we cherish* (pp. 101–102).

First, we must note that we are not taking issue with Bryan's listing of the possible costs of creating a nation of concerned (i.e., altruistic) citizens. The point, of course, is that prosocial acts are costly as they are pitted against a tradition of individualism in which the rights of the individual are held to be supreme. The view that Bryan appropriately summarizes argues that rampant concern for other's welfare might well infringe on individual freedoms to be left alone without the intrusions of others. How much more difficult it must be then to attempt to inculcate altruism into the socialization of children while simultaneously advocating and practicing the merits of this individualistic thesis. Much reticence to get involved in the affairs of others may well stem from our concerns that we be left alone to lead our lives as we wish; if we can rightfully feel that our life is none of their business, then perhaps theirs is none of ours. And this lesson runs to the core of our individualistic values and tradition, thereby facilitating the maintenance of an ambivalence between behaving altruistically or remaining a bystander. It would seem that the idealism expressed in the self-realization view would require a transformation in people's view of themselves away from the individualistic and towards a more collectivistic thesis. It may well be that the era of individualism so vital to the growth and development of civilization will pass or at least lose its intense thrust as the closing boundaries of our total earth's civilization increasingly demand that we be aware of our collective interdependencies. Perhaps, then, a textbook analysis of the roots of altruism written some years from now would not dwell on an ambivalence between egoism and altruism, nor count individual concern for other's welfare as a potential cost to individual freedom. Just as the Kanuri of Nigeria think it abnormal that Western society should feel any deep emotional attachment to others who need help, perhaps Western cultures of the future will think it strange that Western societies of the past thought themselves never to be freer than when they could simply do their own thing and let others do likewise.

The bridge that will carry us from our concern with altruism to the issues of justice that we examine in the next chapter is readily conveyed by Thomas Hobbes's (1651; Also see Ellis, 1971) question of social order and cohesion. How is it that in pursuit of their own self interests persons do not so relate to others who are likewise pursuing their own interests, that society and human relationships disintegrate into a war of all against with benefit to none? In other words, why does there tend to be civil peace rather than civil war? This question draws our attention to the distributive relationship between persons and other social units and to the allocation of resources in ways that achieve mutual satisfaction and a subjective sense of justice.

JUSTICE AND SOCIAL RELATIONSHIPS

10

We might reasonably suppose that issues involving justice have existed in human affairs since that early point in time when a question of resource sharing and distribution arose. I am the hunter who caught the wild beast that will provide meat for supper. How shall the meat be allocated so that all parties involved will feel that it has been distributed fairly? In Chapter 2, the tragedy of the commons was introduced as a vehicle to illustrate the intricate web of interdependencies that characterizes human existence. The tragedy, recall, existed as people pursued their own gains without considering the long-term negative consequences that would occur if others likewise pursued their individual goals, thereby wasting away the resource of the commons for all. The pursuit of just solutions to the problem of the commons and others of its sort draws our attention to stratification systems that regulate the use of the commons by distributing the available resources on the basis of esteemed human qualities: for example, age, sex, race, ability, wealth, power, and so forth. Paralleling the macro-level concern with systems of stratification, we noted in Chapter 9 the more micro-level concern with issues of equity in interpersonal relationships. Resources are allocated equitably, recall, when those whose inputs are greater receive proportionally greater resource outcomes. In this view, the use of equity rules in relationships ensures that order, cohesion, and justice will prevail.

The concern with resource distribution and the related issue of justice are neither idle nor esoteric matters; rather, they take us to the very roots of social cohesion, human survival, and human relationships. Though the Hobbesian problem of social order has been with us for a long time, the issues involved—whether of altruism, cooperation, equity, or stratification—have never seemed as pressing as they do now, when interdependencies tie strangers together into the same resource network, when the abuse of resources for short-term gain has grave long run implications for all, and when an unjust allocation of necessary resources opens up serious questions of both morality and of human survival in a nuclear age.

A version of this material appears in E. E. Sampson, On justice as equality, Journal of Social Issues, 1975.

Our analysis and understanding of the role of justice in human relationships must take place within this broad context. On the input side, concern with justice calls our attention to the nature of the allocation systems that distribute resources; on the output side, our attention is directed towards the social order and cohesion that results when justice is obtained or the distress that follows its nonattainment. We can conveniently summarize this discussion and preview our subsequent concerns by means of the following propositions:

PROPOSITION I:

The distribution of resources among persons or social units poses a fundamental problem, the solution to which determines the degree of social order and cohesion that will prevail. This is termed the *distributive problem* and is involved whenever resources are to be allocated between person and other, as well as among groups within a society or among nation-states.

PROPOSITION II:

Just solutions to the distributive problem promote cohesion and order, including a state of psychological well-being; unjust solutions contribute to both personal and social unrest and disorganization.

PROPOSITION III:

There are two major historical as well as contemporary solutions to the distributive problem. These are the *equity solution* and the *equality solution.* They vary in their understanding of the conditions appropriate to creating harmony, cohesion, and justice and reflect fundamentally different conceptions and assumptions about human nature.

THE NORM OF EQUITY

As we noted in our examination of the equity view of altruism, interpersonal relationships were said to involve an exchange between the participants or between a third party and the participants. As with any exchange relationship, persons bring something to it—their investments or inputs—and receive something from it—their outcomes. In a work or business-type exchange, inputs can include such things as age, skill, seniority, and training, while outcomes primarily involve wages but can also include social support, fringe benefits, status symbols, and so on. According to equity theory, persons are concerned with getting a fair return on their investments where the judgment of fairness is made comparatively. Equity is said to exist whenever the ratio of P's outcomes-to-investments is equal to O's ratio; inequity exists whenever this relative proportionality is violated. Adams (1965) presents three equations defining equity and inequity:

Equity

$$\frac{\text{P's Outcomes}}{\text{P's Inputs}} = \frac{\text{O's Outcomes}}{\text{O's Inputs}}$$

Inequity

$$(1) \quad \frac{\text{P's Outcomes}}{\text{P's Inputs}} < \frac{\text{O's Outcomes}}{\text{O's Inputs}}$$

$$(2) \quad \frac{\text{P's Outcomes}}{\text{P's Inputs}} > \frac{\text{O's Outcomes}}{\text{O's Inputs}}$$

An examination of these equations shows that inequity exists either when P is relatively disadvantaged (1) or relatively advantaged (2) in comparison to O. It is assumed that the subjective quality of injustice that is experienced when P is disadvantaged involves anger or resentment, whereas guilt is the experience of being relatively advantaged.

Equity theory (e.g., Adams, 1965; Walster et al., 1973) makes several further important assumptions. In the first place, equity considerations are involved whenever P and O are in a direct exchange relationship with one another, when each is involved in a relationship with a third party for instance, an employer, or when either is involved in comparing himself or herself to generalized others in similar circumstances. P and O would be in a direct exchange relationship, for example, if the action of each could provide the outcomes desired by the other. For example, if P's behavior can result in O's receiving rewarding outcomes, then P and O are in a direct exchange relationship. In one typical situation, P and O work together on some task and must apportion an award or wage between them. The issue of justice involves who should get what portion of the wage. According to the equity formulation, the person with the greater investments should receive the lion's share. A second important kind of direct exchange relationship involves "a transaction of services or goods" (Burgess & Nielsen, 1974, p. 441): for example, in exchange for P's help, P receives O's approval. The issue of justice that is said to be involved concerns whether O has returned a fair share of rewarding approval for the amount of help that P has given.

A third party or mediated exchange relationship is said to occur whenever someone other than P or O allocates outcomes to them; for instance, an employer pays two employees, P and O, for their work. In the equity formulation, this apportionment creates a sense of justice insofar as it is equitable, giving the greatest outcome to the person with the greatest relative investments. Finally, a generalized other forms the basis for equity comparisons in situations in which "In effect Person asks himself: 'Am I getting as much as other men in some respect like me would get in circumstances in some respect like mine?' " (Homans, 1961, p. 76).

According to a second assumption, inequity is a distressful condition, creating tension that motivates efforts directed towards its reduction. Presumably, the more extreme the inequity the greater the tension and the more intense the efforts to reduce it to achieve a state of equity—that is, justice. Homans (1961) argues that persons will not only seek to establish a fair and equitable exchange, but in addition will avoid activities that would "get them into unjust exchanges" (p. 233). In other words, justice as equity is seen to be a prime value involved in all human relationships.

Thirdly, it is generally assumed that an inequity based on disadvantage is more stressful than an inequity based on advantage. As Adams comments, "a certain amount of incongruity in these cases can be acceptably rationalized as 'good fortune' without attendant discomfort (1965, p. 282). In a similar vein, Homans notes that a person who is relatively advantaged "is less apt to make a prominent display of his guilt . . . Indeed a man in this happy situation is apt to find arguments convincing to himself that the exchange is not really to his advantage after all" (p. 76).

The main thrust of the equity view of justice is based on the contention that inequity creates a sense of injustice that motivates efforts to restore either actual or psychological equity. Actual equity can be restored in any number of ways, all of which involve P's "appropriately altering his own outcomes or inputs or the outcomes or inputs of the other participants" (Walster, Berscheid, & Walster, 1973, p. 154). J. Stacy Adams (1965) proposed several equity restoring possibilities: First, P may vary P's investments to bring them into equitable concord with the outcomes. For example, if P has been working hard and getting little pay as compared with O, who gets the same amount of pay for doing less, P may reduce the work investment by doing less. It also follows that if P is working less hard than O but is getting more pay, P is likely to work harder to more closely approximate an equitable condition. Second, P may vary the outcomes by demanding more pay, greater recognition or fringe benefits befitting someone with P's relative investments. Likewise, if P is overpaid for work relative to O's payment, P may restore equity by redistributing P's own outcomes.

Psychological equity involves processes of perceptual and cognitive distortion. For example, P may not credit O for O's investments by discounting them as a legitimate claim on desirable outcomes. Or people might view their own overcompensation as equitable by exaggerating their own inputs, seeing someone as brilliant as they are deserving the high pay they receive. In these and any number of other specific forms, equity is restored by resorting to distortions of investments or outcomes. We previously noted (Chapter 9), that P maintains a conception of a just world by distorting the perception of the "innocent victim" who gets negative outcomes; P believes that O deserves what O gets; O is the kind of person (i.e., one with investments) who should be punished. Recall the German citizen's response to seeing the concentration camps and its victims (Chapter 8): they must have been very bad persons to have deserved such horrible punishment.

Adherence to an equity solution to the distributive problem is argued by some (e.g., Davis & Moore, 1945) to be functionally requisite to societal survival; only by providing heavily invested persons with proportionality of outcomes, can we ensure that others will be willing to make similar investments later. For example, when the investment involves the time and effort of training to develop skills that are highly valued and necessary to a society, persons must be motivated by the anticipation of later receiving their just proportion of rewards for their effort in training and for their delay in immediate satisfaction. This type of argument was proposed by Davis and Moore in their now-classic analysis of the functionality of social stratification; it has more recently been argued by Hernstein (1973) who suggested that an egalitarian, nonequitable distribution of valued resources ignores the basic importance of genetic differences in ability:

> *If some people have a larger social impact than others, if some people have greater talents than others, then society, for its own sake, should get the able people into the consequential jobs. To do so, no one has found a more humane alternative than [differential] status and income* (p. 404).

And within social psychology proper, Walster, Berscheid, and Walster (1973) have proposed a similar, though not a genetic, functionalist support for a general principle of equity. The equitable allocation of resources (e.g., status and income) according to differential inputs is seen as a necessary tool for maintaining order, promoting social cohesion, and creating justice. Inequity produces a sense of felt injustice—for example, someone is getting more than he or she deserves or one's self is getting less—and motivates actions taken to restore equity and hence justice.

I think that we can readily recognize similarities between this functionalist argument in support of a generalized principle of equity and the late nineteenth century position termed *Social Darwinism.* Inequalities between persons in the receipt of resources were seen to be the outcome of open competition in which those who invested most by way of strength, motivation, ingenuity, skill, native talent, and so forth, received the most favored outcomes; those who were weaker and unfit to compete deserved the lesser outcomes that they received. In its later form, one with which most of us are presently familiar, this perspective stresses the need for all persons to have equal opportunities to compete openly in order to receive the unequal rewards due those who win in this fair and just competitive struggle.

A cornerstone of the democratic conception of equality derives in great part through a seemingly humane interpretation of Social Darwinism. It rests on the concept of equality of opportunity to attain inequality of outcomes, especially economic outcomes. In other words, equality of opportunity paves the way to obtain equity and thus social justice. This is the essence of our contemporary meritocratic principle that believes that all persons are deserving of an equal chance to use their energies and talents to achieve whatever inequality (but equity) of outcomes of wealth, power, and social status they can. Inequality of outcomes within a society is justified on the basis of inequality of merit (i.e., inputs) among persons who have had equality of opportunity to compete individually to achieve these outcomes. This perspective, of course, is simply another way of stating the equity principle but now stressing the importance of differences in motivation and in ability as inputs that provide just claim to differences in outcomes. And in the larger arena of the society, these outcomes, as noted, primarily involve economic wealth, social status or prestige, and power.

Much liberal-versus-conservative debate has centered on the nature of this ability-motivation factor. If it is an inherited matter of intellectual ability, then it makes little sense to speak about equalizing opportunities; persons would be genetically unequal from the beginning. However, if ability is a matter of socializing experiences, then efforts can and should be directed towards their equalization for all persons. Towards this end, many have pressed for legislation that would facilitate an equalization of opportunity, especially in the area of education; educational institutions are a major weeding-out device wherein the meritocratic philosophy is given its major thrust and wherein an equity principle that follows the competitive, marketplace ideology is reinforced.

Yet, the critics of this perspective on equality of opportunity have presented evidence arguing that such equalization has not succeeded and thus while equity prevails it is not based on an equal opportunity.

1. Evidence suggests that in spite of all social legislation created to equalize the opportunity to achieve unequal outcomes, especially wealth, the major source of inequality of wealth within a population is its inequality of inheritance. In other words, equalizing opportunities has not proved to be a satisfactory substitute for having a rich family.

Data bearing on this point come from several sources. The first directly examines the actual distribution of wealth within the United States. The second examines upward mobility among working males by comparing father's education and occupation with son's occupation. Upward mobility would be represented by sons who rose in their occupational ranking as compared with their fathers. Presumably, low mobility opportunities suggest that a person's relative placement within the society remains stable across generations. This issue is also relevant to points 2 and 3 below.

The figures that are most central to the point of economic inequality within the United States are reported in Table 10.1 which shows the income distribution among U.S. families. The data in the table are based on the following formulation. First, all American families are divided into fifths according to their income ranking. Next, each fifth is examined to see what percentage of the total income of the entire nation it receives. If total equality in distribution occurred, then each fifth of the families would receive 20 percent of the total income. Discrepancies from this 20 percent figure indicate the un-

Table 10.1. An Examination of Income Levels, 1950–1970*

	1950	1960	1970
Lowest 5th	4.5%	4.9%	5.5%
Second 5th	11.9%	12.0%	12.0%
Middle 5th	17.3%	17.7%	17.4%
Fourth 5th	23.5%	23.4%	23.7%
Top 5th	42.8%	42.1%	41.6%

*Adapted from Current Population Reports, 1971.

equal nature of the income distribution. An examination of the table indicates that the top fifth of all families receive a disproportionately high share of the national income (e.g., 41 percent in 1970) and that the bottom fifth receive a disproportionately low share (e.g., 5 percent in 1970). The table also indicates that although some shifts have occurred, in general, the inequality that existed in 1950 remains in 1970: those who had the greatest portion of the income pie in 1950 have the greatest portion of the pie in 1970.

A further breakdown of the top fifth of the families is also enlightening. The top 5 percent of U.S. families receive a disproportionate 14 percent of the national wealth; in 1947, that top 5 percent received 17 percent. Though the present figure of 14 percent is down from that of 1947, it still represents a significantly disproportionate share of the nation's wealth. Although cross-national comparisons are difficult, in one such effort (Lydall, 1968), evidence was presented suggesting that the distribution of income was most unequal in the less industrialized and poorer nations (e.g., Brazil, Chile, India, Mexico) and that the United States fell into a cluster along with Denmark, the United Kingdom, Sweden, Canada, and several other nations. This cluster, however, was of lesser overall equality than the top ranked cluster of nations which included Czechoslovakia, New Zealand, Hungry, and Australia: these nations ranked at the top of the list of nations in terms of their relative equality of income distribution.

Mobility data are reported by Blau and Duncan (1967) who provide a valuable insight into the U.S. occupational structure for males. Their data derive from an analysis of occupational mobility patterns between fathers' generation and their sons' generation among a representative sample of U.S. male workers. While their data and conclusions are many and varied, for our present purposes, it is most relevant to note the degree of correspondence they report between a father's occupation and education and a son's occupational attainment. A numerical value of 1.00 would indicate a perfect correspondence: that is, knowing the father's occupational or educational ranking would let one know the exact ranking of the son's eventual occupation. Blau and Duncan's data suggest that these two aspects of the father's life have a *primary* effect on the son's educational attainment (points 2 and 3 below); and these educational attainments, in turn, are the major source of influence over the son's first and subsequent occupation. Father's occupation correlates .28 with son's education; father's education correlates .31. Son's education, in turn correlates .39 with son's present occupational ranking. In comparison, father's occupation only correlates .11 (i.e., very weakly) with son's present occupation. Thus father's occupation and education do not directly affect son's occupation as much as they affect it through the educational opportunities provided to the son. These data are important in showing the role that family background plays in affecting children's opportunity for later upward mobility within the society's stratification systems.

Cross-national comparisons of mobility tend to suggest both national differences as well as similarities between nations in the likelihood of upward mobility. For example, Broom and Jones (1969) find that in three nations studied, the United States, Australia, and Italy, immobility rather than mobility was characteristic of those in both nonmanual and manual occupations. When interviewed for the study, 60 percent of Australian nonmanual workers, 70 percent of U.S. nonmanual workers and 69 percent of Italian nonmanual workers came from backgrounds in which their father's were also nonmanual workers. The figures for manual workers are 65 percent, 62 percent, and 76 percent respectively (i.e., for Australia, United States, and Italy). Overall mobility suggested a higher percentage for the United States as compared with the other two nations, in spite of this tendency for nonmobility to be the predominant pattern.

Another investigation of cross-national mobility patterns (Miller, 1960), suggests that the chances for substantial upward mobility are greater in the United States than the other nations studied, which include Australia, Belgium, Brazil, Denmark, Finland, France, to name but several. It would seem that although inequality may be inherited (i.e., upward mobility not very high), opportunities to break the pattern vary in different nations.

2. Additional evidence suggests that equalization of educational opportunity has not been achieved; those born unequally rich have greater opportunity to move into educational circles that will reinforce their later economic success.

3. There is also evidence that suggests a noncorrespondence between levels of individual motivation and ability (i.e., the inputs of this system) and economic outcomes. Lately we have all been made aware of the truth of this as applied particularly to blacks and women. A Carnegie Commission report examining the opportunities of women in higher education has noted, for example, that "the largest unused supply of superior intelligence in the United States is found among women."

Table 10.2. Chances for Educational Attainment as a Function of Social Origins*

	High Social Class versus Lower Social Class		
Post-high school	2.5	to	1
Access to college	4.0	to	1
Graduate from college	6.0	to	1
Attend graduate or professional school	9.0	to	1

*Adapted from Sewell, 1971.

While the data on which these conclusions are based derive from several sources including the Blau and Duncan work we previously considered, we will provide a summary of some other work both to document and further clarify these last two points. Sewell (1971) summarizes some of the key results of a study of Wisconsin high school students followed up since 1957 when they were seniors. The original sample consisted of some 10,321 seniors; in 1964, follow-up data were obtained on 87 percent of this original group. Of particular relevance to our concerns are those data that suggest the important role of social class factors (e.g., parental income, father's and mother's educational attainment, and father's occupation) as determinants of the individual's own educational attainment. These data strikingly support the contention that not everyone has an equal opportunity for educational attainment: "in their opportunities for higher education the members of this sample . . . seldom escape the influence of their social origins" (p. 796). Table 10.2 provides a summary of some of these findings.

As Table 10.2 indicates, persons from a higher social class background have 2.5 greater chance than someone from a lower background to continue with some kind of post-high school education; they have up to 9 times as great an opportunity to go on to graduate or professional school. Even when Sewell statistically controls the person's academic ability by dividing the total sample into quarters on the basis of their scores on standardized ability tests, the same trend in results is found. Even among students with the same levels of academic ability, those with higher social class backgrounds have a greater chance of obtaining higher levels of educational attainment than those with equal ability but of lower social class origins.

Further analyses from this sample indicate support for the Carnegie Commission's conclusion. Sewell finds that "the educational chances of males are uniformly greater than those of females at every [class] level" (p. 795): As Table 10.3 indicates, at both class

Table 10.3. Relative Advantages in Educational Attainment as a Function of Sex and Social Class*

	High Social Class	Lower Social Class
	Male Advantage over Female	Male Advantage over Female
Post high school	8%	26%
Access to college	20%	58%
Graduate from college	28%	86%
Attend graduate or professional school	129%	250%

*Adapted from Sewell (1971).

levels and for all kinds of educational attainments, the male advantage is greater than the female; this is especially pronounced at higher educational levels, where for example, males have from a 129 percent to a 250 percent advantage over females in attending graduate or professional schools. The trend for male advantage is especially pronounced among those whose origins are of the lower class.

Similar inequality of educational opportunity emerges when one examines figures comparing black versus white educational attainment. For example, in 1970, whereas 65 percent of blacks between 20 to 24 years of age graduated from high school, the figure for whites is 83 percent. In the age grouping, 25 to 29, 7 percent of the blacks and 17 percent of the whites have a college degree. Likewise, in 1970, of all students enrolled in colleges or universities, only 7 percent were black; only 2 percent of those enrolled in graduate schools and 2.5 percent of those enrolled in medical schools were black. Yet, blacks of the relevant age for attendence compose some 12 percent of the total population.

These findings that Sewell reports from his Wisconsin study are not unique to that state. Data reported by others, some of which has been summarized by Collins (1971), provide general confirmation for these same trends in inequality of educational opportunity as a function of inequality of beginnings (i.e., social class origins). That educational opportunity is related to opportunities for attainment of wealth, power, and prestige is also generally true. Collins reports, for example, that "approximately 60 to 70 percent of the American business elite come from upper-class and upper-middle-class families, and fewer than 15 percent from working-class families" (p. 1008).

4. A telling critique of the entire meritocratic-equity approach (e.g., Bowles & Gintis, 1973; Collins, 1971) argues that the system of crediting inputs according to differential ability serves the primary role of legitimizing the existing system of social stratification rather than providing a source for entry into or mobility within that system. In other words, equity interpretations are presented by those with vested interests in maintaining the existing stratification system as a way of legitimizing the system and thereby explaining why justice-as-equity should prevail.

    The radical attack on the equity conception is not satisfied to provide equal opportunities for all to compete openly to obtain unequal rewards; rather, it questions the entire equity principle as a vehicle that will ever allow the achievement of full equality of outcome for all; differential ability—especially as assessed by testing procedures, for example—is seen as an ideological tool for maintaining the status quo rather than as an equalizing device.

I have presented some of these wider implications of the equity conception of justice in order to provide the broadest possible context for our understanding. When we later examine various derivations of the equity model of justice that have been tested by social psychologists we should recall this context; their findings extend well beyond the laboratory within which their research has been done; and as noted, equity theory itself has something very profound to say about the human condition as it is and as it should be.

THE NORM OF EQUALITY

Proposition III indicates a second solution to the distributive problem, involving a principle of equality rather than of equity: differential investments do not provide a legitimate basis for making claims to differential outcomes. Equality does not require an homogenization of persons who may indeed be differentiated in many ways (e.g., age, sex, authority, levels of skill, years of training, etc.); rather, the notion is that these differentiations do not require differential access to resources of wealth, prestige, or power. We might say that equality of resource distribution is seen to be an ideal that is to be approached if never fully achieved in fact.

Proposition III suggests that the equality solution makes different assumptions about human nature and about what justice in human affairs actually should mean as compared with the equity formulation. We must also recognize that these two different perspectives on a just allocation of resources differ as well with respect to the specific input factors that "deserve" corresponding outcomes. Distributing resources differentially on the basis of need or with relative equality among all demands that one accord a minimal salience to the kinds of input factors that an equity formulation views as important. For example, a parent as earner may nevertheless give much to his or her children on the basis of their need rather than according to some equitable input. Or friends may share equally regardless of their variable input characteristics. In essence, an equality norm offers a different mode of dealing with the distributive problem; it does not view all human relationships in marketplace terms and thereby formulates a different conception of justice. A brief historical review of the equality perspective will provide us with a helpful context within which to better understand this alternative to the equity formulation of justice in human affairs.

A BRIEF HISTORY OF THE CONCEPT OF EQUALITY

Greek philosophy (see Brinton, 1931; and Kristol, 1968) in the age of Pericles argued for several kinds of human equality. *Isonomia* referred to an equality before the law, noting that justice is blind. This is a rather profound form of egalitarianism that exists today as a cornerstone of the U.S. legal system: the inscription over the Supreme Court Building reads, "Equal justice under law." *Isotimia* involved equal respect for all persons; *isegoria* focused on equality in the freedom of speech and thus on equality in political action. Some later conceptions were to argue as well for economic equality. The Stoic argument which helped establish the foundation for an egalitarian ethic, maintained that, unlike animals, humans possessed reason; all people were identical in this respect and thereby should receive equal treatment. Given this identity of "humanness," it was everyone's duty to treat all people alike.

Christian doctrine viewed all persons to be equal (i.e., identical) before God; the primitive church also stressed economic equality, with a communalistic sharing of goods. The Middle Ages spoke of the Fall from equality; people were still seen to be equal before God and before the Fall, but unequal after the Fall, here on earth. The Calvinistic doctrine that Max Weber saw to be a major ideological ingredient in the development of capitalism, stressed equality in that all people were required equally to follow a strict moral code, but inequality in that predestination made some persons better or more deserving than others. Calvinism further suggested that we could know these elect persons by their good and hard work. This latter view, of course, is precursor to an equity concept in which "deserving" varies according to differential work input.

The Leveller movement in England (1640–1660) emphasized human equality, including economic equality; all people were felt to be equal by their very nature; none was better than any other. This movement also laid the foundations for a representative government in which equals delegated to others—their representatives— the right to become involved in issues of governance and to exercise authority over them; these representatives, however, were never felt to be better than the people they stood in for as representatives.

The eighteenth century saw the development of most of our modern conceptions of human equality. Brinton (1931) argues that three factors that coalesced in the eighteenth century contributed to this conception. First, the development of a strong physical science argued that behind the surface diversity in physical, and by extension, human things, there lay a fundamental uniformity. This facilitated the development of a belief in the identity of humankind. Just as physical laws required simple material objects, so too did the laws of human political affairs require simple and identical objects (i.e., persons) for their application. And so persons were leveled and made equal. Second, the developing middle classes in both France and England who were achieving economic equality with the aristocracy wished to obtain social and political equality as well; thus they pressed for an egalitarian doctrine that would wipe out the privileges of noble birth. And third, the earlier Stoic notion of human equality and the Christian view of life before the Fall, was reclaimed by Rousseau and others who stressed people's natural goodness rather than their inherent selfishness. Any differentiation among persons was attributed to differential environmental treatment; thus by treating all people alike, they would turn out alike—equal and good. The American creed of "all men created equal" and the French doctrine of "liberty, equality, and fraternity" express this developing eighteenth-century egalitarianism.

It is clear from both the earlier and the eighteenth-century perspective, out of which most of our contemporary Western views have been derived, the equality is the natural state from which inequality is a deviation. In that all persons are of one species, there is no meaningful basis for differentiating them in terms of the resources each should properly receive. It was the fall from this utopian state and the emergence of society, with its differentiations and subsequent hierarchy, that produced an alternative conception of social justice founded on an equity principle: "equal men should get equal rewards." This latter is an alternative ideology concerning the proper solution to the distributive problem; for those adopting the equality position, equity is seen to be the nonutopian present human condition away from which we ought to be moving, rather than a justice-filled condition of bliss and social harmony.

The success of the Western tradition lay in its effort to eliminate the traditional, usually familial bases for human inequality. Its failure (according to some) was in its inability to reclaim full human equality and its substitution of an equity principle for egalitarianism, justifying unequal resource distribution on the basis of unequal investment points of worth, intellect, ability, and so forth.

With respect to certain kinds of equality, the Western democratic tradition has moved towards an equality among all persons. As noted, the principle of equality before the law is the foundation of the system of legal justice, even if the principle is not always honored in its application. If we maintained that the wealthy person or one of political influence should thereby not be accorded the same legal treatment as the poor person, because the former's inputs into the system were greater than the latter's—that is, an equity argument—our sense of justice would be violated. That equality before the law is often violated, as criminal statistics and some recent political events will attest (e.g., it seems likely that the overrepresentation of the poor and the black among prison populations is because of the unequal administration of legal justice), speaks to the failure thus far for this form of egalitarianism to be fully achieved.

Equality within the political arena forms another founding principle of Western democracies, even if, as with equality before the law, the principle is often more honored in the breach than in its observance. Many among us would find a political equity statement to be a violation of our sense of justice; yet, not many years ago political equity and hence justice involved denying women the right to vote. Political equality stresses both universal suffrage and a representative form of democracy, a one-person, one-vote system. We need not have much historical perspective, however, to see how this principle has been violated, in particular (and again) among the poor and minority groups. Yet, it is the pursuit of political equality rather than political equity that conveys a sense of justice.

It is within this arena that the Stoics' early principle, in modern dress, comes to life. While granting differences among persons in their political wisdom, knowledge, sophistication, understanding, or whatever, the essence of the democratic perspective is its argument that in spite of such differences among persons, there exists some absolute quality of being human that grants to each person a right to participate in government through voting. This view suggests that justice is embodied in equality of political action rather than in equity.

Most of us would find it unjust to argue that a person with greater monetary or intellectual investments should rightly have more votes than the poorer or less intelligent person (or would we?). Likewise, few of us would see it as just if persons' social equality, their receipt of dignity and respect, were to follow an equity rather than an equality principle. Most humanitarian protests historically and today have been based on a doctrine of human equality in the social arena, where such inputs as race, religion, sex, and such are not to be taken as legitimate bases for differential social treatment. Again, this is not to deny the unfortunate realities in which social equity more often seems to prevail in practice than social equality. It is to note, however, the transformation in the concept of justice that derives from stating that such a condition is just, right, and proper.

The Stratification Debate

The preceding discussion has suggested that equality conceptions have a substantial history in human affairs, and form the backbone of many Western conceptions of justice. Yet, the major thrust of the Western economic perspective supports a view of justice in terms of equity (e.g., a meritocracy) that serves to legitimate the economic status quo.

The following discussion builds on a far reaching debate within the stratification literature; the arguments raised in this continuing debate help us better understand the meaning and role of equity and equality solutions to the distributive problem; thus we gain a better understanding as well of the broad context within which the social psychological research findings that we will later examine occur.

The essential distinction between an equity and an equality solution to the distributive problem and to social justice has been captured by the debate in the literature on stratification between Davis and Moore (1945) and Melvin Tumin (1953; 1963). Tumin's argument is especially important for the social psychological investigator as it opens to reasonable doubt the inevitability of the base upon which the equity model of justice is founded. Tumin's position can best be summarized in his own words:

> However plagued current societies may be with the demand for unequal rewards for so-called unequal work, and however relatively successful some of those societies may be compared to others, we surely cannot ignore the fact that these cultural orientations and social forms have arisen in very specific historical contexts ... we have never seriously explored the possibilities of alternative forms that might yield much more of the desired values and ideals with much less stratification than is now being practiced (1963, p. 23).

Recall that both equity theory in social psychology and the functionalist approach to social stratification (as proposed by Davis and Moore) maintain that it is functional to a social system to provide unequal rewards for unequal contributions to those tasks that are necessary to insure societal maintenance and survival. In order to insure societal survival, tasks that must be performed and for which few actors are available or for which substantial, effortful training is involved, must receive unequal rewards in order to guarantee that persons will be motivated to undergo the long training period necessary for taking on these kinds of tasks. Inequality, in other words, is fundamental to all social systems; an equity view of justice is right and proper even if all persons will not rest easy with their own inequality: persons whose functional role importance is greater should receive greater rewards. In equity theory terms, the greater one's inputs, now measured by the functional importance of one's role, the greater should be one's outcomes relative to other actors within the same social system.

Tumin questions both the avoidability and the functionality of the kinds of inequality that the Davis and Moore thesis maintains is both inevitable (and hence nonavoidable) and functional. He endeavors to demonstrate that inequality in resource distribution is not necessarily functional to societal survival or maintenance, and that inequality is generally avoidable in most social arrangements. Thus the presence of inequality does not mark a necessary or a functional arrangement that is in some sense natural to or fitting human nature, but rather an arrangement that has historical, ideological, political, and cultural roots. Applying this to equity theory, the argument would be that equity in human relationships, though it may adequately characterize much of contemporary life, is not necessarily natural, but rather is best understood as the outcome of historical, political, ideological and cultural factors, and in particular, the marketplace economic system of Western capitalism.

Both Margaret Mead's pioneering studies of cooperation and competition among primitive peoples (1937) and Ruth Benedict's work on the concept of cultural synergy to which we alluded in Chapter 2, provide some empirical basis for several of Tumin's contentions. Although it would take us too far afield to probe the details of either Mead's or Benedict's works, it is important for us to note that cultures—even fairly complex ones, though admittedly not industrialized societies—have existed in which equality and sharing are more highly valued than individual initiative and individual accumulation of wealth, power, or prestige. And as even our brief overview of more recent analyses has suggested, not all industrialized nations are the same with respect to their inequality of income distribution; some seem to approach an egalitarian ideal more closely than others.

Sources of Inequality. Tumin outlines five sources of social inequality and then demonstrates how each is not the natural-functional-unavoidable state of human social life. These sources generally parallel the inputs of relevance to equity-theorists.

1. Differentiations based on roles (e.g., father, mother, boss, etc.) or attribute specification (e.g., woman, man, etc.)
2. Orderings based on persons' intrinsic characteristics (e.g. taller, prettier, quicker, etc.) or by roles' intrinsic characteristics (e.g., difficult, dangerous, clean, skilled, etc.).
3. Ranking by moral conformity, referring to the ordering of behavior based on the degree to which it is morally acceptable.
4. Ranking by functional contribution, referring both to orderings based on the degree to which behavior or roles exemplify cultural ideals, and to orderings based on the functional contribution of roles in the achievement of necessary social goals.
5. Rankings based on differentials in property, power, and prestige, referring to the continuity over time of inequalities once initiated.

This fifth source of social inequality stresses the generally observed trend for the rich to get richer: that is, for inequalities at one point in time to persist into other points in time. The clear implication is that the inequality we note in a given society may in no way be the result of the rational or equitable allocation of resources to those performing functionally important roles, but rather to the diffusion of inequality via kinship lines (e.g., inheritance of wealth).

It is not necessary for us here to recapitulate Tumin's specific argument regarding the avoidability and the functionality of each of the preceding sources of inequality. For each source his overall thesis is that the inequality we now see, although it is considered equitable, is in no way demonstratably natural or necessary. Thus, the sense of equitable justice that may prevail for any of these sources is a function of history, ideology, or in many cases, the deliberate devices of elites seeking to justify and preserve their own advantageous situation.

> In a culture that trains its people to be motivated by differential rewards and places high value on such differential rewards ... stratification is likely to be at a maximum ... under other cultural circumstances the important cultural tasks can be and will be filled by appropriate personnel without significant differential evaluation and material reward, or, at least, with much less enduring forms of such invidious distinction. To contend otherwise would be to insist that no other motivational schemes and no other cultural themes regarding work and performance are possible, except at great strain to human nature ... Tasks may be highly unequal in many regards without involving judgments of unequal social worth and unequal entitlement to rewards, if people are socialized to view matters in this way (1963, p. 23).

While the preceding passage focuses primarily on inequality deriving from source 4—functional differentiation—the same argument applies with equal vigor to the other sources.

The justice of equity is neither natural nor for that matter even functionally required. That it may prevail in a given culture, at a given time in its history, and among particular persons within that culture, is an important piece of information of social history. Egalitarian socialization, when, where, and if present would override equity pressures and present a countervailing cultural and psychological force that would clearly reveal the nature of the equity-equality solutions to the distributive problem. In other words, existing stratification systems and the applicability of an equity rule to solving distributive issues are not inevitabilities carved in granite or in human nature. But where equity solutions arise and take on special value, for whatever reasons (e.g., maintenance of the elite's status quo), they operate with a forcefulness that may make them seem to be inevitable. And for the person in the street socialized into the equity system, these equity solutions seem completely and irrevocably natural.

Two Conceptions of Justice: Some Systematic Research

We now have sufficient background material to provide a context within which to better understand the empirical investigations of justice that social psychologists and others have undertaken. At this point, it should be apparent that support for an equity conception of justice is more a statement of existing cultural arrangements and preferences than an analysis of something more fundamental in human nature.

If justice prevails when outcomes are allocated in proportion to inputs as the equity formulation suggests, then injustice will occur whenever P gets greater or lesser outcomes than P's investments warrant in comparison with O. To overcompensate someone should prove as distressing as to undercompensate them (but see p. 446 for an exception). The former condition should produce distress from guilt or perhaps even from a fear of retaliation, being caught with more than one rightfully deserves. The latter condition should produce distress from anger or resentment over not receiving one's just rewards. On the other hand, receiving outcomes that are comparatively proportional to one's inputs should be the prime condition of justice and hence should not create distress.

A clear and direct test of the preceding equity idea was reported in 1974 by Austin and Walster. Their subjects were either appropriately compensated for their efforts, receiving an amount of pay they expected as experimental subjects, overcompensated, or undercompensated. Measures of their mood were obtained. Results indicated that "Subjects who were treated equitably were more content and satisfied than were subjects who were either over or underrewarded." It is important for the equity formulation of justice, that overcompensation produces the same distress of injustice as does undercompensation.

Homans (1961) reports several field studies that demonstrate general support for the equity formulation of justice. One study examined two kinds of workers in the accounting department of a utilities company. Cash posters were responsible for recording information regarding customer accounts, while ledger clerks were to deal with all other matters involving customer accounts and service. Within the company, the typical line of promotion was from cash poster to ledger clerk; the latter job tended to have more variety and to be viewed as involving greater responsibility than the cash poster's position. Yet, both received the same pay. As Homans notes:

The investments of the ledger clerks were greater than those of the cash posters: they had put in more time in the company; they had learned to do a more responsible job, one that the cash posters could not do. Distributive justice accordingly demanded that their rewards should be greater than the posters', and some of them were: their work was more varied and interesting. But not all were: they got the same pay as the cash posters, and they were allowed even less autonomy . . . (p. 240).

The response to this injustice was noted primarily in the complaints of the ledger clerks, in particular their concerns that they should be paid more than the posters, given the nature of their investments in their job. The conclusion that Homans reached on the basis of this investigation was that "Only when investments and rewards were all in line would distributive justice reign" (p. 241). In this example, while an alignment existed between investments and outcomes as regards the intrinsic interest of the ledger clerks' job, that was not sufficient to overcome the unjust alignment between their investment of both seniority and responsibility and their pay as compared with the cash posters.

In a different field study involving cashiers and bundlers in a supermarket chain, Homans reports both attitudinal and performance results that are consistent with equity theory formulations of justice. On a comparative basis, the bundler's job is inferior to the cashier's; regular bundlers receive less pay and generally have less responsibility and authority, and more monotony in their work. Homans reports that when employees were asked if they had to help out as a bundler, what kind of a person they would most prefer to bundle for, they replied by indicating someone whose "social investments" of regular work and background were higher than the workers' own. Their preference was for a status arrangement in which persons with the greatest investments should be accorded the job with the greatest rewarding outcomes—namely, the cashier's job—and the person with lesser investments should be given the lesser job of bundler. Discomfort was seen to result from an inequitable arrangement—for example, one in which the bundler had greater investments especially of age and education when compared with the cashier. Homans also reports that misaligned bundler-cashier teams actually performed less efficiently as measured by the number of person-hours used per $100 of sales than equitably aligned teams. In other words, an unjust arrangement led to decreased productivity.

The research that Homans brings to support the equity formulation of justice derives primarily from field investigations. J. S. Adams (1965) has undertaken a series of laboratory studies testing various components of the equity formulation. His research is valuable in suggesting how relative overcompensation can result in P modifying behavior in order to reestablish equity. Recall that Autin and Walster's research showed how distressing overcompensation can be. Presumably, one way to restore the equity that overcompensation creates is to increase one's work investments—for example, by working harder. Adams and Rosenbaum (1962) report a laboratory study in which one group was appropriately paid for their work, given their qualifications, while a second group was relatively overpaid, given their qualifications. Both groups were paid $3.50 per hour for their work, but the second group was made to feel that this was too much considering their lack of experience or training for their job. Results indicated that the overcompensated group averaged 42 percent higher work productivity than the appropriately compensated group. By increasing their productivity, they brought their inputs into equitable alignment with their outcomes.

In order to evaluate the possibility that P's increased work was motivated by equity considerations rather than by feeling underqualified and worried about job security, thus working hard in order to keep the job, Adams and Jacobon (1964) established a different experimental condition in which a presumably underqualified person would be equitably paid: for example, because you are comparatively unqualified to receive a piece rate of $.30 for your work, you will be paid $.20. An examination of the quality of the work produced by the appropriately paid underqualified workers as compared with the overpaid underqualified workers indicated a significantly better quality of work in the latter than the former group. The argument that Adams and Jacobson propose is that both groups of subjects, being underqualified for their jobs, presumably experience the same sense of job insecurity; however, only the overpaid group experiences inequity between investments and outcomes and thus is motivated to reduce that inequity by increasing their work.

In all fairness, it must be noted that there exists a continuing criticism of this preceding work, with Lawler (1968) in particular suggesting and experimentally demonstrating that it is unlikely that insecurity was ever really eliminated from motivating P's performance, thus making an unequivocal confirmation of the equity formulation not possible. Lawler and several of his colleagues, for example, demonstrated how informing subjects that they would not be rehired, thereby presumably eliminating all thoughts of job insecurity, did indeed produce performances consistent with equity theory for the first session of the experimental job situation but failed to do so in a later session. Lawler notes that:

*One explanation for this could be that after the overpaid
subjects were allowed to come back for the second time they
felt relatively secure about holding their job, and hence they
began to behave like the qualified subjects who had felt
secure about holding their job all along* (p. 600).

Essentially, it is Lawler's argument that insofar as it is almost impossible to eliminate the worry of job insecurity and its implications
for a person's sense of self-esteem (i.e., I am a good worker), there
will always be a confounding between equity motivation to work
harder and the motivation to work harder that derives from the
person's efforts to protect one's job and to think well of one's self as
a worker.

Direct Exchange   In addition to the preceding work of Homans and
of Adams on third-party exchanges and justice, there exists an important body of research dealing with more direct exchange relationships involving the allocation of joint rewards.

Various laboratory investigations undertaken by Leventhal and
his associates (e.g., Leventhal, et al., 1969; 1970, 1972; 1973) provide
an examination of the equity principle in these kinds of situations.
Justice as equity is said to be maintained when, for example, P
allocates greater rewards to those who have worked harder than
those who have done less. Several studies have confirmed this general principle. Leventhal and Lane (1970) provided their subjects
with information regarding their own and their partner's task performance, (in actuality a fictituous work partner), and asked the
subjects to allocate the reward that their two-person group earned.
It was expected that subjects would allocate less to the work partner
whose performance was inferior to their own but would take less for
themselves when their own performance was reported to be inferior. The results for male subjects were generally congruent with
these equity theory predictions, as subjects "took more than half the
reward when their performance was superior to that of their partner and less than half when their performance was inferior" (p.
314). Female subjects decided to combine a concern with equity by
taking less than half the reward when their own performance was
inferior, and a concern for their partner's welfare, by taking only a
little more than half the reward when their performance was superior.

Further interesting and informative exceptions to a simple application of an equity norm have also been uncovered. Leventhal, Michaels, and Sanford (1972), for example, demonstrated how
interpersonal conflict is minimized by somewhat increasing the reward given to the worst performer of a pair, in apparent belief that

those are the persons most likely to make trouble. A trade-off of sorts then exists in which a justice of equity yields slightly to a justice of equality in order to prevent too much conflict. This seems also to describe the females' behavior in the Leventhal and Lane study.

Leventhal, Michaels, and Sanford also report the effects of maintaining secrecy about outcomes on the nature of the allocation made. Their data indicate greater adherence to strict equity when participants' outcomes were kept secret than with full disclosure. Thus, the difference between rewards allocated to the best as compared with the worst performer was greater when there was secrecy about the allocation than when everyone knew about it. This laboratory finding has its parallel in the organizational practice of maintaining secrecy regarding employee salaries; secrecy can be seen as a means whereby equity can be obtained without inducing excessive interpersonal conflict. What is so fascinating about this particular study by Leventhal and his colleagues is the degree to which tactics that violate strict equity are needed to create a sense of felt justice. If equity theory were the total picture of justice, then surely persons would have little need to allocate secretly or to elevate the payoffs to the less productive worker. It would appear that subjects sensed that low payoffs, even if deserved according to an equity formulation, were likely to produce a sense of dissatisfaction.

Leventhal, Weiss, and Buttrick (1973) report another factor that is relevant in restricting the degree to which strict equity is sought in a reward allocation situation. Their research demonstrates that P will violate the equity principle by disregarding performance inputs in allocating greater rewards to those persons who are felt better able to use them. Thus, although two O's might have similar inputs, P violates equity by giving greater rewards to the O who is more likely to make good use of it, based on that O's past use of similar rewards.

Leventhal and Michaels provide support for still a further factor influencing equity. Their research demonstrates how external constraints on O's inputs lead P to expect lesser outcomes and thereby to reward O with outcomes proportional to P's expectations for O's performance. For example, if P knows that O's performance is constrained by a stringent time limit, then a person producing a little in a short time is held to be equivalent to a person producing a great deal in a longer time; both should receive equal payment. On the other hand, when both produce the same amount but one takes longer to do so than the other, rewards are allocated equitably such that the longer-time period is taken to mean lower inputs of motivation, for example, and thereby deserving lesser rewards.

IMPLICATIONS OF JUSTICE AS EQUITY VERSUS EQUALITY

Perhaps the best and most direct statement outlining the interpersonal implications of justice as equity or equality is presented by Lerner (1974): "Unit relations require parity [i.e., equality], while nonunit interdependence elicits equity considerations" (p. 549). Briefly, a unit relation exists whenever two or more persons perceive themselves to be part of a cooperating team, community, family, or unit: " 'One for all and all for one' and 'Share and share alike' are the normative expressions of this form of justice" (Lerner, p. 539). Nonunit relations, in which persons view themselves more atomistically and separate from others, are said to promote the institution of an equity perspective of justice in which sharing is accomplished as a function of differential inputs.

While most of the laboratory studies of justice involve persons in a nonunit relationship, thereby loading the case in favor of an equity distribution, several investigations shed some light on this unit-nonunit difference. Lerner systematically varied the degree to which persons felt themselves to be in a unit or nonunit relationship by telling some of the subjects that they were "like a team," finding equity in the allocation of rewards among nonunit persons and equality among unit-related persons. In 1967, Morgan and Sawyer reported an investigation in which subjects involved in bargaining were either friends or first-time acquaintances. The authors contended that friends who wish to maintain a relationship would seek to share more equally than they would seek to fit investments to outcomes. In other words, friends, forming a unit relationship, should be more inclined to adopt an equality strategy than non-friends who would be more concerned with issues of equity. Their data, however, suggested a preference for equality among both friends and non-friends; subjects with initially greater investments and thereby greater likelihood of taking the lion's share of the prize were willing to forego such a share in favor of an equal distribution.

Whether they view greater unit bonds with others or are more concerned with the interpersonal aspects of situations, females appear to more generally prefer an equality distribution to an equity distribution. Some of Vinacke's (1959) work on coalition formation in triads suggested that males are oriented towards individual gain for themselves at any cost—termed an *exploitative strategy*—whereas females are more concerned with establishing harmonious interpersonal relationships—termed an *accommodative strategy*. It is more accommodative to seek an equality of allocation than an equity of allocation. Recall that Leventhal and Lane report sex differences in the division of a group prize that are consistent with this view. Leventhal and Anderson (1970) likewise report a similar sex difference.

Benton's (1971) investigations of the development of equity or equality conceptions of justice demonstrates a similar sex difference. Boys preferred equity solutions and girls equality solutions; consistent with Lerner's perspective on unit relationships, equality was especially important to girls in situations involving their friends. Benton reports the girls as being distressed with an equity solution.

Weinstein, DeVaughn, and Wiley (1969), noting that "a fair repayment of [an] obligation implies equality of status" (p. 1), provide experimental results that show that males seemed more concerned than females with the status implications of their behavior. Through an equity choice males sought to preserve their own relative status advantage; females sought to preserve interpersonal harmony through an equal allocation of resources.

Several investigators have argued that an equality formulation of justice may be adopted and hence inequity maintained for its longer-term benefits to both P and to O. Arnold Kahn's (1972) research demonstrates, for example, a preference for equality of allocation over equity in a direct exchange relationship between P and O. Kahn notes that: "One reason for this preference for equality in direct exchanges may be a desire to maintain a relatively equal-status relationship and assure continuation of a profitable exchange" (p. 122). The status differential that equity produces may prove disruptive to a continuing relationship; that is, if according to an equity formulation, P deserves and actually takes more than O, O may break off the relationship, thus depriving P of what might have been a more rewarding, continuing relationship. So, in the long run, P may get more by accepting an equal distribution; this should be especially the case if there are no alternative relationships with more rewarding possibilities.

A direct experimental test of this idea was reported in 1974 by Burgess and Nielsen. They created a series of separate experiments which demonstrated that subjects would remain in an inequitable direct exchange relationship if that relationship were more rewarding to them than any alternatives that were available. As the authors note: "The occurrence of continued inequitable exchange directly challenges equity and balance theories which predict an effort to reduce inequity even though the effort may be costly to the participants" (p. 438). Although the experimental context was different, a similar conclusion was reached by Kahn, Hottes, and Davis (1971), at least for their male subjects who acted to maximize their own long-term benefit, choosing a strategy of sharing and cooperation if this would accomplish such maximization or one of competition and nonsharing if this was required.

Calling on the concepts employed some years ago by Thibaut and Kelley (1959) in their analysis of small group behavior as social exchange, we note that persons will typically continue in relationships that are less than absolutely satisfying because they provide better outcomes than available alternatives. Thibaut and Kelley introduced the concept, comparison level (CL) to indicate a standard level of outcomes that P employs in evaluating how good a specific outcome is. The concept, comparison level for alternatives (CL-alt) is said to be the standard against which P evaluates outcomes in one relationship in comparison with other relationships that are available, including the alternative of no relationship at all. According to their theoretical statement, P will remain in a relationship that provides outcomes below the CL as long as those outcomes are still greater than P's CL-alt. Thus, P may persist in an inequitable exchange that is less than satisfactory (outcomes less than P's CL) but still greater than P could obtain elsewhere.

A related view maintains that it is important to differentiate between a "comparison equity," an "own equity" and an "other equity." In seeking equity with O, P is concerned with the issue of comparison equity. In seeking an equity between P's present situation and an internal standard derived from past experiences (i.e., CL in Thibaut and Kelley's terminology), P is concerned with the issue of own equity. Finally, P may compare O's investment-outcome ratio with P's own standards regarding equity (i.e., other equity). Lane and Messé (1972) created an experimental situation that would permit an examination of these several different facets of equity. Their data suggest that while P's satisfaction was indeed a function of comparison equity, as the standard equity theory would suggest, the picture is complicated by the finding that comparison equity could be violated as long as own equity or other equity was maintained: that is, P was satisfied with the distribution of rewards as long as the rewards were commensurate with P's expectations, even if the distribution was comparatively inequitable.

The point of the several preceeding studies is to argue that rather than abhorring inequity, P may abhor getting little that is satisfying out of any allocative arrangement. Thus P will accept getting less than equity demands, even sharing equally, if that is better than any alternatives that P is able to obtain; or P will be satisfied with getting a comparatively inequitable cut of the pie as long as that cut provides outcomes at or above P's CL. As Burgess and Nielsen note, in fact P may not feel satisfaction with an inequitable allocation yet will not act to change it. To predict to this latter consequence, we would have to know about alternative possibilities that would provide even better outcomes for P. It may be said that P is willing to operate according to a "bird-in-hand" principle, preferring to maintain an inequitable but known exchange to an unknown future exchange that may or may not be as equitable as the present one.

It is reasonable to speculate even further: what Lerner views as a unit-forming relationship, one that contributes to lesser equity and greater equality, may itself be enhanced by the awareness that P has more to gain by remaining in a relationship with O than is available in any existing alternatives. Thus, a unit relationship may not simply create the conditions for imposing an equality conception of justice but also may emerge as a consequence of an inequitable exchange that is nevertheless more rewarding than P's CL-alt. To put this in another way, the absence of rewarding alternatives may lead P to prefer equality over equity in the hopes that a more equalized exchange will promote a continuation of the rewarding relationship. It may well be that unit relationships (e.g., friendships) evolve on the basis of investing in long-term equal exchanges rather than treating each encounter according to an equity principle, thereby perhaps thwarting the development of the relationship itself. The understanding of justice in human affairs is a complex matter. As we have seen, the equity formulation is too simplistic in that it overlooks varieties of motivations that seem to govern human relationships: life is not simply a marketplace, even in marketplace-oriented social systems.

Differentiating and Integrating Tendencies

Where justice is defined in terms of an equity principle, differentiations between persons are maintained and enhanced; where justice is defined in terms of an equality principle, differentiations are played down and bases for integration are sought and emphasized. We could also phrase this in the reverse, noting that whenever conditions make differentiations between persons salient, then equity considerations will thereby increase; however, where conditions minimize such differences, equality considerations will prevail. The following diagram captures the circularity of these relationships:

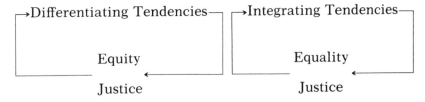

Lerner induced integrating tendencies by means of the team-setting instructions he employed; Morgan and Sawyer accomplished a similar effect by selecting pairs of friends for their research. Kahn's work as well as that of Burgess and Nielsen suggested how P's efforts to maintain an existing, rewarding exchange might lead P to accept an inequitable exchange, with Kahn demonstrating a general preference for equality. As we have previously noted, Leventhal, Michaels, and Sanford's work implied that equity could prove interpersonally costly and so tactics were evolved either to prevent an equitable distribution from gaining too much publicity or to violate strict equity. This concern with the interpersonal consequences of equity is congruent with the several preceding interpretations. Combined they suggest some strong reservations concerning the equity formulation of justice. At least, this perspective suggests that pragmatic considerations make a strict equity view of justice inappropriate. We hasten to note, however, that egalitarian concerns are not necessarily motivated by humanitarian concerns as much as by practical considerations. Thus, the more powerful may accept less than is equitable not because they believe that others deserve more but rather because that is the best way to guarantee that they will continue to get their extra share. Beneath the blindfolds of justice there may yet lurk a pragmatic eye.

The Dialectic.   Perhaps what is needed is a dialectical principle rather than an either-or choice. The question may not be whether persons are motivated by equity or by equality conceptions of justice and fairness; nor even the conditions under which one *or* the other will predominate. Rather, it may be that both conceptions exist, and justice in human affairs is the result of a balancing between these two tendencies. Either extreme violates a conception of proper justice. The research hypothesis would be that as either the differentiating tendencies of equity or the homogenizing tendencies of equality were to become excessive, the opposing process would enter as a kind of self-corrective feedback circuit.

The interpretation of a laboratory experiment conducted by Brandon (1965) is consistent with this dialectical perspective as is the interpretation of several previous studies in which allocation according to strict equity was violated in order to preserve interpersonal harmony. Brandon created small laboratory groups composed of two males differing in age and year in school (graduate student versus college juniors) and one female sophomore. The three were assigned different roles on a task they were given; the roles varied in terms of responsibility and intrinsic interest as well as in their value to the group. The top role, for example, involved a difficult cutting and planning activity whereas the low-status role simply involved folding pieces of paper to be used later. In addition to their job roles, these three individuals were chosen, presumably according to test scores, to serve either in a leadership or understudy role in a later task situation. Brandon so arranged the manner in which tasks and roles on the present task and future task were assigned so that in some groups one person (the graduate male) received all the valued positions while another person (the female) received nothing of value. An assignment of this sort was consistent with an equitable apportionment of jobs according to relevant investments; that is, it was fitting to an equity model that the more qualified graduate male should receive the most valued job and be given leadership on the later task, that the second male be next in line, and be understudy on the later task, and that the female undergraduate receive the least valuable assignments. Yet, groups arranged in this manner were less satisfied than groups with other, even inequitable arrangements. Brandon reasoned that too much equity proved disturbing to the one group; it was simply not fair, even though it was equitable, for one person to get everything and someone else nothing.

Although the preceding investigation does not directly test a dialectical model of justice, it nevertheless offers us a picture consistent with this view. Too much equity in this case and perhaps too much equality in another case create injustice in human relationships, motivating efforts to create a changed state of affairs. And in the view taken here, the change is not towards greater equity or greater equality, but rather involves an increase in the opposing tendency. Thus, too much equity is balanced by moving towards a more equal allocation of resources; too much equality is balanced by moving towards a more equitable allocation of resources. People do not abhor inequity; people abhor an imbalance between equity and equality, between differentiating and integrating tendencies. It is the synthesis of these two opposites into a higher order state of affairs that is sought. The just choice then, is not twofold, but only two facets of one whole. The student will note a similarity between this perspective on justice and our consideration in Chapter 2 of the two opposing interaction tendencies of complementary and symmetrical schismogenesis; too the reader should be able to relate this concept of justice with Bales's analysis of the balancing between instrumental and socioemotional tendencies within small group interaction (Chapter 5).

ALGIMANTAS KEZYS, S.J.

THE PERSON AND MODERNISM

11

The encounter between what C. Wright Mills (1959) termed personal troubles and public issues, which we met in Chapter 2, has been a continuing theme of this text. We have seen the subtle and none-too subtle connections between larger societal trends and the personal joys and sorrows that we all confront in our daily lives. Facing what seem to be the vast complexities and rapid pace of modern life, many persons speak of those good old days when life presumably existed on a simpler, more human scale. Great social thinkers of the past and of today have sought to formulate analyses of the large historical shifts in social life between the premodern and the present modern era and to examine the consequence of those shifts for our lifes (e.g., Durkheim, 1933; Mumford, 1956; Redfield, 1947; 1963; Tönnies, 1887; Weber, 1947). Though their terminology differs and some specific details of their formulations vary, there is general agreement in their broad stroked portrayal of these grand societal transformations from *Gemeinschaft* to *Gesellschaft,* from community to mass society. And most agree that the transformation has been a double-edged sword, at once freeing people from the bonds of kin and tradition that formally held them in place and gave them guidance while casting them adrift alienated, and with a freedom from which, in Fromm's (1941) terms, people now seek escape.

Basically, trends in the growth, diversity, and concentration of population, in particular urbanization, and in the growth of technology and industrialization, including the transformation in the forms of relation to the economic system, have been posited as the prime movers of the transition from community to society and of the many transformations in the lives and psychological character of modern persons. Special attention has been given to each of the following:

1. changes in the patterns of social participation, involvement, and commitment, from active concern to alienated powerlessness;
2. changes in the bonds that tie persons together, from interpersonal attachments founded on primary intimate associations of kin and family, to the more segmented, impersonal bonding of secondary association;

3. changes in the form of social organization from small-scale household groupings to large-scale bureaucratic organizations;
4. changes that produced a mass culture, a form of mass standardization in the midst of apparent diversity.

Melvin Seeman's (1959; 1972) analysis of the concept of alienation captures what many have assumed to be the major consequences of modernism for the individual.

1. *Powerlessness.* The world becomes a place that is too nonresponsive to be influenced by individual needs or desires. Persons are alienated through a loss of control over those forces that shape their life.
2. *Meaninglessness.* The world is experienced as being beyond one's ken; the future is experienced as unpredictable; purpose and direction seem missing.
3. *Normlessness.* The normal regulators of one's behavior seem no longer to hold; one feels unbound by convention or by standards for achieving goals; even once socially unapproved means are accepted.
4. *Cultural Estrangement.* Values that once helped integrate the society are no longer held; persons seek other goals, rejecting those once favored. Cultural roots and traditional heritage are abandoned; there is a loss of common aims and shared values.
5. *Self-Estrangement.* The person becomes separated even from self; work that is unfulfilling and unrewarding is carried out; life itself becomes an unfulfilling, unrewarding ritual.
6. *Social Isolation.* Persons come to expect little inclusion in others' lives and worlds. A feeling of loneliness and despair emerges, of being a stranger in a strange land.

These are said to be the urban alienations, the result of the dramatic transformation of society that one analyst maintained has "produced in the realm of the social the equivalent of a mutation in the realm of the genetic" (Hauser, 1969, p. 8). This mutation is hypothesized to be the result of population explosion, diversification, and implosion (i.e., urban concentration). These results in turn are hypothesized to have produced the chaotic society with its myriad problems ranging from housing, pollution, and resource management to mental illness, crime, and delinquency, to social disorganization, isolation, and the other alienations of modern life. This is Louis Wirth's (1938) classic portrait of "urbanism as a way of life" characterized by an absence of intimate personal relationships and a prevalance of secondary rather than primary bonds. Wirth viewed society as having segmented relationships in which persons relate to one another as parts—that is, as roles—rather than as whole persons; a world of nonpermanence with mobility leading to short-term bonds, instability, and a sense of insecurity; a culture having a mass-like quality in which individual needs must yield to the more generalized demands of the heterogeneous masses.

To help us gain some perspective on these hypothesized connections, it will be helpful for us to examine briefly the nature of the population and technology shifts that are presumed to have triggered our entry into the modern age with its presumed manifold consequences.

POPULATION

We can readily summarize the statistical picture regarding both the population explosion and its implosion or concentration. World population growth has not only increased in absolute size, but as importantly, the rate of growth has itself increased. For example, where it took 350 years—from the time of Columbus to 1850—for the world's population to reach 1 billion, it took only 75 years for that billion to double, some 37 years for the figure to reach 3 billion, some 13 years for nearly 4 billion to be reached, and a projection of some 7 years before 5 billion will be the world's total population. Estimates are that world population will double in 58 years in developed areas of the world, but in only 32 years in the less developed areas of South and East Asia, Africa, and Latin America.

As the sociologist Hauser (1970) has noted, it is not only numbers that have increased, but density as well. He esimates that a density of 1 would be an appropriate density figure for the United States prior to European entry upon the scene. He estimated a density of 50 for the United States in 1960. But more importantly, he notes the implosive concentration of population. He suggests that 8,000 is the probable density for the average central U.S. city, with Chicago having a density figure of 17,000, and 75,000 roughly the density for New York City. Trends in population movement add further to this picture of urban concentration. In 1790 95 percent of the U.S. population was rural with 85 percent involved in agriculture. By 1900, 40 percent lived in places of 2,500 or more and 60 percent were involved in nonagricultural work. In 1960, 70 percent of the population of the United States was urban, occupying only 1 percent of the total land area; the rural 30 percent occupied the remaining 99 percent of land area. Worldwide projections suggest that at present rates of growth and urban movement, 42 percent of the people in the world will live in places of 100,000 persons or more; this contrasts with the 20 percent figure worldwide for 1960 and the 1.7 percent figure for 1900.

The density figures are brought even more into our awareness through Hauser's examination of the number of personal contacts that are possible given a particular population density. He notes that in pre-European America, a person could move within a 10-mile circle and potentially could encounter 313 other persons. Today, that same person can make some 15,699 contacts in the same 10-mile area. In a typical central city, 2.5 million contacts are possible; Chicago alone permits over 5.3 million contacts while in Manhattan, a person has the potential of making over 23.5 million contacts!

The Implications of Density. It is clearly implied, if not always directly stated, that the population density of modern urban life is itself a major contributory cause to the "ills" of persons. If we pause to think about it, I think that we can see how difficult a research issue this hypothesized relationship really is. In the first place, surely we must distinguish between the physical reality of population density, as reflected in the statistical protrait that Hauser has provided, and the psychological experience of density. Density is a function of both numbers of persons and space in which they can move about. While we might expect that many people placed together into little space would provide the most densely populated and stressful arrangement, it is also possible that as a psychological matter, few persons in a small space may be highly stressful to some individuals, while others may find it stimulating and enjoyable, for some purposes, to be crowded together in small quarters. As Hall (1965) has noted, cultural factors also may be critical in evaluating just what level of actual population density is experienced as stressful. What is dense and disturbing in the United States may not be experienced as dense and stressful in India.

In the second place, the direction of causality is often difficult to infer from those studies on human populations that have sought to examine "stressful population density." For example, several investigators have related population density to social pathology—for example, crime rates—controlling for such factors as social class and ethnic group membership (Pessman & Carol, 1971; Winsborough, 1965, Galle et al., 1972). In the typical case, the correlation between density and pathology vanishes with such controls thereby making inferences to density as cause difficult to make. In one study, however, (Galle et al.), a positive relationship was uncovered even with such controls, by defining density in terms of "persons per room" rather than through the more global measure of "persons per acre." Yet, the causal direction still remains cloudy; does density cause the social pathology or do persons inclined towards such pathology converge in high-density areas where crimes are easier to commit, being caught is presumably more difficult, and where criminal support systems may be more prevalent? Other efforts to relate pathology—for example, suicide—to population density, have turned up an inconsistent set of results. Apparently in some cities (e.g., Edinburgh, Scotland) a positive correlation is found, while in others (e.g., London), no relation is found. Lab research has likewise turned up several inconsistencies: Hutt and Vaizey (1966) report more aggressiveness in larger groups of children; Loo (1972), however, reports less aggression among children in a high-density, small room; similarly, Harris and Paluck (1971) report little aggression in crowded public areas, but rather find what they termed a *cocooning effect,* in which persons sought to avoid contact with others. The specific psychological and cultural factors that may mediate between density as a physical fact and stress as a psychological condition obviously need to be specified and systematically examined.

While evidence exists that more clearly and consistently links density to disorder among animal populations (e.g., Goeckner, Greenough, & Mead, 1973), the leap from such findings to humans is one that, if made at all, must be done with great caution. The animal research, nevertheless, is instructive in demonstrating some of the consequences of excessive population density for the animal species studied. Calhoun's (1962; 1970) research with laboratory rats is a classic in this genre. His rats were permitted to increase their population until they reached such an overcrowded condition that severe pathological behavior patterns were noted, thereby restricting their further population growth. Under high-density conditions, the rats became more aggressive; some withdrew into a seemingly catatonic state; others became cannibalistic. Research with cats and monkeys provided confirmatory evidence for these pathological consequences of overcrowding. A field study (Christian et al., 1960) of the behavior of deer reveals some of the bodily consequences of stressful overpopulation. The deer herd's numbers increased until the density was approximately one deer per acre. Suddenly, the death rate began to rise, even though there was plenty of food and water and no apparent externally borne disease. Examinations of the bodies revealed endocrine disorders including greatly enlarged adrenal glands as an apparent response to the stress of overcrowding. Similar to Calhoun's rats, problems with the reproductive system were also noted.

The animal research thus seems to suggest that excessive density, even under conditions of plenty, creates high stress with consequent pathology of normal physiological functioning, resulting both in dramatic behavior changes (e.g., heightened aggressiveness) and death. The problem, however, is to generalize directly from these results on animals to the human situation, and to conclude that overcrowded urban conditions increase the potential for violence, thus explaining increased crime rates in the most crowded areas of the central city (e.g., Lawrence, 1974). While our awareness of the potential problem of density and pathology is now more heightened than ever, we still require much more research to be certain that parallel effects face human populations.

THE TECHNOLOGICAL TRANSFORMATION

Not by bread alone, nor muscle, in fact, but by brains, by tools, and by culture did persons survive and so extend their presence on earth even while reaching for the universe beyond. We think it startling perhaps that the world's population doubles in 37 years; how striking then that in the relatively short period of 60 years people have traveled from the Wright Brothers first flight to setting foot on the moon. With each development and use of a new tool, people extended their capacity for dealing with their environment. They became more efficient hunters or better farmers, allowing a surplus to gather and a more complex form of social organization to evolve. The wheel increased human mobility and power; the domestication of animals and the capturing of winds in sails permitted our horizons to expand. With the development of steam power that was generated from fossil fuels, the Industrial Revolution began, creating machinery run by power that was well beyond human physical capacity but within human reach as a sentient being.

The advent of automation—the cybernetic revolution to some—came into being when technology advanced sufficiently to allow machines to become self-monitoring and self-correcting. Electronic computers took on functions that formerly had to be overseen by people. Entire assembly lines could be run by a few trained technicians who monitored a computer that monitored and controlled operations up and down the line. Communications systems evolved, expanded, and became automated, joining peoples of the world.

Careful documentation is not easy to come by, but it seems reasonable to suggest that modern technology confronts us all with a host of issues that may challenge our capabilities for adjustment. Workers may face considerable stress as they seek to adjust to an automated assembly line or office routine. Each individual error may be magnified; each performance is more observed with an automated technology (Hardin, 1960a; b; Walker, 1957). Personal time schedules become tuned to the time schedule of technology; absence and tardiness are troublesome to the machine world: pressure increases on the person to be punctual, orderly, rational, precise.

The mysteries of technology, especially the awesome abilities of modern computers, may also serve, somewhat paradoxically, to diminish our faith in our own ability to exercise control over our world. Although the forces of technology have in fact provided a greater degree of environmental and human control than ever before, they have created at the same time an alien world that is beyond most people's ken. This new world seems to operate by some incalculable set of economic and social forces that have consequences beyond our personal control or logic; a world of technique that follows its own logic (see Ellul, 1964).

THE ORGANIZATIONAL REVOLUTION

The premodern period of human existence was generally characterized by a fusion into the family or household of activities and forms of relationship that have become separated in the modern era (Bendix, 1974). Specifically, economic activities, social status (i.e., prestige in the community), and power were at one time tied significantly together and resided in the family or household. The household was the owner of property, the unit of production, the giver of status, and the source of power. The individual's own status in the community depended on family ties; even a servant's prestige was a function of his or her master's standing.

Max Weber, (recall his analyses of legitimacy that we examined in Chapter 7), noted how the shift to the modern era (around the sixteeenth and seventeenth centuries) saw the separation of these several functions that once had been fused. Workplace and the family were separated; thus economic activities and relationships occurred in a location and with persons who were no longer necessarily household members. For example, in the premodern era, it was reasonable to keep business records that did not distinguish between household assets and liabilities and those that were connected with business matters; with the separation of work-place and home, a bookkeeping that distinguished between business accounts and home accounts was necessary. The private property that the household might own had to be separated from the property that the partners in business might own; business debts were separate from household debts, and so forth. In similar manner, household servants had to be distinguished from business employees.

Weber notes that one consequence of this evolving separation of household and economic or business functions was the need to develop a legal basis for regulating commercial practices. The traditional bases founded in kinship were not relevant once business activities ceased to involve family and household members. Parallelling this separation of business and household came the separation of status and of authority from household. Where once authority lay in the control over household properties, with the separation of household and business, authority came to lie as well in the administration of business activities as distinct from the possession of properties. The evolution of the large scale formal organization, the bureaucracy, provided the administrative personnel with sources of power that lie within the organization rather than within any personal properties which were owned.

The bureaucracy took over from the traditional household as the major form of modern social organization. Weber's analysis of bureaucracy stands today as a model both of this organizational revolution (i.e., transformation) and of its broader ramifications for all aspects of the life of modern humankind. As societies became larger, more technologically advanced and complex, as the activities that once were within the purview of kin and household were separated, a form of human organization was necessary that could work efficiently to coordinate the activities of many persons whose only relationship to one another was economic. Such an organization could no longer rely on ties based on kin or loyalty, as these had been dissipated by the separation of workplace from household. Its coordination and regulation thus had to follow nontraditional lines; its emphasis had focus upon impersonality of relationships and upon a legalized rationality of governance.

A bureaucracy, according to Weber, designed to achieve maximal efficiency of outcome, was characterized by:

1. its "fixed and official jurisdictional areas," "ordered by rules" so that ordinary work activities become official duties governed by organizational rules and sanctioning apparatus;
2. its office hierarchy with differentiated levels of control and authority;
3. the existence of general and abstract rules that govern categories of individual issues;
4. the separation of the individual as a private person from the office as an organizational role, and the consequent emphasis on the assignment of individuals to roles according to their technical competence; and the emphasis on the priority of the office over the person and thus on impersonality of working relationships;
5. the effort to convert all activities and functions to substantial conformity with clear, written, and generalized rules governing their official handling.

For Weber, bureaucracy was not simply descriptive of the new formal organizations of the modern era, but as importantly, bureaucratization was itself descriptive of the modernizing process whereby all aspects of life were increasingly subsumed under the bureaucratic concerns with rationality, predictability, impersonality, and control. If bureaucratization is the organizational shape of modernism, then rationalization is its driving value. In Weber's view, rationalization involves the conversion of relationships and human values from their primary, communal and kinship-based forms into secondary, impersonal bureaucratized forms. To rationalize a human relationship is to abstract it, generalize it, and thereby make it increasingly less unique and less personal. Bureaucracy as described by Weber is a perfect instrument for rationalizing human organizations by removing the traditional and more personalized bases of human relationships and authority and converting them to secondary forms. Values that were once based on personal feelings were transformed to those based on impersonality

and rationality; emotion and feeling had no place in the bureaucracy of the rationalized modern era.

The historican, Lewis Mumford (1956), in noting the transformations that marked the change from the old to the new world, has
reached a conclusion similar to Weber's, in particular, however,
commenting on the role that the emergence of positive science
played in expressing and giving shape to this rationalized new
being:

> *nothing in life counted except what was countable ... in the*
> *end men were acceptable only when they took on the*
> *attributes of machines"* (p. 99).
>
> *This New World was a product of rationalism,*
> *utilitarianism, scientific positivism ... subjectivity ... had*
> *no place in this new framework ... New World culture*
> *meant organization, standardisation, regularity, control,*
> *applied to every manifestation of life* (p. 96).

And as Mumford, Weber, and others note, this new culture of rationalization and bureaucratization served a freeing and democratiz-
ing function by removing persons from the inevitable bondage that
personal, kin-based traditional forms had carved as their destiny.
Persons were now free to venture forth on their own, to succeed
through their own hard work and efforts to learn those skills that
made them competent to perform jobs within the organization. It is
the other edge of this sword, however, that has caused so much
concern for those who worry about the effects of rationalization on
the human condition. The sociologist, Robert Nisbett (1966) puts it
quite well:

> *So long as the process of rationalization had something to*
> *feed on—that is, the structure of traditional society and*
> *culture that was formed during the Middle Ages—it was a*
> *generally creative and liberating process. But with the*
> *gradual diminution and desiccation of this structure, with*
> *man's increasing disenchantment with the values of this*
> *structure, rationalization threatens now to become, not*
> *creative and liberating, but mechanizing, regimenting, and*
> *ultimately, reason-destroying* (p. 294).
>
> *... It is not disorganization any more than it is catastrophe*
> *that Weber fears, but rather, overorganization, a future*
> *sterilized of the informal ... contexts within which*
> *personality takes on the stuff of resistance to*
> *mass-mindedness and cultural uniformity* (p. 297).

The Modern Chinese Version. The inevitability of bureaucratization and rationalization as processes necessary to efficiently coordinate the efforts of the masses in a modern, technological era, is

opened to some critical question within the context of modern China. Chinese resistance to the full-scale adoption of Western or Soviet style bureaucracies has taken the form of a Chinese-Maoist version of formal organizations which while sharing some features with the Weberian ideal type varies in some significant ways; and it is these variations that call into question the inevitability of Western-style bureaucratization. To briefly discuss some of these Chinese variants, I will borrow significantly from a recently published discussion of M. K. Whyte (1973).

In China, resistance to bureaucratization is not based simply on the Western concerns with its potentially alienating consequences, but rather on the tendency for bureaucracies to breed elite corps of bureaucrats who become increasingly separated from the needs and control of the people they presume to serve. To bureaucratize in a manner that retains roots with the people requires, according to Whyte's analysis, that Weber's version of hiring and promotion based on technical competence (rather than traditional kin lines) be transformed. The Chinese feel technical competence is an important criterion for entry into the bureaucracy, but political purity is equally important: that is, class origins, membership in the party, loyalty, and enthusiasm, and so forth. It is further reasoned that not only would elitism be reinforced by emphasizing technical competence, but also passivity would be encouraged on the part of the masses who would feel "pessimistic about their abilities to compete for higher places" (p. 151). "On the other hand if generalists and the politically pure hold sway, they should be less concerned about establishing their professional prerogatives and more concerned about forging close ties with, and mobilizing the full energy and initiative of, their subordinates" (p. 151).

Whereas the Weberian tradition emphasizes the autonomy of the bureaucracy so it can function more efficiently, the Chinese reject this notion, which they refer to as "localism" and "departmentalism," stressing rather the embeddedness of the organization in the larger community and nation. An autonomous Western organization might make internal decisions without concern for the implications that those decisions have for the larger community. In China, by contrast, it is recognized "that all organizational decisions and actions [have] political implications which extend beyond organizational boundaries" (p. 151); thus, any organization must be open to continuous direction from extraorganizational sources.

Weber's ideal typical bureaucracy emphasizes rational-legal domination which in China is seen as "dulling the initiative of the masses" (p. 152). Thus their forms of bureaucratic authority tend towards the charismatic and the participatory. The Chinese concern with encouraging rather than discouraging mass initiative leads them away from the organizational domination in which subordinates follow simply because they have accepted the legitimacy of their organization and its rules of hierarchy and command (Chapter 7). "The term 'mass line' stands for a large number of procedures organizations are supposed to use to ameliorate the effects of hierarchy" (p. 152). As Whyte notes, in Chinese organizations, participation of subordinates in the decision-making apparatus of the bureaucracy is not simply encouraged but is guaranteed.

While Whyte notes numerous other ways in which the Chinese organization and the Weberian ideal differ (and several ways in which they are similar), we will conclude our own overview of this perspective by noting one further, key contrast. Weber's ideal emphasizes impersonality within the organization, whereas the Chinese emphasis is on comradeship. Furthermore, in order to ensure subordinate involvement and active participation in decision making within the organization, employee groups are urged to form and "are to maintain their form outside the activities and hours of formal organizational life" (p. 153). Employees both inside the organization and on their own time outside are encouraged to relate together as "whole persons" not simply as segmented parts or in office-related roles. A recognition is granted to the merger of organizational and private life, and fellow workers are expected to join together in "a variety of joint activities, helping each other to solve personal problems, while at the same time criticizing those who depart from the official line" (p. 154). Clearly, then, Chinese organizations permeate a greater part of the person's life than the Weberian ideal or the Western and Soviet reality deem desirable.

> *The "partial inclusion" and limited contractual obligations of office-holders which in the bureaucratic ideal type protect participatants from undue exploitation are not basic features of the Maoist ideal. No aspect of the life of an individual is regarded as completely irrelevant to his organizational performance* (p. 155).

The Western view sees a need to separate people's private affairs from their office world so as to minimize intrusions of a nonrational sort, thereby freeing the office-holders to use their technical expertise to the fullest; the Chinese see the need to include the full person so as to promote maximum commitment and involvement.

In Whyte's view, a fundamental difference between the Weberian and the Maoist perspectives on bureaucracies is that whereas the former stresses technical efficiency and control, the latter is concerned with "finding ways to maximize the involvement and commitment of organizational participants, particularly the 'masses' at the bottom of organizations" (p. 156). It would seem likely, therefore, that while isolation and alienation might be the result of the Western style bureaucracy, they would be less likely from the Chinese model with its greater involvement of the total person. Yet, even in its Western form, the emergence and growth of small primary groups within the larger organization, groups that relate together as whole persons both on and off the job, suggest some deviations in reality from the ideal typical model that Weber has offered.

PATTERNS OF PARTICIPATION, INVOLVEMENT, AND COMMITMENT: A THEME OF POWERLESSNESS

One of the consequences attributed to the transformation of society from its premodern to its modern forms involved a change in people's control over their lives and world, and hence their feelings of involvement and commitment to the affairs of their community and their fellow human beings. The alienation of powerlessness to which Seeman referred is a major contemporary theme. It is to this that we now turn our attention, first by means of the fascinating and informative perspective of Roger Barker's psychological ecology (1961; 1965; Barker & Barker, 1963; Barker & Wright, 1955).

Psychological Ecology and Alienation. For many years, Barker and his several coworkers have been involved in the systematic study of the effects of the environment on the individual. In particular, they have been interested in charting the variety of encounters that persons have with their natural daily environment. Barker noted that it is meaningful to discuss the environment in terms of separate units within which sequences of behavior occur. He refers to these units of the environment as *behavior settings.* Examples of behavior settings include such things as baseball games, parties, a classroom, a drugstore, and so forth. For Barker, behavior settings are extra-individual entities that have a structure and an existence apart from any particular individual who happens to be present. A baseball game, for example, involves patterns of relationship that maintain regardless of the characteristics of the individual participants. In a similar manner, there are assumed to be certain ways of relating that are characteristic of a party regardless of who happens to be involved.

A behavior setting not only includes these normative patterns of relationship that define it, but also contains a variety of objects or paraphenalia: for example, walls, chairs, doors, typewriters, and so forth. Behavior settings, furthermore, are thought to be *homeostatic* or self-regulatory systems. This quality, in fact, is a key to Barker's thinking about the relationship between persons and their environment.

If a setting is self-regulatory, this means that it persists with a relative degree of stability in spite of a multitude of forces acting to change it. It has a life of its own, so to speak, governed by principles other than those of individual psychology; forces towards balance are seen to characterize the functioning of the behavior setting.

This view may strike one as a peculiar way of looking at the environment. It makes the environment seem alive, seeking to preserve its stability in the midst of forces acting to produce change. At this point, let us simply assume that behavior settings tend towards homeostasis, balancing pressures from one side with compensating changes on the other.

Take a restaurant as an example of a behavior setting. In the first place, the restaurant is definable as a locale in the environment where a circumscribed set of behaviors is likely to occur. It is a normatively regulated part of the environment. In the second place, the restaurant is definable in its operation independently of who happens to be involved with it. The restaurant is there even if you and I don't patronize it. And if we do, it is still a restaurant governed by its own principles of operation. These principles, in turn, are not the same principles that govern my action or yours.

> *In the functioning of the Pearl Cafe in Midwest, for example, the availability and the price of food, the season of the year, the prevailing temperatures, the size, lighting, and ventilation of the building, the state laws concerning hygenic practices, the customers, and the employees are all involved* [in maintaining a restaurant as a behavior setting] (Barker, 1960, p. 18).

Finally, the homeostatic stability of the restaurant as a behavior setting is maintained within certain limits of pressure to change. Its survival as a behavior setting, for instance, depends on the continued patronage of a certain number of customers; below that number, its life is threatened. Likewise, at the other extreme, too many customers demanding service at the same moment might compel a drastic shift in the organization and functioning of the restaurant. It's life, thus, hangs in balance between extremes. Within those extremes, however, the setting continues to operate in a manner much as it has always done, surviving as a restaurant through lean months and blossoming during peak seasons.

In the preceding example, it is obvious that although persons are interchangable as far as the life of a behavior setting goes, the relationship between people and behavior settings is nevertheless vital. Barker explores several aspects of this relationship: First, Barker notes that people are the most essential component in the functioning of any behavior setting. A classroom, for example, is a setting that can get by without a blackboard, but it is no longer a classroom once the people have vanished. A drugstore may be able to survive without some of its paraphenalia, but without people, it too, vanishes. Second, each behavior setting has an optimal population requirement. This means that each behavior setting has a given number of people necessary before the setting's structure or organization is altered or lost completely. Settings, therefore, may be optimally populated, underpopulated, or overpopulated. We will return momentarily to this crucial matter. Third, Barker assumes that, "of all the equipment and paraphenalia of a setting, people are among the most immediately malleable and adjustable" (1960, p. 22). As he notes, environments do not as easily expand as people "quickly spread out or crowd together, speed up or slow down, write or talk" (p. 22). If a small party is held in a large room, one does not expect the room to contract, but rather expects the people to adjust themselves to the setting, perhaps by spreading around or even by clustering together in one corner of the large setting.

One clear implication of this last point is that behavior settings, in the pursuit of their own self-regulation, can affect a change on the behavior of individuals who enter the setting. Although settings are neither self-conscious nor intentional, their survival is of importance to many persons who get satisfaction out of the setting. A drugstore, for example, gives its owners and its customers a variety of satisfactions. A baseball game or even a classroom provide a host of satisfactions to a host of persons. Maintaining the setting, however, establishes certain of its own requirements, some of which necessitate a change in the behavior of individuals who are involved with it. This point of Barker's is similar to that of a variety of other writers, including, as we have seen, Weber's analyses of bureaucracy, and Karl Marx's (1956) examination of those settings that are directly involved in the means of production. Marx puts forth two specific propositions:

1. People's location in the productive process determines their outlook on a wide variety of personal, social and political matters.
2. There is a logic to the forms of production that is independent of the individuals who are involved. These forms change and develop in accordance with their own principles, creating new functions, new roles, and new demands as they live out their own life. This latter point is congruent with Barker's arguments involving the dynamic of behavior settings.

The point is that once a setting is established and proves pleasing to a number of persons, then its maintenance demands a variety of adjustments on the part of those persons. They must do things now or act in ways now that may be very different than was required of them before the setting came into being. And this is true whether we are discussing the small restaurant in the Midwest studied by Barker or the government bureaucracy headquartered in Washington.

Much of the preceding is preliminary to Barker's main concern which is to relate the population requirements of behavior settings to effects on individual life. To be played properly, a baseball game is said to require eighteen players, nine on each side. The game, in this case, is the behavior setting with its optimal population requirements, at least as far as players go. The maintenance of this setting also has population requirements for paying fans, but for simplicity we will stick to the players. What would happen if instead of eighteen, we would play the game with ten players? We all know that it is possible to play some form of baseball with far fewer than eighteen persons. We might think of this below-optimal number as describing an underpopulated behavior setting. By this we mean that the numbers present to operate the setting are fewer than the optimal number required. But what are the effects of underpopulation on the behavior of the individual participants?

One of the most obvious effects is that all positions cannot be filled in their most ideal form. Some kind of pitcher is usually required; but is a catcher really necessary? Can't one of the members of the team-at-bat become a "neutral" catcher in order to allow more people to be in the field? But what about base and field coverage? A first-baseman is usually required, but surely someone could play center field, short stop and second. Essentially, what occurs is an immediate spreading of the available personnel to cover the several basic requirements of the game setting.

Because all positions cannot be filled, but adequate field coverage is still important, one of the next most obvious consequences in this underpopulated setting is simply that each person must do more work than would be required if he or she were playing under optimal population conditions. If you have to cover both center and short and second base, you must do more work and expend more energy.

Other possibilities, of course, also exist, especially when a setting gets so underpopulated that the game either must be cancelled or its form substantially changed: that is, it becomes a different setting. For example, in a baseball game involving only two or four players, one usually finds extensive rule changes. Whereas, in the first level of underpopulation, persons modify their behavior to meet the population demands of the behavior setting—for example, by spreading themselves around and doing much more—in the second case, the persons modify the setting in addition to their own behavior.

What happens, however, if instead of underpopulation, there is overpopulation, as when thirty people want to join in the game? Here, we would expect a reversal in the effects noted for underpopulation. There will be an excess of personnel: too many fielders, or too many covering the bases, or too many for any position. Under such conditions, each person presumably would have to do much less than would be required in the optimally populated setting. If there are six rather than three outfielders, at minimum, each has less ground to cover. A variety of other effects are also likely given an overpopulated setting. For example, new positions may be created; or unemployment may be institutionalized, benching some persons for a specified period of time. The point is that the size changes relative to setting requirements have consequential effects on the individual participants in the setting.

Barker lists a variety of consequences that follow when a behavior setting is underpopulated. An overpopulated setting would simply reverse the direction of these consequences:

1. Greater effort is required on the part of those persons in the setting. This we have seen in the baseball example; examples from other settings are also obvious. Witness a restaurant that is optimally staffed by three waitresses when it is caught understaffed. Each waitress now works much harder. One would expect less individual effort demanded of persons in an overpopulated setting.

2. Each person must take on more difficult and more responsible tasks and will have to play more roles. Clearly, if the setting's function is to be maintained and fewer persons are around to staff it, people who are around will have to do a greater variety of jobs, often very difficult ones. An underpopulated setting cannot afford the luxury of people sitting around and waiting for the easy job to come along; everyone must pull equally or else everyone and the setting itself fails. By implication, when a setting gets overpopulated, there should be greater specialization of function which would allow for a better match between level of skill and job requirement.

3. There will be less sensitivity and less evaluation of differences among people. With underpopulation of behavior settings, individuals become important regardless of who they are or what they are like; as long as they can pull their own, they're wanted. The implication is that in overpopulated settings, one can afford the luxury of discrimination and sensitization to sex differences, skilll differences, race differences, age differences, and so on. In other words, in an underpopulated setting, men, women, and children all are called on to help keep things going; in an overpopulated setting, women and children may be asked to remain at home or in school, while men—and at that only some kinds of men—enter the work force.

4. Each person's labors have greater functional importance; each person has greater responsibility. Again, the need for personnel that characterizes underpopulated settings means that each person *is* important and each job that he or she performs is one of high responsibility: that is, what each individual does is essential to the maintenance of the behavior setting.

5. There will be a greater functional identity in the underpopulated setting. Barker notes that there will be a shift from "Who are they?" to "What can they do?" In Parsons terms (Parsons et al., 1951; 1953), this is a shift from evaluations based on personal qualities to those based on performances or achievement. The evaluations that others make soon become the criteria for self-evaluations as well. Thus, in the underpopulated setting, persons judge their own worth in terms of what they've done rather than who they are or what personal qualities they have, such as their charm, wit, and possessions. The overpopulated setting, by contrast, shifts the basis both of others' evaluations and subsequently self-evaluations from performances to qualities. Who one is becomes central; in particular, symbols of identity that are little related to one's work roles take on central self-defining importance.

Barker's research examined several interesting implications of this model. One study undertaken with Paul Gump (1964), compared consequences to the individual attending big schools versus attending small schools. A big school was one that had relatively many students per behavior setting—a median of thirty-six—while a small school had a median number of around eleven. Small schools provided the individuals with

more *satisfactions related (a) to the development of competence, (b) to being challenged, (c) to engaging in important actions, (d) to being involved in group activities, (e) to being valued, and (f) to gaining moral and cultural values* (Barker, 1965, p. 11).

Other differences were also noted. For example, those in small schools were involved in 2.5 times more responsible positions and 6 times more leadership roles than students in big schools. Whereas 29 percent of the students in the large schools performed in no particularly important or responsible positions, only 2 percent of the students in the small schools were classed as nonperformers. As expected, students in the small schools experienced greater pressures to participate than their large school counterparts. In concluding his examination of these data, Barker notes that schools as behavior settings, like all behavior settings, are "entities that regulate some aspects of the behavior of their human components" (1965, p. 12). In particular, he comments on how group pressure and negative feedback is employed in the small schools to engage students in performing in those programs established in the setting. For example, teachers were reported to have urged students to participate, or students recognized that the school play needed extra girls in the cast so they felt obliged to try out. In the large schools, by contrast, pressure and negative feedback was brought to bear on selected students—those who showed promise—while others, more marginal, were allowed not to participate.

In another study, Barker examined two towns, one he called Midwest, Kansas, U.S.A., the other, Yoredale, Yorkshire, England. Midwest and Yoredale shared the same kinds of behavior settings. Barker suggested that as far as their content goes, one could transpose the settings of Kansas to England with minimal disruption. However, the Kansas settings were underpopulated, while those in Yoredale were relatively overpopulated. For example, in Midwest, there were 1.25 persons per setting, while in Yoredale, the ratio was 2.63. Each setting in Midwest had almost half the number of persons to maintain it as compared with settings in Yoredale. Given this relation of numbers to setting, one would predict that the citizens of Midwest should be busier, more versatile in the number of different roles they occupied, more responsible, and so forth, than citizens of Yoredale. Results generally confirm these expectations. For example, Midwest citizens participate in the town's behavior settings on the average of 2.5 hours per week more than do the citizens of Yoredale; likewise, they are more involved in responsible positions than are the citizens of Yoredale.

It is among the adolescent population, however, that the most striking differences are uncovered. The adolescents of Midwest, living in a generally underpopulated community, must participate in the running of the community. In general, Midwest's adolescents fill 3.5 times as many responsible positions as do the adolescents of Yoredale: each "acts in a play, works in a store, teaches a Sunday school class, plays in a basketball league game every three weeks; Yoredale adolescents occupy such positions every eleven weeks, on the average" (1960, p. 44). Barker's view is that if adolescents from Yoredale were transported to Midwest, they too would find themselves quickly taking on those higher participation and higher responsibility positions that characterize Midwest's youth; and if Midwesterners went to live in Yoredale, they might soon drop out of such active community involvement. In other words, the setting makes certain differential demands on its inhabitants.

What is equally interesting is Barker's examination of the educational philosophy that characterizes these two communities. In Midwest, education is thought to prepare the youth for adulthood by involving them at an early age in significant community participation. Barker notes that without the involvement of the youth, the town could not maintain its variety of behavior settings; thus, their participation is essential and is encouraged. In Yoredale, by contrast, the school setting is relatively isolated from community participation; children are placed with experts to be trained. They are excluded from responsible positions in the community where their services essentially are not needed.

> *It would be extremely difficult to exchange the educational systems of the two towns. Many Midwest community settings which would be crippled by the* removal *of children would in Yoredale be disrupted by their presence. In fact it appears that the towns could not tolerate such a shift without a major transformation in the whole community system* (1960, p. 47).

A recent analysis of youth in America reported by James S. Coleman (1974) reaches conclusions very similar to Barker's. Coleman notes how schooling today serves to prolong adolescence by legally and socially cutting young persons off from the mainstream of their society, keeping them in a childlike, relatively nonresponsible role often until they are into their mid-20s. We might expect this discrepancy between many facets of physical and psychological maturity on the one hand and the continuation of schoolchild dependency on the other to prove disturbing to modern youth. Coleman notes in particular the loss of motivation and a sense of nonresponsibility that such prolonged dependence may create; hardly a condition conducive to effective functioning in a democratic society. Indeed, the discontinuities that Benedict referred to and which we examined in Chapter 6 seem to be affirmed here both in Barker's and in Coleman's analysis.

Barker's insights reveal the vast system of interdependencies that we too often overlook in our efforts to understand human behavior. For here we have a link between the environment, population, and ideological justification in the form of educational philosophies. We also have a conceptual mapping that helps us gain further insights into both the links between ecology and behavior and the implications of ecological change for transformations in social organization and individual life style. As Barker has indicated, a change in ecology—for example, from an underpopulated setting to a relatively overpopulated setting—has clear-cut consequences for the structure of the community and for the kind of life that the individual will lead. What is further, Barker's outline of the consequences of the overpopulation of behavior settings offers us a mapping of the consequences that exist in contemporary society, where technology and population have combined to change the ecological shape of the nation and increasingly of the world.

Barker suggests that the personal qualities that emerge from an underpopulated setting read like a listing of traditional cultural values, including hard work, difficult tasks, responsibility, and individual dignity, respect, and importance. He notes, however, that:

> We have made a nation's ideal of the fact that these are not imposed *controls in American culture. We sometimes call them self-discipline. In reality they are controls built into the structure and the dynamics of the setting . . . What happens when the ecological environment changes to one of overpopulated settings without intrinsic controls, with the old ideals lingering on, but no longer true?* (1960, p. 48).

It may well be as Melvin Seeman (1972) comments, that this discrepancy between the major American values, especially those of autonomy, mastery, initiative, and responsibility (i.e., the obverse of alienated powerlessness) so important to the survival of democratic social and political institutions, and the realities of everyday life can be taken as an important indicator of the health and well-being of the society. It is to Seeman's and other's work on powerlessness that we now turn our attention.

POWERLESSNESS

The theoretical link between modernism and the individual's alienation of powerlessness as we have seen in Barker's and other's work is relatively straightforward. Modern, mass society is said to bring with it a largeness of scale, an isolation and atomization of persons, and a removal from being instrumental in shaping the affairs of one's life and world. This lack of control over one's life creates a sense of the alienation of powerlessness, thereby threatening to undermine the core values and roots on which democratic institutions are founded. The empirical question, however, is to what extent and for whom is powerlessness an important condition of contemporary existence. Evidence derives from several sources and several different though related conceptions of powerlessness.

Internal-External Control. In 1966, Julian Rotter published a monograph outlining the conception and the measurement of what he termed the locus of control over reinforcement. Rotter suggested that persons had a general tendency, presumably developed on the basis of their past history of success and failure, to attribute the control over reinforcements either to their own efforts or to things beyond their own control—such as fate and luck. He saw those who generally felt that through their own efforts they could receive positive reinforcements or avoid negative reinforcements, as having an internal locus of control; in contrast, were those who generally felt that positive or negative reinforcements were external to their own control. In order to assess the existence of these two general types of control orientation, Rotter developed a paper-and-pencil test in which two alternatives were given for each item, but only one could be checked by the subject. The following items are examples taken from this test:

1.____ Most people don't realize the extent to which their lives are controlled by accidental happenings.
____ There really is no such thing as "luck."
2.____ Sometimes I can't understand how teachers arrive at the grades they give.
____ There is a direct connection between how hard I study and the grades I get.

In both items above, the first choice is the external alternative, while the second is the internal. The test contains twenty-three pairs of items of this sort. (e.g., Lefcourt, 1966; 1972; Phares summarizes this literature.) Extensive programs of research using the I-E scale to measure personal dispositions have suggested several important correlates of internality and externality:

1. Internality tends to be related to resistance to influence.

2. Internality tends to be related to what might best be termed cognitive alertness; that is, the more internal people are, the more attentive they are to information about their environment and the more concerned they are with using that information.

3. There is some indication that externals do not benefit as readily as internals from new learning which give them an experience with success; thus providing a highly external person with success experiences may not alter his or her sense of being in control. There may occur an undoing of the success experience rather than changing the locus of control; the high external may feel that once again chance played out its hand, this time dealing success.

4. In theory, at least, one would expect high externals not to engage in action designed to produce change in their environment because they believe that their efforts are not instrumental anyway; it is the externals, then, that should experience a sense of powerlessness and hence tend to be inactive and nonparticipatory in the affairs of their world. An investigation of civil rights workers at a Southern black college reported by Gore and Rotter (1963) supports this prediction. They find greater involvement by internals as compared with externals. But before we accept this theoretical linkage, we need two additional ingredients to our conceptual and empirical mix. The one comes from close analyses of the I-E test itself; the

second derives from the lengthy and continuing investigations of political efficacy as reported by Converse and his colleagues from the University of Michigan's Survey Research Center.

The Meaning of Internality-Externality.   Although Rotter initially reported that the I–E scale only measured the locus of control factor as he conceptualized it, subsequent work both on the scale and on its use with activist groups suggests a more complex picture than Rotter initially proposed. Mirels, paralleling the work of Gurin's research group (Gurin et al., 1969) reported in 1970 the existence of two factors in the original Rotter I–E scale:
1.   a measure of personal control over the course of one's life;
2.   a measure of system modifiability or the responsiveness of political institutions to personal actions.
One could be internally oriented with respect to personal matters, yet be external as regards system responsiveness, feeling that social and political institutions are beyond one's own control to influence significantly.

Reporting in 1974, Barry Collins suggests that the original I–E scale actually contains four separate factors so that, for example, a highly external orientation could mean:
1.   the world is difficult to comprehend; its rules, though not functioning by chance, are nevertheless often unknown and complex;
2.   the world is not a just place; effort and ability often go unrewarded;
3.   the world is ruled by chance and luck;
4.   the system is unresponsive to change-oriented efforts.
Not only do these detailed analyses of the I–E scale reveal greater complexity of meaning than was initially thought, but analyses of the activities of both black and female militants suggest the important implications of these differences in meaning. Gurin, Gurin, Lao, and Beattie (1969) have argued that for blacks, whose reality is of external control, it would be dysfunctional to believe in internality; to do so would lead to overwhelming self-blame with consequent despair and retreat into apathy. Externality, in this case would serve to motivate innovative programs of change. Their research indicates:

> *that when internal-external control refers to Negroes'*
> *conceptions of the causes of their condition as Negroes, and*
> *these conceptions are related to more innovative coping*
> *criteria, it is the external rather than the internal*
> *orientation that is associated with the more effective*
> *behaviors. When an internal orientation implies self-blame*
> *as a Negro, it also seems to involve a readiness to accept*
> *traditional restraints on Negroes' behavior* (p. 47).

In other words, internality reflects a more traditional, individualistic perspective in which persons hold themselves responsible for either succeeding or failing. While this might work well for persons whose own efforts can actually increase their mobility, for persons whose mobility is systematically thwarted by conditions that are indeed beyond their personal control—including racism and sexism, for example—then to hold self responsible for failure may simply mean to accept the majority's view that one deserves one's subordinate position and thereby to give up efforts to challenge the system. In this case, externality, blaming the system, serves better to motivate action.

Sanger and Alker reported in 1972 a parallel analysis of the relationship between internality-externality and the women's movement. Their factor analysis of the I–E scale indicated a personal control factor and a factor they termed Protestant Ethic Ideology. This latter factor is conceptually similar to the system-blame versus self-blame ideas of Gurin and her colleagues. To score internally on this factor is to accept the ideology of the Protestant Ethic that one's efforts are instrumental to achieving rewards.

Sanger and Alker assessed the scores of members of the women's liberation movement and a matched female control sample on these two factors. Their results indicate that feminists were more internal as regards personal control but more external on the issues of ideological control than nonliberationist females. In other words, paralleling in part the Gurin findings with blacks, more militant feminists were external in system-blame. As before, internality implies accepting a traditional conception of mobility which may be dysfunctional for persons whose race or sex has worked to thwart actual mobility opportunities.

Political Efficacy. In the elections held since 1952, with figures available through the 1968 election, Philip Converse and his several associates (see Converse, 1972) have kept tabs on what they term America's sense of its political efficacy, the obverse of political alienation or a sense of powerlessness. The following four agree-disagree items have formed the backbone of their scale of measurement:

1. I don't think public officials care much what people like me think.
2. Voting is the only way that people like me can have any say about how the government runs things.
3. People like me don't have any say about what the government does.
4. Sometimes politics and government are so complicated that a person like me can't really understand what's going on.

An examination of the trends in response to these questions from 1952 through 1968 demonstrates for all items other than item 2, a decline that Converse attributes to a growing disenchantment with a nonresponsive governmental apparatus. Recalling that the 1960s saw the introduction of ways other than voting to attempt to exert influence over the political system (e.g., civil rights protests, Vietnam war protests, etc.), gives us a sense of both why the voting item (2) was increasingly rejected over time as well as some of the roots of citizen disenchantment. The chaotic quality of life during the 1960s with political assassinations, war escalation, civil protests, and such led many to seriously question their own efficacy to deal with so confusing and difficult a situation.

Another source of national political data that Converse reports (1972), on the other hand, suggests a growth in political participation during this same period in which efficacy was declining. These data are based on analyses of citizen involvement in party work including membership in political clubs, campaign activities, influence attempts, and such. For example, whereas in 1952, approximately 27 percent of the population report trying to influence others' voting behavior, the figure is within the 31 percent to 35 percent range during the 1960s; similarly, whereas only 3 percent report doing party work in 1952, the figure for the 1960s ran up towards 5 percent to 6 percent. While these differences are obviously not great, they represent a consistent trend. And interestingly enough, this trend in actual political involvement and attentiveness shows an increase over time in contrast to the declining sense of political efficacy.

Rightly, we may wonder along with Converse whether we are in fact dealing with a complex conception of efficacy having the two kinds of components we have already noted relevant to the analysis of locus of control.

> *it is useful conceptually to partition gross feelings of political efficacy . . . into at least two components, which might be more precisely labeled "personal feelings of political competence" and "trust in system responsiveness"* (1972, p. 334).

The advantage of this conceptualization is that it permits us to better understand the impact of the dramatic increment in the population's level of education on political participation and competence while not necessarily influencing system trust. Converse and his colleagues report rather consistent correlations between educational level and political attentiveness, sense of competence, and participation. They refer to this as an "education-driven" model and assume that as the population's level of education continues to rise, so too will its sense of political concern and involvement. Thus, one would expect a more highly educated population to be less alienated in terms of powerlessness than an educated population. And, indeed, much data support this contention. However, the sense of inefficacy reported during the 1960s seems to have affected all educational levels. It appears, that the factor of competence is influenced by educational level and in turn influences political participation. However, the factor of trust in the system to be responsive has been declining, leading those less educated to a "response of acquiescence and resignation" (p. 335) and those of higher education to pursue avenues other than voting to try to influence the political apparatus.

In this connection it should be noted that education may not be sufficient to overcome the sense of impotence that derives from a nonresponsive system. An interesting sidelight on this matter was provided by Ralph Turner's (1973) analysis of some survey data obtained in 1969 and 1970 on a sample of college students. His data suggest that a prime contributor to some of the students' sense of powerlessness was not so much that anyone actively thwarted their efforts, but rather that unresponsiveness of the system and of the people around them served to inhibit their behavior. The point is an important one: what Turner's survey data suggests is that when students are asked, for example, if there has been anything that they wanted to say that they haven't felt free to express, almost half of those who answer affirmatively attribute their silence to unresponsiveness: "No one listens; no one cares; no one understands; people have all made up their minds; the system won't change ..." (p. 2). Powerlessness for this group derives not from active efforts by others or by the university system to inhibit their expression, but rather from a climate of uncaring, nonresponsiveness that leads them to feel, "what's the use anyway."

Two factors, a personal control on the one hand and a system control or trust or responsiveness, on the other, emerge in numerous contexts to effect the person's sense of alienation. The disjunctiveness between personal efficacy and trust in the system may speak to a more damaging form of alienation, especially insofar as it threatens to undermine the democratic ideals on which the nation was founded. If the less educated withdraw and some of the more educated seek alternate means to be heard, one can only wonder what the consequences will be to a democratic system in which citizen participation via voting and other related means is assumed to be vital. Apathy may overcome even those of higher education, who in time may abandon all hope of influencing a nonresponsive, nontrustworthy system. Citizen apathy and powerlessness do not sit well with a democratic system of governance; rather, they imply forms of governance that are more totalitarian, at least in the short run.

Interpersonal Attachments

As we have noted, powerlessness is but one of several kinds of alienation presumed to exist in contemporary society. In this section, we will examine several kinds of interpersonal alienation involving self-estrangement, estrangement from others, and what we might best term, a sense of "lost community." As we will see, while the firm empirical evidence begins to grow weaker, the intensity of belief and concern seems never stronger. Serious questions are raised, for example, concerning the factual degree to which the "old community" of the premodern era was the highly integrated, humanizing, and nonalienating setting that our contemporary romanticizing has made it to be; perhaps this is more of our need to idealize the past to contrast it with our sense of the present than an accurate portrayal of our earlier bonds of association and attachment. Still, other serious questions are raised concerning the extent to which modern forms of social organization are as segmented and alienating as many have supposed; do we not find, in fact, many significant social networks and bonds joining person to person even in our seemingly complex urbanized, mass society? A few research examples will help give us both focus and some needed clarity on these several points.

PRIMARY GROUPS IN MODERN LIFE

A primary group, as Charles Horton Cooley (1909) informed us, is characterized by its face-to-face, personal and highly affective quality; it is a form of association that generally occurs in families and among close friends. Mass society theorists (e.g., Tönnies, 1887; Wirth, 1938) have maintained that primary group attachments have been weakened, perhaps even to the point of nonexistence, by contemporary forms of social organization, but especially by urbanization, industrialization, and bureaucratization. Bureaucracy, as we have seen, is concerned primarily with efficiency and impersonality in contrast to the noninstrumental and affective bondings that characterize primary groups. Likewise, the sense of permanence that primary group relationships have presumably cannot survive modern, urban society in which needs for occupational and residential mobility often take persons away from kin and friends, or at best make whatever bonds exist only short term and thereby presumably superficial and alienating.

In contrast to these doom-filled observations, others have argued and demonstrated the survival of primary groups in the midst of the large organization and primary forms of relationship within urban contexts. Melvin Seeman, (see Neal & Seeman, 1964) for example, finds that small work groups within larger organizations serve to insulate the worker from feelings of alienation, in this case, as powerlessness. Another investigator, Form (1972), reports no relationship between the way in which work operations constrain interaction and the worker's sense of alienation; it appears that the worker feels more integrated with other workers, in fact, than he or she may feel with respect to nonwork relationships in society at large.

Eugene Litwak and his colleague, Ivan Szelenyi (1969), formulate the issue in slightly different terms, in asking "what mechanisms permit group cohesion under conditions of limited face to face contact or rapid membership turnover" (p. 466). Their concern is in examining the degree to which primary bonds remain viable even though face to face contacts may be limited and membership turnover increased. Their research focuses on such primary relationships as neighborhood groups, friendships, and kinship bonds. They used sample survey methods to interview persons in Detroit and in two Hungarian cities about where they would turn for help if they needed it or how much help they could expect from their neighbors, friends, or relatives, if, for example, they had a one-day stomach ache, a two-week appendectomy, a three-month broken leg, or needed help in sitting with their children while they were called out.

The authors reasoned that different primary groups would be called on as a function of the urgency and intensity of the person's need. Thus, for example, they expected and found that neighbors would be called on for less urgent or less time-demanding tasks whereas friends and family could be relied on for more serious help-giving activities. As they examined their data, the authors concluded that contrary to much speculation regarding the breakup of all primary groups in modern society, or the survival only of the limited nuclear family, primary groups of different types and servicing different functions are viable and do function well even in technological society; they make life much less alienating and isolating than we might have initially supposed.

The investigations of another group, Kasarda and Janowitz (1974), confirm this same perspective. Janowitz speaks of a community of "limited liability" to indicate

> that in a highly mobile society people may participate extensively in local institutions and develop community attachments yet be prepared to leave these communities if local conditions fail to satisfy their immediate needs or aspirations (p. 329).

Kasarda and Janowitz report an investigation of social networks in Britain; their results confirm those of Litwak and others in showing how both kinship and friendship bonds are not fundamentally weakened in large, densely populated communities. Interestingly enough, their data suggest that the kinds of formal, secondary-type relationships that exist in larger communities do not replace primary bonds, but rather serve to foster increased primary type contacts. Thus, for example, a person who belongs to several formal groups or organizations within the community may thereby develop some close, long-term, primary friendship ties. Mobility, of course, which one may think serves to thwart the maintenance of primary bonds, can obviously also serve to facilitate the maintenance of such bonds. Mobile persons can keep in touch with friends and kin even though they have moved out of their community. The necessity or inevitability of loneliness and isolation of the modern person, thus has been opened to serious question.

ESTRANGEMENT

Estrangement suggests separation; one may be separated from self as well as from others. A key quality said to characterize modern society is the degree to which it contributes to self-estrangement, which in turn, it is argued, lays the foundation for an estrangement from others. Self-estrangement as a circumstance of modernism has several meanings and undoubtedly is not a unitary condition.

Alienated Labor.   Building on Marx's conception of alienated labor, both Seeman (1972) and Fromm (1955) note that self-estrangement may be said to occur when the person engages in activities that are not intrinsically rewarding. Thus, persons who work on an assembly line for eight hours performing an activity that is external to their own interests and needs may be said to be alienated (i.e., self-estranged). And this kind of alienation is often posited as the major problem of contemporary society.

Seeman's (e.g., 1971; 1972) investigations of workers in several different societies (e.g., United States, France, and Sweden) has not found support for this form of alienation. His data suggest that powerlessness is the core of contemporary worker alienation. Yet he is quick to admit that his data on estrangement from work focus specifically on its intrinsic rewards rather than on other outcomes, not measured (e.g., quality of family life, civil strife, etc.), which may be where alienated work takes its toll. On the other hand, investigations reported by Blauner (1964) and by Kornhauser (1959) report how different conditions of work can and do alienate the worker from self, giving him or her a sense of meaninglessness.

Recent studies of worker dissatisfaction in the 1970s (Sheppard & Herrick, 1972), likewise, lend support to the Marxist thesis of alienating labor. National surveys ask workers about their intrinsic job satisfaction, covering such points as their degree of autonomy, the variety of jobs they do versus a routine quality, the degree and nature of their responsibility, and so forth. These measures of work alienation are then related to other factors of satisfaction and other kinds of alienation. Data reported by Sheppard and Herrick suggest that the "happy worker is a myth" and that substantial concern exists over humanizing work by increasing the worker's autonomy and responsibility. Younger workers seem especially alienated in this regard and more insistent than their older counterparts that the workplace become more humanizing. The contemporary syndrome called "blue-collar blues" was found to characterize a substantial proportion of workers, who felt themselves alienated from other aspects of their society, including its political process. This latter finding corresponds to Seeman's own work showing worker powerlessness to be the major form of modern alienation.

It has been argued by some, Herbert Marcuse (1966), for example, that the proof of the extent and intensity of worker self-estrangement is to be found in their very inability to see just how alienated they really are. Thus, when Seeman's investigations turn up results showing that workers do not report significant work-related alienation, others argue that such findings are indicative of just how fundamentally alienated such workers are: that is, they are so estranged from themselves that they are not even in touch with their own needs.

Authenticity. A second sense of self-estrangement captured by several analysts of the modern era, including Eric Fromm (1955) and Amitai Etzioni (1968) among others, is based on the assumption that persons have universal, fundamental needs whose fulfillment may be thwarted by certain contemporary forms of social organization. Alienation as estrangement, therefore, is to be understood as the result of social arrangements that deny the person the fulfillment of his or her basic needs. In a sense, maintaining that work does not permit variety and autonomy, must assume these to be basic to human well-being.

The assumption of basic human needs is important in that it directs us away from an oversocialized view that sees persons as being constituted on the basis of their society's socialization practices and thus as needing only what their culture has taught them to need. A basic human need—Etzioni recommends affection and recognition as two examples—is presumed to be fundamental to humankind, not determined by socialization. What socialization and social structure does determine, however, is the degree to which such basic needs are fulfilled or thwarted.

In this view, adapting to an alienating society—that is, one that thwarts the fulfillment of basic human needs—is a symptom of severe self-estrangement. In this regard, Etzioni suggests that societies and social arrangements can be authentic, inauthentic, or alienating, depending on the relationship between the reality and the appearance of their fulfillment of basic human needs. An authentic social arrangement is one in which both the reality and the appearance are responsive to human needs. An inauthentic arrangement is one in which the reality is not responsive, but the appearance is; an alienating arrangement is one in which both appearance and reality are nonresponsive to human needs. It is Etzioni's speculation that whereas industrialization brought us alienation, where persons were deprived of both the appearance and the reality of fulfillment, postmodern, postindustrial society has brought us inauthenticity: "naked vested interests and power relationships" are covered over "with ideological fig leaves" (p. 883). Etzioni suggests that "front" activities and stage management have become prime features of the inauthentic postmodern era in which the illusion of pleasure is fostered, while the reality is fundamentally frustrating.

But of course, this is much the same kind of conclusion that Marcuse has suggested. In Fromm's terms, our society needs persons who feel themselves to be free and independent (the illusion) but who in reality fit themselves like Mills Cheerful Robots into the "social machine without friction" (p. 110). The data reported by Taviss (1969) are consistent with the idea that these themes of self-alienation (e.g., suppression of or distance from needs) have increased in both frequency and intensity; a content analysis of popular fiction comparing the 1900s and the 1950s reflects this growth in self-estrangement.

Self-denial.   Self-estrangement as a rejection or denial of one's self, while clearly overlapping the other senses of estrangement, nevertheless draws our attention to still another quality posited to describe contemporary forms of alienation. Carl Roger's (1951; 1961) clinical theorizing speaks of the distortions of persons who in the name of achieving positive self-regard try to be pleasing to others even at the cost of rejecting themselves; he thus offers us one view of this modern person. In similar manner, R. D. Laing's (1965) analysis of the divided self offers a view of persons who cut themselves off from a vital part of themselves, their emotions and fantasies, and thereby are diminished as complete people. Modern trends demand-

ing impersonality and rationality are said to have forced this sever-
ing of self, with a consequent rejection of the socially unwanted
parts of self. His analyses of small groups in business, industry,
government, and the university, convinced Argyris (1969) that the
most typical normative pattern of interaction involved rejecting the
affective parts of one's self in favor of playing it safe, keeping cool,
and making no waves that rock the boat of conflict-free consensus.

ANOMIE

The concept of anomie was introduced by Durkheim to discuss one
kind of suicide, the *anomic,* created by a society in which the norms
that typically control and keep desires in check no longer hold sway,
thus casting the person adrift, in despair, to take his or her own life.
A crisis of anomie exists within a society or within segments of a
society whenever the normative rudder that gives it direction, focus,
and a common bond breaks down. Anomie, a state of normlessness,
has been of interest to sociologists, such as Leo Srole (1956) who
have sought its social distribution, and to social psychologists, political scientists, and others, such as McClosky and Schaar (1965), for
whom its psychological aspects have been of greatest interest.

Srole developed five items to assess what he felt to be the variable
of anomie, representing "the individual's generalized, pervasive
sense of 'self-to-others belongingness' at one extreme compared
with 'self-to-others distance' . . . at the other pole" (p. 711):
1. Most public officials are not really interested in the problems of
   the average man.
2. These days a person doesn't really know whom he can count on.
3. Nowadays a person has to live pretty much for today and let
   tomorrow take care of itself.
4. In spite of what some people say, the lot of the average man is
   getting worse, not better.
5. Most people don't really care what happens to the next fellow.
A highly anomic person would agree with those five items. Research
reported by Srole (1956), by Mizruchi (1960; 1964), and by Meier and
Bell (1959) among others suggests a tendency for an inverse relationship between social class and anomie: lower social strata tend
to be more despairing and anomic than the higher strata. Mizruchi,
noting that Roberts and Rokeach (1956) find only a negligible relationship between social class (as assessed by income) and anomia,
when education is held constant, reports no association between
income (i.e., as a measure of social class position) and anomie for
persons whose educational level is below college, but a clear inverse
association for those who have attended college: that is, among the

more highly educated, higher income persons express less anomie than those of lower income. Mizruchi reasoned in a manner reminiscent of the relative deprivation thesis that we considered in Chapter 6, that persons of higher educational levels whose expectancies for success are higher, experience greater anomia when such expectations have not been realized (i.e., when income is low) than persons whose lower educational attainment reduces their expectations for substantial success. The latter seems to expect that they are "stranded in the backwaters" of the cultural success story.

Paralleling both the theory and some prior empirical data, Mizruchi also reports a relationship between social isolation and anomie. Persons who say that they are relatively less involved in formal social participation score higher in anomia than persons whose formal participation is relatively greater. Further analyses suggest to Mizruchi that contrary to a strict urban society thesis that envisions urban persons to be anomic, his data on a relatively small community of 20,000 suggest that over 30 percent of the population report themselves to be anomic, agreeing with three or more of the Srole items.

McClosky and Schaar conceptualized anomie as a psychological state of mind, specifically:

> *the feeling that the world and oneself are adrift, wandering, lacking in clear rules and stable moorings . . . [the anomic person] lives in a turbulent region of weak and fitful currents of moral meaning . . . [he or she has] the feeling of moral emptiness* (p. 19).

They argue that anomie results when normative learning is interfered with, whether such interference derives from social-cultural conditions or from psychological dispositions. Thus persons trapped in poverty will have difficulty in learning the norms of the larger community; but so too will persons whose personality disposes them to have difficulty in learning. In order to assess the connection between personality and anomia, McClosky and Schaar developed an enlarged scale of anomie, which they administered, along with several scales designed to assess psychological functioning, to two general population samples, one based on a cross section of Minnesota (N = 1082), the other a national cross section (N = 1484).

Results of this rather massive investigation suggest that certain personalities are disposed to anomie; cognitive, emotional, and substantive belief factors interfere with their adequate socialization into the mainstream of society. For example, the data suggest that a person's level of cognitive functioning is inversely related to anomie; persons who are cognitively unsophisticated or primitive, who tend to be illogical and mystical in their thinking, are more highly anomic than persons who are better able to reason and comprehend events in their world. Measures of intolerance of ambiguity and manifest anxiety were likewise found to correlate positively with anomie. Furthermore, persons who seemed caught "in the grip of powerful, generalized emotions of rage and fear . . . unable to separate their internal feelings from objective reality" (p. 30) tended towards high anomie.

As regards the relationship between substantive beliefs and anomie, McClosky and Schaar report positive correlations between politically extremist attitudes of totalitarianism, facism, and the extremes of the political right and left, and anomie. "Not only does the anomic feel confused and normless, but he also leans toward values and opinions that are rejected in his society" (p. 33). In like manner, the highly anomic person scores high in attitudes of misanthropy: that is, a generalized distrust of people, suspiciousness, and such.

McClosky and Scharr conclude that anomie is a result of social and psychological factors such that "some social conditions combine with personality to intensify the anomic response, while others combine to diminish it" (p. 35).

> *Our main concern has been to show that within the same society some people are highly resistant to anomy while others are highly vulnerable, and that one's susceptibility may be determined by personality factors quite apart from the state of the society or one's position in it* (p. 39).

I think it valuable for us to note this contribution to the literature on anomie and alienation; it reminds us again of the interactionist perspective that is our heritage as social psychologists. Although this approach cannot inform us whether or not modernism has brought with it the disorders associated with anomic alienation, it has informed us that certain persons are more or less prone to anomie, and that those persons must be understood both sociologically and psychologically; either perspective alone provides only a partial picture of our complex contemporary society.

THE END OR A NEW BEGINNING?

These are indeed the best of times and the worst of times, but whatever, these are our times whose history is ours to make. The modern era of mass society, urbanization, technology and such, as we have seen, is neither so clearly the horrible monster that some have suggested nor the hoped for utopia that others may have imagined. What will become of us and those who follow, however, depends less on whether we subscribe to one view of "Now" or the other, than on those steps we take to exercise the control over the making of history that is humanly possible. Perhaps nothing is as alienating as to abandon our own roles in contributing to this future. Surely, it is part of our role as social scientists not only to chronicle and understand our times (Mills, p. 192) but also to help formulate ways to improve the lot of humankind. While our analysis of the individual and modernism ends here, we close with the realization that this is but the beginning of our work.

We entered social psychology through the eyes of Kurt Lewin's and other's work on interdependence; we leave social psychology mindful of the issues that human interdependence poses and of the courage required of those who would help shape history. The tools of our trade are those concepts and perspectives that we have employed in our efforts to confront the major issues and themes of our day. It is our faith in reason, our values, and our optimism that leads us beyond the crises that seem to abound, in search of a dream.

REFERENCES

Aberle, D. F., Cohen, A. K., Davis, A. K., Levy, M. J., & Sutton, F. X. The functional prerequesites of a society. *Ethics,* 1950, **60,** 100–111.

Adams, D. K., Harvey, O. J., & Heslin, R. E. Variation in flexibility and creativity as a function of hypnotically induced past histories. In O. J. Harvey (Ed.), *Experience, structure and adaptability.* New York: Springer, 1966.

Adams, J. S. Inequity in social exchange. In L. Berkowitz (Ed.), *Advances in experimental social psychology.* Vol. 2. New York: Academic Press, 1965.

Adams, J. S. & Jacobsen, P. R. Effects of wage inequities on work quality. *Journal of Abnormal and Social Psychology,* 1964, **69,** 19–25.

Adams, J. S. & Rosenbaum, W. E. The relationship of worker productivity to cognitive dissonance about wage inequity. *Journal of Applied Psychology,* 1962, **46,** 161–164.

Aderman, D. Elation, depression, and helping behavior. *Journal of Personality and Social Psychology,* 1972, **24,** 91–101.

Aderman, D. & Berkowitz, L. Observational set, empathy, and helping. *Journal of Personality and Social Psychology,* 1970, **14,** 141–148.

Aderman, D., Brehm, S. S., & Katz, L. B. Empathic observation of an innocent victim: The just world revisited. *Journal of Personality and Social Psychology,* 1974, **29,** 342–347.

Adorno, T. W. Freudian theory and the pattern of fascist propaganda. In G. Roheim (Ed.), *Psychoanalysis and the social sciences.* Vol. 3, New York: International Universities Press, 1951.

Adorno, T. W., Frenkel-Brunswik, E., Levinson, D. J., & Sanford, R. N. *The authoritarian personality.* New York: Harper & Row, 1950.

Ajzen, I. & Fishbein, M. Attitudinal and normative variables as predictors of specific behaviors. *Journal of Personality and Social Psychology,* 1973, **27,** 41–57.

Alexander, C. N. & Epstein, J. Problems of dispositional inference in person perception research. *Sociometry,* 1969, **32,** 381–395.

Allport, F. H. The influence of the group upon association and thought. *Journal of Experimental Psychology,* 1920, **3,** 159–182.

Allport, F. H. *Social psychology.* Boston: Houghton Mifflin, 1924.

Allport, F. H. The structuring of events: Outline of a general theory with applications to psychology. *Psychological Review,* 1954, **61,** 281–303.

Allport, F. H. A structuronomic conception of behavior: Individual and collective I. Structural theory and the master problem of social psychology. *Journal of Abnormal and Social Psychology,* 1962, **64,** 3–30.

Allport, F. H. & Odbert, H. S. Trait-names: A psycholexical study. *Psychological Monographs,* 1936, **47,** (Whole No. 211).

Allport, G. W. The historical background of modern social psychology. In G. Lindzey (Ed.), *Handbook of social psychology.* Vol. 1. Cambridge, Mass.: Addison-Wesley, 1954.

Allport, G. W. & Postman, L. J. *The psychology of rumor.* New York: Holt, Rinehart & Winston, 1947.

Almond, G. A. & Verba, S. *The civic culture.* Princeton, N.J.: Princeton University Press, 1963.

Alper, T. & Korchin, S. Memory for socially relevant material. *Journal of Abnormal and Social Psychology,* 1952, **47,** 25–37.

Anderson, L. R. & McGuire, W. J. Prior reassurance of group consensus as a factor in producing resistance to persuasion. *Sociometry,* 1965, **28,** 44–56.

Arendt, H. Reflections on violence. *The New York Review of Books,* February 27, 1969.

Arendt, H. *Eichmann in Jerusalem: A report on the banality of evil.* New York: Viking, 1963.

Argyle, M. *Social interaction.* Chicago: Aldine-Atherton, 1969.

Argyle, M. & Dean, J. Eye-contact, distance and affiliation. *Sociometry,* 1965, **28,** 289–304.

Argyris, C. The incompleteness of social psychological theory. *American Psychologist,* 1969, **24,** 893–908.

Aronson, E. & Carlsmith, J. M. Effect of severity of threat on the valuation of forbidden behavior. *Journal of Abnormal and Social Psychology,* 1963, **66,** 584–588.

Aronson, E. & Mills, J. The effect of severity of initiation on liking for a group. *Journal of Abnormal and Social Psychology,* 1959, **59,** 177–181.

Asch, S. E. *Social psychology,* Englewood Cliffs, N.J.: Prentice-Hall, 1952.

Astin, A. W. An empirical characterization of higher educational institutions. *Journal of Educational Psychology,* 1962, **53,** 224–235.

Astin, A. W. & Holland, J. W. The environmental assessment technique: A way to measure college environments. *Journal of Educational Psychology,* 1961, **52,** 308–316.

Atkinson, J. W. *Motives in fantasy, action, and society: A method of assessment and study.* Princeton, N.J.: Van Nostrand, 1958.

Atkinson, J. W. *An introduction to motivation.* Princeton, N.J.: Van Nostrand, 1964.

Atkinson, J. W. & McClelland, D. C. The projective expression of needs, II. The effect of different intensities of the hunger drive on thematic perception. *Journal of Experimental Psychology,* 1948, **38,** 643–658.

Austin, W. & Walster, E. Reactions to confirmations and disconfirmations of expectancies of equity and inequity. *Journal of Personality and Social Psychology,* 1974, **30,** 208–216.

Backman, C. W. & Secord, P. F. The self and role selection. In C. Gordon & K. J. Gergen (Eds.), *The self in social interaction.* New York: Wiley, 1968.

Bakan, D. The mystery-mastery complex in contemporary psychology. *American Psychologist,* 1965, **20,** 186–191.

Bakan, D. *The duality of human existence.* Chicago: Rand McNally, 1966.

Bales, R. F. *Interaction process analysis: A method for the study of small groups.* Cambridge, Mass.: Addison-Wesley, 1950a.

Bales, R. F. A set of categories for the analysis of small group interaction. *American Sociological Review,* 1950b, **15,** 257–263.

Bales, R. F. Adaptive and integrative changes as sources of strain in social systems. In A. P. Hare, E. F. Borgatta, & R. F. Bales (Eds.), *Small groups: Studies in social interaction.* New York: Knopf, 1955a.

Bales, R. F. The equilibrium problem in small groups. In A. P. Hare, E. F. Borgatta, & R. F. Bales (Eds.), *Small groups: Studies in social interaction.* New York: Knopf, 1955b.

Bales, R. F. Task roles and social roles in problem-solving groups. In E. E. Maccoby, T. M. Newcomb, & E. L. Hartley (Eds.), *Readings in social psychology* (3rd ed.). New York: Holt, Rinehart and Winston. 1958.

Bandler, R. J., Jr., Badaras, G. R., & Bem, D. J. Self-observation as a source of pain perception. *Journal of Personality and Social Psychology,* 1968, **9,** 205–209.

Barker, R. G. Ecology and motivation. In M. R. Jones (Ed.), *Nebraska Symposium on Motivation.* Lincoln: University of Nebraska Press, 1960.

Barker, R. G. Explorations in ecological psychology. *American Psychologist,* 1965, **20,** 1–14.

Barker, R. G. & Barker, L. S. Social actions in the behavior streams of American and English children. In R. G. Barker (Ed.), *Stream of behavior: Explorations of its structure and content.* New York: Appleton-Century-Crofts, 1963.

Barker, R. G. & Gump, P. V. *Big school, small school: High school size and student behavior.* Stanford, Calif.: Stanford University Press, 1964.

Barker, R. G. & Wright, H. F. *Midwest and its children: The Psychological ecology of an American town.* Evanston, Ill.: Row, Peterson, 1955.

Bartlett, F. C. *Remembering: A study in experimental and social Psychology.* Cambridge, Eng.: Cambridge University Press, 1932.

Bateson G. *Naven.* Stanford, Calif.: Stanford University Press, 1936.

Bateson, G., Jackson, D., Haley, J., & Weakland, J. Toward a theory of schizophrenia. *Behavioral Science,* 1956, **1,** 251–264.

Bavelas, A. Communication patterns in task-oriented groups. *Journal of the Acoustical Society of America,* 1950, **22,** 725–730.

Becker, F. D. Study of spatial markers. *Journal of Personality and Social Psychology,* 1973, **26,** 439–445.

Becker, H. S. *Outsiders.* New York: Free Press, 1963.

Becker, H. S. The other side: *Perspectives on deviance.* New York: Free Press, 1964.

Becker, H. S. Art as collective action. *American Sociological Review,* 1974, **39,** 767–776.

Bem, D. J. Self perception: An alternative interpretation of cognitive dissonance phenomena. *Psychological Review,* 1967, **74,** 183–200.

Bem, D. J. Self-perception theory. In L. Berkowitz (Ed.), *Advances in experimental social psychology.* Vol. 6, New York: Academic Press, 1972.

Bem, D. J. & Allen, A. On predicting some of the people some of the time: The search for cross-situational consistencies in behavior. *Psychological Review,* 1974, **81,** 506–520.

Bem, D. J. & McConnell, K. Testing the self-perception explanation of dissonance phenomena: On the salience of premanipulation attitudes. *Journal of Personality and Social Psychology,* 1970, **14,** 23–31.

Bendix, R. Inequality and social structure: A comparison of Marx and Weber. *American Sociological Review,* 1974, **39,** 149–161.

Benedict, R. Continuities and discontinuities in cultural conditioning. *Psychiatry,* 1938, **1,** 161–167.

Benedict, R. *The chrysanthemum and the sword: Patterns of Japanese culture.* Boston: Houghton Mifflin, 1946.

Benedict, R. Patterns of the good culture. *Psychology Today,* 1970, **4,** 53–55; 74–77.

Benjamin, L. S. Structural analysis of social behavior. *Psychological Review,* 1974, **81,** 392–425.

Bennett, E. B. Discussion, decision, commitment, and consensus in "group decision." *Human Relations,* 1955, **8,** 251–273.

Benton, A. A. Productivity, distributive justice, and bargaining among children. *Journal of Personality and Social Psychology,* 1971, **18,** 68–78.

Berelson, B. R., Lazarsfeld, P. F., & McPhee, W. N. *Voting: A study of opinion formation in a presidential campaign.* Chicago: University of Chicago Press, 1954.

Berger, P. L. & Luckman, T. *The social construction of reality.* New York: Doubleday, 1966.

Berke, J. & Wilson, V. *Watch out for the weather.* New York: Viking Press, 1951.

Berkowitz, L. Social norms, feelings, and other factors affecting helping and altruism. In L. Berkowitz (Ed.), *Advances in experimental social psychology,* Vol. 6. New York: Academic Press, 1972.

Berkowitz, L. Reactance and the unwillingness to help others. *Psychological Bulletin,* 1973, **79,** 310–317.

Berkowitz, L. & Daniels, L. R. Responsibility and dependency. *Journal of Abnormal and Social Psychology,* 1963, **66,** 429–436.

Berkowitz, L. & Daniels, L. R. Affecting the salience of the social responsibility norm: Effects of past help on the response to dependency relationships. *Journal of Abnormal and Social Psychology,* 1964, **68,** 275–281.

Berkowitz, L. & Friedman, P. Some social class differences in helping behavior. *Journal of Personality and Social Psychology,* 1967, **5,** 217–225.

Bernard, V. W., Ottenberg, P., & Redl, F. Dehumanization: A composite psychological defense in relation to modern war. In R. Perrucci & M. Pilisuk (Eds.), *The triple revolution: Social problems in depth.* Boston: Little, Brown, 1968.

Berne, E. *Transactional analysis in psychotherapy.* New York: Grove Press, 1961.

Berne, E. *Games people play.* New York: Grove Press, 1964.

Bernstein, B. *Class, codes, and control, I: Theoretical studies towards a sociology of language.* London: Routledge & Kegan Paul, 1971.

Bernstein, B. (Ed.), *Class, codes, and control, II: Applied studies towards a sociology of language.* London: Routledge & Kegan Paul, 1973.

Bernstein, B. Some sociological determinants of perception: An enquiry into sub-cultural differences. *British Journal of Sociology,* 1958, **9,** 159–174.

Berscheid, E. & Walster, E. When does a harm-doer compensate a victim? *Journal of Personality and Social Psychology,* 1967, **6,** 435–441.

Bertalanffy, L. von. *General system theory.* New York: Braziller, 1968.

Bettelheim, B. Individual and mass behavior in extreme situations. In E. E. Maccoby, T. M. Newcomb, & E. L. Hartley (Eds.), *Readings in social psychology* (3rd ed.). New York: Holt, Rinehart and Winston, 1958.

Biddle, B. J. & Thomas, E. J. (Eds.), *Role Theory: Concepts and Research.* New York: Wiley, 1966.

Blake, R. R., Berkowitz, H., Bellamy, R., & Mouton, J. S. Volunteering as an avoidance act. *Journal of Abnormal and Social Psychology,* 1956, **53,** 154–156.

Blau, P. M. & Duncan, O. D. *The American occupational structure.* New York: Wiley, 1967.

Blauner, R. *Alienation and freedom: The factory worker and his industry.* Chicago: University of Chicago Press, 1964.

Block, J. H., Haan, N., & Smith, M. B. Socialization correlates of student activism. *Journal of Social Issues,* 1969, **25,** 143–177.

Block, J. H. Generational continuity and discontinuity in the understanding of societal rejection. *Journal of Personality and Social Psychology,* 1972, **22,** 333–345.

Block, J. H. Conceptions of sex role: Some cross-cultural and longitudinal perspectives. *American Psychologist,* 1973, **28,** 512–526.

Blom, J. P. & Gumperz, J. J. Some social determinants of verbal behavior. In J. J. Gumperz and D. Hymes (Eds.), *Directions in sociolinguistics.* New York: Holt, Rinehart and Winston, 1972.

Blum, A. F. & McHugh, P. The social ascription of motives. *American Sociological Review,* 1971, **36,** 98–109.

Blumer, H. Sociological implications of the thought of George Herbert Mead. *American Journal of Sociology,* 1966, **71,** 535–544.

Blumstein, P. W. Audience, machiavellianism, and tactics of indentity bargaining. *Sociometry,* 1973, **36,** 346–365.

Bourque, L. B. & Back, K. W. Language, society, and subjective experience. *Sociometry,* 1971, **34,** 1–21.

Bowers, K. S. Situationism in psychology: An analysis and a critique. *Psychological Review,* 1973, **80,** 307–336.

Bowles, S. & Gintis, N. I.Q. in the U.S. class structure. *Social Policy,* 1972–1973.

Brackman, J. Onward and upward with the arts: The put-on. *The New Yorker,* June 24, 1967, **43,** 34–73.

Bramel, D. Selection of a target for defensive projection. *Journal of Abnormal and Social Psychology,* 1963, **66,** 318–324.

Brandon, A. C. Status congruence and expectation. *Sociometry,* 1965, **28,** 272–288.

Brehm, J. W. *A theory of psychological reactance.* New York: Academic Press, 1966.

Brehm, J. W. & Cohen, A. R. *Explorations in cognitive dissonance.* New York: Wiley, 1962.

Brehm, J. W. & Cole, A. H. Effect of a favor which reduces freedom. *Journal of Personality and Social Psychology,* 1966, **3,** 420–426.

Brickman, P. & Horn, C. Balance theory and interpersonal coping in triads. *Journal of Personality and Social Psychology,* 1973, **26,** 347–355.

Brinton, C. Equality. *Encyclopedia of the social sciences,* Vol. 5. New York: Macmillan, 1931.

Broom, L. & Jones, F. L. Father-to-son mobility: Australia in comparative perspective. *American Journal of Sociology,* 1969, **74**, 333–342.

Broverman, I. K., Vogel, S. R., Broverman, D. M., Clarkson, F. E., & Rosenkrantz, P. S. Sex-role stereotypes: A current appraisal. *Journal of Social Issues,* 1972, **28**, 59–78.

Brown, R. W. *Words and things.* New York: Free Press, 1958.

Brown, R. W. *Social psychology.* Glencoe, Ill.: Free Press, 1965.

Brown, R. W. & Ford, M. Address in American English. *Journal of Abnormal and Social Psychology,* 1961, **62**, 375–385.

Brown, R. W. & Gilman, A. The pronouns of power and solidarity. In T. Sebeok (Ed.), *Style in language: Conference on Style, Indiana University, 1958.* Cambridge, Mass.: Technology Press of M.I.T., 1960.

Brown, R. W. & Lenneberg, E. H. A study in language and cognition. *Journal of Abnormal and Social Psychology,* 1954, **49**, 454–462.

Bryan, J. H. Why children help: A review. *Journal of Social Issues,* 1972, **28**, 87–104.

Bryan, J. H. & Test, M. A. Models and helping: Naturalistic studies in aiding behavior. *Journal of Personality and Social Psychology,* 1967, **6**, 400–407.

Bryan, J. H. & Walbeck, N. Preaching and practicing self sacrifice: Children's actions and reactions. *Child Development,* 1970a, **41**, 329–353.

Bryan, J. H. & Walbeck, N. The impact of words and deeds concerning altruism upon children. *Child Development,* 1970b, **41**, 747–757.

Buck, R. W., Savin, V. J., Miller, R. E., & Caul, W. F. Communication of affect through facial expression in humans. *Journal of Personality and Social Psychology,* 1972, **23**, 362–371.

Buck, R., Miller, R. E., & Caul, W. F. Sex, personality, and physiological variables in the communication of affect via facial expression. *Journal of Personality and Social Psychology,* 1974, **30**, 587–596.

Bugental, D. E. Interpretations of naturally occurring discrepancies between words and intonation: Modes of inconsistency resolution. *Journal of Personality and Social Psychology,* 1974, **30**, 125–133.

Bugental, D. E., Kaswan, J. W., & Love, L. R. Perception of contradictory meanings conveyed by verbal and nonverbal channels. *Journal of Personality and Social Psychology,* 1970, **16**, 647–655.

Burgess, R. L. & Nielsen, J. An experimental analysis of some structural determinants of equitable and inequitable exchange relations. *American Sociological Review,* 1974, **39,** 427–443.

Byrne, D. & Clore, G. L., Jr. Effectance arousal and attraction. *Journal of Personality and Social Psychology Monograph,* 1967, **6,** 1–18.

Calhoun, J. B. Population density and social pathology. *Scientific American,* 1962, **206,** 139–150.

Calhoun, J. B. The role of space in animal sociology. In H. Proshansky, W. Ittelson, & L. Rivlin (Eds.), *Environmental Psychology.* New York: Holt, Rinehart and Winston, 1970.

Campbell, D. T. Ethnocentric and other altruistic motives. In D. Levine (Ed.), *Nebraska Symposium on Motivation.* Lincoln: University of Nebraska Press, 1965.

Campbell, D. T. On the genetics of altruism and the counter-hedonic components in human culture. *Journal of Social Issues,* 1972, **28,** 21–37.

Campbell, J. P., Dunnette, M. D., Lawler, E. E., III, & Weick, K. E., Jr. *Managerial behavior, performance, and effectiveness.* New York: McGraw-Hill, 1970.

Campus, N. Transituational consistency as a dimension of personality. *Journal of Personality and Social Psychology,* 1974, **29,** 593–600.

Cannavale, F. J., Scarr, H. A., & Pepitone, A. Deindividuation in the small group: Further evidence. *Journal of Personality and Social Psychology,* 1970, **16,** 141–147.

Caplan, N. & Nelson, S. D. On being useful: The nature and consequences of psychological research on social problems. *American Psychologist,* 1973, **28,** 199–211.

Carling, F. *And yet we are human.* London: Chatto & Windus, 1962.

Carmichael, S. & Hamilton, C. V. *Black power: The politics of liberation in America.* New York: Vintage Books, Random House, 1967.

Carroll, J. B. & Casagrande, J. B. The functions of language classifications in behavior. In E. E. Maccoby, T. M. Newcomb, & E. L. Hartley (Eds.), *Readings in social psychology* (3rd ed.). New York: Holt, Rinehart and Winston, 1958.

Cartwright, D. Achieving change in people: Some applications of group dynamics theory. *Human Relations,* 1951, **4,** 381–392.

Cartwright, D. & Harary, F. Structural balance: A generalization of Heider's theory. *Psychological Review.* 1956, **63,** 277–293.

Cassirer, E. *Language and myth.* New York: Harper & Row, 1946.

Cassirer, E. *The philosophy of symbolic forms, Vol. 3: The phenomenology of knowledge.* New Haven: Yale University Press, 1957.

Cassirer, E. *An essay on man.* New York: Bantam, 1970.

Charters, W. W., Jr. & Newcomb, T. M. Some attitudinal effects of experimentally increased salience of a membership group. In E. E. Maccoby, T. M. Newcomb, & E. L. Hartley (Eds.), *Readings in social psychology* (3rd ed.). New York: Holt, Rinehart and Winston, 1958.

Christian, J., Flyger, V., & Davis, D. Factors in the mass mortality of a herd of sika deer (cervus nippon). *Chesapeake Science,* 1960, **1,** 79–95.

Christie, R. & Jahoda, M. (Eds.) *Studies in the scope and method of "The authoritatian personality."* Glencoe, Ill: Free Press, 1954.

Church, J. *Language and the discovery of reality: A developmental psychology of cognition.* New York: Random House, 1961.

Clark, R. D., III & Word, L. E. Where is the apathetic bystander? Situational characteristics of the emergency. *Journal of Personality and Social Psychology,* 1974, **29,** 279–287.

Coch, L. & French, J. R. P., Jr. Overcoming resistance to change. *Human Relations,* 1948, **1,** 512–532.

Cohen, A. R. Cognitive tuning as a factor affecting impression formation. *Journal of Personality,* 1961, **29,** 235–245.

Cohen, A. R. A study in forced-compliance. In J. W. Brehm & A. R. Cohen (Eds.), *Explorations in cognitive dissonance.* New York: Wiley, 1962.

Cohen, M., Freedman, N., Engelhardt, D. M., & Margolis, R. A. Family interaction patterns, drug treatment and change in social aggression. *Archives of General Psychiatry.* 1958, **19,** 50–56.

Cohen, R. Altruism: Human, cultural or what? *Journal of Social Issues,* 1972, **28,** 39–57.

Coleman, J. S. (Ed.) *Youth: Transition to adulthood.* Chicago: University of Chicago Press, 1974.

Collins, B. E. Four components of the Rotter internal-external scale: Belief in a difficult world, a just world, a predictable world, and a politically responsive world. *Journal of Personality and Social Psychology,* 1974, **29,** 381–391.

Collins, R. Functional and conflict theories of educational stratification. *American Sociological Review,* 1971, **36,** 1002–1019.

Comer, R. J. & Piliavin, J. A. The effects of physical deviance upon face-to-face interaction: The other side. *Journal of Personality and Social Psychology,* 1972, **23,** 33–39.

Condon, W. S. & Ogston, M. B. Sound film analysis of normal and pathological behavior patterns. *Journal of Nervous and Mental Disease,* 1966, **47,** 338–347.

Converse, P. E. Change in the American electorate. In A. Campbell & P. E. Converse (Eds.), *The human meaning of social change.* New York: Russell Sage Foundation, 1972.

Cooley, C. H. *Human nature and the social order.* New York: Scribner's 1902.

Cooley, C. H. *Social organization: A study of the larger mind.* New York: Scribner's, 1909.

Coser, L. A. *The functions of social conflict.* Glencoe, Ill.: Free Press, 1956.

Craik, K. H. Environmental psychology. In *New directions in psychology,* Vol. 4. New York: Holt, Rinehart and Winston, 1970.

Crano, W. D. & Cooper, R. E. Examination of Newcomb's extension of structural balance theory. *Journal of Personality and Social Psychology,* 1973, **27,** 344–353.

Crockett, W. H. Cognitive complexity and impression formation. In B. A. Maher (Ed.), *Progress in experimental personality research.* Vol. 2. New York: Academic Press, 1965.

Crockett, W. H. Balance, agreement, and subjective evaluations of the P-O-X triads. *Journal of Personality and Social Psychology,* 1974, **29,** 102–110.

Cronbach, L. J. Proposals leading to analytic treatment of social perception scores. In R. Tagiuri & L. Petrullo (Eds.), *Person perception and interpersonal behavior.* Stanford, Calif.: Stanford University Press, 1958.

Curry, T. J. & Emerson, R. M. Balance theory: A theory of interpersonal attraction? *Sociometry,* 1970, **33,** 216–238.

Darley, J. M. & Batson, C. D. "From Jerusalem to Jericho": A study of situational and dispositional variables in helping behavior. *Journal of Personality and Social Psychology,* 1973, **27,** 100–108.

Darley, J. M., Teger, A. I., & Lewis, L. D. Do groups always inhibit individuals' responses to potential emergencies? *Journal of Personality and Social Psychology,* 1973, **26,** 395–399.

Darley, J. M. & Latané, B. Bystander intervention in emergencies: Diffusion of responsibility. *Journal of Personality and Social Psychology,* 1968, **8,** 377–383.

Davis, K. & Moore, W. E. Some principles of stratification. *American Sociological Review,* 1945, **10,** 242–249.

DeFleur, M. L. & Westie, F. R. Verbal attitudes and overt acts: An experiment on the salience of attitudes. *American Sociological Review,* 1958, **23,** 667–673.

Deutsch, M. Cooperation and trust: Some theoretical notes. In M. R. Jones (Ed.), *Nebraska Symposium on Motivation.* Lincoln: University of Nebraska Press, 1962.

Deutsch, M. Field theory in social psychology. In G. Lindzey & E. Aronson (Eds.), *Handbook of Social Psychology.* Vol. 1 (2nd ed.). Cambridge, Mass.: Addison-Wesley, 1968.

Deutsch, M. Conflicts: Productive and destructive (Kurt Lewin Memorial Address). *Journal of Social Issues,* 1969, **25,** 7–41.

Deutsch, M. & Krauss, R. M. The effect of threat upon interpersonal bargaining. *Journal of Abnormal and Social Psychology,* 1960, **61,** 181–189.

Deutsch, M. & Krauss, R. M. Studies of interpersonal bargaining. *Journal of Conflict Resolution,* 1962, **6,** 52–76.

Dicks, H. V. *Licensed Mass Murder: A socio-psychological study of some S. S. killers.* New York: Basic Books, 1972.

Dillehay, R. C. On the irrelevance of the classical, negative evidence concerning the effect of attitudes on behavior. *American Psychologist,* 1973, **28,** 887–891.

Dittmann, A. T. & Llewellyn, L. G. Body movement and speech rhythm in social conversation. *Journal of Personality and Social Psychology,* 1969, **11,** 98–106.

Doherty, W. F. State high court under Tauro breaking new ground. *Boston Globe,* July 7, 1974, pp. A1–A2.

Dornbusch, S. M., Hastorf, A. H., Richardson, S. A., Muzzy, R. E., & Vreeland, R. S. The perceiver and the perceived: Their relative influence on the categories of interpersonal cognition. *Journal of Personality and Social Psychology,* 1965, **1,** 434–440.

Duncan, S., Jr. Some signals and rules for taking speaking turns in conversations. *Journal of Personality and Social Psychology,* 1972, **23,** 283–292.

Duncker, K. *Zur Psychologie des Produktiven Denkens.* Berlin: Springer, 1935.

Durkheim, E. *The division of labor in society.* G. Simpson translation. Glencoe, Ill.: Free Press, 1933.

Durkheim, E. *Suicide, a study in sociology.* J. A. Spaulding & G. Simpson translation; G. Simpson (Ed.). Glencoe, Ill.: Free Press, 1951.

Durkin, D. The specificity of children's moral judgment. *Journal of Genetic Psychology,* 1961, **98,** 3–13.

Efran, M. G. & Cheyne, J. A. Affective concomitants of the invasion of shared space: Behavioral, physiological, and verbal indicators. *Journal of Personality and Social Psychology,* 1974, **29,** 219–226.

Ekehammar, B. Interactionism in personality from a historical perspective. *Psychological Bulletin,* 1974, **81,** 1026–1048.

Ekman, P. The communication of interview stress through body language. Paper presented at the meeting of the Western Psychological Association, San Francisco, April 1962.

Ekman, P. Body position, facial expression and verbal behavior during interviews. *Journal of Abnormal and Social Psychology.* 1964, **68,** 295–301.

Ekman, P. Communication through non-verbal behavior: A source of information about interpersonal relations. In S. S. Tomkins &

C. E. Izard (Eds.), *Affect, cognition, and personality: empirical studies.* New York: Springer, 1965a.

Ekman, P. Differential communication of affect by head and body cues. *Journal of Personality and Social Psychology,* 1965b, **2**, 726–735.

Ekman, P. A lecture on micromomentary gestures. University of California, Berkeley, 1968.

Ekman, P. & Friesen, W. V. Non-verbal leakage and clues to deception. *Psychiatry,* 1969, **32**, 88–106.

Ekman, P. & Friesen, W. V. Constants across cultures in the face and emotion. *Journal of Personality and Social Psychology,* 1971, **17**, 124–129.

Ekman, P., Friesen, W. V., & Ellsworth, P. *Emotion in the human face: Guidelines for research and an integration of findings.* New York: Pergamon Press, 1972.

Ekstein, R. Psychoanalysis and education for the facilitation of positive human qualities. *Journal of Social Issues,* 1972, **28**, 71–85.

Ellis, D. P. The Hobbesian problem of order: A critical appraisal of the normative solution. *American Sociological Review,* 1971, **36**, 692–703.

Ellison, R. *Invisible man.* New York: Random House, 1952.

Ellsworth, P. C. & Carlsmith, J. M. Effects of eye contact and verbal content on affective response to a dyadic interaction. *Journal of Personality and Social Psychology,* 1968, **10**, 15–20.

Ellul, J. *The technological society,* J. Wilkinson translation. New York: Knopf, 1964.

Endler, N. S. & Hunt, J. McV. Sources of behavioral variance as measured by the S-R inventory of anxiousness. *Psychological Bulletin,* 1966, **65**, 336–346.

Endler, N. S. & Hunt, J. McV. S-R inventories of hostility and comparisons of the proportions of variance from persons, responses, and situations for hostility and anxiousness. *Journal of Personality and Social Psychology,* 1968, **9**, 309–315.

Erdelyi, M. H. A new look at the new look: Perceptual defense and vigilence. *Psychological Review,* 1974, **81**, 1–25.

Erikson, E. H. Identity and the life cycle. *Psychological Issues.* New York: International Universities Press, 1959.

Erikson, E. H. *Gandhi's Truth.* New York: Norton, 1969.

Ervin-Tripp, S. An Issei learns English. *Journal of Social Issues,* 1967, **23**, 78–90.

Ervin-Tripp, S. Sociolinguistics. In L. Berkowitz (Ed.), *Advances in Experimental Social Psychology,* Vol. 4. New York: Academic Press, 1969.

Etzioni, A. Basic human needs, alienation and inauthenticity. *American Sociological Review.* 1968, **33**, 870–885.

Exline, R. V. Explorations in the process of person perception: Visual interaction in relation to competition, sex, and need for affiliation. *Journal of Personality,* 1963, **31,** 1–20.

Exline, R. V. Visual interaction: The glances of power and preference. *Nebraska Symposium on Motivation.* Lincoln: University of Nebraska Press, 1971, 163–206.

Exline, R. V., Gray, D., & Schuette, D. visual behavior in a dyad as affected by interview content and sex of respondent, *Journal of Personality and Social Psychology,* 1965, **1,** 201–209.

Exline, R. V. & Winters, L. C. Affective relations and mutual glances in dyads. In S. S. Tomkins & C. E. Izard (Eds.), *Affect, cognition and personality: Empirical studies.* New York: Springer, 1965.

Feather, N. T. Attitude and selective recall. *Journal of Personality and Social Psychology,* 1969, **12,** 310–319.

Feffer, M. Symptom expression as a form of primitive decentering. *Psychological Review.* 1967. **74,** 16–28.

Feffer, M. Developmental analysis of interpersonal behavior. *Psychological Review,* 1970, **77,** 197–214.

Feffer, M. & Suchotliff, L. Decentering implications of social interactions. *Journal of Personality and Social Psychology,* 1966, **4,** 415–422.

Festinger, L. Motivations leading to social behavior. In M. R. Jones (Ed.), *Nebraska Symposium on Motivation.* Lincoln: University of Nebraska Press. 1954a.

Festinger, L. A theory of social comparison process. *Human Relations,* 1954b, **7,** 117–140.

Festinger, L. *A theory of cognitive dissonance.* Evanston, Ill.: Row, Peterson, 1957.

Festinger, L. & Carlsmith, J. M. Cognitive consequences of forced compliance. *Journal of Abnormal and Social Psychology,* 1959, **58,** 203–210.

Festinger, L., Pepitone, A., & Newcomb, T. Some consequences of deindividuation in a group. *Journal of Abnormal and Social Psychology,* 1952, **47,** 382–389.

Festinger, L., Riecken, H., & Schachter, S. *When prophecy fails.* Minneapolis: University of Minnesota Press, 1956.

Festinger, L., Schachter, S., & Back, K. *Social pressures in informal groups: A study of human factors in housing.* New York: Harper & Row, 1950.

Fishkin, J., Keniston, K., & MacKinnon, C. Moral reasoning and political ideology. *Journal of Personality and Social Psychology,* 1973, **27,** 109–119.

Fishman, J. A. A systematization of the Whorfian hypothesis. *Behavioral Science,* 1960, **5,** 323–339.

Flacks, R. *Conformity, resistance, and self-determination: The individual and authority.* Boston: Little, Brown, 1973.

Flacks, R. The liberated generation: An exploration of the roots of student protest. *Journal of Social Issues,* 1967, **23,** 52–75.

Flavell, J. H. *The developmental psychology of Jean Piaget.* Princeton, N.J.: Van Nostrand, 1963.

Form, W. H. Technology and social behavior of workers in four countries: A sociotechnical perspective. *American Sociological Review,* 1972, **37,** 727–738.

Frankl, V. *Man's search for meaning.* Boston: Beacon Press, 1959.

Frederiksen, N. Toward a taxonomy of situations. *American Psychologist,* 1972, **27,** 114–123.

Freedman, J. L. & Fraser, S. C. Compliance without pressure: The foot-in-the-door technique. *Journal of Personality and Social Psychology,* 1966, **4,** 195–202.

Freedman, J. L. & Sears, D. O. Selective exposure. In L. Berkowitz (Ed.), *Advances in experimental social-psychology.* Vol. 2. New York: Academic Press, 1965.

Freedman, M. B., Leary, T. F., Ossorio, A. G., & Coffey, H. S. The interpersonal dimension of personality. *Journal of Personality,* 1951, **20,** 143–161.

Freedman, N., Blass, T. Rifkin, A., & Quitkin, F. Body movements and the verbal encoding of aggressive affect. *Journal of Personality and Social Psychology,* 1973, **26,** 72–85.

French, J. R. P., Jr. The disruption and cohesion of groups. *Journal of Abnormal and Social Psychology,* 1941, **36,** 361–377.

French, J. R. P., Jr. & Raven, B. The bases of social power. In D. Cartwright (Ed.), *Studies in social power.* Ann Arbor: Research Center for Group Dynamics Institute for Social Research, University of Michigan, 1959.

Fromm, E. *Escape from freedom.* New York: Holt, Rinehart and Winston, 1941.

Fromm, E. *The sane society.* New York: Holt, Rinehart and Winston, 1955.

Fuller, C. H. Comparison of two experimental paradigms as tests of Heider's balance theory. *Journal of Personality and Social Psychology,* 1974, **30,** 802–806.

Gabennesch, H. Authoritarianism as world view. *American Journal of Sociology,* 1972, **77,** 857–875.

Galle, O. R., Gove, W. R., & McPherson, J. M. Population density and pathology: What are the relationships for man? *Science,* 1972, **176,** 23–30.

Gamson, W. A. *Power and discontent.* Homewood, Ill.: Dorsey Press, 1968.

Garfinkel, H. *Studies in Ethnomethodology.* Englewood Cliffs, N.J.: Prentice-Hall, 1967.

Geller, D. M., Goodstein, L, Silver, M., & Sternberg, W. C. On being ignored: The effects of the violation of implicit rules of social interaction. *Sociometry,* 1974, **37,** 541–556.

Gerard, H. B. & Fleischer, L. Recall and pleasantness of balanced and unbalanced cognitive structures. *Journal of Personality and Social Psychology,* 1967, **7,** 332–337.

Gergen, K. J. Personal consistency and the presentation of self. In C. Gordon & K. J. Gergen (Eds.), *The self in social interaction.* New York: Wiley, 1968.

Gerth, H. H. & Mills, C. W. *From Max Weber: Essays in sociology.* New York: Oxford University Press, 1946.

Gerth, H. H. & Mills, C. W. *Character and Social Structure.* New York: Harcourt, Brace, Jovanovich, 1953.

Ghiselli, E. E. & Lodahl, M. Patterns of managerial and group effectiveness. *Journal of Abnormal and Social Psychology,* 1958, **57,** 61–66.

Goeckner, D. J., Greenough, W. T., & Mead, W. R. Deficits in learning tasks following chronic overcrowding in rats. *Journal of Personality and Social Psychology,* 1973, **28,** 256–261.

Goffman, E. *The presentation of self in everyday life.* Garden City, N.Y.: Anchor Books, Doubleday, 1959.

Goffman, E. *Asylums: Essays on the social situation of mental patients and other inmates.* Chicago: Aldine-Atherton, 1961.

Goffman, E. *Behavior in public places: Notes on the social organization of gatherings.* Glencoe, Ill.: Free Press, 1963a.

Goffman, E. *Stigma: notes on the management of spoiled identity.* Englewood Cliffs, N.J.: Prentice-Hall, 1963b.

Goffman, E. *Relations in public.* New York: Harper & Row, 1972.

Goldstein, D., Fink, D., & Mettee, D. R. Cognition of arousal and actual arousal as determinants of emotion. *Journal of Personality and Social Psychology,* 1972, **21,** 41–51.

Goranson, R. & Berkowitz, L. Reciprocity and responsibility reactions to prior help. *Journal of Personality and Social Psychology,* 1966, **3,** 227–232.

Gore, P. M. & Rotter, J. B. A personality correlate of social action. *Journal of Personality,* 1963, **31,** 58–64.

Gordon, C. & Gergen, K. J. *The self in social interaction.* New York: Wiley, 1968.

Gormly, J. A comparison of predictions from consistency and affect theories for arousal during interpersonal disagreement. *Journal of Personality and Social Psychology,* 1974, **30,** 658–663.

Gouldner, A. W. The norm of reciprocity: A preliminary statement. *American Sociological Review,* 1960, **25,** 161–178.

Greaves, G. Conceptual system functioning and selective recall of information. *Journal of Personality and Social Psychology,* 1972, **21,** 327–332.

Green, J. A. Attitudinal and situational determinants of intended behavior toward blacks. *Journal of Personality and Social Psychology,* 1972, **22,** 13–17.

Greenwald, A. G. & Sakumura, J. S. Attitude and selective learning: Where are the phenomena of yesteryear? *Journal of Personality and Social Psychology,* 1967, **7,** 387–397.

Griffitt, W. & Veitch, R. Hot and crowded: Influences of population density and temperature on interpersonal affective behavior. *Journal of Personality and Social Psychology,* 1971, **17,** 92–98.

Grimshaw, A. D. Sociolinguistics and the sociologist. *The American Sociologist,* 1969, **4,** 312–321.

Grimshaw, A. D. On language in society: Part I. *Contemporary Sociology,* 1973, **2,** 575–585.

Gross, N., Mason, W. S., & McEachern, A. *Explorations in role analysis: studies of the school superintendency role.* New York: Wiley, 1957.

Guetzkow, H. & Gyr, J. An analysis of conflict in decision-making groups. *Human Relations,* 1954, **7,** 367–382.

Gumperz, J. J. & Hymes, D. (Eds.) *Directions in sociolinguistics.* New York: Holt, Rinehart & Winston, 1972.

Gurin, P., Gurin, G., Lao, R. C., & Beattie, M. Internal-external control in the motivational dynamics of Negro youth. *Journal of Social Issues,* 1969, **25,** 29–53.

Haan, N., Smith, M. B., & Block, J. Moral reasoning of young adults: Political-social behavior, family background, and personality correlates. *Journal of Personality and Social Psychology,* 1968, **10,** 183–201.

Haber, R. N. Nature of the effect of set on perception. *Psychological Review,* 1966, **73,** 335–351.

Hall, E. T. *The silent language.* Garden City, N.Y.: Doubleday, 1959.

Hall, E. T. Proxemics: The study of man's spatial relations. In L. Galdston (Ed.), *Man's image in medicine and anthropology: Arden House Conference on Medicine and Anthropology, 1961.* New York: International Universities Press, 1963.

Hall, E. T. Human adaptability to high density. *Ekistics,* 1965, **20,** 191–193.

Hall, R. A., Jr. *Hands off pidgin English!* Sydney: Pacific Publications, 1955.

Handel, G. Psychological study of whole families. *Psychological Bulletin,* 1965, **63,** 19–41.

Handel, G. (Ed.) *The Psychosocial Interior of the Family.* Chicago: Aldine-Atherton, 1972.

Hardin, E. Computer automation, work environment and employee satisfaction in an insurance company. *Industrial and Labor Relations Review,* 1960a, **13,** 559–567.

Hardin, E. The reactions of employees to office automation. *Bureau of United States Labor Statistics: Monthly Labor Review.* 1960b, **83,** 925–932.

Hardin, G. The tragedy of the commons. *Science.* 1968, **162,** 1243–1248.

Harris, E. G. & Paluck, R. J. The effects of crowding in an educational setting. *Man-Environment Systems,* May 1971.

Harvey, O. J. System structure, flexibility, and creativity. In O. J. Harvey (Ed.), *Experience, structure, and adaptability.* New York: Springer, 1966.

Harvey, O. J., Hunt, D. E., & Schroder, H. M. *Conceptual systems and personality organization.* New York: Wiley, 1961.

Harvey, O. J. & Ware, R. Personality differences in dissonance resolution, *Journal of Personality and Social Psychology,* 1967, **7,** 227–230.

Hauser, P. M. The chaotic society: Product of the social morphologic revolution. *American Sociological Review,* 1969, **34,** 1–19.

Hays, W. L. *Statistics for psycholigists.* New York: Holt, Rinehart and Winston, 1963.

Haythorn, W. The effects of varying combinations of authoritarian and equalitarian leaders and followers. In E. E. Maccoby, T. M. Newcomb, & E. L. Hartley (Eds.), *Readings in social psychology* (3rd ed.). New York: Holt, Rinehart and Winston, 1958.

Heider, F. *The psychology of interpersonal relations.* New York: Wiley, 1958.

Heider, F. On perception, event structure and the psychological environment. *Psychological Issues,* 1959, **1,** 1–123.

Hemphill, J. K. Job descriptions for executives. *Harvard Business Review,* 1959, **37,** 55–67.

Henry, A. F. & Short, J. F., Jr. *Suicide and homicide: Some economic, sociological, and psychological aspects of aggression.* Glencoe, Ill.: Free Press, 1954.

Hernstein, R. J. Review of inequality. *Contemporary Psychology,* 1973, **18,** 403–405.

Hess, E. H. Attitude and pupil size. *Scientific American,* April 1965, **212,** 46–54.

Hicks, J. D. *A Short History of American Democracy.* Boston: Houghton Mifflin, 1943.

Hobbes, T. *Leviathan.* New York: Meridian, 1966 (orig. 1651).

Hoffman, L. R., Harburg, E., & Maier, N. R. F. Differences and disagreement as factors in creative group problem solving. *Journal of Abnormal and Social Psychology,* 1962, **64,** 206–214.

Hoffman, L. W. Early childhood experiences and women's achievement motives. *Journal of Social Issues,* 1972, **28,** 129–155.

Hoffman, M. L. & Saltzstein, H. D. Parent discipline and the child's moral development. *Journal of Personality and Social Psychology,* 1967, **5,** 45–57.

Hoijer, H. Cultural implications of some Navaho linguistic categories. *Language,* 1951, **27,** 111–120.

Holmes, D. S. & Houston, B. K. Effectiveness of situation redefinition and affective isolation in coping with stress. *Journal of Personality and Social Psychology,* 1974, **29,** 212–218.

Homans, G. C. *Social Behavior: Its elementary forms.* New York: Harcourt, Brace, Jovanovich, 1961.

Horner, M. S. Toward an understanding of achievement-related conflicts in women. *Journal of Social Issues,* 1972, **28,** 157–175.

Hornstein, H. S. Promotive tension: The basis of prosocial behavior from a Lewinian perspective. *Journal of Social Issues,* 1972, **28,** 191–218.

Horwitz, M. The recall of interrupted group tasks: An experimental study of individual motivation in relation to group goals. *Human Relations,* 1954, **7,** 3–38.

Hovland, C. I. & Janis, T. L. (Eds.) *Personality and persuasibility.* New Haven, Conn: Yale University Press, 1959.

Hovland, C. I., Janis, I. L. & Kelley, H. H. *Communication and Persuasion: Psychological studies of opinion change.* New Haven, Conn.: Yale University Press, 1953.

Hovland, C. I., Lumsdaine, A. A., & Sheffield, F. D. *Experiments on mass communications.* Princeton: Princeton University Press, 1949.

Hovland, C. I., & Weiss, W. The influence of source credibility on communication effectiveness. *Public Opinion Quarterly,* 1951, **15,** 635–650.

Hrycenko, I. & Minton, H. L. Internal-external control, power position, and satisfaction in task-oriented groups. *Journal of Personality and Social Psychology,* 1974, **30,** 871–878.

Hutt, C. & Vaizey, M. J. Differential effects of group density on social behavior. *Nature,* 1966, **209,** 1371–1372.

Hyman, H. H., & Sheatsley, P. B. Some reasons why information campaigns fail. In E. E. Maccoby, T. M. Newcomb, & E. L. Hartley (Eds.), *Readings in social psychology* (3rd ed.). New York: Holt, Rinehart and Winston, 1958.

Hymes, D. (Ed.) *Language in culture and society: A reader in linguistics and anthropology.* New York: Harper & Row, 1964.

Hymes, D. (Ed.) *Pidginization and creolization of languages: Proceedings of a conference.* Cambridge, Eng.: Cambridge University Press, 1971.

Isen, A. M. Success, failure, attention, and reaction to others: The warm glow of success. *Journal of Personality and Social Psychology,* 1970 **15,** 294–301.

Isen, A. M., Horn, N., & Rosenhan, D. L. Effects of success and failure on children's generosity. *Journal of Personality and Social Psychology,* 1973, **27,** 239–247.

Jahoda, M. Conformity and independence: A psychological analysis. *Human Relations,* 1959, **12,** 99–120.

James, L. R. & Jones, A. P. Organizational climate: A review of theory and research. *Psychological Bulletin,* 1974, **81,** 1096–1112.

James, W. What is an emotion? *Mind,* 1884, **9,** 188–205.

James, W. *Principles of psychology.* 2 volumes. New York: Holt, 1890.

James, W. *Psychology: The briefer course.* New York: Holt, 1910.

Janis, I. L. Groupthink among policy makers. In N. Sanford & C. Comstock (Eds.), *Sanctions for evil.* San Francisco: Jossey-Bass, 1973.

Janis, I. L. & Gilmore, J. B. The influence of incentive conditions on the success of role playing in modifying attitudes. *Journal of Personality and Social Psychology,* 1965, **1,** 17–27.

Janis, I. L. & Rausch, C. N. Selective interest in communications that could arouse decisional conflict: A field study of participants in the draft-resistance movement. *Journal of Personality and Social Psychology,* 1970, **14,** 46–54.

Jessor, R., Jessor, S. L, & Finney, J. A social psychology of marijuana use: Longitudinal studies of high school and college youth. *Journal of Personality and Social Psychology,* 1973, **26,** 1–15.

Jones, C. & Aronson, E. Attribution of fault to a rape victim as a function of respectability of the victim. *Journal of Personality and Social Psychology,* 1973, **26,** 415–419.

Jones, E. E. *Ingratiation: A social psychological analysis.* New York: Appleton-Century-Crofts, 1964.

Jones, E. E. & Davis, K. From acts to dispositions: The attribution process in person perception. In L. Berkowitz (Ed.), *Advances in experimental social psychology.* Vol. 2. New York: Academic Press, 1965.

Jones, E. E., Davis, K., & Gergen, K. J. Role playing variations and their informational value for person perception. *Journal of Abnormal and Social Psychology,* 1961, **63,** 302–310.

Jones, E. E. & Gerard, H. B. *Foundations of social psychology.* New York: Wiley, 1967.

Jones, E. E. & Kohler, R. The effects of plausibility on the learning of controversial statements. *Journal of Abnormal and Social Psychology,* 1958, **57,** 315–320.

Jones, E. E. & Nisbett, R. E. *The actor and the observer: Divergent perceptions of the causes of behavior.* New York: General Learning Press, 1971.

Jones, H. E. The galvanic skin response as related to overt emotional expression. *American Journal of Psychology,* 1935, **47,** 241–251.

Jones, R. A. Volunteering to help: The effects of choice, dependence and anticipated dependence. *Journal of Personality and Social Psychology,* 1970, **14,** 121–129.

Jones, S. E. & Aiello, J. R. Proxemic behavior of black and white first-third-and fifth-grade children. *Journal of Personality and Social Psychology,* 1973, **25,** 21–27.

Jordan, N. Behavioral forces that are a function of attitudes and of cognitive organization. *Human Relations,* 1953, **6,** 273–287.

Jordan, N. Experimenting with a P-O-Q unit: Complications in cognitive balance. *Journal of Psychology,* 1966, **64,** 3–22.

Jordan, N. Cognitive balance as an aspect of Heider's cognitive psychology. In R. Abelson, E. Aronson, W. McGuire, T. Newcomb, M. Rosenberg, & P. Tannenbaum (Eds.), *Theories of cognitive consistency: A sourcebook.* Chicago: Rand McNally, 1968.

Jordan, W. D. *White over black: American attitudes toward the Negro 1550–1812.* Chapel Hill: University of North Carolina Press & Institute of Early American History and Culture, 1968.

Kagan, J. & Klein, R. E. Cross-cultural perspectives on early development. *American Psychologist,* 1973, **28,** 927–961.

Kahn, A. Reactions to generosity or stinginess from an intelligent or stupid work partner: A test of equity theory in a direct exchange relationship. *Journal of Personality and Social Psychology,* 1972, **21,** 117–123.

Kahn, A., Hottes, J., & Davis, W. L. Cooperation and optimal responding in the prisoner's dilemma game: Effects of sex and physical attractiveness. *Journal of Personality and Social Psychology,* 1971, **17,** 267–279.

Kahneman, D. & Tversky, A. On the psychology of prediction. *Psychological Review,* 1973, **80,** 237–251.

Kaplan, J. A legal look at prosocial behavior: What can happen for failing to help or trying to help someone. *Journal of Social Issues,* 1972, **28,** 219–226.

Kasarda, J. D. & Janowitz, M. Community attachment in mass society. *American Sociological Review,* 1974, **39,** 328–339.

Katz, D. The functional approach to the study of attitudes. *Public Opinion Quarterly,* 1960, **24,** 163–204.

Katz, D. Factors affecting social change: A social-psychological interpretation. *Journal of Social Issues,* 1974, **30,** 159–180.

Katz, D. & Kahn, R. L. *The social psychology of organizations.* New York: Wiley, 1966.

Katz, D., Sarnoff, I., & McClintock, C. Ego-defense and attitude change. *Human Relations,* 1956, **9,** 27–45.

Katz, J. Altruism and sympathy: Their history in philosophy and some implications for psychology. *Journal of Social Issues,* 1972, **28,** 59–69.

Kelly, G. A. *The psychology of personal constructs,* Vol. 1 and 2. New York: Norton, 1955.

Kelly, G. A. *A theory of personality: The psychology of personal constructs.* New York: Norton, 1963.

Kelley, H. H. Salience of membership and resistance to change of group-anchored attitudes. *Human Relations,* 1955, **8,** 275–289.

Kelley, H. H. Attribution theory in social psychology. *Nebraska Symposium on Motivation.* Lincoln: University of Nebraska Press, 1967, 192–240.

Kelley, H. H. Moral evaluation. *American Psychologist,* 1971, **26,** 293–300.

Kelley, H. H. *Causal schemata and the attribution process.* New York: General Learning Press, 1972.

Kelley, H. H. The processes of causal attribution. *American Psychologist,* 1973, **28,** 107–128.

Kelley, H. H. & Stahelski, A. J. Social interaction basis of cooperators' and competitors' beliefs about others. *Journal of Personality and Social Psychology,* 1970, **16,** 66–91.

Kelley, H. H., Thibaut, J. W., Radloff, R., & Mundy, D. The development of cooperation in the "minimal social situation." *Psychological Monographs,* 1962, **76,** 1–19.

Kelman, H. C. Compliance, identification, and internalization: Three processes of attitude change. *Journal of Conflict Resolution,* 1958, **2,** 51–60.

Kelman, H. C. Processes of opinion change. *Public Opinion Quarterly,* 1961, **25,** 57–78.

Kelman, H. C. Violence without moral restraint: Reflections on the dehumanization of victims and victimizers. *Journal of Social Issues,* 1973, **29,** 25–61.

Kelman, H. C. & Barclay, J. The F scale as a measure of breadth of perspective. *Journal of Abnormal and Social Psychology.* 1963, **67,** 608–615.

Kelman, H. C. & Lawrence, L. H. Assignment of responsibility in the case of Lt. Calley: Preliminary report on a national survey. *Journal of Social Issues,* 1972, **28,** 177–212.

Kendall, P. L. & Lazarsfeld, P. F. The relation between individual and group characteristics in The American Soldier. In P. F. Lazarsfeld & M. Rosenberg (Eds.), *The language of social research.* Glencoe, Ill.: Free Press, 1955.

Keniston, K. *The uncommitted: Alienated youth in American society.* New York: Harcourt, Brace, Jovanovich, 1965.

Keniston, K. The sources of student dissent. *Journal of Social Issues,* 1967, **23,** 108–137.

Kilham, W. & Mann, L. Level of destructive obedience as a function of transmitter and executant roles in the Milgram obedience paradigm. *Journal of Personality and Social Psychology,* 1974, **29,** 696–702.

Kimble, G. A. & Perlmuter, L. C. The problem of volition. *Psychological Review,* 1970, **77,** 361–384.

Kluckhohn, C., Murray, H. A. & Schneider, D. M. *Personality in nature, society, and culture.* New York: Knopf, 1956.

Kluckhohn, F. R. Dominant and variant value orientations. In C. Kluckhohn, H. A. Murray, & D. M. Schneider (Eds.), *Personality in nature, society and culture.* New York: Knopf, 1956.

Knowles, E. S. Boundaries around group interaction: The effect of group size and member status on boundary permeability. *Journal of Personality and Social Psychology,* 1973, **26,** 327–331.

Kohlberg, L. The development of modes of moral thinking in the years ten to sixteen. Unpublished doctoral dissertation. University of Chicago, 1958.

Kohlberg, L. The child as a moral philosopher. *Psychology Today,* September 1968, **2,** 24–31.

Kohlberg, L. Stage and sequence: The cognitive-developmental approach to socialization. In D. A. Goslin (Ed.), *Handbook of socialization theory and research.* Chicago: Rand McNally, 1969.

Kohlberg, L. & Kramer, R. Continuities and discontinuities in childhood and adult moral development. *Human Development,* 1969, **12,** 93–120.

Kornahuser, W. *The politics of mass society.* Glencoe, Ill.: Free Press, 1959.

Kristol, I. Equality as an ideal. *International Encyclopedia of the Social Sciences.* Vol. 5. New York: Macmillan, 1968.

Kruglanski, A. W. & Cohen, M. Attributed freedom and personal causation. *Journal of Personality and Social Psychology,* 1973, **26,** 245–250.

Kruglanski, A. W. & Cohen, M. Attributing freedom in the decision context: Effects of choice alternatives, degree of commitment, and predecision uncertainty. *Journal of Personality and Social Psychology,* 1974, **30,** 178–187.

Kuhn, A. *Unified social science.* Homewood, Ill.: Dorsey Press, 1975.

Kuhn, A. *The logic of social systems.* San Francisco: Jossey-Bass, 1974.

Külpe, O. *Versuche Über Abstraktion.* Berlin International Congress of Experimental Psychology, 1904, 56–68.

Kurtines, W. & Grief, E. B. The development of moral thought: Review and evaluation of Kohlberg's approach. *Psychological Bulletin,* 1974, **81**, 453–470.

Kutner, B. & Gordon, N. B. Cognitive functioning and prejudice: A nine-year follow-up study. *Sociometry,* 1964, **27**, 66–74.

Labov, W. *The social stratification of English in New York City.* Washington D.C.: Center for Applied Linguistics, 1966.

Labov, W. *Language in the inner city: Studies in the black English vernacular.* Philadelphia: University of Pennsylvania Press, 1972a.

Labov, W. *Sociolinguistic patterns.* Philadelphia: University of Pennsylvania Press, 1972b.

Laing, R. D. *The Divided Self.* England: Penguin, 1965.

Laing, R. D. *The Politics of Experience.* England: Penguin, 1967.

Laing, R. D. *Knots.* New York: Pantheon, 1970.

Laird, J. D. Self-attribution of emotion: The effects of expressive behavior on the quality of emotional experience. *Journal of Personality and Social Psychology,* 1974, **29**, 475–486.

Laird, J. D. & Crosby, M. Individual differences in self-attribution of emotion. In H. London & R. Nisbett (Eds.), *Cognitive alteration of feeling states.* Chicago: Aldine-Atherton (in press).

Lambert, W. E. A social psychology of bilingualism. *Journal of Social Issues,* 1967, **23**, 91–109.

Lane, I. M. & Messé, L. A. Distribution of insufficient, sufficient, and over-sufficient rewards: A clarification of equity theory. *Journal of Personality and Social Psychology,* 1972, **21**, 228–233.

Lange, C. G. *The Emotions.* Baltimore: Williams & Wilkins, 1922.

Langer, E. J. & Abelson, R. P. The semantics of asking a favor: How to succeed in getting help without really dying. *Journal of Personality and Social Psychology,* 1972, **24**, 26–32.

Lanzetta, J. T. & Kleck, R. E. Encoding and decoding of nonverbal affect in humans. *Journal of Personality and Social Psychology,* 1970, **16**, 12–19.

LaPiere, R. T. Attitudes versus action. *Social Forces,* 1934, **13**, 230–237.

Larsen, K. S., Coleman, D., Forbes, J., & Johnson, R. Is the subject's personality or the experimental situation a better predictor of a subject's willingness to adminsiter shock to a victim? *Journal of Personality and Social Psychology,* 1972, **22**, 287–295.

Latané, B. & Darley, J. M. Group inhibition of bystander intervention in emergencies. *Journal of Personality and Social Psychology,* 1968, **10,** 215–221.

Latané, B. & Rodin, J. A Lady in distress: Inhibiting effects of friends and strangers on bystander intervention. *Journal of Experimental Social Psychology,* 1969, **5,** 189–202.

Lawler, E. E., III. Equity theory as a predictor of productivity and work quality. *Psychological Bulletin,* 1968, **70,** 596–610.

Lawrence, J. E. S. Science and sentiment: Overview of research on crowding and human behavior. *Psychological Bulletin,* 1974, **81,** 712–720.

Lazarsfeld, P. F. & Manzel, H. On the relation between individual and collective properties. In A. Etzioni (Ed.), *A sociological reader on complex organization.* New York: Holt, Rinehart and Winston, 1969.

Lazarus, R. *Psychological stress and the coping process.* New York: McGraw-Hill, 1966.

Lazarus, R. & Alfert, E. Short-circuiting of threat by experimentally altering cognitive appraisal. *Journal of Abnormal and Social Psychology,* 1964, **69,** 195–205.

Lazarus, R., Averill, J. R., & Opton, E. M. Towards a cognitive theory of emotion. In M. Arnold (Ed.), *Third International Symposium on Feelings and Emotions.* New York: Academic Press, 1970.

Lazarus, R., Opton, E., Nomikos, M., & Rankin, N. The principle of short-circuiting of threat: Further evidence. *Journal of Personality,* 1965, **33,** 622–635.

Leary, T. *Interpersonal Diagnosis of Personality.* New York: Ronald Press, 1957.

Leavitt, H. J. Some effects of certain communication patterns on group performance. In E. E. Maccoby, T. M. Newcomb, & E. L. Hartley (Eds.), *Readings in social psychology* (3rd ed.). New York: Holt, Rinehart and Winston, 1958.

Leeds, R. Altruism and the norm of giving. *Merrill-Palmer Quarterly,* 1963, **9,** 229–240.

Lefcourt, H. M. Internal versus external control of reinforcement: A review. *Psychological Bulletin,* 1966, **65,** 206–220.

Lefcourt, H. M. Recent developments in the study of locus of control. In B. A. Maher (Ed.), *Progress in experimental personality research.* Vol. 6. New York: Academic Press, 1972.

Le Furgy, W. G. & Woloshin, G. W. Immediate and long term effects of experimentally induced social influence in the modification of adolescents' moral judgments. *Journal of Personality and Social Psychology,* 1969, **12,** 104–110.

Leinhardt, S. Developmental change in the sentiment structure of children's groups. *American Sociological Review.* 1972, **37**, 202–212.

Lemert, E. *Human deviance, social problems and social control.* Englewood Cliffs, N.J.: Prentice-Hall, 1967.

Lepper, M. R. Dissonance, self-perception, and honesty in children. *Journal of Personality and Social Psychology,* 1973, **25**, 65–74.

Lerner, M. J. Observer's evaluation of a victim: Justice, guilt, and veridical perception. *Journal of Personality and Social Psychology,* 1971, **20**, 127–135.

Lerner, M. J. The justice motive: "equity" and "parity" among children. *Journal of Personality and Social Psychology,* 1974, **29**, 539–550.

Lerner, M. J. & Matthews, G. Reactions to suffering of others under conditions of indirect responsibility. *Journal of Personality and Social Psychology,* 1967, **5**, 319–325.

Lerner, M. J. & Simmons, C. H. Observer's reaction to the "Innocent victim": Compassion or rejection? *Journal of Personality and Social Psychology,* 1966, **4**, 203–210.

Leventhal, G. S. Some effects of having a brother or sister. Paper read at American Psychological Association meeting San Francisco, 1968.

Leventhal, G. S. & Anderson, D. Self-interest and the maintenance of equity. *Journal of Personality and Social Psychology,* 1970, **15**, 57–62.

Leventhal, G. S. & Lane, D. W. Sex, age, and equity behavior. *Journal of Personality and Social Psychology,* 1970, **15**, 312–316.

Leventhal, G. S. & Michaels, J. W. Extending the equity model: Perception of inputs and allocation of reward as a function of duration and quantity of performance. *Journal of Personality and Social Psychology,* 1969, **12**, 303–309.

Leventhal, G. S., Michaels, J. W., & Sanford, C. Inequity and interpersonal conflict: Reward allocation and secrecy about reward as methods of preventing conflict. *Journal of Personality and Social Psychology,* 1972, **23**, 88–102.

Leventhal, G. S., Weiss, T., & Buttrick, R. Attribution of value, equity, and the prevention of waste in reward allocation. *Journal of Personality and Social Psychology,* 1973, **27**, 276–286.

Leventhal, G. S., Weiss, T., & Long, G. Equity, reciprocity and reallocating rewards in the dyad. *Journal of Personality and Social Psychology,* 1969, **13**, 300–305.

Levi, L. D., Stierlin, H., & Savard, R. Father and sons: The interlocking crises of integrity and identity. *Psychiatry,* 1972, **35**, 48–56.

Levine, J. M. & Murphy, G. The learning and forgetting of controversial material. *Journal of Abnormal and Social Psychology,* 1943, **38,** 507–517.

Levine, R., Chein, I., & Murphy, G. The relation of intensity of a need to the amount of perceptual distortion: A preliminary report. *Journal of Psychology,* 1942, **13,** 283–293.

Lewin, K. *Dynamic theory of personality.* New York: McGraw-Hill, 1935,

Lewin, K. Frontiers in group dynamics: Concept, method and reality in social science: Social equilibria and social change. *Human Relations,* 1947a, **1,** 5–41.

Lewin, K. Frontiers in group dynamics, II: Channels of group life; social planning and action research. *Human Relations.* 1947b, **1,** 143–153.

Lewin, K. *Resolving social conflicts.* New York: Harper & Row, 1948.

Lewin, K. *Field theory in social science: Selected theoretical papers.* D. Cartwright (Ed.), New York: Harper & Row, 1951.

Lewin, K. Group decision and social change. In E. E. Maccoby, T. M. Newcomb, & E. L. Hartley (Eds.), *Readings in social psychology* (3rd ed.). New York: Holt, Rinehart and Winston, 1958.

Lewis, H. B. An experimental study of the role of the ego in work: 1. The role of the ego in cooperative work. *Journal of Experimental Psychology,* 1944, **34,** 113–126.

Lewis, H. B. & Franklin, M. An experimental study of the role of the ego in work: II. The significance of task orientation in work. *Journal of Experimental Psychology,* 1944, **31,** 195–215.

Lieberman, S. The effects of changes in roles on the attitudes of role occupants. *Human Relations,* 1956, **9,** 385–402.

Lifton, R. J. *Thought reform and the psychology of totalism: A study of "brainwashing" in China.* New York: Norton, 1961.

Lifton, R. J. *Death in life: Survivors of Hiroshima.* New York: Vintage Books, Random House, 1969.

Linton, R. *The study of man.* New York: Appleton-Century-Crofts, 1936.

Lippitt, R. & White, R. K. An experimental study of leadership and group life. In E. E. Maccoby, T. M. Newcomb, & E. L. Hartley (Eds.), *Readings in social psychology* (3rd ed.). New York: Holt, Rinehart and Winston, 1958.

Little, K. B. Cultural variations in social schemata. *Journal of Personality and Social Psychology,* 1968, **10,** 1–7.

Litwak, E. & Szelenyi, I. Primary group structures and their functions: Kin, neighbors, and friends. *American Sociological Review,* 1969, **34,** 465–481.

Loftis, J. & Ross, L. Effects of misattribution of arousal upon the acquisition and extinction of a conditioned emotional response.

Journal of Personality and Social Psychology, 1974a, **30,** 673–682.

Loftis, J. & Ross, L. Retrospective misattribution of a conditioned emotional response, *Journal of Personality and Social Psychology,* 1974b, **30,** 683–687.

Long, G. T. & Lerner, M. J. Deserving, the "personal contract," and altruistic behavior by children. *Journal of Personality and Social Psychology,* 1974, **29,** 551–556.

Loo, C. M. The effects of spatial density on the social behavior of children. *Journal of Applied Social Psychology,* 1972, **2,** 372–381.

Lydall, H. *The structure of earnings.* London: Oxford University Press, 1968.

Lynch, K. *What time is this place?* Cambridge, Mass.: M.I.T. Press, 1972.

Maccoby, E. (Ed.), *The development of sex differences.* Stanford, Calif.: Stanford University Press, 1966.

Maier, N. R. F. & Solem, A. R. The contribution of a discussion leader to the quality of group thinking: The effective use of minority opinions. *Human Relations,* 1952, **5,** 277–288.

Maier, N. R. F. & Hoffman, L. R. Organization and creative problem solving. *Journal of Applied Psychology,* 1961, **45,** 277–280.

Mandler, G. The interruption of behavior. *Nebraska Symposium on Motivation.* Lincoln: University of Nebraska Press, 1964, 163–219.

Mandler, G. & Watson, D. I. Anxiety and the interruption of behavior. In C. D. Spielberger (Ed.), *Anxiety and behavior.* New York: Academic Press, 1966.

Mannheim, K. *Ideology and utopia: An introduction to the sociology of knowledge.* L. Wirth & E. Shils translation. New York: Harcourt, Brace, Jovanovich, 1936.

Mantell, D. M. The potential for violence in Germany. *Journal of Social Issues,* 1971, **27,** 101–112.

Mantell, D. M. *True Americanism: Green berets and war resisters.* New York: Teachers College Press, 1974.

Marcuse, H. *One-dimensional man: Studies in the ideology of advanced industrial society.* Boston: Beacon Press, 1966.

Marlowe, D., Frager, R., & Nuttall, R. L. Commitment to action taking as a consequence of cognitive dissonance. *Journal of Personality and Social Psychology,* 1965, **2,** 864–867.

Marx, K. *Selected writings in sociology and social philosophy.* T. B. Bottomore & M. Rubel (Eds.). London: Watts, 1956.

Maslach, C. Social and personal bases of individuation. *Journal of Personality and Social Psychology,* 1974, **29,** 411–425.

Maslow, A. H. Deficiency motivation and growth motivation. In R. M. Jones (Ed.), *Nebraska Symposium on Motivation,* 1955. Lincoln: University of Nebraska Press, 1955.

May, R. *Psychology and the human dilemma.* Princeton, N.J.: Van Nostrand, 1967.

Mead, G. H. *The philosophy of the present.* Chicago: Open Court, 1932.

Mead, G. H. *The social psychology of George Herbert Mead.* A. Strauss (Ed.). Chicago: University of Chicago Press, 1934.

Mead, M. (Ed.) *Cooperation and competition among primitive people.* New York: McGraw-Hill, 1937.

Meier, D. L. & Bell, W. Anomia and differential access to the achievement of life goals. *American Sociological Review,* 1959, **24,** 189–202.

Mehrabian, A. Nonverbal Communication. *Nebraska Symposium on Motivation.* Lincoln: University of Nebraska Press, 1971, 107–162.

Mehrabian, A. & Wiener, M. Decoding of inconsistent communications. *Journal of Personality and Social Psychology,* 1967, **6,** 109–114.

Memmi, A. *The colonizer and the colonized.* Boston: Beacon Press, 1967.

Merton, R. *Social theory and social structure.* Glencoe, Ill.: Free Press, 1957.

Milgram, S. Behavioral study of obedience, *Journal of Abnormal and Social Psychology,* 1963, **67,** 371–378.

Milgram, S. Liberating effects of group pressure. *Journal of Personality and Social Psychology,* 1965a, **1,** 127–134.

Milgram, S. Some conditions of obedience and disobedience to authority. *Human Relations,* 1965b, **18,** 57–75.

Milgram, S. & Hollander, P. Murder they heard. *Nation,* 1964, **198,** 602–604.

Miller, D. R. & Swanson, G. E. *The changing American parent: A study in the Detroit area.* New York: Wiley, 1958.

Miller, G. A. Professionals in bureaucracy:Alienation among industrial scientists and engineers. *American Sociological Review.* 1967, **32,** 755–768.

Miller, J. G. The nature of living systems. *Behavioral Science,* 1971, **16,** 1–182.

Miller, R. E. Experimental approaches to the physiological and behavioral concomitants of affective communication in rhesus monkeys. In S. A. Altmann (Ed.), *Social communication among primates.* Chicago: University of Chicago Press, 1967.

Miller, R. E., Caul, W. F., & Mirsky, I. A. Communication of affects between feral and socially isolated monkeys. *Journal of Personality and Social Psychology,* 1967, **7,** 231–239.

Miller, S. M. Comparative social mobility. *Current Sociology,* 1960, **9,** 1–66.

Mills, C. W. *The sociological imagination.* London: Oxford University Press, 1959.

Mintz, A. Nonadaptive group behavior. In G. E. Swanson, T. M. Newcomb, & E. L. Hartley (Eds.), *Readings in social psychology* (2nd ed.). New York: Holt, Rinehart and Winston, 1952.

Mirels, H. L. Dimensions of internal versus external control, *Journal of Consulting and Clinical Psychology,* 1970, **34,** 226–228.

Mischel, W. *Personality and assessment.* New York: Wiley, 1968.

Mischel, W. Continuity and change in personality. *American Psychologist,* 1969, **24,** 1012–1018.

Mischel, W. *Introduction to personality.* New York: Holt, Rinehart and Winston, 1971.

Mischel, W. Toward a cognitive social learning reconceptualization of personality. *Psychological Bulletin,* 1973, **80,** 252–283.

Mischel, W. & Baker, N. Cognitive appraisals and transformations in delay behavior. *Journal of Personality and Social Psychology,* 1975, **31,** 254–261.

Mischel, W., Ebbesen, E. B., & Zeiss, A. R. Cognitive and attentional mechanisms in delay of gratification. *Journal of Personality and Social Psychology,* 1972, **21,** 204–281.

Mizruchi, E. H. Social structure and anomia in a small city. *American Sociological Review,* 1960, **25,** 645–654.

Mizruchi, E. H. *Success and opportunity: A study of anomie.* Glencoe, Ill.: Free Press, 1964.

Monat, A., Averill, J. R. & Lazarus, R. S. Anticipatory stress and coping reactions under various conditions of uncertainty. *Journal of Personality and Social Psychology,* 1972, **24,** 237–253.

Moos, R. H. Sources of variance in response to questionnaires and in behavior. *Journal of Abnormal Psychology,* 1969, **74,** 405–412.

Moos, R. H. Assessment of the psychosocial environments of community-oriented psychiatric treatment programs. *Journal of Abnormal Psychology,* 1972 **79,** 9–18.

Moos, R. H. Conceptualizations of human environments. *American Psychologist,* 1973, **28,** 652–665.

Moos, R. H. & Insel, P. M. (Eds.) *Issues in Social Ecology.* Palo Alto, Calif.: National Press Books, 1974.

Morgan, W. R. & Sawyer, J. Bargaining, expectations, and the preference for equality over equity. *Journal of Personality and Social Psychology,* 1967, **6,** 139–149.

Morse, N. C. & Reimer, E. The experimental change of a major organizational variable. *Journal of Abnormal and Social Psychology,* 1956, **52,** 120–129.

Morse, S. & Gergen, K. J. Social comparison, self-consistency, and the concept of self. *Journal of Personality and Social Psychology,* 1970, **16,** 148–156.

Moulton, R. W., Raphelson, A. C., Kristofferson, A. B., & Atkinson, J. W. The achievement motive and perceptual sensitivity under two conditions of motive-arousal. In J. W. Atkinson (Ed.), *Motives in fantasy, action, and society: A method of assessment and study.* Princeton, N.J.: Van Nostrand, 1958.

Muir, D. & Weinstein, E. The social debt: An investigation of lower-class and middle-class norms of social obligation. *American Sociological Review,* 1962, **27,** 532–539.

Mumford, L. *The transformations of man.* New York: Torchbooks, Harper & Row, 1956.

Murray, H. A. et al. *Explorations in personality.* New York: Oxford University Press, 1938.

Myrdal, G. *An American dilemma: The Negro problem and modern democracy.* New York: Harper & Row, 1944.

McArthur, L. S. The how and what of why: Some determinants and consequences of causal attribution. *Journal of Personality and Social Psychology,* 1972, **22,** 171–193.

McClelland, D. C. *The achieving society.* Princeton, N.J.: Van Nostrand, 1961.

McClelland, D. C. & Atkinson, J. W. The projective expression of needs. 1: The effect of different intensities of the hunger drive on perception. *Journal of Psychology,* 1948, **25,** 205–222.

McClelland, D. C. & Liberman, A. M. The effect of need for achievement on recognition of need-related words. *Journal of Personality,* 1949, **18,** 236–251.

McClosky, H. & Schaar, J. H. Psychological dimensions of anomy. *American Sociological Review,* 1965, **30,** 14–40.

McDougall, W. *Introduction to social psychology.* London: Methuen, 1908.

McGinnies, E. Emotionality and perceptual defense. *Psychological Review.* 1949, **56,** 244–251.

McGuire, W. J. Resistance to persuasion conferred by active and passive prior refutation of the same and alternative counterarguments. *Journal of Abnormal and Social Psychology,* 1961, **63,** 326–332.

McGuire, W. J. Persistence of the resistance to persuasion induced by various types of prior belief defenses. *Journal of Abnormal and Social Psychology,* 1962, **64,** 241–248.

McGuire, W. J. The current status of cognitive consistency theories. In S. Feldman (Ed.), *Cognitive consistency: Motivational antecedents and behavioral consequents.* New York: Academic Press, 1966.

McGuire, W. J. & Papageorgis, D. The relative efficacy of various types of prior belief-defense in producing immunity against persuasion. *Journal of Abnormal and Social Psychology,* 1961, **62,** 327–337.

McGuire, W. J. & Papageorgis, D. Effectiveness of forewarning in developing resistance to persuasion. *Public Opinion Quarterly,* 1962, **26,** 24–34.

McIntosh, D. Weber and Freud: On the nature and sources of authority. *American Sociological Review,* 1970, **35,** 901–911.

McLaughlin, B. Effects of similarity and likeableness on attraction and recall. *Journal of Personality and Social Psychology,* 1971, **20,** 65–69.

Neal, A. G. & Seeman, M. Organizations and Powerlessness. *American Sociological Review,* 1964, **29,** 216–226.

Neisser, U. *Cognitive Psychology.* New York: Appleton-Century-Crofts, 1967.

Newcomb, T. M. *Personality and social change: Attitude formation in a student community,* New York: Dryden, 1943.

Newcomb, T. M. An approach to the study of communicative acts. *Psychological Review.* 1953, **60,** 393–404.

Newcomb, T. M. Attitude development as a function of reference groups: The Bennington study. In E. E. Maccoby, T. M. Newcomb, & E. L. Hartley (Eds.), *Readings in social psychology* (3rd ed.). New York: Holt, Rinehart and Winston, 1958.

Newcomb, T. M. Individual systems of orientation. In S. Koch (Ed.), *Psychology: A study of a science.* Vol. 3. New York: McGraw-Hill, 1959.

Newcomb, T. M. *The acquaintance process.* New York: Holt, Rinehart and Winston, 1961.

Newcomb, T. M. Interpersonal balance. In R. Abelson, E. Aronson, W. McGuire, T. Newcomb, M. Rosenberg, & P. Tannenbaum (Eds.), *Theories of cognitive consistency: A sourcebook.* Chicago: Rand McNally, 1968.

Newcomb, T. M., Koenig, K. E., Flacks, R., & Warwick, D. P. *Persistence and change: Bennington College and its students after twenty-five years.* New York: Wiley, 1967.

Nisbet, R. A., *The sociological tradition.* New York: Basic Books, 1966.

Nisbett, R. E., Caputo, C., Legant, P., & Marecek, J. Behavior as seen by the actor and as seen by the observer. *Journal of Personality and Social Psychology,* 1973, **27,** 154–164.

Nisbett, R. E. & Kanouse, D. E. Obesity, food deprivation and supermarket shopping behavior. *Journal of Personality and Social Psychology,* 1969, **12,** 289–294.

Orne, M. T. On the social psychology of the psychological experiment: With particular reference to demand characteristics and their implications. *American Psychologist,* 1962, **17,** 776–783.

Osmond, H. Function as the basis of psychiatric ward design. *Mental Hospitals,* 1957, 23–29.

Pace, C. R. & Stern, G. G. An approach to the measurement of psychological characteristics of college environments. *Journal of Educational Psychology,* 1958, **49,** 269–277.

Papageorgis, D. & McGuire, W. J. The generality of immunity to persuasion produced by pre-exposure to weakened counterarguments. *Journal of Abnormal and Social Psychology,* 1961, **62,** 475–581.

Parsons, T. & Shils, E. A. (Eds.). *Towards a general theory of action.* Cambridge, Mass.: Harvard University Press, 1951.

Parsons, T. The position of identity in the general theory of action. In C. Gordon & K. J. Gergen (Eds.), *The self in social interaction.* New York: Wiley, 1968.

Parsons, T. Age and sex roles in the social structure of the United States. *American Sociological Review,* 1942, **7,** 604–616.

Parsons, T. *The social system.* Glencoe, Ill.: Free Press, 1951.

Parsons, T., Bales, R. F., & Shils, E. A. *Working papers in the theory of action.* Glencoe, Ill.: Free Press, 1953.

Parsons, T. Family structure and socialization of the child. In T. Parsons & R. F. Bales (Eds.), *Family socialization and interaction process.* Glencoe, Ill.: Free Press, 1955.

Passini, F. T. & Norman, W. T. A universal conception of personality structure? *Journal of Personality and Social Psychology,* 1966, **4,** 44–49.

Patterson, M. Spatial factors in social interaction. *Human Relations,* 1968, **21,** 351–361.

Peterson, R., Centra, J., Hartnett, R., & Linn, R. *Institutional Functioning Inventory: Preliminary technical manual.* Princeton, N.J.: Educational Testing Service, 1970.

Pettigrew, T. F. Social psychology and desegregation research. *American Psychologist,* 1961, **16,** 105–112.

Piaget, J. *The moral judgment of the child.* New York: Harcourt, Brace, Jovanovich, 1932.

Piaget, J. *The psychology of intelligence.* M. Percy & D. E. Berlyne translation. New York: Harcourt, Brace, Jovanovich, 1950.

Piaget, J. *The origins of intelligence in children.* M. Cook translation. New York: International Universities Press. 1952.

Piaget, J. *The construction of reality in the child.* M. Cook, translation. New York: Basic Books, 1954.

Piaget, J. *The language and thought of the child.* New York: Meridian Books, 1955.

Piliavin, I. M., Rodin, J., & Piliavin, J. A. Good samaritanism: An underground phenomenon. *Journal of Personality and Social Psychology,* 1969, **13,** 289–299.

Piliavin, J. A. & Piliavin, I. M. Effect of blood on reactions to a victim. *Journal of Personality and Social Psychology,* 1972, **23,** 353–361.

Platt, J. Social traps. *American Psychologist,* 1973, **28,** 641–651.

Pollack, H. B. Change in homogeneous and heterogeneous sensitivity training groups. Unpublished doctoral dissertation, University of California, Berkeley, 1967.

Pope, L. *Millhands and preachers: A study of Gastonia.* New Haven, Conn.: Yale University Press, 1958.

Porter, L. W. & Lawler, E. E. The effects of "tall" versus "flat" organization structures on managerial job satisfaction. *Personnel Psychology,* 1964, **17,** 135–148.

Postman, L. J., Bruner, J., & McGinnies, E. Personal values as selective factors in perception. *Journal of Abnormal and Social Psychology,* 1948, **43,** 142–154.

Pressman, I. & Carol, A. Crime as a diseconomy of scale. *Review of Social Economy,* 1971, **29,** 227–236.

Price, K., Harburg, E., & Newcomb, T. Psychological balance in situations of negative interpersonal attitudes. *Journal of Personality and Social Psychology,* 1966, **3,** 265–270.

Price, R. H. & Bouffard, D. L. Behavioral appropriateness and situational constraint as dimensions of social behavior. *Journal of Personality and Social Psychology,* 1974, **30,** 579–586.

Proshansky, H., Ittelson, W., & Rivlin, L. (Eds.) *Environmental psychology: Man and his physical setting.* New York: Holt, Rinehart and Winston, 1970.

Pruitt, D. G. Reciprocity and credit building in a laboratory dyad. *Journal of Personality and Social Psychology,* 1968, **8,** 143–147.

Rapoport, A. & Chammah, A. M. *Prisoner's dilemma: A study in conflict and cooperation.* Ann Arbor: University of Michigan Press, 1965.

Raush, H. L. Interaction sequences. *Journal of Personality and Social Psychology,* 1965, **2,** 487–499.

Redfield, R. The folk society. *American Journal of Sociology,* 1947, **52,** 293–308.

Redfield, R. *The social uses of social science: The papers of Robert Redfield.* M. P. Redfield (Ed.). Chicago: University of Chicago Press, 1963.

Redl, F. The superego in uniform. In N. Sanford & C. Comstock (Eds.), *Sanctions for evil.* San Francisco: Jossey-Bass, 1973.

Regan, D. T., Williams, M., & Sparling, S. Voluntary expiation of guilt: A field experiment. *Journal of Personality and Social Psychology,* 1972, **24,** 42–45.

Regan, J. W. Guilt, perceived injustice and altruistic behavior. *Journal of Personality and Social Psychology,* 1971, **18,** 124–132.

Reik, T. *Listening with the third ear.* New York: Farrar Straus & Giroux, 1948.

Reisman, S. R. & Schopler, J. An analysis of the attribution process and an application to determinants of responsibility. *Journal of Personality and Social Psychology,* 1973, **25,** 361–368.

Rest, J., Turiel, E., & Kohlberg, L. Level of moral development as a determinant of preference and comprehension of moral judgements made by others. *Journal of Personality,* 1969, **37,** 225–252.

Roberts, A. H. & Rokeach, M. Anomie, authoritarianism and prejudice. *American Journal of Sociology,* 1956, **62,** 355–358.

Rodin, J. & Slochower, J. Fat chance for a favor: Obese-normal differences in compliance and incidental learning. *Journal of Personality and Social Psychology,* 1974, **29,** 557–565.

Rodrigues, A. Effects of balance, positivity, and agreement in triadic social relations. *Journal of Personality and Social Psychology,* 1967, **5,** 472–576.

Rogers, C. R. *Client-centered therapy: Its current practice, implications and theory.* Boston: Houghton Mifflin, 1951.

Rogers, C. R. *On becoming a person.* Boston: Houghton Mifflin, 1961.

Rogers, C. R. The process of the basic encounter group. In J. F. T. Bugental (Ed.), *Challenges of humanistic psychology.* New York: McGraw-Hill, 1967, 261–276.

Rokeach, M. Political and religious dogmatism: An alternative to the authoritarian personality. *Psychological Monographs,* 1956, **70,** (18, Whole No. 425.)

Rokeach, M. *The open and closed mind: Investigations into the nature of belief systems and personality systems.* New York: Basic Books, 1960.

Rosenbaum, M. & Blake, R. Volunteering as a function of field structure. *Journal of Abnormal and Social Psychology,* 1955, **50,** 193–196.

Rosenthal, A. M. *Thirty-eight witnesses.* New York: McGraw-Hill, 1964.

Ross, E. A. *Social psychology,* New York: Macmillan, 1908.

Ross, L., Rodin, J., & Zimbardo, P. Toward an attribution therapy: The reduction of fear through induced cognitive emotional misattribution. *Journal of Personality and Social Psychology,* 1969, **12,** 279–288.

Rotter, J. B. Generalized expectancies for internal versus external control of reinforcement. *Psychological Monographs,* 1966, **80,** 1–28.

Ruesch, J. & Bateson, G. *Communication: The Social Matrix of Psychiatry.* New York: Norton, 1951.

Sampson, E. E. *Approaches, contexts and problems of social psychology.* Englewood Cliffs, N.J.: Prentice-Hall, 1964.

Sampson, E. E. Studies of Status Congruence. In L. Berkowitz, (Ed.), *Advances in experimental social psychology.* Vol. 4. New York: Academic Press, 1969a.

Sampson, E. E. *Social psychology and contemporary society.* New York: Wiley, 1971.

Sampson, E. E. & Brandon, A. C. The effects of role and opinion deviation on small group behavior. *Sociometry,* 1964, **27,** 261–281.

Sampson, E. E., Fisher, L., Angel, A., Mulman, A., & Sullins, C. Two profiles: The draft resister and the ROTC cadet. Unpublished Report. University of California, Berkeley, 1969b.

Sampson, E. E. & Insko, C. A. Cognitive consistency and performance in the autokinetic situation. *Journal of Abnormal and Social Psychology,* 1964, **68,** 184–192.

Sanger, S. P. & Alker, H. A. Dimensions of internal-external locus of control and the women's liberation movement. *Journal of Social Issues,* 1972, **28,** 115–129.

Sapir, E., *Culture, language and personality: Selected essays.* D. G. Mandelbaum (Ed.). Berkeley: University of California Press, 1956.

Sarbin, T. R. & Allen, V. L. Role Theory. In G. Lindzey & E. Aronson (Eds.), *Handbook of Social Psychology.* Vol. 1 (2nd. ed.). Cambridge, Mass.: Addison-Wesley, 1968.

Schachter, S. Deviation, rejection, and communication. *Journal of Abnormal and Social Psychology,* 1951, **46,** 190–207.

Schachter, S. Cognitive effects on bodily functioning: Studies of obesity and eating. In D. Glass (Ed.), *Neurophysiology and emotion.* New York: Rockefeller University Press & Russell Sage Foundation, 1967.

Schachter, S. & Hall, R. Group-derived restraints and audience persuasion. *Human Relations,* 1952, **5,** 397–406.

Schachter, S., Goldman, R., & Gordon, A. Effects of fear, food deprivation and obesity on eating. *Journal of Personality and Social Psychology,* 1968, **10,** 91–97.

Schachter, S. & Gross, L. P. Manipulated time and eating behavior. *Journal of Personality and Social Psychology,* 1968, **10,** 98–106.

Schachter, S. & Singer, J. S. Cognitive, social, and physiological determinants of emotional state. *Psychological Review,* 1962, **69,** 379–399.

Schaps, E. Cost, dependency, and helping. *Journal of Personality and Social Psychology,* 1972, **21,** 74–78.

Schatzman, L. & Strauss, A. Social class and modes of communication. *American Journal of Sociology,* 1955, **60,** 329–338.

Scheerer, M. Cognitive theory. In G. Lindzey (Ed.), *Handbook of social psychology.* Vol. 1. Cambridge, Mass.: Addison-Wesley, 1954.

Scheff, T. J. *Being mentally ill.* Chicago: Aldine-Atherton, 1966.

Schein, E. H. The Chinese indoctrination program for prisoners of war: A study of attempted "brainwashing." In E. E. Maccoby, T. M. Newcomb, & E. L. Hartley (Eds.), *Readings in social psychology* (3rd ed.). New York: Holt, Rinehart and Winston, 1958.

Schelling, T. The ecology of micromotives. *Public Interest,* 1971, **25,** 61–98.

Scherwitz, L. & Helmreich, R. Interactive effects of eye contact and verbal content on interpersonal attraction in dyads. *Journal of Personality and Social Psychology,* 1973, **25,** 6–14.

Schmidt, C. F. Multidimensional scaling analysis of the printed media's explanations of the riots of the summer of 1967. *Journal of Personality and Social Psychology,* 1972, **24,** 59–67.

Schneider, D. J. Implicit personality theory: A review. *Psychological Bulletin,* 1973, **79,** 294–309.

Schopler, J. & Compere, J. S. Effects of being kind or harsh to another on liking. *Journal of Personality and Social Psychology,* 1971, **20,** 155–159.

Schopler, J. & Thompson, V. The role of attribution process in mediating amount of reciprocity for a favor. *Journal of Personality and Social Psychology,* 1968, **10,** 243–250.

Schroder, H. M., Driver, M. J., & Streufert, S. *Human information processing: Individuals and groups functioning in complex social situations.* New York: Holt, Rinehart and Winston, 1967.

Schur, E. M. *Labeling deviant behavior.* New York: Harper & Row, 1971.

Schutz, A. *The phenomenology of the social world.* Evanston, Ill.: Northwestern University Press, 1967.

Schutz, A. *Collected papers. Vols. 1–3.* The Hague: Martinus Nijhoff, 1970–1971.

Schutz, W. C. *FIRO: A three-dimensional theory of interpersonal behavior.* New York: Holt, Rinehart and Winston, 1960.

Schwartz, S. H. Elicitation of moral obligation and self-sacrificing behavior: An experimental study of volunteering to be a bone marrow donor. *Journal of Personality and Social Psychology,* 1970, **15,** 283–293.

Scott, W. A. Cognitive complexity and cognitive balance. *Sociometry,* 1963, **26,** 66–74.

Secord, P. R. & Backman, C. W. An interpersonal approach to personality. In B. A. Maher (Ed.), *Progress in experimental personality research.* Vol. 2. New York: Academic Press, 1965.

Seeman, M. On the meaning of alienation. *American Sociological Review,* 1959, **24,** 783–791.

Seeman, M. The Urban alienations: Some dubious theses from Marx to Marcuse. *Journal of Personality and Social Psychology,* 1971, **19,** 135–143.

Seeman, M. Alienation and engagement. In A. Campbell & P. E. Converse (Eds.), *The human meaning of social change.* New York: Russell Sage Foundation, 1972.

Sells, S. B. Dimensions of stimulus situations which account for behavior variance. In S. B. Sells (Ed.), *Stimulus determinants of behavior.* New York: Ronald Press, 1963a.

Sells, S. B. An interactionist looks at the environment. *American Psychologist,* 1963b, **18,** 696–702.

Selznick, P. Foundations of the theory of organization. *American Sociological Review,* 1948, **13,** 25–35.

Sewell, W. H. Inequality of opportunity for higher education. *American Sociological Review,* 1971, **36,** 793–809.

Shannon, J. & Guerney, B., Jr. Interpersonal effects of interpersonal behavior. *Journal of Personality and Social Psychology,* 1973, **26,** 142–150.

Sheppard, H. & Herrick, N. Q. *Where have all the robots gone?* New York: Free Press, 1972.

Sher, M. A. Pupillary dilation before and after interruption of familiar and unfamiliar sequences. *Journal of Personality and Social Psychology,* 1971, **20,** 281–286.

Sherif, M. A study of some social factors in perception. *Archives of Psychology,* 1935, **27,** No. 187.

Sherif, M. & Sherif, C. W. *Groups in harmony and tension: An intergration of studies on intergroup relations.* New York: Harper & Row, 1953.

Shils, E. A. Authoritarianism: "Right" and "left." In R. Christie & M. Jahoda (Eds.), *Studies in the scope and method of "The authoritarian personality."* New York: Free Press, 1954.

Shils, E. A. Charisma, order, and status. *American Sociological Review,* 1965, **30,** 199–213.

Sidowski, J. B., Wyckoff, L. B., & Tabory, L. The influence of reinforcement and punishment in a minimal social situation. *Journal of Abnormal and Social Psychology,* 1956, **52,** 115–119.

Sidowski, J. B. Reward and punishment in a minimal social situation. *Journal of Experimental Psychology,* 1957, **54,** 318–326.

Simmel, G. Sociology of the senses: Visual interaction. In R. E. Park & E. W. Burgess (Eds.), *Introduction to the science of sociology.* Chicago: University of Chicago Press, 1921.

Simmel, G. *The Sociology of Georg Simmel.* Translation and edited by K. H. Wolff. Glencoe, Ill.: Free Press, 1950.

Simmel, G. Conflict association. In L. A. Coser & B. Rosenberg (Eds.), *Sociological theory: A book of readings.* New York: Macmillan, 1957.

Simmons, C. H. & Lerner, M. J. Altruism as a search for justice. *Journal of Personality and Social Psychology,* 1968, **9,** 216–225.

Singer, J., Brush, C., & Lublin, S. Some aspects of deindividuation: Identification and conformity. *Journal of Experimental Social Psychology,* 1965, **1,** 356–378.

Skinner, B. F. *Science and human behavior.* New York: Macmillan, 1948.

Skinner, B. F. *Beyond freedom and dignity.* New York: Knopf, 1971.

Smelser, W. T. Dominance as a factor in achievement and perception in cooperative problem solving interaction. *Journal of Abnormal and Social Psychology,* 1961, **62,** 535–542.

Smith, E. E. The power of dissonance techniques to change attitudes. *Public Opinion Quarterly,* 1961, **25,** 626–639.

Smith, H. W. Some developmental interpersonal dynamics. *American Sociological Review,* 1973, **38,** 543–552.

Smith, M. B., Bruner, J. S., & White, R. W. *Opinions and personality.* New York: Wiley, 1956.

Smith, S. S. & Jamieson, B. D. Effects of attitude and ego involvement on the learning and retention of controversial material, *Journal of Personality and Social Psychology,* 1972, **22,** 303–310.

Snyder, M. & Cunningham, M. R. To comply or not comply: Testing the self-perception explanation of the "foot-in-the-door" phenomenon. *Journal of Personality and Social Psychology,* 1975, **31,** 64–67.

Solzhenitsyn, A. I. *The Gulag Archipelago.* Vol. 1. New York: Harper & Row, 1974.

Sommer, R. The distance for comfortable conversation: A further study. *Sociometry,* 1962, **25,** 111–116.

Sommer, R. Further studies of small group ecology. *Sociometry,* 1965, **28,** 337–348.

Sommer, R. Man's proximate environment. *Journal of Social Issues,* 1966, **22,** 59–70.

Sommer, R. Sociofugal space. *American Journal of Sociology,* 1967, **72,** 654–660.

Sommer, R. *Personal space.* Englewood Cliffs, N.J.: Prentice-Hall, 1969.

Sommer, R. & Becker, F. D. Territorial defense and the good neighbor. *Journal of Personality and Social Psychology,* 1969, **11,** 85–92.

Sosis, R. H. Internal-external control and the perception of responsibility of another for an accident. *Journal of Personality and Social Psychology,* 1974, **30,** 393–399.

Sperry, R. W. An objective approach to subjective experience: Further explanation of a hypothesis. *Psychological Review,* 1970, **77,** 585–590.

Srole, L. Social integration and certain corollaries: An exploratory study. *American Sociological Review,* 1956, **21,** 709–716.

Stager, P. Conceptual level as a composition variable in small-group decision making. *Journal of Personality and Social Psychology,* 1967, **5,** 152–161.

Stampp, K. M. *The peculiar institution: Slavery in the antebellum South.* New York: Vintage Books, Random House, 1964.

Staub, E. A child in distress: The influence of age and number of witnesses on children's attempts to help. *Journal of Personality and Social Psychology,* 1970, **14,** 130–140.

Staub, E. Helping a person in distress: The influence of implicit and explicit "rules" of conduct on children and adults. *Journal of Personality and Social Psychology,* 1971, **17,** 137–144.

Staub, E. Instigation to goodness: The role of social norms and interpersonal influence. *Journal of Social Issues,* 1972, **28,** 131–150.

Staub, E. & Baer, R. S., Jr. Stimulus characteristic of a sufferer and difficulty of escape as determinants of helping. *Journal of Personality and Social Psychology,* 1974, **30,** 279–284.

Staub, E. & Sherk, L. Need approval, children's sharing behavior and reciprocity in sharing. *Child Development,* 1970, **41,** 243–253.

Steiner, I. D. Perceived freedom. In L. Berkowitz (Ed.), *Advances in experimental social psychology.* Vol. 5. New York: Academic Press, 1970.

Steiner, I. D. & Field, W. L. Role assignment and interpersonal influence. *Journal of Abnormal and Social Psychology,* 1960, **61,** 239–245.

Steiner, I. D., Rotermund, M., & Talaber, R. Attribution of choice to a decision maker. *Journal of Personality and Social Psychology,* 1974, **30,** 553–562.

Stewart, W. A. Creole languages in the Caribbean. In F. A. Rice (Ed.), *Study of the role of second languages in Asia, Africa, and Latin America.* Washington, D. C.: Center for Applied Linguistics, 1962.

Storms, M. D. Videotape and the attribution process: Reversing actors' and observers' points of view. *Journal of Personality and Social Psychology,* 1973, **27,** 165–175.

Storms, M. D. & Nisbett, R. E. Insomnia and the attribution process. *Journal of Personality and Social Psychology,* 1970, **16,** 319–328.

Stouffer, S. A., Suchman, E. A., DeVinney, L. C., Star, S. A., & Williams, R. M., Jr. *The American soldier. Vol. 1, Adjustment during army life,* Princeton: Princeton University Press, 1949a.

Stouffer, S. A., Lumsdaine, A. A., Lumsdaine, M. H., Williams, R. M., Jr. Smith, M. B., Janis, I. L. Star, S. A., & Cottrell, L. S., Jr. *The American soldier, Vol. 2, Combat and its aftermath.* Princeton: Princeton University Press, 1949b.

Strauss, A. L. *Mirrors and masks.* San Francisco: Sociology Press, 1969.

Sullivan, H. S. *The interpersonal theory of psychiatry.* H. S. Perry & M. L. Gawel (Eds.). New York: Norton, 1953.

Swanson, G. E. Family structure and reflective intelligence. *Sociometry,* 1974, **37,** 459–490.

Tangri, S. S. Determinants of occupational role innovation among college women. *Journal of Social Issues,* 1972, **28,** 177–199.

Tapp, J. L. & Kohlberg, L. Developing senses of law and legal justice. *Journal of Social Issues,* 1971, **27,** 65–91

Taviss, I. Changes in the form of alienation: The 1900's vs. the 1950's. *American Sociological Review,* 1969, **34,** 46–57.

Terhune, K. W. Motives, situation, and interpersonal conflict within prisoner's dilemma. *Journal of Personality and Social Psychology Monograph Supplement,* 1968, **8,** 1–24.

Tesser, A., Gatewood, R., & Driver, M. Some determinants of gratitude. *Journal of Personality and Social Psychology,* 1968, **9,** 233–236.

Thibaut, J. W. & Kelley, H. H. *The social psychology of groups.* New York: Wiley, 1959.

Thibaut, J. W. & Riecken, H. A. Some determinants and consequences of the perception of social causality. *Journal of Personality,* 1955, **24,** 113–133.

Tilker, H. A. Socially responsible behavior as a function of observer responsibility and victim feedback. *Journal of Personality and Social Psychology,* 1970, **14,** 95–100.

Tillich, P. *The courage to be.* New Haven: Yale University Press, 1952.

Titmuss, R. M. *The gift relationship: From human blood to social policy.* New York: Vintage Books, Random House, 1971.

Tönnies, F. *Community & Society.* New York: Harper & Row, Torchbooks, 1963 (orig. 1887).

Torrance, E. P. Some consequences of power differences on decision making in permanent and temporary three-man groups. *Research Studies, Washington State College,* 1954, **22,** 130–140.

Touhey, J. C. Situated identities, attitude similarity and interpersonal attraction. *Sociometry,* 1974, **37,** 363–374.

Triandis, H. C., Loh, W. D., & Levin, L. A. Race, status, quality of spoken English, and opinions about civil rights as determinants of interpersonal attitudes. *Journal of Personality and Social Psychology,* 1966, **3,** 468–471.

Tuckman, B. W. Developmental sequence in small groups. *Psychological Bulletin,* 1965, **63,** 384–399.

Tumin, M. On inequality. *American Sociological Review,* 1963, **28,** 19–26.

Tumin, M. Some principles of stratification: A critical analysis. *American Sociological Review,* 1953, **18,** 387–394.

Turiel, E. An experimental test of the sequentiality of developmental stages in the child's moral judgments. *Journal of Personality and Social Psychology,* 1966, **3,** 611–618.

Turiel, E. Progressive and regressive aspects of moral development. Mimeographed report, University of California., Berkeley, July 1969.

Turner, R. H. The self-conception in social interaction. In C. Gordon & K. J. Gergen (Eds.), *The self in social interaction.* New York: Wiley, 1968.

Turner, R. H. Unresponsiveness as a social sanction. *Sociometry,* 1973. **36,** 1–19.

Uesugi, T. K. & Vinacke, W. E. Strategy in a feminine game. *Sociometry,* 1963, **26,** 75–88.

Valins, S. Cognitive effects of false heart-rate feedback. *Journal of Personality and Social Psychology,* 1966, **4,** 400–408.

Valins, S. & Ray, A. Effects of cognitive desensitization on avoidance behavior. *Journal of Personality and Social Psychology,* 1967, **7,** 345–350.

Vinacke, W. E. Sex roles in a three-person game. *Sociometry,* 1959, **22,** 343–360.

Vinacke, W. E. Variables in experimental games: Toward a field theory. *Psychological Bulletin,* 1969, **71,** 293–318.

Vinacke, W. E. & Gullickson, G. R. Age and sex differences in the formation of coalitions. *Child Development,* 1964, **35,** 1217–1231.

Volkart, E. H. (Ed.) *Social behavior and personality: Contributions of W. I. Thomas to theory and social research.* New York: Social Science Research Council, 1951.

Walker, C. R. *Toward the automatic factory: A case study of men and machines.* New Haven, Conn.: Yale University Press, 1957.

Walker, E. L., & Heyns, R. W. *An anatomy for conformity.* Belmont, Calif.: Brooks/Cole, 1967.

Wallace, J. Role reward and dissonance reduction. *Journal of Personality and Social Psychology,* 1966, **3**, 305–312.

Walster, E., Berscheid, E., & Walster, G. W. New directions in equity research. *Journal of Personality and Social Psychology,* 1973, **25**, 151–176.

Walster, E. & Piliavin, J. A. Equity and the innocent bystander. *Journal of Social Issues,* 1972, **28**, 165–189.

Waly, P. & Cook, S. W. Attitude as a determinant of learning and memory: A failure to confirm. *Journal of Personality and Social Psychology,* 1966, **4**, 280–288.

Warner, L. G. & DeFleur, M. L. Attitude as an interactional concept: Social constraint and social distance as intervening variables between attitudes and action. *American Sociological Review,* 1969, **34**, 153–169.

Watson, J. B. *Psychology from the standpoint of a behaviorist.* New York: Lippincott, 1919.

Watson, J. B. *Behaviorism.* New York: Norton, 1925.

Watts, A. W. *Psychotherapy East and West.* New York: Ballantine, 1961.

Watzlawick, P., Beavin, J. H., & Jackson, D. D. *Pragmatics of human communication.* New York: Norton, 1967.

Weber, M. *The protestant ethic and the spirit of capitalism.* New York: Scribner's, 1930.

Weber, M. *The theory of social and economic organization.* T. Parsons & A. M. Henderson translation. New York: Oxford University Press, 1947.

Weinstein, E. A. & Deutschberger, P. Some dimensions of altercasting. *Sociometry,* 1963, **26**, 454–466.

Weinstein, E. A., DeVaughan, W. L., & Wiley, M. G. Obligation and the flow of deference. *Sociometry,* 1969, **32**, 1–12.

Weitzman, L. J., Eifler, D., Hokada, E., & Ross, C. Sex-role socialization in picture books for preschool children. *American Journal of Sociology,* 1972, **77**, 1125–1150.

White, B. J. & Harvey, O. J. Effects of personality and own stand on judgment and production of statements about a central issue. *Journal of Experimental Social Psychology,* 1965, **1**, 334–347.

White, R. K. Misperception and the Vietnam war. *Journal of Social Issues,* 1966, **22**, (Whole issue).

White, R. W. Motivation reconsidered: The concept of competence. *Psychological Review,* 1959, **66**, 297–333.

Whiting, J. W. M. Sorcery, sin, and the superego: A cross-cultural study of some mechanisms of social control. In M. R. Jones (Ed.),

Nebraska Symposium on Motivation. Lincoln: University of Nebraska Press, 1959.

Whitney, R. E. Agreement and positivity in pleasantness ratings of balanced and unbalanced social situations: A cross-cultural study. *Journal of Personality and Social Psychology,* 1971, **17,** 11–14.

Whorf, B. L. *Language, thought and reality: Selected writings.* J. B. Carroll (Ed.). Cambridge, Mass.: Technology Press of MIT, 1956.

Whyte, M. K. Bureaucracy and modernization in China: The Maoist critique. *American Sociological Review,* 1973, **38,** 149–163.

Wicker, A. W. Attitudes versus actions: The relationship of verbal and overt behavioral responses to attitude objects. *Journal of Social Issues,* 1969, **25,** 41–78.

Wicker, A. W. An examination of the "other variables" explanation of attitude-behavior inconsistency. *Journal of Personality and Social Psychology,* 1971, **19,** 18–30.

Winsborough, H. H. The social consequences of high population density. *Law and Contemporary Problems,* 1965, **30,** 120–126.

Wirth, L. Urbanism as a way of life. *American Journal of Sociology,* 1938, **44,** 3–24.

Witkin, H. A., Dyk, R. B., Faterson, H. F., Goodenough, D. R., & Karp, S. A. *Psychological differentiation: Studies of development.* New York: Wiley, 1962.

Wolfgang, M. *Patterns in Criminal Homicide.* Philadelphia: University of Pennsylvania Press, 1958.

Worchel, S. & Andreoli, V. A. Attribution of causality as a means of restoring behavioral freedom. *Journal of Personality and Social Psychology,* 1974, **29,** 237–245.

Yinger, J. M. *Toward a field theory of behavior: Personality and social structure.* New York: McGraw-Hill, 1965.

Zajonc, R. B. Cognitive theories in social psychology. In G. Lindzey & E. Aronson (Eds.), *The handbook of social psychology* (2nd ed.), Vol. 1. Cambridge, Mass.: Addison-Wesley, 1968.

Zajonc, R. B. The process of cognitive tuning in communication. *Journal of Abnormal and Social Psychology,* 1960, **61,** 159–168.

Zajonc, R. B. Attitudinal effects of mere exposure. *Journal of Personality and Social Psychology, Monograph Supplement,* June 1968, **9,** Part 2, 1–27.

Zajonc, R. B., & Burnstein, E. The learning of balanced and unbalanced social structures. *Journal of Personality,* 1965, **33,** 153–163.

Zanna, M. P. On inferring one's beliefs from one's behavior in a low-choice setting. *Journal of Personality and Social Psychology,* 1973, **26,** 386–394.

Zanna, M. P., Lepper, M. R., & Abelson, R. P. Attentional mechanisms in children's devaluation of a forbidden activity in a forced-compliance situation. *Journal of Personality and Social Psychology,* 1973, **28,** 355–359.

Zimbardo, P. G. The human choice: Individuation, reason, and order versus deindividuation, impulse, and chaos. In W. J. Arnold & D. Levine (Eds.), *Nebraska Symposium on Motivation.* Lincoln: University of Nebraska Press, 1969.

Zimbardo, P. G., Haney, C., Banks, W. C., & Jaffe, D. The mind is a formidable jailer: A Pirandellian prison. *New York Times Magazine,* April 8, 1973, 38–60.

AUTHOR INDEX

SUBJECT INDEX